Deaths and Burials in St. Mary's County, Maryland

Leona Cryer

HERITAGE BOOKS
2008

HERITAGE BOOKS
AN IMPRINT OF HERITAGE BOOKS, INC.

Books, CDs, and more—Worldwide

For our listing of thousands of titles see our website at
www.HeritageBooks.com

Published 2008 by
HERITAGE BOOKS, INC.
Publishing Division
100 Railroad Ave. #104
Westminster, Maryland 21157

Copyright © 1995 Leona Cryer

All rights reserved. No part of this book may be reproduced or transmitted in any form or by any means, electronic or mechanical, including photocopying, recording or by any information storage and retrieval system without written permission from the author, except for the inclusion of brief quotations in a review.

International Standard Book Numbers
Paperbound: 978-0-7884-0173-2
Clothbound: 978-0-7884-7038-7

TABLE OF CONTENTS

ALL FAITH EPISCOPAL CEMETERY	Pg 1
ALL SAINTS EPISCOPAL CEMETERY	Pg 3
CHARLES MEMORIAL GARDENS CEMETERY	Pg 9
CHRIST EPISCOPAL CEMETERY	Pg 47
CHURCH OF THE NAZARENE CEMETERY	Pg 59
EBENEZER METHODIST CEMETERY	Pg 61
EVERGREEN MEMORIAL PARK CEMETERY	Pg 63
FIRST FRIENDSHIP METHODIST CEMETERY	Pg 65
HOLY FACE CATHOLIC CEMETERY	Pg 69
IMMACULATE HEART CATHOLIC CEMETERY	Pg 75
JOY METHODIST CHAPEL CEMETERY	Pg 81
MENNONITE CEMETERY	Pg 93
MT. ZION METHODIST CEMETERY	Pg 95
OLD COMMUNITY CEMETERY	Pg 101
OUR LADY'S CATHOLIC CHAPEL CEMETERY	Pg 103
SACRED HEART CATHOLIC CEMETERY	Pg 113
ST. ALOYSIUS CATHOLIC CEMETERY (OLD)	Pg 157
ST. ALOYSIUS CATHOLIC CEMETERY	Pg 159
ST. ANDREWS EPISCOPAL CEMETERY	Pg 167
ST. FRANCIS XAVIER CATHOLIC CEMETERY	Pg 179
ST. GEORGE'S CATHOLIC CEMETERY	Pg 185
ST. GEORGES EPISCOPAL CEMETERY	Pg 191
ST. GEORGE METHODIST CEMETERY	Pg 195
ST. JAMES CATHOLIC CEMETERY	Pg 197
ST. JOHN FRANCIS REGIS CATHOLIC CEM	Pg 190
ST. JOSEPH'S CATHOLIC CEMETERY (OLD)	Pg 233
ST. JOSEPH'S CATHOLIC CEMETERY	Pg 253
ST. MARKS METHODIST CEMETERY	Pg 269
ST. MARYS EPISCOPAL CEMETERY	Pg 273
ST. MARY'S QUEEN OF PEACE CATHOLIC CEM	Pg 277
ST. MICHAEL'S CATHOLIC CEMETERY	Pg 283
ST. NICHOLAS CATHOLIC CHAPEL CEMETERY	Pg 289
ST. PAULS METHODIST CEMETERY	Pg 299
ST. PETER CLAVER CATHOLIC CEMETERY	Pg 305
TRINITY EPISCOPAL CEMETERY	Pg 309
METHODIST/EPISCOPAL SOUTH CEMETERY	Pg 313
PRIVATE CEMETERIES-BIBLE RECORDS	Pg 315
ST. MARY'S COUNTY MISC. CEMETERIES	Pg 323
ST. MARY'S CO. RESIDENTS' DEATHS	Pg 333
ST. MARY'S CATHOLIC CEMETERY, CHARLES CO.	Pg 351
TRINITY MEMORIAL GARDENS-CHARLES CO.	Pg 353
CEDAR HILL CEMETERY-PR. GEORGES'S CO.	Pg 361

Table of Contents

FORT LINCOLN CEMETERY, PR. GEORGE'S CO.	Pg 367
WASHINGTON NAT'L CEMETERY-PR. GEO'S CO.	Pg 369
MD. STATE MISC. CEMETERIES	Pg 371
OUT OF MD. MISC. BURIALS	Pg 381
VETERANS' CEMETERIES	
MD. VETERANS, PR. GEORGE'S CO.	Pg 389
GARRISON FOREST, BALTO CO.	Pg 397
7TH REG. CIVIL WAR BLACK DEATHS	Pg 399
ARLINGTON NATIONAL CEMETERY, VA.	Pg 401
FLORIDA NAT'L CEM., BUSHNELL, FL.	Pg 406
INDEX BEGINS	Pg 407

PREFACE

I have found that there is little or no information available on deaths and burials in St. Mary's County, Md. While tramping through the local graveyards looking for information for my own use I decided to copy tombstone inscriptions. That is how this book began.

Deaths and burials in this book are from reports in newspapers, the 1860 mortality schedule, mortuary cards, church burial records and tombstone readings. I made most of the tomb-readings myself. Others were by school children as a Bicentenial project and by members of the St. Mary's County Genealogical Society. A lot of information was gleaned from the society's newsletter, "The Generator". Also included are the past five years obituary notices from a local county newspaper, "The Enterprise".

Each cemetery has burials listed alphabetically with wives listed under their maiden name when known. Husbands and wives are cross referenced when possible, known parents are given, and sometimes grandparents. In the cemeteries I physically surveyed, I have noted when it appeared a number of members of the same family were buried side-by-side. I have also indicated by indenting when a tombstone marked more than one grave or that different surnames were together in a burial plot. In the old cemeteries, it is not unusual to find four-sided grave markers with different surnames on each side, or a brother and sister or a parent and child on the same stone.

Since there are many county residents buried in cemeteries located in Charles and Prince Georges Counties as well as Arlington National Cemetery, it was decided to include them. There is also a Miscellaneous section containing deaths of residents who were cremated, buried in cemeteries other than those listed, buried out of the county, and those whose burial place is not known at all. Most of the Miscellaneous Deaths are probably buried in the County. Many of the countians who died in Washington, D.C. were in hospitals there.

Due to factors of age, distance, and time, it was not possible to survey every cemetery in the county, so this book does not claim to be all inclusive. Even those cemeteries which were walked have graves that have not been identified.

Bearing this in mind, it is still my hope that this book will be of some help to the many interested genealogists with roots in St. Mary's County. It is the result of my interest in genealogy and my work on my husband's maternal family, which evolved into a book entitled "Some Johnsons of Southern Maryland," covering three Johnson lines and the Cryer family of St. Mary's County, Md.

ALL FAITH EPISCOPAL CHURCH
Huntersville/Charlotte Hall, Md.
This red brick church was built in 1765 and is the second church built on this site.

ALVEY, Ann Elizabeth "Eliza", 30, bur Apr 26, 1887, wife of John T. Johnson, dau of James H. Alvey.
BRADY, Henryetta Beall, b. Aug 2, 1904, d. Jan 11, 1990, wife of W. Roger Burroughs, Sr., dau of Henry B. and Maude Catherine Gibbons Brady.
BURROUGHS, Henry Preston, b. Nov 17, 1960, d. Oct 15, 1987, son of Ben, Jr, and Joan Hewitt Burroughs.
BURROUGHS, Lawrence, d. Jan 22, 1983, m. 1930 Dorothy Aileen Davis.
BURROUGHS, Lydia Elizabeth, b. Oct 15, 1914, d. Sep 12, 1991, wife of Warren Hancock Burroughs, dau of Robert Stanley and Maude Lillian Davis Burroughs.
CHESLEY, Frederick Smith, b. Jan 5, 1922, d. Jun 23, 1992, m. 12 Apr 1941 Marian Ridgeley, son of William and Cecil Rich Chesley of Hagerstown, Md.
CHESLEY, William Rich, b. Dec 13, 1912, d. Sep 18, 1993, m. (1st) Emily Elizabeth Davis, (2d) Mary Ruth Waring nee Jenkins, son of William and Cecil Rich Chesley. Memorial Mass at Immaculate Conception Ch., Mechanicsville. Md.
COLONNA, Paul, b. Jan 25, 1908, d. Sep 25, 1993, m. 22 Nov 1945 Catherine Abell, son of Thomas H. and Delphia Davis Colonna.
CROPPER, Silas Dale Tilghman, Sr. b. Sep 19, 1906, d. Aug 23, 1993, m. 24 Dec 1932 Mary Florence Davis, son of Samuel and Sarah Gault Cropper.
DAVIS, Dorothy Aileen, b. Jun 30, 1905, d. Aug 24, 1992, wife of Lawrence Burroughs, dau of Joseph Lynwood and Sarah Ann Lewis Davis.
DAVIS, Joseph Bryon, Sr. b. Mar 18, 1918, d. Dec 21, 1990, hus of Eliza Herbert, son of

Joseph Lynwood and Sarah Lewis Davis.
DIXON, May, 94, b. Dec 26, 1897, d. Jul 14, 1992, wife of William Knott, dau of Joseph and Lydia Jones Dixon.
GANDARA, Josette "Josie" Marie, b. Oct 26, 1973 FL, d. Apr 1, 1990, dau of Raul E. and Janet Berger Gandara.
KNOTT, Leo, b. 1885, d. 1929, hus of Ethel Jane Raley (bur St. Joseph RCC), son of James Henry II and Georgianna Davis Knott.
KOGER, Flonnie Hazel, b. Jun 12, 1914 KY, d. Nov 11, 1988, wife of Conrad A. Phillips, dau of Louis and Mary Ann Corder Koger.
MOSSMAN, Dr. David Lothrop, b. Sep 5, 1928 MA, d. Nov 5, 1993, m. (2d) 1980 Mary Maxine Cunningham, son of George A. and Esther Jane Curtis Mossman.
RALEY, Thomas Franklin, b. Nov 2, 1929, d. Feb 20, 1989, son of Arthur E. and Janie Rossetta Raley.
REEDER, Harriet H., b. Dec 10, 1901, d. Sep 17, 1991, dau of John Henry and Mary Dallam Reeder.
SASSER, Mary Turner, 100, b. Nov 25, 1891, d. Oct 24, 1992, wife of Louis Herbert Wise, dau of Clarence DeSales and Marie Turner Sasser.
SULLIVAN, George Michael, USAAC WW11, b. May 31, 1923 OH, d. Oct 2, 1991, hus of Melissa Jayne __, son of George Gamon and Euphenia Docherty Sullivan.
THOMAS, Minnie Odessa, 81, d. Mar 12, 1989, wife of Wilson A. Butler, dau of William and Mollie Thomas.
THOMPSON, Isadore Wilson, b. Oct 31, 1910, d. Apr 12, 1990, son of James Thompson and Bertie Edwards.
WISE, Louis Herbert, d. 1951, hus of Mary Turner Sasser.

ALL SAINTS EPISCOPAL CHURCH
Avenue/Oakley, Md.

This church was built in 1846 and is the second church to be built on this site.

BARNHART, Jason Davis, b. 1900, d. 1983.
BLACKISTONE, Eleanor 'Grace', 93, d. Mar 1959, wife of Dr. Walter Benjamin Dent.
BLACKISTONE, Robert Deminieu, b. Aug 4, 1903, d. Feb 18, 1988 FL, hus of Katherine Porter.
  Listed as Buried
-BLAIR, Mary Gladys, b. May 29, 1906, d. Jul 2, 1970.
-BLAIR, Walter Rayner, b. Dec 13, 193-, d. Feb 13, 1956.
-BLAIR, Bertha L., b. 1874, d. 1954.
-BLAIR, William, b. 1858, d. 1934.
-BLAIR, Ernest, Infant.
-BLAIR, Saxton, Infant.
-BLAIR, William O., b. 1914, d. 1965.
-BLAIR, Jeremiah, b. 1899, d. 1903.
-BLAIR, Charles F., d. Jan 18, 1861, age 1 yr 6 mos 14 das, son of Jerry and Mary R. Blair.
-BLAIR, George W., d. Mar 11, 1866, age 18 yrs 6 mos 5 das, son of Jerry and Mary R. Blair.
-BLAIR, Samuel, d. Apr 23, 1865, age 6 yrs 11 mos 23 das, son of Jeremiah and Mary R. Blair.
-BLAIR, Mary R., b. 1818, d. 1896.
-BLAIR, Jeremiah, d. Feb 22, 1866, age 59 yrs 3 mos 11 das.
-BLAIR, William, b. Mar 15, 1791, d. Apr 5, 1872.
-BLAIR, Agnes E., b. Dec 25, 1852, d. Dec 25, 1922.
-BLAIR, James T., b. 1849, d. 1915, hus of Agnes E. Blair.
-BLAIR, George W., b. 1876, d. 1934.
  Four Sides of One Stone
-GRASON, Thomas, b. 1827, d. 1911, A Friend.
-BLAKISTONE, William W., b. 1870, d. 1927.
-BLAKISTONE, William S., M.D., b. 1907, d. 1938.
-BLAKISTONE, Alice Bohannan, b. 1884, d. 1972.

Four Sides of One Stone-Next 7 Names
- BLAKISTONE, William S., M.D., b. Jan 12, 1834, d. Mar 4, 1890, hus of Kate G. Blakistone.
- BLAKISTONE, Katherine G., b. Feb 20, 1849, d. Sep 13, 1930, wife of Wm. S. Blakistone, M.D.
- BLAKISTONE, Launcelotte, b. Apr 27, 1886, d. Jul 19, 1887, daughter.
- BOIS, Katherine E.B., b. Oct 16, 1875, d. Aug 3, 1969.
- BLAKISTONE, J. Chew, M.D., b. Sep 17, 1880, d. Dec 13, 1918, son of Wm. S. and Kate G. Blakistone.
- BLAKISTONE, Harry, b. Oct 18, 1873, d. Oct 2, 1881, son of Dr. Wm S. and Kate G. Blakistone.
- BLAKISTONE, Ann E., b. Sep 27, 1804, d. Dec 8, 1853, consort of Henry H. Blakistone.
    Four Sided Stone-One Side
- BOWLING, Charles Franklin, b. 1838, d. 1904.
- BOWLING, Merrill Crawford, b. 1897, d. 1924.
    2nd Side of Stone
- BOWLING, Roy Slye and James Lock, b. 1889, d. 1889.
- BOWLING, Robert Slye, b. 1891, d. 1892.
    3rd Side of Stone
- BOWLING, Thomas Benton, b. 1841, d. 1889.
- BOWLING, William Murray, b. 1886, d. 1887.
BRUFF, John Joseph, b. Aug 7, 1908 DC, d. Aug 28, 1992, hus of Eleanor Gibson, son of William and Helen Lyons Bruff.
BRYANT, Annie, b. Sep 26, 1836, d. Aug 30, 1895, wife of Philip H. Dorsey.
BURCH, Elliott Eugene, b. Oct 21, 1894, d. Feb 3, 1991, hus of Ruth Petrie Dent, son of Edw. Albert and Jennie Elise Lomax Burch.
CHESELDINE, Alton Grover, USA WWI, b. Dec 18, 1892, d. Jun 9, 1981.
CHESELDINE, Annie Louise, b. Feb 2, 1907, d. Feb 19, 1990, m. 16 Oct 1967 Robert William Sensenbach, dau of John W. and Mary M. Cheseldine.
CLARKE, Edith, b. Jun 22, 1906, d. Apr 24, 1989, m. (1st)__ Young, (2d)__ Mack, dau of Charlie and Mary F. Woodland Clarke.
CROSS, Virginia, b. Sep 12, 1917, d. Apr 2,

All Saints

1989, m.(1st)__ Blackistone, (2d) George W.
Leopard, dau of Guy and May Ward Cross.
CRYER, Edward Compton, b. Sep 18, 1888, d. Dec
12, 1950, hus of Lillian Caroline __, b. Aug
10, 1889, d. Mar 15, 1978.
DENT, Benjamin Blackistone, b. Jun 24, 1901,
d. Apr 24, 1991, m. (1st) Margaret Chambers,
(2d) Eva Schwienteck, son of Dr. Walter B.
and Grace Blackistone Dent.
DENT, Grace Blackistone, b. Mar 11, 1887, d.
1890, dau of Walter B. and Grace Blackistone Dent.
DENT, Helen Marguerite, b. Nov 21, 1894, d.
Mar 1913, dau of Walter B. and Grace Blackistone Dent.
DENT, Mary Lilla, b. Jul 1, 1885, d. Jun 29,
1984, wife of Arthur F. Reany, dau of Walter
B. and Grace Blackistone Dent.
DENT, Richard Deminieu, b. Nov 23, 1896, d.
Jun 8, 1975, m. 1931 Estelle Drury, son of
Walter B. and Grace Blackistone Dent.
DENT, Walter Benjamin, M.D., b. Feb 2, 1859,
d. Feb 7, 1946, m. 19 Aug 1884 Eleanor
'Grace' Blackistone, son of Walter Levi and
Mary Thoeodosia Mankin Dent.
DENT, Walter Benjamin, Jr., 17, b. Nov 21,
1891, d. 1908, son of Walter B. and Grace
Blackistone Dent.
DORSEY, Amy Ruth, b. Oct 17, 1878, d. Aug 14,
1963, dau of Philip H. and Annie Bryant Dorsey.
DORSEY, Ellen Aletha, b. Oct 13, 1871, d. Sep
17, 1950, wife of Frank T. Gibson, dau of
Phillip H. and Annie Bryant Dorsey.
DORSEY, Philip H., b. Oct 10, 1827, d. Oct 21,
1899, hus of Annie Bryant .
DORSEY, Philip Henry, b. Mar 4, 1870, d. Feb
6, 1945, son of Phillip Henry and Annie Bryant Dorsey.
DORSEY, Richard Luke, b. Apr 12, 1876, killed
by lightning Aug 29, 1895.
DORSEY, Walter Bryant, b. Sep 29, 1866, d. Dec
11, 1923, son of Phillip Henry and Annie
Bryant Dorsey.
DUNN, Joseph Bernard, USA WWII, b. Apr 19,

1916, d. Sep 6, 1983.
DUNN, Pauline V., b. May 29, 1924, d. Mar 23, 1980.
EDWARDS, William Bernard, PFC USA WWII, b. Mar 7, 1920, d. Oct 13, 1979.
GIBSON, Frank Tilton, b. Mar 23, 1859, d. Nov 8, 1939, hus of Ellen Aletha Dorsey, son of Dr. John Chew & Henrietta S. Carroll Gibson of St. Michaels, Md.
GRASON, Thomas, b. 1827, d. 1911, bur in Blakistone Plot.
Double Stone
-GREENE, MARY E., b. Jun 5, 1853, d. Mar 21, 1924.
-YOUNG, Alice E., b. Sep 15, 1860, d. Nov 8, 1928.
HESS, John J., b. 1830, d. 1904, hus of Martha R. ___, b. 1829, d. 1893.
HESS, John J., Jr. b. 1863, d. 1926, 2d hus of Mary Elinor Johnson, son of John and Martha R. Hess.
HESS, William H., b. 1861, d. 1914.
HOLMES, Leonard, Sr. d. Oct 29, 1970, hus of Dorothy Pogue.
HOLMES, Leonard Locke, Jr. b. Jun 10, 1922, d. Jan 6, 1984 GA, hus of Maria B.___.
HUSEMAN, Elsie May "Tut", b. Jul 19, 1899, d. Sep 11, 1991, dau of William T. and Jennie "Jane" Bundick Huseman.
JENIFER, Julia, d. Jun 19, 1884.
JENIFER, Walter, d. Dec 5, 1884 of convulsions, age 6 mos.
JOHNSON, Francis Benedict, b. Nov 30, 1936, d. Feb 17, 1981, hus of Ramona Holmes, son of J. Earnest Hillery and Mary Rosalie Cooper Johnson.
KAUFMAN, Ada M., d. Jun 2, 1892, aged 31 yrs, wife of Ira E. Kaufman.
Double Stone
-KNOTT, George B., b. Nov 8, 1884, d. Mar 15, 1950.
-KNOTT, Julie H., b. Nov 16, 1887, d. Jan 3, 1976.
LINTON, John Hunter, b. Jul 28, 1913 DC, d. Jan 27, 1992 VA, hus of Jane Reaney, son of

All Saints

Hunter B. and Elsie Moore Linton.
MATTINGLY, J. Olin, b. 1912, d. 1978.
MATTINGLY, Muriel M., b. 1911, d. 1983.
MONTFORT, James Brown, Jr. d. Sep 10, 1990, Balto, hus of Barbara F. Curruthers.
PIE, Ellen Douglas, b. Jun 3, 1919 DC, d. Jul 10, 1992 of cancer.
PINES, Benjamin J., b. Mar 24, 1823, d. Aug 8, 1889, hus of Sarah A. __, b. 1824, d. 1901.
POGUE, Robert Elbert Turner, b. May 19, 1910, d. Jun 13, 1988, hus of Lucy L. __, son of Robert Steele and Dorothy Thomas Pogue.
POGUE, Dorothy, d. Feb 12, 1977, wife of Leonard Holmes, Sr.
REEVES, Thomas Billingsly, b. Nov 27, 1900, d. Feb 6, 1989, hus of Mildred Cameron, son of Thomas G. and Katherine Lyon Reeves.
ROWE, Harry Austin, 1st Lt. USA WWII, b. Mar 19, 1919, d. Mar 19, 1980.
SHAW, Alvin Franklin, b. Dec 13, 1899, d. Apr 3, 1989, hus of Viola K. __, son of James Franklin and Laura Johnson Shaw of NC.
SHORT, Henrietta, b. 1860, d. 1954.
ST. CLAIR, Joseph Earl, b. Sep 24, 1908, d. Nov 5, 1991, hus of Mildred Nelson, son of Joseph Francis and Leila Russell St. Clair.
STONE, Nannie D., b. Aug 29, 1868, d. Mar 8, 1926.
WALTEMEYER, Ida B., b. Mar 4, 1897, d. Jul 13, 1974.
WEBB, Harry Cleveland, Sr., 70, d. Sep 22, 1993, hus of Julia St. Clair. Memorial Svc.
WELLS, Susan C., d. Dec 13, 1856 in the 25th yr of her age, consort of E.A. Wells.

CHARLES MEMORIAL GARDENS
Rte. 5
Leonardtown, Md.

ABELL, Ellen Jo, b. Aug 10, 1942, d. Feb 16, 1990. wife of Richard Clyde Shoemaker, dau of Walter B. Sr. and Nora Ellen Driscoll Abell.
ABELL, Gladys Marie, b. Jun 21, 1917, d. Mar 19, 1993, m. 9 Dec 1939 Charles Russell Quade, dau of William Joseph and Mary Maud Norris Abell.
ABELL, Grace Elizabeth, b. Feb 23,1910, d. Jan 29, 1988, wife of J. Testa Johnson, dau of John Combs and Henietta Jane Joy Abell.
ABELL, Mary Hilda, b. Mar 6, 1910, d. Dec 17, 1992, wife of Charles Kennedy Norris, dau of George Edgar and Emma Pauline Bowles Abell.
ABELL, Pauline Elizabeth, b. Feb 17, 1896, d. Dec 23, 1981, m. 18 Nov 1916 Thomas Alvin Johnson, dau of Jack Abell.
ABELL, Walter Bernard. Sr., b. Sep 9, 1922, d. Oct 15, 1988, hus of Nora Ellen ___,son of J. Fulton and Mary Noema Wathen Abell.
ALVEY, Agnes Charlotte, b. Apr 18, 1906, d. Jun 1, 1993, wife of Melvin Morgan Curry, dau of Clarence Hillary and Clora Helen Hayden.
ALVEY, George Kenneth, b. Aug 18, 1934, d. Mar 6, 1989, hus of Ruby Ann ___, son of George Carroll and Margaret G. Hall Alvey.
ALVEY, William Henry, b. Sep 26, 1958, d. Oct 29, 1989, son of Alice Ann Alvey Buckler, stepson of Ralph L. Buckler.
ANDERSON, Emma Liza, b. Jan 16 1917 SC, d. Nov 5, 1993, wife of Elijah Bannister, dau of Willie and Dora Robertson Anderson.
BAKER, John Francis "Fanny", b. Nov 29, 1953, d. May 8, 1991, son of Teresa Baker, gson of James Richard, Sr. and Catherine Louise Countiss Baker.
BAKER, Thomas Frederick, b. May 10, 1948, d. Jan 27, 1990, son of James Richard, Sr. and Catherine Louise Countiss Baker.
BALIUS, John B., b. Dec 31, 1941 MS, d. Apr

6, 1991 VA, hus of Mary Louise "Molly" __,
son of Hypolite William, Sr. and Carroll
Lee Cook Balius.
BANKS, Mary Eleanor, b. Oct 5, 1895 Balto, d.
Mar 31, 1992, m. (1st) Felix A. Somerville,
(2d) John W. Banks.
BARBER, Annie Lucille, b. Sep 1, 1922, d. May
12, 1991, wife of Louis A. Nolan, dau of
John F. and Mary Catherine Whalen Barber.
BARBER, Mary Florence, d. Jul 30, 1981, wife of
Edward Joseph Biscoe.
BARNES, Edith Suvilla, b. Feb 19, 1919, d. Jul
3, 1993, wife of Earl Palmer Tokley, dau of
Joseph Clyde and Rachel Somerville Barnes.
BARNES, Lottie Louise, b. Feb 16, 1926, d.
Feb 4, 1989, wife of Richard White, Sr.,
dau of Dallas and Rosie Barnes.
BEALL, Ada Veronica, b. Feb 7, 1919 DC, d.
Sep 16, 1992, m. 22 Feb 1934 Clyde Elsworth
Ammann, dau of Robert Miller and Caroline
Virginia Loveless Beall.
BEAN, John Stephen, b. Oct 5, 1916, d. Dec 10,
1988, hus of Mary Elizabeth Combs, son of
John Franklin and Ellen Dora Redman Bean.
BEAN, Mary, b. Jul 15, 1909, d. May 23, 1990,
wife of Charles B. Heard, Sr., dau of William G. and Emma May Raley Bean.
BELT, Gregory Loyce "Greg", b. Sep 26, 1963
KY, d. Aug 13, 1991, hus of Veronica Ann
Nelson, son of Janis Faye Jones and Dennis
Paul Belt.
BENNETT, William Isiah "Billy", b. Nov 20,
1942, d. Aug 26, 1992, son of Rhodie Isiah
and Ann Young Bennett.
BENTZ, Kathleen Frances, b. Sep 12, 1927 MA,
d. May 30, 1993, m. (1st) late Wm. Edward
Combs, (2d) John Edward Thomas, dau of James
and Elizabeth Bentz.
BISCOE, Edward Joseph "Shorty B", b. Aug 5,
1922, d. Mar 24, 1991, hus of Mary Florence
Barber, son of Mary Louise Green Biscoe and
stepson of Andrew Sampson.
BLANKENSHIP, Jimmy G., b. Dec 10, 1935, d.
Jul 1, 1989.
BLANKENSHIP, Maxine Edith, b. Jul 4, 1919 WV,

d. Feb 28, 1990, wife of Robert Lee Taylor, Sr., dau of Walter B. and Olie Blankenship.
BOLT, James Frederick, b. Dec 11, 1927, d. May 21, 1992, son of Agnes Vergie Bolt.
BOND, Victoria Elizabeth, b. Feb 27, 1966, d. Nov 13, 1989, dau of Frances Victoria Young and John Henry Bond, Jr.
BONDS, Latisha N., infant, d. Dec 21, 1991, dau of Dinah Marie Bonds and Larry Dickens, gdau of Richley and Mary Miles Bonds; Susie Dickens.
BOWLES, Hazel Rebecca, b. Jan 4, 1924, d. Nov 22, 1989, wife of John Frank Badoniec, dau of Theophilus and Lena Bowles.
BOWLES, Roy Anthony, b. Jun 22, 1934, d. May 5, 1991, hus of Dorothy Knott, son of Joseph Ernest and Mary Edith Bowles.
BOWLING, Glen Richard, Jr, b. and d. Apr 23, 1992, son of Glen Richard and Michelle Lynn Maddox Bowling, gson of Joseph Albert and Patricia A. Bowling; David E. and Carolyn M. Maddox; ggson of Fred Hansborough; Joseph and Anna Lockwood; George and Katherine Lockwood.
BRANSON, Denise Elizabeth, b. and d. Aug 23, 1989, dau of George J. and Janet M. Branson.
BRIDGES, Harry Thomas, b. Dec 13, 1906 ENG, d. Mar 12, 1990, hus of Dorothy R. __.
BRIDGETT, Mary Madeline, b. Sep 26, 1906, d. Mar 17, 1993, wife of James Columbus Reintzell, Sr., dau of George and Anna Pilkerton Bridgett.
BRINDLE, Kathleen Ruth, b. Feb 18, 1915 B.C., Canada, d. Jun 20, 1989, wife of Albert Joseph Fortin, Sr., dau of Joshua and Alice Hurst Brindle.
BRISCOE, James Edward, b. Feb 18, 1915, d. Jun 6, 1990.
BROOKS, Mary Frances, b. Oct 8, 1923, d. Jun 14, 1992 DC, dau of Borden and Mary Brooks.
BROOKS, Robert Alexander "Knute", b. Sep 8, 1927, d. Mar 15, 1993, son of Jas. Richley and Mildred Louise Brooks.
BROWN, Deann Elizabeth, b. Sep 19, 1968, d. Aug 19, 1993 TX, dau of David Edward III and

Rose Darlene Thorington Brown.
BROWN, Jacquelyn Marie "Jackie", b. Nov 15, 1966 RI, d. Sep 17, 1993, dau of Joseph Patrick Brown and Evelyn Jeanette Fenner, step dau of Donald A. Fenner.
BROWN, Joseph Daniel, Sr, b. Apr 26, 1912, d. Jul 8, 1988, hus of Katherine Knott, son of John B. and Mary Ellis Brown.
BROWN, Kathleen Louise, b. Sep 26, 1954, d. Sep 11, 1992 Balto, wife of Joseph F. Marvaso, dau of Elmer and Mary McLeran Brown.
BROWN, Lillian Frances, 84, b. Sep 29, 1906, d. Jan 4, 1991, dau of John Randolph and Mary Elizabeth Coombs Brown.
BRUMBAUGH, James Dean, b. Oct 16, 1946 PA, d. Jun 20, 1991, hus of Ann Dessenberger, son of James D. and Pauline Eamigh Brumbaugh.
BUCKLER, James Martin, b. Feb 22, 1923, d. May 24, 1990, hus of Erma Jane Raley, son of Thomas Lee and Agnes Estelle Williams Buckler.
BURRIS, Louis F., Sr. b. May 27, 1915 OH, d. May 30, 1993, m. 27 Jul 1940 Jean McNey, son of Thomas and Edna Wasser Burris.
BURROUGHS, James Hayden, b. Dec 30, 1926, d. Sep 23, 1989, son of Henry Harvey and Mary Hayden Burroughs.
BUSH, Anson Lee, b. Nov 16, 1972 FL, d. Nov 5, 1991, son of William J. Bush and Nickie J. Bush Youngblood, stepson of David Youngblood.
BUTLER, John Francis, b. Apr 3, 1950, d. Aug 1, 1993, son of William Henry, Sr. and Mary Madeline Jordan Butler.
BUTLER, Joseph John Francis, b. Jan 16, 1925, d. Mar 13, 1988, son of Abraham and Florine Butler.
BUTLER, Phillip Leroy, b. Dec 8, 1926, d. Mar 24, 1988, son of James A. Butler and Cecelia Stevens.
BYRD, Gary Lee, b. May 24, 1949 VA, d. Sep 15, 1991, hus of Brenda Kay Greer, son of James Silas and Bettie Gordon Byrd.
CACCIVIO, Albert Anselmo, Sr. b. Aug 18, 1907 NH, d. May 31, 1992, hus of Vera Miller, son of John and Luiga Donghi Caccivio.

CAMALIER, Ruth Henrietta "Teeny", b. Nov 25, 1933, d. Oct 24, 1992, wife of George Aloysius "Albees" Mattingly, Sr., dau of Charles Henry and Olivia Sewell Somerville Dent Camalier.
CANTER, Carrie Cecelia, b. Aug 21, 1927, d. Jul 12, 1988, wife of Eugene Copsey, dau of Frank W. and Margaret B. Canter.
CAREY, Barbara Ann, b. Jan 7, 1945, d. May 8, 1993 DC, dau of Mrs. Anna Mae Carey; gdau of Mary M. Jenkins.
CARTER, Nina Elizabeth, b. Aug 9, 1929 VA, d. Dec 28, 1993, m. 25 Oct 1964 Joseph Benedict Graves, dau of Orbin and Ella Sexton Carter.
CARTER, Violet Marie, b. Feb 18, 1929, d. Mar 18, 1988, dau of Charles P. and Ellie Marie Hensley.
CHAKALES, Dwight Edward, b. Aug 7, 1938, d. Jun 27, 1992 DC, hus of Linda Perkins, son of Eddie and Blanche Wiggs Chakales.
CHASE, James Matthew, b. Feb 3, 1961, d. Sep 25, 1989, hus of Caroline Young, son of George F. Chase and Ola Mae Carter.
CHASE, Joseph Alvin, b. Jun 3, 1924, d. Jan 31, 1989, hus of Barbara Ann Allen, son of John Henry and Mary Spears Chase.
CHASE, Joseph Francis, Sr, b. May 22, 1930, d. Apr 9, 1991, hus of Mary Catherine Young, son of John Phillip and Mary Catherine Nolan Chase.
CHASE, Kenneth Wayne, b. Nov 11, 1964 Balto, d. Mar 26, 1992, hus of Patricia Ann Stewart, son of Carolyn Cutchember Chase of Mechanicsville and Paul E. Chase of DC.
CHASE, Mary Dorothy, b. Mar 21, 1920, d. Dec 29, 1989, wife of Francis Ford Barber, Sr., dau of John Henry and Mary Rita Spears Chase.
CHAUNG, Michael Cecil, Jr, infant, d. Apr 10, 1992, son of Michael C. Chaung and Ivolene Venus Wiles.
CLARKE, George Willard, Jr. b. Jun 10, 1931, d. Sep 6, 1993, m. 8 Nov 1952 Catherine Marie Combs, son of George W. and Julie Christine Newton Clarke.
CLARKE, John E., Sr. b. Aug 13, 1911, d. Jul

24, 1989, hus of Mildred M. __, son of John
Ralph and Iva Mae Norris Clarke.
CLARKE, John Wilbur, b. Apr 27, 1959, d. Jun
15, 1993, son of George Willard Jr. and
Catherine Marie Combs Clarke.
CLINE, Albert Richard, Sr. b. Nov 21, 1913,
d. Feb 24, 1989, hus of Agnes Raley, son of
John Rubright and Florence Hileman Cline.
COLEMAN, Renee Dottie, b. Nov 7, 1903 NM, d.
Nov 4, 1993, wife of __ Polz, dau of Curtis
and Adelaide Young Coleman.
COLES, Albert Stanley, 69, d. May 10, 1993.
COLLINS, Gertrude Viola, b. Nov 27, 1913, d.
Feb 24, 1989, wife of George N. Collins.
COLLINS, James LeVaughn, Sr. b. Sep 4, 1916,
d. May 13, 1993, m. 27 Oct 1941 Mary Estelle
Scriber, son of James and Daisy Proctor
Collins.
COMBS, James Cox, d. Dec 1985, 2d hus of Helen
Victoria Payne.
CONSTANTINIDES, Kiki, 83, b. Feb 21, 1909,
Turkey, d. May 17, 1992, wife of Augustine
Zissis, dau of George and Mabel Manuelitis
Constantinides.
COOK, Lurty Ray, b. Nov 10, 1899, d. May 5,
1993, son of Laban Scott and Linnie May Bowers Cook.
COPSEY, Christina Marie, b. Sep 25, 1969 VA,
d. Jul 27, 1990, dau of Dick and Jeannie
Copsey; gdau of Lewis Akron and Helen Mae
Copsey; Dorothy W. Costello.
COSGROVE, Maurine, b. Oct 17, 1942 MA, d. Mar
18, 1993, m. 30 Jun 1969 Roger Alan Hammer,
dau of Wm. and Madelyn Rinehart Cosgrove.
COUNTESS, Catherine Louise, b. May 16, 1909,
d. Dec 16, 1992, m. 3 Jan 1926 James Richard
Baker, dau of Ben and Eleanor Holt Countess.
CRAGER, Nicholas Anthony, b. Jan 11, 1993, d.
Mar 15, 1993, son of Tony and Jennifer Pahel
Crager; gson of Robt. A. and Janice Crager;
Robt. E. and Linda K. Pahel.
CRAWFORD, Joyce Irene, b. Oct 3, 1936 OH, d.
Aug 18, 1993, m. PA 13 Aug 1955 Donald
French, dau of Roy G. and Clara Irene Cox
Crawford.

CREGGER, John Phillip, b. Apr 18, 1953 VA, d. Jun 20, 1991 Pensacola, FL, hus of Debra Ann Madison, son of William Henry and June Richardson Cregger.
CROUCH, Jeannette Elizabeth, b. Sep 15, 1924, d. Sep 6, 1989, wife of Joseph Francis Morgan, Sr., dau of Eldridge A. and Mary Bell Crouch.
CURTIS, Catherine Eliza, d Jun 14, 1993, wife of John Steven Hebb.
CURTIS, Charles Leon, b. Jul 27, 1944, d. Jul 25, 1988, hus of Lottie M. ___, son of James G. and Jeanette Curtis.
CURTIS, John Henry, Jr. b. Oct 17, 1937, d. Mar 13, 1993 DC, son of John H. and Helen Rebecca Mason Curtis.
CURTIS, Mary Elizabeth, b. Sep 4, 1918, d. Apr 9, 1987, wife of Joseph Paul Curtis.
CURTIS, Mary Theresa, b. Mar 16, 1927, d. Mar 4, 1991, dau of Charles Henry and Clara Jones Dorsey.
CURTIS, Samuel Albinus, b. Mar 3, 1910, d. Oct 26, 1989, son of Bernard and Mary E. Curtis.
CUTCHEMBER, Donald Izear, b. Nov 11, 1944, d. Feb 18, 1992, hus of Mary Louise Price, son of James Richard, Jr, and Mary Margaret Dyson Cutchember.
CUTCHEMBER, James R., Jr. b. Jun 15, 1915, d. Nov 24, 1991, hus of Mary Margaret Dyson, son of James Richard and Mary Barnes Cutchember.
CUTCHEMBER, Tyreke, b. Oct 8, 1993, d. Oct 22, 1993, dau of Victoria Marie Cutchember, gdau of Vincent R. and Lucille Williams Cutchember
DAVIES, Virginia May, b. Feb 5, 1923, d. Jul 22, 1992, wife of Cecil Marshall St. Clair, Sr., dau of George Brent and Martha America Davies.
DAVIS, Frances Marie, b. Dec 8, 1951, d. Mar 4, 1990, wife of Michael Bailey Farr, dau of Buck and Frances Davis.
DAVIS, Helen Genevieve, b. Feb 14, 1920, d. Feb 25, 1991, wife of Raymond Louis Walker,

Sr., dau of Howard Eugene and Lillian Catherine Payne Davis.
DAVIS, Priscilla Ann "Boots", b. Aug 5, 1922, d. Apr 12, 1992, wife of Charles Carmen "Penny" Pennisi, dau of Howard E. and Lillian C. "Lilly" Payne Davis.
DAVIS, Robert Vernon "Big Bob" "Bobby", b. Oct 8, 1925 DC, d. Apr 12, 1992, hus of Mary Madeline Carter, son of Edward and Sadie Mae Johnson Davis.
DAVIS, William Scott "Bill", b. Dec 10, 1947 TX, d. Apr 8, 1992, son of USN Capt. Hilton K. and Cornelia F. Davis.
DEAN, Doris Marie, b. Jul 1, 1949, d. May 29, 1988, wife of Joseph A. Knight, Sr., dau of Richard Levi and Mary Doreatha Newton Dean.
DEAN, Francis L. "Teddy", b. Dec 10, 1936, d. Apr 13, 1990, hus of Mary Rita __, son of Richard L. and Mary Doreatha Newton Dean.
DEAN, James Luther, b. Mar 17, 1951, d. Apr 6, 1987, son of Chester D. Dean and Alice Ann Buckler, (Mrs. Ralph Earl Buckler).
DEAN, Richard Levi, b. May 2, 1916, d. Jan 28, 1993, hus of Mary Doreatha Newton, son of David Richard and Myrtle Mae Copsey Dean.
DeLOZIER, William Warren "Buddy", Sr. b. Mar 4, 1926, d. Mar 30, 1993, m. 27 Aug 1949 Mary Rita Wathen, son of Anthony and Nellie Cullison DeLozier.
DeMOSS, Harry Alden, b. Jun 29, 1921 IN, d. Dec 4, 1989, hus of Maura Honore Boyle, son of Harry A. and Mary Sweeney DeMoss.
DeMOSS, Mary Kathleen, b. Apr 10, 1961 CA, d. May 7, 1988, dau of Harry Alden and Maura Boyle DeMoss.
DENNIS, Howard Wendell, Sr. b. Dec 24, 1930 PA, d. May 20, 1992, hus of Bessie Christine Hennen, son of Jacob and Nina Brynor Dennis.
DENT, Bernadine, b. Feb 15, 1915, d. May 13, 1988, m. (1st)__ Bush, (2d)__ Fenwick, dau of Francis B. and Nannie R. Talbot Dent.
DENT, Elmer Francis, Sr. 69, d. Aug 4, 1991, hus of Joan Marie Wilson, son of Vivian and Mae Gibbons Dent.
DENT, James Thomas, b. Jul 23, 1939, d. Jul

14, 1990 Balto, son of John E. and Margaret J. Fenwick.
DICKERSON, Ronald Shelton "Ronnie", b. Feb 9, 1969, d. May 6, 1991, hus of Angela Denise Johnson, son of Dianne Thomas and Ronald Shelton Taylor; gson of Francis Aubrey Dickerson.
DINGEE, Wilbur Louis, b. Jan 27, 1925, d. Sep 20, 1988, hus of Mary Bernadette __, son of Louis Edward and Mary Josephine Dingee.
DIXON, Betty J., b. Aug 20, 1965, d. May 4, 1993, wife of __ Osantowski, dau of James E. Dixon Jr. of MI and Carolyn Jean Russell; maternal gdau of Louis and Jean McNey Burris.
DODSON, Joseph Larry, LCPL USMC, b. Nov 14, 1958 Balto, d. Aug 16, 1993, son of late Ernest Joseph Dodson, Jr. and Mary Gwendora Woodland Dodson Holt; gson of Agnes C. Woodland, step gson of Thomas A. Johnson; gson of Eleanor Dodson.
DOOLEY, Stephen Roy, b. Nov 6, 1954, d. Dec 5, 1993, son of Roy and Roberta Miedzinski Dooley.
DORNALL, Margaret Marie, b. Jul 15, 1950, d. Sep 6, 1990, wife of Louis Wilmer Hill, Jr., dau of Charles and Mary Madeline Abell Dornall.
DOUGLAS, James Sherman, b. Dec 7, 1933, d. Sep 7, 1992, son of Anderson and Elizabeth Young Douglas.
DOUGLAS, John Jasper, b. Apr 7, 1916, d. Apr 7, 1991, son of Patrick and Charlotte Cecilia Butler Douglas.
DOUGLAS, Walter, b. Apr 11, 1919, d. Oct 20, 1992, hus of (1st) Mary Estelle __, d. Jul 1, 1981, (2d) Evangeline Effa __, d. Jun 2, 1989, son of Alexander and Jane Douglas.
DOWNS, Herbert Adrian, b. Apr 4, 1910, d. Mar 16, 1989.
DOWNS, Mary Virginia, b. May 13, 1917, d. Nov 18, 1993, m. 1935 Philip Jerome Russell, dau of Charles Benjamin and Mary Linda Wilkinson Downs.
DOWNS, Robert Louis, b. Dec 23, 1952, d. May 26, 1990, son of James Wallace and Doris Marle Downs.

DRISCOLL, Nora Ellen "Driz", b. Sep 6, 1924 DC, d. Sep 23, 1991, wife of Walter Bernard Abell, Sr., dau of late George Alexander Driscoll and Ellen Josephine Gardiner Hefferman.

DUCKETT, James Michael, b. Dec 12, 1965, d. Oct 29, 1988, hus of Kathy L. __, son of Dorothy and David Duckett.

DUDLEY, Danielle Renee, b. and d. Jul 5, 1990, dau of Robert 'Phillip' and Deborah Gibbs Dudley, gdau of Robert S. Jr. and Jeanne Dudley; Ann Gibbs.

DUFOUR, Ronald Andrew, b. Jan 22, 1959, d. Oct 20, 1990, hus of Lorraine S. __, son of Raymond Wilford and Doris May Engles Dufour.

DYSON, Aloin Cornelius, b. Feb 17, 1944, d. Sep 1, 1989, hus of Gladys Marie __, son of James Henry and Jeannette A. Lawrence Dyson.

DYSON, Howard I., b. Apr 14, 1943, d. Oct 9, 1992, hus of Thelma Marie Jones, son of William Howard and Mary Etta Hebb Dyson.

DYSON, James Henry, b. Aug 1, 1918, d. Apr 28, 1993, m. 12 Feb 1939 Jennette Agnes Lawrence, son of Frank and Bell Whalen Dyson.

EDMUNDSON, Mark Douglas, b. Feb 11, 1967 FL, d. May 3, 1991 Balto, son of Kenneth E. and Patricia Nalley Edmundson.

ENGLES, Doris Mae, b. Jun 15, 1925, d. May 13, 1992, wife of Raymond Wilford Dufour, dau of Sara Alice Morgul Posey and late Lester Engles.

FAASS, Esther Vera, b. Oct 12, 1928 DC, d. Mar 31, 1993, wife of Philip M. Long, dau of Carl Frederick and Elsie Bertha Dihlmann Faass.

FABEY, Robert Victor "Bob", b. June 7, 1947, d. Apr 12, 1992, hus of Beth Marlene Rueger, son of Joseph Paul and Martha Mazur Fabey.

FARMER, Matthew "Matt" David, b. Feb 4, 1959, d. Nov 23, 1990, hus of Carol __, son of Charles E. and Mary L. Knott Farmer.

FARMER, Timothy Webster, b. Dec 19, 1964, d. Jul 24, 1993 DC, m. 1993 Bettie Lou Harrell, son of Charles Everett and Mary Louise Knott Farmer.

FARRELL, Agnes Genevieve "Sis", d. Sep 3, 1987, m. 30 Sep 1944 James Albert Thompson.
FARRELL, Katherine Virginia Hall Greene, b. Jul 15, 1918, d. Feb 24, 1991, wife of John William Ellis, dau of Charles Edward and Annie Grace Harris Farrell.
FARRELL, Lee Andrew, b. Mar 18, 1910, d. Dec 21, 1989.
FARRELL, Susan Kathleen "Kitty", b. Jun 30, 1929, d. Sep 2, 1991, wife of Joseph Francis Abell, dau of Benjamin Thomas and Blanche Elizabeth Graves Farrell.
FAUNCE, Henry Sylvester, b. Jul 12, 1932, d. May 17, 1993, m. 1966 Myrtle Estelle Saunders, son of Frank Henry and Pearl Elizabeth Brown Faunce.
FENWICK, Genevieve Marie, b. Aug 11, 1914 OH, d. Dec 17, 1991, wife of James Henry Butler, Sr., dau of Jacob and Marie Slochazki Fenwick.
FENWICK, John Elmore "Big", b. Sep 13, 1913, d. Sep 15, 1991, hus of Margaret Jane Dent, son of James Thurman and Louise Niles Fenwick.
FENWICK, Reginold Anthony, b. Oct 12, 1964 DC, d. Feb 2, 1990, son of Catherine E. Thompson and James C. Fenwick.
FERGUSON, Annie Louise, 88, b. Jul 12, 1901, d. Apr 18, 1990, wife of Thomas G. Jones, dau of James and Rosey Wise Ferguson.
FONNER, Paul Quentin, d. Oct 31, 1957, hus of Violet Augusta Ella Lippert.
FORD, Carlton Allison "Stake", USA, b. Apr 29, 1925, d. Dec 4, 1991, son of Thomas Davis and Lottie Ellen Fox Ford.
FOWLER, John Francis, 89, b. Aug 9, 1899, d. May 5, 1988, son of Mary Lettie Barber.
FRAZIER, Terry W., b. Apr 6, 1940 LA, d. Jan 1, 1991, hus of Katherine ___, son of Paul G. and Bernice Frazier; gson of Mrs. C. M. Franklin.
FRYER, Francis McDurmid, d. May 2, 1992, m. 3 Apr 1933 Hazel Eugenia Wray.
FULKS, Mary Alice, b. Sep 1, 1936 OH, d. Dec 31, 1993, m. 7 Dec 1962 DC, Donald White,

dau of Clarence and Dorothy Bame Fulks.
GARDINER, Lawrence Adrian, Sr. b. Mar 7, 1947, d. May 1, 1992 DC, hus of Sharen Lea Potter, son of Adrian Posey, Jr. and Louise Fowler Parlett Gardiner.
GARNER, Donald Edward, Sr. b. Sep 19, 1912, d. Sep 7, 1988, hus of Emily "Bootsie" Naylor, son of Charles J. and Jennie Waugh Garner.
GASS, Barbara Eloise, b. Jul 2, 1927, d. Sep 4, 1988, m. Apr 1943 Joseph Aloysius Johnson, dau of Joseph Carroll and Ella Mae Cullins Gass.
GASS, Charles Francis "Frank", Sr, b. Oct 27, 1913, d. Jan 7, 1990, m. (1st) 4 Mar 1943 Laura Cecelia Joy, (2d) 1 Oct 1982 Della Christine Turlington, son of Joseph Carroll and Ella Mae Cullins Gass.
GASS, Joseph Herman, b. Sep 3, 1912, d. Feb 23, 1984, m. 10 Oct 1935 Myra Marguerite Meyers, son of Joseph Carroll and Ella Mae Cullins Gass.
GASS, William Cullins, b. Aug 20, 1911, d. Feb 9, 1992, hus of Mary Helen Herbert, son of Joseph Carroll and Ella Mae Cullins Gass.
GATTON, James Herman, b. Jan 23, 1926, d. Dec 25, 1989, hus of Annie Mae __, son of James H. and Elsie M. Gatton.
GATTON, Phillip D., d. Oct 27, 1986, hus of Francis Louise Sweeney.
GLASS, Adrian Joseph, b. Jul 18, 1919, d. Jul 5, 1988.
GODDARD, Candice Ann, b. and d. Jul 28, 1990, dau of Philip Jackson and Agnes Cecelia Guy Goddard; gdau of Clarence, Jr. and Alberta Goddard; Mr. and Mrs. Al Francis Guy.
GODDARD, J. Lloyd, b. Mar 2, 1922, d. Oct 19, 1989, hus of Mary Oliver, son of Stephen B. and Jane Pilkerton Goddard.
GOLDEN, Doris Evelyn, d. Nov 20, 1993, m. 1943 Ralph H. Guenther, Sr.
GOLDSBOROUGH, Elizabeth Gwinnette, 88, b. Oct 10, 1902, d. Sep 17, 1991, wife of John 'Lester' Wible, dau of Charles and Gwinnette Russell Goldsborough.
GOLDSBOROUGH, George Lancaster, 77, d. Nov 16,

1991, hus of Mary Margaret Burrick, son of James Thomas and Lucy Ann Farrell Goldsborough.
GORDON, Jasmine Terrell, b. Apr 4, 1986, d. Jul 31, 1992, son of Geraldine E. Snyder and Ronald E. Gordon, Sr,; gson of Sarah Blackistone and Herbert Snyder; Jeannette and George K. Gordon.
GORDON, Margart Belle "Margie", b. Jan 8, 1926 OH, d. Jul 31, 1992, wife of Louis Hodge Young, dau of William Watson and Ellen Belle Allen Gordon.
GOUGH, Merrill I., b. May 19, 1909, d. Sep 30, 1989, hus of Nellie Virginia __, son of Joseph I. and Roberta H. Gough.
GRAVES, James Bernard, Sr. b. Dec 8, 1909, d. Oct 17, 1991, hus of Rosalie Marie Klear, son of Albert Bernard and Mary Magdalen Jones Graves.
GRAVES, James Kenneth "Bubba", b. Aug 29, 1965, d. Nov 29, 1990, son of James R. W. and Alfretta E. Britton Graves.
GRAVES, Margaret Wilhelmina "Willie", b. May 21, 1945, d. Sep 2, 1991, wife of Francis Greenwell "Clinker" Wood, Sr., dau of Joseph Arthur and Frances Wathen Graves.
GRAY, Andrew Clarence, b. Feb 12, 1918, d. Feb 17, 1990, hus of Catherine Lola __, son of Andrew Jessie and Alice Catherine Gray.
GRAY, Henry Alphonso "Shorty", b. Feb 24, 1909, d. Jul 29, 1991, son of Andrew Jessie and Alice Catherine Gray.
GRAY, Julius "Paul", b. Jun 9, 1914, d. Oct 22, 1989, hus of Nancy E. __, son of Lucy Grey.
GRAY, Lena Magdeline, b. Feb 9, 1903, d. Oct 20, 1992 Balto, wife of George Shiflett, dau of William and Maggie Gatton Gray.
GREEN, Anthony Lydell, Jr. b. Jan 21, 1990, d. Feb 6, 1990, son of Anthony Lydell and Tracy Evette Baker Green.
GREEN, Joseph Aloysius "Joe", b. Oct 24, 1935, d. May 9, 1991, hus of Virginia Lee Talbot, son of Della Ann Berry and Hollsey Green.
GREENWELL, George Daniel, Sr. b. Jul 23, 1922, d. Dec 22, 1993, son of James Thomas and

Phoebe Elizabeth Harden Greenwell.
GREENWELL, Ignatius Valley "Nate", USA WWII, b. May 20, 1917, d. Aug 31, 1992, hus of Laura Mae Alshire, son of Valley Ignatius and Blanche Elizabeth Jones Greenwell.
GREGORY, John Richard, b. July 16, 1920 SC, d. Mar 9, 1991, hus of Pearl McKenzie, son of Marvin and Mary Davis Gregory.
GUY, Berchman Lewis "Bert", b. Jun 24, 1918 DC, d. Dec 26, 1991, hus of Eunice Marie Morris, son of William Alphonsus and Lillian Alice Latham Guy.
GUY, Henry Augustine "Sonny", b. Mar 13, 1930, d. Jan 12, 1990, hus of Cecelia A. __, son of Henry Jerome and Sarah Ann Bowles Guy.
GUY, John 'Ralph', b. Dec 22, 1916, d. Aug 15, 1991 Balto, son of James Francis and Florence G. Latham Guy.
GUY, Sara Catherine, b. Nov 18, 1924, d. May 23, 1990, wife of Emory M. "Buddy" Garrett, dau of William A. "Fonnie" and Lillian Allice Latham Guy.
HALL, Felix Leftwich, b. Dec 9, 1914 VA, d. Dec 10, 1993, hus of Mary Virginia Somerville, son of Joel and Annie Mason Hall.
HALLMARK, Albert Sidney, 97, b. Jan 10, 1891, d. Aug 23, 1988, hus of Lala Carroll.
HAMLET, James Horace, Jr. b. Mar 5, 1927, d. Mar 28, 1988, son of James Horace and Etta Dala Hamlet.
HAMMER, Cora Hazel, b. Feb 6, 1907 ID, d. Oct 29, 1992, m. (1st) Ward Keasts Willoughby, (2d) Claude Russell, dau of Michael and Anna Taysom Hammer.
HAMMETT, Alice Magdalin, b. Jan 7, 1923, d. Oct 21, 1990 DC, m. 9 Jul 1942 Hayden Thomas Alvey, dau of Alfred O. and Mary Therese Wilkerson Hammett.
HANSEN, Christian Funch, b. Nov 14, 1937, Denmark, d. Jan 5, 1992 Balto, son of Mogens and Niels Funch Hansen.
HARPER, Marion O., b. Mar 16, 1936, d. Jun 6, 1988, hus of Helen Gordon, son of Mr. and Mrs. Norman Richardson.
HARRIS, Edward Keith, b. Aug 17, 1964, d. Jul

12, 1988, son of Edward Thomas and Mary Loretta Harris; gson of Rebecca Key.
HARRIS, Edward Thomas, b. Jun 13, 1920, d. Aug 3, 1990, hus of Mary Loretta __, son of Thomas Edward and Katherine Garner Harris.
HARTNETT, Jerome Francis, Jr. b. May 4, 1913, d. Jul 3, 1989, hus of Mary Lillian __, son of Jerome Francis and Eulah Orem Hartnett.
HASSHAW, Jessie Turner, 95, b. Jan 20, 1893, d. Jun 19, 1988.
HAWKINS, John William, b. Oct 11, 1904, d. Nov 5, 1989, son of George and Mary Elizabeth Young Hawkins.
HAYDEN, John Henry, 94, d. Dec 1, 1991, hus of Mary Dorothy Nolan, son of Joshua and Mary Hopkins Hayden.
HAYDEN, Joseph Donald, Sr. b. Oct 19, 1910, d. Apr 28, 1992, hus of Catherine Rosalie Knott, son of Allen and Catherine Johnson Hayden.
HEBB, John Steven, b. Jul 5, 1919, d. Oct 11, 1991, hus of Catherine Eliza Curtis, son of Francis Dominic and Madeline Hebb.
HEBB, Joseph Aloysius, b. May 17, 1950, d. Mar 14, 1990, son of Charles Ignatius and Florence Louise Barber Hebb.
HEBB, William Joseph, b. Jul 9, 1959, d. May 2, 1992, son of Francis and Shirley Nelson Hebb.
HERBERT, Agnes Florine, b. Mar 26, 1946, d. Jul 14, 1991, dau of Josephine Young, stepdau of Joseph H. Young.
HERBERT, Mary Helen, b. Jul 6, 1912, d. Nov 29, 1991, wife of William Cullins Gass, dau of Francis and Blanche R. Mattingly Herbert.
HEWITT, Zackery "Zack" Wilson, infant, d. Jun 14, 1992, son of Carl Wayne and Robin Lynn Rice Hewitt; gson of Cleon W. and Nancy H. Rice; John Stanley, Sr. and Shirley Marie Hewitt.
HIGGS, James Spencer, Sr. b. Oct 23, 1934, d. Dec 3, 1989, hus of Agnes Frances Abell, son of James Spencer and Helen Victoria Combs Higgs.
HILL, Joseph Andrew, Jr. b. Dec 26, 1949, d. Jan 8, 1989, son of Joseph Andrew and Anna

Leitha Hill.
HILL, Kevin Lenwood, b. Nov 24, 1992, d. Nov 29, 1992 DC, son of Charise Hill and Kevin Lenwood Genus, Sr; gson of James and Alena Marie Hill.
HILL, Louis Wilmer "Lee", Jr. b. Jan 23, 1948, d. Mar 7, 1990, hus of Margaret Marie Dornall, son of Louis W. and Helen E. Hill.
HILL, Louis Wilmer III, b. Aug 28, 1968 Balto, d. Apr 24, 1991, son of Louis Wilmer, Jr. and Margaret Marie Dornall Hill; gson of Louis W and Helen E Hill; Charles and Mary Madeline Abell Dornall.
HOFFMAN, Herman Earl, Jr. b. Jul 5, 1963, d. Jun 9, 1988, son of Margaret D. Curry and Richard Curry.
HOLT, Joseph Dallam, b. Oct 2, 1902, d. Aug 19, 1989, hus of Mary A. __, son of Clarence and Mamie Thomas Holt.
HOLT, Mary Alberta, b. Dec 1, 1898, d. May 13, 1993, m. 1915 William Leo Price, dau of Endress and Mary Neale Holt.
HOLTON, Edward LeVern, Sr. b. Jun 9, 1942, d. Oct 19, 1991, hus of Barbara Ann Braxton, son of Edward Jerome and Elsie Irene Woodland Holton.
HOLTON, James Edward, Sr. b. Sep 16, 1902, d. May 22, 1988, hus of Mary Agnes __, son of John Francis and Ada Holton.
HOLTON, Samuel Aaron, b. Sep 7, 1975, d. Oct 19, 1991, son of Edward LeVern and Barbara Ann Braxton Holton; gson of Louis and Chara Braxton.
HOOD, Raymond Leo, Jr. b. Sep 23, 1956 PA, d. May 31, 1988, son of Raymond Leo and Jeanne Hood.
HOOPER, Elva Mollie, b. Aug 23, 1915 DC, d. Aug 13, 1988, wife of James E. Hooper, Sr., dau of Richard A. and Leona G. Riley Hooper.
HOWE, Paul Thomas "Mickey", b. Aug 4, 1950, d. Nov 16, 1993, son of John Sheldon, Sr. and Mary Evelyn Owens Howe.
HOWELL, John Wesley, Sr. b. Aug 11, 1915 VA, d. Sep 17, 1991, hus of Freida Mae __, son of Simon Peter and Lillie Eileen Phillips

Howell.
HUGHES, William Harold, b. Apr 19, 1957, d. Jul 11, 1987, son of Harold W. and Wilma A. Hughes.
HUNT, Thomas Morris Gene "Tom", b. Apr 14, 1932 CA, d. Aug 28, 1992, hus of Shirley Kathleen Klear, son of Walter William and Blanche McKeen Hunt.
HUNTINGTON, Joseph Henry, d. Jun 13, 1985, hus of Lucy Rebecca McGuigan.
JACKSON, Marjorie Ann "Margy", b. Dec 10, 1933 VA, d. Apr 16, 1991, wife of Francis Ira "Jake" Yates, dau of George R. and Frances H. Jackson.
JACKSON, Mildred Regina "Millie", b. Sep 20, 1925 DC, d. Apr 26, 1992, wife of Herbert Sylvester Seek, dau of Frank Ray and Carlotta Lecita Bieber Jackson.
JACOBS, John Wesley "Snake", b. Mar 21, 1929, d. Aug 25, 1991, hus of Mary Theresa Medley, son of Bernard A. and Juanita Hebron Garner Jacobs.
JAYNES, Margaret, b. Nov 4, 1923 TX, d. Oct 7, 1989, wife of Rodney Lee Yoder, dau of Bob and Margaret Sherwood Jaynes.
JENKINS, Anna Mae, b. Mar 27, 1928, d. Mar 30, 1988, wife of __ Carey, dau of James M. and Mary M. Jenkins.
JETER, David James, b. Jan 19, 1977, d. May 11, 1991, son of Harry James Jeter and Debra Lynn Mattingly Jeter Kane; gson of James L. Sr. and Hazel Beatrice Mattingly.
JOHNSON, Edwin Parren, Sr. b. Jul 7, 1901, d. Sep 2, 1989, hus of Florine Agnes Raley, son of George Parren and Charlotte Anne "Lottie" Tennyson Johnson.
JOHNSON, Ernest Hilary, b. Nov 20, 1913, d. May 6, 1993 DC, m. 6 Jan 1944 Mary Elizabeth Milburn, son of James Ernest and Mary Rosalie Cooper Johnson.
JOHNSON, Francis 'Charles', b. Jul 23, 1924, d. Feb 3, 1979, m. 1949 Grace Helen "Sally" Joy, son of Thomas Alvin and Pauline E. Abell Johnson.
JOHNSON, Herbert, d. 1972, hus of Ruth Frances

Lawrence.
JOHNSON, James Alvin, b. 1917, d. Sep 2, 1987, hus of Anna Mae Unkle, son of Thomas Alvin and Pauline E. Abell Johnson.
JOHNSON, James Maurice, b. Feb 4, 1916, d. Jan 30, 1985, hus of Margaret M. Graves, son of James Claude and Martha Russell Johnson.
JOHNSON, Mary 'Elsie', b. Jul 28, 1927, d. Dec 17, 1990, wife of William Howard Toye, dau of Edward Layton and Charlotte A. McPherson Johnson.
JOHNSON, Thomas Alvin, Sr. b. Jul 22, 1895, d. Sep 28, 1988, hus of Pauline Elizabeth Abell, son of Peter H. and Flora Love Johnson.
JONES, Ann Marie, b. Nov 2, 1966, d. Apr 7, 1989, dau of Sherman and Eileen Jones.
JONES, James Andrew, b. Oct 27, 1913 NC, d. Apr 27, 1988, son of George A. Jones.
JONES, James C. "J.J.", Jr., b. Oct 5, 1986, d. Feb 10, 1991, son of James C. and Joyce Breckenridge Jones.
JONES, John Woodley "Bubby", b. Feb 18, 1932, d. Nov 27, 1993, m. 18 Feb 1966 Patricia June Ryan, son of John Hilary and Mazie Elizabeth Pilkerton Jones.
JOY, George Edgar "Jenks", b. Apr 5, 1903, d. Aug 30, 1991 Balto, hus of Anna Wathen, son of George A. and Mary Lillian Love Joy.
JOY, Marion Calvin, Sr. b. Aug 30, 1927, d. Jun 9, 1992, hus of Ada Marie Sheppard, son of Ernest McClellan and Mary Lena Gatton Joy.
JOY, Timothy Paul, b. Dec 1, 1983, d. Dec 18, 1991, son of Robert Lee and Joan Dale Williams Joy; gson of Charles and Betty Joy; John G. and Delores A. Williams.
KANNARKAT, Prestina Pappachan Koithara, b. Oct 3, 1911 India, d. Sep 16, 1993, wife of Pappachan Joseph Kannarkat, dau of Varappan Lonappan Chalissery and Mariam Bramakulam.
KEATING, John Martin, b. Jan 12, 1936 NY, d. Mar 26, 1993, m. 1957 Barbara __, son of Thomas and Mary Fitzpatrick Keating.
KENADY, Stephen, b. Mar 24, 1914 NC, d. Apr

11, 1988, hus of Margaret __, son of Matthew and Hollon Ann Cox Kenady.
KEY, Rebecca Mary, b. Oct 13, 1900, d. Apr 2, 1990, wife of James Eugene Holt, dau of Abraham and Rebecca Miller Key.
KIDD, Theodore Wilson "Cisco", b. Oct 24, 1915 VA, d. Feb 28, 1993, m. 7 Oct 1943 VA Dorothy Vernon Sandidge, son of Milton and Phoebe Campbell Kidd.
KINDER, Curtis Lee, b. Jul 26, 1936 WV, d. Apr 14, 1992, hus of Nancy Rose Russell, son of William Bradley and Grace Sutton Kinder.
KLEGIN, August Fred, b. Aug 19, 1909 MN, d. Jul 27, 1990, son of Ernest and Emma Kahl Klegin.
KNIGHT, Catherine Councell, b. Mar 25, 1928, d. Jun 23, 1992, wife of James Lee Van Devanter, dau of Harold and Janet Agnes Duke Knight.
KNOPE, Edgar C., b. Mar 29, 1901 PA, d. Aug 28, 1990, hus of Margaret A. __.
KNOTT, Dorothy Lee, b. Nov 23, 1934, d. Jun 27 1988, wife of Roy Anthony Bowles, Sr., dau of Ambrose and Ada Goldsborough Knott.
KNOTT, Joseph Louis "Joe", Sr., b. Dec 20, 1928, d. May 10, 1991, hus of Maude E. Tippett, son of Joseph 'Ambrose' and Ada Goldsborough Knott.
KNOTT, William Ernest, Jr., b. Jan 16, 1925, d. Mar 6, 1992 DC, hus of Mary Frances __, son of William and Amanda Knott.
KOSTKOWSKI, Julianna Marie, b. Nov 30, 1943, d. Aug 22, 1993, wife of Douglas Darrell Green, dau of Robert Boleslaw and Julianna Hoppa Kostkowski.
KUEHN, Charles Stephen "Cha", Sr. b. Jun 20, 1925 Balto, d. Sep 29, 1992, hus of Eliette Christina Rossi, son of Ferdinand, Sr. and Johanna Weber Kuehn.
KUHSE, Allen Frederick, b. Jun 9, 1942 IA, d. Jul 12, 1988, hus of Ann __, son of Lorenz R. and Ivanelle Kuhse; gson of Amand Becker.
LACEY, Eleanor Catherine, b. Apr 26, 1925, d. Dec 2, 1988, wife of James Lloyd Russell, Sr., dau of George Albert and Ann Gertrude

Lacey.
LAKE, Kenneth Allen, b. Dec 20, 1975 DC, d. Apr 28, 1990, son of Keith A. and Sandra L. Lake.
LANGSTER, Mary Madlyn, b. Nov 9, 1905, d. Feb 2, 1989, wife of Alfred Lindsey, dau of William and Liza Langster.
LAWRENCE, Charles Bernard "Buck", b. Jun 13, 1935, d. Mar 6, 1993, hus of Doris Cecelia Bowles, son of Francis McQue, Sr. and Anna Mae Nelson Lawrence.
LAWRENCE, Francis Desales "Capt. Frank", b. Jan 18, 1911, d. Mar 13, 1993, m. 2 Jul 1934 Mary Elizabeth Bailey, son of Joseph Francis and Grace Genevieve Thompson Lawrence.
LAWRENCE, Jeannette Agnes, b. Jun 16, 1918, d. Nov 28, 1992, m. 12 Feb 1939 James H. Dyson, dau of Walter and Charity Mason Lawrence.
LAWRENCE, Ruth Frances, b. Mar 1, 1919, d. Apr 24, 1993, m. in DC Herbert Johnson, dau of Frank and Grace Thompson Lawrence.
LAZURE, Herman Arnold, USN, b. Sep 3, 1941 WV, d. Jun 27, 1991, hus of Phyllis Carter, son of Herman Otha and Belva Grooms Lazure.
LEE, Virginia, d. Feb 20, 1989, m. 12 May 1956 Joseph Aloysis Green.
LEVIN, Max, USA WWII, b. Jun 9, 1925 Balto, d. Aug 31, 1992, hus of Sharyn Marie Clark, son of Abraham and Sadie Bass Levin.
LEWIS, Mary Elizabeth, b. Apr 7, 1957 MI, d. Jan 25, 1993, m. 3 Jul 1982 Douglas Adrian Ennels, Sr., dau of Betty Sells and Alton Lewis, Sr.
LIPPERT, Violet Augusta Ella, b. Dec 8, 1910 PA, d. Feb 27, 1993, m. 17 Jul 1934 Paul Quentin Fonner, dau of Charles and Ella Degenkolb Lippert.
LITTEN, Kelly Carson, Sr., d. Dec 29, 1985, hus of Anna Laura Gibson.
LIVINGSTON, Ecessen Quinece, b. and d. Sep 18, 1988, dau of John Davis and Mitchell Denise Livingston.
LOE, Julie Marie, 29, b. Oct 27, 1961, d. Jan 24, 1991, wife of Dennis J. Bahl, dau of Roxanne Matson and Norman Loe.

LOGAN, Jesse Osborn, b. May 25, 1911 DE, d. Jan 12, 1993 DC, m. 4 Oct 1984 Barbara Ellen Stone, son of Harry and Nellie Stoddard Logan.
LONG, Ann Eleanor, 66, d. Dec 22, 1992 DC.
LONG, Elsie Jane, b. Mar 12, 1911, d. Jun 3, 1993, m. 18 Aug 1929 Robert Garrett Russell, dau of Charles Philip and Emma Elizabeth Wise Long.
LONG, Francis Johnson "Bussy", Cpl USA WWII, b. Jul 18, 1922, d. Feb 17, 1978, hus of Pearl H. ___.
LONG, Joseph Albert "Junior" III, b. June 1, 1927, d. May 20, 1988, hus of Mary Susan ___.
LONG, Mary Ann Eleanor, 57, b. Dec 2, 1931, d. Jun 22, 1989, wife of Harold Parker Fowler, dau of Joseph Horace and Josephine Mae Knott Long.
LOVING, Shana Marie, b. and d. Apr 12, 1993, dau of Gerald Weldner Loving and Mary Virginia Graff; gdau of late Harold R. Jr. and Wyona Loving; Geo and Christine Graff; ggdau of Wm. Barrett of VA and May Barrett; Frederick D. Bennett of GA and June L. Brotherton.
LUFFEY, Ethan Michael, infant, d. May 16, 1991, son of Michael Dean and Linda Kathleen Langley Luffey; gson of Charles and Lois Luffey; Charles and Betty Langley.
LUSBY, Alice L., b. Sep 27, 1907 DC, d. Feb 12, 1992, wife of Pinkney A. Earnshaw, dau of Barry W. and Edith Bean Lusby.
LYON, Nathan Alexander, b. Jun 7, 1931, d. Feb 17, 1993, m. 17 Jul 1953 Anna Myrtle Johnson, son of John Franklin and Jennie Oliver Lyon.
MACK, Gladys Marie, b. Apr 11, 1930, d. Nov 9, 1990, wife of Leonard John Walch, dau of Lawrence and Gladys Tydings Mack.
MAGELSSON, Robert Eugene "Bob", b. May 13, 1927 MO, d. Apr 17, 1991, hus of Grayce L. Fritz, son of Peter Christian and Matilda Mae Magelsson.
MAHORNEY, Joseph Bernard, b. Nov 7, 1932 Balto, d. Aug 30, 1988, hus of Ruby I. ___, son of James M. and Alma B. Mahorney.
MALASPINA, Leon Antonio, b. Nov 4, 1922 DC, d.

Mar 31, 1990, hus of Norma Pauline Mills, son of Salvatore and Helen Malaspina.
MANIGAULT, Michael Kyle, infant, d. Feb 26, 1993, son of Linda Sherell Manigault and Kenneth B. Robinson; gson of Regina Moore, Cleveland Moore; Gloria Robinson.
MARINI, Marino, b. Jan 20, 1911, Italy, d. Apr 23, 1990, hus of Marian L. __, son of Batista and Catarina Succhi Marini.
MARSHALL, Anna Elizabeth "Boogie", b. Aug 19, 1940, d. Mar 16, 1992, dau of Elizabeth E. Curtis and William Xavier Marshall.
MASKEE, Edmund Theodore, USM WWII, b. Nov 27, 1912 PA, d. May 5, 1992, m. 1933 Buffalo, NY Pearl __, son of Theodore and Julie Mazuchowski.
MASON, Jeremiah Aloysius, Jr. b. Mar 19, 1939, d. Dec 14, 1991, hus of Mamie LaVerne Lyles, son of Jeremiah A. and Florence Hebb Mason.
MATTINGLY, Agnes 'Naomi', b. Nov 2, 1912, d. Feb 15, 1992, dau of Bernard Eugene and Cliffie Mae Cryer Mattingly.
MATTINGLY, Aloysius, b. Jan 23, 1922, d. Jan 16, 1991, hus of Mary Adele __, stepson of John B. Abell.
MATTINGLY, Andrew Louis "Pee Wee", Jr. b. Apr 29, 1939, d. Apr 16, 1993, m. 6 Jun 1964 Carole Lee Anderson, son of Andrew L. and Mildred Magdaline Hayden Mattingly.
MATTINGLY, Charles Frederick, 17, d. Dec 23, 1968.
MATTINGLY, Daniel Joseph "Dan", b. Apr 24, 1910, d. Jun 8, 1991, hus of Josephine Herbert, son of Robert Allen, Sr. and Estelle Bailey Mattingly.
MATTINGLY, George F., b. Aug 18, 1926, d. Jul 16, 1993 KY, hus of Mary Krupinsky, son of James and Clara Mae Wallace Mattingly.
MATTINGLY, Ida, b. Mar 7, 1916, d. Mar 16, 1990, wife of Lt. Leo Emmett Turley, dau of Clarence and Sarah Blanche Mattingly.
MATTINGLY, J. Louis, Sr., b. ca 1910, d. Jan 15, 1976, m. 20 Jan 1935 Margaret Mary Mattingly.
MATTINGLY, James Latham, Sr. b. Feb 8, 1925,

d. May 26, 1993, hus of Hazel Beatrice Toute, son of William Henry and Mazie Ann Latham Mattingly.
MATTINGLY, James Stanton, d. Dec 24, 1992, hus of Laura Evelyn Yates.
MATTINGLY, James Virgil "Booker", Sr., b. Sep 5, 1912, d. Jul 6, 1992, hus of Fayrene Hallmark, son of Andrew Johnson and Nettie Eulia Wise Mattingly.
MATTINGLY, Margaret Mary, b. May 9, 1915, d. Mar 30, 1993, wife of J. Louis Mattingly, Sr., dau of Bernard Eugene and Cliffie Mae Cryer Mattingly.
MATTINGLY, Mary E., b. Sep 9, 1915, d. Mar 22, 1991, wife of __ Tague, dau of Adrian Thomas and Mary Aline Gibbons Mattingly.
MATTINGLY, Robert Paul, b. Jun 19, 1910, d. Jan 9, 1991, hus of Marguerite Attaway Thompson, son of William Urah Bishop and Noema Clara Hayden Mattingly.
MATTINGLY, Taylor Brooke, b. and d. Jan 4, 1992, dau of Thomas Aloysius and Susan Lynn McKay Mattingly.
MATTINGLY, W. Clarke, b. Nov 9, 1919, d. Dec 11, 1987.
MAYOR, Robert Earl "Bob", b. Mar 31, 1939, d. Jul 23, 1993 DC, hus of Elaine Wofford, son of Joseph L. Sr. and Myrtle Ridgell Mayor.
McCABE, William Marcus "Mac", b. Aug 15, 1918 OH, d. Jun 24, 1992, hus of Mary Roberta Rice, son of Joseph Alexander and Mabel Margaret Conroy McCabe.
McGUIGAN, Lucy Rebecca, b. Mar 4, 1917, d. Oct 1, 1992, wife of Joseph Henry Huntington, dau of Michael F. and Susan Rebecca Adams McGuigan.
McWILLIAMS, Nelson LeRoy, b. Oct 7, 1911, d. Sep 17, 1988, hus of Mabel Payne, son of Edward L. and Hanna M. McWilliams.
MEADE, George Willard, b. Jul 26, 1912 VA, d. Sep 30, 1991, hus of Lillian Sylvania Carter, son of Clark and Nannie Sayler Meade.
MEREDITH, Raymond Reith, b. Mar 15, 1910 VA, d. Apr 24, 1993, m. 19 Jul 1952 Gerdie Beatrice Thomas, son of Isaac and Mary Meredith.

MIEDZINSKI, William Benedict "Billy", b. Jul 26, 1941, d. Jan 16, 1992, hus of Agnes Delores Insley, son of Robert and Mary Lillian Hayden Miedzinski.
MILES, John Paul, Sr. b. Mar 10, 1917, d. Mar 27, 1989, hus of Elizabeth Rosetta Holt, son of Louis Benedict and Laura Elizabeth Yorkshire Miles.
MILES, Lawrence Eugene, Sr. b. Aug 25, 1950, d. Oct 5, 1991, son of John Paul, Sr. and Elizabeth Rosetta Holt Miles.
MILLER, Charles William, b. Jan 5, 1930 PA, d. Jul 3, 1991, hus of Joan Schiller, son of late Charles Alexander Miller and Dorothea Eaton Meck.
MILLS, Norma Pauline, b. May 28, 1923, d. Aug 28, 1991, wife of Leon Antonio Malaspina, dau of Nathan T. and Ella Reed Mills.
MILSTEAD, Joseph Whittier, b. Apr 21, 1912, d. Jan 23, 1991, hus of Mary D. __, son of Elizzie Mae and Josephus Milstead.
MITCHELL, Barbara, b. Nov 24, 1930 NC, d. May 15, 1988, wife of Victor O. Baird, dau of Joseph W. and Edith Pichard Mitchell.
MOLDEN, Thomas Rodney, 96, b. May 2, 1892, d. Feb 3, 1989, hus of Mary L. __, son of Nathan and Sarah Molden.
MOORE, Robert Lee "Bobby", Sr. b. Feb 3, 1945, d. June 9, 1992, hus of Sandra Louise Capps, son of Charles Hedges Moore, Sr, and Delores Elizabeth Knott Goodwin; gson of Ruth E. Knott.
MORGAN, Charles Henry, 76, b. 1911/12, d. Apr 7, 1988, son of Stephen and Thurrella Burch Morgan.
MORGAN, DeVante Tavelle, b. Nov 3, 1991, d. Jan 29, 1992, son of Scott Trevor and Jennifer Louise Barnes Morgan; gson of Joseph and Gloria Morgan; Brenda Barnes.
MORGAN, James Carroll, b. Apr 16, 1923, d. Aug 29, 1992, hus of Ruby Pegg, son of William and Carrie Thompson Morgan.
MORGAN, James Lester, Jr. b. Jul 4, 1960, d. Jan 24, 1992, son of James Louell Morgan, Sr, and Dorothy Elizabeth Wilson Barnes.

MORGAN, John Mitchell, Sr, b. Jun 6, 1915, d. Nov 18, 1993, m. 6 Mar 1935 Elizabeth Victoria Quade, son of Stephen S. and Thurella Burch Morgan.
MORRIS, Charles Leroy, Sr. b. Dec 18, 1936, d. Nov 17, 1989, hus of Shirley Ann __, son of Charles S. "Buster" and Ruth Alma Morris.
MORRIS, Joseph Earl "Popeye", b. Apr 9, 1911, d. Oct 19, 1988, son of Foster and Eva Morris.
MURPHY, Bette Romaine, b. Jan 10, 1921 NY, d. Aug 30, 1989, wife of __ Rudigier, dau of Avery Lue and Bessie Magner Murphy.
NALLEY, Fred Earl, Jr., b. Jun 3, 1919 DC, d. Jun 24, 1992, son of Fred and Inez Rowze Nalley.
NELSON, James Carter "J.C.", b. Jan 12, 1956, d. Aug 9, 1991 DC, son of William Albert and Virginia Hall Nelson.
NELSON, Joseph Elmer, Sr. b. May 1, 1915, d. Mar 5, 1991, hus of Mary Lucy Brown, son of Francis Benton and Catherine Elizabeth Tennyson Nelson.
NEWELL, Kathryn Eve, b. Jun 18, 1981, d. Mar 28, 1990, dau of Keith and Helen Newell.
NEWKIRK, Jacobi Manilito, b. Feb 4, 1972, d. Jun 23, 1991, son of Stuart and Deborah Brooks Newkirk.
NEWTON, Franklin Theodore, d. Jan 10, 1974, hus of Goldie Elouise Tasker.
NOLAN, Mary Dorothy, d. Jun 22, 1981, m. 4 Jan 1920 John Henry Hayden.
NORRIS, Charles Kennedy "Bap", b. Aug 11, 1915, d. Jun 5, 1993, son of Joseph Wellington and Lucy Pauline Thompson Norris.
OLIVER, Mary, b. Aug 2, 1923, d. Dec 25, 1989, wife of J. Lloyd Goddard, dau of Edward I. and Sally Lynn Oliver.
OLSON, Axil Hjalmar, b. Dec 23, 1906 CT, d. Oct 14, 1993, m. 1969 Balto, Ann Hopson, son of John and Anna Hansen Olson.
OTT, Bertha W. L., b. Apr 19, 1917 SD, d. Nov 11, 1992 IL, wife of Sollie Heinz, dau of Adolph Ott.
OWEN, Mary Virginia "Sis", b. Nov 2, 1935 DC,

d. Oct 1, 1991, wife of John Manley Owen, dau of late Cecil Wilbur Owen and Mary Martha Dodd Owen White.
OWENS, Lakia Donisha, b. Feb 16, 1988, d. Oct 28, 1988, dau of Yvette Thompson and Bruce Owens.
OWENS, Theresa Valerie, b. Jul 3, 1932, d. Jan 11, 1993, m. 30 Dec 1965 Marion, SC, Gaylord O. Stalker, Sr., dau of Richard Benj. and Mary Alberta Pilkerton Owens.
PAINTER, Jarverise "Jerry" Elizabeth, b. Aug 14, 1909, d. Jun 17, 1988, wife of Charles Frederick "Fred" Painter.
PARHAM, Lewis Wiley, b. Apr 25, 1956, d. Jan 23, 1990, son of Carroll W. Parham and Nina Carter Parham Graves, stepson of Joseph B. Graves, Sr.
PARKER, Louis Henry, b. Jul 28, 1917, d. Oct 8, 1989, hus of Alice Cecelia __, son of John J. and Mary 'Elizabeth' Shelton Parker.
PARKER, Samuel Leonard, b. Jan 5, 1924, d. Jun 26, 1988, son of John Joseph and Mary 'Elizabeth' Shelton Parker.
PARTIN, Amelia Gertrude, b. Jan 11, 1946 Balto, d. Jun 13, 1993, m. 16 Mar 1981 Rev. John C. Hilbert, dau of Joseph Milton and Margaret Rudroff Partin.
PASSMORE, Vance Jackson "Jackie", b. Nov 24, 1959 TN, d. Jun 16, 1993, m. 26 May 1979 Cynthia Theresa Oliver, son of Vance Woodrow and Annie Jane Brooks Passmore.
PAYNE, Helen Victoria, b. Feb 13, 1913, d. Mar 4, 1991, m. (1st) James Spencer Higgs, (2d) Jimmy Cox Combs, dau of John Abell and Ann Victoria Quade Payne.
PAYNE, Mabel, b. Jan 4, 1910 VA, d. Jun 13, 1989, wife of Nelson LeRoy McWilliams, dau of Oliver and Marie Young Payne.
PAYNE, Michelle Denise, b. Sep 23, 1968, d. Aug 21, 1982, dau of Francis X. and Loretta Cox Payne; gdau of Vernon H. and Thelma Cox; George and Grace Johnson Payne.
PEACOCK, Anna Mae, b. Apr 2, 1903, d. Mar 30, 1989, dau of James Harry and Daisy Mary Longmore Peacock.

PENNISI, Charles Carmen "Pennie", b. Jul 18, 1921 NY, d. Jul 20, 1991, hus of Priscilla Ann "Boots" Davis, son of Mariano and Carmella Pennisi.
PHILIPPY, Thelma Elizabeth, b. May 10, 1908 Balto, d. Feb 14, 1992, Honolulu, wife of George Washington Morgan, dau of John and Fannie Tase Philippy.
PIERAS, Dago Antonio, M.D., b. Jun 9, 1917, Cuba, d. Oct 9, 1991, hus of Juana E. __, son of Antonio and Modesta Barbas Pieras.
PILKERTON, William Joseph "Willie", b. May 31, 1919, d. Feb 12, 1993, m. 23 Mar 1940 Agnes Rosalee __, son of Harry Arthur and Rena Paulene Owens Pilkerton.
PLATER, Spencer Edward "Peanuts", Jr. b. Dec 20, 1961, d. Aug 24, 1989, son of Spencer Edward and Margaret E. Plater.
PLOWDEN, Lawrence Eugene, b. Mar 22, 1914, d. Apr 8, 1989, hus of Agnes Melissa __, son of Charlie and Eva Reddin Plowden.
POORMAN, John Clarence, b. Sep 6, 1912, d. Jul 20, 1989, hus of Ruth B. __, son of Simian and May Rich Poorman.
PORRETTI, Samantha Marie, b. Feb 12, 1990, d. Feb 18, 1990, dau of Douglas V. and Helen L. Porretti; gdau of Alton and Mary Cartwright; Francis and Dorothy Shay; Louis Porretti; ggdau of Warren and Helen Kidwell; Dorothy Price.
POSEY, Thurman Wilson, USN, b. Sep 1, 1925, d. Nov 14, 1992, m. 18 May 1962 Edith McGhee, son of Thomas and Susie Bowie Posey.
POWELL, Donetta Crickett, 37, d. Sep 13, 1993 CA, dau of Patty Lee Dean of Laurel, Md. and Claude Powell of Dameron, Md; gdau of Eva Burnside of Dry Creek, WV; Vivian Powell of NC.
PRICE, George Francis, b. Jul 6, 1912, d. Dec 26, 1989, hus of Mary Agnes __, son of John Henry and Florine Anna Price.
PRYOR, Charlotte Ann, b. Jun 26, 1942, d. Jan 9, 1993, m. 9 Mar 1963 Salisbury, MD Richard Floyd Jones, dau of William Thomas Pryor and Margaret Hilda Welch Lynch.

QUADE, Ann Eleanor, b. Jun 16, 1926, d. Dec 22, 1992 DC, m. 1954 Samuel J. Long, dau of Joseph Lansdale and Annie Gertrude Williams Quade.
QUADE, Bobby Lee, b. Mar 10, 1993, d. Mar 21, 1993, son of Robert Lewis Quade, Jr, and Brenda Lee Hill Strippey; gson of Robt. L. Quade and Rose Ruby Ferris; Lewis Roger, Sr. and Patricia Hill; ggson of Rhodie and Louise Quade; Lewis L. and Elizabeth Hill.
QUADE, Charles Russell, Sr. d. Nov 1, 1987, hus of Gladys Marie Abell.
RALEY, Florine Agnes, b. Jan 13, 1902, d. Aug 28, 1987, wife of Edwin Parren Johnson, Sr., dau of Joseph A. and Anna Florence Guy Raley.
RAVAGO, Michael Anthony, b. Jan 13, 1962 DC, d. Jun 9, 1992 FL, son and stepson of Monika Elizabeth Weart Kopel and Carl Kopel; Arando and Kathleen Ravago; gson of Dita Katterla of Berlin, Germany.
REDMOND, Agnes Violet, b. Nov 30, 1900, d. Dec 31, 1991, wife of Theodore Herbert Russell, dau of Joseph and Lucy Pilkerton Redmond.
REED, Christopher Lamont, Sr. b. Jun 7, 1973, d. Dec 16, 1992, son of Francis LaVerne and Anna Gertrude Brown Reed; gson of Mary Elizabeth Reed; Anna G. Brown.
REED, Francis Octavius, b. Jun 28, 1909, d. Sep 21, 1990, hus of Mary Elizabeth __, son of Andrew Spitaler and Mary Ella Reed.
REED, James Wheatley, 36, d. Feb 16, 1989, son of Carroll E. and Lillian Lucille Butler Reed.
REID, Annie Elizabeth, b. Aug 7, 1944 DC, d. Aug 28, 1990, dau of Joseph P. and Henrietta C. Countess
REINTZELL, James Columbus, Sr., d. Jan 25, 1969, hus of Mary Madeline Bridgett.
RICE, Francis Noble, b. May 31, 1922, d. Dec 7, 1990, hus of Louise G. __, son of Charles Noble and Ethel Beatrice Chesser Rice.
ROBERTS, George Walter, b. Oct 7, 1925 DC, d. Feb 26, 1991, m. 18 May 1946 Theresa Hayden, son of Flourney C. and Elsie Mattingly

Roberts.
ROBERTS, Mary Patricia "Patsy", b. Apr 25, 1936, d. Jan 20, 1992, dau of late Albert Brooks and Sarah Elizabeth Milburn Somerville.
ROBINSON, Randolph John, b. May 9, 1937, d. Jan 28, 1990, hus of Gloria Thomas, son of Ella Robinson and Roland Briscoe.
ROESSLER, Ethel Gertrude, b. Apr 27, 1906 NY, d. May 6, 1992, wife of Norman Frederick Textor, dau of Adolph and Louise Meyers Roessler.
ROGERS, Burress Franklin, Sr. b. Jan 5, 1909 NC, d. Oct 2, 1992, m. 1948 Dillon, SC Leila __, son of Ernest Preston and Marie Rogers.
ROGERS, Reba Anita, b. Jul 9, 1933, d. Jul 25, 1988, wife of Evan Leo Perisho, dau of Willie M. and Sibyl A. Rogers.
RUSSELL, Betty Lou, b. Dec 18, 1938, d. Jan 16, 1993 DC, m. 12 Apr 1958 J. Franklin Harris, dau of Philip and Mary Virginia Downs Russell.
RUSSELL, Claude, d. 1987, 2d hus of Cora Hazel Hammer.
RUSSELL, James Bernard, Sr. USA WWII, b. Sep 1, 1919, d. Jan 17, 1992, son of George C. and Rose Suite Russell.
RUSSELL, Joseph Leonard, b. Nov 6, 1935, d. Oct 14, 1988, son of George C. and Rose A. Suite Russell.
RUSSELL, Robert Garrett "Gary", b. Jun 30, 1907, d. Aug 8, 1992, hus of Elsie Jane Long, son of Edward and Mary Alice Cheseldine Russell.
RUSSELL, Sharon Ann, b. Nov 20, 1947, d. Aug 29, 1993, wife of Thomas Aloysius Vallandingham, dau of Phillip Jerome and Mary Virginia Downs Russell.
RUSSELL, Theodore Herbert, d. Dec 31, 1961, hus of Agnes Violet Redmond.
RYCE, Ashley Nicole, b. Sep 8, 1990, d. Dec 14, 1990, dau of Thomas Levin Ryce and Rebecca Marie Quade.
SAPP, Sara Marie, b. Jul 20, 1967 DC, d. Jun 26, 1992 (spina bifida), dau of Raymond and

Carolyn Sue Vance Sapp.
SAYRES, Sarah Elizabeth, b. Feb 28, 1914, d. Nov 17, 1989, wife of Thomas Peter Guy, dau of Silas E. and Ruhannah I. Sayres.
SCANLON, Agnes Rose, b. Jun 24, 1917 Balto, d. May 28, 1991, wife of Clarence Grey Poe, dau of John M. and Esther Mary Goddard Scanlon.
SCOTT, Albert Francis, b. Feb 5, 1950, d. Apr 18, 1988, hus of Darlene Harrison, son of David and Frances M. Scott.
SCOTT, Charles Earl, b. Jan 31, 1948 NC, d. Apr 22, 1993, m. 7 Jul 1984 Mary Frances __ Norris, son of Charlie Mac and Betty Mae Baker Scott.
SCRIBER, Bruce Clayton, b. Aug 30, 1958, d. Mar 27, 1992, son of Joseph Randolph and Rosa Dorsey Scriber.
SCRIBER, Jackie Rochelle, b. Mar 10, 1973, d. Jun 21, 1991, dau of Arthur J. Robinson and Frances E. Scriber.
SCRIBER, Timothy Mark, b. Oct 24, 1960, d. Jul 18, 1992, hus of Karen __, son of Joseph Randolph and Rosa Dorsey Scriber.
SEBASTIAN, Margaret Abel, b. Oct 20, 1915, d. Feb 19, 1989, wife of Edgar Knope, dau of John and Jessie Dent Turner Sebastian.
SECORA, Walter Michael, Jr. b. Aug 7, 1936 PA, d. May 14, 1990 VA, hus of Donna Marie Pilkerton, son of Walter Michael and Mary Ann Summits Secora.
SELLERS, Cassie Nell, b. Mar 1, 1933, d. Jul 16, 1989, wife of Henry "Hank" Underwood, dau of Bertie Moore and Dallas Sellers.
SEXTON, Ella, b. Mar 1, 1895 VA, d. Dec 20, 1991, m. (1st) Orbin H. Carter, (2d) Joseph Moore, (3d) Berg G. "Buck" Hall, dau of Bill and Mary Sexton.
SHAFFER, Lewis Michael, b. Jul 26, 1969 Balto, d. Feb 17, 1991, son of Gary N. and Mary Ann Miller Shaffer; gson of Carl G. and Mae G. Shaffer; William J. and Edith L. Wallace.
SHAIKEWITZ, Morris George, b. Jan 7, 1900, d. Dec 7, 1990, hus of Agnes M. __, son of Samuel and Emma Shaikewitz.
SHIRLEY, Ferne Darlene, b. Jul 1, 1937 PA, d.

Sep 13, 1991, wife of Jack Linn McLane, dau of John Earl and Helen Woods Walker Shirley.
SHORT, Glenn, infant, d. Jun 29, 1991, son of Glenn Albert Short and Joan Melanie Butler.
SHOTWELL, Thomas "Tom" Edward, b. Apr 14, 1913, d. Nov 18, 1989, hus of Agnes E. Quade, son of Edgar and Lillie Mooney Shotwell.
SHUPE, Earl Robert, b. Apr 21, 1966, d. Jun 9, 1993, hus of Kristin N. __, son of Barbara Springirth Follin of Mechanicsville and Henry S. Shupe of Lexington Park.
SIMONS, Helen, b. Apr 29, 1924 NC, d. Jul 7, 1989, wife of James S. Buckler, dau of Fred and Minnie Simons.
SIZEMORE, Gary Wayne, b. Feb 9, 1962 CA, d. Dec 29, 1989, son of Jack and Mary Sizemore.
SMALLWOOD, Mary Estelle, b. Mar 4, 1917, d. Jun 15, 1990, dau of Joseph and Mary Louise Spears Smallwood.
SMITH, Joshua Lee, b. Oct 24, 1982, d. Apr 22, 1992, son of Kenneth Lee Smith, stepson of Kurri Smith; gson of Henry A. "Buck" and Patricia A. Smith; Jack and Patricia Gumtow.
SMITH, Phillip Adair, b. Mar 27, 1936 NC, d. Sep 9, 1993 DC, m. 10 Aug 1954 SC, Billie Ann Crawford, son of Willie Warren and Nellie Small Smith.
SMITH, Phyllis Ann, b. Jun 11, 1955 NC, d. Mar 24, 1990, wife of __ Tolson, dau of Phillip Adair and Billie Ann Crawford Smith.
SMITH, Sandra Kay Abell, b. Dec 9, 1913, d. Apr 7, 1987, dau of John and June Jones.
SMITH, Terrance J., b. Dec 15, 1965, d. Feb 9, 1991, son of William Merrill and Sandra Nightman Smith.
SOMERVILLE, Francis Xavier, b. Jul 30, 1958, d. Sep 4, 1992, son of James "Link" and Ann Dyson Somerville.
SOMERVILLE, James Randolph III, b. and d. Feb 21, 1990, son of James Randolph and Mary Doris Swales Somerville.
SOMERVILLE, Kelly Watson, b. Apr 7, 1968 NC, d. Sep 24, 1993 DC, m. 2 Aug 1968 DC, Barbara Blackwell, son of William and Pattie Powell Somerville.

SOMERVILLE, Mary 'Beatrice', b. Jun 9, 1923, d.
May 20, 1991, wife of John Henry Stewart, dau
of Mary E. Banks and Felix Albert Somerville.
SOMERVILLE, Phyllis Diane, 36, b. Apr 24,
1956, d. Jul 11, 1992, dau of James Foley
and Sarah Dyson Somerville.
SOMERVILLE, Robert Lance III, b. and d. Jul 2,
1993, son of Giovanna Shandella Bush and Robert L. Somerville; gson of Linda Ann Bush
and Robert E. Moore; Robert Lang and Austine
E. Somerville; ggson of Janet Moore; Chas.
and Vergie Dyson.
SPARKS, James Dallas, 42, b. May 7, 1947, d.
Nov 12, 1989, hus of Barbara Ann Quade, son
of George and Ethel Cleo Sparks.
SPAULDING, James Robert "Bob", Sr, 61, b. Mar
16, 1931, d. Aug 10, 1992, hus of Bonnie Lee
Edwards, son of George and Mary Louise Raley
Spaulding.
SPEARS, Joseph Cornelius, Sr, 80, b. Mar 30,
1911 Balto, d. Dec 31, 1991, son of Jimmy
and Florene Holt Spears.
ST. CLAIR, Virginia May, 69, d. Jul 22, 1992.
STONE, Elmer A., Sr. 77, b. Apr 11, 1911, d.
Nov 29, 1988, hus of Elizabeth Anne __,
son of Alfred and Mary M. Stone.
STONE, Ernest Leo, Jr. 67, USN, b. Dec 15,
1923, d. Jul 4, 1991, hus of Ruth Agnes Peacock, son of Ernest Leo and Dorothy Elizabeth Hammett Stone.
STONE, Joseph Ford "Joe", Jr. b. May 5, 1919,
d. Jan 26, 1983, hus of Elsie Johnson, son
of J. 'Ford' and Mary Catherine "Mamie" Godwin Stone.
STRICKLAND, Elizabeth Frances, b. Aug 27,
1920 NC, d. Mar 22, 1992, wife of J. Foley
Mattingly, Jr, dau of Thomas George and
Rosa Franklin Howell Strickland.
SUITE, John Irwin, b. Jun 11, 1939, d. May 7,
1992, son of Andrew Johnson and Catherine
Lavata Quade Suite.
SWEENEY, Frances 'Louise', b. Aug 26, 1908
DC, d. Jun 23, 1991, wife of Philip D. Gatton, dau of Ralph E. and Frances Taylor
Sweeney.

SWEENEY, Thelma Maxine, b. Sep 11, 1921 IL, d. Sep 24, 1989, wife of Donald W. Cronkite, dau of Charles F. and Edna J. Sweeney.
SWIDERSKI, Florence Caroline, b. Feb 24, 1930 PA, d. Mar 26, 1990, wife of __ Balsbaugh, dau of John and Caroline Swiderski.
TALBOT, Virginia Lee, b. Apr 12, 1933, d. Feb 20, 1989, wife of Joseph A. Green, dau of Mary Talbot.
TASKER, Goldie Elouise, b. Oct 19, 1916, d. Nov 10, 1993, m. 20 May 1944 Franklin Theodore Newton, dau of Osborne and Melinda Ann Switer Tasker.
TATE, Carrie Bell, b. Feb 9, 1920 SC, d. Jun 22, 1992 NY, wife of Pat Jefferies, dau of Ernestine Littlejohn Tate.
TAYLOR, George Raymond, b. Apr 5, 1903, d. Feb 11, 1989, hus of Mary Alice __, son of George Washington and Millie E. Taylor.
TENNYSON, Cecelia Beatrice, b. Sep 12, 1922, d. Apr 22, 1989, wife of James Andrew "Toots" Nelson, dau of Ira F. and Mary Alberta Guy Tennyson.
TENNYSON, Kevin Patrick, b. Aug 13, 1988, d. Jan 16, 1990, son of Joseph Donald and Barbara Lynn Norris Tennyson; gson of Rodman and Janis Tennyson; William R. and Mary Norris.
TESERMAN, Evelyn Margaret, d. May 6, 1992 DC, m. Feb 1956 NC, Kenneth Milo Wiles.
TEXIERA, Raymond Allen "Ray", Jr. USN, b. Jan 15, 1970 CA, d. Mar 30, 1991 DC, son of Raymond A. and Alma Louise Clements Texiera, g-son of Martin L. and Evelyn Clements.
THOMAS, Eugene Preston, b. Jun 5, 1966, d. Feb 4, 1989, son of Catherine C. Briscoe and Francis Paul Bonds, Sr.
THOMAS, George Francis, b. Dec 15, 1911, d. Mar 6, 1989, hus of Agnes Lucretia Briscoe, son of Louis Alfred and Mary Louise Marshall Thomas.
THOMAS, Hillary Truman "Bub", b. Nov 28, 1928, d. Sep 3, 1990, son of Harry Alexander and Mary Madeline Countiss Thomas.
THOMAS, Imogene, d. Aug 5, 1993.

THOMAS, Joseph Frank, Jr. b. Jul 29, 1913, d. Jun 10, 1992, son of Joseph Frank and Elizabeth Rebecca Thompson Thomas.
THOMAS, Kelly Anthony, b. Nov 19, 1938, d. May 31, 1990, son of George Francis and Agnes Briscoe Thomas.
THOMAS, Robert Lee, b. Jul 31, 1915 VA, d. Aug 27, 1993, m. 5 Mar 1948 Clara Mae Mattingly, son of James Wesley and Alice Flippo Thomas.
THOMAS, Walter Randolph, b. Jul 25, 1915 VA, d. Mar 22, 1992, hus of June A. __, son of Harris Randolph and Ida Catherine McCrae Thomas.
THOMPSON, Dorothy Marie, b. Mar 2, 1939, d. May 9, 1990, wife of John Raymond Williams, Sr., dau of George B. and Agnes Rosie Somerville Thompson.
THOMPSON, Joseph Henry "Harry", b. Oct 30, 1925, d. May 20, 1991, son of Joseph Henry and Alice Downs Thompson.
THOMPSON, Kenneth Eugene and Kristin Marie, d. Dec 3, 1993 Balto, infant twins of Kenneth Eugene and Cheryl Marie Nelson Thompson, gchildren of Albert and Genevieve Thompson; George and Jean Nelson.
THOMPSON, Morgan Ignatius "Tex", b. Jul 10, 1927, d. May 19, 1988, son of Harry and Alice Thompson.
THOMPSON, Robert Henry, b. Nov 27, 1919 CT, d. Feb 9, 1990, hus of Barbara A. __.
TIPPETT, Annie Mae, b. Nov 25, 1935, d. Jul 24, 1988, wife of James F. Gatton, dau of John Walter and Mary Eva Tippett.
TIPPETT, Mabel Ann, b. May 12, 1926, d. Aug 10, 1993, m. 19 May 1946 James Gregory "Buck" Curry, Sr., dau of Joseph Raymond and Elizabeth Morgan Tippett.
TOUTE, Hazel Beatrice, b. ca 1925, d. Jan 31, 1987, wife of James Latham Mattingly.
TRAUB, Benjamin Harry, b. Nov 1, 1908 NY, d. Jul 16, 1991, hus of Marian Brown, son of Benjamin and Ethel Walsch Traub.
TROSSBACH, Warren Ignatius, Sr. b. Mar 1, 1927, d. Dec 29, 1992, hus of E. Frances Aud, son of William and Rosalie Hammett Trossbach.

TURLEY, Leo Emmett, Lt USN, b. Sep 16, 1910 KS, d. Nov 27, 1992, hus of Ida Catherine Mattingly, son of Phillip Turley and Minnie Bird Turley Gold.
TURNER, Jeffrey Raymond "Jeff", b. May 22, 1938 DC, d. Apr 27, 1992, hus of Jane Elizabeth Lawrence, son of Elmer Rudolph and Ivy Ann Fittall Turner.
TURNER, Keith Lerron, Jr, infant, b. May 4, 1992 DC, son of Keith and Sharon Morgan Turner; gson of Mary E. Morgan; Vivian Turner and Leonard Evans, KY.
TUTT, Helen Marie, b. Jan 4, 1922 MI, d. Nov 17, 1993, wife of _ Rasmussen, dau of George and Eva Winkle Tutt.
UNKLE, Anna Mae, b. May 1, 1929, d. Jun 28, 1991, wife of James Alvin Johnson, dau of William Alvin and Pearl Marie Morgan Unkle.
UNDERWOOD, Henry Maurice, b. Nov 5, 1927 NC, d. Jun 15, 1989, son of Ada D. and Bernard M. Underwood.
VAN DEVANTER, James Lee, d. Dec 14, 1992 DC, m. 1957 VA Catherine Councell Knight.
VAN HOUSEN, LeRoy E., b. Jul 7, 1924 NY, d. Jan 31, 1992, hus of Evelyn O. __, son of Charles Grant and Edna Ward Van Housen.
VAN PELT, Alma Bessie, b. Dec 18, 1908 DC, d. Feb 4, 1993, m. 8 Aug 1927 James Melemorth Mahorney, dau of Edw. and Bessie Bassford Van Pelt.
VARNER, William Donald, Sr. b. Jun 2, 1930 PA, d. Dec 31, 1992 DC, m. 1972 Cumberland, MD Doris Jane Myers, son of Wm. Francis and Minnie Best Varner.
WAGNER, Howard Pershing, b. Aug 16, 1919 NJ, d. Dec 28, 1989.
WALLACE, Frederick Wayne, b. Jan 12, 1960 VA, d. Oct 17, 1991, hus of Maria Pauline Shatzer, son of Lou and Audrey Hawks Wallace.
WALLACE, James Woodrow Wilson "Frogie", b. Mar 23, 1918 Balto, d. Aug 1, 1993, hus of Estelle Marie DeVaughn, son of Joseph and Barbara Jones Wallace.
WALLIS, Frederick Richard, b. Jun 19, 1909 PA, d. Apr 9, 1990, hus of Margaret Sweeney,

son of James F. and Mary Reith Wallis.
WARD, Elva M., b. Feb 28, 1910, d. Apr 2, 1993, wife of James K. Smith, dau of Wm. C. and Maude Belle Gallion Ward.
WARE, Mary Elizabeth, b. Jan 29, 1907, d. Sep 30, 1989, wife of Walter W. Daye, dau of John E. and Lottie Kidwell Ware.
WATHEN, Anna M., b. Feb 15, 1905, d. Oct 25, 1979, m. 6 Sep 1924 George Edgar Joy.
WATHEN, Frances, b. Feb 23, 1911, d. Nov 16, 1990, wife of Joseph Arthur Graves, dau of Raley and Frances Wathen.
WATHEN, James 'Wayne', Sr, b. Mar 21, 1952, d. Sep 4, 1992, son of James 'Tilton' and Frances 'Theresa' Owens Wathen.
WATHEN, John Wellington "Jack", Jr. b. Oct 13, 1925, d. Jan 8, 1990, hus of Mary R. Hammett, son of John W. and Anna Mae Long Wathen.
WATHEN, Michael Leonard, b. Dec 22, 1964, d. Nov 7, 1991, son of Albert Leonard, Jr. and Mary Martha Morgan Wathen.
WATSON, Richard Lyle, b. June 22, 1916 WA, d. Apr 4, 1988, hus of Lois M. Hogan, son of Robert Mitchell and Ethel Newell Watson.
WEST, Donald Lee, Jr. b. Jul 13, 1955 Annap, MD, d. Feb 21, 1993 VA, son of Donald L. and Melvina Jane Rawlings West.
WHALEN, Lettie Bell, b. Jan 26, 1898, d. Oct 2, 1988, wife of Frank Dyson, dau of George and Sarah Whalen.
WIBLE, John 'Lester', b. Nov 17, 1902, d. Dec 27, 1991, hus of Elizabeth Gwinnette Goldsborough, son of William Martin and Susan Roberta Ellis Wible.
WILLIAMS, Lucille, b. May 20, 1949 NC, d. Dec 31, 1989, wife of Vincent Cutchember.
WILLOUGHBY, Ward Keasts, d. 1940, 1st hus of Cora Hazel Hammer.
WILLS, James Lorenza "Lightning", Sr. b. Jan 17, 1908, d. Oct 8, 1992, hus of Rose Elizabeth Farmer, son of James Earl and Susie Agnes Yorkshire Wills.
WILSON, Ella Louise, b. Mar 14, 1925, d. Aug 24, 1992, wife of James I. Price, dau of William Henry and Ella Mae Turner Wilson.

Charles Memorial

WILSON, Joseph Elmer, b. Apr 12, 1925, d. Apr 12, 1993, son of Jas. Wm. and Nellie Alberta Young Wilson.
WILSON, Mary Juanita, b. Feb 6, 1922 PA, d. Apr 6, 1993, wife of Louis John Debbis, dau of George and Emma Chapman Wilson.
WINDSOR, James Berry, b. Oct 28, 1944, d. Nov 10, 1990, hus of Dorothy Dorene __, son of Robt. Vincent and Ida Natalie Berry Windsor.
WINDSOR, Nelson E., b. Apr 12, 1919, d. Dec 13, 1989.
WOOD, James Greenwell, Sr. b. May 25, 1923, d. Aug 29, 1991, hus of Mary M. __, son of Henry A. and Martha L. Graves Wood.
WOOD, James Irving "Boonie", b. Mar 10, 1911, d. Jun 6, 1988.
WUNDER, Linda Marie, b. Jun 20, 1952 Phila, PA, d. Jun 15, 1990, wife of Anthony M. Pompizzi, dau of Frank and Dorothy Wunder.
WYWICK, Gleason G., b. Nov 6, 1911 VA, d. Nov 17, 1990, hus of M. Ruth __, son of Henry A. and Louise J. Hunter Wywick.
YATES, Francis Ira "Jake", b. Apr 22, 1930, d. Sep 19, 1991, hus of Marjorie "Margy" Jackson, son of Joseph Louis and Agnes Jeannette Tennyson Yates.
YATES, Joseph Aloysius "Slewfoot", b. May 28, 1912, d. Jan 27, 1990, hus of Lois R. __, son of Charles Joseph and Frances Ruth Bailey Yates.
YATES, Laura Evelyn, b. Jun 17, 1914 DC, d. Jul 19, 1993, m. DC 23 May 1941, James Stanton Mattingly, dau of Joseph Lewis and Laura Evelyn Graves Yates.
YORKSHIRE, Kevin Darnell, b. Sep 3, 1962, d. Feb 1, 1992, son of James Timothy and Ada Theresa Holton Yorkshire.
YOUNG, Darrell Benedict, b. Jul 23, 1963, d. Aug 29, 1988, son of John B. and Rosanna Young.
YOUNG, George Antonio, b. Dec 5, 1963, d. Feb 24, 1990 DC, son of Mary Rose Young and George Albert Curtis.
YOUNG, James Aloysius, b. Sep 12, 1949, d. Jul 10, 1992, son of Mary Cecelia Young and James

L. Cooper.
YOUNG, Joseph Givens, WWII, b. Jan 23, 1927, d. Jun 2, 1991, hus of Jane Frances __, son of Joseph T. Suter and Maizie Young.
YOUNGER, Robbi B., b. Aug 8, 1914, d. Jan 13, 1989, wife of Willie E. Younger.

CHRIST EPISCOPAL CHURCH
Chaptico, Maryland

1st Church built 1642, 2d Church built 1737 on plaque in front of church. The 1642 church was built by Thomas Gerrard. The 1737 church is of brick, Georgian style. It has a semi-circular chancel, a high arched ceiling over the nave, and round-headed windows and doors. Inside, it had high-back walnut pews, a center and cross aisle, and three doors; one on the end and one on each side. The windows were many paned. The interior of the church has now lost much of its original appearance.

Most of these are tombstone readings through 1975 as sent in to St. Mary's County Genealogical Society by member David Roberts. Many of the tombstones do not give a birthdate or age, and relationships are not shown.

ALEXANDER, Randolph F., b. 1903, d. 1932.
BARNES, Jane Llewellyn Key, d. 1816.
BARNS, Mary, b. 1824, d. Sep 11, 1862.
BEECHAM, Catherine Ann Waring, b. 1876, d. 1960.
BEECHAM, Oscar, b. 1875, d. 1941.
BILLINGSLEY, Jennie Reeder, b. Oct 20, 1874, d. Dec 9, 1956 DC, m. 25 Feb 1897 at Christ Epis. Ch., Richard Morris Abell.
BLED, Stuart L., b. Feb 19, 1884, d. Nov 3, 1886.
BOND, Ann, b. Feb 21, 1801, d. Sep 29, 1885.
BOND, John Thomas, b. 1763, d. Nov 2, 1814.
BOND, Lorenzo D., b. 1827, d. 1890.
BOND, R. Garner, b. 1861, d. 1932.
BOND, Rebecca A., b. 1836, d. 1884.
BOYD, Walter Mathew, b. Mar 24, 1898, d. Jun 24, 1967.
BRISCOE, Gustavis Brown, b. Mar 27, 1832, d. Jun 24, 1860.
BRISCOE, John, b. 1818, d. May 29, 1899.
BRISCOE, Marvin, b. Dec 8, 1790, d. Feb 12, 1863.

BRISCOE, Philip, b. Nov 9, 1786, d. Sep 26, 1842.
BROOKBANK, James, b. 1799, d. Sep 16, 1862.
BULLARD, Thomas Edmund, b. Aug 11, 1949, d. Nov 19, 1954.
BURCH, Elizabeth, b. 1843, d. May 26, 1843.
BURCH, Henry Dade, b. Jul 17, 1817, d. Sep 19, 1850.
BURCH, Henry Dade, b. Jul 28, 1850, d. Jun 6, 1854.
BURCH, J. Chew, b. Nov 27, 1847, d. Oct 22, 1883.
BURCH, L. Whittingham, b. 1846, d. May 28, 1870.
BURROUGHS, ___, b. Nov 13, 1854, d. Jun 1, 1934.
BURROUGHS, Anne Lillian, b. 1887, d. 1955.
BURROUGHS, Anne Rebecca, b. Jul 30, 1846, d. Dec 27, 1928.
BURROUGHS, Annie, b. 1888, d. 1934.
BURROUGHS, Annie Alma, b. 1880, d. 1946, wife of William Oscar Swann.
BURROUGHS, Aquila, b. 1806, d. Jun 9, 1882.
BURROUGHS, B. Webster, b. Mar 13, 1858, d. Aug 25, 1931.
BURROUGHS, Cardine Alice, b. Jan 7, 1862, d. Jul 22, 1900.
BURROUGHS, Carlisle "Barney" Herriman, b. May 16, 1916 PA, d. May 13, 1990, hus of Leola Simpson, son of William Barker and Annie Herriman Burroughs.
BURROUGHS, Caroline Marian, b. 1830, d. Jul 10, 1864.
BURROUGHS, Edna, b. Nov 2, 1888, d. Nov 18, 1888.
BURROUGHS, Effie Barber, b. Mar 7, 1864, d. Jan 28, 1941.
BURROUGHS, Eliza T., b. Feb 25, 1810, d. Nov 4, 1831.
BURROUGHS, Elizabeth E., b. 1799, d. Jul 21, 1855.
BURROUGHS, Henry, b. 1851, d. Nov 5, 1855.
BURROUGHS, John A., b. Mar 20, 1802, d. Feb 17, 1872.
BURROUGHS, Mary Amanda, b. Mar 25, 1886, d. May 29, 1886.

Christ Church

BURROUGHS, Mary Estelle, b. Mar 22, 1913, d. Dec 29, 1913.
BURROUGHS, Maude Davis, b. 1891, d. 1957.
BURROUGHS, Robert Davis, b. 1927, d. 1932.
BURROUGHS, Robert S., b. 1890, d. 1954.
BURROUGHS, Susan E., b. 1818, d. Mar 20, 1843.
BURROUGHS, Virginia H., b. Nov 13, 1854, d. Jun 1, 1934.
BURROUGHS, William, b. Oct 10, 1839, d. Sep 1, 1906.
BURROUGHS, William L., b. 1876, d. 1930.
BURROUGHS, William McK., b. Sep 7, 1840, d. Feb 15, 1923.
BURROUGHS, Zadok, no dates on stone.
BUSH, Monty Herman, b. Aug 17, 1972.
BUTLER, Georgianne E., b. 1882, d. 1967.
CARPENTER, Annie Clarinda, b. 1879, d. 1927.
CARPENTER, George Alexander, b. 1875, d. 1958.
CARPENTER, Capt. John, b. 1735, d. 1803.
CARPENTER, Mildred, b. 1892, d. 1974, wife of William S. Donaldson, Sr.
CARPENTER, Susannah Turner, d. Sep 26, 1805.
CAWOOD, B. Hezekiah, b. Feb 27, 1800, d. Oct 4, 1887.
CAYWOOD, Evans, b. 1908, d. 1966.
CAYWOOD, Mary Arlene, b. 1918, d. 1966.
CHESLEY, Abraham L., d. Dec 17, 1935, m. 9 Aug 1918 Maud M. "Sookie" Mills.
CHING, Hammett, b. Mar 2, 1892, d. May 3, 1967.
CHING, John F., d. Jul 13, 1893.
CHING, John Regis, b. Feb 2, 1934, d. May 7, 1981.
CHING, Mary Gwynette, b. Jan 4, 1897, d. Feb 10, 1988.
CHING, Pauline Lyon, d. May 19, 1973.
CHING, Sarah, d. Jul 21, 1893.
CHING, Thomas Aloysius, d. Jun 11, 1975.
CLAGETT, Octavious S., b. Mar 19, 1841, d. Feb 27, 1922.
CLAGETT, Richard H., b. Oct 17, 1888, d. Sep 19, 1917.
CLARK, Eliza C., b. 1893, d. 1974.
CLARKY, William H., b. Dec 19, 1889, d. Sep 3, 1949.

COOKE, Chloe R.B., d. Dec 8, 1913.
COOKE, James, b. 1760, d. Mar 13, 1820.
COOKE, John Llewellen Briscoe, b. 1841, d. Oct 16, 1852.
COOKE, Mary, d. Apr 11, 1818.
COOKE, Zora Columbia Zalute, b. Sep 8, 1833, d. Mar 9, 1846.
DAVIS, Anne Dorothea, b. 1898, d. 1967.
DAVIS, Annie E.C., b. Apr 9, 1860, d. Mar 6, 1940.
DAVIS, Carroll, b. 1880, d. 1889.
DAVIS, Carroll Lee, b. 1901, d. 1960.
DAVIS, Charles Francis, b. Oct 25, 1835, d. Sep 7, 1912.
DAVIS, Chesley, b. 1884, d. 1889.
DAVIS, Dosia, b. 1901, d. 1901.
DAVIS, Dosia S., b. Oct 25, 1876, d. Apr 26, 1964.
DAVIS, Elizabeth C., b. Jun 26, 1837, d. May 19, 1923.
DAVIS, Francis Dudley, b. 1868, d. 1941.
DAVIS, Gertrude, b. 1882, d. 1889.
DAVIS, Henry Albert, b. 1896, d. 1967.
DAVIS, James Burgess, b. 1910, d. 1961.
DAVIS, James Edward, b. 1865, d. 1951.
DAVIS, Lewis H., b. Jan 1, 1852, d. May 22, 1930.
DAVIS, Louisa, b. Jan 30, 1825, d. Feb 17, 1901.
DAVIS, Mary E., b. May 5, 1859, d. Dec 22, 1835 (as transcribed, may be 1885 or 1935).
DAVIS, Mary P. Love, b. Mar 12, 1858, d. Jan 4, 1937.
DAVIS, Montie M., b. 1893, d. 1958.
DAVIS, Oscar H., b. Jul 4, 1843, d. Aug 27, 1907.
DAVIS, Robert, b. Mar 13, 1811, d. Mar 23, 1890.
DAVIS, Robert Lee, b. Jun 19, 1864, d. Dec 28, 1932.
DAVIS, Robert Simms, b. Sep 12, 1876, d. May 31, 1936.
DAVIS, Thomas Lee, b. 1864, d. 1945.
DONALDSON, William Stanley, Jr, LCOL USAF, b. Sep 4, 1921 Balto, d. Jul 24, 1993, m. 1984

Christ Church 51

Roberta Shields, son of William S. and Mildred Carpenter Donaldson.
EDMONDS, Blanche Wood Garner, b. Apr 8, 1885, d. Nov 21, 1962.
EDMONDS, Charles Sidney, b. Jun 24, 1917, d. Jan 21, 1958.
EDMONDS, Stuart Hobbs, b. Oct 25, 1876, d. May 13, 1948.
EDSON, Dorothy Lincoln, d. Apr 12, 1969, wife of J. Compton Swann.
EDWARDS, Louise Natalie, b. Dec 31, 1916 Balto, d. Jul 2, 1992 MA, wife of Truman Lawrence Mills.
EGARTON, Susan, d. Aug 14, 1820.
FORBES, Charles Ernest, Jr. b. Aug 6, 1935 VA, d. Oct 7, 1993, m. 16 Nov 1963 Margaret Louise Hughes, son of Charles and Mandie Dawson Forbes.
FOWLER, Lucy B., b. Mar 3, 1857, d. Feb 10, 1893.
FULLER, Bonnie Lou, b. Mar 5, 1959, d. Sep 19, 1988, wife of James Curtis Woodrum, dau of Carl R. Sr, and Thelma C. Fuller.
FULLER, Carl Rhuben, b. 1872, d. 1963.
GANTT, Chesley, b. Nov 9, 1884, d. Sep 16, 1908.
GANTT, Ernest Gibson, b. 1882, d 1889.
GANTT, Laura, b. 1843, d. 1924.
GANTT, Laura Valinda, b. Oct 4, 1851, d. Jan 7, 1883.
GARNER, Catherine Ann Reeder, d. Oct 6, 1877.
GARNER, George Reeder, b. Sep 24, 1843, d. Dec 29, 1916.
GARNER, Henry Green, b. Mar 19, 1789, d. Feb 25, 1862.
GARNER, Henry Green, b. 1870, d. 1935.
GARNER, John Henry, b. 1815, d. Oct 11, 1819.
GARNER, John Henry, b. Oct 9, 1851, d. Dec 4, 1926.
GARNER, John Turner, b. Apr 4, 1882, d. Sep 30, 1883.
GARNER, Juliet Reeder, b. 1792, d. Oct 22, 1837.
GARNER, Lola Wood, b. 1869, d. 1950.
GARNER, Mary Thomas, b. Feb 12, 1848, d. Mar

1, 1893.
GARNER, William Henry, b. Dec 26, 1872, d.
  Nov 30, 1899.
GIBSON, Elva Jennings, b. 1879, d. 1949.
GIBSON, Emily Patterson, b. Aug 28, 1907, d.
  Feb 15, 1929.
GIBSON, Joseph Patterson, b. 1870, d. 1934.
GIBSON, Joseph Patterson, b. 1913, d. 1933.
GLADSTONE, William Edward, b. 1891, d. 1955.
GOOD, Thomas W., b. Feb 10, 1840, d. Feb 24,
  1901.
GOODE, Douglas, b. Nov 22, 1893, d. Mar 7,
  1971.
GOODE, George Hatcher, b. Nov 22, 1867, d. Feb
  20, 1897.
GOUGH, Rebecca Hayden, b. Sep 1, 1855, d. Jun
  20, 1924.
GOUGH, Wilfred, b. Jun 4, 1850, d. Sep 14,
  1898.
GOUGH, William H., b. Apr 2, 1889, d. Apr 19,
  1889.
GREEVES, Eleanor Catherine, b. May 9, 1903, d.
  Oct 20, 1918.
GREEVES, John William Courtney, b. Jan 4, 1905,
  d. Aug 17, 1919.
HALL, Arthur William, Jr. b. Oct 13, 1929, d.
  Mar 29, 1971.
HARRISON, B. Arthur, b. 1888, d. 1944.
HARRISON, Robert L., b. 1890, d. 1966.
HAYDEN, Ann Waring, b. Feb 29, 1854, d. Mar 1,
  1944.
HAYDEN, Catherine A., b. 1841, d. Dec 26, 1872.
HAYDEN, E. Somerset, b. 1862, d. 1936.
HAYDEN, Eliza Burroughs, d. Apr 8, 1881.
HAYDEN, Eliza C., b. Sep 17, 1823, d. Jan 20,
  1893.
HAYDEN, Francis D., b. 1878, d. 1943.
HAYDEN, George, b. 1842, d. Sep 23, 1863.
HAYDEN, Hegeckinda G., b. 1813, d. Feb 23,
  1858.
HAYDEN, Jonathan, b. Oct 1, 1770.
HAYDEN, Katherine M., b. May 21, 1892, d. Mar
  11, 1898.
HAYDEN, Katherine Maddox, b. 1854, d. 1930.
HAYDEN, Lillian Keech, b. Jul 20, 1807, d. Aug

Christ Church

1, 1897.
HAYDEN, Mary Amanda, b. 1852, d. Jan 12, 1863.
HAYDEN, Mary Elizabeth, d. Dec 22, 1868.
HAYDEN, Nannie, b. Jun 3, 1849, d. Aug 5, 1891.
HAYDEN, Oscar G., b. 1839, d. 1903.
HAYDEN, Oscar George, b. Jul 1, 1830, d. Jul 18, 1888.
HAYDEN, Oscar Maddox, b. 1889, d. 1915.
HAYDEN, Peregrine, b. 1764, d. Feb 29, 1848.
HAYDEN, Perry, b. May 3, 1853, d. Jun 21, 1932.
HAYDEN, R. Ford, d. 1940.
HAYDEN, Samuel, b. Oct 3, 1850, d. Jun 1, 1933.
HAYDEN, Samuel Bond, b. May 9, 1864, d. Aug 27, 1946.
HAYDEN, Sarah, b. Mar 29, 1846, d. Oct 3, 1933.
HAYDEN, Sarah Lee., b. Sep 10, 1880, d. Jun 18, 1882.
HERBERT, Clarion W., b. Sep 19, 1859, d. Aug 24, 1882.
HERBERT, Elizabeth C., b. Sep 23, 1865, d. May 1, 1923.
HERBERT, Elizabeth S., b. Nov 17, 1828, d. May 30, 1891.
HERBERT, May, b. Mar 17, 1799, d. Mar 25, 1870.
HERBERT, Nettie H., b. 1898, d. 1971.
HERBERT, S., b. Sep 5, 1895, d. Oct 6, 1963.
HERBERT, Washington P., b. 1828, d. Sep 24, 1888.
HERBERT, Webster B., b. Jul 15, 1856, d. Mar 19, 1916.
HERBERT, Webster Guy, b. Dec 22, 1889, d. 1975.
HERRIMAN, Albert, b. 1888, d. 1966.
HERRIMAN, Ella Yates, b. 1888, d. 1965.
HERRIMAN, Mary E., b. Jul 8, 1893.
HERRIMAN, Melvin H., b. Oct 31, 1833, d. Feb 25, 1913.
HERRIMAN, Vivian A., b. 1882, d. 1962.
HIGGS, George C., b. 1909, d. 1945.
HIGGS, Gerald P., b. Apr 27, 1896, d. Nov 7, 1915.
HIGGS, Hattie M., b. 1912, d. 1926.
HIGGS, James Roland, b. 1906, d. 1974.
HIGGS, Mary L., b. May 13, 1836, d. Dec 23, 1907.
HIGGS, Maude, b. 1873, d. 1935.

HIGGS, Nirva A., b. 1880, d. 1943.
HIGGS, Preston, b. 1863, d. 1956.
HIGGS, R.E., b. 1910, d. 1944.
HIGGS, Walter A., b. 1872, d. 1944.
HIGGS, Webster L., b. 1877, d. 1946.
HILL, James W., b. Feb 20, 1845, d. Nov 11, 1895.
HILL, Julia C., b. Dec 21, 1854, d. Mar 25, 1930.
HUNTINGTON, Francis Cleveland, b. Sep 23, 1892, d. Feb 25, 1970.
JOHNSTON, Helen Roberta, b. 1923, d. 1961, wife of LLoyd E. Johnston, Jr.
JOHNSTON, Lloyd E. Jr, b. 1922.
JOHNSTON, Lloyd E., b. 1894, d. 1969, hus of Nellie H. __.
KIRK, Ida, b. 1859, d. 1933.
KIRK, Martha E., b. Oct 29, 1839, d. Feb 28, 1925.
KIRK, William A., b. Sep 21, 1821, d. Sep 5, 1895.
KNOTT, Alice T., b. 1902, d. 1971.
KNOTT, Harry J., b. 1898, d. 1966.
KNOTT, James Woodley, b. 1875, d. 1943.
KNOTT, Mrs. Mary, b. Dec 4, 1778, d. Feb 7, 1849.
KNOTT, Mary Ella, b. 1874, d. 1941.
LOWERY, Edith Cushman, b. 1911, d. 1972.
LOWERY, Louise Davis, b. 1878, d. 1955.
LOWERY, Lloyd C., b. 1904, d. 1944.
LOWERY, Robert Lee, b. 1909, d. 1968.
LUNCEFORD, Mary Anne, b. Apr 20, 1917 VA, d. Jul 26, 1990 VA, wife of Everett C. Cooper, Sr., dau of Robert and Annie Creel Lunceford.
LYLES, Cecelia Brown, b. 1788, d. 1828.
LYNCH, Elizabeth Slye, b. 1875, d. 1932.
LYON, Agnes R., b. 1890, d. 1907.
LYON, Alice R., b. Sep 21, 1870, d. Sep 12, 1957.
LYON, Eliza, b. Jan 13, 1847, d. Jun 25, 1933.
LYON, Elizabeth Waring Hayden, b. Sep 25, 1894, d. Nov 5, 1931.
LYON, J.B., b. Jan 13, 1850, d. Dec 25, 1932.
LYON, James A., b. 1876, d. 1939.

Christ Church

LYON, Jennie Oliver, b. Apr 18, 1898, d. Sep 8, 1950.
LYON, John B., b. Mar 8, 1887, d. May 9, 1969.
LYON, John Franklin, b. Apr 26, 1891, d. Dec 1, 1971.
LYON, Margaret I., b. 1894, d. 1960.
LYON, Samuel Carpenter, b. Dec 15, 1877, d. Mar 1944, hus of Agnes Russell.
LYON, Stonten Warren, b. 1870, d. Sep 30, 1911.
LYON, West Russell, b. Feb 10, 1916, d. Dec 22, 1988, hus of Anne Townsend of Swindon, Eng., son of Samuel Carpenter and Agnes Russell Lyon.
LYON, William Elmer, b. 1889, d. Oct 15, 1914.
MADDOX, George F., b. Oct 4, 1802, d. Jan 9, 1880.
MADDOX, George William, b. 1863, d. 1947.
MADDOX, James Francis, b. 1848, d. 1928.
MADDOX, Lucy Virginia Lancaster, b. Nov 25, 1868, d. Feb 22, 1949.
MADDOX, Mary Elizabeth, b. Aug 24, 1814, d. Jan 1, 1895.
MADDOX, Rebecca Dent, b. 1847, d. 1924.
MADDOX, Verlinda G., b. Sep 13, 1874, d. Jul 9, 1920.
MILLS, Lottie R., b. Dec 3, 1901, d. Jan 7, 1932.
MILLS, Truman Lawrence, b. Dec 1, 1898, d. Feb 10, 1993, m. Feb 1939 Louise Natalie Edwards, son of Thomas and Ellen Bush Mills.
MORGAN, Hennie S., b. Feb 13, 1829, d. May 24, 1855.
NELSON, Catherine A., age 75, no dates, wife of George T. Nelson.
NELSON, George T., age 73, no dates.
NELSON, Obadiah, b. 1883, d. 1975, hus of Mary A. __, b. 1892, d. 1964.
OLIVER, Bob Cecil, b. 1902, d. 1969.
OLIVER, Elias E., b. 1890, d. 1952.
OLIVER, Francis L. "Pete", b. Feb 25, 1907, d. Nov 30, 1988, hus of Catherine Eugene __, son of Luke William and Susan Irene Oliver.
OLIVER, James B., d. Apr 28, 1973.
OLIVER, Luke William, b. 1854, d. 1936.
OLIVER, Susan Irene, b. 1870, d. 1940.

OLIVER, William T., b. 1888, d. 1924.
PARKER, Deshaw, b. 1891, d. 1974.
PATTERSON, Emily, b. Aug 28, 1907, d. Feb 15, 1929.
PENN, Sadie Herriman, b. 1883, d. 1960.
PENN, William, b. Sep 21, 1895, d. Jan 13, 1927.
PENNINGTON, Marjorie Maddox, b. Feb 28, 1890, d. Mar 16, 1971.
POFF, Raymond William, b. Jul 23, 1922, d. Mar 27, 1989, hus of Ruire Mae __, son of Archie Blane and Trellanice Esther Poff.
PURKS, Roderick H., b. 1906, d. 1968.
RECOS, Samuel Sprigg, b. 1869, d. 1932.
REDMOND, W. Howard, b. 1885, d. 1961.
REED, Lillian, b. 1906, d. 1944.
REEVES, Elizabeth Eleanor, b. Sep 20, 1838, d. Apr 18, 1869.
REEVES, Florence, d. 1908.
REEVES, Garner, b. 1861, d. 1937.
REEVES, J.R.T., b. Oct 8, 1832, d. Apr 19, 1911.
REEVES, John Courtney, b. Oct 31, 1867, d. Feb 16, 1912.
REEVES, Katherine, b. 1872, d. 1956.
REEVES, Lucie Beall, b. May 18, 1925, d. Aug 28, 1969.
REEVES, Mary C., b. Feb 17, 1879, d. Aug 17, 1919.
REEVES, Ralph, d. 1908.
REEVES, Samuel S., b. Jun 23, 1930, d. Apr 9, 1954.
REEVES, Samuel Sprigg, b. Mar 30, 1905, d. May 1, 1973.
REEVES, Virginia Sargent, b. Sep 8, 1906, d. May 2, 1952.
REEVES, William P., b. 1871, d. 1943.
RIPPIE, Ammon Syril, b. 1900, d. 1962.
RUSSELL, John Carroll, b. Sep 14, 1911, d. Mar 8, 1966.
RUSSELL, Joseph Solomon, Jr. b. Jan 3, 1919, d. Aug 31, 1992 VA, hus of Jane Welsh.
RUSSELL, Sarah Lyon, b. Apr 2, 1882, d. Jul 9, 1941.
SCHUHART, Harrison, b. Oct 2, 1891, d. Oct 22,

1950.
SCHUHART, Jacob, b. Feb 24, 1821, d. Apr 3, 1875.
SCHUHART, Magaret Wiener, b. Dec 2, 1774, d. Sep 22, 1875.
SCHUHART, Magaret Wiener, b. Dec 30, 1854, d. Jun 16, 1934.
SCHUHART, William H., b. Jan 19, 1840, d. Oct 8, 1919.
SELLMAN, Laurel Hayden, b. 1855, d. 1905.
SHEKELL, Annie Pinkney Hayden, b. 1883, d. 1957.
SHEKELL, Forrest Leon, b. 1875, d. 1938.
SLYE, Francis Augustus, b. Apr 5, 1915, d. Oct 26, 1920.
SOLOMON, Joseph, b. Aug 6, 1877, d. Aug 3, 1958.
SOTHORON, Eleanor Somerset, b. 1847, d. 1936, wife of __ Smith.
STAHL, Julia Maddox, b. 1892, d. 1973.
STODDERT, Mary, b. Nov 1, 1801, d. Apr 9, 1822.
SWANN, Benjamin W., b. May 1, 1888, d. Jul 19, 1907.
SWANN, Frank Davis, b. 1870, d. 1932.
SWANN, J. Compton, d. Nov 24, 1977, hus of Dorothy Lincoln Edson.
SWANN, Mildred E., sister, b. Feb 12, 1873, d. Feb 5, 1932.
SWANN, Mildred Lowery, b. 1918, d. 1965.
SWANN, R. Mattingly, b. 1853, d. 1946.
SWANN, Susan Marie, b. Jan 2, 1857, d. May 26, 1927.
SWANN, William Frank, Sr. b. Jan 25, 1915, d. Dec 5, 1990, hus of Annie Mildred __, son of William O. and Annie Burroughs Swann.
SWANN, William Oscar, b. 1868, d. 1943, hus of Annie Alma Burroughs.
THOMAS, Clare, b. May 14, 1861, d. Jan 2, 1889.
THOMAS, Eleanor Mackubin, b. Jun 12, 1827, d. Aug 28, 1901.
THOMAS, Matilda, b. 1852, d. Feb 9, 1908.
THOMAS, Truman H., b. 1856, d. 1941.
THOMPSON, Edward Charles, b. Jan 30, 1895, d. Nov 15, 1917.
THOMPSON, Francis Edgar, b. Oct 27, 1895, d.

Aug 26, 1959.
THOMPSON, Houten, b. 1874, d. 1962.
THOMPSON, Laura, b. 1874, d. 1952.
THOMPSON, Lessie G., b. 1905, d. 1969.
TURNER, Dorothy A., b. Oct 15, 1819, d. Aug 19, 1883.
TURNER, Elizabeth A., b. 1795, d. Dec 26, 1818.
TURNER, John H., b. Aug 18, 1816, d. Jun 13, 1882.
TURNER, Margaret V., b. 1879, d. 1964.
TURNER, Marion T., b. 1873, d. 1958.
TURNER, Walton E., b. 1907, d. 1962.
VONHEIN, Mabel Hayden, b. 1884, d. 1963.
WARING, Ethel Kapy, b. 1889, d. 1961.
WARING, James, b. Mar 26, 1841, d. Sep 25, 1878.
WARING, James, b. 1878, d. 1970.
WARING, James, b. 1920, d. 1932.
WARING, Maria Reeder Garner, b. Apr 8, 1848, d. Oct 8, 1922.
WEST, Emily Stuart Maddox, b. 1914, d. 1967.
WINDSOR, Charles E., b. 1887, d. 1967.
WINDSOR, Valerie Dixon, b. Mar 4, 1899, d. Dec 2, 1928.
WOLFE, Elberta, b. Oct 11, 1904, d. Feb 19, 1990, wife of William Reed Hayden, dau of Thomas Melville and Lydia Dent Wolfe.
YOUNG, Rachel Ann, d. 1859.

CHURCH OF THE NAZARENE
Hollywood, Md.

BREWER, Louis John, b. Dec 11, 1907 Balto, d. May 11, 1990, hus of Ella May Joy.
CHESELDINE, Grace Mae, d. Nov 24, 1961, wife of Frederick L. Davis.
DAVIS, Frederick L. "Stubby" Sr. b. Nov 25, 1903 NC, d. Aug 7, 1991, hus of Grace Mae Cheseldine, son of Georgette Davis.
GATTON, William Raymond, b. Sep 3, 1914, d. Mar 24, 1989, hus of Ruth Evelyn ___, son of Oscar S. and Elizabeth Dean Gatton.
GREEN, Charles Joseph, d. 1987, hus of Dorothy Derwent Martin.
JOY, Sherman Wilson, Sr. USA WWII, b. Mar 3, 1913, d. Mar 16, 1992, hus of Dorothy O. ___, son of Everett and Annie Dean Joy.
MARTIN, Dorothy Derwent, b. Mar 30, 1911 VA, d. Aug 12, 1988, wife of Charles Joseph Green, dau of John Todd and Rebecca Jo Creasey Martin.
SUTPHIN, Paul Irvin, b. Sep 10, 1918 VA, d. Aug 16, 1989, hus of Rosetta V. ___, son of Elijah and Alrendia Sutphin.

EBENEZER METHODIST CHURCH
Lexington Park/Charlotte Hall, Md.

Apparently there are two churches by this name in St. Mary's County. The local paper does not always identify which one is referred to in their obituaries, so they have been combined and are listed alphabetically.

CALVERT, Michael Ray, b. Oct 27, 1953, d. May 9, 1988 NY, son of John Milliken and Alberta Hupp Calvert.
CHESSER, Hazel Elizabeth, b. Sep 15, 1913, d. Apr 1, 1988, wife of Emerson M. Chesser.
CLEMENTS, Charles Louis, b. Sep 13, 1911, d. Nov 8, 1990, hus of Eileen O. __, son of Walter D. and Sarah L. Vallandingham Clements.
GARDNER, Leonard Marsden, 91, b. Apr 1, 1900 TN, d. Sep 12, 1991, divorced from Alice Gardner, son of George W. and Jessie E. Foote Gardner.
HAZEL, Earl Hezekiah, b. Aug 15, 1913, d. Nov 3, 1988, hus of Agnes __, son of Lee and Julia Saulk Hazel.
HELMS, Katherine, b. Dec 6, 1912 NY, d. Nov 26, 1993, wife of __ Benjamin, dau of Fred and Fannie Longworth Helms.
HOWELL, Rosa Franklin, b. May 1, 1900, d. Jul 18, 1989, wife of Thomas 'George' Strickland, dau of Robert H. and Mary Elizabeth Creech Howell.
LANTZ, Allen Ward, b. Aug 22, 1918 VA, d. Mar 30, 1988, hus of Dana J. Witburn, son of Jasper A. and Dorothy Dove Lantz.
LONG, Willard B., Jr. b. Dec 18, 1926, d. Aug 9, 1988, hus of Mary Ellen __, son of Willard B. and Bertie "Barefoot" Long.
LOUDEN, John Bertram, d. Jan 5, 1983, m. 7 Oct 1931 Barbara Catherine Dean.
NEWKIRK, Rebecca, d. 1979, m. 1962 Roscoe Lee Strickland.
PARRIS, Hilary Jane, d. at birth Jul 9, 1992, dau of Alan and Cheryl Martin Parris; gdau

of Marvin and Miriam Parris of SC; William and Colleen Martin; ggdau of Lola Quilliam of LaFayette, LA. and Lela G. Martin of Wolcott, IN.

PEGG, Carrie Rebecca, 89, d. Aug 4, 1991, wife of James Biscoe, dau of James Luther and Sarah Ellen Purcell Pegg.

PEGG, Helen Genevieve, b. Oct 26, 1911, d. Apr 4, 1988, wife of Cecil G. Strickland, dau of William F. and Drucy Gatton Pegg.

PULLIAM, Jane Wilda, b. Jan 12, 1903 TX, d. Sep 13, 1989, wife of Ted O. Stroud, dau of Rev. Theodore and Talley Mullins Pulliam.

STEWART, George Thomas, b. Apr 19, 1934, d. Feb 13, 1990, hus of Mary __, son of Joseph R. and Florence Stewart.

STRICKLAND, Mahartney F., Sr. b. Mar 31, 1926 NC, d. Jan 2, 1992 NM, hus of Hilda Long, son of Thomas George and Rosa Franklin Howell Strickland.

STROUD, Fran, b. Aug 23, 1927 TX, d. Jan 22, 1991, wife of __ Cawood, dau of Ted O. and Jane Pulliam Stroud.

TAWNEY, Ralph Arthur, Sr. b. Aug 13, 1939 DC, d. Mar 8, 1991, hus of Joan Ann __, son of James Merriman II and Catherine Mary Tawney.

WILLENBORG, Bush Foley, b. Jun 7, 1902, d. Mar 11, 1988, hus of Odie L. __.

WISE, Robert Calvin, Jr. b. Jan 30, 1911, d. Sep 7, 1990, hus of Agnes Enola Twilley, son of Robert C. and Nettie Graves Wise.

WOODLAND, Elsie Irene, b. Dec 5, 1919, d. Nov 16, 1989, wife of Edward Jerome Holton, dau of Willie and Eleanora Braxton Woodland.

WOODSON, Julia E., b. Aug 3, 1920 VA, d. Jul 9, 1990, wife of William H. Brown, Sr., dau of Nathaniel and Moriah Woodson.

EVERGREEN MEMORIAL PARK
Chancellor's Run Road
Lexington Park. Md.

BADALAMENTI, Joseph Natoli, b. Oct 13, 1905 NYC, d. Nov 23, 1993, hus of Eva Miller, son of Andrew and Frances Badalamenti.
BROWN, Margaret Virginia, b. Oct 26, 1911 NC, d. Jan 14, 1992, wife of Marion Leroy Huff, dau of John Henry and Sally Locke Rice Brown.
CARTER, Orbin Hans III, b. Sep 28, 1963, d. Jan 23, 1992, m. 28 Sep 1984 Terrie Lynn Blackistone, son of Orbin II and Delie Jeannette Anderson Carter.
GASSMAN, Anne Elizabeth, b. April 20, 1915 PA, d. Nov 29, 1989, wife of __ Stewart, dau of Joseph and Anna Gassman.
GIBSON, Ruth Louise, b. Apr 28, 1926 NY, d. Dec 13, 1992 DC, wife of William Joseph Gray, dau of Hiram and Georgianna Jones Gibson.
GOLDER, Margaret Hartline, d. Oct 29, 1988, wife of John Kenneth Shrey.
GRAY, William Joseph, d. Dec 15, 1967, m. 11 Jan 1948 NY Ruth Louise Gibson.
HIDALGO, Allan Sagun, Jr. b. Sep 16, 1969 Italy, d. Nov 16, 1993, son of Allan S. and Margaret Powell Hidalgo.
HUFF, Marion Leroy, d. 1981, hus of Margaret Virginia Brown.
MINNICK, Ethel Betty, b. Nov 29, 1915 VA, d. Mar 30, 1993, wife of Royal Wilford "Roy" Cyrus, dau of John W. and Ellie Bell Minnick.
MONEYMAKER, Lloyd Albert, Sr. b. Mar 20, 1929 VA, d. Nov 21, 1993, m. 16 Feb 1950 Blanche Duke Parrish, son of Sidney Bailey and Annie Pearl Henderson Moneymaker.
QUADE, Elizabeth Agnes, b. Nov 24, 1919, d. Mar 28, 1988, wife of Lewis Clements Bowles, Sr., dau of Richard C. and Alice Russell Quade.
RANDOLPH, John Joseph Leroy Paul, b. May 1, 1988, d. Jun 16, 1988, son of John Clifford and Kelly Denise Willenborg Randolph; gson

of Leroy and Vernon Willenborg; Shirley Ann Johnson of TN; ggson of Odie Willenborg; Randy Paul Randolph.

RATLIFF, Sandy, b. Jan 30, 1953 VA, d. Oct 15, 1993, wife of Kevin W. King, dau of Roy Ratliff and Dorothy Twilley Ratliff Russell.

SEXTON, Christine Marie, b. Jul 4, 1933 VA, d Jul 3, 1991, wife of __ Biscoe, dau of Orbin and Laura Phillips Sexton.

SHEPHERD, Barkley, USN, b. Dec 16, 1938 KY, d. Dec 27, 1993, m. (2d) 5 Jul 1991 Mary Lee Fitzpatrick, son of Juanita Shepherd and the late Bueren Marcum.

SHREY, John Kenneth "Kenny", b. Sep 14, 1915 PA, d. Mar 15, 1993, hus of Margaret Hartline Golder, son of Luther and Esther Bastian Shrey.

SULLIVAN, Madeline L., b. Oct 31, 1923 CT, d. Mar 6, 1989, wife of William H. Mann, dau of Eugene and Nellie Clark Sullivan.

SUTHERLAND, Eva Mae, b. Dec 12, 1897, d. Apr 21, 1989, wife of John C. Dugan, dau of Ira and Nancy Wallace Sutherland.

TAYLOR, Stephanie Mae, b. Oct 26, 1943 KY, d. Jun 19, 1988 PA, wife of Larry D. Borg, dau of Steve and Willena Morris Taylor.

THEODOSSIOU, Helen, b. Dec 28, 1907 Cyprus, d. Feb 17, 1991, wife of Pandelis Samaras, dau of Steliane and Chara Sambos Theodossiou.

THORNE, Paul Eugene, Sr. b. Apr 16, 1915 OH, d. May 1, 1988 TX, m. 1944 Faye Slacum, son of Orrie Eugene and Gladys Wagoner Thorne.

TRAN, Khiem "Kim" Thi, 30, d. Dec 29, 1993, wife of __ Hinton.

VAN METER, Vina, b. Dec 12, 1909 WV, d. Nov 20, 1992, wife of William Henry Shaffer, dau of Tilden and Bertha Evans Van Meter.

WILLIS, Clarence Robert, Jr. b. Apr 5, 1968, d. Jan 1, 1994, son of Clarence R. Willis and Betty Lou Carson Willis Carter.

WOOD, Christine Monica, b. Nov 16, 1988, d. Feb 5, 1989, dau of Michael D. and Julie Morgan Wood.

FIRST FRIENDSHIP METHODIST CEMETERY
Ridge, Maryland

Unmarked graves identified by research of Mrs. Pat Biondi, Ridge, Md.

ALLGOOD, Thelma Beatrice, b. Sep 16, 1909, d. Jan 2, 1978, wife of Thomas H. Fenwick.
BAECHTOLD, Mary Helen, d. Apr 10, 1974, wife of Ralph Baechtold.
BAECHTOLD, Ralph, no dates.
BARNES, William M., b. Sep 30, 1864, d. Oct 11, 1915.
BISCOE, Sallie Ann, b. Aug 4, 1828, d. Jan 30, 1882.
BISHOP, Benjamin F., b. 1886, d. 1972.
BOYD, Virginia, b. 1904, d. 1971, wife of Robert F. Somers.
BRADBURN, Lloyd V., d. Feb 7, 1922.
BROWN, Horace Clement, b. 1885, d. 1965.
BROWN, Melissa S., b. 1888, d. 1966.
BUSH, Harry, d. 1859, 42nd year of his age.
CAREY, Mr., unmarked grave.
CAREY, Mrs., unmarked grave.
CHERRY, Benjamin W., b. Apr 16, 1903, d. Mar 10, 1969.
COURTNEY, Lewis F., b. 1869, d. 1957, hus of Lucy B. Abell.
DAVIS, Jemima, d. Jul 11, 1837, aged 75 years.
DIZE, Fannie Price, unmarked grave.
ETHRIDGE, ANNA P.E., b. Aug 26, 1914, d. Mar 24, 1972.
FENWICK, Elizabeth B., b. 1857, d. 1934, wife of Thomas E. Fenwick.
FENWICK, Lottie A., b. Sep 17, 1885, d. Mar 3, 1889.
FENWICK, Marie S., b. 1896, d. 1954.
FENWICK, Thomas E., b. 1856, d. 1926.
FENWICK, Thomas H., b. May 20, 1889, d. Mar 9, 1965, hus of Thelma Beatrice Allgood.
FIELDS, Abraham P., b. Aug 28, 1870, d. Aug 12, 1889, son of Dr. A.P. and Susannah Fields.
FORREST, Dr. John Wesley, b. Mar 17, 1819, d. Apr 29, 1871, hus of Ann White Price.

FOXWELL, John L., b. May 4, 1839, d. Jan 30, 1881.
GREENWELL, Albert E., b. Aug 8, 1874, d. Jul 14, 1938.
GREENWELL, Albert E., Jr. b. Feb 28, 1909, d. Apr 19, 1977.
GREENWELL, Amy M., b. Jan 6, 1874, d. Dec 16, 1961.
GREENWELL, Marian Ann, unmarked grave.
HAMMETT, Mary E., b. 1874, d. 1935, wife of Thomas Hammett.
HANEY, W.A., b. 1870, d. 1926.
JONES, Mollie F., b. Oct 8, 1886, d. Dec 11, 1967.
LANG, Joseph A., b. Sep 22, 1922, d. Jul 19, 1974.
LANG, Margaret Ann, d. 1963.
LETAU, Evelyn Irene, b. Mar 21, 1915 Balto, d. Oct 24, 1992, wife of William Christopher Nichalson, Jr., dau of August Frederick and Elizabeth Lillian Schefere Letau.
LETTAU, Charles August, b. 1942, d. 1964.
LETTAU, Mary C., b. 1952, d. 1952.
MAJORS, Leslie Andrew, 86, d. Oct 26, 1991.
MAYOR, Edward, b. 1854, d. 1933.
MAYOR, Edward D., b. Aug 8, 1898, d. Nov 14, 1977.
MAYOR, Margie M., b. Jan 12, 1898, d. Apr 2, 1974, wife of Edward D. Mayor.
McKENNEY, Balsorrah H., b. Jan 10, 1855, d. Jan 29, 1878.
MESSICK, Ralph, unmarked grave.
MOOR, John, d. Dec 9, 1859, 40th year.
MOTTLER, Shirley Ann Coffman, b. Dec 14, 1951, d. Jun 25, 1973.
NELSON, James H. O'Niell, b. 1881, d. Jan 11, 1884, 2 yr 5 mos, son of W.J. and Roxey A. Nelson.
NELSON, Marcillious R., b. 1883, d. Oct 1883, 8 mos, son of W.J. and Roxey A. Nelson.
NELSON, Roxey Ann, b. Jul 10, 1855, d. Apr 14, 1889, wife of W.J. Nelson.
NELSON, Sabrie, b. Feb 28, 1896, d. Oct 31, 1965.
NICHALSON, Alton Lee, d. May 5, 1981.

First Friendship

NICHALSON, John Harold, b. Dec 2, 1964, d. Mar 5, 1968, son of Alton L. Nichalson.
PRICE, Ann White, b. Mar 25, 1827, d. Mar 3, 1876, wife of Dr. John W. Forrest.
REDMOND, Mr., unmarked grave.
RIDGELL, Charles E., b. Feb 5, 1900, d. Aug 30, 1970.
SAUNDERS, Janie F., b. 1890, d. 1967.
SAUNDERS, Wilber W., b. 1875, d. 1963.
SAUNDERS, Wilbur Wesley, b. Oct 3, 1917, d. Nov 15, 1989, hus of Irene Thumbsur, son of Wilbur W. and Jane Sanner Saunders.
SHAW, Raymond Herold, b. Jun 9, 1925, d. Apr 23, 1969.
SISSON, Mary Lamb, unmarked grave.
SISSON, Will, unmarked grave.
SMITH, infant, child of Charles T. and Cherry F. Smith, unmarked grave.
SOMERS, Robert F., b. 1902, d. 1982, hus of Virginia Boyd.
SOMERS, Wesley Harrison, b. 1913, d. 1965.
SOUDER, Roland Atwood, unmarked grave.
THARPE, W. Terry, b. 1951, d. 1976.
THARPE, Claude Daniel, b. Oct. 31, 1949, d. Apr 15, 1993, son of Claude and Laura Hatcher Tharpe.
TODD, Mary M., b. Mar 1, 1844, d. Jan 2, 1908, wife of George Todd.
UGLOW, Norman Ray, USN WWII, b. Oct 13, 1923 PA, d. Jan 9, 1992, m. 1944 Eleanor Hendrick, son of Walter Van and Blanche Bittinger Uglow.
VALDENAR, William Ronald, b. Aug 24, 1942, d. Oct 27, 1974.
WEST, Anna Maria, b. Apr 4, 1835, d. Dec 9, 1903, wife of William T. West.
WEST, Hattie D., d. Jun 4, 1890, 16 yrs 11 mos, wife of Jerry Wrightson, dau of W.T. and Annie West.
WEST, Charles, d. 1972.
WEST, Theodore, unmarked grave
WEST, William, d. 1968.
WILSON, Alice Mae, b. 1893, d. 1962.
WILSON, James Walter, b. Mar 1, 1871, d. Mar 25, 1951.

WISE, John Albert, b. Oct 15, 1877, d. Jan 19, 1952, son of Robert McK and Lydia Wise.
WISE, Mary Custis, b. Aug 25, 1876, d. Nov 2, 1884.
WOOD, Elfreda Lillian, b. Nov 7, 1921, d. Aug 19, 1978.
WRIGHTSON, James D., b. Nov 6, 1886, d. Jul 11, 1906.
WRIGHTSON, Jennie M.S., b. Feb 4, 1859, d. no date on stone, wife of John B. Wrightson.
WRIGHTSON, John B., b. Oct 28, 1860, d. May 12, 1923.
WRIGHTSON, John W., b. Nov 13, 1827, d. Mar 29, 1887.
WRIGHTSON, Mary Jane, b. Oct 29, 1829, d. Mar 1, 1897.
YEATMAN, Ann Maria, unmarked grave.
YEATMAN, Cora Elizabeth, unmarked grave.
YEATMAN, Helen E., b. Aug 12, 1914, d. Apr 8, 1977, Memorial stone, buried in Balto., Md.
YEATMAN, W.M., b. Oct 1, 1830, d. May 31, 1908, hus of A.M. Yeatman.

HOLY FACE RCC CEMETERY
Great Mills. Md.

ADAMS, George Parren, b. Sep 18, 1904, d. Dec 28, 1993, m. 15 Feb 1926 Sarah Massie Shepherd, son of Columbus O. and Mary Indiana Edwards Adams.

ALVEY, Clayton Edward "Reds", Sr. b. Nov 12, 1903, d. Feb 20, 1991, hus of Edna Leigh Cullison, son of George E. and Clara S. Hayes Alvey.

BARBER, Mary Ella, b. Dec 20, 1925, d. Jun 25, 1988, wife of __ Warner, dau of Walter and Mary Toney Barber.

BARNARD, Raymond Herbert, b. May 12, 1906 NY, d. Oct 23, 1992, m. 1946 CT Matilda Marian Salvioli, son of Amie Pollifetti and Maude Alice Barnard.

BEAL, Thomas Henry, b. Aug 10, 1912, d. Mar 13, 1987, hus of Alice __, son of Matthew and Lucy Barber Beal.

BOWLES, James Lloyd, b. Jan 15, 1910, d. Jul 24, 1989, hus of Julia __, son of Wilson and Bertha Mae Airey Bowles.

CECIL, James Eugene, b. Oct 17, 1892, d. Mar 18, 1988, son of George Perry and Susanna Armsworthy Cecil.

COLLEARY, Paul Thomas, b. Jan 21, 1962, d. Jun 17, 1988, son of John E. and Shirley Evans Colleary.

COMBS, Margaret Mary, b. Feb 14, 1914, d. May 25, 1988, wife of John N. Cullison, Sr.

COMBS, Mary Rose, b. Feb 26, 1924, d. Jan 15, 1989, wife of Capt. Leonard Louis Kohl, USA, 4th child of William Parran and Blanche Victoria Redman Combs.

COMBS, Robert William "Bobby", b. Jul 26, 1952 DC, d. Jul 29, 1992, son of William Clayton and Mary Virginia Crump Combs.

COMBS, Thomas E., Sr. b. Mar 19, 1920, d. Jan 4, 1992, son of James T. and Annie May Cecil Combs.

CRYER, Mary 'Maude' Louise, b. Dec 7, 1916, d. Dec 20, 1991, wife of Richard Theodore Nelson, Sr., dau of Francis Leslie and Rosetta

Jarboe Cryer.
DEAR, Grace, b. April 5, 1913 MS, d. Oct 31, 1993, m. Oct 1929 MS Howard W. Evans, dau of Sam and Sarah Richardson Dear.
DENIS, Wendy Marie, b. Oct 10, 1973, d. Aug 27, 1990, dau of Tom and Linda Brown.
DYSON, Brent, b. Jun 14, 1908, d. Jan 17, 1991, hus of (1st) Vi Hammett, (2d) Hilda Louise Mauck, son of Oden M. and Margaret Watts Dyson.
EVANS, Howard W., d. 1975, hus of Grace Dear.
EVANS, Thomas Rowland, b. Apr 24, 1909, d. Jul 9, 1988, son of Louis R. and Margaret Long Evans.
FORREST, Margaret Sandra "Sandy", b. Jan 17, 1944, d. Jan 19, 1991, wife of Alfred Knott, dau of Ernest Matthew and Jeanette Allen Greenwell Forrest.
GARDINER, Kevin Daniel, Sgt USA, b. Jun 16, 1967, d. May 3, 1992 FL, hus of Tammy Treadwell, son of Edward Gerald and Dianne Finch Gardiner; gson of Harry and Helen Finch; Imogene Gardiner.
GODDARD, Robert Luke, Sr. b. Aug 19, 1917, d. Jul 6, 1992, hus of Evelyn Gatton, son of Luke and Elvie Pilkerton Goddard.
HAMMETT, Charles Somerset, b. Jan 14, 1889, d. Jan 10, 1968, hus of Rose Jones, son of David and Henrietta Cox Hammett.
HAMMETT, Laurence Matthews, Sr., b. Jul 23, 1911, d. Dec 16, 1988, hus of Alberta Catherine Combs.
HAMMETT, Ruth, b. Feb 3, 1913, d. Jun 4, 1990, wife of Ernest L. Coombs, Sr., dau of Richard T. and Margaret Jones Hammett.
HAMMETT, Vi, d. 1980, 1st wife of Brent Dyson.
HAMMETT, Virginia, d. 1984, wife of T. Melvin Jarboe.
HASKELL, Bruce Bailey, b. May 25, 1948 GA, d. Mar 27, 1988, son of Warren B. and Ann B. Gasparovic Haskell.
HASKELL, Warren Bailey, b. Nov 5, 1917 MN, d. Aug 21, 1990, hus of Ann Beatrice Gasparovic, son of James Madison and Ida Catherine Bailey Haskell.

HAYFORD, Lyle David, b. Apr 14, 1916 MN, d. Oct 11, 1993, m. 27 May 1965 (late) Margaret "Pegg" Harden Randall, son of David A. and Blanche B. Tynan Hayford. Memorial Mass.
HEWITT, Christopher Francis, b. Jul 8, 1989, d. Jul 21, 1989, son of William F. and Sharon Pilkerton Hewitt.
HEWITT, William 'Franklin', b. May 18, 1922, d. Apr 14, 1991, hus of Elizabeth 'Ellen' Hill, son of William Vernon and Lettie Ann Vallandingham Hewitt.
HEWITT, Willim Vernon. d. Jan 25, 1967, hus of Lettie Ann Vallandingham.
JARBOE, T. Melvin, b. Jun 18, 1910, d. Feb 12, 1992, hus of Virginia Hammett, son of J. Clyde and Minnie Fenhagen Jarboe.
JOHNSON, John M., MD TEC 5 316 BASE UNIT AAF WWII, b. Nov 30, 1919, d. Jan 21, 1966.
JOHNSON, Peter William, d. Oct 14, 1971.
JOHNSON, Thomas Henry, b. Jan 31, 1920, d. Apr 14, 1989, 2d hus of Mae Virginia Mattingly, son of Thomas Alvin and Pauline Abell Johnson.
JUROVATY, Catherine Anna, b. May 12, 1919, d. Jun 7, 1992, Patuxent NAS Hospital, wife of Michael William Lang, dau of John and Katherine Simonchi Jurovaty.
KNOTT, Dorothy Magdalene, b. Oct 13, 1917, d. May 28, 1992, wife of William E. Winters, Sr., dau of John "Gonzie" and Annie Maria Goddard Knott.
KNOTT, Joseph Irving, Sr. b. Jan 2, 1927, d. Aug 6, 1990, hus of Hazel T. __, son of John "Gonzie" and Annie Maria Goddard Knott.
LANG, Michael William, d. Apr 13, 1970, m. 20 Sep 1936 Catherine Anna Jurovaty.
MATTINGLY, Mae Virginia, b. Jun 6, 1910, m. (1st)__ Mattingly, (2d) Henry 'Thomas' Johnson.
MAYNARSKY, Diane, b. Nov 28, 1938 NY, d. May 10, 1992, m. 17 May 1959 John Joseph Healy, dau of John and Joanne O'Donnell Maynarsky.
MAYOR, Charles Edward, b. Jan 13, 1927, d. Sep 14, 1993, m. 28 Jul 1951 Mary Teresa Goldsborough, son of Joseph and Myrtle

Ridgell Mayor.
MAYOR, Joseph Leonard, Sr. b. Sep 19, 1897, d. Feb 1, 1991, hus of Marie Norris Guy, son of Charles Henry and Annie Amanda Cullison Mayor.
MAYOR, Joseph Leonard "Lenny", Jr. b. Oct 17, 1942, d. Mar 16, 1987, son of Joseph Leonard and Myrtle E. Ridgell Mayor.
MAYOR, Richard David, b. Feb 2, 1955, d. Jan 13, 1990, hus of Barbara J. Purdy, son of Richard B. and Regina Goldsmith Mayor; gson of Leonard and Myrtle Ridgell Mayor.
MIESOWITZ, William Joseph, b. Aug 26, 1904 Poland, d. Sep 22, 1988, hus of Marie Harriet __.
NELSON, Richard Theodore "Dick", Sr. b. Jun 4, 1909, d. Dec 13, 1988 DC, m. 1936, Maude Louise Cryer, son of Zepheniah and Elizabeth Woodburn Nelson.
NORRIS, Catherine Eloise, b. Jul 12, 1922, d. Apr 16, 1990, wife of George E. Combs, dau of Joseph and Lucy Norris.
NORRIS, Charles Aubrey, d. Dec 17, 1975, m. 1949 Margaret Laverne Unkle.
NORRIS, Daniel Thomas, b. Jul 20, 1957, d. Jun 29, 1989, son of Thomas Ed and Theresa Ann Norris.
NORRIS, Joseph Jenifer, b. Jun 8, 1921, d. Mar 11, 1988, hus of Delores __, son of Joseph Brennan and Lula Abell Norris.
NOVOTNY, Robert Thomas, b. Nov 22, 1924 NY, d. Dec 20, 1988, hus of Mary H. __, son of Robert William and Mae Hickey Novotny.
OWENS, James Allen, Sr. b. Feb 8, 1916, d. Jul 28, 1993, m. 29 Apr 1930 Frances Mary Russell, son of Leo Dudley and Vertie Victoria Redman Owens.
RANDALL, Margaret Hardey, b. Dec 18, 1916, d. Feb 23, 1992, wife of Lyle David "Bud" Hayford, dau of Louis and Martha L. Washington Randall.
RUSKIN, James A., Sr. b. Jun 13, 1912, d. Apr 15, 1990, hus of Mary Elizabeth __, son of Jas. Henry and Rosa Marie Butler Ruskin.
SCHERNE, Josephine Elizabeth, b. Dec 5, 1909,

d. Jan 20, 1991, m. (2d) __ Schorn, dau of Frank and Anna Bender Scherne of NY.
SHEPHERD, Sarah Massie, d. Feb 13, 1979, wife of George Parren Adams.
STALLMAN, Peter Edward, 68, b. MI, d. Jul 8, 1992, son of Joseph Bernard and Mary Estelle Williams Stallman.
STONE, Dorothy H., b. 1902, d. 1968, wife of Ernest L. Stone.
STONE, Ernest L., b. 1904, d. 1977, hus of Dorothy H. Stone.
TARLETON, Luther Reginold, b. Aug 30, 1905, d. Apr 18, 1990, hus of Mary Josephine __, son of Samuel Cleveland and Maggie Josephine Purcell Tarleton.
UNKLE, Margaret Lavern "Peggy", b. Oct 16, 1932, d. Mar 24, 1992, wife of Charles Aubrey Norris, dau of James William and Thelma Regina Thompson Unkle.
UNKLE, Robert William, Sr. b. Mar 14, 1937, d. Nov 11, 1989, hus of Sara F. __, son of James William and Thelma R. Thompson Unkle.
VALLANDINGHAM, Lettie Ann, b. Apr 5, 1897, d. Mar 23, 1984, wife of Wlliam Vernon Hewitt.
ZHAN, Eileen Deloris, b. May 5, 1922 SD, d. Jul 29, 1989, wife of John Antonovitch, dau of John and Pauline Hoffman Zhan.

IMMACULATE HEART OF MARY RCC
Rte 235,
Lexington Park, Md.

ANDERSON, George L., b. May 12, 1937 DC, d. Aug 1, 1992, hus of Rosalie Stewart, son of Norman and Anna Hildenberg Anderson of Clinton, Md.
AWKWARD, Thomas Jefferson, Sr. b. Nov 24, 1924 VA, d. Sep 19, 1992, hus of Theodoris Nolan, son of Joseph and Cora Jackson Awkward.
BARNES, Catherine Ann, b. Jan 24, 1932, d. Aug 29, 1988, dau of John Douglas and Annie Somerville Barnes.
BARNES, John Warren, b. Jan 23, 1928, d. Feb 11, 1989, hus of Mary Louise Barber, son of Francis Xavier and Queenie Viola Barnes.
BARNES, Marie Heldegarde, b. Mar 14, 1913, d. Feb 24, 1993, m. 22 Mar 1937 Benjamin Edward Lynch, dau of James and Annie Egerton Barnes.
BARNES, Thomas Parren, b. Jun 8, 1935, d. Apr 6, 1991, hus of Shirley Mary Frances __, son of Joseph Shepaly and Mary Rozenia Edgertson Barnes.
BAULT, Barbara Anne, b. Jan 7, 1947 MI, d. Aug 5, 1992, wife of Jerome Richard Sochowski, dau of Ralph and Eva Coleman Bault of Roseville, MI.
BEAUREGARD, Madeline Lena (Mrs), d. Feb 4, 1991.
BECKERT, Randolph William, b. Nov 5, 1929 Balto, d. Nov 11, 1988, hus of Marjorie O'Brien son of William R. and Mary E. MacFarron Beckert.
BISCOE, Joseph William, b. May 30, 1933, d. Dec 28, 1989, son of William Thomas and Mary Margaret Biscoe.
BRISCOE, Stephen Alexander, b. Mar 1, 1965, d. Nov 16, 1989, son of Pauline J. Briscoe and James W. Handy.
BURKETT, Wendy Lee, b. Jun 29, 1941, d. Oct 13, 1988, wife of Lawrence J. Gallagher, dau of Dorothy E. and Charles M. Burkett, Sr.
CALDWELL, John Benjamin "Jack", b. Dec 13, 1898, d. Jun 19, 1989, hus of Kathryn Gene-

vieve "Kitty" __, son of Charles W. and Julia A. Mahoney Caldwell.
CALLIHAM, Alice M., b. Apr 29, 1928 OK, d. Feb 11, 1989, wife of Ralph E. Dresher, dau of Alec David and Annie Vaught Calliham.
CAMPBELL, Bernice Elizabeth, b. May 1, 1911 Balto, d. Oct 25, 1991, wife of __ Nolan, dau of Blake and Elizabeth Campbell.
CHASE, Joseph Bernard, USA WWII, b. Feb 14, 1914, d. Mar 16, 1992, hus of Mary Jones, son of Joseph and Edith Biscoe Chase.
CHASE, Lawrence Vincent, b. Jul 16, 1916, d. Dec 1, 1988, hus of Sarah G. __.
CHASE, Marion Levinalee, b. Nov 5, 1954, d. Mar 17, 1993, dau of Lawrence and Sarah Thomas Chase.
CHASE, Raymond Emory, Sr. b. Aug 7, 1922, d. Nov 28, 1988, hus of Elizabeth Toney, son of Arthur and Edith Briscoe Chase.
COLLINS, Francis Cleon, Sr. b. Sep 9, 1935, d. Apr 21, 1988, hus of Mary Alice __, son of Henry J. Sr. and Thelma T. Collins.
COOK, Edward Joseph, b. Nov 5, 1924 Balto, d. May 15, 1991, hus of Maxine O. Waters.
DEXTER, John Brett, b. Feb 22, 1909, d. Jul 2, 1988, hus of Regina Dorothy Gams, son of John Nelson and Kate Ingersol Dexter.
DYSON, Aloysius Chester, b. Sep 18, 1920, d. Nov 21, 1988, son of Margaret Dyson; gson of John and Louise Dyson.
EISGRAU, Alexander Edward "Al", b. Feb 8, 1910 NY, d. Dec 14, 1991, hus of Margaret Susan O'Hearn, son of Jacob Eisgrau.
FENWICK, Mary Elizabeth, b. Jul 4, 1911, d. Apr 13, 1990, dau of Frank and Maggie Barber Fenwick.
FISHER, Allen Charles, b Jan 21, 1909 OH, d. May 18, 1988, hus of Catherine M. __.
FLEISSNER, William Howard "Willie", b. May 19, 1915 NY, d. Sep 19, 1990, hus of (2d) Helen J. __, son of Edward and Anna Ruhlman Fleissner.
GAMS, Regina Dorothy, b. Mar 9, 1919, d. Sep 8, 1988, wife of John Brett Dexter, dau of Frank and Anna Droschak Gams.

Immaculate Heart

GEORGE, Margaret Catherine, 71, d. Jun 23, 1989, wife of Bill George.
GRINDER, Raymond M., d. 1964, m. 1923 Theodora Catherine Pilkerton.
HART, Evelyn, b. Dec 29, 1913 MO, d. Apr 3, 1993, wife of James Ora Hills, dau of Laurence and Glenn Talbert Hart.
HEARD, Joseph Matthew, b. Jul 7, 1911, d. Apr 9, 1987, hus of Agnes Norris.
HILLS, James Ora "J.O.", d. Feb 16, 1980, hus of Evelyn Hart.
HINZ, Cleo Lloyd, b. Feb 20, 1924 MN, d. Apr 14, 1993, hus of Lillian Gertrude __, d. Jan 8, 1984, son of Robert Hinz.
HOLLEY, Angel Alexandria, infant, d. Oct 26, 1992, dau of Rita Hebb and Gary Holley; gdau of Joseph and Mary Hebb; Richard Holley and Lena Gough.
JOHNSON, Sonya Elise, b. Dec 15, 1967, d. Mar 18, 1988, dau of Francis R. and Teresa E. Johnson.
JORDON, Mary Ethel, b. 1897, d. Apr 14, 1971, wife of John A. Johnson, dau of Mrs. Mary Estelle Carroll.
KANE, James Leonard, b. May 1, 1910, d. May 12, 1990, son of Joseph Francis and Daisy Ann Washington Kane.
KANE, William Francis, b. Aug 10, 1908, d. Jul 26, 1989, hus of Mary Margaret __, son of Joseph Francis and Daisy Ann Washington Kane.
LAIGLE, Lowell Wayne, b. Apr 9, 1957 San Diego, CA, d. Jun 24, 1989, hus of Tracy Bast, son of Paul David and Charlene Mary Laigle.
LATHAM, Timothy Brian "Tommy", b. Nov 5, 1964, d. Mar 5, 1993, m. 1990 Eve Walker, son of James and Carolyn Latham.
LYNCH, Benjamin Edward, d. 1964, hus of Marie Heldegarde Barnes.
McLAUGHLIN, Agnes, b. Mar 23, 1899 Co. Derry, Ireland, d. Feb 17, 1993, dau of James and Annie McDermott McLaughlin.
MEYERS, Theodore Thomas, 57, d. Sep 28, 1992 Largo, FL.
MOORCONES, Joseph John, b. Jul 29, 1902, d. Oct 16, 1988, hus of Mary Winifred Short.

NORRIS, Agnes Pearl, b. Sep 28, 1910, d. Mar 19, 1993 DC, m. 18 Apr 1934 Joseph Matthew Heard, dau of Bernard M. and Leila Hayden Norris.
NOYES, Clifford Lewis, Sr. b. Mar 23, 1915 MI, d. Jul 7, 1992 DC, m. 20 June 1942 Wandau Rayniak, son of Lewis and Rebecca McAllister Noyes.
O'BRIEN, Marjorie Anne, b. Jun 6, 1934 DC, d. Oct 29, 1992, wife of Randolph W. Beckert, dau of William and Marguerite St. Peter O'Brien.
PRICE, Brent Matthew, b. Jan 6, 1928, d. Apr 18, 1993, m. 25 Oct 1953 Mary Catherine Adams, son of Claude and Bertha Gordon Price.
PRICE, Claude Sylvester, 85, b. Aug 28, 1903, d. Jan 9, 1989.
RABBITT, Ruth Lee, b. Nov 12, 1913 DC, d. Jul 7, 1992, wife of Edward J. Sumstine, dau of Harry and Fannie Yeatman Rabbitt.
RASPA, Joseph A., b. Aug 10, 1961 TN, d. Aug 2, 1988 IA, son of Sal and Myra Raspa. Memorial Service.
REDMOND, Jeffrey Leland "Jeffy", b. Nov 1, 1987 DC, drowned Jul 26, 1991, son of Charles A. and Mary Diane Aud Redmond; gson of Charles B. and Dorothy Redmond; George and Mary Aud.
RIDDELL, William Anthony, b. Dec 11, 1964, d. Apr 6, 1989, son of William Allen and Marie Makin Riddell.
ROITH, John George, 91, b. 1897 WI, d. Oct 13, 1988, hus of Marium Laurene ___.
SANCHEZ, Jacqueline, b. and d. Mar 19, 1992, dau of Alex and Ramona Cartagena Sanchez; gdau of Ana Sanchez of C. Amer. and Basilio Sanchez of NY; Iris Cartagena of NJ and Angel Cartagena of Elizabeth, NJ.
SAXON, Oliver, b. Mar 15, 1924, d. Jan 20, 1993, m. Apr 1950 Catherine M. Coates, son of Thomas and Leola Ennels Saxon.
SHADE, Joseph Edward, Sr. b. Jun 25, 1923, d. Jun 2, 1992, hus of Lillian Ellen Somerville, son of William, Sr. and Lillian Thomas Shade.

Immaculate Heart

SHORT, Mary Winifred, d. 1967, wife of Joseph John Moorcones.
STEVENS, Francis Ralph, b. May 18, 1909, d. Apr 27, 1989, hus of Margaret E. Snyder, son of Samuel Joseph and Mary Kelly Stevens.
THOMAS, Virginia Elene Bavely, b. Mar 5, 1918, d. Aug 18, 1988.
THOMPSON, Helen Rebecca, b. Oct 21, 1922, d. Jul 12, 1988, wife of Morris F. Jordon, dau of John Louis and Cora Johnson Thompson.
THOMPSON, James Harry, Sr. b. Jun 27, 1910, d. Nov 21, 1989, hus of Ann Elizabeth Lloyd, son of John Louis and Cora Rebecca Johnson Thompson.
THOMPSON, Nellie Elizabeth, b. Feb 2, 1907, d. Jan 6, 1991, dau of John Louis and Cora Rebecca Johnson Thompson.
TORNEY, James Richard, b. Apr 12, 1920, d. Apr 22, 1992 DC, son of Francis and Martha Hayden Torney.
TORNEY, Joseph Parran, b. Sep 15, 1930, d. Nov 25, 1988, son of Francis and Martha Hayden Torney.
WATTS, Stephen, 99, b. Jun 1, 1890, d. Dec 2, 1989, hus of Mary Idora ___, son of John and Lizza Watts.
WILKINS, Eugene Hamilton "Gene", b. Mar 31, 1927, d. Nov 21, 1992, m. 20 Aug 1955 Joyce W. Rudd, son of Carl and Bertha Ketterman Wilkins.
WRIGHT, Brian David, b. Dec 18, 1973, d. Nov 29, 1993, work accident, son of David Lee Wright and Yvonne Potter Wright Moss; gson of Edsel and Angie Malueq Potter; Berkley D. Wright of TN.
ZAWISLAK, Florence Marie, b. Jan 7, 1920, d. Aug 21, 1988, wife of Nicholas Thomas Potts, dau of Walter Edward and Mary Elizabeth Bubniak Zawislak.

JOY CHAPEL METHODIST CEMETERY
Joy Chapel Road
Hollywood, Md.

The first church was built in 1868 on land donated by James Joy. It was rebuilt in 1894 and burned to the ground in 1931. The present chapel was built by Mervel Dean in 1966 as a memorial to his wife and her parents.

Many of these dates were read from tombstones as a Bicentennial Project. Names were listed in alphabetical order and relationships were not shown.

ADAMS, Lee B., Sr. b. Feb 14, 1908, d. Sep 27, 1976.
ADAMS, Lee B., b. Jun 26, 1930, d. Mar 24, 1955.
ADAMS, Margaret L., b. 1910, d. 1973.
ALVEY, Tonia Lynn, infant girl, d. Apr 13, 1974.
ALVEY, Zonia Faye, d. Nov 11, 1972.
BAKER, John Edgar, Sr. b. Jan 2, 1899, d. Feb 16, 1958, 2nd hus of Irma Jones.
BARBER, Hazel, b. 1899, d. 1924, wife of Francis D. Johnson.
BARBER, J. Perry, Sr. b. 1875, d. 1933.
BARBER, Perry Duvall, b. 1906, d. 1906.
BECK, Albert L., b. 1909, d. 1968.
BIRTWISTLE, Leonard Roy, b. 1946, d. 1972.
BOND, Elizabeth T., b. Sep 21, 1873, d. Nov 30, 1932.
BOND, Hayden Benjamin, b. Mar 23, 1901, d. Sep 9, 1990, hus of Gertrude Copsey, son of Benjamin H. and Elizabeth Hayden Bond.
BOND, Hilda L., b. Aug 1, 1903, d. Oct 6, 1910.
BOND, Ira Joy, b. 1869, d. 1895.
BOND, John H., b. Sep 25, 1874, d. Jan 7, 1919.
BOND, Samuel Wylie, b. 1855, d. 1913.
BOYER, Wayne Allen, b. Jan 23, 1946, d. Jul 10, 1974.
BUCKMASTER, John Wallace, b. Feb 27, 1913, d. Oct 10, 1968, 3rd hus of Sylvia Eleanor Buckmaster.

BUCKMASTER, Philip D., b. Oct 30, 1904, d. May 9, 1972.
BUCKMASTER, Sylvia Eleanor, b. Sep 25, 1911, d. Sep 12, 1990, m. (1st) Albert I. Tracy, (2d) __ Melvin, (3d) John Wallace Buckmaster, dau of John Wesley and Effie Mae Parks Buckmaster.
BURR, I.E., b. 1906, d. 1963.
CALLIS, Clifton, b. 1882, d. 1938.
CALLIS, Eleanor May, b. Dec 18, 1912, d. Dec 10, 1918.
CALLIS, Frances H., b. 1926, d. 1964, wife of __ Bowles.
CALLIS, Laura, b. 1884, d. 1967.
CALLIS, Mable E., b. Jan 6, 1890, d. Jun 14, 1974.
CALLIS, Noah W., b. 1885, d. 1967.
COMBS, Virginia A., b. Feb 4, 1884, d. Aug 26, 1955, wife of Pirley C. Weeks.
DARE, Nathaniel H., b. 1886, d. Jul 21, 1981, hus of Myrtle Ruth Taylor.
DAVIS, Joseph King, b. 1890, d. 1961.
DAVIS, Mary A., b. 1886, d. 1962.
DAVIS, Sarah Bell, b. 1865, d. 1960.
DAVIS, Thomas Warn, b. Feb 18, 1888, d. Feb 4, 1972.
DEAKINS, Martha Ann, b. 1837, d. 1881, wife of __ Joy.
DEAKINS, Mary Emma, b. Oct 22, 1862, d. May 1, 1888, wife of N. R. Hales, dau of __ Deakins and Lydia C. __ Deakins Magill.
DEAN, Albert Levi, b. Sep 26, 1881, d. Apr 6, 1946, hus of Annie Mary Evans.
DEAN, Arthur R., b. May 4, 1881, d. Feb 13, 1911.
DEAN, B. Gladys (Mrs), b. Sep 12, 1899, d. May 11, 1988.
DEAN, Carrie B., b. 1879, d. 1959.
DEAN, Chester, no dates.
DEAN, David Chester, b. Oct 19, 1926, d. Dec 19, 1956.
DEAN, Elizabeth Catherine, b. Aug 15, 1845, d. Sep 24, 1928.
DEAN, Gary, b. and d. Dec 1, 1944.
DEAN, George Wilson, b. Dec 24, 1872, d. Jul

Joy Chapel

4, 1943, hus of Effie L. Graves.
DEAN, Irma M., b. 1914, d. Aug 19, 1915.
DEAN, James J., d. Jun 5, 1907.
DEAN, John A., d. Apr 22, 1919.
DEAN, John Caleb, b. Jun 15, 1855, d. Jun 12 1921, hus of Lydia A. Joy.
DEAN, Joseph Albert, b. Feb 6, 1920, d. Jan 9, 1980.
DEAN, Joseph Andre, b. Sep 5, 1970, d. Sep 7, 1970.
DEAN, Joseph R., b. 1844, d. Feb 26, 1906.
DEAN, June, b. Sep 20, 1923, d. May 29, 1993, m. 7 Aug 1943 John Gram Fletcher, dau of George W. and Effie Graves Dean.
DEAN, L. Maude, b. 1893, d. 1941, wife of ___ Smith.
DEAN, Mamie, b. 1875, d. 1896, wife of Robert H. Spedden.
DEAN, Mervell Miller, b. Dec 13, 1904, d. Feb 8, 1968, son of George and Effie Graves Dean.
DEAN, Nelson C., b. Oct 14, 1911, d. Mar 13, 1971.
DEAN, Raymond Levi, b. Nov 5, 1912, d. Jul 17, 1956.
DEAN, Roger H., b. Jun 13, 1899, d. Sep 22, 1978.
DEAN, Ruth, no dates.
DEAN, Sheldon M., b. Oct 31, 1902, d. Oct 14, 1908.
DEAN, Sterling Wilson, b. Sep 4, 1906, d. Dec 30, 1993, m. 12 Jul 1931 Grace Martha Taylor, son of George and Effie L. Graves Dean.
DEAN, Wilbur H., b. 1884, d. 1946.
DEAN, William Columbus, b. 1858, d. 1915.
DENT, Rosalie Ashton, d. 1889, wife of Archibald Pierce Maddox.
DILLON, Goldie G., b. Sep 30, 1915, d. May 19, 1955.
DOHRMAN, Wilbur Charles, b. Jul 13, 1927, d. Jan 17, 1992, hus of Oneita Sommerkamp, son of Wilbur J. and Eva Grace Darst Dohrman.
ELLIOTT, Roger, b. Jan 21, 1917, d. Jan 26, 1950.
EVANS, Abraham, b. 1894, d. 1900.
EVANS, Ann D., b. 1850, d. 1908.

EVANS, Annie Mary, b. Aug 24, 1892, d. Dec 25, 1947, wife of Albert Levi Dean.
EVANS, Eva G., b. 1914, d. 1914.
FORT, Doris Josephine, b. May 26, 1913, d. Mar 7, 1989, wife of Clifford D. Greig, dau of Sewell Thomas and Ella Simpson Fort.
FULTON, John "Scotty", b. Sep 9, 1909, d. May 9, 1963, m. 1932 NY Estelle Howland.
GATTON, Alice Victoria, b. Jul 28, 1868, d. Aug 29, 1965.
GATTON, Anna B., b. 1898, d. 1958.
GATTON, Charles M., b. Oct 22, 1859, d. Jul 30, 1942.
GATTON, Elizabeth M., b. Apr 12, 1892, d. Jan 2, 1975.
GATTON, Ernest E., b. 1887, d. 1963.
GATTON, Flossie M., b. 1892, d. 1930, wife of __ Wallace.
GATTON, J.C., b. Jul 28, 1875, d. Aug 4, 1911.
GATTON, Jackie J., b. and d. Aug 4, 1945.
GATTON, John W., b. Oct 7, 1835, d. Oct 13, 1908.
GATTON, Joseph E., b. Apr 27, 1862, d. Aug 26, 1927.
GATTON, June L., b. Jul 17, 1943, d. Dec 1943.
GATTON, Margaret E., b. 1900, d. 1923.
GATTON, Mary Jane, b. 1840, d. Dec 21, 1903, wife of W. W. Gatton.
GATTON, Oscar S., b. Aug 17, 1884, d. Apr 13, 1964, hus of Oster May __, b. Jun 11, 1886, d. Jun 19, 1957.
GATTON, Pirly I., b. 1887, d. Jan 29, 1959.
GATTON, Rebecca, b. 1875, d. 1939.
GATTON, Solomon R., b. Jun 11, 1909, d. Jun 12, 1934.
GATTON, Sommie W., b. 1864, d. 1929.
GATTON, Sterling L., b. Sep 18, 1911, d. Mar 24, 1976.
GODDARD, Lollie N., b. Aug 13, 1929, d. Mar 21, 1976.
GOULD, Madeline J., b. 1916, d. 1969.
GRAVES, Effie L., b. Nov 6, 1880, d. Dec 18, 1938, wife of George W. Dean.
GRAVES, Florence, b. 1867, d. 1945, wife of Hilary Eccleston Jones.

Joy Chapel

GRAVES, John Franklin, b. 1877, d. 1922.
GRAVES, Margaret D., b. 1875, d. 1963.
GREENWELL, Arabella, b. 1843, d. 1916, wife of __ Spedden.
GREIG, Clifford D., b. Jun 23, 1911, d. Jul 10, 1980, hus of Doris J. Fort.
GREIG, Miriam, b. Oct 11, 1948, d. Jun 19, 1968, wife of __ Roberts, dau of Clifford D. and Doris Josephine Fort Greig.
HAMMETT, Lida J., b. 1872, d. 1947, wife of __ Jones.
HAMMETT, Minnie M., b. Nov 20, 1856, d. Jun 26, 1882, wife of __ Jones.
HARROVER, George Jackson, b. Sep 7, 1869, d. Nov 3, 1959.
HARROVER, Lena Elizabeth, b. Jun 27, 1899, d. Aug 5, 1980.
HARSH, Robinson H., b. Oct 9, 1894, d. Oct 9, 1968.
HAYDEN, Alexander, b. 1880, d. 1967.
HAYDEN, Alice L., b. 1871, d. 1904.
HAYDEN, Annie, b. 1876, d. 1907, wife of __ Joy.
HAYDEN, Annie M., b. 1882, d. 1899.
HAYDEN, Charles W., b. 1890, d. 1892.
HAYDEN, Elizabeth, b. 1809, d. 1879, wife of __ Joy.
HAYDEN, J. Alex., b. 1880, d. 1907.
HAYDEN, James Alexander M., b. 1843, d. 1893, hus of Mary J. __.
HAYDEN, Lena M., b. 1867, d. 1888.
HAYDEN, M. Germa, b. 1875, d. 1962.
HAYDEN, Marion R., b. 1887, d. 1973.
HAYDEN, Mary Ellis, b. 1846, d. 1934, wife of __ Joy.
HAYDEN, Mary I., b. 1848, d. 1926.
HEARD, M. Blanche, b. Sep 17, 1882, d. Mar 8, 1922, wife of __ Joy.
HOFFMAN, Mildred M., b. Aug 12, 1920, d. Mar 8, 1922.
HOFTIEZER, John, b. 1904, d. May 1983.
HOLTZ, John W., b. Nov 17, 1899, d. Aug 24, 1979, hus of Audry Wible.
HOOPER, Ella A., b. Jun 18, 1870, d. Aug 26, 1890.

HOOPER, John E., b. Nov 23, 1886, d. Jun 2, 1916.
HOOPER, William T., b. Mar 18, 1859, d. Jan 15, 1922.
HOWLAND, Estelle, b. Oct 9, 1911 NJ, d. Mar 28, 1992, m. 1932 NY, John "Scotty" Fulton, dau of Bordon Sanford and Jennie E. Lucas Howland.
INSLEY, Carl Deshield, b. Apr 5, 1887, d. Apr 6, 1971.
INSLEY, Harrison, b. 1894, d. 1895.
INSLEY, John Benjamin, b. Jan 6, 1845, d. Sep 24, 1914, hus of Martha Ellen Jones.
INSLEY, Mattie, b. Aug 14, 1889, d. Jul 15, 1982, wife of __ Bond.
INSLEY, Millard, b. 1889, d. 1892.
INSLEY, Patricia Lee, b. and d. Dec 4, 1968.
INSLEY, Preston Estee, b. Jul 29, 1896, d. Jul 15, 1993, m. 1928 Rosalie Jones, son of John Benjamin and Martha Ellen Jones Insley.
INSLEY, Wilmer, b. 1891, d. 1892.
JACKSON, John Carol, b. Jul 1, 1939, d. Aug 6, 1959.
JACKSON, Kate, b. Aug 3, 1886, d. Oct 28, 1972, wife of James Dammon Owen.
JOHNSON, Ada H., b. 1922, d. May 1984.
JOHNSON, Francis D., b. 1896, d. 1954, hus of Hazel Barber.
JONES, Alice L., b. Dec 23, 1869, d. May 7, 1894.
JONES, Amy, d. 1890.
JONES, Amy V., b. and d. Jan 3, 1894.
JONES, Annie W., b. 1862, d. 1892.
JONES, Beth Sheba, b. Aug 29, 1869, d. Mar 9, 1911, wife of __ Taylor.
JONES, Chester H., b. Sep 9, 1893, d. Jun 14, 1894.
JONES, D. Whitfield, b. 1854, d. 1892, hus of Minnie M. __.
JONES, Edward S., b. 1832, d. 1904, hus of Catherine E. __, b. 1837, d. 1926.
JONES, Edward S., b. Jul 4, 1905, d. Jul 19, 1905.
JONES, Elizabeth A., b. May 23, 1884, d. Aug 21, 1959.

Joy Chapel

JONES, Emma F., b. 1864, d. 1939, wife of C. Dean.
JONES, G. Jestina, b. 1862, d. 1884, m. Apr 26, 1881 F. A. Breeden.
JONES, Hilary, Co. D 3d MD Inf USA, b. Apr 11, 1837, d. Jun 27, 1865 while returning home by boat two months after Civil War ended, son of Milely Jones.
JONES, Hilary Eccleston "Eck", b. Oct 10, 1867, d. Sep 15, 1961, hus of Florence Graves.
JONES, Irma, b. Oct 18, 1897, d. Sep 6, 1993, m.(1st) __ Wilson,(2d) John Edgar Baker, Sr. dau of Hilary "Eck" and Florence Graves Jones.
JONES, James, d. Feb 3, 1881, hus of Rebecca __.
JONES, Katherine Ruth, b. 1887, d. 1970, (metal plate marker).
JONES, Layman W., b. Feb 23, 1900, d. Apr 6, 1902.
JONES, Lemuel W., b. 1861, d. 1933.
JONES, Lida Esther, b. Apr 10, 1895, d. Dec 6, 1992, m. 18 Dec 1913, Paul Joy Mosher, dau of Hillary "Eck" and Florence Graves Jones.
JONES, Marion V., d. Aug 10, 1874.
JONES, Martha Ellen, b. May 9, 1866, d. Jul 9, 1955, wife of John Benjamin Insley.
JONES, Mary, no dates.
JONES, Miley, b. Feb 22, 1805, d. Nov 26, 1868.
JONES, Minnie S., b. 1885, d. 1892.
JONES, Naomi, b. Feb 20, 1903, d. Oct 16, 1989, wife of Francis E. Johnson, dau of Hilary E. and Florence Graves Jones.
JONES, Pamelia D., b. Sep 19, 1803, d. Dec 23, 1868.
JONES, Samuel Elijah, b. 1855, d. 1938.
JONES, Spencer M., b. Apr 5, 1892, d. Aug 7, 1892.
JONES, Thomas, b. 1828, d. 1907, hus of Martha Stone.
JONES, Thomas, infant, d. 1860.
JONES, Thomas Jarret, b. 1893, d. 1943.
JONES, Zachariah 'Taylor', b. 1842, d. 1914, hus of Georgeanna __.

JOY, Alice M., b. 1877, d. 1965.
JOY, Angel and Candance, b. and d. Mar 27, 1983.
JOY, Annie Elizabeth, b. Aug 18, 1905, d. Jun 29, 1981.
JOY, Edna, b. 1886, d. 1913, wife of __ Mattingly.
JOY, Ella, b. Dec 23, 1869, d. Jul 9, 1962, wife of __ Dean.
JOY, Emma U., b. Feb 6, 1862, d. Sep 26, 1886.
JOY, Ernest M., b. May 26, 1897, d. Aug 13, 1966.
JOY, Eva M., b. 1870, d. Oct 8, 1960.
JOY, Fannie Eva, b. 1913, d. 1913.
JOY, Herbert W., b. 1922, d. 1970.
JOY, James, b. Apr 10, 1815, d. Sep 12, 1871, hus of Elizabeth __.
JOY, James Summerfield, b. Apr 1, 1838, d. Mar 24, 1882, hus of Mary E. __.
JOY, John F., b. 1842, d. 1873.
JOY, Lena M., b. Aug 9, 1900, d. Jul 18, 1978.
JOY, Lydia A., b. 1860, d. 1886, m. 26 Dec 1878 John Caleb Dean.
JOY, Manley Lounge, b. Nov 6, 1895, d. Sep 11, 1965.
JOY, Milton C., b. 1880, d. 1946.
JOY, Paul, b. Jun 22, 1902, d. Mar 21, 1983.
JOY, Permelia Ann, b. 1835, d. 1891.
JOY, Ruth M., b. 1891, d. 1892.
JOY, Sherman Wilson, d. Mar 27, 1992, m. 1981, Dorothy Kirby nee Smith.
JOY, Thomas Franklin "Frank", b. 1828, d. 1895, hus of Ann __.
JOY, Walter B., b. 1876, d. 1963.
JOY, William Gwinn, b. Nov 4, 1871, d. Mar 26, 1959.
JOY, William Wallace, b. 1847, d. 1919, hus of Charlotte E. __, b. 1849, d. 1924.
KEMP, Robert E., b. 1913, d. 1970.
KIRBY, John C., Sr., b. 1910, d. 1963.
KIRST, Lois P., b. Apr 29, 1917, d. Apr 14, 1986
LAWRENCE, William T., b. Aug 5, 1906, d. Apr 24, 1959.
LUNDREGAN, infant, d. 1968.

Joy Chapel

LUNDREGAN, Jeanette, b. 1917, d. 1969.
MADDOX, Archibald Pierce, d. 1918, hus of Rosalie Ashton Dent.
MAGILL, Charles A., b. Apr 21, 1839, d. Jan 13, 1911, 2d hus of Lydia C. (__) Deakins, b. May 15, 1840, d. Nov 27, 1908.
MARTIN, Jess Samuel, b. 1925, d. 1974.
MASON, Nelson E., d. 1928.
McCRADY, Mary, b. 1824, d. 1859, wife of __ Joy.
McDANIEL, Florence, b. 1883, d. 1967.
McLEOD, Hershel V., Sr., b. Feb 22, 1917, d. Jan 19, 1983, hus of Nellie Elizabeth Pfiel.
MILANO, Bobby Robert Benny, b. Oct 6, 1937, d. Aug 25, 1985.
MORGAN, infant, d. May 31, 1972, child of Deborah Sue Wheeler Morgan.
MORRIS, James H., b. 1839, d. Feb 5, 1872.
MOSHER, Paul Joy, b. Aug 1, 1892, d. Jan 1, 1960, m. 18 Dec 1913 Lida Esther Jones.
MOSHER, William Edward Jones, b. Sep 14, 1920, d. Dec 14, 1987, son of Paul J. and Lida Jones Mosher.
NEILL, Joseph Howard, Jr., b. Nov 25, 1906, d. Feb 21, 1986.
NORRIS, Joseph Francis, b. Jul 10, 1929, d. Jun 19, 1986.
OGDEN, Betty Lewis, b. 1926, d. 1981.
OLSON, Ivar Karl, b. 1901, d. 1977, hus of Daisy Iola Weeks.
OWEN, James Dammon, b. Apr 3, 1882, d. Nov 22, 1966, hus of Kate Jackson.
OWEN, Richard "Dickie", b. 1936, d. Oct 1990.
OWEN, Tammy L., b. Nov 9, 1962, d. Nov 18, 1962.
PHIEL, Nellie Elizabeth, b. Aug 10, 1921 DC, d. May 22, 1992, wife of Herschel V. McLeod, Sr., dau of Walter and Maude Dishman Pfiel.
PINGLETON, Elizabeth A., b. Jun 24, 1880, d. Feb 4, 1962.
PINGLETON, John B., b. Mar 12, 1913, d. Apr 4, 1986.
PINGLETON, Joseph Elijah, b. Nov 13, 1879, d. Apr 21, 1961.
READMOND, James Philip "Sumpy", b. Mar 14,

1932, d. Dec 21, 1990, hus of Joy S. __, son of James Leonard and Emma Estelle Wallace Readmond.
ROBESON, Bernice S., b. May 20, 1881, d. Mar 21, 1917.
ROBESON, Mary Bernice, b. Nov 23, 1911, d. 1913.
ROBESON, Robert C., b. Sep 15, 1914, d. Jan 22, 1915.
ROBINSON, Marge, b. Dec 13, 1915, d. Jun 12, 1977, ashes bur Oct 1984.
ROWE, Allan and Bryon, b. and d. 1952.
SHENTON, Ernest D., b. Jun 8, 1874, d. Jun 2, 1895.
SHENTON, John D., b. Oct 3, 1839, d. Feb 2, 1892.
SHENTON, Mary A., b. Sep 17, 1840, d. May 3, 1903.
SIMS, Gloria V., b. 1921, d. 1989.
SIMS, Robert Lee, b. 1916, d. 1973.
SMITH, J. Cynthia, b. 1893, d. 1921, wife of __ Elliott.
SMITH, J. Winfield, b. 1846, d. 1912.
SMITH, Sarah Mae (Mamie), b. Oct 15, 1889, d. Jun 9, 1978.
SMITH, Umphrey Winfield, b. Apr 14, 1884, d. Mar 21, 1977.
SPARKES, Marion M., b. 1895, d. 1985.
SPARKES, Walter, b. 1890, d. 1965.
SPEDDEN, J. Bruner, b. 1885, d. 1934.
SPEDDEN, Levin, b. Feb 26, 1828, d. Jul 9, 1913, hus of Mary A. __.
SPEDDEN, Robert H., b. 1873, d. 1935, hus of Mamie Dean.
SPENCER, Melville W., b. Oct 31, 1903, d. Aug 14, 1973, hus of Ruth Winn.
STARKWEATHER, Modena M., 101, b. 1867, d. 1968.
STARKWEATHER, Rolo J., b. 1862, d. 1938.
STONE, Martha, b. 1830, d. 1916, wife of Thomas Jones.
STONE, Robert Phillip, Jr., b. Jan 29, 1952, d. d. Nov 5, 1986.
STROUD, Clayton Rufus "Slim" b. Aug 13, 1906 OK, d. Aug 9, 1993, m. 30 Dec 1933 OK, Sibyl McDaniels, son of Raleigh Hampton and Bennie

Edith Matthews Stroud.
TAYLOR, Orem Jones, b. Oct 4, 1888, d. Nov 25, 1896.
TAYLOR, Myrtle Ruth, b. Mar 15, 1896, d. Jun 27, 1993, wife of Nathaniel H. Dare, dau of John and Pamela Jones Taylor.
THOMPSON, James Ronald "Dick", b. Jun 10, 1959, d. May 25, 1990, son of Lamen Samuel and Alma Teresa Thompson.
THOMPSON, Jennie D., b. Feb 5, 1887, d. Jun 3, 1957.
THOMPSON, Lamen Samuel, b. Aug 11, 1915, d. Apr 29, 1990, hus of Alma Teresa __, son of P. Briscoe and Daisy C. Thompson.
THOMPSON, P. Briscoe, b. 1884, d. 1963, hus of Daisy C. __, b. 1888, d. 1966.
THOMPSON, P. Rosco, b. Dec 13, 1908, d. Oct 6, 1978.
THOMPSON, Robert Phillip, b. Oct 20, 1934, d. Jul 8, 1988, son of Phillip O. and Margaret Dean Thompson.
TRACY, Lollie M., b. Aug 13, 1929, d. Mar 21, 1976.
TRIBLE, Jennifer Lynn, b. Dec 2, 1973, d. Jul 13, 1974, dau of Robert and Barbara Dean Trible.
TRIGGER, William C., b. 1911, d. 1973.
TUCKER, Charles M., b. 1888, d. 1964.
TUCKER, Katie M., b. 1889, d. 1949.
VAN SISE, Theodore M., b. May 16, 1905, d. Sep 25, 1983.
WALLACE, Effie E., b. Aug 25, 1888, d. May 3, 1975.
WEEKS, Daisy Iola, b. Dec 28, 1905 Balto, d. Dec 15, 1990, wife of Ivor Karl Olson, dau of Pirley C. and Virginia A. Combs Weeks.
WEEKS, Melvin L., b. Mar 13, 1908, d. Dec 26, 1956.
WEEKS, Pirley C., b. 1876, d. 1962, hus of Virginia A. Combs.
WEEKS, Violet May, b. May 7, 1911 Balto, d. Jan 4, 1993, m. 1945 in Brooklyn, NY George Stirling Greenwell, dau of Pirley C. and Virginia A. Combs Weeks.
WHEELER, Deborah Sue, b. Aug 9, 1951, d. May

31, 1972, wife of __ Morgan.
WHITAKER, Robert Chester, b. Dec 31, 1934, d. Oct 3, 1971.
WIBLE, Audry, b. 1901, d. 1971, wife of John W. Holtz.
WINN, Ruth, b. 1907, d. Jul 1986, wife of Melville W. Spencer.
WISE, Nancy, b. 1808, d. 1845, wife of __ Joy.
WOODS, Elmer Guy, b. Jun 25, 1918, d. Dec 23, 1981.
YOUNG, Kharmine Hudson, b. Aug 29, 1921, d. Jul 16, 1975.
YOUNG, Walter Hopkins, b. Dec 23, 1903, d. Aug 16, 1981.

MENNONITE CEMETERY
Loveville, Md.

BRUBACHER, David G., d. Nov 5, 1984, m. 1951 Elizabeth Stauffer.
GRICE, Basil Eugene, d. Feb 11, 1979, hus of Lucy Stauffer.
MARTIN, Celeste Fay, b. Apr 15, 1990, d. Feb 27, 1991, dau of Edward Lee, Sr. and Susie S. Brubacher Martin.
MARTIN, Charles Richard, b. Oct 24, 1983, d. Oct 26, 1992, son of Marvin S. and Debbie Lou Stauffer Martin; gson of Walter S. and Katherine A. Martin; Marvin and Elsie Stauffer of Stone Creek, KY.
STAUFFER, Ammon Witmer, b. Oct 25, 1902 PA, d. Apr 30, 1992, hus of Barbara Zimmerman, son of David B. and Elizabeth B. Stauffer.
STAUFFER, Anna, b. Jun 7, 1903 IA, d. Apr 5, 1991, wife of Reuben Stauffer, dau of John S. and Veronica M. Brubacher Stauffer.
STAUFFER, Elizabeth, b. Sep 16, 1930 PA, d. Dec 1, 1991 wife of David G. Brubacher, dau of Ammon W. and Barbara S. Zimmerman Stauffer.
STAUFFER, Esther, d. 1979, wife of Noah R. Wenger.
STAUFFER, Lucy, b. Sep 9, 1929 PA, d. Sep 7, 1993, m. Nov 1966 Basil Eugene Grice, dau of Reuben S. and Anna B. Stauffer.
STOLTZFUS, Rebecca D., b. May 28, 1914 PA, d. Aug 29, 1992, wife of Isaac Hertzler, dau of John B. and Sarah Isaac Hertzler, bur Hertzler Cem., Mechanicsville, Md.
WEAVER, Barbara Brubacher, b. May 11, 1989, d. Jul 14, 1989, dau of Elvin Martin and Elva Brubacher Weaver.
WENGER, Ammon Reich, 92, b. PA, d. Nov 22, 1991 MO, hus of Civilla Zimmerman.
WENGER, Noah R., 90, d. Aug 4, 1988, hus of Esther Stauffer.

MT. ZION UNITED METHODIST CHURCH
Rte. 235
Laurel Grove, Md.

BALL, Richard L., b. Jun 5, 1925, d. Apr 7, 1988, son of Frank and Cecelia Lee Ball.
BALL, Rev. Swope Acker, b. Apr 25, 1908, d. May 9, 1993, hus of Lillian Maywood Wells, son of John and Nettie Washington Ball.
BEAL, Laura Blanche, 104, b. Jun 7, 1885, d. Nov 5, 1989, wife of Samuel Kane, dau of James and Catherine Dyson Beal.
BLACKWELL, Timothy Tyrone, b. Jul 16, 1991 DC, d. Jul 26, 1991, son of Timothy and Cheryl Barnes Blackwell; gson of William and Geneva Blackwell; Bernard and Lorraine Smith Barnes.
BOND, Nettie Maude, 105, b. Oct 16, 1887, d. Mar 15, 1993, m. 9 Dec 1916 Phila,PA, Arthur Morrison Woodburn, Sr., dau of John Benjamin and Mary Graves Bond,
BUCKLER, Edward St. Clair, Jr. b. 1910, d. Oct 6, 1983, m. 1934 Balto, Eleanor Craig Hough.
BUCKLER, Hamilton Ethelbert, Jr. b. Nov 29, 1905, d. Jan 13, 1990, hus of Mabel Elizabeth Graves, son of Hamilton E. Sr. and Mary Graves Buckler.
BUCKLER, Roy Vernon, b. May 24, 1907, d. Mar 17, 1993, son of Hamilton E. Sr. and Mary Eleanor Graves Buckler.
DAVIS, William Phillip "Bog", Sr. b. Feb 4, 1924, d. Jul 30, 1991, son of William Gorman and Blanche Leila Morgan Davis.
DIEHL, Edward Lafayette, b. Mar 14, 1928, d. Aug 19, 1992, hus of Mary Evelyn Anderson, son of Albert R. and Mabel Elizabeth Diehl.
DILL, Phyllis Mae, b. Nov 28, 1931, d. Aug 28, 1990, wife of Harvey Burroughs, dau of Wilbur J. and Mabel E. Davis Dill.
DIXON, Mrs. Phyllis G., d. Feb 3, 1991.
DIXON, William Reck, d. 1968, 1st hus of Rebecca Wallace.
DORSEY, Lillian Lucille, b. Aug 5, 1929, d. Apr 14, 1993, wife of Joseph F. Milburn, dau of William and Lucy Bolt Dorsey.
FOX, Anna Stahl, b. Oct 16, 1920 PA, d. Nov

13, 1990, wife of Ezra S. Stauffer, dau of John S. and Elizabeth Stahl Fox.
GALLAGHER, Thomas Stuart, b. Mar 23, 1908 PA, d. Jan 8, 1990, hus of Eva __, son of Patrick and Ann Brislin Gallagher.
GORDON, Virgie Mary, b. May 30, 1911, d. Oct 13, 1989, wife of Charles Biscoe, dau of Columbus and Ida Bolt Gordon.
GRAVES, Edith Elizabeth, b. Jan 23, 1913, d. Aug 16, 1988, dau of Zackariah and Jane Elizabeth Graves.
GRAVES, Lawrence Walter "John", b. May 14, 1895, d. Oct 18, 1988, hus of Anita Higgs, son of Zackariah S. and Jane E. Graves.
GRAVES, Mabel Elizabeth, b. Aug 11, 1904, d. Jun 17, 1989, wife of Hamilton E. Buckler, dau of Lafette and Eleanor Graves.
GRAVES, Martha Harding, b. Aug 13, 1906, d. Oct 17, 1991, wife of Herman E. Hensel, dau of Phillip Thomas and Carrie M. Harding Graves.
GRAY, Daniel Benjamin "Ben", b. Dec 25, 1919, d. Nov 15, 1991 DC, hus of Teresa Mae Flora, son of Isaac Daniel and Ethel C. Thompson Gray.
GREEN, Estelle Lilly Page, b. May 28, 1923, d. Dec 19, 1989, wife of Isaac Chisley, dau of Jeremiah and Cecelia Biscoe Green.
HANCOCK, Norman Hubert, Jr. b. Apr 26, 1946, d. Nov 24, 1992, son of Norman H. and Mary Erva Curry Hancock.
HAWKINS, John Lindsey, b. May 30, 1905, d. Nov 25, 1991, hus of Carrie Scofield, son of John Thomas and Mary Agnes Ball Hawkins.
HENZEL, Harman E., d. 1979, hus of Martha Harding.
HILL, Mary Etta, b. Sep 24, 1922 VA, d. Oct 26, 1992, m. (1st) John H. Smith, d. 1976, (2d) William Barber, d. 1986, dau of Moses and Pearl Usual Hill.
HINZMAN, Earl A., b. Nov 26, 1921 IA, d. Apr 12, 1990, hus of Lorena L. __, son of Frank Fred and Frances D. Hinzman.
HOLT, Thelma, b. Mar 16, 1913 VA, d. Jan 28, 1990, wife of __ Keller, dau of Robert H.

Mt. Zion

and Florence E. Young Holt.
HOUGH, Eleanor Craig, d. March 3, 1989, wife of Edward St. Clair Buckler, Jr.
HOWLIN, Thelma Louise, b. Sep 19, 1921 DC, d. Dec 24, 1990, wife of __ Archer, dau of Bernard and Mary Howlin.
INGLIS, William Elbert "Hank", d. Oct 19, 1986, hus of Eugenia Pearson.
JARVIS, Gladys Elsie, b. Mar 14, 1904 MA, d. Aug 5, 1991, wife of George Frederick Darney, Jr., dau of Edward James and Ida Hawks Jarvis.
JONES, Amy V., d. Oct 31, 1886, wife of Oscar Jones.
JONES, John Henry, b. Jan 1, 1914 NC, d. Apr 24, 1991, hus of Mary Molly __.
JONES, Lee Etta, b. Oct 24, 1920, d. Aug 21, 1993, wife of John Nelson, Sr., dau of Charles and Madeline Blake Jones.
KEELING, Irene Beatrice, b. Jul 14, 1920, d. Jun 25, 1989, m. (1st) Norman Edward Bailey, Sr.,(2d) 1985 Wilson W. Williams, dau of Harrison and Annie Cuffee Keeling.
KEISTER, Richard William, b. Aug 31, 1952, d. Aug 27, 1992, son of Lelon Clifford and Nellie Rose Sean Keister.
KENYON, Laura L., b. Oct 8, 1946, d. Jan 30, 1991, wife of Allen C. Haukland, dau of Harry and Mildred Harrington Kenyon.
KNOTT, Joseph Howard "Pat", b. Jun 26, 1905, d. Oct 26, 1991, hus of Agnes Marie Connelly.
MARSH, Sandra Lee, b. Jan 7, 1943, d. Aug 9, 1988, dau of Jesse L.and Eva G. Grove Beatty.
MARSHALL, Everett Layton, b. Mar 28, 1912, d. Jan 18, 1991, hus of Harriet Anne Graves, son of Robert Richard and Flora Augusta Layton Marshall.
MARSHALL, Laura Melissa, b. May 6, 1903, d. Sep 9, 1993, dau of Robert and Flora Layton Marshall.
MC FARLEN, William "Mack", USMC WWII, b. Sep 15, 1920 MO, d. Oct 5, 1993, m. 23 Sep 1967 Murna Josephine Cornthwaite, son of William Preston and Innis Rainey McFarlen.
MILBURN, Joseph F., d. Nov. 16, 1971, hus of

Lillian Lucille Dorsey.
MOORE, Norman, b. Nov 2, 1924, d. Jul 3, 1993, m. 25 Dec 1948 Janet Hazel Johns, son of Mabel Keen and late Fred R. Waters.
MOORE, Robert Wilkins, b. Jul 31, 1913 DC, d. Jun 8, 1992, hus of Sarah Carson, son of Silas Sr. and Alice Yingling Moore.
PEARSON, Eugenia, b. Aug 20, 1903 TX, d. Dec 27, 1993, wife of William Elbert Inglis, dau of Joseph and Eula James Pearson.
QUARLES, Clarence Earvin, Sr. b. Feb 11, 1934, d. Feb 22, 1989, hus of Marion C. __, son of George and Minnie McCowan Quarles.
REAM, Edith, b. Sep 1, 1905, d. May 4, 1991, wife of Paul Jones Bennett, dau of John W. and Alberta Gilpen Ream.
RETTSTATT, Zane Oliver, Sr, "Zeke", b. Oct 10, 1930 DC, d. May 19, 1991, hus of Frances E. Sheridan, son of late Wendell P. Rettstatt, Sr. and Edna Grace Cummings. Mem. Serv.
RYCE, Elsie L., 78, d. Aug 7, 1993 FL, wife of T. C. Ryce. Memorial services at Union Park Chapel, Orlando, FL and Mt. Zion Church.
SEWELL, Brother Marvin Eric, b. Aug 16, 1953, d. Apr 17, 1988, son of Robert, Sr. and Geraldine Sewell.
SMITH, Ann Rebecca, b. Aug 23, 1822, d. Mar 8, 1911, m. (1st) Mathias Oster, (2d) James Jones, dau of George Arthur Smith of SC and Vienna, Md.
TENNISON, Harry Aloysius, d. 1984, 2d hus of Rebecca Wallace.
VAN WART, Alice Maude, b. Dec 15, 1895, d. May 2, 1990, wife of James Earl Curry, dau of Thomas Ashbury and Elizabeth Laura Brookband Van Wart.
WALLACE, Charlotte, b. May 1, 1904, d. Jul 14, 1993, wife of John Dennis Dean, Sr., dau of William Biscoe, Sr. and Charlotte Ledley Wallace.
WALLACE, Rebecca, b. Mar 29, 1912, d. Oct 19, 1993, m. (1st) Jun 1933 William Reck Dixon, (2d) 1971 Harry Aloysius Tennison, dau of William Biscoe, Sr. and Charlotte Ledley Wallace.

WELLS, Lillian Maywood, b. Jul 24, 1919 VA, d. Jun 29, 1990, wife of Rev. Swope A. Ball, dau of Rufus and Lara Pugh Wells.
WOOD, George Freets, 97, d. Oct 20, 1988, hus of Mattie __.
WOODBURN, Arthur Morrison, Sr. d. Jul 8, 1959 Balto, hus of Nettie Maude Bond.

OLD COMMUNITY CEMETERY
St. George Island, Md.

Memorial at St. Francis Xavier Church on St. George Island giving names of persons known to be buried in Old Community Cemetery. I have found a few missing dates and a few additional names of persons buried there, also a few relationalships.

BALL, Ann, b. 1855, d. 1884, wife of __ Evans.
BALL, Benjamin, b. 1884, d. 1909.
BALL, Catherine, b. 1843, d. 1861.
BALL, George Allen, b. 1878, d. 1906.
BALL, Joseph, b. 1890, d. 1902.
BALL, Warren, b. 1887, d. 1901.
BALL, Richard T., b. 1827, d. 1903, hus of Elizabeth Chesser.
CHESSER, Elizabeth, b. 1830, d. 1891, wife of Richard T. Ball.
CHESSER, Richard, b. 1840, d. 1867.
COURTNEY, Adeline, b. 1835, d. 1865.
CROWDER, Thomas, b. 1815, d. ca 1885.
CROWDER, Thomas B., b. 1845, d. 1865.
CROWDER, Walter Franklin, b. Jun 24, 1842 VA, d. Apr 13, 1892 St. Georges Isl., MD.
GIBSON, Alonzo, b. 1844, d. ca 1905.
GIBSON, Anna, b. 1820, d. 1867.
GIBSON, Elizabeth W., b. 1851, d. 1875.
GIBSON, Emma, b. 1839, d. 1900.
HAZZARD, Cathy, b. 1845, d. ca 1903, wife of __ Moore.
HENDERSON, Charles Edward, b. 1858, d. 1909.
HENDERSON, Edward P., pilot, b. 1819, d. Oct 1859 of ship fever, married.
HENDERSON, Eva May, b. ca 1891, d. 1897.
HENDERSON, Lula, b. 1861, d. 1912.
HOBBS, Joseph C., b. 1836, d. 1897.
HOBBS, Mary, b. 1798, d. ca 1875.
LEWIS, Elenor Parke, b. Apr 18, 1819 VA, d. Aug 7, 1886/88 St. Georges Isl, Md. wife of __ Franklin.
MESSICK, George, b. 1815, d. 1879.
MESSICK, Mary, b. 1810, d. ca 1885.
MESSICK, Virginia Jane, b. Mar 27, 1842, d.

Aug 7, 1873 St. Georges Isl, Md.
MIDDLETON, William, b. 1869, d. 1913.
MOORE, George A., b. 1853, d. 1865.
MOORE, James, b. 1845, d. 1908/10.
MOORE, Jerome, b. 1843.
MOORE, John R., b. 1837, d. ca 1890.
MOORE, Minerva, b. 1844.
PEARSON, Mary, b. 1830, d. ca 1895.
PEARSON, William, b. 1825, d. ca 1890.
POE, John of George, b. 1849, d. 1937.
POTTER, Elizabeth, b. 1832, d. ca 1901.
POTTER, Francis, b. 1830, d. ca 1896.
POTTER, William, b. 1875, d. ca 1890.
ROBRECHT, John H., b. 1815 Germ.(?), d. 1865.
ROBRECHT, Sarah, b. 1829.
SIMPKINS, Mary, b. ca 1840, d. 1891.
SIMPKINS, William, b. 1835, d. 1891.
THOMAS, Harriet, b. 1855, wife of __ Twilley.
TWILLEY, Mariah, b. 1825, d. 1897.
TWILLEY, Sara, d. 1893, wife of __ Hobbs.
TWILLEY, William, b. 1818.
TWILLEY, Infant son of William and Eva, b. ca 1915.

OUR LADY'S ROMAN CATHOLIC CHAPEL
Route 244
Medley's Neck, Md.

The original chapel was built on a high hill, ca 1766, possibly by FR James Walton, S.J. In 1911 FR William J. Stanton had it pulled down and another chapel was built on the same spot. The words, "The General Armstrong Memorial", are above the main entrance.

ABELL, Anna, d. Oct 8, 1902, aged 32 years, wife of C. Benedict Greenwell.
Next two tombstones in enclosure
-ABELL, Mrs. B. Wilson Bond, b. Aug 1876, d. Sep 1953.
-BOND, B. Wilson, b. Jan 22, 1866, d. May 26, 1903.
Four-sided Stone
-ABELL, Bennett M., d. Apr 25, 1902, aged 47 years.
-ABELL, Bennett R., d. Sep 4, 1896, aged 67 years, his wife Philomena Roach, d. Jan 12, 192-, aged 83 yrs.
-ABELL, James Roach, b. May 20, 1866, d. Mar 16, 1915, his wife Margaret Krause, d. May 2, 1950, age 71 years.
-ABELL, Margaret C., d. Oct 2, 1901, age 3 days.
ABELL, Enoch, Sr., 60 yrs, bur Apr 2, 1881.
ABELL, James F., d. Sep 7, 1858, aged 1 yr, 4 mos and 24 days, son of James F. and Maria James Abell.
ABELL, John Harold, Sr., b. 1895, d. 1952, m. 7 Jan 1939 Anne "Anna" Eliza Mattingly.
ABELL, Lillian, b. 1872, d. 1955, wife of Joseph Maguire Mattingly.
ABELL, Mary C., d. Dec 11, 187-, aged 10 mos and 23 days, dau of James F. and Maria J. Abell.
ABELL, Nellie Ann, enfant (sic) daughter of J. F. and M. J. Abell, no dates.
ABELL, Susan B., b. Feb 11, 1860, d. Sep 17, 1862, dau of James F. and M. J. Abell.
ABELL, Thomas Benedict "Dick", b. Jun 10, 1909, d. Mar 30, 1993, m. 6 Jan 1933 Mary Eva

Higgs, son of Thomas Benjamin and Mary Vannah Curry Abell.
ABELL, William, 19, bur Oct 5, 1870.
BARNS, Mr. Watt, 45, bur Dec 31, 1869.
BARNES, J. Rhody, b. 1885, d. 1967, hus of Alice Poteete.
BARNES, James Andrew, PFC USA WWII, b. 1912, d. 1976, 2d hus of Addie Anne Watts Taylor.
BARNES, Joseph F., MD Pvt, CO F, 2 Dev BN WWI, b. May 2, 1897, d. Apr 26, 1953.
BARNES, Joseph Henry, MD TEC 5, USA WWII, b. May 16, 1919, d. Nov 15, 1973.
BARNES, Thomas L., b. 1924, d. 1963, hus of Mary L. __, b. 1924, d. 1978.
BEAN, Mary Emily, b. May 2, 1872, d. Dec 23, 1928, wife of Charles A. Heard.
BEVAN, John Walter, 74, bur Oct 17, 1872.
BLACKISTON, J. William, 80, bur Aug 16, 1872.
BOWLES, Violet, b. Nov 14, 1890, d. Mar 11, 1981, wife of Arthur V. Evans.
BOGIE, James Edward "Jim", USN WWII, b. Oct 10, 1923 MN, d. Dec 23, 1993, m. 19 Feb 1949 Mary Elizabeth Floyd, son of Charles and Ione Sonestogard Bogie.
BOWMAN, George O., Sr. b. Mar 22, 1894.
BOWMAN, Robert H., MD TEC/S USA WWII.
BROOKS, Charles Aloysius, USA Korea, b. 1936, d. 1977.
BROOKS, Estelle Elizabeth, b. Aug 19, 1910, d. Jan 20, 1992, wife of Joseph Aloysius Thomas, dau of Francis and Mary Elizabeth Barnes Brooks.
BURGESS, Lawrence William, b. May 7, 1899 ME, d. May 17, 1991, hus of Beulah C. __, son of Lincoln and Eva Rioux Burgess.
COLE, John Aloysius, 30, bur Feb 22, 1873.
COMBS, Dr. Charles, 50, bur Aug 18, 1886.
COMBS, Helen Isabelle, b. Nov 11, 1909, d. Jan 5, 1992, wife of Edwin Granger Pritchard, Sr., dau of Francis Joseph and Susie Madeline Abell Combs.
COMBS, Isabelle J., d. Aug 22, 1909, age 2 yrs, 11 mos and 16 days, dau of Francis Joseph and Susie Madeline Abell Combs.
COMBS, James G., d. Sep 5, 1907, aged 5 yrs,

Our Lady's Chapel

5 mos, son of Francis Joseph and Susie Madeline Abell Combs.
COPSEY, Cody Holland, infant, b. Jul 22, 1989, d. Mar 8, 1990, son of James Hilary, Jr, and Susan Vandergrift Copsey; gson of James H. and Frances Goldsmith Copsey; Raymond and Delores Holland Vandergrift.
CRYER, Charles Ignatius, b. Jan 26, 1907 DC, d. Jan 18, 1965, hus of Alberta A. Stone, son of William Baptist and Martha Lucinda Johnson Cryer.
CRYER, James Bertram "Bert", b. Oct 1, 1901 DC, d. Jul 1, 1987, hus of Jessie May Latham, son of William Baptist and Martha Lucinda Johnson Cryer.
CRYER, Thomas 'Leonard', Sr. b. May 19, 1904 DC, d. Jan 12, 1985, hus of Mary 'Grace' Stone, son of William Baptist and Martha Lucinda Johnson Cryer.
CRYER, Walter Elmer "Teddy", b. Nov 20, 1905 DC, d. Oct 18, 1975 Balto, hus of Leona Alva Dewey, son of William Baptist and Martha Lucinda Johnson Cryer.
CURTIS, Annie Mae, b. Dec 30, 1911, d. Aug 28, 1992, wife of James William Butler, dau of John Martin and Mary Nettie Thomas Curtis.
DAFFRON, Florence, b. 1904, d. 1981, wife of C. Benedict Greenwell.
DAVIS, James R., b. Mar 26, 1904, d. Dec 15, 1972.
DAVIS, Mary Teresa, b. Apr 3, 1898, d. Oct 1, 1991, wife of Joseph Johnson, dau of Mary Cecelia Davis.
DeCORDANI, Mary Victoria, b. May 30, 1901 Italy, d. Dec 1, 1993, wife of John Ferrari (d. May 1976), dau of Jack and Rose DeCordani.
DOWNS, Rebecca, 70, bur Aug 5, 1872.
DRURY, John R., Sr., d. 1975, 2d hus of Mary Goode.
DYER, Robert Ignatius, b. Dec 5, 1912, d. Feb 26, 1992, hus of Mabel Marie Smith, son of Edward and Bertha Smith Dyer.
DYER, William, no dates.
ERICH, Floyd Francis, d. Jan 16, 1966.
One stone

-EVANS, Alice E., b. 1917, d. 1951.
-EVANS, Annie E., b. 1891, d. 1952.
-EVANS, Charles H., b. 1886, d. 1944.
EVANS, Alice, b. 1856, d. 1940, wife of Joseph Benedict Norris.
EVANS, Arthur V., b. Feb 7, 1883, d. Dec 12, 1936, hus of Violet Bowles.
EVANS, James Nelson, b. 1835, d. 1893, hus of Eliza Norris.
EVANS, Roy V., b. Oct 17, 1921, d. Sep 3, 1922.
FARRELL, James, d. 1955, 1st hus of Mary Goode.
FEATHERS, Reba Dorcus, b. Nov 4, 1909 NY, d. Jun 8, 1993, m. (1st) __ Page, (2d) 8 Nov 1969 William Leo Pilkerton, dau of Miles Alden and Mary Eva Boulton Feathers.
FORD, C. Ridgeley, b. 1882, d. 1928.
FORD, J. Frank, d. Feb 26, 1901, age 56 years, hus of Ida C. Manning, erected by Members of the Bench and Bar of Md. in recognition of his services as Clerk of the Court of Appeals of Md.
GALLANT, Beatrice Martha, b. Oct 18, 1903, Pr. Edw. Isl., Can., d. Aug 5, 1990, wife of Fabien Breau, dau of Isidore and Ursule Gallant.
GATTON, John, 45, bur Jan 1, 1870.
GATTON, Mary Elizabeth, b. Nov 28, 1913, d. Jan 6, 1989, wife of Calvert Ignatius Norris, dau of William Robert and Ada Elizabeth Gatton.
GODDARD, Benjamin S., b. Feb 29, 1922, d. May 24, 1982.
GODDARD, Clarence A., Sr. d. Feb 13, 1966, hus of Mary 'Josephine' Spaulding.
GODDARD, Clarence Alfred, Jr. b. Aug 20, 1923, d. Jun 27, 1989, hus of Mary Alberta Trossbach, son of Clarence A. and Mary 'Josephine' Spaulding Goddard.
GODDARD, Debra Lynn, infant, d. Nov 4, 1993 DC, dau of Clarence and Elizabeth Abell Goddard, gdau of Clarence A. Jr. and Mary Alberta Trossbach Goddard; J. Perry and Shirley Nelson Abell.
GODWIN, Mary Catherine "Mamie", b. Jun 21, 1877, d. Sep 15, 1966, wife of Joseph 'Ford'

Stone.
GOLDSBOROUGH, Andrew J., d. Sep 27, 1970, hus of Susie C. __, b. Apr 22, 1905, d. Feb 16, 1986.
GOLDSBOROUGH, Anne Combs, b. Jan 6, 1931, d. Aug 30, 1932, dau of A. J. and Susie Goldsborough.
GOLDSBOROUGH, Clyde, b. 1890, d. 1981, hus of V. C. __, b. 1897, d. 1983.
GOLDSBOROUGH, Veronica E. "Bootsie", b. Apr 9, 1908, d. Jul 1, 1993, m. (1st) John Bernard Mattingly, (2d) Webster "Hutch" Hutchins, dau of J. Francis and Florence Victoria Yates Goldsboroough.
GOODE, Mary, b. Jul 31, 1894, d. Mar 8, 1991, wife of (1st) James Farrell, (2d) John R. Drury, Sr., dau of Marion Francis and Rose Cecelia Tippett Goode.
GORDON, Ruth Naomi, d. Sep 1943.
GOUGH, Ann, 67, bur 1886.
GOUGH, Jane, b. Apr 18, 1904, d. Oct 18, 1977, wife of __ Mattingly.
GOUGH, Miss Jennie Maude C., 16, bur Oct 13, 1887.
GOUGH, Mrs. Marion, 28, bur Oct 9, 1899.
GOUGH, Stephen, b. Mar 15, 1785, d. Apr 15, 1835.
GRAVES, Richard Harold, d. May 28, 1976, m. 29 Dec 1924 Violet Lucy Norris.
GREEN, Nettie B., d. Mar 1950.
   One Stone
-GREENWELL, Anna Abell, d. Oct 8, 1902, aged 32 years, wife of C. Benedict Greenwell.
-GREENWELL, C. Benedict, d. Feb 10, 1934, aged 67 years.
-GREENWELL, Mary Slater, d. Oct 19, 1902, aged 1 mo 8 days, infant daughter of C. B. and Anna Greenwell.
-GREENWELL, J. Franklin, b. Dec 29, 1899, d. Jan 1, 1939.
-GREENWELL, James C., b. Dec 29, 1899, d. Apr 20, 1946.
-GREENWELL, C. Benedict, b. Jan 10, 1898, d. May 12, 1966.
GREENWELL, C. Benedict, b. 1898, d. 1966, hus

of Florence Daffron.
GREENWELL, Charles B., MD Pvt STU Army TNG Corps, WWI, b. Jan 10, 1898, d. May 12, 1966.
GREENWELL, Joseph J., 42, bur Feb 22, 1907.
GREENWELL, Mrs. Mary A., 72, bur Dec 3, 1905.
GREENWELL, Robert Benedict, PFC USA WWII, no dates.
GREENWELL, William George, 20, bur Apr 11, 1882.
HAMMETT, John Jones, b. Jul 28, 1907, d. 1939.
HANSON, Betsie, 1 da, bur Jan 13, 1872.
HANSON, Priscilla, 35, bur Mar 19, 1872,
One Stone
-HEARD, Alex, b. 1853, d. 1925.
-HEARD, Ann M., b. 1870, d. 1932
-HEARD, Son Harry, no date.
HEARD, Ann E., b. Dec 21, 1816, d. Apr 3, 1849.
HEARD, James D., b. Aug 7, 1909, d. Jan 14, 1934.
HEARD, John, b. Aug 2, 1854, d. Feb 23, 1856, son of James M. and Jane M. Heard.
HEBB, George Ferdinand, b. 1879, d. 1962.
HODGES, Thomas Allen "Al" Duckett, b. Mar 7, 1905, d. Jul 9, 1991, hus of Anna C. Combs, son of Ramsey and Lucy Duckett Hodges.
HOLLY, Nancy, 22, bur Jan 23, 1871.
HOLLY, Thomas E., b. Jan 26, 1948, d. Jul 23, 1966.
HOLLY, William Jackson, Pvt USA WWI, b. 1896, d. 1975.
HOLMES, Alexander B., 53, bur Feb 19, 1872.
HOLMES, Mrs. Alexander B., 62, bur Jun 4, 1890.
HOLMES, Frank N., 45, bur Aug 10, 1896.
HUTCHINS, Webster "Hutch", d. Mar 24, 1974, 2d hus of Veronica E. Goldsborough.
JAMES, Maria, b. Sep 24, 1828, d. Jun 17, 1862, wife of James F. Abell.
JOHNSON, Elizabeth Loraine, b. Jun 16, 1908, d. Jan 19, 1991, wife of T. Frank Latham, dau of Daniel Phillip "D.P." and Mamie Harden Johnson.
JOHNSON, John, d. Nov 1959.
JOHNSON, Mary 'Mildred', b. Mar 7, 1915, d. Apr 24, 1976, m. (1st) Joseph Vernon "Jack" Stone, (2d) Joseph Raymond Adams, dau of

Earnest and Mary Rosalie Cooper Johnson.
JONES, Mrs. Sophia, 57, bur Apr 1, 1906.
JORDAN, John Louis, 20 das, bur Jan 13, 1871.
KAUFMANN, Helena K. 91, b. May 2, 1889 PA, d. Dec 1, 1990, wife of William Franklin Combs, dau of Harry S. and Martha Mae Adams Kaufmann.
KNOTT, Annie Elizabeth, b. 1873, d. 1962, wife of Richard Theodore Latham.
KRAUSE, Margaret, d. May 2, 1950, age 71 years, wife of James Roach Abell.
LATHAM, Mary 'Virginia', b. Sep 24, 1909, d. Jul 25, 1988, m. (1st) "Freddy" St. Clair, (2d) Charles Berkman "Buck" Wise, dau of Richard Theodore and Annie Knott Latham.
LATHAM, Richard Theodore, b. 1872, d. 1912, hus of Annie Elizabeth Knott.
LATHAM, Theodore 'Frank', b. Dec 17, 1902, d. Sep 21, 1973, hus of Elizabeth Loraine Johnson, son of Richard T. and Annie Elizabeth Knott Latham.
LOKER, Frances M., b. Apr 24, 1908, d. Aug 17, 1988, wife of George P. Wigginton, dau of William Meverell and Mabel Ford Loker.
LOKER, William Alexander "Aleck", Sr, b. Jul 26, 1909, d. Jul 25, 1992, hus of Margaret Belle Wigginton, son of Judge William Meverell and Mabel Ford Loker.
LONGMORE, Susanna, 19, bur Oct 17, 1872.
LONGMORE, Y. Abell, d. May 1, 1973.
MANNING, Ida C., b. Feb 22, 1851, d. Dec 24, 1924, wife of J. Frank Ford.
MANNING, James H. C., d. Mar 14, 1855 aged 22 yrs, 3 mos and 8 days.
MANNING, Mary Priscilla, d. Dec 12, 1854, aged 10 mos and 10 days, dau of James H. and Eliz. Manning.
MANNING, Robert, d. Aug 2, 1839, aged 42 yrs, 10 mos and 2 days.
MASON, Pauline, b. Feb 22, 1889, d. Jun 17, 1958.
MATTHEWS, William Francis, Our Father, b. Nov 1, 1859, d. May 20, 1943.
MATTINGLY, 1914, infant sons of Joseph M. and Lillian A. Mattingly.

MATTINGLY, Anne Eliza "Anna", b. Mar 7, 1903, d. Feb 25, 1992, wife of John Harold Abell, Sr., dau of Joseph Maguire and Lillian Benedicta Abell Mattingly.
MATTINGLY, Ann Sophia, our mother, b. Feb 22, 1837, d. Mar 26, 1895.
MATTINGLY, Eleanor Ann, b. Oct 5, 1928, d. Dec 25, 1990, wife of __ Newton, dau of Marshall and Mary M."Madge" Williams Mattingly.
MATTINGLY, Harry I., d. Oct 14, 1909, aged 2 yrs, 3 mos, son of J.M. and L.B. Mattingly.
MATTINGLY, James F.A., b. Jan 21, 1907, d. Oct 7, 1919.
MATTINGLY, James 'Maguire', Jr, b. Dec 8, 1927, d. May 7, 1992, hus of Mary Ann Edwards, son of James Maguire and Helen Marie Barrett Mattingly.
MATTINGLY, John Bernard, d. Oct 12, 1931, 1st hus of Veronica E. Goldsborough.
MATTINGLY, John Simpson "Jack", b. May 15, 1909, d. Feb 20, 1985, hus of Ella Roberta Latham.
MATTINGLY, Joseph Maguire, 91, b. 1869, d. Mar 6, 1961, hus of Lillian Abell.
MATTINGLY, Mary Catherine, 1958.
MATTINGLY, Sophia, 50, bur Jun 2, 1872.
MATTINGLY, Thomas W., 59, d. Jul 30, 1991 NY, hus of Adele __.
MILBURN, James W., b. 1915, d. 1973.
MILLS, George Daniel, Sr. b. Oct 20, 1891, d. Dec 9, 1973.
MORGAN, J. W. J., 47, bur Aug 11, 1869.
NORRIS, Eliza, b. 1839, d. 1891, wife of James Nelson Evans.
NORRIS, Elsie Marie, b. Jul 25, 1919, d. Feb 8, 1992, wife of Francis Abell Woodburn, Sr., dau of Joseph and Lucy Thompson Norris.
NORRIS, John, 35, bur Sep 8, 1869.
NORRIS, John Baptista, 65, bur Jul 30, 1872.
NORRIS, Joseph Benedict, b. 1859, d. 1921, hus of Alice Evans.
NORRIS, Joseph Warren, b. May 31, 1912, d. Sep 11, 1988, son of Joseph Ward and Lucy Norris.
NORRIS, Violet Lucy, b. Jan 13, 1906, d. Sep 22, 1991, wife of Richard Harold Graves, dau

Our Lady's Chapel

of Joseph and Lucy Thompson Norris.
NOY, Patrick, 60, bur Sep 2, 1872.
POTEETE, Alice, b. 1889, d. 1968, wife of J. Rhody Barnes.
PRITCHARD, Edwin Granger, Sr., d. May 2, 1968, hus of Helen Isabelle Combs.
QUADE, Cora G., b. 1932, d. 1967.
ROACH, Philomena, d. Jan 12, 192-, aged 83 years, wife of Bennett R. Abell.
RUSSAVAGE, Arthur Joseph, b. Nov 19, 1946 PA, d. Oct 10, 1993, son of Arthur J. and Mary Sipko Russavage.
RYON, Jane, b. DC., d. Jun 14, 1993, m. 11 Aug 1962 Bert Abell, dau of Allison F. and Caroline Goldsmith Ryon.
SAMSON, Martha Ann, 30, bur Oct 22, 1871.
SCHINDLER, Joanne, b. Sep 6, 1957, d. Nov 30, 1988, wife of David M. Guyther, dau of William Charles and Dorothy Aud Schindler.
SELF, Catherine, 33, bur Sep 24, 1872.
SMITH, Elizabeth, 74, bur May 16, 1890.
SOMERVILLE, d. Oct 25, 1975.
SPAULDING, Mary 'Josephine', d. Feb 1, 1967, wife of Clarence A. Goddard, Sr.
STONE, Alberta Agnes, b. Feb 16, 1908, d. Apr 22, 1977, m. (1st) Charles I. Cryer, (2d) William "Rhodie" Cryer, dau of Joseph 'Ford' and Mary "Mamie" Godwin Stone.
STONE, Joseph "Ford', b. Apr 13, 1871, d. Apr 2, 1956, hus of Mary Catherine "Mamie" Godwin.
STONE, Joseph Vernon "Jack", b. Jun 21, 1904, d. Jul 8, 1949 Balto, hus of Mary 'Mildred' Johnson, son of Joseph 'Ford' and Mary "Mamie" Godwin Stone.
STONE, Mary 'Grace', b. Feb 11, 1906, d. Jun 1, 1986, wife of Thomas 'Leonard' Cryer, Sr., dau of Joseph 'Ford' and Mary "Mamie" Godwin Stone.
SWALES, Edward, d. May 19, 1977.
SWALES, George, d. Aug 20, 1976.
TANEY, Lucy Eline, 2 yrs, bur May 4, 1871.
TENNESON, Dorothy, d. Jul 23, 1851, aged 18 yrs, 3 mos and 22 days, wife of William H. Tenneson.

THOMAS, Patrick Eugene, b. 1949, d. 1965.
TRENT, Annie Marie, b. Dec 3, 1923, d. Nov 11, 1990, wife of Joseph Benedict Neal, dau of Alfred and Edwina Dorsey Trent.
WATTS, Addie Anne, b. Jul 5, 1904, d. Apr 8, 1993, m. (1st) Arthur Taylor, (2d) 1933 James Andrew Barnes, dau of Ben Watts.
WEBB, Adeline, 47, bur Apr 30, 1881, wife of __ Jenkins.
WHEELER, Mrs. 68, bur Apr 19, 1870.
WHITE, Theodore William, b. Dec 12, 1938, d. Feb 22, 1989, hus of Mary Rita Garner, son of Theodore Eli White.
WIGGINTON, George Peter, b. May 25, 1905 PA, d. Dec 25, 1990, hus of Frances M. Loker, son of George Peter and Margaret Heasly Wigginton.
WIGGINTON, Margaret Belle, b. Mar 1, 1914, d. Dec 11, 1982, m. 18 Nov 1934 William Alexander "Aleck" Loker, Sr.
WILSON, Helen Cora, Mother, b. Aug 5, 1879, d. Jan 14, 1952.
WILSON, Lloyd Randolph, b. Jan 5, 1928 Balto, d. Apr 21, 1988, hus of Margaret Ann __, son of John Joshua and Madelene Ferrell Wilson.
WISE, Charles Berkman "Buck", d. Jan 8, 1965, hus of Mary 'Virginia' Latham.
WOODBURN, Francis Abell "Whitey", Jr., b. Dec 23, 1938, d. May 30, 1982, son of Francis Abell and Elsie Marie Norris Woodburn.
YATES, Thomas Benedict, MD CPL USA, b. Oct 11, 1930, d. Dec 25, 1963.
YOUNG, Mary F., b. Dec 17, 1911, d. Nov 14, 1966, wife of Stephen R.L. Young.
YOUNG, Philip Francis, b. May 8, 1887, d. Sep 20, 1967.
YOUNG, Stephen R.L., b. Jan 14, 1908, d. Sep 9, 1982, hus of Mary F. __.
YOUNG, Stephen Robert Leo, USA Vietnam, b. Nov 3, 1941, d. Aug 29, 1976.

SACRED HEART ROMAN CATHOLIC CHURCH
Bushwood, Md.

A wooden chapel was built near the Bushwood Manor House nearly a hundred years before Sacred Heart was established in 1755. In 1770 FR James Walton, S.J. built a sizable church. It caught fire and burned to the ground in 1946. The present brick and mortar church was constructed on the same foundation by Fr Johnson. Trunks of very old trees in the oldest section of this cemetery are covered with carvings and the most readable are as follows:

R.V. n---	L.S. 98	That
Bern (born?)		is
3. Day of	S.H. boxed	Sweet
Nov. 1882		H.A.
	R.Q.	(inverted N.)A.
D.A.F. boxed	T.Q. 78	L.H.
J.M.	T.M. 1760	J.M.
B.C.	M. circled	boxed A.L.
W.R.)	A.R.	F.W.
J.D.E)boxed	At Rest	L.R.
N 3)		
J.D.W. age ?3	F.W.	F.W.
Jun 26, 1830	L.R.	A.B.
G.W.	40	
A.W. E.W.	Met	
L.W.	J.W.	
L.W.	R.W.	

Little Lucy, on small cross, no other marking, located on front edge of cemetery.
ABELL, Robert Peery "Bob", Sr. b. Oct 20, 1925 Balto, d. Nov 10, 1991, hus of Ann Lawrence, son of Benjamin Kennedy, Sr. and Adelaide M. Lynch Abell.
ALVEY, Helen Mor, d. Oct 12, 1832, aged 10

mos, dau of James and Ann Alvey.
ALVEY, Ignatius, d. Aug 27, 1828, aged 7 days, son of James and Ann Alvey.
ALVEY, James, d. Jun 12, 1832, aged 42 years and 4 mos.
ALVEY, James L., 59, bur May 10, 1889.
ALVEY, James R., b. Nov 16, 1831, d. May 6, 1889.
ALVEY, Peter H., Husband, b. Dec 8, 1864, d. Sep 14, 1894.
ALVEY, Zorah Colomber, d. Oct 29, 1832, aged 3 years and 3 mos, dau of James and Ann Alvey.
ARMSTRONG, Henry W., 6 mos, bur Jan 30, 1870.
ARNOLD, Elizabeth Frances, b. Oct 31, 1907, d. Aug 7, 1990 VA, dau of Richard Lee and Frances Elizabeth Harden Arnold.
ONE STONE
-ARNOLD, Garnett L., b. 1894.
-ARNOLD, Cora M., b. 1901, d. 1961.
ARNOLD, Mrs. Mary C., bur Feb 11, 1892.
One Stone
-ARNOLD, Regina H., Mother, b. Aug 8, 1861, d. Nov 13, 1927.
-ARNOLD, Mary M., Daughter, b. Sep 12, 1885, d. Feb 13, 1967, wife of __ Tate.
G(?).B., hand carved field stone adjacent to Charles Rock tombstone.
BAILEY, Agnes Estella, b. 1880, d. 1955, wife of Robert Allen Mattingly.
BAILEY, Ann Marie, d. Mar 26, 1884, aged 8 mos and 5 days, dau of James and K. E. Bailey.
BAILEY, Charles, b. Feb 5, 1905, d. Aug 31, 1976.
BAILEY, DeSales Cleveland, b. Oct 23, 1884, d. Apr 20, 1971, hus of S. Madeline Woodburn.
BAILEY, Dorothy, b. Feb 6, 1913, d. Apr 6, 1993, wife of Andrew John Kucher, dau of Cpt. Matthew Roosevelt and Clara Sadonia Meushaw Bailey.
BAILEY, Dorothy "Dorie" Rebecca, b. Jun 21, 1907, d. Oct 16, 1991, wife of John Haverman Banagan, Jr., dau of Joseph Fenwick and Mazie Rebecca Cheseldine Bailey.
BAILEY, Eleanor Beatrice "Beezie", b. Jul 12, 1922, d. Jan 3, 1991 DC, wife of Richard

Dennis Tippett, Sr., dau of Samuel Matthew
and Minnette Collins Bailey.
BAILEY, Ella, b. Dec 2, 1865, d. Dec 22, 1881,
consort of John H. Russell, dau of James H.
and Eliza A. Bailey.

Double Stone
-BAILEY, F. Harvey, b. Feb 20, 1890, d. Jan
14, 1973.
-BAILEY, Marie M., b. Jan 12, 1892, d. Aug 31,
1969.
BAILEY, Genevieve, b. Oct 10, 1911, wife of
William Francis Herbert.

One Stone
-BAILEY, George C., b. 1854, d. 1899.
-BAILEY, Lucy S., b. 1854, d. 1898.
-BAILEY, John E., b. 1887, d. 1910.
BAILEY, Helen, b. 1901, wife of J. Clifton
Downs.

Side By Side
-BAILEY, James C., b. 1869, d. 1932, hus of
-BAILEY, Grace E., b. 1873, d. 1940.
-BAILEY, James T., b. 1898, d. 1931.
-BAILEY, Grace, b. Apr 22, 1902, d. Apr 15,
1962, wife of Thomas J. Kennedy.
-BAILEY, Charles, b. Feb 5, 1905, d. Aug 31,
1976.
-BAILEY, Joseph F., MD Pvt, CO C 312 MG BN
WW I, b. Sep 23, 1875, d. Jul 30, 1955.

Side By Side
-BAILEY, James H., d. Oct 14, 1911, aged 78
years.
-BAILEY, Julia C., b. Feb 22, 1858, d. Aug
25, 1920.
BAILEY, James Mitchell, b. 1876, d. 1955, hus
of Blanche Yates.
BAILEY, James Theodore, b. Jan 15, 1860, d.
Dec 13, 1916, hus of Catherine E. __, b.
Apr 21, 1868, d. Aug 28, 1902.
BAILEY, Joseph David "Dave", USA WW II, b. Jun
11, 1909, d. Jan 29, 1992, hus of Mary Theresa Gibson, son of Joseph Fenwick "Fennie"
and Mazie Rebecca Cheseldine Bailey.
BAILEY, Joseph Fenwick, b. 1885, d. 1958,
hus of Mazie Rebecca Cheseldine.
BAILEY, Joseph Lester, d. Jul 31, 1890, aged

3 years and 16 days, son of James H. and
Julia C. Bailey.
     Side By Side
-BAILEY, Matthew R., MD CMAA USNRF WW I, b.
 Jun 7, 1875, d. Sep 24, 1959.
-BAILEY, Bessie E., b. Feb 19, 1917, d. Sep
 30, 1919.
-BAILEY, Edith, b. Jun 29, 1883, d. Oct 25,
 1909, wife of __ Gass.
     Double Stone
-BAILEY, Matthew R., b. 1875, d. 1959.
-BAILEY, Clara S., b. 1876, d. 1944.
BAILEY, Maud, d. Nov 18, 1885, aged 1 year 1
 mo and 10 das, dau of Jas. H. and Julia C.
 Bailey.
BAILEY, Mildred, b. 1902, wife of Herman G.
 Blair.
     One Stone
-BAILEY, Norman M., b. Nov 26, 1898, d. Aug
 16, 1899.
-BAILEY, S.B., d. Sep 7, 1899.
BAILEY, Thomas 'Elmer', USA WW II, b. Apr 25,
 1919, d. Oct 1, 1991, hus of Mary Agnes
 Downs, son of Joseph Fenwick and Mazie Rebecca Cheseldine Bailey.
BAILEY, Thomas Woodburn, b. 1907, d. 1931.
BAKER, Raymond Lloyd, b. Dec 20, 1915 DC, d.
 Oct 6, 1990, hus of Margarette Cleo __, son
 of Raymond Franklin and Mary Ethel William
 Baker.
BANAGAN, George P., b. 1878, d. 1944.
BANAGAN, George 'Marshall', Sr. b. Jul 7,
 1908, d. Sep 28, 1992, hus of Hilda Veronica
 Morris, son of George Palmer and Susan Lily
 Herbert Banagan.
BANAGAN, John Haverman, Jr. d. Apr 27, 1970,
 m. 25 Dec 1925, Dorothy "Dorie" Rebecca
 Bailey.
     One Stone
-BANAGAN, Havie, b. 1872, d. 1936, hus of
-BANAGAN, Birdie, b. 1875, d. 1953.
-BANAGAN, Louise, b. 1914, wife of Perry A.
 Gibson.
BANAGAN, Joseph S., d. Mar 11, 1907, aged 2
 years, son of Havey J. and Bertie M. Banagan.

Sacred Heart

BANAGAN, Loretta A., "Ditty", b. Jul 30, 1902, d. Dec 16, 1989, wife of C. Frederick Mattingly, dau of George Palmer and Susan Lilly Banagan.
BARNES, Annie Lucille, b. Feb 23, 1908, d. Nov 28, 1988, wife of Robert Curtis, dau of Willie and Annie Brown Barnes.
BARNES, John Francis, b. Oct 17, 1911, d. Sep 20, 1988, hus of Pearl Butler, son of Willie and Annie Brown Barnes.
                Double Stone
-BEITZELL, A. Clement, b. 1898, d. 1976,
-BEITZELL, Rose Lee, b. 1898, d. 1976.
                ONE STONE
-BEITZEL, Charles H., b. Sep 13, 1873, d. Jan 6, 1967.
-BEITZEL, Ida C., b. Jun 4, 1882, d. May 5, 1947.
-BEITZELL, George L., Father, b. 1875, d. 1952, hus of Susie V. Houck.
BEITZELL, Elsie C., b. Oct 1, 1902, d. Jun 2, 1971. Bur in Andrew Freeman Cheseldine plot.
BEITZEL, Ida Grace, d. May 30, 1914, age 9 mos.
BEITZEL, no given name on stone, b. Oct 22, 1876, d. July 23, 1914.
BEITZELL, Joshire, (sic) d. Oct 23, 1884, aged 50 years, husband of Mary __, d. Apr 14, 1890, aged 54 years. (Church record gives her age as 55, bur Apr 18, 1890.)
                Double Stone
-BEITZELL, Joshiah E., b. 1867, d. 1959.
-BEITZELL, Mary E., b. 1865, d. 1925.
BLAIR, no given name, 3 mos, bur Jan 2, 1870.
BLAIR, Catherine D., b. Apr 4, 1925, d. Oct 12, 1934.
BLAIR, Herman G., b. 1896, d. 1971, hus of Mildred Bailey.
BLAIR, Laura, b. Jan 27, 1846, d. Nov 18, 1887, wife of J. F. Mattingly, dau of Wm. and Mary Elizabeth Blair.
BLAIR, Mary E., d. Sep 16, 1850, aged 28 years and 20 days, consort of Wm. Blair.
BLAIR, Susan, d. Mar 12, 1883, aged 77 years.
BLAIR, William H., d. Mar 10, 1862, aged 20

years 4 mos and 7 days, son of Wm. and Mary Blair.
?? Ignatius Bernard, b. Feb 19, 1888, d. Sep 23, 1888, aged 7 mos and 4 days. (Couldn't find a surname, stone was next to William H. Blair.)
BOLLING, Mary 'Evelyn', wife of __ Danos, no dates.
BOLLING, Mary Jeannette, d. April 1973, wife of __ Goetz, sister of Mary 'Evelyn' Danos.
                    Side By Side
 -BOSTWICK, Mother, d. Jun 25, 1909.
 -BOSTWICK, Frank, b. 1872, d. 1944.
 -BOSTWICK, Margaret, b. 1878, d. 1953.
                    Double Stone
 -BOSTWICK, Theodore, b. 1877, d. 1946.
 -BOSTWICK, Fannie O., b. 1875, d. 1960.
BOSTWICK, Dorothy Ione, b. Sep 8, 1904, d. Sep 11, 1919, dau of Theo and Fannie Bostwick.
BOSTWICK, John L., MD BM1 USN WW II, b. Dec 17, 1911, d. Feb 12, 1971.
BOWLES, John Ralph, b. Feb 5, 1912, d. Jul 20, 1993, m. 19 May 1940 Anna Marie Hill, son of Daniel Webster and Laura Frances Kennan Bowles.
                    Double Stone
 -BOWLES, John W., Father, b. Mar 22, 1860, d. Feb 7, 1927.
 -BOWLES, Mrs. John W., Mother, b. Feb 11, 1861, d. Jun 23, 1944.
BOWLES, William Bryant, MD SSGT USA WWII, b. Jun 1, 1910, d. Jul 4, 1972, BSM.
BOWLING, Mrs. Benjamin, 40, bur Jul 17, 1887.
BROWN, Infant son of Geo. Edward and Grace C. Heard Brown, d. Mar 11, 1930.
BROWN, George 'Edward', b. 1901, d. 1973, hus of Grace C. Heard.
BROWN, Margaret Mary, b. Oct 24, 1908, d. Nov 19, 1991, wife of Thomas McGuire Lacy, Sr., dau of Joseph Morgan and Mary Louise Gorman Brown.
BROWN, Rose Belle, b. 1883, d. 1932.
BROWN, Ruth Alma, b. Feb 26, 1915, d. Jun 2, 1989, wife of Charles "Buster" Morris, dau of Samuel F. and Rosa Belle Tyler Brown.

Sacred Heart

BUCKLER, Catherine "Kitty", b. Jan 11, 1944, d. Jan 5, 1990, wife of __ Van Wert, dau of Richard Warren and Marie Ryce Buckler.
BUCKLER, J. Woodley, b. May 11, 1874, d. Jul 5, 1930, hus of Effie R. __, b. May 2, 1879, d. Aug 28, 1952.
BUCKLER, Marie R., d. Apr 4, 1974.
BUCKLER, R. Warren, d. Apr 1, 1973.
Side By Side in this Order
-BURCH, Addie C., d. Apr 15, 1873, aged 28 years 4 mos and 4 days, wife of Dennis C. Burch.
-BURCH, Dennis C., Dr., b. Nov 18, 1802, d. Oct 23, 1878, My Husband.
-BURCH, Elizabeth T., Mother, b. Jan 19, 1844, d. Dec 11, 1909, wife of Dennis C. Burch.
BURCH, Albert, b. Sep 23, 1866, d. Oct 10, 1886.
Double Stone
-BURCH, Ann R., b. May 16, 1840, d. Jun 15, 1934.
-BURCH, Mary J., b. Feb 8, 1842, d. Jan 10, 1920.
BURCH, C. Whittingham, b. May 27, 1870, d. Mar 23, 1943, dau of Charles A. and L. Whittingham Burch.
BURCH, Charles A., b. Oct 29, 1845, d. Jul 23, 1902, hus of Josephine Walter.
BURCH, Charlotte Alberter (sic), d. Feb 5, 1855, aged 3 years 9 mos and 11 days, dau of Albert and Amanda Burch.
BURCH, Dennis Constantine, d. Dec 28, 1873, aged 4 years and 22 days, son of D. C. and A. C. Burch.
BURCH, Ernest DeSales, b. Feb 25, 1878, d. Dec 29, 1934, hus of Lorena Foxwell.
BURCH, George, d. Mar 13, 1876, aged 4 years and 19 days, son of D. C. and A. C. Burch.
BURCH, J. Walter, Dr., b. Nov 23, 1876, d. Oct 2, 1903.
BURCH, Mary Amanda, d. Aug 31, 1850, aged 42 years 6 mos and 3 days, consort of Albert Burch.
BURCH, Mary Lilius, 7 mo 20 das, bur Sep 17, 1871.

BURCH, Robert Ludwell, d. Dec 13, 1873, aged 5 years 9 mos and 22 days, son of D. C. and A. C. Burch.
BURROUGHS, Susan, see Robert Dean stone.
BUTLER, Alice Frances, b. May 9, 1900, d. Aug 12, 1992, dau of John and Mary Elizabeth Collins Butler.
BUTLER, Kate, d. Jun 30, 1927.
BUTLER, Maria, 6 das, bur Feb 1870.
BUTLER, Pearl Elizabeth, b. Apr 15, 1901, d. Aug 25, 1993, m. 4 Jul 1948 John F. Barnes, Sr., dau of John and Elizabeth Collins Butler.
BUTLER, Susan, 7 yrs, bur Sep 7, 1869.
CARTER, Francis I., b. 1885, d. 1948.
CARTER, James Oscar, 9 mos, bur Mar 9, 1870.
CARTER, Josephine, Mother, d. Dec 7, 1919, aged 70 years.
CARTER, Marc Antonio "Tony", Sr. b. Oct 28, 1964, d. Apr 25, 1993, son of Ernest S. Carter and Martha Jane Carter Abell.
CARTER, Mary Ann, 40, bur Jan 30, 1870.
    Double Stone
-CHESELDINE, Andrew Freeman, b. 1874, d. 1935.
-CHESELDINE, Annie Maude, b. 1880, d. 1962.
    Double Stone
-CHESELDINE, Andrew Jackson, Father, b. Feb 14, 1836, d. May 11, 1923.
-CHESELDINE, Annie Marie, Mother, b. Apr 15, 1841, d. Nov 29, 1916.
CHESELDINE, Miss Beatrice, 17, bur Jan 2, 1890.
CHESELDINE, Doris, b. May 26, 1900, d. Jun 26, 1976, wife of Charles Henry Gibson.
CHESELDINE, Elmer Bennett, d. Apr 17, 1974, hus of Hope Imelda Wheeler.
CHESELDINE, Everett A., Sr. b. 1910, d. 1983, hus of Sarah Margaret Mullen.
    Four Stones Side By Side
-Double Stone
 -CHESELDINE, Garrett, b. 1883, d. 1952.
 -CHESELDINE, Mary L., b. 1886, d. 1975.
-CHESELDINE, Garrett, b. May 19, 1883, d. Dec 21, 1952.
-CHESELDINE, Robert G., MD S1 USNR WW II, b. Feb 3, 1917, d. Nov 28, 1967.

-CHESELDINE, Anne Marie, b. Jan 13, 1914, d. Nov 12, 1983.
CHESELDINE, Capt. George, 55, bur Jan 18, 1887.
CHESELDINE, Gladys Mae, b. May 24, 1900, d. Dec 26, 1992, m. 1918 John William Hall, dau of John Keneluam and Mary Virginia Long Cheseldine.
CHESELDINE, Isabel G., b. 1909, d. 1968.
CHESELDINE, John A., b. Jul 13, 1865, d. Sep 25, 1865, son of A.J. and Ann M. Cheseldine.
CHESELDINE, Joseph Seneca, b. 1860, d. 1930, hus of Nellie Norris.

Double Stone
-CHESELDINE, John K., b. 1847, d. 1930.
-CHESELDINE, Mary V., b. 1864, d. 1945.

CHESELDINE, Mary Beatrice, b. Dec 26, 1870, d. Jan 1, 1890, dau of A. J. and Ann M. Cheseldine.
CHESELDINE, Mary Jane, d. Sep 23, 1873, aged 3 years 9 mos and 21 days, dau of John K. and Frances Cheseldine.
CHESELDINE, Mazie Rebecca, b. 1887, d. 1948, wife of Joseph Fenwick "Fennie" Bailey.
CHESELDINE, Nelson, 55, bur Feb 10, 1885.
CHESELDINE, Robert, 40, bur Oct 9, 1896.
CHESELDINE, Robert, b. Jan 15, 1872, d. Sep 29, 1896, son of A. J. and Ann Cheseldine.
CHESELDINE, Robert A., b. Dec 13, 1859, d. Oct 1, 1865, son of A. J. and Ann M. Cheseldine.
CHESLEY, Abram, b. 1853, d. 1933.

One Stone
-CLARKE, Grace A., b. 1885, d. 1925.
-CLARKE, Julia P., b. 1863, d. 1935.
-CLARKE, Julia B., b. 1895, d. 1970.

CLARKE, John Lincoln, b. Jan 2, 1917, d. Feb 13, 1990, hus of Grace__, son of Charles and Mary Frances Clarke.
COAD, Delia C., 64, bur Aug 12, 1890.
COAD, Matilda, 5 mos, bur Aug 16, 1872.
COAD, Mrs. Mollie, 31, bur Nov 21, 1895.
COADE, John, 2 yrs 6 mos, bur Apr 9, 1870.
COLLINS, Mrs. Jane, d. Dec 9, 1907, aged 75 years, relict of Hannibal Collins.
COLLINS, John Abraham, b. Oct 16, 1863, d. May 8, 1885.

COLLINS, John Dickerson, b. Dec 29, 1904, d. Feb 10, 1989, hus of Mary Louise __, son of Robert Henry and J. Frances Collins.
                    One Stone
-COLLINS, Robert H., b. 1866, d. 1948.
-COLLINS, Jane F., b. 1869, d. 1918.
-COLLINS, Daisy R., b. 1891, d. 1927.
-COLLINS, J. Edward, b. 1890, d. 1980.
-COLLINS, Margaret Regina, b. 1942, d. 1945.
COOPER, Peter, 4 das, bur Apr 3, 1870.
COUNTISS, William Edward, b. Jul 26, 1929, d. Jul 27, 1993, son of Joseph and Mary Lee Countiss.
CRISMOND, Ethel Virginia, b. Jul 7, 1895, d. Jan 18, 1968, m. (1st) William Stuart Morris, (2d) Paul J. Walker. Buried next to Wm. S. Morris.
CROWDER, Robert Vaughn, b. Jan 30, 1925, d. Nov 6, 1989, hus of Dorothy Hayden, son of Sylvan Robert and Gracia Poe Crowder.
CULLINS, Ella Mae, b. May 17, 1886, d. Mar 6, 1968, m. 17 Jul 1910 Joseph 'Carroll' Gass, dau of William Edward and Mary Elizabeth Russell Cullins.
CULLINS, George Henry, b. June 3, 1880, d. Jan 25, 1960, hus of M. Belle Deane.
CULLINS, T. Clifford, b. Jul 21, 1894, d. Dec 5, 1954.
CULLINS, William Edward, b. Jan 30, 1857, d. Jun 3, 1909, hus of Mary Elizabeth Russell.
                    Side By Side
-CULLISON, Celania C., b. Mar 29, 1825, d. Jun 28, 1897.
-CULLISON, John 'Henry', b. Oct 21, 1820, d. Mar 24, 1892.
CURTIS, James Dunbar III, b. Apr 20, 1945, d. Feb 2, 1992, son of Dorothy Louise Scriber Bowman.
CURTIS, John L., 5 mos, bur Oct 24, 1869.
CURTIS, Mary S., b. 1851, d. 1913, wife of Wm. J. Curtis.
DAVIS, John Robert, Sr. b. Nov 25, 1914, d. Jan 17, 1991, hus of Helen T. Morris, son of Nathaniel B. and Mittie Deadman Davis.
DAVIS, Sarah, b. Aug 27, 1848, d. Jul 13,

1939, wife of John Johnson Deane.
   One Stone
-DEAN, James Allen, b. May 10, 1961, d. May 11, 1961.
-DEAN, Robert Francis, b. May 6, 1963, d. Oct 16, 1963.
DEAN, James Levi, MD Pvt BTRY B 33 FIELD ARTY WW I, b. Jul 15, 1896, d. May 20, 1961.
   One Stone
-DEAN, Robert
-BURROUGHS, Susan
-DEAN, James Levi, b. Jul 15, 1896, d. May 20, 1961.
-HALL, Loretta, b. May 19, 1904, d. Jan 5, 1985.
-GARNER, John Francis, Aug 17, 1980.
-GARNER, Stephen Levi, b. Jun 17, 1981, d. Jun 18, 1981.
DEANE, John Johnson, b. Jun 10, 1855, d. Feb 22, 1925, hus of Sarah Davis.
DEANE, M. Belle, b. Jul 27, 1883, d. Apr 21, 1972, wife of George Henry Cullins.
DEANE, Ruth, b. 1892, d. 1984, wife of __ Thrall.
DEL ROSSI, Philomena J. "Peggy", b. Feb 3, 1902 Phila, PA, d. Sep 17, 1991, wife of William John Toland, dau of Michael and Rose Del Rossi.
DICKERSON, Earl Benedict, Sr. b. Aug 7, 1930, d. Oct 5, 1992, hus of Violena Frances Wheeler, son of George Allen and Betty Elizabeth Rich Dickerson.
DICKERSON, Mary, few mos, bur Feb 1870.
DICKERSON, Wanda Denise, b. Apr 12, 1966, d. Aug 17, 1988, dau of Mr. and Mrs. John Francis Dickerson.
DIGGS, Jane, d. Oct 15, 1889, aged 50 years.
DINGEE, Margaret Ruth, b. Sep 8, 1923 NJ, d. Jun 23, 1991, wife of Thomas Horace Wise, dau of Harry and Laura Jones Dingee.
DORSEY, Joanna, Mother, b. 1863, d. 1937, wife of Thomas Thomas.
DOWNS, J. Clifton, b. 1902, d. 1970, hus of Helen Bailey.
DOWNS, Mary Eva, b. Sep 12, 1908, d. Dec 4,

1989, wife of Joseph Irving Norris, dau of
Alec and Mary E. Downs.
Double Stone
-DOWNS, Stephen, b. 1882, d. 1941.
-DOWNS, Mary Agnes, b. 1887, d. 1950.
DRURY, Bessie L., b. Apr 1897, d. Dec 1973,
Mother, bur in George H. Long plot.
DRURY, Eleanor Catherine, b. Sep 30, 1949, d.
Sep 1, 1989, wife of Robert Patrick Gill,
Sr., dau of Thomas Harry and Mary B. Drury.
DYER, Alexander, drowned May 1860, age 27 yrs.
DYER, Jane C., 33, bur Feb 11, 1886, wife of
__ Gough.
Double Stone
-DYSON, Alfred F., d. Sep 12, 1910, age 17.
-DYSON, Mary J., d. Sep 27, 1911, age 14 yrs.
DYSON, Annie, b. Jan 26, 1869, d. Mar 18,
1946, wife of __ Herbert.
DYSON, George A., 4 yr 6 mos, bur Dec 11, 1869.
DYSON, Isaac Alexander, b. Oct 3, 1918, d. Aug
2, 1993, son of John Clement and Mary Pearl
Butler Dyson.
Double Stone
-DYSON, Isaac F., b. Mar 7, 1864, d. Nov 29,
1932.
-DYSON, Susie A., b. Jun 11, 1867, d. Apr 1,
1959.
DYSON, Robert (colored), 60, bur Sep 17, 1889.
DYSON, Samuel, 70, bur Mar 29, 1872.
EDELIN, Susan L., 10 mos 18 das, bur Mar 9,
1870.
Double Stone
-ELLIS, Benjamin H., b. 1877, d. 1934.
-ELLIS, Annie E., b. 1892, d. 1971.
Double Stone
-ELLIS, Charles E., b. 1876, d. 1945.
-ELLIS, Esther L., b. 1896, d. 1973.
ELLIS, Charles Gilbert, b. Sep 27, 1903, d.
Oct 3, 1988, hus of Ida Catherine Mattingly,
son of Thomas D. and Mary Ella Ellis.
ELLIS, Charles McDonald, infant son of Chas.
A. and Mary F. Long Ellis. (No dates)
ELLIS, Frances Cabrini, Baby, 1946.
ELLIS, Joseph C., b. 1909, d. 1954.
ELLIS, Joseph Lee "Joe Boy", Sr. b. Nov 16,

1934, d. Oct 24, 1993 VA, m. 26 Dec 1959 Nancy Ryder, son of John Edward Jr. and Viola Rose Wathen Ellis.
ELLIS, Paul, b. May 9, 1902, d. Oct 17, 1990, son of George W. and Mary Magdalene Norris Ellis.
One Stone
-ELLIS, R. Carroll, b. 1884, d. 1975, hus of Ella Mary Russell.
-ELLIS, Ellen M., b. 1886, d. 1967.
-ELLIS, Frances M., no dates.
Double Stone
-ELLIS, Richard H., b. Apr 1828, d. Dec 1893.
-ELLIS, Luvenia M., b. Mar 1849, d. Jul 1889.
Double Stone
-ELLIS, Thomas D., b. 1871, d. 1944.
-ELLIS, Mary E., b. 1883, d. 1953.
EVANS, Clarence Leo, b. Sep 4, 1897, d. Sep 21, 1970, hus of Gertrude Pilkerton.
One Stone
-FARR, Joseph J., Sr. b. 1863, d. 1935.
-FARR, Sarah P., b. 1864, d. 1941.
-FARR, George L., b. Feb 16, 1905, d. Jul 19, 1929.
FARR, Martha Ann, 45, bur Dec 10, 1881.
FARR, Martha Ann, b. 1936, d. 1978, wife of __ Lacey.
FARR, Martha D., b. Nov 16, 1898, d. Oct 8, 1968.
FARR, Mary L., b. Oct 25, 1834, d. Feb 27, 1922.
FARR, William P., b. Sep 25, 1893, d. May 1, 1965.
FARRELL, Charles E., MD Pvt CO E 164 INF WW I, b. May 9, 1891, d. Apr 8, 1970, hus of Ann Grace Hill.
FARRELL, James Bernard, b. Sep 26, 1949, d. Apr 7, 1993, hus of Carolyn Mae Guy, son of Jos. Bernard and Mary Agnes Harden Farrell.
FARRELL, Lillian Frances, b. 1884, d. 1953, wife of Philip Dominick Gatton.
FARRELL, Minnie Margaret, b. Aug 13, 1906, d. Sep 2, 1991, wife of James Walter Lacey, dau of Charles C. and Susan C. Knott Farrell.
FARRELL, Peter Henry, b. 1860, d. 1930, hus

of Jane Morgan.
FARRELL, T. C., b. Dec 24, 1891, d. Nov 11, 1929.
                Double Stone
-FARRELL, William J., b. 1892, d. 1953.
-FARRELL, E. Mabel, b. 1900, d. 1973.
                One Stone
-FAUNCE, Conrad E., b. 1859, d. 1932.
-FAUNCE, Infant Mary, Oct 18, 1910.
-FAUNCE, Emma G., b. 1885, d. 1971.
                One Stone
-FEENEY, Eleanor A., b. 1851, d. 1924, wife of John W. Renehan.
-FEENEY, James, b. 1820, d. 1908.
FENWICK, George James John, 1 da, bur Aug 4, 1869.
FERGUSON, Bernard Andria, MD CPL CO 5 ENGRING REGT WW I, b. Mar 1, 1887, d. Feb 7, 1963.
FERGUSON, Florence L., b. Feb 26, 1898, d. May 31, 1990, wife of Lawrence S. McGrath, dau of James Bernard and Ann Rebecca Thompson Ferguson.
FORD, infant, 3 das, bur Aug 6, 1870, child of Henry and Catherine O'Moore Ford.
FRANCIS, William H., b. 1850, d. 1923, hus of Sarah __.
FREDERICK, John F., b. 1880, d. 1952, hus of Lena C. __, b. 1882, d. 1956.
FREDERICK, John H., b. 1908, d. 1930, age 22.
FREDERICK, Dorothy E., b. 1920, d. 1944, our daughter.
FREEMAN, Emily, b. 1880, d. 1942, wife of William F. Herbert.
FREEMAN, Col. John D., 69, bur Aug 22, 1891.
FREEMAN, Josephine, b. 1836, wife of __ Plowden.
FREEMAN, Josephine, b. Jan 14, 1848, d. Feb 14, 1912, wife of Wm. M. Freeman.
                Double Stone
-FREEMAN, Robert M., b. 1841, d. 1913.
-FREEMAN, Cecelia H., b. 1862, d. 1940.
                Adjacent Stone
-Marker "Deo Vindice 1881-1885"
-Stone "SON" no name or date.
                Double Stone

Sacred Heart

-FREEMAN, William M., b. 1878, d. 1966.
-FREEMAN, Ida M., b. 1880, d. 1957.
GARDNER, James Frederick, b. Jan 3, 1912 WV, d. Oct 4, 1993, m. 1938 Margarite Kenny, son of Wallace Ambrose and Ethel Mae Ott Gardner.
GARNER, Stephen Levi, b. Jun 17, 1981, d. Jun 18, 1981, (see Robert Dean stone).
Double Stone
-GASS, Claude D., b. 1906, d. 1977.
-GASS, Emma R., b. 1918.
Side By Side
-GASS, George W., b. 1852, d. 1927.
-GASS, Marie, b. 1860, d. 1930.
-GASS, G.H. Garry, b. Aug 18, 1878, d. Nov 4, 1954.
GASS, Joseph 'Carroll', b. May 26, 1882, d. Jan 8, 1945, m. 17 Jul 1910 Ella Mae Cullins.
Double Stone
-GASS, William H., b. 1896, d. 1969.
-GASS, Jessie A., b. 1900, d. 1972.
GATTON, Arthur Francis, b. Oct 21, 1907, d. Jul 21, 1993 DC, son of Phillip Dominick and Lillian Frances Farrell Gatton.
GATTON, Esther, b. Jul 28, 1879, d. Jan 18, 1974, wife of William Francis Pilkerton.
Side By Side
-GATTON, John Cleveland, b. 1885, d. 1954.
-GATTON, Cecelia Jennie, b. 1850, d. 1950.
GATTON, Philip Dominick, b. 1866, d. 1954, hus of Lillian Frances Farrell.
Side By Side
-GIBSON, Burch C., b. Oct 8, 1901, d. Jul 24, 1944, has Amer. Legion Aux. Marker.
-GIBSON, Annie G., b. 1898, d. 1959.
GIBSON, Charles Henry, b. June 8, 1898, d. Nov 14, 1979, hus of Doris Cheseldine.
Double Stone
-GIBSON, G. Garner, b. 1900, d. 1981.
-GIBSON, Ida R., b. 1897, d. 1977.
GIBSON, George, b. 1866, d. 1947, hus of Mary I. Goode.
GIBSON, George W., b. 18--, d. 18--, hus of Sarah E. Lawrence, believed buried beside wife but stone cannot be found.
GIBSON, James H., d. Apr 28, 1856, aged 26

years 7 mos and 7 days, son of Rodolph M. and Susan Gibson.
GIBSON, Jeremiah, b. 1847, d. 1935, hus of Sarah J. C. __, b. 1851, d. 1929.
Six Stones Side By Side
-GIBSON, Annie Alberta, b. Jan 1, 1892, d. Dec 1, 1900, dau of Jeremiah and Sara C. Gibson.
-GIBSON, Edwin Elmer, b. Sep 25, 1900, d. Jan 11, 1901, son of J. E. and M. A. Gibson.
-GIBSON, M. Blanche, b. Oct 24, 1878, d. Nov 13, 1970.
-GIBSON, Jeremiah, Jr. b. Nov 8, 1888, d. Aug 18, 1960.
-GIBSON, Ella C., b. Dec 29, 1885, d. Jun 20, 1953.
-GIBSON, Virginia, b. May 27, 1876, d. Oct 16, 1948, wife of Thomas G. Hodges.
One Stone
-GIBSON, John J., b. 1849, d. 1932.
-GIBSON, Sarah M., b. 1859, d. 1943.
-GIBSON, William, Jr. b. 1914, d. 1917.
GIBSON, John David, Sr. b. Apr 6, 1911, d. Apr 20, 1993, m. 19 Apr 1942 DC Mary Dora Morris, son of George and Mary I. Goode Gibson.
GIBSON, Joseph Benjamin "Ben", b. Feb 12, 1911, d. Jun 12, 1991, son of Benjamin and Rebecca Hill Gibson.
Double Stone
-GIBSON, Joseph E., b. 1890, d. 1961.
-GIBSON, Mary E., b. 1890, d. 1982.
GIBSON, Joseph Richard "Jack", b. Apr 4, 1905, d. Nov 19, 1993, m. (2d) 26 Dec 1983 Grace Elder, son of Edwin and Mary Beitzell Gibson.
GIBSON, Mary A., d. Oct 1859 of sore throat, age 3 yrs.
GIBSON, Mary Ida, d. Sep 17, 1887, aged 1 year 1 mo and 17 days, dau of John J. and Sarah M. Gibson.
GIBSON, Nellie, b. Aug 27, 1891, d. Jun 30, 1916.
GIBSON, Perry A., b. 1909, d. 1972, hus of Louise Banagan.
GIBSON, Rodolph M., d. Dec 14, 1850 in 49th year.

Double Stone
-GIBSON, William Thomas, b. 1892, d. 1935.
-GIBSON, Catherine B., b. 1897, d. 1973.
GOLDSBOROUGH, Ruth Cynthia, b. Feb 17, 1902, d. May 21, 1981, In Loving Memory from children and grandchildren.

Square Monument
-GOODE, James H., b. 1845, d. 1929, his wife
-GOODE, Julie R., b. 1858, d. 1910.
-GOODE, Arthur L., b. 1892, d. 1918, killed in action in France.
GOODE, Joseph Henry, d. 1984, m. 1926 Ethel Mae __, d. May 18, 1993 at age 89 yrs.
GOODE, Julia A., b. Nov 23, 1875, d.--, wife of (1st) G. F. Thompson, (2d) John F. Hill.
GOODE, Lydia May, b. May 31, 1891, d. Feb 7, 1920.
GOODE, Mary I., b. 1873, d. 1955, wife of George Gibson.
GOODE, Maude V., b. Nov 14, 1922, d. Dec 13, 1992, m. 6 Jan 1941, Joseph Clyde Vallandingham, dau of Walter B. and Mary Jane Hill Goode.
GOODE, Mrs. Thomas, 43, bur Nov 4, 1892.
GOODE, Walter Alexander, b. Feb 26, 1897, d. Oct 16, 1990, hus of Anna Tutwiler, son of Thomas W. and Cora Woodburn Goode.

Side By Side
-GOODE, Capt. Walter B., b. Sep 20, 1896, d. Nov 25, 1955.
-GOODE, Mary Jane, b. Jan 31, 1893, d. Sep 27, 1966.
GOODE, Wilson Perry, b. Feb 23, 1873, d. Feb 9, 1938.
GOODWIN, Alice Teresa, d. Mar 20, 1919, age 5 years 6 mos.
GRAGAN, Alice Elizabeth, b. Jun 24, 1918, d. Nov 7, 1986, wife of Lewis Lorenzo Hill, dau of Mr. Gragan and Josephine Quade Gragan.
GRASON, James B., 62, bur May 21, 1888.
GRAVES, Arthur F., b. Feb 19, 1866, d. Jul 13, 1924.
GRAVES, Blanche Elizabeth, b. Jul 14, 1902, d. Sep 7, 1989, wife of Benjamin Thomas Farrell, Sr., dau of John Morris and Annie Elizabeth

Hall Graves.
GRAVES, John L., b. Jun 8, 1947, d. Sep 4, 1967.
Double Stone
-GRAVES, Joseph H., b. Mar 10, 1907, d. Jun 6, 1979.
-GRAVES, Evelyn F., b. Feb 27, 1915, d. Sep 28, 1982.
GREENWELL, James C., 54, bur May 14, 1885.
GUY, Mattingly, b. 1910, d. 1982.
GUY, Rose Marie, b. 1953, d. 1968.
Double Stone
-HALL, Eugene, b. 1858, d. 1944, Father.
-HALL, Alice E., b. 1860, d. 1929, Mother.
HALL, Francis Elmer, b. Jun 12, 1921, d. Jun 24, 1978, m. 14 Sep 1943 Mary Elizabeth Vallandingham.
HALL, Helen Veronica, b. Jan 8, 1923, d. Jul 12, 1992, wife of James B. Norris, Sr. dau of John F. and Helen S. Hall.
HALL, J. Frank, b. Jul 8, 1852, d. Sep 6, 1901.
Double Stone
-HALL, J. Henry, Father, b. Jan 18, 1873, d. Apr 12, 1943.
-HALL, Lillian G., Mother, b. Jan 9, 1875, d. Aug 10, 1931.
HALL, James Henry, b. 1908, d. 1976, hus of Catherine Quade.
HALL, Loretta, b. May 19, 1904, d. Jan 5, 1985, see Robert Dean stone.
HALL, Myrtle Pauline, b. Jul 3, 1900, d. Sep 3, 1989, wife of Harry Thomas St. Clair, dau of James Henry and Lillian Gertrude Tennyson Hall.
HALL, Mary A., b. Feb 20, 1875, d. Feb 24, 1901, wife of Augustus Anderson, USN.
HAMILL, Mary G., b. Mar 1886, d. Nov 1927.
HAMMERSLY, Janet, b. 1759, d. 1804, wife of Edmund Plowden.
HAMMETT, Louis Valentine, b. Aug 12, 1918, d. May 3, 1992, hus of Elizabeth Wallace, son of George David and Minnie Beatrice Watts Hammett.
HARDEN, Robert Dent, 5 mos 20 das, bur Apr 18, 1879.

Sacred Heart

HARDIN, Mary, b. 1870, d. 1914, wife of Capt. John H. Long.
HARRISON, Ann M., d. Aug 16, 1849, aged 22 yrs 3 mos and 13 das, leaving a husband and little boy.
HARTNETT, Carmen Louisa, b. Dec 28, 1909, Trinidad, West Indies, d. May 16, 1992, dau of Henry and Louisa Ferreira De Freitas.
HAWKINS, James Henry, abt 6 yrs, bur Jun 19, 1870.
Double Stone
-HAYDEN, E. Howard, b. Feb 19, 1898, d. Jul 20, 1942.
-HAYDEN, Pearl Q., b. Jan 7, 1908, d. Mar 25, 1972.
HAYDEN, E. Mildred and Olive M., no dates, on one stone.
Double Stone
-HAYDEN, Edward H., b. 1856, d. 1941.
-HAYDEN, Susie E., b. 1868, d. 1902.
HAYDEN, Franklin C., b. 1889, d. 1934, hus of Mary Simpson.
Double Stone
-HAYDEN, George C., b. 1865, d. 1943.
-HAYDEN, Mary Louise, b. 1864, d. 1950.
Square Monument
-HAYDEN, J. M., b. Sep 8, 1839, d. Dec 15, 1900.
-HAYDEN, N. H., his wife, b. Mar 4, 1850.
-HAYDEN, W. D., b. Nov 19, 1875, d. Oct 4, 1926.
-HAYDEN, M. E., no dates.
-HAYDEN, Nellie M., Our Mother, Mar 4, 1850.
-HAYDEN, James M., Our Father, b. Sep 8, 1841, d. Dec 15, 1900.
-W. D. H., son, b. 1875, d. 1926.
-N. C. H,, dau, b. 1873, d. 1935.
One Stone
-HAYDEN, James E., b. Feb 19, 1898, d. Jul 28, 1978.
-HAYDEN, Daisy E., b. May 5, 1901, d. Aug 19, 1966.
-HAYDEN, James E., Jr. our son, b. Oct 12, 1929, d. Feb 1, 1930.
HAYDEN, James M., b. Apr 20, 1860, d. Aug 12,

1865.
HAYDEN, Maria B.A., b. Aug 20, 1838, d. Nov 26, 1867, consort of A. Hayden.
HAYDEN, Mary Violet, d. Mar 1974, m. 1923 William Albert "Dusty" Graves.
HAZELL, William, d. Jan 6, 1854, aged 36 yrs 2 mos.
HEARD, Grace C., b. 1905, d. 1963, wife of George 'Edward' Brown.
HEARD, Mary Grace, b. Nov 28, 1905, d. Jan 29, 1991, wife of Henry Tester Woodburn, dau of Charles Abell and Mary Emily Bean Heard.
HEBB, Priscilla, b. Dec 29, 1830, d. Jul 4, 1877, relict of John L. Lancaster.
HERBERT, Bernard, Sr, d. March 8, 1993, m. (1st) Lillian E. __; (2d) Charlotte __.
HERBERT, Mrs. Clarence, 44, bur Jan 3, 1893.
HERBERT, Clarence C., d. Apr 7, 1919, aged 73 years 2 mos and 11 das.
Side By Side
-HERBERT, Frank, b. Feb 14, 1877, d. Apr 2, 1946.
-HERBERT, Blanche L., b. Aug 9, 1879, d. Jan 17, 1965.
-HERBERT, Gilbert Francis, MD SSML2 USN WW II, b. Apr 18, 1908, d. Feb 27, 1974.
Side By Side
-HERBERT, George F., b. Aug 1, 1850, d. Jan 8, 1929.
-HERBERT, William F., b. 1884, d. 1936, hus of Emily Freeman.
-HERBERT, William Francis, b. Jan 20, 1912, d. Nov 17, 1979, hus of Genevieve Bailey.
HERBERT, George M., b. and d. Sep 28, 1911, son of George F. and Elsie R. Maddox Herbert.
HERBERT, James P. C., 9 mos, bur Aug 4, 1869.
HERBERT, Mrs. Jere, 45, bur Dec 3, 1872.
HERBERT, John P., d. Nov 27, 1912, aged 61 years, hus of Mary E. __, b. Mar 18, 1853, d. Feb 7, 1910.
HERBERT, Mary, b. 1878, d. 1911, wife of John Francis Thompson.
HERBERT, William "Gonnie", b. 1906, d. 1980, hus of Edith Eileen __.
HERBERT, William Thomas, b. Nov 4, 1877, d.

Jan 23, 1897, son of John P. and Mary E. Herbert.
HESSE, Selma Teresa, b. 1867 Ger., d. 1956, wife of Joseph Renschke.
HIGGINS, Robert Thomas, b. Sep 21, 1927, d. Jun 19, 1989, hus of Sharon Mae __, b. Sep 14, 1929, d. Jul 26, 1988, son of Thomas A. and Mildred Higgins.
HILL, Agnes Marie, b. Oct 28, 1912, d. Jan 2, 1994, wife of Joseph Hampton Somerville, Sr. dau of Thomas Edwin and Sarah L. Barber Hill.
HILL, Ann Grace, b. Sep 24, 1897, d. Mar 10, 1974, wife of Charles E. Farrell.
HILL, Edward Maurice, b. Apr 15, 1961 Balto, d. Nov 6, 1991 DC, son of Helen Josephine Hill Johnson; gson of Susie Hill.
HILL, Grace, b. Sep 6, 1879, d. Nov 11, 1956, wife of Andrew Jackson Morris.
HILL, James W., b. 1905, d. 1948.
HILL, John F., b. 1868, d. 1929.
HILL, John F., b. Sep 12, 1860, d. May 27, 1929, (2d) hus of Julie A. Goode.
HILL, John Wilmer, b. Apr 30, 1901, d. Jan 19, 1979.

Side By Side
-HILL, Joseph Edward, b. 1861, d. 1945, hus of Kate Knott.
-HILL, Joseph Gibbons, b. 1908, d. May 1, 1970, hus of Mary Helen Vallandingham.
-HILL, Alice Irene, Feb 24, 1951, infant of Mr. and Mrs. J. G. Hill.
-HILL, William, MD PFC USA WW I, b. Feb 10, 1893, d. Jan 19, 1973.
HILL, Joseph Gibbons, d. May 1, 1970, hus of Mary Helen Vallandingham.
HILL, King Henry, b. 1874, d. 1943, hus of Rose Emily Lacey.
HILL, Lewis Lorenzo, b. Nov 11, 1911, d. Apr 21, 1982, hus of Alice Elizabeth Gragan.
HILL, Mary Edith nee Hill, b. Nov 17, 1913, d. Mar 4, 1988, wife of Zackery Joseph Hill, Sr.
HILL, Mazie Rose, b. Jun 6, 1910, d. Feb 12, 1992, wife of Clarence Edward Lacey, dau

of King Henry and Rose Emily Lacey Hill.
Double Stone
-HILL, Samuel B., b. May 11, 1883, d. Apr 14, 1946.
-HILL, Ada I., b. Aug 24, 1888, d. Feb 24, 1939.
HILL, Susan A., b. 1883, d. 1962. (in Andrew A. Morris plot)
HILL, William E., b. 1910, d. 1984.
HODGES, Delia, 26, bur May 13, 1884, wife of __ Plowden.
HODGES, Edwin Joseph "Ed", Sr. b. Nov 16, 1906, d. Oct 4, 1990, hus of Mary Helene __, son of Thomas G. and Virginia J. Gibson Hodges.
HODGES, Lewis, b. Nov 30, 1872, d. Dec 16, 1927, hus of Anna Rush.
IMMEDIATELY next is a hand carved field stone
-A. D. 1783.
HODGES, Sarah Katherine, b. Oct 30, 1900, d. Jun 17, 1933, dau of Thomas G. and Virginia Gibson Hodges. (Buried in Jeremiah Gibson plot.)
HODGES, Thomas G., b. Jul 15, 1855, d. Oct 19, 1939.
HODGES, Thomas R., 60, bur May 26, 1886.
HODGES, Zora, d. Jun 15, 1915, aged 50 years, wife of Frederick M. Thomas.
HOLLY, Beatrice M., b. Dec 25, 1909, d. Aug 30, 1956, bur in John F. Frederick plot.
HOLMES, Edmond Alexander, aged 2 ys 9 mos, eldest son of H. B. and Maria D. Holmes.
HOLMES, Jackson, 40, bur Apr 21, 1872.
HOLT, Mabel Virginia, b. Nov 5, 1916, d. Jan 3, 1990, wife of Paul Benjamin Wise, dau of Clayton E. and Mabel A. Holt.
HOLTON, Andrew, Sr. d. Feb 22, 1990, hus of Pearl __, son of James and Agnes Holton.
HOOD, Arvilla Elizabeth "Billie", b. Feb 8, 1907 VA, d. Apr 10, 1992, wife of Benjamin Lee, dau of Abner Toune and Olive Gertrude Richards Hood.
HOUCK, Henry M., b. Nov 24, 1909, d. Dec 5, 1973.

Sacred Heart

HOUCK, Susie V., Mother, b. 1872, d. 1944, wife of George L. Beitzell.
HOWE, Leander, 27 yrs 7 mo, bur May 25, 1870. Double Stone
-HUNTINGTON, Robert B., b. Sep 20, 1884, d. Nov 14, 1967.
-HUNTINGTON, Jeannette M., b. Dec 12, 1898, d. Dec 25, 1981.
HURRY, John C., 60, bur Sep 9, 1888.
HURRY, Mrs. John C., 50, bur Apr 9, 1885.
HURRY, Johnson, 16, bur Jun 14, 1891.
HUSEMAN, Mary E., Mother, b. Dec 10, 1869, d. Aug 13, 1947, wife of John M. Quade.
HUTSON, Agnes J., b. 1915, wife of George W. Joy, Jr., died after 1985.
HUTSON, Thomas O. "Speedy", b. Apr 15, 1899 SC, d. May 20, 1991, m. 11 Mar 1978, Jane Agnes Gatton, son of Dr. Thomas O. and Annie Owens Hutson.
JENKINS, Jason, d. Sunday Feb 25, 1821 from a fall from a horse on his way home from church, in his 28th year.
JOHNSON, J. Leonard, b. Feb 16, 1923, d. Nov 16, 1962, son of Julius J. and Lillian Mattingly Johnson.
JOHNSON, James Ignatius, b. Apr 30, 1921, d. Jul 29, 1921, son of Julius J. and Lillian Mattingly Johnson.
JOHNSON, J. L., d. Sep 22, 1865, age 18 years, 5 mos and 6 days, son of Joseph and Ellen Johnson.
JOHNSON, Joseph, b. Mar 21, 1812, d. Nov 23, 1871, hus of (1st) Eleanor "Ellen" Lawrence, (2d) Ruth Ann __, son of Philip and Mary Thomas Johnson.
JOHNSON, Ruth Ann, d. May 4, 1871, aged 54 years, 2 months and 4 days, 2d wife of Joseph Johnson.
JOHNSON, Joseph 'Julius', b. Dec 7, 1891, d. Oct 24, 1978, m. (1st) M. Lillian Mattingly, (2d) Anna Swann Wills, son of Zackariah and Missouri Woodburn Johnson.
JONES, Anna Louise, b. Mar 26, 1917, d. Sep 8, 1992, dau of James Darby and Anna Elizabeth Hobb Jones.

JONES, Mary, 50, bur Apr 30, 1872.
JORDON, Elizabeth, d. Jun 10, 1861, aged 53 years, wife of Edmund S. T. Maddox.
JOY, George W., Jr. b. 1891, d. 1973, hus of Agnes J. Hutson.
Side By Side
-KEENAN, George A., Father, b. 1891, d. 1973.
-KEENAN, Gladys C., Mother, b. 1903, d. 1973.
-KEENAN, John D., MD Pvt 30 RCT CO GEN SVR INF WW 1, b. Dec 2, 1893, d. May 30, 1963.
-KEENAN, Roberta, b. 1863, d. 1942.
KENNAN, Laura Frances, b. Jan 8, 1889, d. Jun 2, 1913, wife of Daniel Webster Bowles.
KENNEDY, Thomas J., b. 1925, d. 1976, hus of Grace Bailey. Bur in James C. Bailey plot.
Double Stone
-KENNETT, John K., b. 1902, d. 1983.
-KENNETT, Catherine L., b. 1903.
KNIGHT, William Johnson "Bill", b. Feb 14, 1905, d. Oct 4, 1989, hus of Ella Mae Wathen, son of Benjamin 'Carroll' and Mary 'Nannie' Knight.
Side By Side
-KNOTT, Clarence Guy, b. Nov 18, 1909, d. Jun 15, 1941.
-KNOTT, John L., b. July 12, 1882, d. Jan 8, 1945.
-KNOTT, Katie M., b. Jul 28, 1883, d. Dec 25, 1943.
KNOTT, Kate, b. 1865, d. 1929, wife of Joseph Edward Hill.
KNOTT, Margaret, Our Aunt, b. 1885, d. 1937.
KNOTT, Mary Elsie, b. Oct 20, 1904, d. Dec 23, 1989, wife of William Dudley Lacey, dau of John Louis and Katie Maria Quade Knott. M. L., hand-carved field stone, next to Elizbeth Pilkerton plot.
Double Stone
-LACEY, Daniel V., b. 1899, d. 1976.
-LACEY, Francis V., b. 1900, d. 1980.
Double Stone
-LACEY, Eleanor Teresa, 1925-1926.
-LACEY, William Luke, 1925-1926.
Double Stone
-LACEY, George Albert, b. 1892, d. 1976.

-LACEY, Ann Gertrude, b. 1899, d. 1965.
LACEY, James W., Father, b. Sep 10, 1924, d. May 12, 1977, hus of Minnie Margaret Farrell.
LACEY, Linda Ellen, b. Mar 19, 1894, d. Mar 24, 1993, dau of Charles Henry and Mary Edmonia Gatton Lacey.
LACEY, Mary, b. Jul 31, 1865, d. Oct 9, 1951, wife of John Joseph Quade.
LACEY, Rena Elizabeth, Mother, b. Dec 26, 1889, d. Oct 25, 1956.
LACEY, Rose Emily, b. 1875, d. 1953, wife of King Henry Hill.
LACEY, Samuel T., b. Jun 6, 1895, d. May 20, 1919.
LACEY, Thomas Maguire, Sr., d. Oct 1962, m. 10 Jul 1930 Margaret Mary Brown.

Double Stone
-LACEY, Walter B., b. 1900, d. 1979.
-LACEY, Mary Ada, b. 1902, d. 1959.
LACY, Annie Florence, Mother, b. Nov 1, 1878, d. Jan 2, 1926, wife of Joseph F. Lacy.
LACY, Robert L., b. Dec 20, 1835, d. May 7, 1905.

Double Stone
-LANCASTER, John, b. 1846, d. 1904.
-LANCASTER, Jane, b. 1854, d. 1926.
LANCASTER, John L., b. Mar 15, 1817, d. May 7, 1876, hus of Priscilla Hebb.
LATHAM, Josephine 'Ella', b. Aug 11, 1876, d. Mar 17, 1946, wife of Ernest J. Wheeler, (tombstone shows Ella J.)

Double Stone
-LATHAM, James A., Father, b. 1880, d. 1945.
-LATHAM, Alice M., Mother, b. 1881, d. 1954.
LAWRENCE, Arthur Bernard, Jr., m. (1st) 1925 Emma Marie __, she d. Feb 14, 1964, m. (2d) Gertrude Marie Scherer.
LAWRENCE, Eleanor "Ellen", d. Oct 3, 1853, age 36 years, (1st) wife of Joseph Johnson, dau of Monica Lawrence, widow.
LAWRENC(E), Elizabeth, b. Dec 7, 1776, d. Mar 29, 1862.

Side By Side
-LAWRENCE, Francis McH., b. 1879, d. 1903.

-LAWRENCE, Joseph A., b. 1856, d. 1928.
-LAWRENCE, Susan C., b. 1859, d. 1941.
LAWRENCE, George L., b. 1886, d. 1952, hus of Pauline F. Long.
LAWRENCE, George L., Jr. b. Apr 22, 1923, d. Jun 21, 1923, son of Geo. L. and Pauline F. Long Lawrence.
LAWRENCE, Sarah Elizabeth, b. Jan 1813, d. Apr 16, 1882, wife of George W. Gibson, dau of Monica Lawrence, widow. Stone broken in half and laying in Joseph Johnson plot. Footstone S.E.G. in row containing J. Johnson and Charles Rock plots.
Side By Side
-LAWRENCE, Thomas J. N., b. Aug 10, 1858, d. Aug 2, 1940.
-LAWRENCE, Elizabeth C., b. Sep 15, 1855, d. Mar 23, 1921, wife of T. J. N. Lawrence.
-LAWRENCE, William S., b. Sep 18, 1884, d. Jul 3, 1905, son of T. J. N. and Mary J. Lawrence.
LEE, Benjamin, d. Mar 1988 DC, hus of Arvilla Elizabeth "Billie" Hood.
Double Stone
-LONG, George H., b. Oct 15, 1849, d. Jun 26, 1915.
-LONG, Georgianna L., b. May 25, 1868, d. Jan 26, 1955.
LONG, Mrs. Jane, 60, bur Mar 17, 1897.
Side By Side
-LONG, John, d. Dec 12, 1828, aged 60 years.
-LONG, Ann, d. Jan 13, 1856, aged 76 years.
Side By Side
-LONG, Capt. John H., b. 1863, d. 1940.
-LONG, Mary Elsie, b. 1902, d. 1919.
-LONG, Hattie, b. Jul 31, 1899, d. Jun 8, 1978, wife of __ Fix.
Double Stone
-LONG, Louis W., b. 1882, d. 1965.
-LONG, Lala M., b. 1888, d. 1915.
LONG, Lucy M., b. May 2, 1862, d. Feb 2, 1885, wife of Lewis K. Mattingly, dau of J. B and S. A. Long.
LONG, Mary F., d. Apr 29, 1887, aged 29 years and 24 days, wife of Charles A. Ellis, dau

of J. B. and S. A. Long.
LONG, Pauline F., b. 1890, d. 1957, wife of George L. Lawrence.
LONG, Richard, 29, bur Feb 5, 1871.
LYON, Albert Lawrence, "Speedy", Jr. b. Jul 22, 1972, d. Oct 7, 1990, son of Albert L. and Donna Lee Pierce Lyon; gson of Albert Vivian and Lucille Thompson Lyon; Lester Eugene and Robbie Jewel Pierce.
LYON, Virgie, b. Nov 9, 1903, d. Dec 28, 1992, wife of John Marshall Gragan, dau of Alexander and Josephine Quade Lyon.
MACK, Andrew Aloysius, b. Aug 9, 1910, d. Nov 29, 1989, son of Stephen and Rosetta Mack.
MADDOX, Elsie R., b. Feb 24, 1892, d. Aug 3, 1922, wife of George F. Herbert.
MADDOX, James Columbus, Jr. b. Dec 29, 1904, d. Feb 10, 1989, son of James C. and Mary C. Neale Maddox.
MADDOX, John Nathaniel, Sr. b. Feb 11, 1919, d. Sep 15, 1991, hus of Mary Delia __, son of James Columbus and Mary Neale Maddox.
MASON, Jane E., d. May 16, 1830 in her 19th year, leaving an infant son, L. S. Mason, consort of Nehemiah H. Mason.

Square Monument

-MASON, Miss Nancy, 80, bur Jun 1881, friend of family,
-MATTHEWS, Dr. Thomas, b. Apr 18, 1813, d. Feb 21, 1857.
-MATTHEWS, Thomas, Jr. b. Aug 25, 1849, d. Jul 16, 1863.
-MATTHEWS, Harriet Ann, b. Feb 21, 1854, d. Nov 11, 1861.
MATTINGLY, Alice A., b. 1856, d. 1920.
MATTINGLY, Bernard Joseph, Pvt USA, b. 1902, d. 1977.
MATTINGLY, Elizabeth C., b. Aug 14, 1913, d. Sep 1, 1914, dau of Wm. H. and Agnes M. Mattingly.
MATTINGLY, Evelyn Cecelia, b. Mar 2, 1908 DC, d. Nov 30, 1992, m. (1st) Walter T. Morris, Sr. (2d)__ Barry, dau of Clarence Zackariah and Sarah Blanche Vallandingham Mattingly.

MATTINGLY, Florence, d. Apr 11, 1884, aged 3 mos and 3 days, dau of L. K. and L. M. Mattingly.
Double Stone
-MATTINGLY, Ignatius E., b. Sep 4, 1845, d. Jan 29, 1897.
-MATTINGLY, Susan B., his wife, b. Apr 19, 1847, d. Jan 30, 1927.
MATTINGLY, J. Gibbons, b. Mar 18, 1920, d. Nov 11, 1922, son of Wm H. and Agnes M. Mattingly.
MATTINGLY, John, 79, d. Jan 17, 1854.
MATTINGLY, John, 60, bur Jan 15, 1871.
MATTINGLY, Joseph B., b. 1899, d. 1969, hus of Mazie Morgan.
Double Stone
-MATTINGLY, Joseph W., b. 1864, d. 1941,
-MATTINGLY, Mary E., b. 1877, d. 1934.
MATTINGLY, J. Clyde, b. May 7, 1899, d. Jan 3, 1928.
MATTINGLY, Julia, b. Sep 15, 1889, d. Jun 8, 1973.
MATTINGLY, Mrs. La---, 46, bur Nov 21, 1887.
Double Stone
-MATTINGLY, Lewis K., d. May 2, 1913, aged 55 years.
-MATTINGLY, Elizabeth C., d. Apr 30, 1912, aged 44 years.
MATTINGLY, Loretta, b. Mar 17, 1906, d. after 1985, wife of Francis Gwynn Swann.
MATTINGLY, M. Lillian, b. Aug 25, 1884, d. Aug 23, 1954, 1st wife of Joseph 'Julius' Johnson, dau of Ignatius E. and Susan B. Mattingly.
Double Stone
-MATTINGLY, R. Allen, b. 1878, d. 1965.
-MATTINGLY, Agnes Estella, b. 1880, d. 1955.
MATTINGLY, Sarah Elizabeth, b. Feb 5, 1917, d. Jun 12, 1991, wife of William Paul Russell, Sr., dau of Robert Allen, Sr. and Estelle Bailey Mattingly.
MATTINGLY, Thomas Arthur, MD Pvt CO K 4 INF WW I, b. Sep 15, 1886, d. Feb 9, 1959, has American Legion Auxiliary marker.
MATTINGLY, Tina Marie, infant, d. Jun 26, 1971,

Sacred Heart

dau of Donald and Phyllis L. Johnson Mattingly.
MATTINGLY, W. Leonard, b. 1893, d. 1972.
MATTINGLY, William, 55, bur Feb 15, 1872.
    Side By Side
-MATTINGLY, William, Father, b. Jun 11, 1820, d. Feb 25, 1872.
-MATTINGLY, Maria, Mother, b. Aug 30, 1820, d. Aug 30, 1888, wife of William Mattingly.
MATTINGLY, William Francis, b. Jan 13, 1915, d. Nov 12, 1964.
MATTINGLY, William H., b. Apr 23, 1851, d. Aug 5, 1887.
    Double Stone
-MATTINGLY, William H., b. 1890, d. 1977.
-MATTINGLY, Agnes M., b. 1891, d. 1945.
    Double Stone
-MATTINGLY, William T., b. 1865, d. 1917.
-MATTINGLY, Mary E., b. 1871, d. 1954.
MAUPAI, Donald Wayne, b. Nov 26, 1957 Balto, d. Aug 28, 1992 Balto, son of William and Lillian Schonhart Maupai.
McCORMICK, Lionel, PA Pvt 2 CO COAST ARTY CORPS WW I, b. Jul 15, 1896, d. Oct 19, 1972.
McGRATH, Lawrence S., FL Pvt QMC WW I, b. Jun 28, 1892, d. Sep 7, 1962, hus of Florence L. Ferguson.
    One Stone
-McWILLIAMS, Claudia G., b. 1874, d. 1914.
-McWILLIAMS, George, b. 1884, d. 1980.
-McWILLIAMS, Mary G., b. 1874, d. 1929.
McWILLIAMS, Mrs. Cora, 45, bur Jul 28, 1888.
McWILLIAMS, Corinne, b. 1860, d. 1895, 1st wife of Thomas G. Hodges.
McWILLIAMS, Edwin J., b. Jun 18, 1875, d. Nov 29, 1890, only child of James and Mary L. McWilliams.
McWILLIAMS, Emeline, Our Mother, b. Feb 24, 1798, d. Mar 23, 1879 in her 82th year, (Church record gives her age as 65 and bur Feb 23, 1879.) wife of James McWilliams.
    One Stone
-McWILLIAMS, Frederick J., b. May 28, 1869, d. Jan 9, 1955.
-McWILLIAMS, Bessie G., b. Aug 12, 1870, d.

Feb 21, 1962.
McWILLIAMS, George, Jr. b. Oct 3, 1913, d. Nov 5, 1992, m. 1933 Phila, PA, Mary Alice Beitzell, son of George and Claudia Grayson McWilliams.
One Stone
-McWILLIAMS, James, b. 1836, d. 1907. (See Mary Pratt, is this her husband?)
-McWILLIAMS, Thomas, b. 1836, d. 1892.
-McWILLIAMS, Mary Queen, b. 1838, d. 1914, dau of James and Emeline McWilliams.
Double Stone
-McWILLIAMS, John G., b. Oct 15, 1910.
-McWILLIAMS, Mary Edna, b. Jan 2, 1911, d. Sep 12, 1978.
McWILLIAMS, Mary, m. Jan 1796, Dr. Elijah Jackson, he d. Aug 25, 1805.
McWILLIAMS, Mrs. Mary, 44, bur Mar 27, 1898.
McWILLIAMS, Thomas, 58, bur Nov 11, 1882.
Side By Side
-MEDLEY, Charles, b. Sep 5, 1806, d. Sep 20, 1873, AND CHILDREN (not named)on one stone.
-Footstone I.B.M.
-MEDLEY, Elizabeth G., d. Jan 9, 1836, in her 33d year, consort of Charles Medley.
MEDLEY, Miss Louise, 18, bur Apr 12, 1892.
MILES, Mary E., d. Aug 18, 1834, age 28 years, 8 mos and 8 days, wife of Dent H. Miles.
MILES, Mary S., 65, bur Feb 21, 1889.
MILES, R. H., Col., d. Aug 7, 1889 in his 87th year, hus of Mary B. ___, d. Jan 17, 1886, aged 72 years.
MILES, Richard H., 89, bur Aug 7, 1887.
MILLS, Pattie, 65, bur Jun 20, 1870.
MOORE, Thomas G., AK1 USN WW II, b. Mar 31, 1910, d. Sep 19, 1975, hus of Grace M. ___.
Double Stone
-MORGAN, Bernard St.P., b. Sep 27, 1904, d. Dec 3, 1929.
-MORGAN, Abbie L., b. Nov 18, 1902, d. Jun 17, 1926.
MORGAN, Eugene B. "Buck", Sr. b. (worked Washington Navy Yard pre WWII), d. Oct 19, 1988, hus of Lil ___, son of Eugene C. and Cora B.

Morgan.
MORGAN, James, 39, bur Mar 3, 1897.
MORGAN, James Roy, Sr. b. Oct 23, 1923, d.
Sep 3, 1988, hus of Margaret L. __, son of
William Lee and Anna Morgan.
MORGAN, Jane, b. 1866, d. 1915, wife of Peter
Henry Farrell.
Double Stone
-MORGAN, Kingsley J., b. 1891, hus of
-MORGAN, Mary G., b. 1903, d. 1924.
MORGAN, Mazie, b. 1905, d. 1960, wife of Joseph B. Mattingly.
MORGAN, Susan, b. 1862, d. 1947.
MORGAN, Susanna, d. Nov 12, 1795, aged 34
years, wife of James Morgan.
Sufanna by thy worth, Remembered by the
juft and be thy Frailities Buried in the
duft, A friend this verfe Beftowe by Honour
led (rest buried)
MORGAN, Mrs. Thomas, 55, bur Apr 11, 1893.
MORGAN, William Douglas, b. Nov 18, 1876, d.
Nov 30, 1943, hus of Cora E. Tippett.
MORRIS, Andrew Jackson, b. Mar 25, 1870, d.
Jan 14, 1935, hus of Grace Hill.
MORRIS, Charles B., b. Mar 31, 1894, d. Jul 21,
1921, Amer. Legion marker, hus of Blanche __.
MORRIS, Charles Stuart "Buster", b. Sep 5,
1915, d. Apr 24, 1991, m. 29 Jun 1936 Ruth
Alma Brown, son of Wm. Stuart Morris and
Ethel Virginia Crismond Morris Walker.
Three Stones Side By Side
-MORRIS, Conrad B., b. Jan 28, 1891, d. Jul
12, 1930.
-Double Stone
-MORRIS, William T., b. 1861, d. 1917.
-MORRIS, Dora O., b. 1865, d. 1915.
-MORRIS, Walter Thomas, Sr. b. 1902, d. 1974,
1st hus of Evelyn Cecelia Mattingly.
MORRIS, Joseph F., b. Apr 12, 1875, d. May 21,
1951.
MORRIS, Thelma Virginia, b. Nov 18, 1921, d.
Mar 7, 1989, wife of Carl J. Huseman, Sr.,
dau of William Stuart Morris and Ethel Virginia Crismond Morris Walker.
MORRIS, Walter Thomas, Jr. b. Mar 31, 1928,

d. Jul 8, 1988, hus of Nellie Hutton, son of late Walter T. Morris and Evelyn Mattingly Morris Barry.

Side By Side
- MORRIS, William Stuart, b. Jan 30, 1889, d. Dec 8, 1924, hus of Ethel Virginia Crismond.
- MORRIS, George Elwood "Biggie", b. Jun 1, 1920, d. Jan 6, 1940.
- MORRIS, James LeRoy, MD CO K 339 INF 85 INF DIV WW II, b. Oct 11, 1917, d. Dec 6, 1956, BSM & OLC.

MULLEN, Sarah Margaret, b. Feb 22, 1918, d. May 15, 1991, wife of Everett A. Cheseldine, Sr., dau of Samuel and Sarah Margaret Gladstone Mullen.

MURPHY, Patricia A., d. May 13, 1926, age 6 days.

J.A.N. and E.N., Two small crosses.

NEALE, Mary Jane, d. Oct 11, 1906, aged 56 years, wife of James Neale.

Side By Side
- NEALE, Susana, d. Sep 24, 1854, in her 82d year, wife of Cpt. Thomas G. Neale.
- NEALE, Thomas G., Cpt., d. Mar 22, 1835, aged 55 years, hus of Susana __.

NELSON, Joseph Herman, Sr. b. Feb 3, 1948, d. Oct 13, 1991, hus of Laverne __, son of Josephine Nelson and Walter Bowman.

NELSON, Mary B. "Connie", b. Jan 31, 1906, d. Oct 24, 1988, wife of John Herman Nelson, Sr.

NELSON, Mary Rose, b. Oct 4, 1906, d. Jun 9, 1992, dau of Joseph and Mary Catherine Butler Nelson.

NEVITT, Charles F., b. Mar 28, 1848, d. Dec 21, 1925.

Double Stone
- NORRIS, Bernard E., b. Jul 11, 1903, d. Mar 1, 1970.
- NORRIS, Mary E., b. Dec 21, 1903, d. Nov 3, 1975.

Side By Side
- NORRIS, John Leo., Sr. b. Apr 11, 1877, d. Aug 1, 1958,
- NORRIS, Mary Noema, b. May 25, 1881, d. May 29, 1920.

NORRIS, Joseph Cunningham, "Connie", b. Jul 1, 1913, d. Mar 23, 1990, hus of Susie Bell Perry, son of Stewart and Alice Wise Norris.
              Side By Side
-NORRIS, Joseph S., b. 1872, d. 1925.
-NORRIS, Alice S., b. 1883, d. 1955.
NORRIS, Nellie, b. 1872, d. 1935, wife of Joseph Seneca Cheseldine.
NORRIS, Susan K., b. 1862, d. 1932, in Joseph Seneca Cheseldine plot.
OLIVER, Agnes Janette, b. Dec 5, 1897, d. Mar 27, 1988, wife of George Lawrence Hayden, dau of John Henry and Margaret Davis Oliver.
OLIVER, Joan Catherine, b. Mar 7, 1935 DC, d. Jul 30, 1992, wife of Joseph Melvin Blair, Sr., dau of Joseph Aloysius and Gertrude Elizabeth Zornek Oliver.
OLIVER, Mrs. John H., 41, bur Jun 20, 1889.
              Double Stone
-OLIVER, John H., b. Jan 4, 1914, d. Dec 26, 1968, hus of Mary W. __, b. May 4, 1886, d. Jan 24, 1968.
              Side By Side
-OLIVER, John H., b. 1860, d. 1939, hus of Margaret J. __, b. 1862, d. 1935.
-OLIVER, Mary Estelle, b. Aug 1, 1894, d. Oct 21, 1962.
-OLIVER, Martin Lamar, MD COX USNRF WW I, b. Mar 30, 1891, d. Jan 28, 1959.
OLIVER, Joseph Aloysius, b. Aug 17, 1912, d. Jul 10, 1992, m. 12 Mar 1934 Gertrude Elizabeth Zornek, son of John and Daisy Ellis Oliver.
              One Stone
-OLIVER, Sarah, b. 1846, d. 1921.
-OLIVER, Raymond, b. 1887, d. 1923.
-OLIVER, Vick, b. 1885, d. 1943.
O'MOORE, Catherine, 22, bur Aug 4, 1870, wife of Henry Ford.
OWENS, Annie Rebecca, b. Oct 3, 1917, d. Aug 2, 1990, wife of Albert Russell, dau of William Lee and Catherine Dove Owens.
              Double Stone
-OWENS, Benjamin I., b. 1859, d. 1935.
-OWENS, Lucy N., b. 1867, d. 1931.

OWENS, John W., Father, b. 1862, d. 1910.
OWENS, Joseph S., b. Nov 16, 1918, d. Jan 23, 1923, son of Chas. M. and Eva Owens.
OWENS, Louis Matthew, b. Oct 8, 1910, d. Apr 21, 1992, son of George Webster and Agnes Lacey Owens.
OWENS, Margaret Elizabeth, b. Mar 16, 1941, d. Dec 31, 1942.
OWENS, Mary Delia, b. Oct 2, 1905, d. May 3, 1993, wife of Henry L. Wathen, dau of Geo. Webster and Mary Agnes Lacey Owens
Double Stone
-OWENS, Zachariah, b. 1848, d. 1933.
-OWENS, Eliza, b. 1858.
Double Stone
-PALMER, Harry D., b. Aug 31, 1872, d. Jan 10, 1948.
-PALMER, Rena C., b. Mar 13, 1888, d. Jan 3, 1967.
PARKER, Augusta M., b. Sep 11, 1909, d. Apr 14, 1990, wife of James Henry Scriber, dau of John and Lucy Armstrong Parker.
PARKER, Julia Alberta, b. Jan 1, 1903, d. May 2, 1993, m. 1978 John Stanley, dau of George Columbus and Jane Elizabeth Hill Parker.
Side By Side
-PAYNE, Daniel J., 65, d. Nov 24, 1904.
-PAYNE, Mary Susan, d. suddenly, Jul 12, 1881, aged 29 years and 10 mos, 1st wife of Daniel J. Payne.
-PAYNE, Richard Bernard, b. Jul 19, 1876, d. Dec 28, 1893, son of D. J. and M. S. Payne. A gift from his stepmother Sophia M. Payne.
-PAYNE, Mary Rhenia, drowned in Thompson's Hollow, St. Clements Bay, Sep 26, 1880, aged 10 years, 11 mos and 3 days, dau of Daniel J. and M. Susan Payne.
Side By Side
-PEACOCK, J. Horace, b. 1905, d. 1959.
-PEACOCK, Alberta M., b. Sep 10, 1906, d. Dec 19, 1981.
PILKERTON, David Lee, Sr. b. Feb 21, 1936, d. May 7, 1993, son of John Henry and Mary Lillian Quade Pilkerton.
PILKERTON, Elizabeth, b. Sep 29, 1812, d. Dec

Sacred Heart

29, 1882, wife of Joseph Pilkerton.
PILKERTON, Gertrude, b. Dec 19, 1902, wife of Clarence Leo Evans.
PILKERTON, Harry Victory, Sr. b. Feb 6, 1910, d. Jan 31, 1993, hus of Lessie Marie Farrell, son of Ernest Mitchell and Margaret Eleanor Gatton Pilkerton.
Double Stone
-PILKERTON, John H., b. Dec 2, 1889, d. Sep 1, 1938.
-PILKERTON, Mary L., b. Feb 12, 1894, d. Oct 16, 1979.
PILKERTON, Magdalene Gertrude, b. Dec 19, 1902, d. Jul 6, 1992, wife of Clarence Leo Evans, dau of Robert Alexander and Eleanora Pilkerton.
Double Stone
-PILKERTON, Robert A., b. 1869, d. 1951.
-PILKERTON, Eleanora P., b. 1877, d. 1951.
PILKERTON, Theresa, b. Apr 24, 1915, d. May 26, 1973, wife of __ Floyd.
PILKERTON, William Francis, b. Jan 8, 1861, d. Dec 17, 1932, hus of Esther Gatton.
Side By Side
-PLOWDEN, Agnes D., b. 1869, d. 1959.
-PLOWDEN, Edmund J., b. 1855, d. 1934.
-PLOWDEN, Mary, b. 1866, d. 1933.
-PLOWDEN, Josephine Freeman, b. 1836.
PLOWDEN, Edmund, b. 1751, d. 1804, hus of Janet Hammersly.
PLOWDEN, Edmund J., 63, bur Feb 6, 1872.
PLOWDEN, Mary Ann, d. Jun 27, 1827 at "Clamber Hill", age 42 yrs 8 mos 21 das, wife of John J. Jenkins, dau of Edmund and Jane Plowden.
PRATT, Mary L., d. Mar 9, 1898 in her 54th year, wife of James McWilliams, dau of Edwin and Elizabeth Pratt.
PRICE, Andrew Aloysius, 2 das, bur Jun 21, 1870.
PRICE, Mary Magdaline, 8 das, bur Jun 25, 1870.
QUADE, Bessie Mae, b. 1889, d. 1977, wife of William 'Lawrence' Vallandingham.
QUADE, Catherine, b. 1916, wife of James Henry Hall.
QUADE, Dorothy Irene, b. Nov 21, 1924, d. Sep

27, 1993, wife of John F. "Popeye" Quade, dau of James Carroll, Sr. and Grace Irene Lacey Quade.
QUADE, Freeman, no dates.(Funeral Home marker)
QUADE, James E., DC Pvt 315 INF WW II, b. Dec 29, 1924, d. Jul 4, 1944.
QUADE, John Joseph, b. Jan 24, 1862, d. Oct 21, 1926, hus of Mary Lacey.
QUADE, John M., b. 1867, d. 1928, hus of Mary E. Huseman.
QUADE, William R., b. May 9, 1910, d. Feb 24, 1941.
M. R., Hand carved field stone adjacent to Charles Rock tombstone, also two unmarked field stones are adjacent.
RALEY, John M., b. 1870, d. 1935, hus of Mary Elizabeth __, b. 1870, d. 1933.
RALEY, Thomas Arthur, b. Mar 31, 1910, d. Mar 7, 1986, hus of Margaret Lucille __, b. Feb 18, 1920, d. Jun 25, 1981, son of Daniel and Minnie Iowa Hazel Raley.
            Side By Side
-RALEY, Walter G., b. Jul 9, 1908, d. Oct 23, 1960,
-RALEY, Nellie L., b. Jul 16, 1910, d. Aug 31, 1965.
RAUTERBERG, Mary Augusta, b. 1858, d. 1913.
RENEHAN, John W., b. 1846, d. 1915 hus of Eleanor A. Feeney.
RENSCHKE, Joseph, b. 1870 Ger., d. 1960, hus of Selma Teresa Hesse.
RENSCHKE, Gertrude Marie, b. Oct 20, 1894 Ger., d. Apr 10, 1991, dau of Joseph and Selma Teresa Hesse Renschke.
RICHARDSON, Rex B., NC Pvt USA Korea, b. Apr 1, 1931, d. Nov 9, 1970.
ROCK, Charles, d. Jan 27, 1842 in the 80th year of his age.
RUSSELL, Miss Agnes, 17, bur Jul 25, 1898.
RUSSELL, Edward, b. 1860, d. 1941, FATHER, hus of Alice __, b. 1867, d. 1950, MOTHER.
RUSSELL, Ella Bayley, 20, bur Dec 19, 1884.
RUSSELL, Ella Mary, b. 1889, d. 1932, wife of R. Carroll Ellis.
RUSSELL, Mrs. Frank, 40, bur Jul 19, 1890.

Sacred Heart

RUSSELL, James Douglas, b. Sep 17, 1923, d. Jun 2, 1993, son of John Daniel and Rose Ann Morgan Russell.
RUSSELL, Jeb Stuart, Husband, b. Dec 25, 1862, d. Jul 11, 1895. Adjacent footstone J.B.R.
Double Stone
-RUSSELL, John L., b. Jun 20, 1892, d. Nov 23, 1946.
-RUSSELL, Pearl R., b. Sep 13, 1897, d. Oct 24, 1984.
Side by Side
-RUSSELL, John "Tom", b. Nov 30, 1923, d. Jan 24, 1983.
-RUSSELL, John H., d. Mar 15, 1923, aged 62 years.
-RUSSELL, Sarah Frances, Mother, b. Dec 30, 1870, d. Nov 4, 1948.
-RUSSELL, Effie F., b. May 18, 1894, d. Jul 7, 1949.
-RUSSELL, George Gibson, b. Nov 8, 1881, d. Oct 11, 1918.
-RUSSELL, Thomas A., b. Jul 7, 1894, d. Jul 23, 1928.
-RUSSELL, Joseph Burroughs, b. 1908, d. 1957.
-RUSSELL, William L., d. Jan 3, 1916, aged 61 years.
-RUSSELL, Cora B., b. 1875, d. 1962.
RUSSELL, Lelia Maria, b. 1888, d. 1910, wife of Joseph F. St. Clair.
RUSSELL, Louise A., b. Jan 20, 1899, d. Mar 28, 1920, wife of Charles Froesch.
RUSSELL, Mary Elizabeth, b. Nov 17, 1862, d. Apr 22, 1921, wife of William Edward Cullins.
RUSSELL, Patrick 'Edward', b. Apr 22, 1911, d. Jan 18, 1993, hus of Mary Estelle Hill, son of George Wilson and Elizabeth Norris Russell.
RUSSELL, Rebecca, d. Dec 29, 1899, age 39 yrs.
RUSSELL, Ruth Ann, b. Aug 17, 1865, d. Sep 2, 1885, dau of J.F. and S.A. Russell.
RUSSELL, Wm. H., my beloved husband, d. Jul 7, 1878, in the 46th year of his age.
SCHERER, Gertrude Marie, d. May 30, 1982, m. 1964 Arthur Bernard Lawrence, Jr., 2d wife.
SCORAH, Baby Girl, Jul 26, 1965.
SCOTT FAMILY, Memorial Stone, no names.

SCOTT, Patty, faithful nurse, b. 1834, d. 1917, wife of William Holly.
SCRIBER, Martha Elizabeth, b. Mar 10, 1935, d. Apr 18, 1988, wife of James A. Tyer, dau of James H.and Augusta M. Scriber.
Double Stone
-SEYMOUR, George W., WVA SGT USA, b. Apr 25, 1914, d. Sep 13, 1969, has American Legion Aux. Marker.
-SEYMOUR, Mary Helen, b. 1918.
SHORT, Mabel, b. Feb 21, 1908, d. Jul 6, 1993, wife of William Matthias Thompson, dau of James Henry and Catherine Fenwick Short.
SIMPSON, Florence C., b. Jun 12, 1893, d. Jul 13, 1974.
Double Stone
-SIMPSON, John F., b. 1855, d. 1947.
-SIMPSON, Mary M., b. 1857, d. 1939.
SIMPSON, Mary, b. 1883, d. 1972, wife of Franklin C. Hayden.
SMITH, Hodges, 17, bur Jun 25, 1885.
ST. CLAIR, Agnes Genevieve, b. Jun 14, 1906, d. Jan 18, 1990, m. (1st)__ Wise, (2d) T. Grover Stone, dau of William E. and Annie Violet Wise St. Clair.
ST. CLAIR, Eliza J., b. Jun 17, 1833, d. Nov 3, 1892, wife of Thomas W. Good.
ST. CLAIR, George M., b. Mar 11, 1868, d. Apr 19, 1908.
ST. CLAIR, Mary Elizabeth "Mae", b. Jan 29, 1908, d. Mar 7, 1990, wife of __ Abell, dau of William E. and Annie Violet Wise St. Clair.
ST. CLAIR, Rezin, 61, bur Nov 11, 1888.
ST. CLAIR, William E. and Annie W. and Family, no dates. Memorial Stone.
STEWART, Elizabeth, d. Dec 1, 1921, aged 88 years.
STONE, F. G., b. 1862, d. 1942.
STONE, Mrs. Fannie, 18, bur Feb 16, 1890.
STONE, Francis J., Fond Husband, Devoted Father, b. Mar 27, 1826, d. Apr 20, 1889.
STONE, James J., b. Nov 25, 1859, d. Aug 17, 1931.
STONE, Lewis B., b. May 25, 1845, d. Feb 19,

1926, hus of Mary E. __, b. Aug 30, 1854, d. Nov 15, 1951.
STONE, Matthew Xavier, Sr. b. Jun 16, 1898, d. Jan 15, 1988, hus of Dorothy Cameron.
STONE, Nellie C., b. 1875, b. 1959.
SUITE, Andrew "Andy" Raymond, b. Oct 23, 1930, d. Oct 26, 1990, hus of Shirley Ann __, son of Andrew Johnson and Catherine Lavada Suite.
SUITE, Arthur Guy, b. May 2, 1899, d. Sep 10, 1916, son of Edward and Alice Suite.
SUITE, Raymond A., MD Pvt USMC WW I, b. Jul 14, 1898, d. May 22, 1965.
SWANN, Francis Gwynn, b. Dec 11, 1904, d. after 1985, hus of Loretta Mattingly.
SWANN, Iona Gertrude, b. Jun 8, 1911, d. Apr 28, 1993, dau of Frank Davis and Fannie Dyson Swann.
SWANN, Olive Ann, b. Mar 18, 1902, d. Jul 22, 1902, infant dau of F. D. and Fannie Swann.

Side by Side

-SWANN, Oscar Z., b. Dec 9, 1909, d. Nov 14, 1926.
-SWANN, Fannie G., b. June 3, 1879, d. Sep 12, 1961.
SWANN, Samuel W., b. Feb 3, 1861, d. Aug 13, 1900, hus of Lucy M. __, b. 1864, d. 1938.
SWEENEY, Edward A., b. Jun 9, 1897, rest of stone buried.
TARLTON, John Sothern, d. Feb 29, 1825, aged 4 yrs, 2 mos and 18 days, son of George and Mary Tarlton.
THOMAS, James Bruce, Sr. b. Mar 26, 1911, d. Feb 12, 1991, hus of Mary Ethel Ellis, son of Joseph Frank and Rebecca Thompson Thomas.
THOMAS, James Louis "Wallace", b. Jun 17, 1938, d. May 6, 1990, hus of Barbara A. __, son of Harry Alexander and Mary Madeline Countiss Thomas.
THOMPSON, G. F., b. Mar 10, 1863, d. Aug 9, 1894, 1st hus of Julia A. Goode.
THOMPSON, Mr. and Mrs. Gratian, bur May 29, 1888.

One Stone

-THOMPSON, Harriet M., b. 1846, d. 1918.
-THOMPSON, Joseph O., b. 1873, d. 1935.

-THOMPSON, Ann Teresa, b. 1900, d. 1913.
Double Stone
-THOMPSON, J. Bruce, b. 1858, d. 1941.
-THOMSON, Eleanor, b. 1868, d. 1934.
THOMPSON, J. Lester, Sr., b. Mar 17, 1910, d. Jan 22, 1972, In memory of Greg, Donna and Jay.
THOMPSON, John B., b. Jan 1, 1896, d. Mar 5, 1958, hus of Teresa M. Greensfelder.
Side by Side
-THOMPSON, Joseph, b. Apr 5, 1884, d. May 4, 1911, son of James V. and Elima Thompson.
-THOMPSON, Mary Ozella, b. Jun 25, 1918, d. Mar 11, 1935.
THOMPSON, Joseph A., Apr 1924, infant son of Rhody and Helen Thompson.
Side by Side
-THOMPSON, Thomas Bertram, b. 1908, d. 1946.
-THOMPSON, John Francis, b. 1870, d. 1967, hus of Mary Herbert.
-THOMPSON, Mary Herbert, b. 1878, d. 1911.
-THOMPSON, Mary Margaret, d. Feb 28, 1932, aged 1 year.
-THOMPSON, Deborah Lynn, Mar 17, 1965.
-THOMPSON, Joan Victoria, b. and d. 1947.
THOMPSON, Leonard Allen, d. Apr 8, 1982, hus of Mary Edith Mattingly.
THOMPSON, Thomas V., b. Aug 6, 1873, d. Nov 3, 1945, hus of Eliza S. __, b. Jun 26, 1881, d. Aug 25, 1920.
One Stone
-THOMPSON, William E., b. 1870, d. 1955.
-THOMPSON, Frances Louise, b. 1870, d. 1926.
-THOMPSON, Edgar, b. 1893, d. 1965.
-THOMPSON, Elsie, no dates.
THOMPSON, William Matthais, d. Oct 30, 1946, hus of Mabel Short.
TIPPETT, Cora E., b. Jul 8, 1886, d. Oct 18, 1966, wife of William Douglas Morgan.
TIPPETT, Richard Dennis, Sr. b. Feb 24, 1920, d. Jan 1, 1989, hus of Eleanor B. Bailey, son of James O. and Gertrude Tippett.
TIPPETT, Susan E., b. Mar 4, 1832, d. Dec 16, 1906, wife of R. Bruce Tippett.
TOLAND, William John, d. Dec 25, 1943, hus of

Philomena J. DelRossi.
TRUXILLO, Mary, b. Dec 12, 1910 LA, d. Dec 24, 1990, wife of __ Hill, dau of John F. Sr. and Henietta Folse Truxillo.
TURNER, Edwin, b. Aug 23, 1838, d. June 3, 1853, son of Lewis E. and June Maria Turner.
TURNER, Emily, dau of Lewis E. and June Maria Turner. (Bottom of stone broken off.)
TURNER, Lewis E., d. Dec 20, 1860, aged 5 years.
TURNER, Lewis E., Jr. b. Oct 16, 1853, d. Apr 12, 1855, son of Lewis E. and June Maria Turner.
Side by Side
-VALLANDINGHAM, James Parren, b. 1913, d. 1961.
-VALLANDINGHAM, Henry B., b. Aug 18, 1915, d. Jun 17, 1965.
VALLANDINGHAM, Joseph Clyde, Sr., d. Aug 29, 1982, m. 6 Jan 1941 Maude V. Goode.
VALLANDINGHAM, Mary Helen, b. Oct 6, 1908, d. May 1, 1992, wife of Joseph Gibbons Hill, dau of William Martin and Mary Eva Guy Vallandingham.
VALLANDINGHAM, Samuel Edward, b. 1918, d. 1959.
VALLANDINGHAM, William 'Lawrence', b. 1884, d. 1949, hus of Bessie Mae Quade.
VALLANDINGHAM, William Lawrence "Willie", Jr. b. Apr 22, 1909, d. Nov 5, 1992, hus of Mary Helen Thomas, son of William L. and Bessie Mae Quade Vallandingham.
VAN WERT, Mabelle, Feb 22, 1907, 5 years, dau of William and Arabelle Van Wert. (I could not read part of inscription.)
VAN WERT, Webster W., b. 1868, d. 1949, m. (1st) Ann Ellen __, b. 1868, bur Oct 21, 1890, (2nd) Arabelle __, b. 1871, d. 1942.
WALTER, Josephine, b. 1850, d. 1916, wife of Charles A. Burch.
WATHEN, Joseph Lawrence, Sr. b. Oct 26, 1920, d. Sep 29, 1991, hus of Lillie Jane Mullen, son of Arthur Mitchell and Mary Effie Lacey Wathen.
WHEELER, Ernest J., b. Feb 25, 1874, d. Apr 27, 1958, hus of Josephine 'Ella' Latham,

(dau's obit shows name as Justin Ernest).
WHEELER, Hope Imelda, b. Feb 15, 1909, d. Mar 30, 1993, wife of Elmer Bennett Cheseldine, dau of Justin Ernest and Josephine Ella Latham Wheeler.
WICKER, John William, b. Feb 5, 1930 VA, d. Feb 5, 1990, hus of Frances Louise __, son of Harry and Lillian V. Soper McFarland.
WILKINSON, George N., d. Jul 19, 1852, aged 23 yrs.
WILKINSON, George H., d. Mar 18, 1852, aged 10 mos, son of George N. Wilkinson.
WILLIAMS, Alice Louise, d. May 19, 1973.
Side by Side
-WILLIAMS, Charles C., b. Apr 2, 1910, d. Nov 30, 1965.
-WILLIAMS, Mildred L., b. 1903, d. 1911.
WILLIAMS, Elinor A., d. Jun 29, 1836 in her 67th year, wife of Ja. W. Williams.
WISE, Elisa, 32, bur Mar 9, 1870.
WISE, Paul Benjamin "Flee", Sr. USA WW II, b. Sep 12, 1917, d. Nov 19, 1992, m. 15 May 1937 Mabel Virginia Holt, son of Thomas Matthew and Frances Ann Long Wise.
WISE, Thomas Horace, d. Dec 16, 1982, m. 19 Jan 1949 Margaret Ruth Dingee.
WOODBURN, Lucy Florence. b. Jul 2, 1887, d. Jun 29, 1939, wife of Wm. M. Russell.
Side by Side
-WOODBURN, M.D., b. 1862, d. 1937.
-WOODBURN, J.B., b. 1862, d. 1933.
WOODBURN, S. Madeline, b. Sep 23, 1885, d. May 18, 1963, wife of DeSales Cleveland Bailey.
WOODLAND, Henry F., 5 mos, bur Jun 2, 1870.
WOODLAND, Juanita Frances "Neats", b. May 18, 1921, d. Oct 30, 1992, wife of John William Tyer, dau of Richie and Annie Carter Woodland.
WOODLAND, Mary E., b. Mar 17, 1860, d. Jun 24, 1892, wife of John C. Woodland.
WOODLAND, Nellie, 85, bur Oct 17, 1869.
YATES, Blanche, b. 1875, d. 1949, wife of James Mitchell Bailey.
YATES, James E., b. Jan 8, 1859, d. Feb 4, 1914.

Sacred Heart

One Stone
-YATES, Chas. J., b. Dec 10, 1864, d. Dec 11, 1921, hus of Francis (sic) Ruth Yates.
-YATES, Mary Veronica, b. Feb 20, 1914, d. Jun 28, 1916, dau of Chas. J. and Francis Ruth Yates.
-YATES, Francis (sic) Ruth, b. Oct 30, 1880, d. Dec 29, 1960.
YOUNG, Alice C., b. Aug 15, 1873, d. May 23, 1919.
Double Stone
-YOUNG, George H., b. 1861, d. 1927.
-YOUNG, Jennie V., b. 1873, d. 1948.
YOUNG, James Leo "Jamie" Jr. b. Jul 13, 1979, d. Apr 25, 1993, son of James L. Young of Lovev'le and Mary Theresa Dickerson, Waldorf.
YOUNG, Phillip, 55, bur Jun 28, 1870.

OLD ST. ALOYSIUS RCC
Rt. 245
Leonardtown, Md.

DUKE, Janet Agnes, b. Mar 31, 1903, d. Oct 29, 1992, wife of Harold Knight, dau of J. Roland and Catherine Councell Duke.

HEBB, Joseph Franklin, b. May 7, 1909, d. Feb 18, 1991, son of Allie and Sarah Jane Ashton Hebb.

SWALES, Bertha, b. Apr 10, 1893, d. Sep 29, 1989, wife of John Gresham, dau of William Francis and Jane Frances McWilliams Swales.

SWALES, James 'Virgil', b. Mar 21, 1902, d. Dec 10, 1991, m. (1st) Mary Ella __, (2d) Minerva Gertrude Thompson, son of Frank and and Jane Frances Gunn Swales.

SWALES, Ella Mignonette, b. Mar 24, 1900, d. Jan 6, 1990, wife of Raymond G. Barnes, dau of Francis and Jane McWilliams Swales.

YOUNG, David Aloysius, b. Jul 3, 1952, d. Sep 3, 1989, son of James R. and Theresa Swales Young.

ST. ALOYSIUS RCC
Rt 5
Leonardtown, Md.

The first church was completed in 1766 on land donated by Mrs. Ann Thompson. By 1844 it was in ruins and in 1846 permission was obtained to erect a new church within the town limits. The new church was made of rose brick and cost $3555. It was completed in December, 1846. By 1960, yet another St. Aloysius was again being planned. It was dedicated 18 March 1962. There are no remains of the first two churches. The cemeteries of the first and second churches are still in use. One is located on Rte. 245 and the other is on the opposite side of Rt. 5 and to the south of the present church.

BARNES, Andrew David, b. Oct 25, 1988, d. Jan 9, 1989, son of David and Daren Barnes.
BLACKISTONE, James M, 9 mos, bur Aug 17, 1871.
BOCKSKO, Anne Victoria, b. Jan 4, 1917 OH, d. Apr 14, 1993, wife of Louis Joseph Morvick, dau of Geo. and Elizabeth Banovak Bocksko. Memorial Service.
BOWLES, Helen Elizabeth, b. Mar 14, 1910, d. Jan 19, 1993, wife of James Robert Nelson, dau of William Henry and Julia Mae Adams Bowles.
BROWN, Alice Blanche, b. 1909 DC, d. Jan 5, 1979, m. (1st) Oscar M. Cryer, (2d) Leo Peter Klear.
BROWN, Mrs. Charles, 35, bur Aug 13, 1870.
BROWN, John Richley, d. May 27, 1973, hus of Rosalie Hewitt.
BUTLER, James William, d. Dec 5, 1979, hus of Annie Mae Curtis.
CAGNEY, Helen Theresa, b. Mar 7, 1913 NY, d. Jun 14, 1991, wife of Edward Henry Farrell, dau of Michael J. and Ellen Fitzgibbon Cagney.
CAMALIER, Charles, 40, bur Sep 28, 1870.
CAREERRY, Aloysius, 14, bur Aug 21, 1870.
CLEMENTS, Frances Eileen, b. Jun 10, 1916, d. Aug 13, 1988, dau of Walter Dawkins, Sr.

and Sarah Louis Clements.
COFFMAN, Francis Hunter, 52, d. Sep 21, 1993. Memorial service.
COMBS, Henry, 60, bur Nov 15, 1870.
CONNELLY, Annie 'Eliza', b. 1886, d. Oct 8, 1970, m. (1st) Jack Abell, (2d) Peter Henry Johnson, dau of James L. and Sarah Bradburn Connelly.
CONNELLY, George Aloysius, b. Dec 25, 1919, d. Oct 26, 1989, son of Millard Philmore and Mary Maude Connelly.
CREIGHTEN, Phillis, 55, bur Jan 5, 1871.
CRYER, James Henry "Jim", b. Dec 1854, d. 1937, m. (1st) Noema C. Goldsborough, (2d) Mary Victoria Johnson, son of William Henry and Elizabeth Ann Thompson Cryer.
CRYER, Oscar Melvin "Jack", b. Jul 1898 DC, d. 1940, hus of Alice Blanche Brown, son of James H. and Mary Victoria Johnson Cryer.
CRYER, Oscar Melvin "Skip", b. Dec 11, 1927 DC, d. Mar 25, 1978 VA, m. (1st)__ Bragg, (2d) 23 Jul 1965, Mary Link Rivers, son of late Oscar M. "Jack" Cryer and Alice Brown Cryer Klear.
DOWNS, Mary Virginia Mildred, 18 mos, bur Sep 14, 1872,
DUKE, George, bur June 6, 1901.
DUKE, Mrs. John K., bur Mar 13, 1897.
DUKE, Kenneth B., Jr., USN, b. Mar 21, 1923, d. Dec 12, 1991 OK, hus of Elizabeth M. __, son of Kenneth B. and Lorraine Hodges Duke. Mem. Serv.
FARR, Michael, 80, bur Sep 20, 1879.
FARRELL, Edward Henry, d. 1985, hus of Helen Therese Cagney.
FENWICK, Aloysius Francis, III, d. Sep 1968, m. 20 Jun 1936 Anabel "An" Barto.
FENWICK, Charles Edward, Sr. b. Oct 15, 1910, d. Nov 10, 1993, hus of Anna LaVerne Miller, son of Aloysuis Francis, Jr. and Ann Rebecca "Nannie" Greenwell Fenwick.
FENWICK, James Baron "Barry", Sr. b. Aug 11, 1936, d. Mar 2, 1993, son of Cuthbert Ignatius, Sr. and Hilda Louise Martin Fenwick.
GOLDSBOROUGH, Noema, b. Dec 29, 1855, d. Jun

St. Aloysius

27, 1878, 1st wife of Jas. Henry Cryer, dau of Geo. Washington and Clara Bowes Abell Goldsborough.
GOUGH, Alfred Fabian "Tick", Sr. b. Feb 1, 1907, d. Nov 13, 1993, m. 1 May 1937 Ada Bartol, son of Fabian Ferdinand and Margaret Greenwell Gough.
GRAND, Louise Marie Lasserre, 76, b. Jun 16, 1916 DC, d. Sep 5, 1992, dau of George and Agnes Gerlich Lasserre.
GRAY, Emily, d. Nov 3, 1993, dau of Albert Joseph III and Debra Jones Gray; gdau of Albert Jr. and Betty Ann Gray; Carl and Betty Jones of CO; ggdau of James and Ruby Cheseldine; Bessie Gray.
GREENWELL, French, 62, bur Jul 12, 1887.
GREENWELL, Margaret 'Christine', b. Nov 26, 1903, d. Jun 2, 1990, wife of John F. Gardiner, dau of William F. Greenwell, Jr. and Henrietta Knight Greenwell Wilmer. Memorial Service.
GUY, Holland Ignatius "Jr." 60, b. May 9, 1929, d. Feb 14, 1990, son of George F. and Mary Ellen "Mae" Guy.
HARDEN, Mamie, b. May 1879, d. 1961, wife of "D.P." Johnson, dau of Thomas Harden.
HARRIS, Francis Michael, 71, b. Jan 3, 1917, d. Dec 15, 1988, hus of Norma Jean Rogers, son of George and Jennie Mendelis Harris.
HERBERT, Mary Katherine, d. Dec 5, 1986, m. 1 Jan 1931 William Gray Holley.
HEWITT, Rosalie, b. Aug 15, 1908, d. Oct 25, 1993, m. 9 Feb 1935 John Richley Brown, dau of Benjamin and Blanche Emily Redman Hewitt.
HOFMANN, Earl Francis, b. Mar 11, 1928 Balto, d. Sep 29, 1992, hus of Jean Nordstrom, son of Earl Henry and Mary Jarboe Hofmann.
HOLLEY, William Gray "Bill", b. Mar 9, 1909 NC, d. Aug 24, 1993, hus of Mary Katherine Herbert, son of Thomas and Annie Gray Mason Holley.
HUNT, Robert Murray, Jr., d. Mar 6, 1968, m. 24 Nov 1923 Marie Elizabeth "Johnnie" Greenwell.
HUNTT, George Enoch, b. Apr 22, 1921, d. Jun

29, 1989, hus of Mary Agnes __, son of George, Jr. and Catherine N. Huntt.
JARBOE, Mrs. Ann V., 55, bur Mar 19, 1899.
JOHNSON, Daniel Phillip "D.P.", b. Oct 1866, d. 1957, m. 13 Apr 1898, Mamie Harden, son of Hillery and Ann Marie Thompson Johnson.
JOHNSON, Francis Franklin "Frank", b. Mar 12, 1873, d. May 3, 1947, hus of Rose Frances "Fannie" Spalding, son of Hillery and Ann Marie Thompson Johnson.
JOHNSON, Joseph Albert, b. Apr 26, 1915, d. May 7, 1983, son of Wm. A. and Lula E. Wathen Johnson.
JOHNSON, Mary Gladys, b. Feb 16, 1899, d. Feb 12, 1987, wife of Joseph Leroy McNey, dau of "D.P." and Mamie Harden Johnson.
JOHNSON, Mary Victoria "Tora", b. Mar 1867, d. 1960, wife of James Henry Cryer, dau of Wm. Edward and Mary "Liza" Raley Johnson.
JOHNSON, Peter Henry, b. Oct 1873, d. 1962, m. (1st) Flora Catherine Love, (2d) Otelia S. __, (3d) Annie 'Eliza' Connelly, son of Joseph S. and Eliza C. Mattingly Johnson.
JOHNSON, William Albert "Alfred", b. Nov 1871, d. 1957, m. (1st) Mary Adeline Adams, (2d) Lula Elizabeth Wathen, son of William Edward and Liza Raley Johnson.
JOHNSON, William Robert "Sonny", b. 1921, d. 1968, hus of Eva Lucretia nee Johnson, son of Earnest and Mary Rosalie Cooper Johnson.
KILGO, Charity, 75, bur Sep 12, 1872.
KING, A.N., 34, bur Mar 19, 1872.
KLEAR, Leo Peter, Sr. b. Jan 9, 1907, d. Feb 24, 1989, (2d) hus of Alice Brown Cryer, son of George and Theresa Zenz Klear.
KNOTT, James 'Francis', Sr. b. Dec 9, 1932, d. Sep 1, 1991, hus of Mary Alice Norris, son of late Clarence Guy Knott and Ella Louise Harris Knott Hemming.
LANGLEY, Mary Elizabeth, b. Mar 2, 1896, d. Dec 7, 1988, wife of James Edward Burch, dau of William and Katie Abell Langley.
LONG, William, 13, bur Sep 8, 1870.
MADOX, Hon. Fred, 44, bur Jan 4, 1871.
MATTINGLY, Charles Jenkins, Sr. b. Aug 9,

St. Aloysius

1900, d. Jun 30, 1989, hus of Agnes Gertrude __, son of William Clement and Mary Margaret Mattingly.
MATTINGLY, Elizabeth, b. and d. Nov 12, 1992, dau of Robert, Jr. and Susan Aud Mattingly; gdau of Robert G. and Virginia Mattingly; Benedict and Anna Mae Aud; paternal ggdau of Laura Chesser.
MATTINGLY, James Vernon, Jr. d. Feb 23, 1974, son of James Vernon and Dorothy H. Milford Mattingly; gson of S. Lawrence Vallandingham.
MATTINGLY, Katherine Sophia, b. May 27, 1898, d. Jul 12, 1993, m. (1st) Benedict Booth Love, Jr, (2d) W. Haverman Mattingly, dau of William Clement and Margaret Hayden Mattingly.
MATTINGLY, Leila M., b. Feb 11, 1893, d. Feb 16, 1990, wife of __ Hodges, dau of William Clement and Mary Margaret Hayden Mattingly.
McCULLY, Mary Elizabeth, b. 1904, d. 1970, m. (1st) Clyde M. Johnson, (2d) Eugene S. Spurlock.
McNEY, Joseph Leroy "Mac", b. Jul 13, 1899, d. Aug 27, 1975 DC, hus of Gladys Johnson.
MILLARD, Joseph, 30, bur Nov 20, 1872.
MILLER, Anna LaVerne, d. Dec 1, 1983, wife of Charles Edward Fenwick, Sr.
MILLS, Charlotte, 27, bur Oct 14, 1869.
MILLS, William Joseph, 1 yr, bur Sep 13, 1872.
MITCHELL, Daisy P., d. Jun 22, 1993.
MORGAN, Joseph F., 62, bur Jul 20, 1906.
MORGAN, Louis Columbus "Little Bud", Jr. b. Dec 8, 1972, d. Feb 8, 1993, son of Louis C. and Kathleen Marie Connelly Morgan.
MURRAY, Robert, Jr., d. Mar 6, 1968, m. 24 Nov 1923 Maria Elizabeth "Johnnie" Greenwell.
NAKRASEIVE, Anne Frances, b. May 8, 1913 NY, d. Jul 5, 1993, m. 8 Sep 1940 NY Alfred T. Passarelli, dau of Peter and Benedicta Belakavitch Nakraseive. Memorial service.
NORRIS, Joseph Harry, Jr. b. Jul 21, 1923, d. Feb 11, 1992, hus of Patricia Anne Mertz, son of late Joseph Harris Norris and Sarah Anita Camalier Norris Thrift.
NUTHALL, Susie Mae, b. May 16, 1907, d. Jun

15, 1988, dau of J. Gregory and Dorothy E. Nuthall.
PASSARELLI, Naomi Elizabeth, 83, d. Jul 21, 1992 FL.
PAYNE, Jannese, b. Aug 17, 1916 VA, d. Jun 9, 1992 FL, wife of Victor E. Marine, dau of J. Winston and Blanche Donovan Payne.
RUSSELL, Lillian Mary, b. Nov 6, 1904, d. Dec 11, 1989, wife of Charles Reginold Clements, dau of George Wilson and Alice Maud Elizabeth Norris Russell.
SCHUELE, James David, b. Jul 1, 1940, d. Apr 3, 1989, son of Margaret Sullivan Schlang and late James M. Schuele.
SMITH, Harriet, 70, bur Nov 14, 1870.
SMITH, James Robert, 6 mos, bur Oct 18, 1871.
SPAULDING, Bernard Leo, Jr. b. Mar 23, 1925, d. Dec 15, 1989, son of Bernard L. and Mildred Rose Spaulding.
SPAULDING, Mildred Rose, b. Sep 4, 1905, d. Jan 12, 1987, wife of Bernard L. Spaulding Sr.
SPAULDING, Rose Frances "Fannie", b. Jul 20, 1877, d. Jul 27, 1954, wife of Francis Franklin Johnson, dau of James and Jane Ann Mattingly Spaulding.
STONE, Mary Magdeline, b. Oct 9, 1894, d. Nov 5, 1993, m. 26 Dec 1922 George Wilson Russell, dau of William Henry and Margaret Bradburn Stone.
STONE, Matthew Xavier, Sr. b. Jun 16, 1898, d. Jan 15, 1988, hus of Dorothy Cameron.
SWALES, Mary Agnes, b. Apr 17, 1909, d. Aug 9, 1991, wife of James M. Curtis, dau of George Henry and Emma Young Swales.
SWALES, Vincent McWilliams, Sr. b. Dec 6, 1912, d. Aug 26, 1988, hus of Hester Irene __, son of William F. and Frances M. Swales.
TANEY, Ignatius, 75, bur Apr 5, 1871.
TURNER, Mary Ellen 'Mae', b. Jun 9, 1893, d. Sep 12, 1988, wife of George E. Guy, dau of Stouten and Catherine Turner.
WALLY, Phillip, 40, bur Jan 23, 1871.
WATHEN, Charles, 13, bur Dec 3, 1870.

St. Aloysius

WATHEN, Janice, b. Jul 5, 1922, d. Dec 10, 1988, wife of Thomas A. "Mac" McGuyre, dau of Henry and Anna Mae Yates Wathen.

WATHEN, Lula Elizabeth, b. 1895, d. Jan 9, 1989, wife of Wm. "Alfred" Johnson, dau of John T. and Margaret Edwards Wathen.

WOOD, Charles Henry, b. Feb 15, 1921, d. Dec 16, 1991, son of Henry Arthur and Martha L. Graves Wood.

YATES, Anna Mae, b. May 20, 1903, d. Nov 2, 1991, wife of Henry Wathen, dau of Norman and Ruth Abell Yates.

ZELLER, Kathleen, b. Apr 18, 1918 NY, d. May 1, 1990, wife of Murray E. Jackson, dau of Chester A. and Mary Cooney Zeller.

ST. ANDREWS EPISCOPAL CHURCH
St. Andrews Church Road
California, Md.

St. Andrews was established in 1744 and built of brick in 1767. It is the oldest Protestant Church in the state still in regular use and is considered one of the outstanding architectual gems in the country.

ABELL, E. Thompson, d. Aug 15, 1855, age 37 yr.
                    Side by Side
-ABELL, Ann, d. Apr 25, 1852, age 63 years 1 mo and 11 das.
-ABELL, Francis, b. Dec 17, 1790, d. Jul 26, 1867.
ABELL, Francis J., d. Jun 4, 1852, aged 19 yrs 11 mos and 29 das.
ABELL, Harriet, Mother, d. Nov 9, 1855, aged 61 years 6 mos.
                    One Stone
-ABELL, Martha H., b. Feb 27, 1830, d. Dec 22, 1969, wife of William C. Abell.
-ABELL, Nina, their daughter, b. Jan 27, 1866, d. Feb 1, 1869.
                    One Stone
ABELL, Children of Wm. C. and Martha H.:
-ETTA, d. Aug 17, 1857, aged 7 mos.
-FRANK, d. Nov 4, 1862, age 7 yrs 2 mos.
-HETTIE, d. Nov 4, 1862, aged 2 years 10 mos.
-ANNA, d. Nov 11, 1862, age 4 yrs 7 mos.
ABELL, Matthew, d. May 13, 1830, aged 40 years 7 mos and 15 das.
ARMSWORTHY, Mary V., d. Jan 23, 1881, age 24 yrs 9 mos and 9 das., wife of John E. Armsworthy.
ARMSWORTHY, Thos. B., d. Sep 13, 1867, aged 59 years 11 mos and 13 days.
BALLARD, Wm. Bryant, AZ1 USN Vietnam, b. Nov 16, 1941, d. Apr 27, 1986.
BARLEY, Frank J., b. Mar 12, 1905, d. Oct 28, 1980, hus of Evelyn Esch.
BARLEY, Sharon Tiare, b. Nov 10, 1960, d. May 21, 1982.
BARNES, Earl, Jr. b. Jan 21, 1942, d. Jan 28, 1942.

Double Stone
-BARNES, Earl, b. Jul 24, 1903, d. Dec 3, 1965.
-BARNES, Flossie H., b. Aug 11, 1907, d. Jul 17, 1983.
BEAN, Charles T., b. Aug 7, 1912, d. Jun 24, 1987, hus of Elizabeth Cary.
BENNETT, Blanche I., d. Feb 6, 1962.
One Stone
-BENNETT, Delmar Milburn, b. Jan 4, 1917.
-BENNETT, Thomas Oliver, MD SP4 USA Vietnam, b. Sep 21, 1950, d. Jun 5, 1972.
-BENNETT, Thomas W., b. Nov 28, 1899, d. Aug 9, 1974.
BENNETT, John C., d. Jun 1, 1974.
BENNETT, John Roland, USA, b. Feb 13, 1922, d. JUN 9, 1987.
BENNETT, Rollins, b. Oct 26, 1902, d. Oct 23, 1977.
BENNETT, Thomas F., b. 1904, d. 1964.
BENNETT, Woodrow Wilson, b. Nov 6, 1912, d. Mar 8, 1990, hus of Dorothy Wise, son of Richard Henry and Blanche Nash Bennett.
BENNETT, Woodrow Wilson, Jr. b. Jan 17, 1937, d. Dec 28, 1970, son of Woodrow Wilson and Dorothy Wise Bennett.
BENTZ, Mary, b. Jul 23, 1893 PA, d. Jun 24, 1989, m. (1st) Thornton Rollens Burns, (2d) __ McCall, dau of John Andrew and Ellen Celesta Smith Bentz.
BOND, Briscoe, b. Mar 12, 1872, d. Oct 3, 1893.
BOND, Duke, b. 1869, d. 1953, Judge of the Supreme Bench of Baltimore City, 1922-1938.
BOND, John 'Douglas', Sr. b. Feb 2, 1916, d. Nov 18, 1991, hus of Frances Jacqueline Goldsborough, son of John Thomas and Mary Evelyn Parran Bond.
BOND, John Thomas, b. 1876, d. 1946.
BOND, Mary Adelaide, b. Oct 4, 1905, d. May 16, 1980.
BOND, Thomas Holdsworth, b. Feb 19, 1840, d. May 1, 1922.
BOND, Thomas Holdsworth, b. Dec 25, 1911, d. Jul 29, 1990, hus of Marguerite Mattingly, son of John Thomas and Mary Evelyn Parran Bond.

St. Andrews

BOYD, Rosalie, Mother, b. Sep 30, 1938, d. Apr 15, 1985.
BRADY, Rosalie S., d. Mar 2, 1899 in her 77th year, wife of John F. Harris, dau of Rev. John H. Brady, former Rector of this parish.
BRAUN, Ellen Leigh, b. Apr 22, 1921, d. Sep 13, 1969, wife of __ Duke. (Bur in Dawkins fenced plot).
BRAUN, Roswell Bascom, Jr. 1st LT USA WW I, b. Aug 31, 1889, d. Aug 31, 1976.
BRILL, Paul Alexis, MD Pvt AIR SERV WW I, b. Feb. 20, 1891, d. Jan 21, 1974.
BRISCOE, Jeannette, b. Apr 16, 1827, d. Nov 10, 1881, wife of James R. Thomas, dau of Dr. W. H. and E. Briscoe.
BRISCOE, Jeannette Eleanor, b. Apr 20, 1802, d. Jul 4, 1893, dau of William and Sarah Stone Briscoe.
BRISCOE, Lucretia Leeds, b. Nov 6, 1818, d. Mar 11, 1871, wife of __ Carroll, dau of Phillip Briscoe, Esq.
BRISCOE, Margaret Ann, b. Jan 27, 1829, d. Aug 7, 1902, wife of Robert Hanson Wise, dau of Dr. Walter H. S. and Emeline W. Briscoe.
BRISCOE, Mary Ella, b. Sep 15, 1849, d. Aug 15, 1875, dau of Dr. W. H. and Emeline W. Briscoe.
BRISCOE, Salie Emeline, b. Sep 18, 1842, d. Jun 4, 1918, wife of Thomas H. Bond.
BRISCOE, Susan Adelade, b. Sep 16, 1844, d. Dec 29, 1882, wife of Thomas H. Bond, dau of Walter H. S. and Emeline Briscoe.
BRISCOE, Walter Hanson Stone, b. Aug 21, 1854, d. Aug 22, 1922, son of Dr. Walter D. S. and Emmeline Dalton Briscoe.
One stone
-BRISCOE, Walter S., b. Mar 20, 1801, d. Dec 30, 1887.
-BRISCOE, Emeline W., b. Jul 12, 1809, d. Sep 9, 1887.
BROWN, James Hardin, b. Jul 29, 1903, d. Apr 26, 1989, hus of Laura M. Wise, son of James M. and Helen Watts Brown.
BURNS, Roland Earl, b. Dec 31, 1916, d. Aug 23, 1988, son of Thornton Rollens Burns and

Mary Bentz Burns McCall.
CARY, Elizabeth, b. Jun 14, 1912, living in 1987, wife of Charles T. Bean.
CHAMNESS, Jean Delores, b. Jun 19, 1927 DC, d. Aug 30, 1990, wife of Joseph B. LeCompte, Jr., dau of David I. and Mildred Ball Chamness.
CLARK, Stephen Benjamin, b. Jun 17, 1978, d. Jan 6, 1982.
CLARK, Baby, 1978.
CLEMENTS, Della Reed Ching Connelly, b. Feb 22, 1887, d. Mar 21, 1983.
CLEMENTS, William M., MD SFC MED CO 512 ENG WW I, b. Dec 24, 1886, d. Nov 28, 1967.
CONNELLY, Edith Norine, b. Mar 20, 1905, d. Oct 31, 1983, wife of James Alfred Johnson, dau of James L. and Sarah Bradburn Connelly.
CONNELLY, William F., b. Feb 28, 1917, d. Mar 7, 1963.
COMBS, Sarah J., b. Jan 5, 1850, d. Jun 30, 1887, wife of John F. Combs.
COWAN, Dr. Horace F., b. 1854, d. 1918, hus of Rebecca S. Hammett.
CRANE, Edwardina, Deaconess, b. Jan 7, 1879, d. Oct 9, 1940, dau of J. Parran and Laura A. Crane.
CRANE, James Parran, b. Aug 6, 1838, d. Jan 5, 1916.
CRANE, Katherine, b. Jul 2, 1873, d. Feb 4, 1953, wife of Robert Combs Loker.
CRANE, Laura A., b. Aug 29, 1848, d. Aug 19, 1885, wife of J. Parran Crane.
CRANE, Laura A., b. Oct 7, 1888, d. Apr 8, 1968.
CRANE, Mollie Dent, b. Aug 6, 1855, d. Jun 27, 1938.
DAUGHERTY, Rev. Charles R.C., corner markers.
DAUTRICH, Nancy E., b. Mar 2, 1932, d. Dec 12, 1986, wife of ___ Gillette.
DAVIDSON, John Carlos, b. Dec 9, 1907 OH, d. Feb 18, 1990, hus of Vera Cooksey, son of Charles Steele and Mary Waite Davidson.
DAVIS, Paul R., b. Jun 13, 1904, d. Oct 9, 1962, hus of Mattie Tippett.
DEAN, Mary Louise, Mother, b. Jun 10, 1878,

St. Andrews

d. Mar 4, 1965, wife of Nicholas Pussler.
DENT, Benjamin, aged 5 years 3 mos and 9 das, no dates. (This stone is very old.)
  One Stone
-DENT, Charles S., b. Mar 5, 1827, d. Apr 17, 1876, his wife
-DENT, Sarah A., b. Jun 15, 1828, d. Dec 12, 1882.
DENT, Francis H., b. 1896, d. 1979.
DENT, G. Frank, b. 1869, d. 1946.
DENT, George, Rev. War Capt; War of 1812 Col., b. 1757, d. 1842, hus of Elizabeth T. Mills.
DENT, George B., d. May 1907,(no other info).
DENT, Lucy Adele, b. 1866, d. 1939.
DENT, Martha A., aged 17 years 8 mos and 7 das, no dates.
DENT, Patty, b. 1860, d. 1944, wife of Walter Hanson Briscoe Wise.
DENT, Susan, b. Jan 13, 1803, d. Dec 17, 1857, wife of Thomas E. Dent.
DENT, Susan S., b. Sep 28, 1860, d. Mar 10, 1925.
DENT, Thomas E., d. Sep 6, 1853, aged 48 yrs 2 mos and 8 das, hus of Susan ___.
DODSON, Henry Lee, b. Feb 16, 1891, d. Oct 5, 1977, hus of Elizabeth G. ___, b. May 31, 1893, d. Feb 12, 1974.
DODSON, Robt. Curtis, b. Nov 28, 1944, d. Jan 2, 1965.
  Fenced Plot, "DAWKINS' Over Gate
This plot is overgrown, unable to open gate, from outside fence only able to read four of the eleven tombstones contained therein, as follows:
-DORSEY, Barberry B., b. Aug 8, 1825, d. Aug 2, 1852, aged 22 yrs 11 mos and 20 das, dau of Walter and Ann Dorsey of Calvert County.
-DORSEY, Philip Henry, Chief Judge 7th Judicial Circuit, b. Jul 15, 1901, d. Jun 6, 1976, hus of Dorothy Rule Stewart, son of Walter B. and Elizabeth Turner Dorsey.
-DORSEY, Dorothy Stewart, b. May 28, 1905, d. Jan 16, 1985, dau of Dr. John B. and Helen Rule Stewart.
-DUKE, Ellen Leigh Braun, b. Apr 22, 1921, d.

Sep 13, 1969.
EICHNER, Kathryn Pearl, b. Apr 26, 1892, d. May 1, 1981.
ERWIN, Bessie, Mother, b. Oct 23, 1889 TX, d. May 15, 1988, wife of Robert L. Hurt.
ESCH, Evelyn, b. Jun 4, 1907, d. Aug 7, 1975, wife of Frank J. Barley.
EVANS, Andrew Clark, b. Aug 21, 1898, d. Jul 30, 1986.
EVANS, E. R., b. Mar 1, 1823, d. Jun 8, 1907, hus of Mary L. ___, d. Jul 27, 1896, aged 55 yrs.
EVANS, George W., b. May 29, 1869, d. Oct 13, 1957, hus of Amanda M. ___, b. Sep 11, 1870, d. Jul 18, 1921.
EVANS, John A., b. Apr 18, 1853, d. Jan 7, 1919, hus of Mary E.___, b. Jun 21, 1861.
EVANS, John F., b. Jan 3, 1810, d. Mar 20, 1878, hus of Mary J. L. ___, d. Feb 14, 1902 in the 74th year of her life, wife of John F. Evans.
EVANS, Joseph F., b. Nov 28, 1857, d. Aug 21, 1883, son of John F. and Mary J. L. Evans.
GERLICH, Augusta, no dates, mother of Agnes M. Gerlich Lassere. I O A
           All Together
-GILLIAMS, Ann Elizabeth, b. Sep 15, 1843, d. Sep 22, 1843, dau of Louis S. and Charlotte A. Gilliams.
    Between Ann E. Gilliams and J. S. Gough
-MILLIE, our daughter, b. Dec 1, 1850, d. Dec 28, 1853.
-GOUGH, J. S., d. Apr 28, 1833, son of B. and A. L. Gough.
-GOUGH, Benjamin Franklin, d. Jan 25, 1850 in the 15th year of his life.
Fenced enclosure, no tombstones or dates, one large stone with the following:
"Within this enclosure repose the remains of"

B. GOUGH	A.L. GOUGH
R.M. MILLS	E.B. MILLS
L.S. GILLIAMS	C.L. GILLIAMS
R.T. GOUGH	E.A. GOUGH
M.L. GOUGH	E.D. MILLS

GOUGH, Oscar William, b. 1905, d. 1960.

GREENWELL, Clement G., d. Mar 30, 1855, aged 55 yrs.
GREENWELL, Rebecca, d. Sep 13, 1843, aged 76 years and 7 mos.
GUSTAFSON, Maj. Carl, d. 1955, m. 1938 Mabel Violet __, b. Oct 15, 1901 ND, d. Feb 29, 1992.
HAMMETT, Enoch, d. Dec 4, 1855, aged 75 yrs, hus of Anne __, d. Aug 24, 1870, aged 82 yrs 9 mos and 5 das.
HAMMETT, George E., d. Feb 25, 1878, aged 53 years, hus of S. Sophia __, d. Oct 5, 1855, aged 26 years.
HAMMETT, Helen, b. Feb 20, 1878, d. Sep 21, 1928.
Side by Side
-HAMMETT, Capt. J.A., b. Sep 20, 1818, d. Sep 15, 1890.
-HAMMETT, Samanda, b. Jun 13, 1818, d. Sep 5, 1893.
HAMMETT, Jas. S., Father, b. Mar 15, 1820, d. Aug 29, 1897, hus of Ann L. __, Mother, b. Sep 18, 1819, d. Oct 5, 1906.
HAMMETT, James, b. Aug 28, 1857, d. May 18, 1948, hus of Helen Revely Hammett.
HAMMETT, Littleton S., b. Apr 17, 1850, d. Jun 17, 1884, hus of Jennie W. __.
HAMMETT, Lucia C., b. Apr 20, 1848, d. Feb 19, 1908.
HAMMETT, Mary L., b. Aug 3, 1878, d. Feb 10, 1909.
Two Small Head Stones Side by Side
-HAMMETT, R. W., d. 1858
-HAMMETT, P. M., d. Aug 4, 1973.
HAMMETT, Rebecca S., b. 1853, d. 1931, wife of Dr. Horace Cowan, dau of J. S. B. and Ann L. Hammett.
HAMMETT, S. Lafayette, b. May 9, 1855, d. Feb 3, 1910.
HARBISON, Harriet H., b. Mar 1, 1908 NY, d. Nov 24, 1990, wife of Albert G. Richardson, dau of Clarence Brown and Nellie Atkinson Harbison.
HARRIS, John F., b. 1824, d. 1903, hus of Rosalie S. Brady.

HARRIS, John Walton, b. 1851, d. 1933.
HARRIS, Josephine, b. 1853, d. 1942, wife of
 __ Shepherd.
HARRISON, Sarah M., d. Jul 14, 1855, aged 26
 years 6 mos and 17 das, leaving a husband.
HAW, Dr. Henry, d. Dec 7, 1878 in his 81st yr.
HILL, Allen B., PFC CO III Machine Gun BN WW I,
 b. Oct 5, 1892, d. Jun 26, 1958.
HILL, Minnie, b. 1889, d. 1955.
HORNE, Clyde Newton, Pvt USA WW I, b. 1900, d.
 1983.
HOUSER, Dr. Allen D., b. May 12, 1916, d. Sep
 2, 1972, hus of Alice A. __, b. Nov 1, 1918.
HOWE, A. F., b. Feb 12, 1800, d. Aug 16, 1842.
HURLBURT, James S., b. 1906, d. 1983.
JOHNSON, Agnes 'Iva', b. May 3, 1910, d. Jul
 11, 1989, dau of Ignatius 'Stanley' Johnson
 and Julie Connelly.
JOHNSON, Geo. Washington Doane, b. Mar 27,
 1844, bur Sep 29, 1846, son of W. P. C. and
 Ann E. Johnson. W. P. C. Johnson was Rector
 of St. Andrews Parish.
JOHNSON, James Alfred "Jack", 65, b. 1906, d.
 Jan 16, 1972, hus of Edith Norine Connelly,
 son of Charles and Agnes Hayden Johnson.
KAUFMAN, Eugene A., b. 1925, d. 1951.
KING, John, d. Oct 3, 1852,
 Square Stone
-KNIGHT, Grace W., Mother, b. 1888, d. 1962.
-KNIGHT, George M. Jr. Son, b. 1909, d. 1956.
LIVINGSTON, Charles B., b. 1900, d. 1982.
LOKER, George Peabody, Jr. b. Oct 23, 1904,
 d. Nov 11, 1975.
LOKER, James Lamdin, b. Jul 4, 1910, d. Aug 7,
 1926.
LOKER, James Parren Crane, b. Apr 1, 1916, d.
 May 13, 1918, son of Robert Combs and Kathe-
 rine Crane Loker.
LOKER, Sara Lamdin, b. Feb 7, 1872, d. Jul 29,
 1949.
LORE, G. T. Rupert, b. Mar 19, 1904, d. Nov 1,
 1982, hus of Dora D. __, b. Jan 12, 1909, d.
 Dec 10, 1976.
MADSEN, Valvard A., Pvt USA WW II, b. Nov 26,
 1905, d. Apr 7, 1975, hus of Grace Hazel Mc-

St. Andrews

Whirt.
MATTINGLY, Marguerite, b. Apr 16, 1911, d. Oct 12, 1978, wife of Thomas Holdsworth Bond.
McCALL, Mary B., b. 1898, d. 1989.
    Side by Side
-McCALLUM, James, d. 1881.
-McCALLUM, Margaret, d. Sep 4, 1887.
McELHINEY, Rev. George, D.D., Rector of St. Ann's Parish, Annapolis, MD., May 9, 1841 in his 43d year. (Stone erected by his widow.)
McGREEVY, Joseph T., Pvt USA, b. Apr 10, 1915, d. Sep 16, 1975.
McWHIRT, Grace Hazel, b. Apr 6, 1911 VA, d. Jan 10, 1992, wife of Valvard A. Madsen, dau of Harry and Mary Beach McWhirt.
MILBURN, C. Briscoe, b. Jun 24, 1833, d.-, hus of Sarah J. __, b. Jan 29, 1842, d. --.
MILBURN, Lucia J., b. Aug 29, 1870, d. Aug 26, 1880, dau of C. B. and S.J. Milburn.
MILBURN, Myrtle B., b. Feb 7, 1867, d. Sep 21, 1870, dau of C. B. and S. J. Milburn.
MILLS, Elizabeth T., wife of Col George Dent, no dates on stone, bur with him.
MOORE, Charles Robert, PFC USMC, b. Mar 8, 1928, d. Dec 9, 1982, m. 28 Jan 1949.
    One Stone
-MOORE, Olive D., d. Oct 23, 1898.
-MOORE, M. Mignette, d. Jun 4, 1894.
L.S.M., adjacent foot stone.
OLIVERA, Clifford Emil, NY LT USNR, b. Dec 30, 1937, d. Feb 14, 1968.
PADGETT, Elma P., b. Aug 21, 1914 SC, d. Jan 18, 1992, wife of Frederick Robert Sternkopf, dau of Luther G. and Sallie Padget Padgett.
PICKRELL, Eloise N., b. 1911, d. 1986.
    Double Stone
-PICKRELL, Raymond D., b. 1879, d. 1960.
-PICKRELL, Florence V., b. 1885, d. 1952.
PRICE, Edna E., b. 1903, d. 1968, wife of __ Pugh, dau of Maggie A. Price.
PRICE, Maggie A., Mother, b. 1864, d. 1947.
PRICE, Mary V., b. 1897, d. 1915, dau of Maggie A. Price.
PUSSLER, Bessie Victoria, b. Apr 3, 1898, d.

Aug 11, 1988, dau of Nicholas and Mary Louise Dean Pussler.
PUSSLER, Edna, b. Aug 1, 1912, d. Jun 14, 1913.
PUSSLER, Jacob Melvin, b. Jan 13, 1923 Balto, d. Dec 14, 1992, hus of Lillian __, son of Nicholas and Mary Louise Dean Pussler.
PUSSLER, John, b. Jul 25, 1840, d. Mar 18, 1923.
PUSSLER, Nicholas, b. Dec 26, 1871, d. Dec 4, 1936, hus Mary Louise Dean.
PUSSLER, Wilmer, b. Sep 4, 1905, d. Sep 28, 1992, son of Nicholas and Mary Dean Pussler.
RAMSEY, Bennetta E., b. Jul 10, 1908 NJ, d. Oct 21, 1991, wife of Thomas F. Bennett, Sr. dau of Richard A. and Mary E. Rumbol Ramsey.
RAPP, Elizabeth C., b. 1904, d. 1956.
Double Stone
-RATLEDGE, Thomas F., b. 1907,
-RATLEDGE, Deborah H., b. 1911, d. 1967.
REDMOND, James R., b. 1869, d. 1897.
REEDER, H. Ann E., d. Oct 10, 1878.
ROSE, Andrew Thomas, b. May 14, 1918, d. Jan 20, 1986.
ROTH, Diane, b. Jun 23, 1960 IL, d. Feb 27, 1992, wife of Allen L. Peterson, Capt. USA, dau of Julius and Elsie Tesar Roth.
SANDIDGE, Mosby Brown "Moe", b. May 23, 1935, d. Oct 17, 1993, hus of Joyce Ann Latham, son of Cecil Truette and Nellie Evanola Wills Sandidge.
SANNER, Ann, d. Sep 4, 1856.
SANNER, Mathias, d. Mar 25, 1882, age 74 years.
SAUNDERS, James H., b. Aug 28, 1806, d. Mar 12, 1879.
SHEPHERD, Rhodes, b. 1836, d. 1922.
SHIRCKLIFF, Phoebe, b. Dec 1838, d. Oct 21, 1918, age 80 years.
SILVER, Mary Lou, b. Sep 21, 1928 MT, d. Jun 8, 1989, dau of Francis A. and Elizabeth Booth Silver.
SILVER, Robert F., b. Jul 1, 1931, d. Sep 11, 1984.
SKIDGEL, Gerald Thomas, MARINE LT USN, b. Dec 30, 1937, d. Feb 14, 1968.
Double Stone
-SMITH, James Howard, SGT USA WW II, b. Oct

15, 1913, d. Mar 17, 1985.
-SMITH, Doris E., b. Sep 2, 1915.
SOMERVILLE, Cecelia, b. Dec 25, 1862, d. Feb 13, 1961.
SPENCER, Catherine M., d. Aug 20, 1908 in her 87th year.
SPENCER, Thomas O., d. Oct 15, 1880 in his 65th year.
SQUIRES, Rebecca Beth, b. Jul 7, 1970, d. Aug 14, 1973, dau of Wayne E. and Margaret Bennett Squires.
STEWART, Dorothy Rule, b. May 28, 1905, d. Jan 16, 1985, wife of Philip Henry Dorsey, dau of Dr. John B. and Helen Rule Stewart. (Bur in Dawkins fenced plot).
STONE, Jemima, d. Jul 11, 1847, aged 67.
STRINGER, Francis William, Jr. b. Sep 2, 1912, d. May 21, 1973, hus of Dorothy M. Tinsley.
THOMAS, James Richard, b. Jan 11, 1826, d. Jan 6, 1885, hus of Jeannette Briscoe.
THOMAS, Roger, d. Sep 15, 1842 in his 76th yr.
THOMAS, Waring, b. 1866, d. 1927, son of James Richard and Jeannette Briscoe Thomas.
Double Stone
-THROCKMORTON, Roy E., b. 1907,
-THROCKMORTON, Alice I., b. 1908, d. 1975.
TIPPETT, Mattie, b. Sep 10, 1904, d. Jan 1, 1985, wife of Paul R. Davis.
WARD, Thomas C., d. Nov 7, 1841 in his 55th yr.
WATSON, Douglas C., MD CPL HQ & SVC TRP 8 CAV, b. Jul 17, 1906, d. Jul 11, 1971.
WATSON, Esther Elizabeth, b. Jun 29, 1903 Balto, d. Apr 9, 1991, dau of Dr. William Topping and Esther E. Barnard Watson.
WATTS, Catherine Hebb, d. Jun 30, 1843, aged 18 years 9 mos and 17 das.
Double Stone
-WELLS, Robert P., b. 1919.
-WELLS, Beverly J., b. 1926, d. 1987.
WILLIAMS, Arthur L., b. 1891, d. 1961, hus of Dorothy B. __, b. 1900, d. 1968.
WISE, Jane M. L. C., b. Apr 16, 1856, d. Aug 4, 1860, dau of John H. and Eleanor D. Wise.
WISE, John A., b. Mar 22, 1847, d. Jun 13, 1847, son of John H. and Joanna Wise.

WISE, Laura M., b. 1908, d. 1972, m. 1929 James Hardin Brown.
WISE, Lottie Mae, b. 1892, d. 1982.
WISE, Lydia A., b. Jun 19, 1856, d. Apr 10, 1942.
WISE, Robert Hanson, b. Nov 25, 1823, d. Apr 19, 1884, hus of Margaret Ann Briscoe, son of John C. and Mary H. Wise.
WISE, Robert McKinsey, b. Nov 7, 1845, d. Mar 5, 1915.
WISE, Sarah, b. Apr 12, 1879, d. Apr 18, 1969, wife of __ Soboleft.
WISE, Walter Hanson Briscoe, b. 1862, d. 1938, hus of Patty Dent.

Double Stone
-WISE, William Oliver, b. Apr 29, 1887, d. Nov 15, 1968.
-WISE, Mary Elizabeth, b. Sep 19, 1890, d. Jul 3, 1974.

WOLFORD, Fred Leon III, b. Sep 25, 1967 IL, d. Dec 21, 1990, son of Fred L. and Martha "Marty" Vaupel Wolford.
WOLFORD, Patrick Christopher, b. Dec 23, 1968, d. Sep 20, 1986.

Double Stone
-YOUNG, Alvah Horace, D.C. MECH USA WW I, b. Jul 4, 1892.
-YOUNG, Myrtle D., b. May 9, 1890 DC, d. Jun 16, 1974.

YOUNG, John Phillip, Jr. b. Jun 9, 1961, d. Mar 7, 1991, son of John P. and Eleanora Agnes Price Young.
Foot Stones: H.F., R.H.(H may be Hurt), G.B.M., T.F.W.

ST. FRANCIS XAVIER RCC
Compton, Md.

Originally known as Newtown Neck, the Newtown Mission was established between 1638 and 1640. St. Francis Xavier Chapel was built in 1662 on land donated by the Bretons. The Jesuit priests lived here, raising field crops and their food. The Chapel was located then where the cemetery is now. In 1704, St. Francis Xavier Church was built, and it was rebuilt in 1766. The present vestry is the only portion of that church that remains unchanged. Even the stained glass windows have been replaced by small paned windows.

This cemetery was bulldozed ca 1975 and plots are being resold. I have recorded a few of the old burials.

ABELL, Mrs. Susan, abt 45, bur Nov 1869.
BAILEY, Samantha Jo, b. and d. Nov 30, 1989, dau of John Robert III and Karen Leigh Williams Bailey; paternal gdau of John R. and Alice Bailey; ggdau of Mary Agnes Bailey; maternal gdau of Clark and Ella Williams; ggdau of Stephen Laurence Jr. and Eleanor Guy Fortney Vallandingham; gggdau of Joseph M. and Mary Alma Hancock.
BLAIR, Mrs. Mary, 75, bur Sep 11, 1870.
BRAZEAU, Bernice "Bunny", b. Dec 21, 1913 WI, d. Jun 9, 1990, wife of Jacob van Aernam VIII, dau of James Edward and Katherine Young Brazeau.
BULLOCK, Mrs. James, 40, bur Oct 2, 1894.
BULLOCK, Marie T., d. Oct 13, 1907 DC, wife of Joseph T. Cryer.
BUSSLER, Agnes Ruth, b. Nov 30, 1919, d. Jul 17, 1991, wife of Norman A. Pilkerton, Sr., dau of Frank and Agnes Bussler.
BUTLER, Catherine Rosalie, b. Sep 14, 1913, d. Jul 11, 1991, dau of Dominick W. and Bernadette Holly Butler.
CHASE, Barbara Ann, b. Dec 22, 1925 MA, d. Dec 12, 1988, wife of Charles W. Chase.
CHOPORIS, Demosthenes Paul, b. Oct 21, 1928,

d. Jun 21, 1991, hus of Jo Anne Greenwell, son of William G. and Angeline Comuntzis Choporis.
COOMBS, Amelia, 55, bur Mar 30, 1872.
CREIGHTON, Mrs. Anne M., b. Jul 6, 1902, d. Nov 24, 1988 FL.
CROSWELL, Albert Francis, d. Jul 30, 1883 Balto, age 4 mos 20 das, son of John and Mary F. Cryer Croswell.
CRYER, Agnes Maude, d. 8 Oct 1896, age 7 yrs, dau of Wm. T. and Ann E. "Bettie" Mattingly Cryer.
CRYER, Albert Frank, d. Apr 14, 1887, age 1 yr 10 mos, oldest child of John C. and A. Mary Leach Cryer.
CRYER, Ella, b. Feb 1870, d. Oct 1, 1873, dau of Wm Henry and Elizabeth Ann Thompson Cryer. Tombstone shows birthdate as May 13, 1869, the 1870 Census shows her age as 4 mos.
CRYER, John C., b. 1858, d. 1891/92, hus of A. Mary Leach, son of Wm. Henry and Eliz. Ann Thompson Cryer.
CRYER, Joseph Walter, b. Aug 7, 1907, d. Nov 19, 1974, hus of Christine Dinenna, son of James Walter and Bessie Delores Cryer.
CRYER, Joseph Tilden, b. Nov 7, 1875, d. Apr 10, 1960, m. (1st) Marie T. Bullock, (2d) Pearl___, son of Wm. T. and Ann E. "Bettie" Mattingly Cryer.
CRYER, Margaret Theresa, b. Jan 5, 1907 DC, d. Feb 12, 1993, m. 1941 Thomas Bernard Johnson, dau of Joseph Tilden and Marie T. Bullock Cryer.
CRYER, Mary Frances, b. 1855/56, d. Mar 13, 1883 Balto, wife of Cpt. John W. Croswell, Jr., dau of Wm. Henry and Elizabeth Thompson Cryer.
CRYER, Mary Tayler, d. Aug 24, 1853, aged 14 years 5 mos 14 das, dau of William H. and Elizabeth A. Thompson Cryer.
CRYER, William Henry, d. Feb 12, 1873, age 55 yrs, hus of Elizabeth Ann Thompson.
CRYER, William T., b. 1847/48 DC, d. May 26, 1902, hus of Ann Elizabeth Mattingly, son of Wm. Henry and Elizabeth Ann Cryer.

St. Francis Xavier

CUSIC, Robert, 25, bur Oct 31 1871.
DAVIS, Eugene Howard "Buck" Jr, b. Feb 22, 1907, d. May 2, 1993, m. 1935 Helena Martha Hendrick, son of Eugene H. and Blanche Virginia Payne Davis.
DAVIS, Mrs. Kate, 46, bur Sep 21, 1898.
DEAN, Raymond Anthony, Sr. b., Jul 20, 1915 DC, d. Dec 29, 1993, hus of Agatha Theresa Kern, son of Spencer Joseph and Sybil Beatrice Hall Dean.
DILLOW, Alfred, 62, bur Jun 6, 1901.
EDWARDS, Iola, b. Sep 14, 1910 DC, d. Aug 30, 1993, m. 30 Apr 1930 Eugene Francis Quigley, dau of William and Annie Gray Edwards.
ELDER, Frances Cordelia, b. Oct 29, 1923, d. Oct 28, 1989, wife of Paul C. Wentzell, dau of Albert Leo and Agnes Genevieve Elder.
EPPARD, Mary Louise, b. Mar 14, 1926 DC, d. Sep 15, 1991, dau of George I., Sr. and Louise Anna Eppard.
FOLEY, John Dennis, 18, b. 1953, d. Jan 3, 1972, son of Charles W. and Mary Cryer Foley.
GARDINER, Thomas Richard II, b. Nov 10, 1921, d. Nov 1, 1991, hus of Beatrice Marie Ringling, son of Hugh Charles, Sr. and Mary Isabelle Middleton Gardiner.
HARDEN, Capt. John, 35, bur Aug 1869.
HARDIN, Robert Lee, 59, bur Nov 3, 1901.
HAZEL, Mrs. 70, bur Jan 2, 1870.
HAZEL, John, 60, bur Mar 9, 1899.
HENDRICK, Helena Martha, b. May 17, 1913 Balto, d. Dec 23, 1991, wife of Eugene Howard "Buck" Davis, dau of Francis and Mary Martha Goldberg Hendrick.
HERBERT, William C., 9 mos, bur Apr 15, 1870.
HERMANN, Ladyne M. "Deane", b. Apr 28, 1920, d. Nov 23, 1989, dau of Victor H. and Rose Loichot Hermann.
HIGGS, John Leon "Happy", b. May 7, 1902, d. Jan 13, 1989, hus of Helen Victoria Pilkerton, son of James Mitchell and Julia Mae Bush Higgs.
HOWARD, Mrs. Ann, 64, bur Sep 24, 1870.
HOWARD, James, 89, bur Oct 2, 1871.
HUDSON, Jeanne C., b. Dec 12, 1942 DC, d. Jul

10, 1988 DC, wife of William O. Tuite, dau of Francis J. Hudson and Catherine Hudson Pope.
JOHNSON, Thomas 'Bernard', b. 1902, d. 1975, hus of Margaret T. Cryer, son of John Andrew and Mary "Cassie" Mattingly Johnson.
JOHNSON, Thomas W., b. Apr 2, 1897, d. Jan 4, 1899, son of John T. and Maggie A. Johnson.
LEACH, A. Mary, b. 1865, d. after 1892, wife of John C. Cryer, dau of Wm. Francis and Mary E. Yates Leach.
LEE, Mary Etta Glovina, 103, b. Apr 13, 1887, d. May 16, 1990, wife of Ira Gunnell, dau of James Fitzhugh and Mary Frances Nelson Lee.
MacDONNELL, George Anthony, b. Feb 17, 1907 MA, d. Sep 11, 1992, m. (1st) Unice Nilsen (2d) Vera Hurt, son of Joseph and Ann Coughlin Larr MacDonnell. Mem. Service.
MARSHALL, Daniel, 80, bur Nov 19, 1869.
MATTINGLY, Ann Elizabeth "Bettie", b. 1853/54, bur Sep 3, 1894, wife of Wm. T. Cryer.
McWILLIAMS, Dr., 65, bur May 20, 1898, hus of Adria E. __, 24, d. Mar 1860 of brain disease.
McWILLIAMS, Emily, 30, bur Nov 6, 1872.
MERRYMAN, James Alexander, 52, bur Jan 8, 1872.
MOORE, Gabriel Jerome, b. May 29, 1919, d. June 22, 1990.
MORGAN, James Bernard, Sr. b. Feb 21, 1907, d. Mar 11, 1992, hus of Marie Clothilda __, son of Joseph and Ida Morgan.
NEALE, Enoch, 80, bur Aug 22, 1869.
PADGETT, Emma Adelaide, b. Sep 17, 1900 DC, d. Mar 18, 1991, wife of James Z. "Pappy" Mattingly, dau of James L. and Emma Wedding Padgett.
PAYNE, David 'Alan', b. Jun 14, 1946, d. Nov 23, 1971, hus of Dorothy Anne Martin, son of Johnson and Genevieve Raley Payne.
PAYNE, Joseph Brennan, b. Sep 26, 1914, d. Aug 2, 1988, m. (1st) Frances Tayloe (d. 1982), (2d) Myrtle N. "Polly" Morgan, son of Oswald Eugene and Mary Lillian Evans Payne.
PILKERTON, Norman A., Sr. b. Oct 13, 1912, d. Nov 2, 1981, hus of Agnes Ruth Bussler.

POE, Albert Franklin, d. May 2, 1977, hus of Eva Estelle Knott.
POE, James Roland, Sr. b. May 15, 1926, d. Mar 26, 1992, hus of Suzanne Burch Knott, son of Albert Franklin Sr. and Eva Estelle Knott Poe.
POPE, Daisy Agnes, b. Aug 19, 1916, d. Jul 15, 1990, dau of John Clinton and Mary Ida Mills Pope.
QUIGLEY, Eugene Francis, d. Feb 24, 1988, hus of Iola Edwards.
RAMSEY, Joseph W., b. Jun 13, 1962, d. Nov 19, 1988 FL, hus of Rita Faye __, son of Joseph DeLano and Phyllis Evelyn Ramsey.
RUSSELL, John, 25, bur Sep 21, 1869.
RUSSELL, John Franklin, few das, bur Feb 13, 1870.
SESTAN, Mary, b. Feb 7, 1909 LA, d. Aug 14, 1992, wife of George H. Ely, dau of Samuel and Sofia Matitiavich Sestan.
SMITH, Ann, 65, bur Nov 4, 1871.
SOMERVILLE, Eleanor Cecelia, b. Oct 2, 1931, d. Mar 8, 1988, dau of Albert and Eleanor Banks Somerville.
SPAULDING, Daniel, 61, bur May 25, 1899.
STEWART, Mrs., abt 40, bur Nov 3, 1869.
STONE, Dr. Thomas Jefferson, bur Dec 3, 1869.
TAYLOR, Frances, d. 1982, m. 1959, 1st wife of Joseph Brennan Payne.
TEACHEM, Capt. James, 50, bur Nov 4, 1871.
THOMPSON, Elizabeth Ann, d. Oct 6, 1873, age 74 yrs 9 mos, wife of Wm. Henry Cryer, dau of widow Ann Thompson.
THOMPSON, Ignatius, 80, bur Dec 8, 1872.
THOMPSON, Richard Emmett, b. Oct 25, 1892, d. Jul 1, 1989, hus of Madge __, son of Richard and Isabel Thompson.
TIPPETT, Mary Glovenia "Sally", b. Sep 24, 1941, d. Apr 16, 1991, wife of __ Brown, dau of Thomas Parren and Agnes Juanita Pope Tippett.
TIPPETT, Thomas Parren, d. Feb 8, 1972, hus of Agnes Juanita Pope.
TURNER, Mary Florine, b. Nov 8, 1904, d. Apr 19, 1989, wife of Horace M. Robinson, dau of George and Florence Coombs Turner.
WATHEN, Robert, 36, bur Sep 8, 1871.

WESTURA, Edwin Eugene, M.D., b. Aug 29, 1930 NJ, d. Jul 2, 1989, hus of Elizabeth Ann Richards, son of Andrew J. and Teresa Marie Westura.

YATES, Maude, b. Dec 12, 1898, d. Oct 25, 1988, wife of Francis Compton Heard, dau of Robert Norman and Ruth Abell Yates.

ST. GEORGE CATHOLIC CEMETERY
Valley Lee, Md.

ABELL, Calvin T., Sr. b. Oct 17, 1924, d. Dec 24, 1991, hus of Agnes Rosalie Franck, son of Walter Eugene and Eleanor Louise Clarke Abell.

ABELL, Joseph Walter, Sr. b. Jan 4, 1955, d. Nov 29, 1993 work accident, m. 29 Sep 1979 Barbara Jean Crook, son of Calvin T. and Agnes Franck Abell.

ADAMS, Lillian Agnes, b. Mar 8, 1902, d. Dec 2, 1993, wife of Charles Melchoir Herrmann, dau of Oliver Lee and Laura Ann Bean Adams.

AUD, Rosalie Virgie, b. Mar 26, 1925, d. Dec 22, 1990, wife of Philip Gregory Redman, dau of Joseph Jeff and Emma H. Johnson Aud.

BEAN, Edward Andrew "Ned", b. Dec 7, 1944, d. Feb 18, 1992, hus of Rose Marie Woodburn, son of James Aloysius, Sr. and Isabelle Coates Bean.

BEAN, James Aloysius, Sr. b. Dec 18, 1919, d. Feb 8, 1992, hus of Isabelle Coates, son of John Stephen and Violet Agnes Goodwin Bean.

BEAN, Joseph Lee, d. May 29, 1960, hus of Helen Genevieve Redman.

BEAN, Lucy Madeleine, b. Jan 4, 1891, d. Jul 5, 1978, wife of Jessie Andrew Redman.

BISCOE, Mary Christine, b. Jul 30, 1929, d. Apr 29, 1989, wife of Walter A. Lloyd, dau of William Thomas and Mary Margaret Butler Biscoe.

BLACKWELL, Morris Elmore, USN, b. Mar 25, 1915, d. Nov 15, 1992, m. 1938 Grace Cecelia Lawrence, son of Saint Elmore and Mary Wilson Blackwell.

BOWES, Jason Mark, Infant, b. May 15, 1992, son of Mark and Bonnie Wise Bowes; gson of Robert and Patricia Usilton Bowes; Wayne and Brenda Gay Wise; ggson of Joseph and Audrey Cranston Bowes; David and Kathleen Shannonhouse Usilton; Charles Gay; Wayne and Anna Parks Wise.

BRADBURN, Mary Madeline, b. May 22, 1903, d. May 12, 1988, wife of Charles Bernard Brad-

burn.
BRISCOE, Benjamin Lewin "Ben", b. Mar 4, 1910, d. Jul 12, 1993, hus of Angeline Dickens, son of Carroll Alexander and Lugitta Strong Briscoe.
BRISCOE, Harold Benjamin, b. Feb 6, 1936, d. May 14, 1993, m. 8 Mar 1969 Catherine Estelle Lawrence, son of Benjamin and Angeline Dickens Briscoe.
BRISCOE, Irene Frances, "Rene", b. Jun 5, 1909 Balto, d. Jun 29, 1991, wife of Joseph Vincent Briscoe.
BRISCOE, Joseph Vincent, d. Jun 17, 1972, m. 1930 Irene Francis __.
BROWN, Lettie Estelle, b. Oct 6, 1926, d. Jan 13, 1992, wife of Francis Oliver Maddox, dau of James Aaron and Lillie Hendnick Brown.
BUSSLER, Catherine Gwinnette, b. May 14, 1912, d. Aug 31, 1989, wife of Clarence C. Adams, dau of William James and Ada Cecelia Bussler.
CASIMANO, Mary Santa, 75, b. NY, d. Apr 19, 1992, wife of Dominick Paul Logalbo, dau of Joseph and Angela Messina Casimano.
CECIL, Annie Marie, b. Mar 2, 1904, d. Sep 28, 1993, m. 12 Feb 1927 Thomas Eugene Springer, dau of George and Annie Raley Cecil.
CECIL, Margaret, b. Jun 10, 1910, d. Nov 27, 1993, m. 3 Sep 1940 Robert G. Dean, dau of George and Annie Raley Cecil.
COMBS, Joseph 'Earl', b. Jun 30, 1910, d. Sep 25, 1991, son of Joseph Franklin, Sr. and Margaret L. Redman Combs.
CUTCHEMBER, Patrick Brian, b. Feb 7, 1964 Balto, d. Jun 6, 1991, hus of Felicia Young, son of Francis Buck and Rosie Sewell Cutchember.
DICKENS, James Orville, d. 1979, hus of Viola Matilda Greene.
DYSON, Thomas Joseph, b. May 9, 1925, d. Oct 27, 1992 MI, son of John and Mary Calvary Dyson.
ECHOLS, Garyton C., Sr. b. Jun 8, 1910 DC, d. May 9, 1992, hus of Christine Combs, son of late Garyton C. Echols and Ella Johnson Echols Chambers.

St. George Catholic

ESLIN, George Adelbert, Sr. b. Mar 10, 1904 DC, d. Jun 26, 1988, hus of Mary Grace __.
ESLIN, Mary Grace, b. Aug 31, 1904, d. Feb 9, 1989, wife of George Adelbert Eslin, Sr.
FARR, Dorothy Lucille, b. Mar 17, 1919, d. Oct 22, 1991, wife of Edward Leo Springer, Sr., dau of William P. and Martha E. Davis Farr.
FITZGERALD, Marion Frances, b. Jul 11, 1908 NY, d. Jun 10, 1993, m. 1941 NY Victor Anthony Orsini, dau of John and Mary Sullivan Fitzgerald. Memorial Service.
GOUGH, Esther Merle, b. Oct 1, 1915 Balto, d. Mar 7, 1993, wife of James A. Redman, dau of William Vernon and Mary Priscilla Neilson Gough. Memorial Service 3/25/1993.
GREENE, Agnes Evelyn, 70, d. Nov 15, 1989, m. __ Jordon, dau of John Q. and Lottie Cecelia Mason Greene.
GREENE, Viola Matilda, b. Oct 5, 1912, d. Oct 24, 1992, wife of James Orville Dickens, dau of John Q. and Cecelia Mason Greene.
GREENE, Violet Cecelia, d. Dec 21, 1988, wife of Frederick Rudolph Robinson, dau of John Q. and Cecelia Mason Greene.
HARDMAN, Oscar Howard, b. Mar 19, 1931 WV, d. Aug 16, 1990, hus of Shirley Adams, son of Oscar Carrey and Freda O. Hardman.
HERN, Ethel Mae, b. Jun 12, 1903 VA, d. May 30, 1991, wife of Mulry Joseph Thompson, dau of Heath Hern.
HERRMANN, Charles Melchoir, d. Mar 10, 1968, hus of Lillian Agnes Adams.
HERRMANN, Charles Paul, b. Nov 18, 1931 Balto, d. May 6, 1993 ME, son of Charles M. and Lillian Agnes Adams Herrmann.
HIGGS, Catherine Gladys, b. Sep 16, 1923, d. Oct 20, 1988, wife of Cornelius Knott, dau of Herbert and Bessie Higgs.
KEATLEY, Paul William Jenkins, b. Dec 12, 1924 DE, d. Aug 1, 1991, m. 22 May 1948 Robena McKay, son of late Millard F. Keatley and Helen Keatley Williams.
KNOTT, Harry Rudolph, Jr. b. Jan 10, 1911 DC, d. Sep 4, 1991, hus of Frances Marie Wahler,

son of Harry Rudolph and Lucy Reynolds Martin Knott.
LAWRENCE, Morris Andrew, Jr. b. Oct 8, 1933, d. Nov 7, 1989, hus of Mary Nellie Mason, son of Morris and Janie Lawrence.
LOGALBO, Dominick Paul, b. Apr 10, 1913 NY, d. Jul 8, 1989, hus of Mary Santa Marie Casimano, son of Frank and Constance Labou Logalbo.
LORD, Robert Alfred "Bobby", "Pussy Cat", b. Mar 16, 1927 NY, d. Mar 2, 1991, hus of Krystyna Korbeka, son of Clarence and Vera Russell Lord.
MARSHALL, Joseph Genesee, b. Sep 17, 1921, d. Apr 17, 1992, hus of Agnes Rebecca __, son of James and Maud Blair Marshall.
MASON, Mary Alberta, b. May 14, 1905, d. Jul 28, 1988, m. (1st) John Joseph Saxton, (2d) George Henry Toney.
MASON, Robert, 102, b. Apr 20, 1886, d. Aug 17, 1988, hus of Amanda __, son of Joseph T. and Lottie Taylor Mason.
McKAY, William Ford, Sr. b. Jul 10, 1903, d. Aug 16, 1990 FL, hus of Hilda Rae __.
MILBURN, James Manning "Peaches", Jr. b. Apr 11, 1924, d. Dec 21, 1993, m. 13 May 1930 Alice Briscoe, son of James M. and Beatrice A. Holland Milburn.
MORONEY, Gertrude Rose, b. Dec 15, 1904 DC, d. Jan 3, 1993, m. 6 Dec 1924, John M. Shepherd Sr., dau of William Webb and Exzelda Rosanne LaFlame Moroney.
NEALON, Jeanne, b. Jan 27, 1922, d. Sep 8, 1988, wife of Charles Seymour Kimball, Jr., dau of George Ambrose and Loretta Lakearn Nealon.
ORSINI, Victor Anthony, d. Oct 24, 1988, hus of Marion Frances Fitzgerald.
RANDOLPH, Paul Raymond, 85, b. Youngstown, OH, d. Jan 9, 1989, m. (1st) Pearl __,(2d) Nelle __, son of Frank and Agnes Randolph.
REDMAN, Helen Genevieve, b. May 27, 1913, d. July 2, 1993, m. 31 Dec 1932 Joseph Lee Bean, dau of John Bean and Sarah Neadurra Abell Redman.
REDMAN, James Andrew, b. Mar 6, 1915, d. Jan

St. George Catholic

26, 1991, hus of Esther Merle Gough, son of Benjamin F. and Annie Elizabeth Bean Redman.
REDMAN, Philip Gregory, b. Jan 30, 1927, d. Mar 31, 1990, hus of Rosalie Virgie Aud, son of Jessie Andrew and Lucy M. Bean Redman.
ROBERTS, Sean Christopher, b. Nov 12, 1973 VA, d. May 17, 1991, son of John Donald and Patrice Joan Howell Roberts; gson of Utley W. and Wilma K. Roberts; Wilford D. and Patrice Howell.
ROBINSON, Doris Marie, b. May 15, 1955, d. Feb 9, 1990, dau of George Henry and Margaret Marie Robinson.
ROBINSON, Joseph Sidney, b. Jul 18, 1940, d. Sep 27, 1991 DC, son of Frederick Rudolph and Violet Cecelia Greene Robinson.
SAUNDERS, Albert Edward Vernon, Sr. b. Nov 20, 1911, d. Sep 4, 1991, hus of Viola Redman, son of Wilbur Wesley and Janie Fish Sanner Saunders.
SLADE, David Lloyd, b. Oct 27, 1947, d. Dec 27, 1992, son of John Frank, Jr. and Marian Gass Slade.
SMOOT, Eleanor Myrtle, b. Dec 23, 1915 VA, d. Jun 14, 1992, wife of John Thomas Scrivener, dau of Howard and Stella Vietch Smoot.
SPRINGER, Adeline Cecelia, b. Sep 18, 1907, d. Jan 15, 1991, wife of William Paul Cecil, dau of Benjamin M. and Mocky Jeannette Combs Springer.
SPRINGER, Thomas Eugene, d. Sep 20, 1977, hus of Annie Marie Cecil.
STEPHENSON, Edna, b. Mar 11, 1909 DC, d. Sep 19, 1989, wife of Arthur C. Morse, dau of Edmund V. and Anna Elizabeth McGee Stephenson.
STREBE, Annette Taylor, b. Jan 1, 1936 CA, d. May 8, 1991, wife of James E. Hughes, dau of Vincent and Helen McDonald Strebe. Mem.Serv.
THOMPSON, Veronica Rose "Ronnie", b. Jun 2, 1918 NJ, d. Feb 26, 1993, dau of late Eugene Mason and Sophia Thompson.
THOMPSON, William Manuel III, b. May 19, 1971 MA, d. Apr 25, 1992 VA, son of William and Mary Blackwell Thompson of Ithaca, NY; gson

of Morris and Grace Blackwell.
WAHLER, Frances, b. Aug 4, 1912, d. Dec 21, 1990, wife of Harry R. Knott, Jr., dau of Francis and Maud Richards Wahler.
WILEY, John, CPO USN, b. May 5, 1934 NJ, d. Dec 31, 1993, m. 29 Sep 1957 NJ Mary Elizabeth McCormack, son of John and Genevieve Hoffman Wiley.

ST. GEORGE EPISCOPAL CEMETERY
Valley Lee, Md.

ADAMS, Louise Virginia, b. 1886, d. 1964, wife of Oliver Burton Milburn.
ALBRIGHT, Celestine Margaret "Fess", NSDAR, b. Oct 1, 1901 MO, d. Aug 5, 1991, wife of Charles Reginold Adams, dau of Daniel Kinsley and Margaret Link Albright.
ALLWINE, Robert Thomas, b. Oct 18, 1930 DC, d. Nov 27, 1992, m. 28 Dec 1979 Nancy Lee, son of Oscar and Nell Chesser Allwine.
BISCOE, Clarence Jefferson "Capt. Clarence", 103, b. Apr 13, 1890, d. Oct 15, 1993, m. 1913 Gertrude Edwards, son of William Walter and Mary Elizabeth Trice Biscoe.
BISCOE, Ethel J., b. Nov 1, 1894, d. Feb 26, 1991, dau of William Lee and Mary P. Biscoe.
BISCOE, Hattie Ann, b. Mar 8, 1901, d. Oct 24, 1989, wife of William Duke Coppage, dau of William Lee and Mollie Biscoe.
BLACKWELL, James Dale, USN Korea, b. Apr 22, 1932, d. Dec 20, 1986, hus of Lucy Dement.
BRYAN, Thomas Brooke, b. Oct 28, 1905, d. Oct 1, 1989, son of James Brooke and Mary Rooker Bryan.
COMBS, Hiltrude Victoria, b. Sep 29, 1908, d. Mar 3, 1993, m. 1 Mar 1930 Alphonso Hewitt, dau of J. Frank and Blondell Fenhagen Combs.
COPPAGE, Elizabeth, "Betty" b. Jun 25, 1919, d. Jan 1, 1993, wife of Edward Lloyd Bunch (bur VA, see Misc.), dau of George Herman and Clementine Howard Craddock Coppage.
COPPAGE, Martha Priscilla, b. Dec 5, 1898, d. Dec 27, 1992, dau of John Benjamin and Susan Elizabeth Duke Coppage.
CRITCHFIELD, Ruth, 77, d. May 12, 1992, wife of Walter S. Reid.
DAMERON, Charles E., Sr. d. 1976, hus of Margaret Davis.
DAVIS, Margaret, b. Jan 8, 1906, d. Jul 18, 1989, wife of Charles E. Dameron, dau of Robert and Charlotte Baden Davis.

Double Stone
-DEMENT, George R., b. May 14, 1870, d. Sep

25, 1944.
-DEMENT, Monica A., b. Jun 6, 1875, d. Jul 12, 1957.
Double Stone
-DEMENT, Harry Lee, b. 1895, d. 1955.
-DEMENT, Clara Maude, b. 1905, d. 1985.
DEMENT, Harry W., Our Darling, 1946.
DEMENT, Lucy, b. 1936, wife of James Dale Blackwell.
DONALDSON, Charles Hudson, 60, d. Jan 22, 1993, son of Charles and Eleanor Hudson Donaldson.
DONALDSON, Charles Suehle, b. Mar 11, 1909, d. Jan 28, 1991, hus of Mary 'Eleanor' Hudson, son of Harry Thomas and Bertha Suehle Donaldson.
DOYEN, Fay, b. 1901, d. 1984, wife of V.Adm. Felix Johnson.
EDWARDS, Austin, d. Oct 24, 1985, hus of Alberta Hewitt.
EDWARDS, Gertrude, d. 1987, wife of Capt. Clarence Biscoe.
FELDMAN, Herman O., d. 1972, hus of Thelma Marie Wiggington.
FORD, Everett Raymond, Jr. b. Jan 17, 1941, d. Dec 16, 1989, hus of Deane E. ___, son of Everett R. and Thelma Ford.
FRANKS, Algernon Earl, d. Mar 3, 1976, hus of Catherine Alice Hughes.
GENGE, Enid, 78, b. ME, d. Sep 10, 1993, wife of Ernie Slusser, dau of Rev. Q. Quenton and Alma Scott Genge. Memorial Service.
GODDARD, Gladys Lorraine, b. Dec 10, 1940, d. Sep 27, 1992, wife of George L. Goodwin, dau of Thomas Albert and Grace Elizabeth Smith Goddard.
GODDARD, Joan Elizabeth, b. May 20, 1937, d. Sep 12, 1992, m. 22 Oct 1965 Ronald Clark Melendy, dau of Thomas Albert and Grace Elizabeth Smith Goddard.
GODDARD, Mary Jean, b. Apr 20, 1945, d. Sep 25, 1991 Balto, wife of William Gary Robrecht, dau of Joseph Benjamin and Ruby Mary Thompson Goddard.
GRAHAM, J. Gordon, b. Nov 22, 1928 OH, d. May 15, 1993, m. DC 19 Apr 1947 Shirley M. Rich-

St. George Episcopal

ardson, son of Thomas and Patricia Stout Graham.
HANSON, Norris Orville, b. Jan 23, 1926 ND, d. Mar 2, 1993, m. 1951 Lucy Mae Russell, son of Guslave Victor and Ina Alice Tostenson Hanson.
HEINZMAN, Karl W., d. 1967, hus of Louise __. b. Mar 23, 1896, d. Feb 21, 1991.
HENDERSON, Charles 'Lynwood' Sr. b. Dec 13, 1908, d. Apr 15, 1992 DC, hus of Alice Marie Shorter, son of William Clinton and Addie R. Twilley Henderson.
HENDERSON, James Marion, Jr. b. Nov 5, 1918 DC, d. Jun 28, 1993, m. DC 15 Feb 1941 Myrtle Leizear, son of James M. and Mary R. Taylor Henderson. Memorial Service.
HEWITT, Alberta, b. Dec 7, 1907, d. Mar 17, 1993, m. 24 Sep 1942 Austin Edwards, dau of Herman W. and Pearl Harris Hewitt.
HEWITT, Herman Walter, Jr. b. Sep 9, 1909, d. Apr 6, 1989, hus of Regina Redman, son of Herman W. and Pearl Harris Hewitt.
HUGHES, Catherine Alice, b. Oct 10, 1900 DC, d. Sep 8, 1991, wife of Algernon Earl Franks, dau of Simon I. and Emily Belle Burgess Hughes.
JOHNSON, Felix, V.Adm. USN, b. 1897, d. 1981, hus of Fay Doyen.
JOHNSON, John, b. 1857, d. 1929.
KELLER, Joseph Leonard, d. 1952, hus of Margaret Aileen Sheler.
LARSON, Ryan Nathaniel, b. Jul 24, 1975, d. Aug 7, 1992 (car accident), son of David and Mary Hildebrand Larson; gson of E.J. and Betty Hildebrand; Donald and Margaret Larson; ggson of Lucinda Potter, all of MI.
LINGER, Josephine Mary, b. Oct 4, 1908 NY, d. Apr 23, 1990, wife of Hoye N. Linger.
MILBURN, Clarence, b. Nov 2, 1872, d. May 18, 1912.
MILBURN, G. Elizabeth, Mother, b. 1850, d. 1923.
MILBURN, James E., d. Jul 6, 1849 in his 18th year, son of John L. and Ann S. Milburn.
MILBURN, Oliver Burton, b. 1885, d. 1962, hus

of Louise Virginia Adams.
MILBURN, Stephen Oliver, b. Oct 31, 1911, d. Mar 4, 1989, son of Oliver Burton and Louise Virginia Adams Milburn.
PHILLIPS, Edgar Curtis "Ed", Jr. b. Dec 27, 1973 VA, d. Dec 5, 1993 in Chesapeake Bay, son of Edgar and Betty Drury Phillips.
RADCLIFFE, William Eugene, USA WW II, b. Jan 23, 1914 VA, d. Jan 20, 1992 FL, hus of Mary Mills, son of Victor Moore and Gladys Miller Radcliffe.
RUSSELL, George Houston, Sr. b. May 16, 1947 Balto, d. Jun 28, 1991, hus of Betty Ann __, son of Houston Charles and Goldie E. Saunders Russell.
SHELER, Margaret Aileen, b. Apr 6, 1903 IN, d. Dec 6, 1993, wife of Joseph Leonard Keller, dau of Henry and Elizabeth Marshall Sheler.
SHORTER, Alice Marie, d. Jan 16, 1974, m. 3 Oct 1953 Charles 'Lynwood' Henderson.
THOMPSON, Ella Irene, b. Feb 9, 1911, d. Sep 15, 1991 DC, wife of Chester Blackwell, dau of William and Ella Thompson.
TURNER, Louise Elizabeth, b. Jan 1, 1899 ENG, d. Oct 2, 1988, wife of Herbert T. Giddings, dau of William Henry and Mary Elizabeth Helcomb Turner.
WAIKART, Frank W. II, b. Apr 13, 1913 DC, d. Oct 9, 1991, hus of Jean Tolson, son of Harry W. and Maude Orton Waikart.
WARD, Hoge, b. Jan 23, 1939 VA, d. Jun 12, 1990, hus of Poda N. __, son of W. S. and Janie Baldwin Ward.
WIGGINGTON, Thelma Marie, b. Feb 20, 1917 Balto, d. Apr 7, 1988, wife of Herman O. Feldman, dau of Howard Wharton and Minnie Cannoles Wiggington.
WILLIAMS, Phyllis Louise, b. Nov 30, 1937, d. Jul 3, 1988, wife of Lawrence G. Mann, dau of Forrest E. Sr. and Marie Nemecek Williams.

ST. GEORGE METHODIST CEMETERY
St. George Island, Md.

BARBAGALLO, Andrew, d. Mar 20, 1983 FL, hus of Jane Rebecca Smith.

BEAVERS, Everett John, Sr. b. Sep 23, 1913 DC, d. Jul 21, 1991, hus of Kathryn Ruth Hall, son of Everett Jackson and Flora P. Knott Beavers.

BOWIE, Drucilla Louise, b. Jan 9, 1898, d. Feb 19, 1992, wife of Walter Graydon Stephens, dau of John Richard and Sarah A. Tucker Bowie.

BROWN, Pearl E., b. Sep 5, 1928, d. Sep 23, 1991, wife of Albert William Dickens, dau of James Aaron and Lillie Hendrick Brown.

BURKE, Kinsey Wilson, b. Sep 27, 1913 VA, d. Oct 10, 1990, hus of Mary Ellen McKenney, son of Henry and Louise Welch Burke.

DICKENS, Albert William, d. Sep 30, 1976, m. 1946 Pearl E. Brown.

HALL, Katheryn Ruth, d. Aug 26, 1985, wife of Everett John Beavers.

HIGGINS, James Edward, b. Aug 17, 1924, d. Dec 10, 1990, hus of Yolanda Tiburzi, son of Henry U. and Thelma Kew Higgins.

KNOTT, Eva Estelle, b. Mar 23, 1901, d. Apr 19, 1991, wife of Albert Franklin Poe, dau of William Henry and Anna Mae Goddard Knott.

McGOWAN, Margaret J. "Peggy", b. Feb 26, 1929 MI, d. Oct 10, 1993, m. 5 Apr 1952 Jack Isaac Parcel, dau of Wesley James and Mary Agnes Aud McGowan.

McKENNEY, Mary Ellen, b. Sep 19, 1925, d. Mar 23, 1990, wife of Kinsey Wilson Burke, dau of David A. and Lottie Poe McKenney.

McNEELY, Loretta Mae Fannin, b. Mar 10, 1920 KY, d. Aug 7, 1990, wife of David F. Sayre, dau of George and Bessie Mae Fannin McNeely.

NELSON, Joseph Edward, Jr. b. Nov 28, 1923 WV, d. Apr 4, 1993, hus of Elizabeth Gene Poe, son of Joseph E. and Bertha Elizabeth Palmer Nelson.

POE, Edward Raleigh, b. Apr 28, 1918 VA, d. Aug 12, 1990, son of Leonard and Eva Bell

Poe.
POE, Lottie Roena, 98, b. Apr 7, 1890, d. Jul 26, 1988, wife of David A. McKenney, dau of George W. and Mary Ellen Poe.
POTTER, Leona Mae, b. Jan 25, 1907, d. Jul 4, 1991, m. (1st) Charles Edward Lavender, (2d) Robert Golden Clarke, dau of Edward Richard and Clara Mae Twilley Potter.
PRINGLE, William Robertson, b. Jun 3, 1914 IA, d. Sep 6, 1991 FL, hus of Margaret Langford Thomas.
SHEAFFER, John Mitchell, b. Jun 29, 1924 DC, d. Jul 31, 1990, hus of Grace Merryman, son of John M. and Lillian A. Sheaffer.
SMITH, Jane Rebecca, b. May 6, 1901 DC, d. Mar 12, 1991 FL, m. 19 Oct 1922 Andrew Barbagallo, dau of Parker W. and Laura V. Satterfield Smith.
STEPHENS, Walter Graydon, d. Nov 23, 1970, hus of Drucilla Louise Bowie.
THOMAS, Margaret, b. Oct 20, 1914, d. Jun 16, 1990 FL, wife of William Pringle, dau of George W. and Lollie Stephens Thomas.

ST. JAMES CATHOLIC CEMETERY
Lexington Park, Md.

BALTA, Paul R., Sr. b. Mar 29, 1921, d. Jul 15, 1990 FL, hus of Jennie C. Adams.

BUTLER, William Cornelius, b. Jan 9, 1923, d. Dec 28, 1990, son of John Francis and Nettie R. Fenwick Butler.

CARROLL, Allen Edward, b. Oct 22, 1946, d. Mar 22, 1989, hus of Betty J. Hayden, son of Bernard and Edna Ridgell Carroll.

CULLISON, Helen Elizabeth, b. Jun 26, 1945, d. Apr 6, 1993 DC, m. 16 Apr 1966 George Herman Angle, dau of Leo Vincent and Madeline Ridgell Cullison.

HALL, Webster William, b. May 20, 1904, d. Dec 8, 1992, m. 23 Apr 1924 Mary Frances Hawkins, son of John and Bertha Jackson Hall.

KNOTT, Francis J. "Stix", b. Nov 7, 1927, d. Apr 7, 1991, hus of Goldia C. Sexton, son of James I. and Bertha Bohannon Knott.

KNOTT, James Ignatius, Jr. USA WW II, b. Sep 24, 1925, d. Sep 22, 1991, hus of Juliana Mayor, son of James I. and Bertha Marie Bohannon Knott.

LEWIS, William Edward, USN, b. Jul 6, 1920 NY, d. Feb 11, 1991, hus of Justina Angerame, son of William Henry and Phoebe Parezo Lewis.

LUKAC, Pauline, b. Oct 12, 1903, d. May 22, 1993, wife of Paul Sivak, dau of John and Juliana Lukac.

OLIVER, John Wilmer "Bob", b. Mar 13, 1914, d. Nov 3, 1993, m. 16 Nov 1938 Oceanta Rachel Bayless, son of John and Daisy Ellis Oliver.

POPE, Lisa Suzanne, b. May 3, 1968, d. Aug 7, 1988, wife of Kenneth Joseph Knott, dau of Edward and Grace Zidek Pope.

RALEY, Maude Alberta, b. Feb 22, 1909, d. Dec 28, 1990, wife of Charles Francis Purcell, dau of Joseph A. and Anna Florence Guy Raley.

ROLLINS, Robert Shane, b. Oct 16, 1966, d. Oct 15, 1989, son of Robert Michael and Beatrice L. Angle Rollins.

SEXTON, Goldia C., b. May 18, 1932 VA, d. Jun 7, 1991, wife of Francis J. "Stix" Knott, dau of Samuel Patton and Nancy M. Sluss Sexton.

SHADE, William A., Sr. b.(was a ggfather), d. Sep 23, 1989, hus of Mary Rebecca __, son of William and Lillian Thomas Shade.

SIVAK, Charles David, b. Dec 5, 1954, d. Jun 9, 1990, hus of Sharon Ann Langley, son of John and Mary Trossbach Sivak.

SIVAK, Paul, d. May 22, 1976, hus of Pauline Lukac.

TARLETON, Brian Joseph, Jr. b. Dec 13, 1990, d. Feb 1, 1991, son of Brian J. and Marie Taylor Tarleton.

ST. JOHN FRANCIS REGIS CATHOLIC CEMETERY
St. John's Road at Rt. 235
Hollywood, Md.

In 1690 the Church was established and was dedicated to a 16th century French Jesuit priest, St. John Regis. The first church was built near a natural spring along Three Notched Road about one mile south of present Hollywood. The second church, built in 1780, was about 100 yards west of the original church. The present church, located on the corner of St. John's Road and Rt. 235 (formerly Hickory Hill and Three Notched Roads) was built in 1898.

In 1980, tombstone inscriptions were copied in one section of this cemetery by schoolchildren as a Bicentennial Project.

___, "Uncle Ben", at Poor House, abt 110 yrs, bur May 19, 1870.
___, Dallas, at Poor House, 25, bur May 26, 1870.
ABELL, Agatha, b. 1914, d. 1964, 1st wife of Joseph 'Raymond' Adams.
ABELL, Ann, dau of Geo. and Eva Abell. No dates.
ABELL, Beatrice, b. 1874, d. 1954, wife of ___ Courtney.
ABELL, Beatrice Catherine "Bea", b. Oct 29, 1903, d. Sep 19, 1991, wife of Thomas Benjamin Combs, dau of George Franklin and Alice Victoria Hammett Abell.
ABELL, Bennet, b. Jan 7, 1793, d. Oct 9, 1828, in his 36th year.
ABELL, Claude Leo, b. Jul 20, 1903, d. Mar 3, 1988, hus of Catherine Marie ___, son of John Lewis, Sr. and Jane Loretta Abell.
ABELL, Elizabeth, b. Mar 20, 1939, d. May 31, 1972, wife of ___ Wathen.
ABELL, Emma, b. Sep 27, 1884, d. Dec 5, 1964, wife of G. Harry Bowles.
ABELL, French M., b. Nov 3, 1846, d. Sep 5, 1922, hus of Hannah G. ___, b. Jan 30, 1852, d. Oct 27, 1921.
ABELL, George F., b. 1865, d. 1943, hus of

Alice Victoria Hammett.
ABELL, G. Claude, b. Jul 4, 1874, d. Mar 22, 1928.
ABELL, Grace Elizabeth, b. Feb 23, 1910, d. Jan 29, 1988, wife of J. Testa Johnson, dau of John and Henerietta Abell.
ABELL, Hannah, b. Aug 11, 1870, d. Jan 24, 1954, wife of John L. Brown.
ABELL, J. Benedict, b. Feb 4, 1910, d. Sep 20, 1969, hus of Mary M. __.
ABELL, James Dawkins, b. Aug 13, 1947, d. May 31, 1967.
ABELL, James Vernon, b. 1960, d. 1964.
  Side by Side
-ABELL, John of Theo, d. Jul 26, 1851, aged 74 years.
-ABELL, Alexander, d. Jul 26, 1851, aged 38 years.
ABELL, John Combs, b. May 5, 1868, d. Jun 28, 1933, hus of H. Jane Joy.
  Double Stone
-ABELL, John L., b. 1872, d. 1949.
-ABELL, Janie L., b. 1879, d. 1962.
ABELL, John Vivian, b. Mar 27, 1900, d. Jul 15, 1933, 1st hus of E. Gwinnette Russell.
ABELL, Joseph Alvin, b. Dec 8, 1908, d. Dec 1, 1972.
ABELL, Joseph Andrew, b. 1889, d. 1980, hus of Mabel L. __, b. Dec 23, 1886, d. Mar 26, 1979.
  Double Stone
-ABELL, Joseph F., b. 1855, d. 1936.
-ABELL, Mary Emma, b. 1856, d. 1937.
ABELL, Joseph Horace, b. Jun 18, 1916, d. Mar 18, 1960.
ABELL, Leila, b. Mar 20, 1921, d. Apr 20, 1966, wife of __ Hanobeck.
ABELL, Leila C., b. Jun 10, 1881, d. Aug 7, 1969.
ABELL, Louis Spencer, b. Feb 15, 1895, d. Jul 9, 1969, hus of Lillian M. Long.
ABELL, Martha Ann, d. Dec 26, 1840, aged 18 years.
  One Stone, part missing
-ABELL, Martha Ann, d. Dec 26, 1810.

St. John Francis Regis

-ABELL, Ann, dau of Thos. and Ann Abell.
ABELL, Mary A., b. Sep 22, 1781, d. Dec 1, 1854.
ABELL, Mary Henrietta, d. Sep 11, 1813, aged 23 years.
ABELL, Mary 'Lillian', b. Jul 15, 1885, d. Feb 3, 1970, wife of Benjamin Clarence Johnson.
ABELL, Regina, b. 1915, d. 1970, wife of __ Thompson.
ABELL, Richard Thomas, b. Nov 27, 1927, d. Aug 6, 1990, son of William Joseph and Jane Rose Anna Norris Abell.
ABELL, Robert A., d. Jan 25, 1813, in his 17th year, son of Geo. and Harriett Abell.
    Side by Side
-ABELL, Robert A., b. Jun 6, 1818, d. Apr 24, 1898.
-___, Elizabeth Serera, (rest of headstone missing), footstone E.S.A.
ABELL, Robert A., b. May 29, 1861, d. Jan 22, 1944.
ABELL, Robert W., b. 1912, d. 1961.
ABELL, Susan P., infant dau of J. B. and S. R. Abell.
ABELL, Susan R., b. Jan 18, 1866, d. Feb 2, 1935.
ABELL, Susan Rebecca, b. Mar 6, 1832, d. Dec 25, 1857, aged 25 years 7 mo and 19 days, wife of John B. Abell.
ABELL, Timothy Wayne, Sr. b. Jun 29, 1968, d. Dec 21, 1993 Balto, m. 24 Dec 1991 Jeannette Marie Quade, dau of James Thomas Abell, Sr. and Helen Elizabeth Goodwin Abell Lawson.
ABELL, W. W., b. Jul 4, 1861, d. Jan 1, 1933.
ABELL, William H., b. May 29, 1846, d. Jul 14, 1853, aged 7 years 1 mo and 14 days.
ABELL, William W., b. Jul 20, 1904, d. Jul 10, 1927.
ADAMS, Edith, b. Dec 5, 1915, d. Nov 10, 1973, wife of __ Snider.
ADAMS, G. Thomas, b. 1919, d. 1980.
    Double Stone
-ADAMS, Howard B., b. 1886, d. 1966.
-ADAMS, Minnie C., b. 1883, d. 1961.

ADAMS, Jonathan Dale, b. Apr 29, 1958, d. Jul 6, 1989 DC, son of Robert S. and Rose E. Adams. Mem. Serv.
ADAMS, Joseph 'Raymond', Sr. b. 1909, d. Feb 20, 1976, m. (1st) Agatha Abell, (2d) Mildred Johnson Stone.
ADAMS, Miss Katie, 17, bur Feb 17, 1870.
ADAMS, Robert Smith, b. 1920, d. 1978.
ALVEY, Elizabeth A., b. Aug 13, 1872, d. Apr 30, 1943.
     Double Stone
-ALVEY, Joseph M., b. 1901, d. 1966.
-ALVEY, Louise E., b. 1904, d. 1970.
ALVEY, Richard T., b. Oct 24, 1894, d. May 29, 1917.
ALVEY, William A., b. Sep 5, 1866, d. Oct 10, 1930.
ANGEVINE, George Edward, b. Nov 1, 1907, d. Mar 14, 1969, hus of Mary Ellen Thompson.
ANGEVINE, George Edward, b. Sep 8, 1941, d. Jun 8, 1974.
ANTHONY, James, b. 1951, d. 1979.
ARMSWORTHY, Louise J., b. May 21, 1866, d. May 26, 1926.
AUD, G. Gregory, b. Mar 22, 1908, d. Jan 3, 1973, hus of Catherine Goddard.
BANKINS, Blanche, b. 1875, d. 1963, wife of John Whalen Fenwick.
BANKINS, James L., b. Nov 4, 1890, d. Feb 11, 1970.
BARBER, J. Bernard, b. 1909, d. 1971, hus of A. Ruth Somerville.
BARBER, James Walter, Jr., b. Mar 4, 1923, d. May 13, 1993, son of James and Harriet Dyson Barber.
BARNES, James Thomas, b. 1905, d. 1973.
BARNES, Joseph Andrew, b. 1913, d. 1974.
BARNES, Mary Catherine, b. 1889, d. 1969.
BARRETO, Margaret L., b. Feb 26, 1885, d. Dec 12, 1969.
BASSFORD, Catherine Jean, b. 1963, d. 1964.
BASSFORD, James Manning, b. Nov 20, 1925, d. Feb 7, 1956.
BASSFORD, Joseph Elmer, b. Mar 24, 1919, d. Sep 18, 1958.

St. John Francis Regis

BASSFORD, Lemial Thomas, b. Nov 28, 1921, d. Nov 24, 1971.
BASSFORD, Philip Donald, b. 1935, d. 1960.
BASSFORD, William Francis, b. 1886, d. 1963, hus of Anna Ruth Norris.
BAXTER, William Ashley, b. Apr 17, 1916, d. Apr 24, 1975, hus of Lillian Gorham.
BEAN, Joseph O., b. 1911, d. 1964.
BEAN, Margaret V., b. 1895, d. 1972.
BEANDER, Francis, b. 1929, d. 1979.
BEANDER, Mary M., b. Dec 25, 1889, d. Feb 22, 1976.
BELL, Margaret A., b. Sep 13, 1836, d. Mar 30, 1856.
BELLINI, Emerick, d. Jul 9, 1963.
BERTRAND, William James, b. May 10, 1923, d. Jul 31, 1971, hus of Louise Simmons.
BLACKISTON, Mary Alberta, b. Oct 31, 1905, d. Aug 25, 1967.
BOWLES, Dominic S., b. Nov 6, 1841, d. Jan 10, 1921.
BOWLES, Francis Oswald, b. 1904, d. 1980.
BOWLES, James Enoch, b. Dec 17, 1900, d. Oct 10, 1966.
BOWLES, Joseph Francis, b. Dec 3, 1846, d. Feb 14, 1928, hus of Mary S. Tippett.
BOWLES, Mary Alice, b. 1860, d. 1942.
BOWLES, Thomas Richard, b. Feb 28, 1937, d. Apr 25, 1971.
BOWLES, William I., b. Feb 25, 1907, d. Oct 11, 1978, (2d) hus of Mary Louise Wood.
BOWLES, William W., b. Jul 20, 1873, d. May 27, 1958, hus of Ellen J. Hayden.
BRADBURN, Thomas Webster, b. 1906, d. Feb 12, 1970, m. 1931 Bertha Mae Ridgell.
BRADBURN, Thomas Webster, Jr. b. Aug 19, 1942, d. Apr 24, 1988, hus of Donna Marie __, son of Thomas W. and Bertha Bradburn.
BRAWLEY, Frances W., b. 1927, d. 1955.
BREWER, George V., b. Jan 1, 1858, d. Mar 23, 1928.
BRICK, Imogene 'Jeanne', b. Oct 9, 1909 MN, d. Nov 4, 1993, m. 31 Oct 1939 Balto, John W. Garner, dau of Thomas Benedict and Elizabeth Harty Brick.

BROOKS, Joseph Patrick, d. Aug 8, 1973.
BROWN, James Richley, b. 1928, d. 1974.
BROWN, John Lewis, b. Apr 1, 1872, d. Jul 16, 1952, hus of Hannah Abell.
BROWN, Thomas Aubrey. No dates.
BRUMBAUGH, Susan Stake, b. 1881, d. 1955, wife of Maurice Chapman Thompson.
BURCH, Cora Columbia, b. Oct 19, 1912, d. Nov 3, 1988, wife of Joseph Johnson Morgan, dau of Joseph E. and Betty Elizabeth Knott Burch.
BURCH, Ruth Delma, b. 1919, d. 1954.
BURKE, Mary E., b. Dec 5, 1831, d. Dec 1, 1854.
BURROUGHS, Blanche, b. Mar 16, 1893, d. Feb 22, 1925, wife of James A. Burroughs.
BURROUGHS, Everett B., b. 1897, d. 1975.
BURROUGHS, Georgianna M., b. 1833, d. 1926, wife of J. F. Marion Burroughs.
BURROUGHS, Helen M., b. Jan 27, 1905, d. Jan 7, 1911, dau of L. W. and W. A. Burroughs.
BURROUGHS, James Howard, b. 1923, d. 1979.
BURROUGHS, James W., b. 1895, d. 1979.
BURROUGHS, John R., b. Mar 13, 1925, d. Jun 28, 1972.
BURROUGHS, John Richard "Junior", b. Mar 14, 1947, d. Nov 29, 1992, m. 4 Oct 1968 Linda Ellen Marshall, son of late John Richard Burroughs and Bessie Elizabeth Russell Twilley.
BURROUGHS, Joseph McQuillian, b. Aug 16, 1897, d. Apr 5, 1921, son of William A. Burroughs.
BURROUGHS, William A., b. Oct 5, 1861, d. Oct 23, 1952, hus of Lettie W ___, b. Dec 12, 1861, d. Apr 3, 1925.
BURROUGHS, William Philip, b. Jan 17, 1966, d. Jun 2, 1973.
BUTLER, James. No dates.
BUTLER, James C., b. 1915, d. 1975.
BUTLER, James Joseph, b. Nov 21, 1925 NJ, d. Dec 10, 1992, m. 17 Jul 1948 Mary Ernell Nolan, son of late James Joseph Butler and Annie Mae Smallwood Butler Bell.
BUTLER, James R., b. Aug 12, 1944, d. May 26, 1974.
CAMERON, Bernard E., b. 1907, d. 1936.
CECIL, Alice A., b. Nov 13, 1850, d. Feb 10,

St. John Francis Regis

1929, wife of __ Russell.
CHANCE, Dorothy E., b. Jun 19, 1914, d. Dec 5, 1990, wife of Charles Alfred Jarboe, dau of Thomas Roy and Elma Chance.
CHANDLER, Henry Moody, b. Sep 8, 1921, d. Jan 25, 1960.
CLARKE, Agnes, b. 1912, d. 1966, wife of __ Swifflett.
CLARKE, Ann Hope, b. Jul 31, 1929, d. Aug 7, 1991, wife of Joseph B. Abell, dau of George Willard, Sr. and Julia Christine Newton Clarke.
CLARKE, Charles K., b. Jan 25, 1878, d. Apr 15, 1947.
CLARKE, Charles M., b. Apr 6, 1901, d. Jan 25, 1924.
CLARKE, Charles M., b. 1957, d. 1960.
CLARKE, Delia A., b. Aug 29, 1876, d. Oct 23, 1944.
CLARKE, Francis B. No dates.
CLARKE, Hattie S., b. Oct 20, 1886, d. Jan 4, 1980.
CLARKE, Henrietta, b. 1909, d. 1936, wife of __ Martin.
CLARKE, J. George, b. Mar 1, 1895, d. Jul 28, 1979, hus of Helen __, b. Feb 2, 1905, d. Jan 13, 1977.
CLARKE, James Clarence, b. 1886, d. 1963.
CLARKE, John 'Ralph', Sr. d. Jul 11, 1987, hus of Shirley A. Hutcheson, son of Joseph Aubrey and Agnes Copsey Clarke.
CLARKE, Joseph A., b. Jul 18, 1903, d. Jan 25, 1945.
CLARKE, Louise, b. Mar 28, 1920, d. Apr 15, 1970, wife of Joseph N. Jarboe.
CLARKE, Mary, b. May 29, 1801, d. Dec 26, 1862 or 1867, consort of Philip Clarke.
CLARKE, Mary Olive, b. 1894, d. 1965, wife of Joseph Clarence Clarke.
CLARKE, Mary Thelma, b. Apr 1, 1918, d. Sep 9, 1993, m. 28 Dec 1940 Francis Marcellus Abell, dau of Philip Paul and Mary Helen Norris Clarke.
CLARKE, Philip Paul, b. Jul 31, 1893, d. Mar 11, 1991, hus of Mary Helen Norris, son of

Thomas Ignatius and Dora Dawkins Clarke.
CLARKE, R. King, b. Aug 4, 1832, d. May 4, 1908, hus of Ellen R. __, b. 1840, d. 1926.
CLARKE, Richard A., b. Oct 10, 1874, d. Jun 8, 1977.
CLARKE, Richard A., b. 1907, d. 1961.
CLARKE, Robert W., b. 1969, d. 1977.
CLARKE, Thomas Ignatius, b. 1865, d. 1945, hus of Dora Dawkins.
CLARKE, William E., b. 1895, d. 1963, hus of Louise Hayden.
CLEMENTS, James Finnie, b. Aug 19, 1890, d. Dec 17, 1970, hus of Ethel Newton.
CLEMENTS, Ronald W., b. Nov 30, 1958, d. Apr 13, 1964.
CLYBURN, Monica C., b. 1964, d. 1969.
COLLISON, Julia A., b. 1888, d. 1979.
COMBS, Charles A., b. Feb 7, 1866, d. Mar 3, 1891, son of W. F. and Sarah A. Combs.
COMBS, George E., b. 1863, d. 1940, hus of Lucy L. __, b. 1879, d. 1967.
COMBS, Mrs. Rebecca, 45, bur Jan 10, 1870.
COMBS, Sarah A., b. Nov 29, 1828, d. Jun 4, 1898, wife of William F. Combs.
COMBS, William, 60, bur Mar 30, 1872.
COOK, Mary Veronica, b. 1883, d. 1963, wife of Joseph I. Habig.
COPSEY, Peggy, b. Jan 12, 1945, d. May 15, 1970, wife of __ Alvey.
COX, Archie Joseph, b. Jan 28, 1923 DC, d. Jan 12, 1992, hus of Blanche E. Henrickson, son of Archie Samuel and Lottie Nalley Cox.
CUNNINGHAM, Harold Benson, b. Jul 29, 1911 MA, d. Jan 16, 1990, hus of Juliette F. __, son of Harold B. and Nellie Fitzgerald Cunningham.
CURTIS, Mary Ella, b. 1918, d. 1966.
CURTIS, Paul F., b. 1944, d. 1974.
CUSIC, Cecelia, 74, d. Jun 5, 1988, wife of George Leonard Van Wert.
CUSIC, James Aubrey, b. 1915, d. 1974, hus of Rose 'Bernette' Mattingly.
CUSIC, James Carroll, b. Jul 25, 1943, d. Apr 25, 1956.
CUSIC, Joseph E., b. Oct 2, 1935, d. Jan 12,

1980, hus of Julia M. ___.
CUSIC, Joseph Ronald, b. Feb 17, 1946, d. Apr 9, 1988, son of James Carroll and Gertrude B. Cusic.
CUSIC, Robert Allan, b. Mar 3, 1956, d. Jul 9, 1972.
CUSIC, Tammy Sue, b. Mar 1, 1971, d. Sep 20, 1971.
CUSICK, Hurley, b. Dec 27, 1876, d. Dec 12, 1950.
CUSICK, Laura, b. Mar 10, 1879, d. Jan 4, 1951.
CUSICK, Lawrence Michael, b. Jul 22, 1913, d. Apr 14, 1972.
DAVID, Karoly, b. May 10, 1913 Hungary, d. Oct 14, 1993, hus of Maria Horvath, son of David Imre and Zanyik Erzsebet.
DAVIS, Agnes Leola, b. Jan 20, 1917, d. Jun 6, 1973, 1st wife of William Aloysius Raley, dau of Louis Daniel and Frances Ruth Newton Davis.
DAVIS, Charles Daniel "Buck", Sr. b. Feb 2, 1922, d. Dec 20, 1992, m. 15 Jan 1946 Frances Catherine Raley, son of Louis Daniel and Frances Ruth Newton Davis.
DAVIS, Franklin Melvin, b. Jun 21, 1919, d. Apr 10, 1987, son of John William and Annie Mae Davis.
DAVIS, John W., b. Feb 21, 1921, d. Apr 19, 1964.
DAVIS, Nancy, b. May 20, 1950, d. Jan 22, 1970, wife of C. William Knott.
DAVIS, Thomas Joseph, b. Jan 5, 1923, d. May 28, 1970.
DAWKINS, Dora, b. 1859, d. 1943, wife of Thomas Ignatius Clarke.
DEAN, Catherine R., d. Dec 13, 1972, wife of John Philip Russell.
DEAN, John Philip, b. Sep 1, 1923, d. Apr 7, 1990, hus of Mary Catherine ___, son of Albert Levi and Annie Mary Dean.
DENNIS, Michael Robert, b. Jun 5, 1968, d. Aug 28, 1988, son of Vernon R. and Geraldine Clorise Buckler Dennis.
DILLOW, Charles Richards, b. 1925, d. 1926.
DILLOW, Joseph A., b. 1900, d. 1978, hus of

Roberta G.___, b. 1900, d. 1972.
DILLOW, Robert E., b. Mar 5, 1932, d. Nov 8, 1955.
DIXON, Ellen Rebecca, 101, b. Jul 24, 1890, d. Sep 21, 1991, wife of Joseph N. Colton, dau of Daniel T. and Sarah Floyd Payne Dixon.
DODSON, Herbert J., b. 1935, d. 1974.
DORSEY, Mrs., 40, bur May 12, 1870.
DORSEY, Annie M., b. 1892, d. 1980.
DORSEY, John I., b. Dec 13, 1885, d. Nov 25, 1964.
DORSEY, Mary, 36, and infant, bur Jun 16, 1890.
DOWNS, Johnson A., b. May 12, 1909, d. Dec 16, 1953.
DOWNS, Mrs. Robert, bur Nov 5, 1888.
DRURY, Susan Rebecca, b. 1861, d. 1942, wife of ___ Buckler.
DRURY, Sarah Marthalina, 72, b. 1799, bur Jun 30, 1872, wife of John Johnson, dau of Michael Drury.
DRURY, Wilson L., 42, bur Dec 21, 1899.
DUGAN, Michael Hugh, b. Oct 20, 1923 WV, d. May 31, 1993, m. 26 Dec 1945 WV Shirley Ann Wren, son of Michael and Mahala Henderson Dugan.
DUPONT, George Thomas, b. Feb 19, 1913, d. Oct 23, 1990, hus of Geneva Samples, son of Moses and Valida Robidas Dupont.
EDWARDS, Benedict, d. Jun 19, 1971.
ENNELS, John Daniel, b. 1902, d. 1968.
ERVIN, Edward Sterling "Chuck", Jr. b. Feb 22, 1961, d. Feb 27, 1991, son of Edw. S. and Ellen Webster Mattingly Ervin.
ESTEP, James, d. Jul 12, 1973.
ETHERTON, Donna Marie, b. Mar 23, 1958 Balto, d. Jun 12, 1992, wife of ___ Dubreuil, dau of Albert and Doris Etherton. Mem. Serv.
EVANS, George A., b. Nov 8, 1910, d. Mar 2, 1977.
EVANS, George W., b. Mar 27, 1874, d. Jul 1, 1946, hus of Mary Agnes ___, b. May 5, 1873, d. Sep 9, 1942.
EVANS, Joseph Webster, 85, d. Jul 6, 1987, hus of Mary Madeline Russell.
EVANS, Mary Evelyn, b. Jan 17, 1934, d. Dec 30, 1992 Balto, wife of Elmo Jackson Hicks,

St. John Francis Regis

dau of Joseph Webster and Mary Madeline Russell Evans.
FABRIZIO, Karen Ann, d. 1974, dau of Mary E. Fabrizio.
FABRIZIO, Mary Evelyn, b. May 17, 1939, d. Nov 21, 1974.
FELLENCHER, Marie D., b. 1889, d. 1980.
   Side by Side
-FENWICK, Ellen Rebecca, b. Sep 19, 1821, d. Dec 11, 1898, wife of John F. Fenwick.
-FENWICK, Felix, b. Sep 8, 1819, d. Dec 1, 1886.
-FENWICK, Charlie Rose, b. Sep 18, 1863, d. Jul 21, 1864, dau of John F. and Ellen R. Fenwick.
-FENWICK, Mary M., consort of J. F. Fenwick (rest of stone missing).
FENWICK, John Francis, d. Feb 13, 1979.
FENWICK, John Whalen, b. 1870, d. 1963, hus of Blanche Bankins.
FENWICK, Nannie, b. 1921, d. 1979.
FENWICK, Sylvester Neal, b. Mar 21, 1889, d. Jul 9, 1972.
FERGUSON, Bernard X., b. 1898, d. 1954, hus of Essie M. __, b. 1896, d. 1970.
FERGUSON, Bernard X., b. Jul 26, 1923, d. Apr 7, 1966.
FERGUSON, R. Ditman, b. 1889, d. 1949, hus of Myrtle Newton.
FERGUSON, R. Luke, b. 1926, d. 1963, hus of A. Mildred __.
FERRALL, Cecelia S., b. Nov 1, 1924, d. May 14, 1974, wife of T. Newton Ferrall.
FINCH, Harry Chandler, Sr. b. Jul 26, 1925 AL, d. Mar 25, 1993, hus of Helen Marian __, son of George and Lonnie Knighton Finch.
FLOYD, James R., b. Aug 9, 1797, d. Dec 8, 1851.
FLOYD, Mary Ellen, b. Oct 18, 1823, d. Aug 12, 1882.
FLOYD, Mary L., Mother, b. Jun 30, 1884, d. Jun 30, 1912, her children: John C., Bessie A., Richley.
FLOYD, William, b. Oct 4, 1783, d. Jan 23, 1868, hus of Ellen __, b. Mar 3, 1794, d.

May 3, 1854.
FLOYD, William G., b. Oct 9, 1820, d. May 17, 1860.
FORD, Jason E., b. 1918, d. 1978.
FREEMAN, Alice Elizabeth, b. Apr 11, 1908 DC, d. Nov 13, 1991, wife of Joseph Elmer Young, dau of John and Susie Freeman.
GARNER, Cecelia, b. Jan 25, 1906, d. Jun 15, 1965, wife of ___ Saunders.
GARNER, Anne Elizabeth b. Jul 18, 1920, d. Nov 15, 1952, wife of William Lemuel Russell.
GARNER, Edward Andrew, b. 1910, d. 1972, hus of Jane Thompson.
GARNER, Edward Andrew, Jr. b. 1939, d. 1958.
GARNER, Francis Louis, Sr. b. Jun 4, 1912, d. Nov 17, 1961, hus of Ethel Regina Woodburn.
GARNER, John W., b. Jan 8, 1902, d. Aug 10, 1962, hus of Imogene Brick.
GARNER, Louis D., b. Dec 16, 1875, d. Oct 28, 1941, hus of Elizabeth H. ___, b. Nov 20, 1882, d. Nov 14, 1952.
GARNER, Martha S., b. 1892, d. 1974.
GARNER, Robert I., b. Mar 17, 1916, d. Sep 14, 1966.
GATTON, Benjamin Webster, b. Jul 1, 1886, d. Jul 21, 1962.
GATTON, Danna Michelle, b. Sep 22, 1964, d. Jan 19, 1980.
GATTON, James Hayden, b. Jul 20, 1903, d. Oct 24, 1989, hus of Elsie Marie ___, son of Joseph E. and Rebecca Gatton.
GATTON, John Phillip, b. Jul 19, 1958 DC, d. Nov 25, 1988, hus of Laura Miedzinski, son of Frank and Margaret Harris Gatton.
GATTON, Joseph Gorman "Hoss", b. Mar 23, 1914, d. Apr 6, 1991, hus of Ida Mae Chaffins, son of John and Osta Gatton.
GATTON, Marshall L., b. Apr 6, 1898, d. Mar 17, 1977.
GATTON, Rose Catherine, 12, bur Feb 19, 1870.
GAUS, Helen M., b. Jul 12, 1902, d. Jan 7, 1960.
GEORGE, Elizabeth Ann, b. and d. Jul 10, 1987, dau of Michael and Rebecca George.
GIBBS, Anna, b. Nov 9, 1898, d. Jan 2, 1979,

wife of Bernard C. Jarboe.
GODDARD, Catherine, b. Aug 13, 1913, d. Jun 10, 1970, wife of G. Gregory Aud.
GODDARD, Stephen, b. 1887, d. 1931.
GOLDSBOROUGH, Camillus Paul, b. 1879, d. 1947.
GOLDSBOROUGH, Charles Delmas, b. 1913, d. 1970, hus of Loretta H. __.
GOLDSBOROUGH, Charles M., b. Oct 15, 1874, d. Oct 22, 1935, hus of E. Gwinette Russell.
GOLDSBOROUGH, Lucille Sophia, b. Feb 6, 1900, d. May 24, 1987, wife of John David Stone, Sr., dau of Benjamin and Adriana Norris Goldsborough.
GOODWIN, Eva M., b. Jun 24, 1895, d. Apr 28, 1968, wife of James C. Schindler.
GOUGH, Sarah E., d. Aug 20, 1976.
GRANADOS, Luis, b. Apr 11, 1904 Cuba, d. Aug 1, 1992, hus of Anne Maria Waters, son of Ramon Granados and Maria Concepcion Rey Marquez.
GRAVES, Lewis G., b. Dec 27, 1901, d. Apr 13, 1970.
GRAY, Gladys Catherine, b. Feb 21, 1921, d. Oct 3, 1988, wife of George William Tippett, dau of Isaac Daniel and Ethel Thompson Gray.
GRAY, Luke Manning, b. 1916, d. 1956.
GRAY, Matthew Ford Earl, b. May 24, 1912, d. Jul 27, 1988, m. (1st) Mary Ellen __, (2d) Bertha T. __.
GRAY, Mary Ellen, b. Sep 24, 1902, d. Aug 9, 1965.
GREENWELL, Albert Warren, b. Jan 17, 1885, d. May 7, 1957, hus of Catherine Copsey.
GREENWELL, Annie D., b. Jul 22, 1884, d. Feb 22, 1916.
GREENWELL, Elizabeth, b. Jan 15, 1792, d. Jun 27, 1859.
GREENWELL, Elizabeth, b. Jul 23, 1920, d. May 28, 1960, wife of __ Jameson.
GREENWELL, Frances Fidelis, b. Jan 8, 1903, d. Mar 27, 1990, wife of T. Joseph Burch, 3d dau of Dr. Francis Floyd and Margaret Linehan Greenwell.
GREENWELL, Henry Chester, b. 1921, d. 1955, son of Valley I. Greenwell.

GREENWELL, John of Philip, b. Aug 19, 1801, d. Nov 2, 1850.
GREENWELL, John Charles, b. Dec 15, 1907, d. May 25, 1988, son of John Joseph and Annie L. Greenwell.
GREENWELL, John Joseph, b. Dec 25, 1879, d. Mar 12, 1958, hus of Annie L. __.
GREENWELL, Joseph Frederick, b. Sep 2, 1913, d. Apr 28, 1988, hus of Kate Magee, son of John Joseph and Annie L. Greenwell.
GREENWELL, Julianna, d. Oct 28, 1835, aged 32 years.
GREENWELL, Margaret L., b. 1870, d. 1939.
GREENWELL, Marietta, b. Nov 21, 1837, d. Apr 10, 1867, m. 26 May 1859 James B. Hopper of Baltimore, Md.
GREENWELL, Martha, 21, bur Sep 7, 1872.
GREENWELL, Mary Helen, d. by 1992, wife of Joseph Archie Wood.
GREENWELL, Mrs. Sarah, 61, bur Aug 8, 1901.
GREENWELL, Sarah Marie, b. 1897, d. 1980.
GREENWELL, Thomas, d. Aug 15, 1975.
GREENWELL, Thomas, d. Nov 16, 1826, aged 38, left a mournful widow.
GREENWELL, Valley I., b. 1889, d. May 9, 1969, m. 14 Apr 1912 Blanche Elizabeth Jones.
GREENWELL, Violet Elizabeth, b. Nov 13, 1910, d. Nov 24, 1991, wife of John Walter Norris, dau of Joseph Warren and Catherine Elizabeth Copsey Greenwell.
GREENWELL, William F., d. Dec 27, 1842, aged 63 years.
GUY, J. Elmer, b. 1897, d. 1966.
GUY, Paul Daniel, b. Sep 4, 1943, d. Aug 1, 1969.
GUY, Paul L., b. 1903, d. 1973.
GUY, Rosalie, b. Feb 2, 1906, d. Aug 13, 1962, wife of __ Clarke.
HEH, no other data on stone.
HABIG, Joseph I., b. 1882, d. 1960, hus of Mary Veronica Cook.
HABIG, Mary Elizabeth, b. May 27, 1910, d. Jan 13, 1991, wife of __ Farrell, dau of Joseph I. and Mary Veronica Cook Habig.
HAMMETT, Alice Victoria, b. 1873, d. 1960,

St. John Francis Regis 213

wife of George Franklin Abell.
HARRIS, George W., b. 1907, d. 1980.
HARTER, Winfield E., b. 1904, d. 1976.
HAYDEN, Angeline, b. Oct 3, 1813, d. May 27, 1849.
HAYDEN, Annie C., b. Nov 21, 1851, d. May 7, 1914, wife of Robert E. Hayden.
HAYDEN, Charles, b. May 20, 1892, d. Mar 18, 1958.
HAYDEN, Eliza, d. Jul 13, 1884, aged 30 years.
HAYDEN, Ellen J., b. Jan 3, 1880, d. Nov 18, 1936, wife of William W. Bowles.
HAYDEN, Eva, b. Sep 4, 1889, d. Aug 12, 1972, wife of __ Curtis.
HAYDEN, Francis Roger, b. 1889, d. 1944, hus of Mary Gertrude Wells.
HAYDEN, George F., b. 1930, d. 1977.
HAYDEN, J. Thomas, b. 1900, d. 1973, hus of A. Lucille __, b. 1902, d. 1973.
HAYDEN, John E., b. Jun 16, 1842, d. Jul 26, 1858.
HAYDEN, Louise, b. 1895, d. 1936, wife of William E. Clarke.
HAYDEN, Marie L., b. Nov 19, 1884, d. Feb 12, 1975.
HAYDEN, Philomena G., b. 1901, d. 1975, wife of J. Claude Hayden.
HAYDEN, Robert C., b. Feb 9, 1848, d. Oct 20, 1920.
HAYDEN, Robert Wells "Toots", b. Mar 1, 1923, d. Apr 14, 1990, hus of Barbara Jean __, son of Francis Roger and Mary Gertrude Wells Hayden.
Side by Side
-HAYDEN, S. Mills, b. Dec 10, 1854, d. Mar 29, 1894.
-HAYDEN, Marcellus N., b. Jun 1, 1844, d. Dec 15, 1863.
-HAYDEN, Stephen, b. Nov 6, 1809, bur Dec 4, 1871, age 61 yrs.
-HAYDEN, Maria V., b. Jun 20, 1812, d. Feb 17, 1877.
HAYDEN, Stephen, 61, bur Dec 4, 1871.
HAYDEN, Thomas Alvin, b. Jan 30, 1892, d. Dec 16, 1966.

HAYDEN, Thomas Alvin, Jr. b. Aug 28, 1928, d. Aug 6, 1929.
HAYDEN, William Alvin, b. Jun 2, 1938, d. Jun 6, 1976.
HAYWARD, Laura G., b. 1873, d. 1953.
HEARD, Edmund, b. Mar 1, 1798, d. Apr 5, 1860 of heart disease, hus of Teresa __, b. Feb 10, 1793, d. Oct 23, 1856.
HEARD, Mrs. Ellen Rebecca, 25, bur Dec 15, 1869.
HEARD, Frank Ignatius, b. 1932, d. 1979.
HEARD, James Benedict, b. Mar 21, 1950, d. Feb 27, 1970.
HEARD, Mary Blanche, b. Mar 10, 1924, d. Sep 20, 1989, wife of Frank Brooks, dau of Jas. K. and Rosie C. Heard.
HEARD, Rebecca L., b. Mar 6, 1783, d. Nov 20, 1859.

Double Stone
-HEBB, A. Alexander, b. Apr 5, 1865, d. Jul 17, 1953.
-HEBB, Angelica C., b. Jun 6, 1867, d. Nov 11, 1937.

HEBB, George Alexander, b. Mar 4, 1889, d. Nov 3, 1965.
HEBB, George Benjamin, b. May 26, 1890, d. Apr 5, 1973, son of John Benjamin Hebb.
HEBB, George W., b. 1860, d. 1925.
HEBB, John B., b. 1857, d. 1940, hus of Mary Inez __, b. 1858, d. 1933.
HEBB, John W., b. 1892, d. 1949, hus of Amanda Grace __, b. 1891, d. 1957.
HEBB, William A., b. Nov 19, 1894, d. Oct 3, 1975.
HEMMING, Mary C., b. Oct 22, 1954, d. Oct 24, 1954.
HERBERT, George C., b. 1875, d. 1925, hus of Nellie __, b. 1877, d. 1949.
HERBERT, Stephen Webster, b. Sep 2, 1921, d. May 26, 1975.
HICKS, Elmo Jackson, b. May 15, 1927, d. Jun 28, 1989, hus of Mary Evelyn Evans, son of Bernie C. and Ethel B. Hicks.
HIGGS, Thomas M., b. Jan 24, 1882, d. Jun 18, 1944, hus of Florine L. __, b. Aug 8, 1881,

d. Sep 23, 1945.
HILL, Elsie, b. Apr 29, 1912, d. Apr 29, 1979, wife of M. Woodley Newton.
HILL, Emma Elizabeth, b. Apr 3, 1908, d. Dec 1, 1989, m. 20 Feb 1928 Elmer James Brown, dau of Lafayette and Mary Mattingly Hill.
HILL, Mary Lettie, b. Sep 7, 1921, d. Sep 22, 1992, wife of William Richard Stevens, dau of Charles and Sara Barber Hill.
HOLT, Albert W., b. 1931, d. 1974.
HOOPER, Mary J., d. Mar 19, 1858, aged 20 mos and 14 days.
HOPKINS, Eva M., b. 1883, d. 1962.
HOPPER, John Philip, b. Mar 13, 1860, d. Aug 7, 1861, son of James B. and Marietta Greenwell Hopper.
HOPPER, Mary Elizabeth, b. Jan 3, 1862, d. Aug 5, 1863, dau of James B. and Marietta Greenwell Hopper.
HORVATH, Maria, b. Jan 23, 1915, d. Apr 27, 1979, wife of Karoly David.
HUNTT, George, b. 1948, d. 1976.
HOWE, George Samuel, 24, bur May 18, 1890.
INSLEY, George E., b. 1871, d. 1942, hus of M. Edith __, b. 1878, d. 1962,
JACKSON, Attaway E., b. 1889, d. 1970.
JACKSON, Thomas E., d. Jun 10, 1973.
JARBOE, Bernard C., b. Aug 29, 1896, d. Jan 10, 1970, hus of Anna Gibbs.
JARBOE, Ernest T., b. 1871, d. 1948.
JARBOE, James 'Carroll', b. 1879, d. 1947, hus of Annie E. Stone.
JARBOE, Joseph Nathaniel, b. Mar 26, 1917, d. Mar 22, 1988, hus of Louise Clarke Stone, son of Carroll and Annie Stone Jarboe.
JARBOE, Sarah Alice, b. 1854, d. 1927.
JOHNSON, Alice, d. by 1992, wife of Joseph Aubrey Johnson, dau of Joseph Richley and Elizabeth Latham Johnson.
JOHNSON, Benjamin Clarence, b. Aug 6, 1879, d. Aug 23, 1965, hus of Mary Lillian Abell, son of Hillery and Ann Marie Thompson Johnson.
JOHNSON, John, 80, d. Feb 1860, hus of Sarah "Martha" Drury, son of Leonard and Mary Howard Johnson.

JOHNSON, Joseph Aubrey, b. Oct 13, 1906, d.
Jan 7, 1969, hus of Alice nee Johnson, son
of Benjamin Clarence and Lillian Abell Johnson.
JOHNSON, Joseph Hebb, b. Oct 16, 1900, d. Dec
31, 1984, hus of Margaret Payne, son of
"Rhodie" and Marie Hebb Johnson.
JOHNSON, Joseph Norman, b. Sep 17, 1927, d.
May 24, 1990, hus of Gladys L. Lacey, son of
John Norman and Queenie Mae Bowles Johnson.
JOHNSON, Lillie Magdlin, b. Aug 15, 1907, d.
Apr 27, 1992, wife of Wm. 'Abell' Johnson,
dau of Joseph Richley and Elizabeth Latham
Johnson.
JOHNSON, Marie Elizabeth, b. Nov 4, 1891 (1892
on tombstone) d. Aug 31, 1943, wife of William Elmer Raley, dau of Joseph Richley and
Elizabeth Latham Johnson.
JOHNSON, Rose Marie, b. Oct 4, 1964, d. Oct 1,
1992, wife of Harold Haynes Emory, Jr., dau
of Charles Maurice Johnson of Hollywood and
Elizabeth Virginia Holsinger Johnson Goddard
of Leonardtown.
JOHNSON, William Abell, b. Sep 4, 1907, d. Jun
6, 1985, hus of Lillie Magdlin nee Johnson,
son of Benjamin Clarence and Lillian Abell
Johnson.
JONES, Annie E., Mother, b. 1865, d. 1938.
JONES, Blanche Elizabeth, 100, b. Mar 7, 1891,
d. Jan 2, 1992, wife of Valley I. Greenwell,
dau of Samuel E. and Annie E. King Jones.
JONES, Donald Mason, b. 1955, d. 1975, son of
Frederick W. Jones.
JONES, James Alfred, d. May 20, 1978.
JONES, Jeffrey Alan, b. Nov 11, 1961, d. Apr
15, 1974, son of Frederick W. Jones.
JONES, Patricia Dale, b. Feb 20, 1957, d. __
23, 1957.
JORDAN, Essie, b. 1910, d. 1965.
JORDAN, Joseph M., b. Jul 24, 1895, d. Feb 22,
1972.
JOY, H. Jane, b. Jun 23, 1877, d. Aug 25, 1929,
wife of John Combs Abell.
KANE, Dereck Adrian, b. 1971, d. 1975.
KANE, Mary, b. Sep 14, 1903, d. Sep 7, 1978,

St. John Francis Regis

wife of John Henry Taylor.
KELLEY, James Alfred, b. Aug 28, 1928, d. Nov 18, 1989, hus of Agnes Deloris __, son of Robert Lee and Mary Benita Scriber Kelley.
KELLY, Andrew, b. 1915, d. 1977.
KELLY, Louise W., b. Apr 17, 1914, d. Nov 27, 1978.
KELLY, Robert L., b. 1905, d. 1976, hus of Mary V. __, b. 1907, d. 1976.
KING, Annie E., b. 1865, d. 1938, wife of Samuel E. Jones.
KING, James I., 101, b. Feb 10, 1817, d. May 13, 1918.
KING, Joseph Oster, b. 1872, d. 1940.
KING, Joseph Oster, b. Oct 18, 1906, d. Aug 28, 1907.
KING, Mary F., b. May 27, 1851, d. May 17, 1934.
KIRCHNER, Mary Rosina, b. Jul 31, 1909 PA, d. Aug 22, 1992, wife of John Franklin Davis, dau of John and Annie Warner Kirchner.
KIRK, James J., b. 1888, d. 1954 hus of Clara H. __, b. 1885, d. 1975.
KNIGHT, George Morgan, b. 1877, d. 1949.
KNIGHT, John W., b. 1926, d. 1952.
KNOTT, Aubrey Raymond, b. Apr 11, 1903, d. Sep 20, 1977.
KNOTT, Ernest William, b. Nov 3, 1887, d. Oct 19, 1955, hus of Amanda Sarah __, b. Oct 29, 1889, d. Oct 8, 1946.
KNOTT, India L., b. Sep 18, 1891, d. Jun 19, 1975.
KNOTT, Joseph Edward, b. May 21, 1945, d. Oct 26, 1946.
KNOTT, Julie Ann, b. Oct 21, 1951, d. Jan 28, 1957.
KNOTT, Louis Guy, b. Jul 19, 1937, d. Apr 21, 1976.
KOSEL, Anna Marie, b. Jun 23, 1906 CT, d. Apr 25, 1992, wife of Walter James Murr, dau of Joseph John and Maria Annie Wick Kosel.
KRUG, Charles Leo, b. Dec 30, 1892, d. May 15, 1967.
LACEY, Gladys L., b. Oct 9, 1928, wife of Joseph Norman Johnson, dau of Wm. Dudley and

Mary Elsie Knott Lacey.
LACEY, Mary Lucille, b. Jun 29, 1924, d. Dec 20, 1993, car accident, m. (1st) John Joseph Magill, (2d) 1989 Curtis Junior Bushell (bur Trinity Memorial Gardens, Waldorf, Md.), dau of William Dudley and Mary Elsie Knott Lacey.
LANDAU, Guy W., b. Nov 11, 1933, d. Mar 15, 1970.
LANGLEY, Mary Julia, b. 1879, d. 1964.
LANIFER, Peter, 75, bur Nov 19, 1869.
LATHAM, Benjamin C., b. Oct 9, 1894, d. Feb 25, 1974.
LATHAM, Owen. No dates.
LATHROUM, Jos. Kilgore, b. Apr 1895, d. Dec 1925.
LEE, Cherry Anna, 2 mos, bur Jun 5, 1890.
LEE, Mildred Maretta, b. Aug 28, 1900 Balto, d. Jun 20, 1993, wife of __ Pickens, dau of Anthony and Sally Christmas Lee.
LLOYD, Eileen V. "Sally", b. May 25, 1927 VA, d. Apr 22 1993 DC, m. 25 Sep 1948 Thomas Joseph Burks, Sr., dau of Wm. Bernard and Mary Patricia McCarthy Lloyd.
LOCHNER, Arthur Thomas, b. 1928, d. 1965.
LONG, Amy Gertrude, d. Feb 15, 1970, wife of James Robert Long.
LONG, John B., b. 1892, d. 1965.
LONG, Joseph O., b. 1935, d. 1951.
LONG, Lillian M., wife of Louis Spencer Abell.
MAC WILLIAMS, Grace Mae, b. Mar 21, 1902, d. Apr 9, 1972, wife of James Richard MacWilliams.
MADDOX, Elizabeth, b. May 6, 1896, d. Sep 29, 1988, wife of Seward Bacon, dau of John Joseph and Adrianna Gough Maddox.
MADDOX, James Samuel, b. Nov 28, 1941, d. Aug 1, 1969.
MADDOX, John J., Jr. b. Aug 6, 1936, d. Nov 2, 1988, hus of Barbara C.__, son of John J. and Marjorie Hill Maddox.
MAGILL, John Joseph, b. Oct 26, 1925, d. Aug 14, 1975, 1st hus of Mary Lucille Lacey.
MAGILL, Rosa Mae, b. Apr 11, 1907, d. Jun 8, 1978.

MARTIN, Charles J., b. 1863, d. 1935, hus of Mary V. __, b. 1870, d. 1935.
MARTIN, Charles Spencer, Sr. b. Aug 25, 1937, d. Jul 9, 1989, hus of Kelly __, son of Joseph Spencer and Mary Estelle Clarke Martin.
MARTIN, Thomas F., b. Apr 9, 1941, d. Aug 1, 1969.
MARTIN, William E., b. 1943, d. 1969.
MASON, William Nathaniel, b. 1900, d. 1972, hus of Mary Florence __.
MATTHEWS, James William "Zigzag", b. Nov 29, 1954 C.Z., d. Aug 3, 1992, son of Orville Dale and Jean Marie Norris Matthews.
MATTINGLY, Grace, d. Jan 8, 1976.
MATTINGLY, John Leo, b. 1878, d. 1966.
MATTINGLY, Joseph A., b. 1922, d. 1942.
MATTINGLY, Joseph Elmer, b. 1937, d. 1958.
MATTINGLY, Luke, b. 1874, d. 1950.
MATTINGLY, Luke Gorman "Dick", b. Jun 7, 1916, d. Apr 27, 1988, hus of Margaret A. Warwick, son of Luke W. and Ivy E. Greenwell Mattingly.
MATTINGLY, Rose Bernette "Nicky", b. Jan 15, 1920, d. Oct 3, 1989, wife of James Aubrey Cusic, dau of Mary B. Wallace Mattingly.
McGEE, Agnes Marie, b. Jul 29, 1935, d. May 6, 1936, dau of Stephen H. McGee.
McGEE, Charles L., d. Feb 14, 1975.
McGEE, Mary Leatha, b. Oct 15, 1909, d. Aug 29, 1988, wife of Bernard S. Norris, dau of Stephen A. and Estelle M. McGee.
McGEE, Stephen Henry, b. Jun 2, 1911, d. Sep 5, 1962, hus of Marie Hill.
McGEE, William Edward, d. Jun 13, 1956, hus of Thelma Sara Newton.
McKAY, George F., b. 1872, d. 1955, hus of Mary Blanche __, b. 1882, d. 1955.
McKAY, Joseph Norman, b. Aug 26, 1904, d. May 21, 1988, hus of Mary Helen Stone, son of Lee and Mamie Raley McKay.
McTHOMPSON, Tommy T., b. Sep 6, 1930, d. Feb 6, 1978.
MIEDZINSKI, Doris C., b. Apr 1, 1935, d. Jul 19, 1979, wife of __ Johnson, dau of Edward and Mary I. Miedzinski.

MIEDZINSKI, Francis X., b. 1940, d. 1959.
MIEDZINSKI, Joseph, b. 1935, d. 1951.
MIEDZINSKI, Philip Herbert, b. Oct 17, 1943, d. Jun 22, 1960.
MIEDZINSKI, Thomas, b. Mar 13, 1924, d. Jan 8, 1989, hus of Mary Margaret __, b. 1926, d. 1966, son of Wm. Vincent and Frances M. Miedzinski.
MIEDZINSKI, Wm. Vincent, b. 1869, d. 1970, hus of Frances Mary __, b. 1882, d. 1953.
MILES, Frederick, b. 1932, d. 1975.
MILES, James Perry, b. 1948, d. 1970, son of John and Edna May Miles.
MILES, Joseph Henry, b. 1898, d. 1971.
MILES, Madeline, b. Apr 5, 1906, d. Jun 9, 1973.

One Stone
-MILLS, John J., b. Sep 18, 1806, d. Feb 18, 1850.
-MILLS, Catherine, b. Aug 28, 1799, d. Mar 16, 1826.

MILLS, Elizabeth C., d. Apr 10, 1852, aged 27 years 6 mos and 20 days.
MILLS, William, d. Oct 20, 1852, aged 74 yrs 4 mos and 5 days.
MORAN, Ollie W., b. Jun 28, 1895, d. Apr 19, 1973, hus of Lillian A. __.
MORGAN, Benjamin, b. 1910, d. 1965.
MORGAN, Charles Henry, 76, d. Apr 7, 1988, son of Stephen and Thurrella Burch Morgan.
MORGAN, Joseph Johnson, b. Jan 2, 1910, d. Dec 12, 1972, hus of Cora Columbia Burch.
MORGAN, Lucille, b. 1925, d. 1974.
MORGAN, Mary Edith, b. Dec 15, 1873, d. Feb 9, 1958, wife of Dr. Leonard B. Johnson.
(Memorial Stone, she is bur St. Joseph RCC.)
MORRIS, Francis Wayne, b. 1959, d. 1961.
MOSHER, Stanley E., b. Jan 3, 1915, d. Sep 12, 1993, hus of Mary Pilkerton, son of Paul and Lida Mosher.
MUGG, James Shepherd, b. 1905, d. 1976.
MURPHY, Harry C., b. 1908, d. 1946.
MURPHY, Kay Cecelia, b. Jan 14, 1966, d. Jan 15, 1966.
NEWTON, Ann Elizabeth, b. 1923, d. 1952.

St. John Francis Regis

NEWTON, Ethel, b. Aug 20, 1891, d. Apr 3, 1971, wife of James Finnie Clements.
NEWTON, Louise H., b. Oct 13, 1900, d. May 4, 1979.
NEWTON, M. Woodley, b. 1903, d. 1974, hus of Elsie Hill.
NEWTON, Myrtle, b. 1898, d. 1979, wife of R. Ditman Ferguson.
NEWTON, T. Parren, b. 1910, d. 1967, hus of Lorraine P. __.
NEWTON, Thelma Sara, b. Jul 10, 1910, d. Apr 6, 1992, wife of William Edward McGee, dau of James Edward and Ruth Estelle Goldsborough Newton.
NEWTON, Theodore, b. 1912, d. 1974.
NEWTON, William Lee, b. Feb 6, 1893, d. Oct 22, 1965.
NICHOLSON, Frances E., b. Jun 19, 1918, d. Nov 24, 1974, wife of Vincent Nicholson.
NOLAN, William F., b. Nov 16, 1904, d. Oct 10, 1967.
NORRIS, baby girl. No dates.
NORRIS, Anna Ruth, b. Nov 30, 1898, d. Jul 12, 1989, wife of William Francis Bassford, dau of Jim and Ella Norris.
NORRIS, Edith, b. May 27, 1901, d. Dec 3, 1922, wife of Robert L. Bennett.
NORRIS, Grace Ann, b. Oct 1, 1970, d. Feb 11, 1972.
NORRIS, J. Elbert, b. Mar 20, 1906, d. May 25, 1972, hus of Violet H. __.
NORRIS, Jane Rosa Anna, b. Sep 30, 1890, d. Jan 8, 1979, wife of William Joseph Abell.
NORRIS, John "Snake", b. Jan 4, 1935, d. Oct 19, 1988, hus of Betty Lou Smith, son of Carroll and Edith Heard Norris.
NORRIS, John E., d. Mar 8, 1802 in his ?5 yr.
NORRIS, John F., b. Aug 15, 1893, d. Oct 14, 1918.
NORRIS, John F.A., b. 1863, d. 1942.
NORRIS, John Walter, Jr., b. Sep 20, 1958, d. Jun 10, 1980, son of John W. and Violet Elizabeth Greenwell Norris.
NORRIS, Lucy Ada, b. 1866, d. 1964.
NORRIS, Manning Joseph, b. 1957, d. 1976, son

of Robert and Gertrude Clarke Norris.
NORRIS, Mary Helen, b. Jul 13, 1895, d. Aug 25, 1979, m. 1917 Philip Paul Clarke.
NORRIS, Mildred Agnes, b. Nov 8, 1899, d. Mar 3, 1917.
NORRIS, Norman A., b. Aug 26, 1902, d. Dec 22, 1972.
NORRIS, Robert W., b. 1864, d. 1930.
NORRIS, Susan Marie, b. 1959, d. 1979.
NORRIS, William Bernard "Jim", USA WW 11, b. Jul 13, 1927, d. Jul 28, 1991, hus of Doreen Anne Miles, son of Bernard StC. and Mary Letha Norris.
NORRIS, William Richley, b. 1898, d. 1964.
OBERAITIS, Simon S., d. 1929.
PARENT, Raymond A., b. Jan 27, 1935, d. May 22, 1972.
PAYNE, Cornelius, d. Oct 9, 1877, aged 58 yrs.
PAYNE, Margaret E., b. Oct 30, 1912, wife of Joseph 'Hebb' Johnson, dau of Oswald Eugene and Mary Lillian Evans Payne.
PAYNE, Mary A., d. Sep 25, 1856, aged 6 years 6 mos and 10 das.
PEACOCK, John S., 56, d. May 15, 1860 of lung inflamation, hus of Anne __, d. Feb 11, 1882, aged 71 years 9 mos and 16 days.
PEAK, Ignatius, d. May 27, 1844, aged 69 yrs.
PERRY, Richard Neal "Rick", b. Dec 4, 1937 MI, d. May 15, 1993 VA, m. 4 Jun 1962 CA, Linda Lou Baumgartner, son of Richard Lloyd and Loretta V. Ayotte Perry.
PETER, Will E., no dates.
PILKERTON, Christopher Alan, b. Apr 23, 1967, d. May 29, 1967.
PILKERTON, Helen Patricia, b. May 24, 1945, d. Apr 16, 1967.
PILKERTON, Joseph S., b. 1916, d. 1973.
PILKERTON, Mary Alberta, b. 1873, d. 1945.
PLATER, Joseph Wilson, b. Dec 31, 1932, d. Jan 10, 1971.
PLOWDEN, Charles Herman, d. 1968.
PLOWDEN, Elizabeth, b. 1919, d. 1968.
PORTER, Agnes Marie, b. 1897, d. 1969.
QUADE, Richard Claude, Jr. b. Jan 1, 1929, d. Mar 26, 1993, m. 1981 Margaret Cecelia Hall,

son of Clarence Richard and Alice Russell Quade.
QUADE, Thomas Edward, b. 1910, d. 1970.
RAILEY, M. Virginia, Mother, b. Apr 1, 1879, d. Apr 30, 1933, wife of Benjamin M. Garner.
RALEY, Agnes Leola "Sue", b. Mar 1, 1944, d. Oct 27, 1992, m. (1st) 16 Aug 1966 Charles J. Mattingly, (2d) 18 Jul 1976 Dennis Maher, dau of William Aloysius and Agnes L. Davis Raley.
RALEY, Bernadine, b. 1882, d. 1967.
RALEY, Carol Anne, b. Jun 26, 1943, d. Aug 20, 1965, dau of William Aloysius and Agnes Leola Davis Raley.
RALEY, Catherine, 6 wks, bur Feb 24, 1871.
RALEY, John B., b. Mar 21, 1804, d. Nov 5, 1879, hus of Jane M. __, b. Dec 31, 1822, d. Sep 16, 1871, age 48 years 18 mos and 15 days.
RALEY, Joseph A. "Spanky", Sr. b. Oct 17, 1938, d. Mar 2, 1990, divorced from Patricia Mac-Williams, son of William Aloysius and Agnes Leola Davis Raley.
RALEY, Rev. Joseph E., b. Jul 28, 1914, d. Mar 31, 1988, son of William Elmer and Marie Elizabeth Johnson Raley.
RALEY, Lawrence Y., b. Aug 5, 1885, d. Nov 24, 1968.
RALEY, Leonard C., b. Jul 12, 1891, d. - 26, 1964.
RALEY, Thomas David, b. Jan 30, 1860, d. Feb 13, 1950.
RALEY, William Aloysius "Sally", b. Oct 10, 1916, d. Nov 10, 1990, m. (1st) Apr 1938 Agnes Leola Davis, (2d) Dorothy Wible Garner, son of Wm. Elmer and Marie E. Johnson Raley.
RALEY, William Elmer, b. Jan 6, 1893, d. Dec 1949, hus of Marie Elizabeth Johnson, son of John Leo and Harriet Elizabeth Goodwin Raley.
READMOND, Emma W., b. Feb 1, 1877, d. Sep 23, 1955.
READMOND, Philip C., b. Sep 20, 1885, d. May 10, 1948.
READMOND, James L., b. 1904, d. 1961.
REDMOND, James O., b. 1897, d. 1963, hus of Mary E. __, b. 1892, d. 1976.

REDMOND, James Francis, b. Jan 16, 1936, d. Oct 17, 1957.
REDMOND, John Millard, b. 1900, d. 1979.
RITCHIE, Frederic E., b. Feb 21, 1910, d. Nov 8, 1972.
ROLLER, Jessica Elizabeth, b. Dec 7, 1911, d. Mar 4, 1980.
ROLLER, John Harrison, b. 1915, d. 1980.
ROSSON, Eleanor Louise, b. Nov 28, 1916, d. Apr 13, 1989, wife of Frank Charles "Dutch" Van Dalsum, dau of John Carl and Eleanor Winkfield Rosson.
ROSSON, John Carl, b. Oct 13, 1890, d. Feb 21, 1973.
RUSSELL, Donald Abell, b. 1946, d. 1977.
RUSSELL, E. Gwinnette, b. Nov 4, 1875, d. Feb 2, 1967, m. (1st) John Vivian Abell, (2d) Charles M. Goldsborough.
RUSSELL, J. Wilmer, b. 1893, d. 1930.
RUSSELL, John Philip, b. 1905, d. 1965, hus of Catherine Regina Dean.
RUSSELL, L. Cecil, b. 1890, d. 1961.
RUSSELL, Mae B., b. 1883, d. 1974.
RUSSELL, Mary Ann, b. and d., 1926.
RUSSELL, Mary Theresa, b. Apr 24, 1904, d. Oct 8, 1991, wife of J. Frank Wilkerson, dau of William Mason and Lucy Florence Woodburn Russell.
RUSSELL, William Jennings "Bill", b. Feb 7, 1936, d. Jul 5, 1992, son of John Phillip and Catherine Regina Dean Russell.
RUSSELL, William Lemuel, b. May 29, 1917, d. Jul 14, 1993, hus of Anne Elizabeth Garner, son of William Mason and Florence Lucy Woodburn Russell.
SALTER, Margaret E., b. 1924, d. 1966.
SAXTON, Mary Kate, b. Apr 11, 1859, d. Feb 23, 1913.
SCHINDLER, James C., b. May 1, 1900, d. May 31, 1971, hus of Eva M. Goodwin.
SCHINDLER, William C., b. 1923, d. 1968.
SCRIBER, James Edward "Tice", Sr. b. Sep 21, 1906, d. Nov 28, 1991, hus of Alice Ruth Somerville, son of James Edward and Nettie Lyle Scriber.

One Stone
-SCRIBER, James V., 103, b. 1878, d. 1981.
-SCRIBER, J. Sanders, b. 1908, d. 1981.
SCRIBER, Joseph Stanbury, b. 1915, d. 1967.
SCRIBER, Mary Gertrude, b. Dec 12, 1912, d. Sep 24, 1966.
SCULLY, Albert T., b. Jun 25, 1924, d. May 28, 1960.
SHEA, Agnes, b. 1880, d. 1963.
SHEA, John, b. 1886, d. 1953.
SMALLWOOD, Joseph Howard, b. 1918, d. 1964.
SNIDER, George T., b. Jul 9, 1892, d. Feb 20, 1977, hus of Audrey L. __, d. Sep 5, 1993.
SOMERVILLE, George Webster, d. Oct 12, 1976.
SOMERVILLE, J. Mitchell, d. Jan 3, 1978.
SOMERVILLE, Joseph A., b. Sep 17, 1924, d. Nov 2, 1971.
SOMERVILLE, Joseph S., b. Mar 16, 1919, d. Oct 9, 1963.
SPAULDING, Dr. A. Jackson, b. Sep 10, 1826, d. Oct 5, 1897, hus of Margaret Ann __, b. Jun 10, 1832, d. Sep 3, 1863.
SPAULDING, Alethea E., b. Oct 22, 1860, d. Jul 12, 1861, only dau of J. J. and M. A. Spaulding.
SPAULDING, Elizabeth T., b. 1907, d. 1940.
SPAULDING, Francis X., b. 1901, d. 1968.
SPAULDING, Karen Ann, b. Aug 13, 1961, d. Mar 14, 1973.
SPAULDING, Dr. Samuel E., 63, bur May 1, 1899.
SPAULDING, William B., b. Sep 11, 1855, d. Jul 27, 1861, eldest son of J. J. and M. A. Spaulding.
SPEARS, Idola Marie, b. 1908, d. 1965.
SPEARS, Joseph A., b. 1899, d. 1970.
SPENCER, Louis, b. Feb 15, 1895, d. Jul 9, 1969.
SPINNER, Larnie Burke, USMC WW II, b. Mar 25, 1917 VA, d. May 14, 1992, hus of Grace Evelyn Stevens, son of Charles and Marion Powell Spinner.
ST. CLAIR, Joan, b. Sep 14, 1937, d. May 11, 1971, wife of James F. Ferguson.
STEVENS, Barbara, b. 1907, d. 1980.
STEVENS, Catherine A., b. 1901, d. 1964.

STEVENS, Charles William, b. Apr 3, 1910, d. Jun 19, 1991, hus of Rose Holt, son of Robert and Mary 'Nellie' Barnes Stevens.
STEVENS, Frank, b. 1872, d. 1950.
STEVENS, Joseph Ignatius, b. Oct 8, 1911, d. Oct 14, 1989, hus of Nettie Scriber, son of Robert and Mary 'Nellie' Barnes Stevens.
STEVENS, Joseph Roy, b. Dec 1, 1896, d. Mar 12, 1962.
STEVENS, Lee Aloysius, b. Aug 19, 1900, d. Jul 5, 1976.
STEVENS, Priscilla, b. 1873, d. 1945.
STEVENS, William Richard, Sr. d. 1987, hus of Mary Lettie Hill.
STEWART, Alice. No dates.
STEWART, Florence Marie "Lucy", b. Oct 19, 1949, d. Oct 11, 1990, wife of George Vernon Maddox, Sr., dau of Clara Louise Young and late James Edward Stewart, Sr.
STEWART, James. No dates.
STEWART, William Joseph, MD SGT 5532 QM TRR CO WW II, b. Apr 7, 1920, d. Jul 27, 1965.
STONE, Alice, b. 1876, d. 1939.
STONE, Annie E., b. 1874, d. 1925, wife of James Carroll Jarboe.
STONE, Elizabeth M., b. Jan 8, 1934, d. Aug 30, 1978.
STONE, Francis A., b. Sep 8, 1904, d. Jan 28, 1967.
STONE, J. Elmer, b. 1911, d. 1970.
STONE, John D., b. 1896, d. 1963, hus of Lucille Sophia Goldsborough.
STONE, Joseph Xavier, b. Feb 26, 1928, d. Jan 21, 1968.
STONE, Mary Helen, b. Sep 29, 1908, d. Apr 3, 1991, wife of Joseph Norman McKay, dau of Edward and Sarah Frances Pegg Stone.
SUMMERVILLE, Mary, (French-col.) 17, bur Jun 21, 1890.
SUNDERLAND, James E., b. 1889, d. 1964.
SUNDERLAND, Nellie E., b. 1891, d. 1960.
SWAINE, Ester, d. Mar 3, 1976.
SWALES, Joseph Chester, "Erby" "Bird", b. Jan 6, 1920, d. Dec 3, 1991 DC, hus of Elizabeth R. Stevens, son of Frank and Jane Frances

Gunn Swales.
SWALES, Joseph G., b. Jan 5, 1943, d. Mar 18, 1963.
SWEENEY, Agnes M., b. Sep 19, 1905, d. May 9, 1980.
SYDNOR, Mary Helen, b. Oct 19, 1927, d. Mar 14, 1975, wife of Bradley G. Sydnor.
TAVEY, Lois Rees, b. Nov 1913, d. Jul 1970.
TAYLOR, Frank I., d. Dec 5, 1978.
TAYLOR, John Henry, b. Oct 24, 1902, d. Dec 3, 1958, hus of Mary Kane.
TAYLOR, Mary Cornelius, b. 1880, d. 1963.
THOMAS, Carl George, b. Jul 16, 1908, d. Sep 15, 1973.
THOMAS, Gregory, b. 1950, d. 1979.
THOMPSON, _innet_ied, b. Apr 1, 1777, d. Feb 17, 1856, aged 78 years 10 mos and 12 days. (Stone very worn.)
THOMPSON, Mrs. Alice, 19, bur Nov 16, 1869.
THOMPSON, Benjamin Clyde, b. Nov 17, 1909, d. Mar 18, 1943.
THOMPSON, George Clarence, b. Mar 12, 1907, d. Aug 20, 1972.
THOMPSON, Jane, b. 1915, d. May 29, 1971, wife of Edward A. Garner.
THOMPSON, Joseph Edwin "Ed", Sr. b. Feb 2, 1911 Balto, d. Dec 18, 1990, hus of Josephine Georgius __, son of Charles E. and Mary Virginia Pomeroy Thompson.
THOMPSON, Joseph Upton, b. Sep 17, 1937, d. Dec 10, 1967.
THOMPSON, Katherine Stake "Kitty", b. Oct 23, 1905, d. Dec 13, 1987, dau of Maurice Chapman and Susan Stake Brumbaugh Thompson.
THOMPSON, Mary Catherine, b. Jan 21, 1873, d. Feb 8, 1942.
THOMPSON, Maurice Chapman, b. 1874, d. 1960, hus of Susan Stake Brumbaugh.
THOMPSON, Maurice Chapman, b. Sep 21, 1904, d. Apr 3, 1971, son of Maurice Chapman and Susan Stake Brumbaugh Thompson.
THOMPSON, Upton, b. 1909, d. 1979, son of Maurice C. and Susan S. Brumbaugh Thompson.
THOMPSON, William W., b. Nov 21, 1912, d. Dec 7, 1972.

TIPPETT, James Anthony "Tony", Sr. b. Aug 22, 1966, d. Sep 1, 1990, hus of Sue __, son of Richard D. and Mary Louise Norris Tippett; gson of Richard D., Sr. and Eleanor B. Tippett; Jetson J. and Mary L. Norris.
TIPPETT, Mary S., b. Apr 6, 1841, d. Mar 25, 1932, wife of Joseph Francis Bowles.
TIPPETT, William 'Roger', b. Sep 27, 1939, d. Jan 21, 1992, hus of Doris Marie Thompson, son of George William and Gladys Catherine Gray Tippett.
TRAYNOR, Frances L., b. Nov 1, 1924, d. Sep 1, 1975.
TUCKER, Alethea, b. Feb 9, 1836, d. Jan 25, 1876, wife of W. B. Tucker.
TUCKER, Emma C., b. Sep 25, 1856, d. Sep 21, 1857, dau of W. B. and Mary F. Tucker.
TUCKER, James Herman, MD PFC USA WW II, b. Jan 21, 1922, d. Jun 10, 1969, hus of Jeannette G. __.
TUCKER, Mary F., b. Mar 9, 1832, d. Mar 14, 1863, wife of W. B.Tucker.
                Double Stone
 -TUCKER, Osborne, b. 1894, d. 1950.
 -TUCKER, Lillian, b. 1900.
TURNER, Sarah Elizabeth, b. Mar 7, 1909, d. Aug 4, 1993, wife of William "Rhody" Barnes, dau of John Henry and Mary Eliza Adams Turner.
UHLER, David Joseph, b. Apr 19, 1937, d. Oct 12, 1972.
VAN DALSUM, Frank Charles "Dutch", d. 1981, hus of Eleanor Louise Rosson.
VAN WERT, George Leonard, b. Jun 27, 1911, d. Apr 27, 1979, hus of Cecelia Cusic.
WALKER, Raina Marlene, d. Oct 9, 1971.
WALLACE, Edna, b. 1903, d. 1979, wife of __ Redmond.
WALLACE, Joseph 'Glen', b. Nov 5, 1898, d. Jun 18, 1973, hus of Mary B. __, b. May 2, 1901, d. Jan 16, 1974.
WALLACE, Louis Grant, b. Oct 4, 1914, d. Dec 11, 1992, hus of Rosalie Combs, son of Andrew Grant and Rose Elizabeth Redmond Wallace.
WARRENTON, Rose, (col) 14, bur Jun 17, 1890.
WATHEN, Joseph Charles, Jr. b. Mar 24, 1926, d.

Jun 30, 1990, hus of Dorothy E. __, son of Joseph C. and Alma Elizabeth Abell Wathen.
WATHEN, Leonard McGuire, b. Sep 11, 1927, d. Nov 11, 1973, hus of Susan Dodson, son of Ignatius Truman and Mary Genevieve Mattingly Wathen.
WATHEN, Melvin Aloysius, b. Nov 21, 1929, d. Apr 16, 1976.
WATSON, Wendell, b. May 6, 1963, d. Dec 25, 1975.
WELLS, Mary Gertrude, b. 1891, d. ca 1974, wife of Francis Roger Hayden.
WHEELER, James Thomas, b. Feb 28, 1862, d. Dec 17, 1933.
WHITE, Paul Wayne, b. 1921, d. 1978.
WHITINGER, Melvin Arnold, b. May 6, 1939, d. Sep 27, 1962.
WIBLE, Frances Cecelia, b. Mar 9, 1926, d. Nov 27, 1989, wife of Thomas Hillery Dean, Sr., dau of John M., Sr. and Ella Mae 'Nora' Woodley Wible.
WIBLE, J. Edward, b. Mar 4, 1884, d. Aug 24, 1960.
WIBLE, John Martin, b. 1880, d. 1966, hus of Ella Mae 'Nora' Woodley.
WIBLE, John Martin, Jr., d. Jan 31, 1984, hus of Martha Aline Payne, son of John M. and Ella Mae "Nora" Woodley Wible.
WIBLE, M. Lillian, b. May 19, 1885, d. May 28, 1958.
WIBLE, Ruth Mae, b. Mar 7, 1908 PA, d. Jul 28, 1992, wife of Lloyd Willis Copsey, Sr., dau of John Martin, Sr. and Ella 'Nora' Woodley Wible.
WIBLE, Raymond Spencer "Ray", b. Sep 24, 1913, d. Feb 11, 1993, m. 1936 Margaret Virginia __, son of John Martin, Sr. and Ella 'Nora' Woodley Wible.
WIBLE, William M., Father, b. 1838, d. 1915, hus of Catherine H. __, Mother, b. 1842, d. 1916.
WIDMAN, Joseph W., b. 1899, d. 1976, hus of Elizabeth C. __, b. 1901, d. 1975.
WIELAND, Lee V., b. Apr 24, 1903, d. Sep 20, 1972.

WILKERSON, Eleanor J., b. 1882, d. 1970.
WILKERSON, G. Alexander, b. Apr 24, 1882, d. Jul 30, 1970.
WILKERSON, J. Frank, d. Jan 20, 1987, m. 25 Dec 1925 DC, Mary Theresa Russell.
WILKERSON, John McCall, b. Aug 20, 1909, d. Mar 5, 1939.
WILKERSON, John P., b. Sep 7, 1869, d. Apr 11, 1935.
WILKERSON, Joseph P., b. 1873, d. 1970.
WILKERSON, May P., b. Mar 1, 1878, d. Nov 26, 1956.
WILKERSON, Nannie L., b. Jan 23, 1867, d. Sep 11, 1935.
WILKERSON, Noema L., b. Aug 18, 1883, d. Mar 13, 1951.
WILKERSON, Washington, d. Oct 4, 1917.
WILKERSON, William T., d. Mar 6, 1917.
WILKINSON, Miss Henrietta, 22, bur Feb 11, 1870.
WILKINSON, Wilmer E., b. 1898, d. 1976, hus of Violet A. __.
WILLIAMS, Henry Vernon, b. Jan 1, 1920, d. Aug 20, 1989, hus of Mary E. __, son of Joseph Henry and Rosa Mary Paddy Williams.
WILLIAMS, Wigie, b. Aug 29, 1880, d. Aug 10, 1956.
WISE, Helen, b. 1886, d. 1965.
WISE, Mary Inez, b. 1885, d. 1948.
WISE, Mary J., b. 1861, d. 1927, wife of __ Elliott.
WISE, Vincent A., b. 1877, d. 1946.
WISE, Walter A., b. 1881, d. 1969.
WOOD, Joseph Archie, b. Apr 18, 1907, d. Feb 13, 1992, hus of Mary Helen Greenwell, son of William Albert and Mary Alice Thompson Wood.
WOOD, Mary Helen, b. 1914, d. 1975.
WOOD, Mary Louise, b. May 5, 1905, d. Feb 27, 1992, m. (1st) Joseph Ethelbert Abell, (2d) William I. Bowles, dau of William Albert and Mary Alice Thompson Wood.
WOODBURN, Ethel Regina, b. Sep 5, 1920, d. Aug 23, 1992, wife of Francis Louis Garner, Sr., dau of Walter Leonard and Clotilda Lee Abell

Woodburn.
WOODBURN, James Frederick "Jimmy", d. before 1971, hus of Constance Catherine __.
WOODBURN, John Dwight "Doc", b. Jul 18, 1947, d. Mar 21, 1988, m. (1st) __, (2d) Carol Ann Stone, son of late James Frederick "Jimmy" Woodburn and Constance Catherine Woodburn Copsey.
WOODLEY, Ella Mae 'Nora', b. Apr 30, 1884, d. Dec 4, 1978, wife of John Martin Wible, Sr.
YATES, Jennie, b. 1861, d. 1935.
YATES, Martin J., b. 1860, d. 1937.
YATES, Mary, b. Jul 17, 1863, d. Jan 6, 1927, wife of __ Raley.
YATES, Warren, b. 1884, d. 1954.
YOUNG, Bernard William, b. May 18, 1912, d. Aug 6, 1972.
YOUNG, Enoch Bernard, b. 1897, d. 1980.
YOUNG, James R., b. Oct 18, 1867, d. Mar 27, 1941.
YOUNG, James Richley, d. Feb 22, 1988, m. 1933 Gladys Elizabeth Somerville.

OLD ST. JOSEPH RC CEMETERY
Busy Corner Road at Rt. 5
Morganza, Md.

In 1983 when I was working on the genealogy of the St. Mary's County Johnsons I was told many of them were buried in old St. Joseph Catholic Cemetery. It was hard to find exactly where it was located. When found it was overgrown with trees, brush and vines. It had even been logged since being out of use. I did hack my way through it with a hand sickle and found as many stones as I could. Many had fallen down and the loggers had removed the ones in their way and dumped them in a pile, breaking many. Not long after my trek through it, a man from Calvert Co., Md. who was searching for his great grandfather's grave started to clear the cemetery. Today St. Mary's County Genealogical Society has adopted and is maintaining it. In 1990 they began "Records of Known Burials at Old St. Joseph's Cemetery, Morganza, Md." in their newsletter, "The Generator". Many are vastly different from the visual readings of the headstones as deciphered by me. Many of these old stones are very worn and are difficult to read. There is always a possibility that the data has been misread. I have combined them together in this listing and hopefully if there is a discrepancy on the one you are working with, you will have enough information to know which is correct.

Row of footstones, no headstones.
P.M.S
T.M.
L.J.G.
W.M.S.
J.B.M.
J.H.M.
ADAMS, Mary Alice, d. Nov 13, 1889, age 15 yrs.
ADAMS, Morgan, b. Jan 18, 1890, d. Dec 9, 1901, son of Wilson and Mary Lulu Adams.
ALVEY, Elizabeth, d. Mar 28, 1827, age 23 yrs.
ALVEY, George N., d. May 2, 1870, age 60 years.

ALVEY, Joel, bur Mar 15, 1872, age 63 years.
ANDERSON, Jennie, b. Feb 6, 1861, d. Sep 27, 1912.
E.A.B., Footstone.
BAILEY, Alberta Maud, d. Aug 18, 1880, age 3 years 5 mos and 18 das.
BAILEY, Ann, b. May 10, 1802, d. Dec 19, 1888.
BAILEY, Ann G., b. Dec 8, 1834, d. Feb 17, 1872.
BAILEY, Bessie, b. Jan 22, 1878, d. Aug 11, 1879, dau of James H. and Julie C. Bailey.
BAILEY, Bettie, d. Oct 3, 1876, age 28 years.
BAILEY, Charles C., b. Aug 15, 1835, d. Oct 6, 1889.
BAILEY, Charlotte Ann, bur Feb 12, 1872, age 35 years.
BAILEY, E. Albert, b. Oct 5, 1891, d. Aug 15, 1892, son of Wm T. and Rosie C. Bailey.
BAILEY, Eliza A., d. Apr 9, 1869, age 27 yrs, late consort of Jos. H. Bailey.
BAILEY, Elizabeth, b. Jun 14, 1885, d. Dec 17, 1909.
BAILEY, Elizabeth A., d. Jul 14, 1881, age 59 years 8 mos and 9 das.
BAILEY, Felix Albert, b. Oct 5, 1891, d. Aug 15, 1892.
BAILEY, Gracie, b. 1882, d. 1886, may be bur. St. Joseph.
BAILEY, Jennie, d. Jul 15, 1886.
BAILEY, John J., d. Mar 7, 1894, age 63 years.
BAILEY, John L., b. Oct 12, 1816, d. Aug 22, 1860, hus of Elizabeth A. ___, d. Jul 14, 1881, aged 59 yrs 8 mos and 9 das.
BAILEY, Mary V., d. Aug 25, 1894, age 45 yrs, dau of Jno J. and Sarah J. Bailey.
BAILEY, Noah, d. May 27, 1858, age 72 yrs, m. (1st) Mary Wheatley, (2d) Ann Shercliffe Tennison.
BAILEY, Sarah J., d. Mar 26, 1893, age 37 years, wife of Jno J. Bailey.
BARNES, James, bur Jan 11, 1872, age 40 yrs.
BARNES, Plowden, bur Aug 5, 1871, age 25 yrs.
BARNES, Primus, d. Aug 3, 1821 in his 25th year.
BATEMAN, Catherine E., d. Jul 13, 1903, age 80

Old St. Joseph

years.
BENNETT, Charles E., d. Jul 26, 1905.
BISCHOP, H., b. 1914, d. 1916.
BLACKISTONE, Maud, b. Dec 7, 1895, d. Dec 17, 1899, dau of A. E. and S. A. Blackistone.
BOND, Betsie, bur Nov 26, 1871, age 56 yrs.
BOND, Catherine S., b. Apr 11, 1848, d. Mar 24, 1884.
BOND, R. P., d. Mar 13, 1902.
BOND, Sarah "Sallie", d. Nov 20, 1869, age 75 years.
BONN, J. S., CO H, I MD INF. No dates.
BOWLES, Daniel, bur Dec 10, 1906, age 52 yrs.
BOWLES, Mrs. Daniel, bur Jun 13, 1872, age 35 years.
BOWLES, George W., b. Apr 13, 1860, d. Apr 20, 1894.
BOWLES, Mabel Frances, b. Dec 9, 1892, d. Feb 13, 1896, age 3 years.
BOWLES, William, bur Oct 11, 1870, age 67 yrs.
BRADBURN, Edward R., b. Aug 29, 1789, d. Apr 18, 1854, age 64 yrs 7 mos and 20 das, hus of Sarah __, d. Sep 11, 1871, age 81 years.
BRADBURN, Anna Elizabeth, b. Dec 25, 1829, d. Mar 9, 1869, wife of Thomas L. Harrison, dau of Edw. R. and Sarah Bradburn.
BRADBURN, Sarah, bur Sep 12, 1871, age 80 yr.
BRADBURN, William E., d. Nov 22, 1851, age 19 years and 12 das.
BRANSON, Olivia, bur May 6, 1872, age 22 years.
BROOKBANK, Catherine, b. Jul 26, 1801, d. Feb 19, 1875.
BROOKE, Emma, cross, d. Feb 29, 1920, age 32.
BROWN, Dorothy, d. Jan 26, 1869, age 68 years.
BUCKLER, Gracie, no dates.
BUCKLER, Jane Catherine, no dates.
BUCKLER, Mary J., b. Feb 5, 1824, d. Jul 18, 1894, wife of Richard Long.
BUCKLER, Rebecca, b. - 14, 1852, d. Mar 1909.
BURROUGHS, Cecelia M., d. Jan 29, 1855, age 28 years.
BURROUGHS, Grosven(or), d. Dec 19, 1902.
BURROUGHS, Jane P., b. Jan 20, 1892, d. Jun 5, 1892.
BURROUGHS, John, bur Dec 23, 1870, age 25 yrs.

BURROUGHS, John A., b. Aug 1, 1818, d. Sep 23, 1900.
BURROUGHS, Rosa E., d. Jun 14, 1896, age 59.
BUSH, Benedict, bur Aug 18, 1869, age 65 yrs.
BUTLER, Charlotte, bur Sep 7, 1869, age 1 yr.
BUTLER, Henry, b. 1870, d. 1924.
BUTLER, Lucy Ann, bur Apr 21, 1870, age 35 yrs.
BUTLER, William Frank, bur Sep 4, 1869, 2 yrs.
CARPENTER, George, bur Jul 13, 1870, age 45.
CARROLL, Laura E., b. Feb 26, 1874, d. Jan 17, 1899, wife of Francis M. Carroll.
CARROLL, Paul M., b. Dec 15, 1898, d. Jan 21, 1899.
CHESELDINE, Katherine, b. Apr 19, 1852, d. Oct 24, 1898, wife of __ Burroughs.
CLARKE, Sarah Jane, bur Mar 15, 1870, age 22.
CLARKE, William H., bur Apr 3, 1870, age 4 years 3 mos and 10 das.
COATES, Carter, bur Sep 13, 1871, age 75.
COATS, F., cross with no dates.
COATS, James, cross with no dates.
COLE, Charity, bur Jun 16, 1870, age 85 yrs.
COLE, James E., PVT 16th CO 154th DEP BRIG, b. Dec 5, 1896, d. Camp Meade, MD, Oct 11, 1918.
COLE, Peter, bur Apr 30, 1872, age 22 yrs.
COLE, Richard Henry, 5 wks, bur Aug 4, 1870.
COMBS, James C., d. Nov 22, 1900.
COMBS, Maria M., wife of Geo. W. Combs; sons Zack M. and James C. Combs. Memorial Stone.
COOPER, Annie, bur Jan 19, 1870, age 70 yrs.
COOPER, Jane, d. Feb 13, 1871.
COPSEY, Mrs. Charles, bur May 19, 1872, age 45 years.
CULLINS, John T., d. Sep 3, 1903.
CULLINS, John Thomas, bur Sep 12, 1871, age 4 years 3 mos.
CURTIS, Ann, bur Nov 20, 1872, age 33 yrs.
CURTIS, George H., bur Jul 22, 1870, age 25.
CURTIS, Jane, bur Oct 17, 1869, age 30 yrs.
CURTIS, William H., bur March 8, 1872, age 18.
DAVIS, J. H. McKennie, b. Feb 16, 1862, d. Nov 1, 1870, son of John K. and Ann L. Davis.
DAVIS, J. Perry, b. Jun 2, 1872, d. May 2, 1875, son of John K. and Ann L. Davis.
DAVIS, Katie, d. Aug 1, 1887, age 14 years.

Old St. Joseph 237

DAVIS, Kenrick, bur Nov 14, 1870, age 10 yrs.
DAWSON, David L., d. Feb 2, 1896, age 27 yrs.
DAWSON, Lucy Roberta/Rebecca, d. Oct 14, 1870, age 3 years.
DAWSON, Mary E., d. Mar 10, 1904.
DICANDY, Mary Ann, d. in 1856, age 55 years, wife of George Mattingly of John.
DILLAHAY, Miss Elizabeth, d. Aug 3, 1871, age 43/55 years.
DILLAHAY, John, Father, b. Sep 8, 1825, d. Jun 12, 1885, hus of Anna C. __, Mother, b. May 11, 1840, d. Mar 28, 1875.
DILLAHAY, Lottie, d. Oct 9, 1866, age 35 years, wife of Francis Dillahay.
DILLAHAY, Mollie, bur Oct 4, 1870, age 6 years.
DORSEY, Juliet, bur Mar 22, 1970, age 60 yrs.
DOWNS, Catherine, no dates.
DOWNS, Rosa Catherine, b. 1853, d. Jul 4, 1914.
DRURY, Agnes Marie, d. Nov 11, 1889, age 2 yrs 4 mos and 2 das.
DYSON, Harriet, bur Oct 30, 1870, age 65 yrs.
EDELEN, John, bur Nov 5, 1870, age 50 yrs.
EDLY, Mary, (field stone) bur Jul 7, 1804.
EDWARDS, Eliza C., b. Nov 1, 1837, d. Aug 5, 1853, dau of Henry S. and Mary R. Edwards.
EDWARDS, Elizabeth E., b. Sep 27, 1839, d. Oct 27, 1848, dau of Henry S. and Mary R. Edwards.
EDWARDS, Henry S., d. Jan 7, 1862, age 55 years, hus of Mary R. __, d. Mar 15, 1881, age 75 yrs, left three children.
EDWARDS, Margaret J., b. Oct 27, 1832, d. Aug 3, 1853.
Footstone, J.E.E.
FARR, John, d. Feb 8, 1895.
FORBES, Jacob, b. Aug 25, 1828, d. Jul 7, 1906.
FORD, Jane A., b. Jul 13, 1819, d. Jan 3, 1882.
FORD, Mary A., d. Oct 5, 1846, in her 42 year.
FORD, William Henry, d. Aug 12, 1893, age 39.
FOWLER, Jane H., b. Feb 18, 1835, d. Apr 19, 1902.
FOWLER, Mary C., b. Jul 1, 1862, d. Jan 2, 1869.
FOWLER, Mary H. C., b. Jul 1, 1868, d. Jan 21, 1869.

FOWLER, Rebecca, b. Mar 8, 1825, d. Jun 25, 1853, wife of John W. Fowler.
GEADY, ___, b. Mar 10, 1900, d. Mar 30, 1901.
GODDARD, Elizabeth, d. Aug 5, 1858, age 60.
GODDARD, William B., d. Feb 10, 1886, age 62 years.
GOLDEN, Matilda, bur Sep 10, 1871, age 80 yrs.
GOLDSBOROUGH, Creston Leroy, b. Sep 9, 1899, d. Jun 26, 1900, son of Chas. E. and Mary Goldsborough.
GOLDSBOROUGH, Frances V., b. Nov 3, 1893, d. Jun 11, 1894, dau of Chas. E. and Mary C. Goldsborough.
GOLDSBOROUGH, Joseph R., b. Dec 4, 1890, d. Sep 12, 1891, son of Chas. E. and Mary C. Goldsborough.
GOLDSBOROUGH, Leonard Johnson, b. Jul 11, 1902, d. Nov 20, 1902, son of Charles E. and Mary C. Goldsborough.
GOLDSBOROUGH, Lily M., b. Oct 19, 1895, d. Jul 26, 1896, dau of Chas E. and Mary Goldsborough.
GOLDSBOROUGH, Mary O., b. Dec 17, 1854, d. May 21, 1886, wife of George W. Goldsborough.
Row of Footstones - S.A.H.
J.R.G.
F.A.G.
M.A.R.
F.A.M.
E.A.B.
GOUGH, Emily, d. Mar 13, 1844, age 3 years.
GOUGH, James, d. Jul 2, 1848, age 51 years.
GOUGH, Sarah C., d. Nov 16, 1873, age 68 yrs.
GRAVES, Ann, b. Mar 16, 1772, d. Jun 28, 1865.
GRAVES, Ann A., b. Jan 7, 1851, d. Jul 13, 1860, dau of Lewis and Ina Graves.
GRAVES, Anna May "Annie", d. Jul 16, 1869, age 1 yr 2 mo and 16 days.
GRAVES, Barbara, bur Jul 29, 1870, age 66 yrs.
GRAVES, Catherine P., d. Mar 25, 1896, 83 yrs.
GRAVES, Ellen E., b. Sep 1, 1834, d. Dec 1, 1899.
GRAVES, George A., b. May 6, 1848, d. Apr 6, 1860, son of Lewis and Ann Graves.
GRAVES, J. Jackson, b. Mar 25, 1828, d. Nov

27, 1882.
GRAVES, James T. No other markings.
GRAVES, John Maguire, bur Jun 8, 1872, 2 yrs.
GRAVES, John Peter, bur Mar 1, 1872, 70 yrs.
GRAVES, John Spencer, b. Jan 1, 1886, d. Nov 17, 1886, 3d son of John A. and Mary A. Graves.
GRAVES, John T., d. Feb 19, 1860, age 53 yrs 3 mos and 3 days.
GRAVES, Joshua T., d. Jun 6, 1872, age 25 yrs.
GRAVES, Lewis, b. Oct 9, 1808, d. Dec 27, 1872, age 64 years, hus of Ann __, b. Dec 22, 1816, d. Jul 16, 1859, age 42 yrs 6 mos and 24 das, consort of Lewis Graves.
GRAVES, Teresa, b. Aug 16, 1772, d. Jul 7, 1858.
GRAVES, Wm. Jennings Bryant, b. Sep 21, 1896, d. Feb 21, 1897, son of Chas. F. and Lucy Graves.
GRAY, Uriah, bur Dec 2, 1870, age 60 years.
GREENFIELD, James, bur Oct 15, 1870, 50 years.
GREENFIELD, Mary, d. Sep 3, 1886, age 70 yrs.
GREENWELL, John L., b. Sep 8, 1818, d. Jul 23, 1906.
GREENWELL, Mary Jane, d. Feb 17, 1872, 45 yrs.
GREENWELL, Phillip, b. Mar 3, 1898, d. Apr 8, 1898.
GUY, Alphonsus, b. Oct 29, 1886, d. Feb 20, 1890, son of Peter H. and Jane Guy.
GUY, Ann R., Our Mother, b. Nov 22, 1825, d. Sep 29, 1904.
GUY, Felix A., b. Oct 10, 1871, d. Apr 4, 1888.
GUY, Jane A., b. Nov 11, 1836, d. Jul 4, 1907.
GUY, Margaret E., bur Jul 12, 1869, age 25 yrs.
GUY, Peter Columbus, bur Feb 11, 1873, 16 yrs.
GUY, Peter H., b. Feb 11, 1827, d. Aug 20, 1906.
GUY, Richard, b. May 4, 1816, d. Jun 25, 1901.
GUY, William Henry, d. Nov 9, 1892, age 52 yrs.
J.R.G., F.A.G., Footstones.
HANCOCK, Maria. Rest of facing missing.
HANCOCK, Otha, b. Jun 30, ----.
HANDY, Charlotte, bur Feb 20, 1870, age 25 yrs.
HANDY, Doshia, b. Aug 3, 1858, d. Nov 9, 1919.
HANDY, James A., b. Jan 12, 1888, d. Jan 16, 1896.

HANDY, Jefferson P., b. Mar 13, 1860, d. Apr 22, 1906, hus of Jane R. ___.
HARRIS, Rose, bur Dec 31, 1871, age 20 yrs. S.A.H., Footstone.
HARRISON, Thomas L., b. Jan 10, 1820, d. Oct 12, 1883, hus of Anna Elizabeth Bradburn.
HAWKINS, Jaine, b. Jan 1853, d. Nov 1912.
HAWKINS, John W., d. Jan 2, 1903, age 28 years, son of J.A. and J. Hawkins.
HAWKINS, ___gen, b. May 8, 1878, d. May ___.
HAYDEN, Edgar Poe, d. Jul 16, 1828 age 22 yrs.
HAYDEN, Elizabeth J., d. Jun 27, 1853, 30 yrs.
HAYDEN, Gladys, b. Mar 10, 1900, d. Mar 30, 1901, dau of S. E. and W. M. Hayden.
HAYDEN, Joanna, d. Feb 25, 1902.
HAYDEN, Mary E., d. Jan 19, 1844, age 24 yrs.
HAYDEN, Mary E., d. Feb 28, 1901.
HAYDEN, Mary Susan, bur Nov 18, 1869, 2 mos.
HAYDEN, Phyllis, bur Dec 31, 1871, 7 das.
HAYDEN, Thomas Henry Joseph, bur Nov 25, 1869, age 4 mos.
HAZEL, Elizabeth, bur Nov 12, 1870, age 80 yrs.
HEARD, Col. Benedict I., d. May 13, 1864, age 74 yrs.
HEARD, James M., d. Mar 24, 1864, age 45 years and 11 das.
HEARD, Sarah A., d. Jul 7, 1865, age 35 years.
HERBERT, Annette Estelle, b. Jun 17, 1864, d. Oct 9, 1905, wife of Lewis Chapman Johnson.
HERBERT, Catherine V., my sister, b. Apr 23, 1863, d. Jan 13, 1896.
HERBERT, Chloe Rebecca, d. Jun 20, 1870, 7 mos.
HERBERT, S., CO K, 7 US CAV.
               Memorial Stone
  -HERBERT, Samuel
  -HERBERT, Jane M.
  -HERBERT, Georgia A.,
  -HERBERT, Catherine V.
  -HERBERT, Warren
  -HERBERT, S. Stanley
HERBERT, William H., d. Apr 12, 1886, age 65 years.
HILL, James, bur Nov 4, 1871, age 55 years.
HOLT, Alice, bur Jan 14, 1870.
HUNTINGTON, Mrs., bur Sep 1, 1871, age 65 yrs.

JACKSON, Lucy, d. Apr 21, 1870, age 52/60 yrs.
JARBOE, James B., d. Mar 2, 1882, age 34 yrs.
JENKINS, George Columbus, (col), bur Aug 24, 1870, age 16 yrs.
JOHNSON, Alen T., b. Feb 3, 1827, d. Sep 5, 1888, hus of Mary Cecelia Moreland, son of Joseph and Mary E. Yates Johnson.
JOHNSON, Allen "Allie", b. 1882, d. Sep 6, 1889, age 6 yrs 10 mos, eldest son of Zackariah and Missouri Woodburn Johnson.
JOHNSON, Eleanor, b. 1830, d. 1868, 1st wife of John Michael Joy, dau of John and "Martha" Drury Johnson.
JOHNSON, Mrs. Elizabeth, bur Dec 4, 1869, age 60 years.
JOHNSON, Elizabeth Ann, b. Feb 15, 1839, d. May 14, 1886, wife of James L. Milburn, dau of Joseph and Roseann Knott Johnson.
JOHNSON, Harry, d. Oct 17, 1879, age 2 yrs 6 mos, son of Hilary and Ann Thompson Johnson.
JOHNSON, Herbert Pernell, b. Jul 16, 1890, d. Oct 9, 1890, infant son of Lewis Chapman and Annette Estelle Herbert Johnson.
JOHNSON, John, b. 1901, d. Dec 1903 son of Peter Henry and Flora Love Johnson.
JOHNSON, John Spencer, b. Jan 1, 1886, d. Nov 17, 1886, son of John A. and Mary A. Johnson.
JOHNSON, John T., d. Nov 7, 1853, age 31 years.
JOHNSON, Jos. R. Taylor, b. Sep 1, 1847, d. after 1926, hus of Mary Emily Mattingly, son of Joseph and Roseann Knott Johnson.
JOHNSON, Joseph Stephen, b. Dec 26, 1830, d. Apr 1, 1901, hus of Eliza C. Mattingly, son of John and Martha Drury Johnson.
JOHNSON, Lewis Chapman, b. Aug 28, 1859, d. Jan 1, 1934, hus of Annette Estelle Herbert, son of Jos. S. and Eliza C. Mattingly Johnson.
JOHNSON, Mary, d. Mar 8, 1880, age 80 years, consort of John Leach, dau of James and Mary Johnson.
JOHNSON, Mary Eleanor, b. Mar 25, 1850, d. Jun 19, 1857, dau of Uriah and Clarissa E. Sherkley Johnson.
JOHNSON, Mary Madgalene, b. Jun 30, 1902, d.

Jul 5, 1902, infant dau of Lewis Chapman and Annette E. Herbert Johnson.
JOHNSON, Mary Nettie, b. Feb 16, 1897, d. Jul 12, 1897, twin dau of John A. and Mary Ann Johnson.
JOHNSON, Mary Rose 'Catherine', b. Feb 4, 1841, d. Feb 21, 1911, 2nd wife of Benjamin H. Swann, dau of Joseph and Roseann Knott Johnson.
JOHNSON, Myrtle Violet, b. Oct 1886, d. Feb 2, 1926, age 39 yrs, dau of Lewis C. and Annette E. Herbert Johnson.
JOHNSON, Rose Ann, b. Jul 1874, d. Oct 12, 1876, age 2 yrs 3 mos and 12 days, dau of J. R. Taylor and Mary Emily Mattingly Johnson.
JOHNSON, Uriah, b. Mar 25, 1821, d. Apr 23, 1896, a loving father, hus of Clarissa E. "Clara" Sherkley, son of John and "Martha" Drury Johnson.
JONES, infant of Wm. Jones, few das, bur Feb 1870.
JOY, John Michael, b. 1821, d. Jun 22, 1879, m. (1st) 18 Jan 1855 Eleanor Johnson, (2d) Amanda A. Mattingly, son of Ignatius III and Dorothy Drury Joy.
JOY, Joseph, b. Sep 27, 1869, d. Jan 16, 1937, son of John M. and Eleanor Johnson Joy.
KING, Jane Elizabeth, Mother, b. Mar 7, 1816, d. Feb 3, 1900, wife of James E. King.
KNIGHT, James H., d. Oct 18, 1880, age 2 yrs and 14 das, son of Henry B. and Henrietta Knight.
KNOTT, Henry, b. Jan 4, 1814, d. Feb 25, 1904, hus of Julia Ann __, b. Jan 17, 1817, d. Nov 1, 1894, son of William and Elizabeth Johnson Knott.
KNOTT, J. Frank, b. Apr 13, 1841, d. Nov 5, 1906, son of Henry and Julia Ann Knott.
KNOTT, Luke William, b. 1849, d. 1897, son of Henry and Julia Ann Knott.
KNOTT, Martha Catherine, b. Jun 7, 1841, d. Dec 8, 1862.
R.L. on stone.
LATHAM, Ann Elizabeth, d. Apr 26, 1869, 20 yrs.
LATHAM, Ann Priscilla, b. May 3, 1812, d. May

1, 1875.
LATHAM, Endres, b. Apr 7, 1853, d. May 13, 1885.
LATHAM, Matthew, bur Aug 5, 1869, age 75 yrs.
LATHROUM, Geo. W., b. May 23, 1825, d. Aug 31, 1882.
LATHROUM, John B., b. Jun 1, 1821, d. Sep 14, 1885.
LATHROUM, Margaret N., Our Mother, d. Oct 8, 1896, age 82 yrs 5 mos and 21 days.
LATHROUM, Susie E., b. Aug 21, 1858, d. Jun 13, 1891.
LLOYD, Nellie A. P., b. Mar 21, 1848, d. Jun 23, 1886, wife of John M. Lloyd.
LONG, Emma, bur Mar 1, 1870, age 3 yrs.
LONG, J. T., no dates, son of J. M. and Mary Long.
LONG, Judson J., d. May 2, 1901.
LONG, Laura V., b. Jun 22, 1876, d. Jan 27, 1907.
       Side by Side
-LONG, Mary E., d. Oct 30, 1843, age 40 yrs.
-J.M.L., very small stone
-J.T.L., very small stone
-LONG, Jos. M., d. Nov 18, 1876, age 76 yrs.
LONG, Mary E., no dates, dau of J. M. and Mary Long.
LONG, Richard, b. Feb 29, 1820, d. Aug 15, 1899, hus of Mary J. Buckler.
LONG, Thomas (J), bur May 6, 1872, age 30 yrs.
LONG, William R., bur Nov 23, 1870, age 26 yrs.
LOVE, Flora Catherine b. Nov 1873, d. Oct 12, 1901, 1st wife of Peter Henry Johnson, (he bur St. Aloysius) dau of Dr. Samuel Turner and Charlotte Catherine Chunn Love.
LOVE, Henrietta, bur Dec 7, 1871, age 69 yrs.
LOVE, William Charles, d. Jan 7, 1885, 60 yrs.
J.T.M., Small Tombstone.
S.M., Footstone.
       Row of Small Square Slabs
       J.J.M.   R.P.M.
       E.A.M.   T.P.M.
       T.W.M.   H.J.M.
MATTINGLY, Amanda A, b. Jul 29, 1838, d. Jun 22, 1897, 2nd wife of John Michael Joy.

MATTINGLY, Ann, d. Aug 8, 1874, age 76 years.
MATTINGLY, Anne E., d. Mar 17, 1868, in her 19th year.
MATTINGLY, Elinor, d. Jul 25, 1858, age 68 years, wife of Francis Mattingly.
MATTINGLY, Eliza C., b. Mar 30, 1834, d. Oct 26, 1909, wife of Joseph Stephen Johnson, dau of John Mattingly.
MATTINGLY, Elizabeth, infant, dau of Wm L. J. and Sophia Johnson Mattingly. No dates.
MATTINGLY, Elizabeth, d. Jun 16, 1894, age 31, wife of J. Walter Mattingly. F.A.M., Footstone.
MATTINGLY, Francis, bur Jun 13, 1872, age 81.
MATTINGLY, Francis L., d. Mar 17, 1878, age 56 years 7 mos and 7 das, m. Dec 28, 1843, Mary Ellen ___, b. Jul 29, 1822, d. Jul 23, 1881.
MATTINGLY, George of John, d. Feb 6, 1869 in his 77th year, hus of Mary Ann Dicandy.
MATTINGLY, George Armston, b. Sep 8, 1866, d. Apr 12, 1888.
MATTINGLY, George D., b. Sep 25, 1877, d. Aug 31, 1901.
MATTINGLY, George E., b. Nov 20, 1850, d. Dec 18, 1907.
MATTINGLY, George G., d. Dec 24, 1864.
MATTINGLY, George H., b. Feb 26, 1818, d. Nov 17, 1887, hus of Martha M. ___, Mother, b. Oct 8, 1835, d. Jan 6, 1916.
MATTINGLY, George S., b. Jul 20, 1810, d. Aug 23, 1874.
MATTINGLY, Geo. Thompson Keating, b. Apr 12, 1887, d. Jun 29, 1887, age 2 mos 19 das, son of Thomas D. and Mary E. Johnson Mattingly.
MATTINGLY, Geo. W., Father, b. Mar 25, 1825, d. Sep 14, 1870.
MATTINGLY, Gonzaga C., d. 10 Mos and 11 days, no dates.
MATTINGLY, Henry, bur Sep 15, 1869, age 56 yrs.
MATTINGLY, Henry J., d. Jun 13, 1898, age 21 years, son of Wm L. J. and Sophia Johnson Mattingly.
MATTINGLY, J. Frank, d. Feb 23, 1887, 17 yrs, eldest son of Wm. L.J. and Sophia Mattingly.

MATTINGLY, J. Godfrey, b. Nov 12, 1891, d. Mar 2, 1893.
MATTINGLY, J. Harriet, b. May 24, 1856, d. Apr 24, 1924.
MATTINGLY, J. Levis, b. Apr 9, 1888, d. Apr 13, 1896.
MATTINGLY, J. Wilmer, b. Apr 24, 1891, d. Dec 27, 1897.
MATTINGLY, James A., d. 1872.
MATTINGLY, James F., b. Sep 19, 1819, d. Feb 16, 1851.
MATTINGLY, James S., d. Oct 15, 1837, age 6 years 9 mos and 17 das, son of Sylvester Mattingly and Ann his wife.
MATTINGLY, James T., b. Oct 13, 1835, d. Nov 20, 1902.
MATTINGLY, James T., b. Oct 13, 1863, d. Nov 23, 1902 on tombstone.
MATTINGLY, Jane E., d. May 17, 1868, 49 yrs.
MATTINGLY, Jane H., b. Aug 28, 1828, d. Nov 18, 1896.
MATTINGLY, John B., b. Aug 1, 1861, d. May 27, 1889.
MATTINGLY, John Freeman, bur Jul 9, 1870, 4 mos.
MATTINGLY, John L., b. May 19, 1867, d. Jan 24, 1897.
MATTINGLY, John S., b. Oct 31, 1822, d. Aug 2, 1887.

Side by Side
-MATTINGLY, Joseph W., Husband, b. May 1, 1836, d. Apr 12, 1897.
-MATTINGLY, Lettie A., Mother, Aug 25, 1842, (rest of stone buried).
MATTINGLY, Leonard Johnson, d. Nov 20, 1902.
MATTINGLY, Levis M., b. Jul 18, 1885, d. Apr 5, 1887.
MATTINGLY, Lewis Johnson, b. Apr 9, 1888, d. Apr 18, 1896, son of Jas E. and Maggie C. Johnson Mattingly.
MATTINGLY, Mary, Mother, b. Mar 1815, d. Mar 20, 1886.
MATTINGLY, Mary A., b. Jan 20, 1824, d. Oct 1, 1888.
MATTINGLY, Mary Emily, b. Feb 11, 1847, d. May

8, 1926, wife of Jos. R. Taylor Johnson, dau of George W. Mattingly.
MATTINGLY, Mary J., d. Sep 2, 1865, age 2 yrs 6 mos and 5 days.
MATTINGLY, Mrs. Mary Jane, d. Sep 19, 1882, age 53 years.
MATTINGLY, Mary O., d. Jun 21, 1893, age 42.
MATTINGLY, Matilda, d. Oct 17, 1843, age 2 yrs 6 mos and 28 days.
MATTINGLY, Prissilla, d. 1873.
MATTINGLY, Robert Paul, d. Nov 10, 1884, age 10 mos, son of Wm L. J. and Sophia Johnson Mattingly.
MATTINGLY, Sarah A., d. Jun 2, 1868, age 19 years, 8 mos and 2 das.
MATTINGLY, Stephen, bur Sep 8, 1871, 23 yrs.
MATTINGLY, Sylvester, b. Jun 3, 1792, d. Jan 1, 1872, age 79 years, hus of Ann ___.
MATTINGLY, T. Webster, b. Oct 19, 1866, d. Nov 24, 1900.
MATTINGLY, Thomas Dominick, b. Feb 1, 1835, d. May 17, 1899, 63 years, hus of Martha __, d. Apr 2, 1885.
MATTINGLY, Theolphus, b. Oct 29, 1862, d. Nov 30, 1888.
MATTINGLY, Victor Baynard, b. Nov 1895, d. Mar 29, 1896, age 5 mos, son of Jas E. and Maggie Johnson Mattingly.
MATTINGLY, William H., d. Oct 8, 1837, age 4 years 7 mos and 10 days.
MATTINGLY, William Thomas Harrison, who d. Sep 11th A.D. 1812, aged 2 yrs 9 mos and 6 das. Z.W.M., corner stones.
MATTINGLY, Z., Jr. d. Dec 20, 1881, age 28 years.
MATTINGLY, Z. T., b. Sep 1, 1849, d. Jul 3, 1891.
MATTINGLY, Zac, d. Feb 16, 1890, age 72 yrs, hus of Anne M."Annie" __, d. Jun 21, 1885, age 64 yrs.
McKENNIE, J. H., b. Feb 16, 1862, d. Nov 1, 1870.
MEDLEY, Martha M., b. Sep 16, 1823, d. Apr 3, 1885, wife of ___ Mattingly.
MILBURN, James T., b. Aug 16, 1835, d. May 5,

Old St. Joseph

1900, hus of Elizabeth Ann Johnson.
MILBURN, Joseph J., d. May 10, 1880, age 20 years, eldest son of J. T. and E. A. Johnson Milburn.
MILBURN, Susan, d. Jan 14, 1887, age 77 years.
MORELAND, Mary Cecelia, b. Jun 30, 1835, d. Sep 12, 1888, wife of Alen T. Johnson, dau of George W. Moreland.
MORGAN, Alice, bur Sep 10, 1870, age 14 years.
MORGAN, Ann C., d. Jul 23, 1828, age 27 years.
MORGAN, Ann M., d. Dec 20, 1852, age 27 years.
MORGAN, Ann P., d. Dec 17, 1839, age 51 years.
MORGAN, Attaway, d. Mar 10, 1854, age 71 yrs.
MORGAN, Blanche, d. Aug 24, 1863, age 17 yrs.
MORGAN, Cecelia, d. Apr 2, 1826, age 21 years.
MORGAN, Cecelia E., b. Nov 6, 1851, d. Jul 28, 1853, dau of Daniel T. and Mary C. Morgan.
MORGAN, Charles, d. May 17, 1855, age 57 years.
MORGAN, Daniel T., b. 1823, d. 1891, hus of Mary C. __, b. Jul 29, 1828, d. Jul 5, 1857.
MORGAN, Dorothy, bur Feb 18, 1872, age 14 yrs.
MORGAN, Mrs. Elizabeth, d. Nov 10, 1836, age 22 years.
MORGAN, Elizabeth, d. Feb 18, 1830, age 70 yrs.
MORGAN, Elizabeth C., b. Mar 18, 1854, d. Aug 17, 1855, dau of Danl T. and Mary C. Morgan.
MORGAN, Elizabeth M., d. Nov 10, 1836, 22 yrs.
MORGAN, Geo. H., d. Nov 8, 1836, age 35 yrs.
MORGAN, George H., d. Apr 10, 1870, age 52 yrs.
MORGAN, Henry, bur Oct 9, 1870, age 50 years.
MORGAN, J. Benjamin A., b. Jul 23, 1901, d. Nov 4, 1901.
MORGAN, James Alexander, bur Dec 7, 1871, age 63 years.
MORGAN, John LL., d. Dec 18, 1855 in the 52nd year of his age.
MORGAN, Joseph, Sr. d. May 8, 1845, age 82.
MORGAN, Joseph E., b. Oct 29, 1836, d. Aug 8, 1855. (Has two stones side by side, same)
MORGAN, Martha Ellen, bur Aug 27, 1871, 30 yrs.
MORGAN, Mary, d. Apr 9, 1847.
MORGAN, Mary, d. Dec 21, 1855, age 65 years.
MORGAN, Mary C., d. Sep 14, 1891, age 52 yrs.
MORGAN, Mary D., d. Mar 28, 1857, age 6 mos and 21 days.

MORGAN, Mary Genevieve, b. Jan 28, 1867, d.
  Aug 3, 1869, dau of D.T. and Mary C. Morgan.
MORGAN, Mary L., d. Jun 4, ----, age 39 years.
MORGAN, Sarah B., bur. Aug 25, 1869, age 17.
MORGAN, Thomas W., b. Feb 9, 1796, d. Feb 25,
  1856, age 60 years.
MORGAN, W. M., d. May 15, 1858, 8 yrs 9 mos.
MORGAN, Wilhelmiria T., d. Jun 29, 1851, age
  32 years, consort of Thos. W. Morgan.
MORGAN, William S., d. Jan 13, 1872, age 70 yrs.
MORGAN, William S., bur Jan 12, 1872, age 75.
NEALE, Francis, d. Jan 26, 1871, age 40 yrs.
NELSON, Attie, b. Aug 4, 1888, d. Oct 18,
  1889, dau of Obediah and Lula Hayden Nelson.
NELSON, Mary Lula, b. Sep 25, 1870, d. Apr 15,
  1900.
PARSONS, James Thomas, b. May 18, 1839, d. Jan
  24, 1901.
PAYNE, Ann M., d. Nov 20, 1898, age 81 years,
  headstone has A.M.P. only, plot has corner
  stones "G.H. PAYNE".
       Memorial Stone-Erected Mar 4, 1918
  -PAYNE, Ella B., Jane C. and John M.
PAYNE, Jane Cornelius, d. Aug 1, 1907.
PAYNE, John L., d. Jan 27, 1867, age 18 yrs.
PLOWDEN, Mrs. James, abt 40, bur Dec 12, 1869.
PONTON, C. Frederick, d. Feb 18, 1819, aged 35
  years.
POWER, Thomas, bur Feb 18, 1871, age 78 yrs.
PRICE, Edward A, d. Dec 7, 1816, 40 yrs 10 da.
PRICE, Nellie Ann, bur Sep 20. 1871, age 11.
QUAID, Emonia, bur Sep 20, 1871, 7 mos.
RALEY, Bennet R., bur Jan 17, 1872, 6 mos.
RALEY, James, d. Nov 8, 1875, age 19 years.
RALEY, James, d. Jan 25, 1871, age 27 years.
RALEY, James T. M., b. Jun 12, 1826, d. Mar
  19, 1895, age 69 years.
RALEY, Julia A. B., b. Dec 26, 1831, d. May
  20, 1918.
RALEY, Lucy Maria Lucretia, b. Sep 11, 1851,
  d. Aug 5, 1852.
RALEY, Sarah Catherine, d. Mar 6, 1870, age 3
  years 7 mos.
RALEY, W. R. L., b. Sep 16, 1858, d. Feb 7,
  1893.

Old St. Joseph 249

REEDER, Jane Henrietta, d. Aug 12, 1871, 6 yrs.
REEDER, William T. A., d. May 2, 1887, 26 yrs.
RUSSELL, Ann L., b. Feb 14, 1846, d. Dec 2, 1878.
RUSSELL, Ann R., b. Sep 2, 1822, d. Nov 11, 1878.
RUSSELL, Benjamin Donatus, b. Aug 30, 1871, d. May 15, 1872, son of L. R. and C. Russell.
RUSSELL, C.L., b. Dec 13, 1792, d. Jan 6, 1868.
RUSSELL, Catherine, d. Dec 30, 1873.
RUSSELL, Charles Ignatius, b. Aug 12, 1870, d. Oct 6, 1870.
RUSSELL, Donatus Benjamin, bur May 8, 1872, 8 mos.
RUSSELL, Mrs. Edgar, d. Aug 1897.
RUSSELL, J. Lambert, b. Dec 5, 1828, d. Feb 4, 1883.
RUSSELL, James M., b. Oct 28, 1819, d. Apr 23, 1901, hus of Elizabeth A. __, b. Aug 26, 1826, d. Apr 22, 1883.
RUSSELL, James M., b. Sep 1, 1853, d. Nov 9, 1884, son of James M. and Elizabeth Russell.
RUSSELL, John A., b. Oct 31, 1824, d. Feb 27, 1863.
RUSSELL, John Farr, b. Sep 14, 1892, d. Feb 8, 1895, son of J. P.. and M. A. Russell.
(M.A.R. foot stone, no headstone.)
RUSSELL, Joseph E., b. Jan 13, 1848, d. Sep 17, 1894, hus of Fannie S. ___.
RUSSELL, Joseph P., b. Mar 16, 1832, d. Aug 5, 1912.
RUSSELL, Julia Frances, bur May 1872, age 9 mos.
RUSSELL, Julia Ruth, b. Jul 6, 1873, d. Aug 26, 1873, dau of J. P. and C. Russell.
RUSSELL, Lucy A., b. Jun 1, 1874, d. Jun 30, 1874.
RUSSELL, Margaret E., Mother, b. Nov 25, 1828, d. May 24, 1894.
RUSSELL, Mary Ann, b. Jun 28, 1796, d. Apr 15, 1861.
RUSSELL, Mary J., b. Jul 11, 1837, d. Dec 23, 1872.
RUSSELL, T. Edgar, b. Jun 4, 1865, d. Jun 3, 1908, hus of Susan J. __, b. Sep 16, 1868, d. Sep 4, 1901.

RUSSELL, William A., b. Feb 21, 1828, d. Jun 29, 1864.
J.E.S., very small headstone.
L.S., footstone.
M.A.S., footstone.
SAXTON, Joseph, b. May 18, 1818, d. Jan 11, 1866, eldest son of Geo and Sarah A. Saxton. (Tombstone)
(b. May 18, 1848, October 1990 Generator)
SAXTON, Henrietta, bur March 2, 1872, age 80.
SAXTON, Lucretia, d. May 8, 1878, age 48 yrs.
SCOTT, William, d. Jul 17, 1873, age 70 yrs.
SHERCLIFFE, Elizabeth A., b. ca 1824, d. Jul 14, 1881.
SHERKLEY, Clarissa E. "Clara", b. Jan 14, 1828, d. Nov 17, 1895, a loving mother, wife of Uriah Johnson.
SIMMS, Francis, d. Jan 17, 1853, age 75 yrs 6 mos and 17 das.
SIMMS, Ignatius, b. Mar 5, 1809, d. Nov 20, 1882.
SMITH, Agnes Cusic, cross with no dates.
SOMER_____, Ernest, cross with no dates.
SOMERVILLE, Jennie E., b. May 3, 1860, d. May 18, 1897, on cross.
SPAULDING, Cecelia, d. Nov 19, 1869, 77 yrs.
SPAULDING, Mrs. Cornelia, bur Nov 22, 1869, age 77 yrs.

Side by Side
-SPAULDING, Edward, d. Feb 28, 1823 in the 46 year of his age.
-SPAULDING, Mary C., d. May 24, 1819, age 31.
SPAULDING, Edward Dyer, b. Feb 20, 1846, d. Aug 27, 1864.
SPAULDING, James G., b. 1814, d. 1889.
SPAULDING, John O., d. Oct 27, 1858, age 22 yrs 11 mos.
SPAULDING, Joseph, d. Feb 16, 1859, age 52 yrs.
SPAULDING, Mary Ann, d. Mar 5, 1859, age 29 yrs.
SPAULDING, May, b. Jul 30, 1873, d. Aug 2, 1876, dau of Dr. J. T. and L. J. Spaulding.
SPAULDING, Sylvester, d. Jan 16, 1852, age 41 yrs 10 mos.
STONE, Willie, b. Nov 20, 1871, d. Jun 29,

Old St. Joseph

1872, son of L. B. and M. U. Stone.
SWANN, Benjamin H., b. Jul 31, 1827, d. Apr 6, 1908, m. (1st) Lucinda Mattingly, (2d) Mary Rose 'Catherine' Johnson.
TABBS, Lewis, b. Dec 25, 1858, d. Jun 13, 1920.
TANEY, Elizabeth, d. Jul 26, 1824, age 60 yrs.
TENNISON, Edmond, d. Dec 29, 1820, age 29 yrs.
TENNISON, Elenor, d. Sep 8, 1829.
TENNISON, Elizabeth, d. Jan 3, 1835, age 33 yrs.
TENNISON, Frances Etta, b. Oct 27, 1872, d. May 5, 1893, wife of Charles W. Bowles, eldest dau of George F. and May C. Tennison.
TENNISON, Leo, d. Sep 14, 1870, age 14 years.
TENNISON, Mary C., b. Apr 11, 1817, d. Jun 22, 1871, wife of John G. Tippett, dau of J. E. and Elizabeth Tennison.
THOMAS, Ann Mary, bur Oct 8, 1870, age 24 yrs.
THOMAS, Catherine, b. 1760, d. 1812.
THOMAS, George, bur Sep 19, 1869, age 75 yrs.
THOMAS, Ignatius, bur Feb 12, 1871, 6 wks.
THOMAS, Mary Elizabeth, d. Feb 6, 1857, 26 yrs.
THOMAS, Teressa Emily, d. Mar 4, 1862, age 25 yrs 2 mos, dau of J. U. and Catherine Thomas.
THOMAS, William, d. Mar 11, 1841, age 52 years.
THOMAS, William M. D., b. Mar 8, 1793, d. Sep 30, 1849.
THOMPSON, Ann Mary, d. Oct 6, 1870, age 25 yrs.
THOMPSON, Catherine, d. Jul 10, 1818, 57 years.
THOMPSON, Clements, d. Jan 16, 1872, age 80 yrs.
THOMPSON, Donatus Wellington, d. Mar 25, 1893, age 25 years.
THOMPSON, Mary Catherine, bur Dec 21, 1870, 4 mo 21 da.
THOMPSON, Mary Ellen, bur Jun 25, 1870, 17 mo.
THOMPSON, Mary Jane, d. Dec 21, 1870, age 4 mos 21 das.
TIPPETT, Abbie J., b. Nov 2, 1886, d. --.
VALLANDINGHAM, Samuel, d. Mar 11, 1872, 46 yrs.
VAN WART, George Abraham, b. Feb 6, 1873, d. Oct 20, 1888.
VAN WART, William H., b. Oct 3, 1820, d. Feb 18, 1903.
WELCH, Catherine, d. Jun 3, 1879, age 41 yrs.
WELCH, John, d. Sep 14, 1883, age 82 years.

WELCH, Martin, no dates.
WILLIAMS, Albred, no dates.
WILLIAMS, Eliza Catherine, d. Jan 18, 1871, age 32 years.
WILLIAMS, George, d. Feb 5, 1870, age 21 yrs.
WILLIAMS, Georgiana, d. Feb 23, 1871, 14 yrs.
WOOD, Francis C., d. Jan 23, 1895, age 22 yrs 10 mos and 17 das.
WOOD, Henry Edward, no dates.

ST. JOSEPH CATHOLIC CEMETERY
Rt. 5
Morganza, Md.

This church dates from 1759 when the original wooden building and cemetery were located on the corner of what is now Rt.5 and Busy Corner Road. The present brick church was built in 1860 on the south side of Rt. 5 approximately 1/2 mile west of the old location. The land for the cemetery was purchased in May 1904 and is directly across Rt. 5 from the church.

ABELL, Geo.'Donald', b. Feb 4, 1904, d. Oct 28, 1989, hus of Ethel 'Gertrude' Payne, son of George Edgar and Emma Pauline Bowles Abell.
ABELL, Janet, b. Jul 11, 1924, d. Jan 12, 1991, m. (1st) Hugh H. Marshall, (2d) Walter E. Wilson, dau of Bernard and Florine Delahay Abell.
ABELL, John Lee, 70, d. Sep 19, 1974, hus of Agnes T. Johnson, son of John B. and Mary Alma Mattingly Abell.
ABELL, John Ralph, Sr. 83, d. Mar 24, 1977, hus of Pauline Hayden.
ANDERSON, Charles E., d. 1973, hus of Effie Matilda Curry.
ANDERSON, James Herman, b. Apr 24, 1917, d. Dec 23, 1993, m. Dec 29, 1940 Ethel Cecelia "Dolly" Long, son of John Briscoe and Cora Eva Williams Anderson.
ARNDT, Gail Louise, d. Dec 26, 1992, Balto.
BLANK, Anna, 103, b. Mar 27, 1888 PA, d. Oct 20, 1991, wife of Egon Bohle, dau of Martin and Anna Oeller Blank.
BOWLES, John Ignatius "Nace", Sr. b. Jun 10, 1909, d. Dec 1, 1992, hus of Susan Alberta Ellis, son of Dr. Ruther Ignatius and Noema Catherine Stewart Bowles.
BOWLES, Queenie Mae, b. Mar 4, 1903, d. Apr 19, 1990, wife of J. Norman Johnson, dau of William Charles and Violet Woodburn Bowles.
BRIDGETT, Dorothy E., b. 1921, d. 1985, wife of Thomas Geo. Johnson, dau of Dennis O. Bridgett.

BROOKS, James Kerrick "Tot", b. May 5, 1922, d. May 30, 1992, hus of Mary Martha Hall, son of James Richley and Mildred Louise Butler Brooks.
BURKE, Bernadine Elizabeth, b. Jul 11, 1912 DC, d. Jul 19, 1992, wife of Geo. Frederick Boyd, Sr., dau of Peter Paul and Mary Magdalen O'Connor Burke.
BURCH, Charles Webster, d. Feb 27, 1963, hus of Jessie Marie Tennison.
BURCH, Lillian Elizabeth, b. Jun 6, 1902, d. Jun 22, 1992, wife of Freeman Edward Copsey, dau of Geo. W. and Mary Elizabeth Knott Burch.
BURROUGHS, George DeBracy, Sr. d. Apr 24, 1975, hus of Clara Elizabeth Thompson.
BURROUGHS, Thomas Maddox "Mac", Sr. b. Apr 6, 1912, d. Mar 9, 1992 DC, hus of Mary Magdalen Pilkerton, son of Turner Ashby and Madeline Maria Turner Burroughs.
CAWOOD, Carrie M., b. Oct 13, 1897, d. Aug 7, 1990, wife of Alfred E. Lewis, dau of J. Clement and Alice Raley Cawood.
COLLINS, Jane Frances, b. Jan 7, 1926, d. Sep 19, 1992, m. 19 Apr 1952 Joseph Givens Young, dau of Joseph and Thelma Harper Collins.
COLTON, Joseph N., d. Oct 1968, m. DC Ellen Rebecca Dixon.
COOPER, Mary Rosalie, b. May 17, 1892, d. Apr 27, 1964, wife of J. Ernest H. Johnson.
COPSEY, Freeman Richard, b. Jun 15, 1931, d. Nov 29, 1991, hus of Mary Jeannette Lacey, son of Freeman Edward and Lillian Elizabeth Burch Copsey.
COPSEY, Louis A., d. 1960, m. 1928 Balto, Helen Mae Lupus.
COUNTISS, Joseph Walter, Sr. b. Apr 9, 1898, d. Feb 29, 1988, hus of Rachel Reid.
CUSIC, Catherine, b. Feb 26, 1927, d. Nov 27, 1986, m. Nov 1945 Raymond Raley, dau of Quincy and Nora Bussler Cusic.
CRYER, Cliffie Mae, b. 1876, d. 1943, wife of Bernard Eugene Mattingly, dau of James H. and Noema C. Goldsborough Cryer.
CRYER, James Lowell, b. Apr 19, 1914, infant,

St. Joseph

son of Wm. B. and M. L. Johnson Cryer.
CRYER, John Spencer, b. 1916, d. 1926 DC, son of Wm. B. and M. L. Johnson Cryer.
CRYER, Joseph Mitchell, b. Dec 25, 1903, d. Jan 26, 1919, son of Wm. B.and M. L. Johnson Cryer.
CRYER, Marguerite Mae, b. 1911, d. Jan 21, 1919, dau of Wm. B. and M. L. Johnson Cryer.
CRYER, William Baptist, b. Apr 24, 1874 NY, d. Feb 29, 1948, hus of Martha Lucinda Johnson.
CURRY, Effie Matilda, b. Mar 19, 1909, d. Jul 6, 1993, m. DC 1967 Charles E. Anderson, dau of John Randolph and Susan Hall Curry.
CUSIC, Nora Catherine, b. May 24, 1895, d. Feb 9, 1990, wife of John Quincy Cusic, dau of John and Catherine Knott Cusic.
DEAN, Mabel, b. Apr 3, 1917, d. Jan 8, 1989, wife of William J. Owens.
DELAHAY, Lillian L., b. 1887, d. 1969, wife of Louis Johnson Mattingly.
DINGEE, Alice E., b. Feb 3, 1921, d. Feb 15, 1989, wife of Albert Tippett, dau of Louis Edward and Mary Josephine Long Dingee.
DIXON, Mary Agnes, 104, b. Dec 5, 1888, d. Oct 3, 1993, dau of Daniel and Sally Floyd Dixon.
DOWNES, Agnes Lorena, b. Dec 13, 1917, d. May 12, 1988, wife of Charles L. Mattingly.
DRURY, Catherine Elizabeth "Bessie", b. Nov 10, 1897, d. May 16, 1956, wife of Mattingly Gibbons Johnson.
DRURY, Daniel Maguire, b. 1907, d. 1929, hus of Agnes G. Johnson.
ELLIS, Susan Alberta, d. Nov 12, 1967, wife of John Ignatius Bowles.
ESTEP, Charles Richard, d. 1959, hus of Ruth Eleanor Johnson.
FLORA, William Elmer, b. Dec 5, 1928, d. Oct 28, 1993, m. 8 Aug 1973 Betty Lou __, son of Charles Edward and Cora Virginia Pilkerton Flora.
FOWLER, Ann Elizabeth, b. Dec 26, 1900, d. Nov 7, 1990, dau of Thomas Henry and Charlotte A. Burch Fowler.
FOWLER, Henry J. Sr. 79, d. Jul 23, 1989, hus of Susan Ficklin, son of John Aquilla and

Pearl Love Fowler.
FOWLER, Zack Morgan, Sr. b. Mar 10, 1896, d. May 22, 1990, hus of May Reeder, son of Zackariah M. and Martha Barber Fowler.
GRAVES, Ellen Sophia, b. Jun 22, 1902, d. Jun 21, 1992, wife of Bernard Arthur Bowles, dau of Leonard Thomas and Mamie Mattingly Graves.
GRAVES, Francis Wilmer "Greybutt", Sr. b. Mar 3, 1909, d. Aug 26, 1993, son of James Earnest and Martha Ellen Long Graves.
GRAVES, Mary 'Ethel', b. Mar 3, 1905, d. Dec 20, 1993, wife of Warren S. Thompson, dau of Richard Bernard and Mary Florence Nelson Graves.
GRAVES, Stephen Xavier "Uncle Peter", b. Mar 11, 1911, d. Apr 21, 1992, son of James Earnest and Martha Ellen Long Graves.
GRAY, Frederick Carroll, b. Dec 8, 1909, d. Oct 12, 1990, hus of Mary Elizabeth Anderson, son of Charles McKenny and Lucy Ann Pilkerton Gray.
GREEN, Hallsey Francis, b. Mar 22, 1906, d. May 13, 1992, son of Stephen and Annie Young Green.
GUY, Joseph Clyde, d. May 14, 1989, hus of Dorothy D. Jones.
GUY, Margaret Eleanor, b. Nov 24, 1912, d. Nov 25, 1989, wife of Charles W. Fortney, dau of Clarence N., Sr. and Margaret T. Rose Mattingly Guy.
GUY, Rebecca Catherine, b. Oct 4, 1991, d. Oct 8, 1991, dau of Walter Lawrence and Glenda Catherine Spaulding Guy.
HANCOCK, Frances Fowler, b. Sep 18, 1906, d. Sep 22, 1988, dau of Leonard H. and Mary Burroughs Hancock.
HANCOCK, Mary H., b. 1876, d. 1954, wife of Benedict B. Love.
HARDING, Joseph Samuel, b. Mar 3, 1919, d. Dec 24, 1992, m. 30 Jan 1944 Mary Catherine __, son of Samuel Wm. and Sarah Jane Tippett Harding.
HAYDEN, Agnes Adele, b. Jun 9, 1866, d. Jan 24, 1954, wife of Charles Llewellyn Johnson,

dau of Zackariah and Mary Sophia Johnson Hayden.
HAYDEN, James Aloysius 'Allen', b. 1863, d. May 15, 1926, hus of Catherine Emma (Katie) Johnson.
HAYDEN, Joseph J., b. 1852, d. 1909.
HAYDEN, Joseph L., "Len", Sr., MD PVT 122 CO TRANS CORPS, b. May 3, 1896, d. Mar 3, 1965, hus of Mary Verna Wood.
HAYDEN, Mary, b. Jun 24, 1909, d. Feb 19, 1989, wife of Henry Harvey Burroughs, dau of Joseph Dent and Mary Priscilla Bowles Hayden.
HAYDEN, Zachariah, b. 1892, d. 1938.
HAZEL, Minnie Iowa, b. 1874, d. 1956, m. 26 Jan 1891 Daniel Raley, dau of James T. and Eleanor S. Evans Hazel.
HEALY, John Edward, b. Aug 27, 1908 DC, d. Mar 17, 1988, hus of Agnes Emily Hurry, son of Dennis L. and Mary Brightwell Healy.
HEBB, Mary Lillith "Marie", b. ca 1880, d. Aug 11, 1963, wife of Thomas "Rhodie" Johnson, dau of John Benjamin Hebb.
HERBERT, James Andrew, b. Mar 28, 1931, d. Oct 7, 1989, son of Joseph Alton Herbert and Bessie Rebecca Herbert Buckler.
HERBERT, Julia F. M., b. Dec 16, 1853, d. May 25, 1936.
HOWE, Joseph C., Sr. b. Jan 3, 1928, d. May 27, 1991, 7th child of Parren Martin and Mary Agnes Harris Howe.
HURRY, Agnes Emily, b. Mar 31, 1911, d. Jan 31, 1993, wife of John Edward Healy, dau of Joseph and Agnes Raley Hurry.
JOHNSON, Agnes N., b. Oct 22, 1885, d. Mar 23, 1968, wife of Joseph Johnson Swann, dau of Zackariah and Missouri Woodburn Johnson.
JOHNSON, Agnes T., b. Oct 1908, wife of John Lee Abell, dau of Parren and Lottie Tennison Johnson.
JOHNSON, Beatrice, b. Feb 12, 1914, d. Aug 27, 1918, dau of Andrew and Cassie Johnson.
JOHNSON, Catherine Emma "Katie", b. 1870/71, d. after 1910, wife of James A. Hayden, dau of Joseph S. and Eliza C. Mattingly Johnson.
JOHNSON, Charles Llewellyn, b. Feb 19, 1865,

d. Jun 8, 1931, hus of Agnes Adele Hayden.
JOHNSON, Clara "Eva", b. 1882, d. 1919, wife
of George Morgan Payne.
JOHNSON, Clara 'Elaine', b. Apr 1892, d. 1976,
dau of Charles and Agnes Hayden Johnson.
JOHNSON, Claude Chester, b. Jun 7, 1917, d.
Jul 3, 1917, son of James Claude and Martha
Russell Johnson.
JOHNSON, Edward Garry, b. Jan 1897, d. 1953,
son of George Edw. and Johanna Long Johnson.
JOHNSON, Ella Pauline, b. May 1883, d. Oct 18,
1973, wife of J. Hanson Wathen, dau of Hillery and Ann Marie Thompson Johnson.
JOHNSON, Catherine 'Ethel', b. Nov 1889, d.
1971, wife of Wilbert W. Lloyd, dau of Geo.
Edw. and Johanna Long Johnson.
JOHNSON, Francis Edward, b. Jul 30, 1915, d.
Sep 1, 1919, son of Francis V. and Annie
Williams Johnson.
JOHNSON, Francis Desales, b. 1893, d. 1939,
hus of Lucy C. ___, b. 1897, d. 1983.
JOHNSON, Francis Vernon, b. Apr 3, 1892, d.
Nov 13, 1957, m. 7 Oct 1914 Annie Myrtle
Williams.
JOHNSON, Francis Xavier, b. 1916, d. 1938,
son of George Webster and Elinor T. Payne
Johnson.
JOHNSON, George Edward, b. 1854, d. 1930, hus
of Johanna Long.
JOHNSON, George Moreland, b. 1871, d. 1934,
son of Allen T. and Mary Cecelia Moreland
Johnson.
JOHNSON, George 'Parren', b. 1874, d. 1943,
hus of Charlotte Anne Tennison, son of Wm.
Edward and Liza Raley Johnson.
JOHNSON, George Webster, b. 1880, d. 1920, hus
of Elinor T. Payne.
JOHNSON, Hilary E., b. Apr 22, 1832, d. Apr 27,
1915, hus of Ann Marie Thompson, son of John
and Martha Drury Johnson.
JOHNSON, Isaac Lester, b. 1899, d. 1919, son
of Geo. Edward and Johanna Long Johnson.
JOHNSON, J. Andrew, b. 1871, d. 1951, hus of
Mary C. Mattingly.
JOHNSON, J. Bernard, b. 1910, d. 1979, son of

Parren and Lottie Tennison Johnson.
JOHNSON, J. Claude, b. 1891, d. Dec 31, 1980, hus of Martha Marie Russell, son of John A. and Mary Ann Johnson.
JOHNSON, J. Keating, b. Dec 17, 1885, d. Nov 21, 1967.
JOHNSON, J. Norman, b. Oct 19, 1905, d. Aug 22, 1979, hus of Queenie Mae Bowles, son of John Andrew and Mary "Cassie" Mattingly Johnson.
JOHNSON, James Claude, Jr. b. Sep 24, 1932, d. Nov 28, 1932, son of Jas. and Martha Russell Johnson.
Inf. son of Mr. and Mrs. Johnson, Apr 6, 1925.
Inf. son of Mr. and Mrs. Johnson, Feb 3, 1921.
JOHNSON, James 'Ernest' H., b. Oct 28, 1882, d. Feb 17, 1956, hus of Mary Rosalie Cooper, son of Hillery and Ann Marie Thompson Johnso.
JOHNSON, James H., b. Sep 25, 1920, d. Aug 11, 1940, son of Francis V. and Annie Williams Johnson.
JOHNSON, James Kennedy, b. Feb 19, 1903, d. Sep 1, 1979, son of Parren and Lottie Tennison Johnson.

Three Sides of Square Column
-JOHNSON, John Alexander, b. Dec 28, 1861, d. Oct 3, 1947, hus of Mary Ann nee Johnson.
-JOHNSON, Mary Ann Hays "Molly", b. Oct 13, 1860, d. Mar 4, 1939, wife of John Alexander Johnson.
-JOHNSON, Keating, b. Mar 7, 1888, d. Aug 5, 1907, son of J. A. and M. A. Johnson.
-JOHNSON, Bessie M., b. Apr 15, 1895, d. Feb 16, 1964, dau of J. A. and M. A. Johnson.
-JOHNSON, J. Sidney, b. Feb 6, 1890, d. Dec 31, 1912, son of J. A. and M. A. Johnson.
JOHNSON, Joseph Adrian, b. 1905, d. 1919.
JOHNSON, Joseph Bernard, b. Dec 29, 1910, d. Nov 17, 1979, son of Geo. P. and Charlotte Tennison Johnson.
JOHNSON, Joseph Spencer, Sr. SGT USA WW II, b. Dec 20, 1914, d. Oct 10, 1987, hus of Susan Claire Thompson, son of James Claude and Martha Russell Johnson.
JOHNSON, Joseph Spencer, Jr. b. Aug 31, 1948,

d. Jan 10, 1990, hus of Janice Elaine Taylor, son of Joseph S. and Susan Claire Thompson Johnson.
JOHNSON, Leonard B., M.D., b. Jun 9, 1867, d. Nov 28, 1962, hus of Mary Edith Morgan.
JOHNSON, Martha, b. Apr 3, 1887, d. Dec 29, 1974, wife of Thomas Allen McKay.
JOHNSON, Martha Lucinda "Lula", b. Mar 1870, d. Jan 23, 1919, wife of William Baptist Cryer, dau of Wm. Edw. and Mary Eliza Raley Johnson.
JOHNSON, Mary 'Grace', b. Feb 29, 1912, d. Jan 7, 1957, wife of George X. Payne, Sr., dau of Rhodie and Marie Hebb Johnson.
JOHNSON, Mary Sophia, b. Mar 9, 1839, d. May 25, 1925, wife of Zackariah Hayden, dau of Bennet and Mary A. Johnson.
JOHNSON, Mary Virginia, b. 1884, d. 1932, dau of Geo. Edward and Johanna Long Johnson.
JOHNSON, Mattingly 'Gibbons', b. Apr 3, 1887, d. Nov 10, 1973, hus of Catherine "Bessie" Drury, son of Geo. Edw. and Johanna Long Johnson.
JOHNSON, Ruth Eleanor, b. May 9, 1918, d. Apr 10, 1992, wife of Charles Richard Estep, dau of Layton Edward and Charlotte Alberta McPherson Johnson.
JOHNSON, Sophie, b. Oct 13, 1847, d. Mar 19, 1924, wife of Wm. L. J. Mattingly, dau of Uriah and Clarissa Sherkley Johnson.
JOHNSON, Thomas George, b. 1913, hus of Dorothy E. Bridgett.
JOHNSON, Thomas Keating, b. Mar 5, 1919, d. Oct 10, 1919, son of Desales and Lucy C. Johnson.
JOHNSON, Thomas Rudolphus "Rhodie", b. Oct 1878, d. 1968, hus of Mary Lilith "Marie" Hebb, son of William Edward and Mary "Liza" Raley Johnson.
JOHNSON, William E., Jr. b. Jan 3, 1943, d. Mar 2, 1943.
JOHNSON, Zackariah, b. 1852, d. 1932, hus of Missouri Woodburn, son of Uriah and Clarissa Sherkley Johnson.
JONES, Dorothy Dillard, b. Jun 22, 1924 NC, d.

St. Joseph   261

Jul 16, 1993 DC, m. 15 Jan 1944 Joseph Clyde
Guy, dau of William Doyle and Daisy Ellen
Gowens Jones.
KNOTT, Ann Laura, b. Mar 27, 1881, d. Mar 31,
1906, wife of J. Spencer Knott.
KNOTT, Gladys Madeline, b. 1895, d. 1977, wife
of ___ Raley, dau of Luke Knott and Eleanor
Payne Knott Johnson. (Tombstone reads "dau of
Eleanor Payne and Knott Johnson".)
KNOTT, James D., b. Nov 28, 1914, d. Dec 20,
1918, son of Leo and Ethel Jane Raley Knott.
KNOTT, Louise Cecelia, b. Dec 11, 1896, d.
Mar 31, 1992, wife of Benjamin Clyde Raley,
dau of Henry and Georgianna Davis Knott.
LE CLERE, Lt. William Earl, USN, b. Jun 16,
1919, d. Nov 9, 1976 FL, hus of Marie
Johnson.
LLOYD, Wilbert W., b. 1892, d. 1923, hus of
Catherine 'Ethel' Johnson.
LONG, Amy Gertrude, b. Feb 3, 1901, d. Feb
15, 1970.
LONG, Charles Franklin, b. Dec 31, 1906, d.
Nov 19, 1991, hus of Margaret Evelyn Cusic,
son of Charles Philip and Emma Elizabeth
Wise Long.
LONG, Eleanor Rebecca, b. Oct 18, 1914, d. Feb
2, 1990 Balto, dau of Charles Philip and
Emma Elizabeth Wise Long.
LONG, J. Fred, b. 1865, d. 1947, hus of Lucy
M. ___, b. 1870, d. 1962.
LONG, J. Matthew, b. 1881, d. 1957.
LONG, J. Robert, b. Jul 29, 1855, d. Jan 10,
1931.
LONG, James J., b. Mar 25, 1846, d. Apr 30,
1901, hus of Annie E. ___, b. 1843, d. 1921.
LONG, James Robert, b. Nov 2, 1900, d. Apr
16, 1941.
LONG, James Thomas, b. 1849, d. 1916, hus of
Jane Harriet ___, b. 1851, d. 1928.
LONG, Johanna, b. 1859, d. 1927, wife of
George Edward Johnson.
LONG, John R., b. Aug 14, 1891, d. Apr 27,
1919.
LONG, Julie Theodora, b. Aug 28, 1887, d. Mar
29, 1977.

LONG, Katy, b. 1872, d. 1962.
LONG, Martin S., b. 1888, d. 1956, hus of Mary E. __, b. 1892, d. 1973.
LONG, Mazie Lou Theresa, b. May 3, 1911, d. Jun 20, 1992, wife of __ Cargill, dau of Richard Pelham and Rachel Ann Buckler Long.
LONG, Nannie C., b. Mar 16, 1868, d. May 27, 1935.
LONG, R. P., b. Oct 15, 1878, hus of Rachel Ann __, b. Jan 6, 1889, d. May 22, 1943.
Double Stone-Relationship Unknown
-LONG, Richard J., b. 1857, d. 1947.
-LONG, Mary Eulalia, b. 1898, d. Dec 10, 1975.
LOVE, Albert K., b. 1870, d. 1951, hus of Nora T. __, b. 1868, d. 1963.
LOVE, Benedict B., b. 1872, d. 1959, hus of Mary H. Hancock.
LOVE, Benedict Parren, d. Nov 14, 1974, hus of Mary Gibbons, son of Philip Dunbar and Madeline Johnson Love.
LOVE, Cecelia May, b. Apr 9, 1896, d. Jul 21, 1896, dau of Benedict B. and Mary Hancock Love.
LOVE, James Wilson, b. Jun 18, 1904, d. Oct 25, 1933.
LOVE, Linda, b. Dec 9, 1906, d. Jun 23, 1993, wife of Joseph D. Montedonico, dau of A. Kingsley and Nora Tippett Love.
LOVE, Mary J., d. Jan 18, 1920, age 75 yrs.
LOVE, May C., b. 1871, d. 1947.
LOVE, Miss Mazie, d. Oct 18, 1918, age 22 yrs.
LOVE, Philip, b. 1903, d. 1953.
LOVE, Philip G., Father, b. 1826, d. 1892.
LUPUS, Helen Mae, b. Sep 10, 1910 Balto, d. Mar 12, 1992, wife of Louis A. Copsey, dau of William and Catherine Lupus.
MARSHALL, Wilson Alexander, b. Nov 17, 1915, d. Feb 7, 1992, hus of Alice Miles, son of William Patrick and Anna Marie Mason Marshall.
MASON, Agnes T., b. Nov 17, 1917, d. Mar 10, 1987, wife of ___ Hazel, dau of Joseph and Lena Sommerville Mason.
MATTINGLY, Bernard Eugene, b. 1872, d. 1934, hus of Cliffie Mae Cryer.

St. Joseph

MATTINGLY, C. Cleopatra, b. 1880, d. 1950.
MATTINGLY, Clara E., b. Aug 12, 1899, d. Aug 7, 1991, wife of Samuel A. Nelson, dau of Eugene B. and Cliffie M. Cryer Mattingly.
MATTINGLY, Genevieve Hilda, b. Jan 21, 1918, d. Nov 18, 1992, m. 1935 John Francis Wood, dau of Louis Johnson and Lillian Delahay Mattingly.
MATTINGLY, Horace I., b. Apr, 1898, d. 1971, hus of Annie A.___, b. 1898, son of Bernard Eugune and Cliffie Cryer Mattingly.
MATTINGLY, J. Freeman, b. Feb 12, 1891, d. Jun 3, 1965, hus of Agnes E.___, b. Sep 6, 1898.
MATTINGLY, James Ignatius, b. Dec 20, 1899, d. May 25, 1944.
MATTINGLY, Louis Johnson, b. 1888, d. 1956, hus of Lillian L. Delahay.
MATTINGLY, Mary Amelia, b. Jul 19, 1903, d. Oct 25, 1987, wife of Joseph Richard Cheseldine, Sr, dau of Bernard Eugene and Cliffie Cryer Mattingly.
MATTINGLY, Mary C., b. 1876, d. 1940, wife of J. Andrew Johnson.
MATTINGLY, Mary Madalin, b. Aug 26, 1884, d. Aug 7, 1977.
    One Stone
-MATTINGLY, Mary Sophia, Dec 26, 1921.
-MATTINGLY, Mary Jane, Oct 21, 1921.
-MATTINGLY, Doris T. Lee, infant.
    One Stone
-MATTINGLY, Peter H., b. 1842, d. 1917.
-MATTINGLY, Eleanora, b. 1843, d. 1926.
-MATTINGLY, Fannie, b. 1848, d. 1933.
-MATTINGLY, Bettie J., b. 1850, d. 1909.
MATTINGLY, T. Lee, b. 1864, d. 1941.
MATTINGLY, Thomas Richley "Tommy", b. Jan 30, 1965, d. Aug 21, 1991, son of Schercliffe B. "Tholly" and Agnes C. "Sis" Mattingly.
MATTINGLY, Wm. B., b. Feb 22, 1873, d. Sep 25, 1925, hus of C. Noema ___, b. Apr 29, 1882, d. Jan 3, 1960, stone also reads "children
  MATTINGLY, E. Paul, b. Jun 19, 1910.
  MATTINGLY, Margaret T., b. Dec 12, 1909."
MATTINGLY, Wm. L. J., b. Mar 17, 1845, d. Jun 8, 1926, hus of Sophie Johnson.

One Stone
-MATTINGLY, Wm. Sylvester, b. Sep 22, 1901, d. Oct 4, 1982.
-MATTINGLY, Geo. Goddard, b. Jul 12, 1903, d. Aug 23, 1974.
-MATTINGLY, Mary Virgina, b. Jun 10, 1909, d. Jun 20, 1958.
MATTINGLY, Wm. Wallace, b. Oct 27, 1876, d. Jul 1, 1939, hus of Ada Virginia __, b. Sep 8, 1874, d. Jan 31, 1962.
McKAY, Thomas Allen, b. Sep 30, 1881, d. May 24, 1974, hus of Martha Johnson.
McQUADE, George Henry, b. Apr 19, 1926 DC, d. Jun 7, 1993, son of John Marshall and Lillie V. Morgan McQuade.
McQUADE, John Marshall, Jr. b. May 23, 1923 DC, d. Oct 27, 1992, son of John Marshall and Lillie V. Morgan McQuade.
MIDDLETON, Christine, b. Jan 3, 1911, d. Dec 11, 1988, m. (1st) Dr. Aloysius C. Welch, (2d)__ Healy, dau of Arthur R. and Christina Murray Lloyd Middleton.
MILES, John Henry, d. Jan 18, 1974, hus of Helen Australia Thomas.
MITCHELL, Virginia, b. Mar 25, 1901 MN, d. Jul 10, 1991, wife of Richard F. Barber, Sr.
MONTEDONICO, Joseph D., Sr. d. Mar 24, 1993, hus of Linda Love.
MORGAN, John Nelson, b. Mar 8, 1918, d. Jan 31, 1989, son of Woodley and Mertie Morgan.
MORGAN, Joseph Johnson, d. Dec 11, 1972, hus of Cora C. __.
MORGAN, Mary Edith "Mamie", b. Dec 15, 1873, d. Feb 9, 1958, wife of Leonard B. Johnson, M.D., also has Memorial Stone in St. John's Cemetery.
NELSON, Benjamin, d. Dec 21, 1974, m. 1931 Rosalie Short.
NELSON, Edna Mae, b. Feb 25, 1908, d. Oct 17, 1911, dau of F. Benton and Elizabeth Tennyson Nelson.
NELSON, Francis Benton, b. Oct 6, 1885, d. Sep 7, 1938, hus of C. Elizabeth Tennyson.
NELSON, Francis P., b. 1910, d. 1974, hus of Kathleen __, b. 1912, d. 1984.

St. Joseph

NELSON, John Benton, CPL USA WW II, b. Aug 14, 1913, d. Dec 12, 1959.
NELSON, Samuel A., b. Feb 21, 1892, d. May 24, 1979, hus of Clara E. Mattingly.
NORRIS, Annie Gertrude, b. Jul 6, 1903, d. Jun 19, 1988, wife of ___ Cusic.
O'HARA, Esther Miriam, 96, b. May 14, 1894 Phila, d. Sep 6, 1990 DC, wife of James Bernard Naughton, dau of Henry and Catherine O'Connell O'Hara.
OWENS, William James, b. Apr 5, 1912, d. Sep 1, 1990, hus of Mabel Dean, son of Robert A. and Lena Rebecca Russell Owens.
PAYNE, Eleanor T., b. 1876, d. 1965, m. (1st) 1892 Luke Knott, (2d) 1902 George Webster Johnson, dau of Thos and Sarah E. Long Payne.
PAYNE, Ethel 'Gertrude', b. Jul 17, 1905, d. Apr 26, 1971, wife of Geo. Donald Abell, dau of Morgan and Eva Johnson Payne.
PAYNE, George H., b. 1932, d. 1954, son of Geo. X. and Mary G. Johnson Payne.
PAYNE, George Morgan, b. 1872, d. 1946, hus of Clara Johnson.
PAYNE, George X., Sr. b. Jul 28, 1911, hus of Mary 'Grace' Johnson.
PAYNE, John A., b. 1861, d. 1927, hus of Annie Q. ___, b. 1878, d. 1918.
PILKERTON, William A., Sr. d. Jan 1983, hus of Helen Mae Wood.
QUADE, Earl Matthew, b. Mar 21, 1921, d. Jun 28, 1992, m. 21 Jun 1958 Sue Ann Lowe, son of Joseph Francis and Annie Marie Morgan Quade.
QUADE, Martin A., Jr. 58, d. Jun 19, 1990, hus of Nancy I. ___, son of Martin Quade and Margaret Quade Gray.
QUADE, Thomas Elmer, Sr. b. Jul 28, 1912, d. Nov 7, 1989, hus of Mary Josephine ___, son of Joseph "Jody" and Sarah Frances Quade.
RALEY, Benjamin 'Clyde', b. Nov 9, 1897, d. Jun 4, 1985, m. 19 Jan 1920 Louise Cecelia Knott, son of Daniel and Minnie Hazel Raley.
RALEY, Daniel, b. 1863, d. 1951, hus of Minnie Iowa Hazel, son of John B. and Jane M. Drury Raley.

RALEY, Daniel Leroy, b. Oct 9, 1921, d. Jan 4, 1922, son of Alvah and Mary Magdaline Henderson Raley.
RALEY, Donald, b. Oct 1922, d. Aug 1923, son of Benj. 'Clyde' and Louise Cecelia Knott Raley.
RALEY, Earl, b. 1902, d. 1964, hus of Frances __, son of Daniel and Minnie Hazel Raley.
RALEY, Ethel Jane, b. Oct 27, 1894, d. Dec 20, 1918, wife of Leo Knott (bur All Faith RCC), dau of Daniel and Minnie Hazel Raley.
RALEY, Franklin "Teddy", b. Sep 29, 1936 Pr. Geo. Co., MD, d. Mar 31, 1937 Pr. Geo. Co., MD, son of Alvah and Mary M. Henderson Raley.
RALEY, John E., b. Apr 25, 1925 DC, d. Nov 2, 1925 DC, son of Alvah and Mary M. Henderson Raley.
RALEY, Leo Elmer, b. Dec 19, 1916, d. Oct 23, 1918, son of Daniel and Minnie Hazel Raley.
RUSSELL, James Victor, b. Dec 14, 1906, d. Feb 11, 1993, hus of Violet G. __, son of William and Theresa Woodburn Russell.
RUSSELL, Martha Marie, b. 1890, d. Feb 4, 1974, m. 6 Jan 1914, James 'Claude' Johnson, dau of William and Willie Lee Russell.
RUSSELL, Mary Elvie, b. Jan 22, 1904, d. Apr 5, 1990, wife of Bernard H. Russell.
RUSTIN, James Aloysius, Sr. b. Jun 13, 1912, d. Apr 15, 1990, hus of Mary Elizabeth __, son of James Henry and Rosa Marie Butler Rustin.
RYAN, Matthew George, b. Jul 17, 1898 Balto, d. Mar 4, 1988.
SHORT, Rosalie, b. Apr 24, 1915, d. Dec 19, 1991, wife of Benjamin Nelson, dau of James Henry and Catherine Fenwick Short.
SWANN, Joseph Johnson, b. Mar 20, 1892, d. Oct 10, 1970, hus of Agnes N. Johnson.
TENNISON, Mrs. Alice O., b. April 20, 1847, d. Apr 12, 1923.
TENNISON, Charlotte Anne "Lottie", b. 1874, d. Feb 4, 1962, wife of Geo. Parren Johnson.
TENNISON, Endress Clem, b. 1887, d. 1965.
TENNISON, George F., b. Oct 27, 1816, d. Oct 31, 1906.

St. Joseph

TENNISON, Jessie Marie, 101, b. Nov 24, 1889, d. Apr 10, 1991, wife of Charles Webster Burch, dau of Geo. Francis and Mary Cornelia Latham Tennison.
TENNYSON, Agnes Jeannette "Nettie", b. Feb 17, 1909, d. Aug 3, 1990, wife of Joseph Louis Yates, dau of Ira F. and Mary Alberta Guy Tennyson.
TENNYSON, C. Elizabeth, b. June 24, 1890, d. Dec 20, 1976, wife of Francis B. Nelson.
THOMAS, Helen Australia, b. Jan 24, 1923, d. Jul 24, 1993 DC, m. 20 Feb 1938 John Henry Miles, dau of William and Sarah Countiss Thomas.
THOMAS, Mary Teresa, b. Mar 20, 1921, d. Dec 8, 1992, m. 7 Jun 1947 William Edwin Young, dau of Aquila Thomas and Cecelia Young Thomas Reed, stepdau of James M. Reed.
THOMAS, Rosetta, b. Apr 4, 1907, d. Dec 2, 1988, wife of __ Briscoe, dau of Theodore and Hattie Thomas.
THOMPSON, Brent Allen, b. Aug 2, 1908, d. May 4, 1990, hus of Theresa Somerville, son of William B. and Ella Hawkins Thompson.
THOMPSON, Catherine June, b. Jun 21, 1943, d. Aug 4, 1990, dau of Joseph G. and Mary Agnes Nelson Thompson.
THOMPSON, Clara Elizabeth, b. Sep 27, 1908, d. Jan 2, 1994, wife of George DeBracy Burroughs, dau of William James and Sarah Helen Swann Thompson.
THOMPSON, John William, b. Oct 24, 1896, d. Nov 29, 1992, son of James Bruce and Eleanor Pilkerton Thompson.
THOMPSON, Joseph Henry, b. Nov 23, 1930, d. Aug 19, 1989, hus of Mary Alice __, son of Joseph and Maidee Cusic Thompson.
THOMPSON, Susan Claire, b. Dec 6, 1913, wife of Joseph Spencer Johnson, Sr.
VALLANDINGHAM, Dorothy Irene, d. Feb 14, 1978, m. 27 Feb 1938 Robert Aloysius Guy.
WALKER, Helen Genevieve, 71, d. Feb 25, 1991, wife of Raymond Louis Walker, Sr.
WATHEN, Ignatius Trueman, b. 1879/80, d. May 18, 1970, hus of Mary Genevieve Mattingly.

WATHEN, James Thomas, b. Apr 13, 1937, d. Sep 16, 1990, son of Ignatius Trueman, Sr. and Mary Genevieve Mattingly Wathen.

WATHEN, Mary Imelda, b. Nov 24, 1910, d. Mar 2, 1993, wife of Leonard Bethleham Johnson, dau of Ignatius and Mary Genevieve Mattingly Wathen.

WELCH, Joseph Carney "Connie", b. Jun 26, 1934, d. Jan 11, 1991, hus of Mary Joyce Tennyson, son of Herman and Bessie M. Garner Welch.

WILLIAMS, Anna Myrtle "Annie", b. Mar 18, 1898, d. Nov 15, 1977, wife of Francis V. Johnson.

WOOD, Elvie Ann, b. Nov 22, 1919, d. Oct 8, 1992, wife of Elwood Cusic, Sr., dau of James Clarence and Mary Etta Long Wood.

WOOD, Helen Mae, b. Mar 22, 1901, d. Dec 16, 1992, m. 1919 William A. Pilkerton, Sr., dau of William Leonard and Mary Melvina Wood.

WOOD, Henry A., d. Feb 25, 1967, hus of Martha L. __.

WOOD, Johnson B., Sr. b. May 29, 1912, d. Dec 14, 1989, hus of Catherine M. __, son of Henery (sic) A. and Martha L. Wood.

WOOD, Mary Verna, b. Dec 5, 1902, d. Apr 3, 1992, wife of Joseph L. Hayden, Sr., dau of Wilson and Fannie Payne Wood.

WOODBURN, Catherine P., b. Feb 16, 1897, d. Jun 21, 1965.

WOODBURN, Missouri, b. 1854, d. 1932, wife of Zackariah Johnson.

YATES, Claudia Lynn, b. Sep 28, 1943, d. Dec 19, 1992, m. 2 Jun 1962 George G. Burroughs, Jr., dau of J. Lewis and Claudia "Bugs" Abell Guy Yates.

YOUNG, William Edwin, Sr. d. Apr 15, 1975, m. 7 June 1947 Mary Teresa Thomas.

ST. MARK'S METHODIST CEMETERY
Valley Lee, Md.

Cemetery Records submitted to St. Mary's Co. Genealogical Society by member David Roberts in observance of "Black History Month" 1983.

BENNETT, Louise, b. 1868, d. Feb 16, 1948.
BISCOE, Arthur, b. 1878, d. 1968.
BISCOE, Enoch Mansfield, b. 1906, d. 1975.
BISCOE, Henry A., b. 1878, d. 1958.
BISCOE, Raymond G., b. Nov 8, 1896, d. Oct 7, 1918.
BRISCOE, Clarence Enid, b. Sep 10, 1945, d. Dec 2, 1993, son of William Alexander and Mary Catherine Fenwick Briscoe.
BRISCOE, Flora Christine, b. Dec 16, 1921, d. Nov 6, 1967.
BRISCOE, James A., b. Jan 12, 1892, d. Dec 28, 1951.
BRISCOE, James Franklin, d. Jul 28, 1940.
BRISCOE, Joseph S., b. Mar 9, 1919, d. Dec 26, 1958.
BRISCOE, Joseph X., b. 1950, d. 1969.
BRISCOE, Rebecca, b. 1897, d. 1964.
BROWN, Ethel Genevieve, b. May 1, 1922, d. Aug 18, 1993, m. 18 Nov 1939 John Cornelius Jordon, Sr., dau of James Aaron and Lillie Hendrickson Brown.
BROWN, Lettie Ann, b. Nov 21, 1897, d. Oct 5, 1988, wife of John Waters, dau of Joseph and Annie Brown.
BROWN, Vernon A., b. Aug 31, 1907, d. Sep 30, 1965.
CASTER, Annie E., b. 1873, d. 1952.
CASTER, Isaac, b. 1867, d. 1932.
CUTCHEMBER, Jeremiah A., b. 1886, d. 1957.
DAILEY, Juanita, b. 1901, d. 1969.
DICKENS, Paul Leon, b. 1940, d. 1966.
DYSON, Frank, b. 1884, d. 1962.
GLADDEN, Elsie Nona, b. Feb 18, 1930, d. May 18, 1993, dau of Charles Alexander and Ruth Allen Morgan Gladden.
GROSS, Annie A., b. May 1, 1910, d. Aug 8, 1989, wife of Holton R. Briscoe, dau of

William and Maggie Cook Gross.
GROSS, Maggie M., b. 1874, d. 1968.
HOLLAND, Rosemary "Sally", b. Jul 7, 1921, d. Jul 29, 1991, wife of __ Morgan, dau of Catherine Holland.
JORDON, Lorenzo, b. 1899, d. 1969, divorced from Mary Myrtle Statesman.
LANCASTER, E., b. Apr 8, 1864, d. Aug 5, 1918.
LAWRENCE, Adolph Donald, b. 1930, d. 1964.
LAWRENCE, Dennis William, b. 1895, d. 1969.
LAWRENCE, James Arthur, b. 1964, d. 1969.
LAWRENCE, Jesse Cornelius, b. Nov 11, 1903, d. Nov 30, 1968, hus of Bertha M. Jordon.
LAWRENCE, Maggie Louise, b. Dec 28, 1931, d. Mar 8, 1989, wife of Russell L. Haywood, Sr., dau of Jesse C. and Bertha M. Jordan Lawrence.
LAWRENCE, Maurice, b. Apr 3, 1893, d. Jun 11, 1963.
LEE, James Richard, b. Nov 15, 1913, d. Sep 4, 1992, hus of Ruth __, son of Joseph and Julie Greenwell Lee.
MORGAN, Arthur R., b. 1887, d. 1949.
MORGAN, Blanche, b. 1875, d. 1961.
MORGAN, Daniel, b. 1885, d. 1974.
MORGAN, Daniel, b. 1943, d. 1975.
MORGAN, Dora E., b. 1871, d. 1948.
MORGAN, Joseph A., b. 1880, d. 1956.
MORGAN, Kendall O., b. 1911, d. 1964.
MORGAN, Patsy Ann, b. 1850, d. 1925.
PECK, Emma V., b. 1895, d. Apr 7, 1949.
ROACH, George W., d. May 6, 1972.
SEARIGHT, Dorothy Mae, b. Nov 9, 1939 AL, d. Dec 31, 1991, wife of __ Terry, dau of Zollie and Lurline Perdue Searight.
STATESMAN, Rev. Joseph S., b. 1874, d. 1943, hus of Ida R. __, b. 1877, d. 1963, son of Rev. Hezekiah Statesman.
STATESMAN, Mary E., b. 1910, d. 1937.
STATESMAN, Mary Myrtle, b. Oct 5, 1898, d. Nov 1, 1988, divorced from Lorenzo Jordon, dau of Rev. Joseph S. and Ida R. Statesman, gdau of Rev. Hezekiah Statesman.
THOMPSON, Elizabeth Mary Jane, b. May 1, 1904, d. Apr 16, 1993, wife of Arthur Thompson,

St. Marks

dau of William and Ellen Hawkins Thompson.
THOMPSON, Helen, b. 1909, d. 1966.
THOMPSON, W. John, b. Jan 10, 1888, d. Feb 20, 1953.
THOMPSON, William B., b. 1861, d. 1954.
TRAVERS, Charles C., b. May 5, 1917, d. Apr 19, 1968.
TRAVERS, James W., b. 1886, d. Sep 6, 1948.
WHALEN, Dora Lennett, b. Dec 29, 1929, d. Jul 1, 1991, wife of Frank D. Travers, dau of G. Raymond and Helen Morgan Whalen.
WHALEN, Rev. Frances Leona, b. Sep 7, 1928, d. Aug 1, 1991, wife of Thomas Cornelius Morgan, dau of Geo. Raymond and Helen Morgan Whalen.
WHALEN, Henry Alexander, b. Jun 8, 1933, d. Aug 23, 1961.
WHALEN, James Limon, 90, d. Oct 24, 1993.
WHALEN, Marion Adelaide, b. Sep 10, 1919, d. Nov 11, 1991, wife of Aaron Eugene Brown, dau of George and Sarah Gladden Whalen.
WIGGINS, Audrey B., b. 1914, d. 1970.

ST. MARY'S EPISCOPAL CHAPEL
Rt.6 E
New Market, Md.

This Chapel was built in 1887 for the black members of All Faith Parish. These records are in the St. Mary's Chapel Registers 1906--1975. The Chapel was closed in 1960. Since then, the black members have joined the congregation of the Parish church. Those who had burial sites continued to use them.

BARNES, Jno. Samuel, d. Oct 1923, no age given.
BRISCOE, Elizabeth, d. Oct 19, 1927, 42 yrs.
BRISCOE, Mrs. Margaret, d. Jun 18, 1921, age 82 yrs.
BRISCOE, Nannie, d. Jul 16, 1957, age 41 yrs.
BRISCOE, Robert, d. May 1923, no age given.
BRISCOE, Rufert, d. Feb 8, 1919, age 8 mos.
BROOKS, Frank, d. 1909-1911, no other info.
BROOKS, Mrs. Harriett Mahalie, d. May 27, 1911, age 67.
BROOKS, Jean Elizabeth, d. May 26, 1947, age 8 yrs 11 mos 10 das, tombstone standing 1976.
BROOKS, Mary Jane Adelaide, d. Aug 11, 1935, age 1 yr 5 mos.
BUSH, Alice, d. May 15, 1937, age 59 yrs 10 mos 14 das, tombstone standing in 1976.
DENT, Samuel, d. May 6, 1937, age 77 or 80 yrs.
DORSEY, Nellie, d. 1909-1911, no other info.
DUNCAN, Infant, d. 1955-1957, son of James and Irine Duncan.
FORD, John, d. after Oct 1962, no info. given.
FORD, Infant, d. Nov 24, 1945, son of John P. and Mary Ford.
FORD, Mary Ann Lee, d. Mar 29, 1948, age 30 yrs 14 das, wife of __ Campbell.
FORD, Mary Laura Lee, d. Jan 18, 1957, age 72.
FORD, Robert Lee, d. Aug 1, 1970, age 83 yrs.
FORD, Vinie Elizabeth, d. Jan 31, 1969, age 81 yrs.
HAWKINS, Georgiana, d. Jun 12, 1935, age 59 yrs 3 mos and 2 das, wife of __ Holly.
HOLLEY, Thomas Claude, 79, d. Feb 25, 1975.
HOLLY, Jane, d. Jun 4, 1906, age 80, wife of

___ Carter.
HOLLY, Laura Catherine, d. Jun 11, 1940, age 51 yrs, wife of ___ Somerville, tombstone standing in 1976.
HOLLY, Mary Anetta, d. Apr 13, 1936, age 50 yrs.
HOLLY, Marion, (male) d. Sep 15, 1907, age 20.
HOLLY, Oscar, d. 1929, no age given.
HOLLY, Rosa Gertrude, d. Apr 25, 1944, age 50 yrs 5 mos 6 das.
JACKSON, Rebecca, d. Mar 1923, age 55 yrs.
JENIFER, Alfred A., d. Oct 22, 1941, 52 yrs.
JENIFER, Gertrude, d. Oct 23, 1909, age 37.
JENIFER, Ida, d. 1909-1911, no other info.
KEY, Benjamin, d. 1909-1911, no other info.
LYLES, Sarah Maria, d. Jan 21, 1950, age 85 yrs 1 mo 10 das, wife of ___ Holley, tombstone standing in 1976.
LYLES, William Isaac, d. Feb 19, 1955, 54 yrs.
MACK, Thomas, d. 1909-1911, no other info.
MARTIN, Edward O., d. Oct 31, 1962, age not given.
MARTIN, Henry Joseph, d. Apr 21, 1972, age 61 yrs.
MARTIN, Mary Charlotte, d. May 27, 1940, age 50 yrs 1 mo, tombstone standing 1976.
MARTIN, Merrick, d. Apr 19, 1927, 105 yrs.
MOLDEN, James Thomas, d. Camp Dix, NJ Oct 6, 1918, age 26. Tombstone standing 1976.
PENN, Samuel, d. Jul 29, 1918, age 65.
PLATER, Edward, d. Jan 16, 1937, age 78 yrs 7 mos.
PLATER, Hattie Virline, d. Apr 12, 1949, age 58 yrs 3 mos 5 das, wife of ___ Woodland.
PLATER, Robert S., d. Jul 24, 1954, 54 yrs.
SOTHORON, James, d. Nov 5, 1907, age 26.
SPEEKS, Mollie Ann, d. Mar 18, 1951, age 78 yrs 7 das, wife of ___ Thomas.
THOMAS, Ann, 1893. Only date given.
(From All Faith Parish Register, appears to be first burial recorded for this cemetery.)
THOMAS, Mrs. Ann, d. Feb 5, 1909.
THOMAS, Elmer, d. Camp Meade, MD Oct 19, 1918, age 22. Tombstone standing 1976.
THOMAS, Henry, d. 1929, no age given.
THOMAS, Joseph Wadsworth, d. Oct 31, 1941, age

St. Marys Episcopal

39 yrs 1 mo 16 das, tombstone standing 1976.
THOMAS, Julia Eileen, d. Aug 12, 1936, 35 yrs, wife of __ Briscoe.
THOMAS, Louise, d. 1907, age 6 yrs.
THOMAS, William, d. Mar 17, 1927, no age given.
TOLSON, Ida, d. 1918/1919, no other info.
TOLSON, Ida, d. Jul 11, 1935, age 7 yrs 6 mos 13 das.
TOLSON, Mary, d. May 1, 1936, age 37 yrs.
TOLSON, Thomas Alfred, d. Oct 2, 1942, age 56 yrs 8 mos.
TOLSON, Webster, d. Nov 19, 1957, no age given.
TYLER, Ada, d. 1918/1919, no other info.
TYLER, William, d. 1918/1919, no other info.
WARREN, George, d. 1927? tombstone standing in 1976.
WARREN, Grace, d. Feb 6, 1919, tombstone standing in 1976.
WEEMS, Charles, d. Jun 16, 1950, age 42 yrs 2 mos 18 das.
YATES, Mary, d. 1927, no age given.
YOUNGE, Jno. W., d. Dec 1924, no age given.

ST MARY'S QUEEN OF PEACE CATHOLIC CEMETERY
Dr. Johnson Road
Helen, Md.

ATLAS, David Marlowe, Jr. b. Apr 3, 1970, d. Dec 21, 1993, Phila, PA, m. 10 Jul 1993 Mary Helen Rose, son of David and Katherine Bell Atlas; gson of T. Webster, Sr. and Mary Catherine Sterling Bell; Harry and Mary Jo Atlas.

BAILEY, John Franklin, Jr. b. Mar 31, 1918, d. May 27, 1990, hus of Shirley Theresa Fuller, son of John Frank and Alberta "Vertie" Marie Bailey.

BARNES, Joseph Bernard, Sr. b. Jan 21, 1923, d. Nov 7, 1991 NY, son of Charles Henry and Agnes Short Barnes.

BARNES, Mary Catherine "Katie", b. Dec 17, 1901, d. Apr 10, 1993, wife of John A. Young, dau of James Samuel and Lucy Young Barnes.

BEAN, Olive Marie, b. Apr 22, 1907, d. Oct 5, 1988, wife of Leon Hill, dau of Thomas W. and Elizabeth Evans Bean.

BERRY, Frank Saint, b. Aug 4, 1913, d. Mar 2, 1993, m. 1930 Mary Cecelia Trent, son of Milton and Annie Gray Berry.

BERRY, James Henry "Luke", b. Jan 9, 1924, d. Oct 15, 1990 DC, son of Joseph Walker, Sr. and Lena Somerville Mason Berry.

BERRY, Joseph Edward, Sr. b. Dec 20, 1922, d. Feb 24, 1990, hus of Elsie Frances __, son of Joseph Walker, Sr. and Lena Pauline Mason Berry.

BOND, Mary Lola, b. Mar 22, 1916, d. Apr 14, 1988, wife of __ Plater, dau of Joseph and Nannie Bond.

BOWMAN, Walter Marshall, Jr. b. Jan 20, 1927, d. Mar 6, 1993, m. 4 Feb 1950 Ann Mills, son of Walter and Grace Hawkins Bowman.

BOYD, William Dunbar III, b. Jul 27, 1972, d. Jul 31, 1988, son of Dr. Wm. D. and Carmel O. "Duffy" Boyd.

BUCKLER, Elizabeth V., d. Jul 1976, wife of F. Elliott Burch.

BURCH, F. Elliott, b. Dec 21, 1908, d. Dec

12, 1992, m. 1923 Elizabeth V. Buckler, son
of Samuel Bernard and Sarah Adams Burch.
BUTLER, Joseph Ignatius "Sam", Jr. d. Jul 25,
1987, m. 27 Dec 1947 Laura Lee Holt.
CHASE, James Leroy, b. Sep 7, 1927, d. Jun 3,
1992, hus of Martha Louise Holt, son of
John and Catherine Nollan Chase.
COYLE, John A., b. Mar 11, 1914, d. Nov 15,
1993 NY, hus of Mary Agnes Liddy, son of
John and Ruby Haddow Coyle.
CROLL, Mathilda C., b. Oct 5, 1911, d. May 15,
1990, wife of Bartlett E. Frere, dau of
August and Anna Adams Croll.
CUMMINGS, Robert John "Bob", USM Vietnam, b.
May 5, 1944 NY, d. Jul 31, 1993, son of John
Joseph and Katherine Mary Anderson Cummings.
CURTIS, Joseph B., Sr. b. Nov 24, 1910, d. Sep
23, 1988, hus of Jane C. __, son of James
Curtis and Regina Wade.
DALY, Richard Anthony, b. Dec 12, 1958, d. May
7, 1991, hus of Carol Marie __, son of Jack
Lloyd and Elizabeth Ann Baxter Daly.
DICKERSON, Francis Aubrey, Sr. b. Jul 11, 1920,
d. Feb 24, 1993, m. (1st) Agnes Loretta __,
(2d) 28 Jun 1980 Shirley Theresa Briscoe,
son of George Allen and Elizabeth Dickerson.
DYSON, Mary Elizabeth "Doris", b. Dec 26,
1927, d. Jun 27, 1992, dau of Edward and
Josephine Jordon Dyson.
DYSON, Mary Hilda, b. Dec 1, 1932, d. Apr 10,
1990, dau of Wm Edw.and Mary Josephine Dyson.
FAUNCE, Dorothy Ann, b. 1923, d. 1981, wife of
George Thomas Johnson.
FENWICK, John Leonard, b. Apr 27, 1944, d. Oct
24, 1990 DC, hus of Edna __, son of James
Earl and Lillian T. Fenwick.
FORBES, Joseph William, b. Dec 24, 1930, d.
Aug 25, 1991, hus of Ethel Elizabeth __, son
of Richard E. and Rose Hance Forbes.
FULLER, Shirley Theresa, b. Feb 25, 1922, d.
Feb 25, 1978, wife of John Franklin Bailey.
GOLDRING, Earl Bernard, b. Jan 27, 1940, d.
Mar 26, 1991 OH, hus of Mary Frances Barnes,
son of John P. and Janie E. Goldring.
GOLDRING, John Philip, b. Mar 28, 1907, d. Apr

6, 1989, hus of Julia Dorothy __, son of Grant and Mary Liza Coates Goldring.
GRAY, Martin Goddard, b. Oct 9, 1905, d. Nov 29, 1990, hus of Josephine Quade, son of Charles McKenny and Lucy Ann Pilkerton Gray.
HERBERT, Edward Lee, b. Dec 25, 1918, d. Feb 10, 1989, son of Lee and Mary Elizabeth Thomas Herbert.
HILL, Nicholas, b. Jun 2, 1906, d. Feb 19, 1988, hus of Flora E. Lyon, son of Zackary and Elizabeth Hill.
HILL, Woodrow Wilson, Sr. b. Dec 22, 1916, d. Feb 19, 1989, hus of Mary Agnes __, son of King Henry and Rose Emily Lacey Hill.
HOLLAND, Melvin, b. Oct 27, 1932 GA, d. May 13, 1988, hus of Evelyn L. __, son of Allen and Gertin Holland.
HOLT, Helena Melissa "Missy" b. Jul 9, 1969, d. Sep 22, 1993 Germany, dau of Philip Irvin and Mary Teresa Holt.
HOLT, Laura Lee, b. Sep 20, 1929, d. Nov 6, 1991, wife of Joseph Ignatius "Sam" Butler, Jr., dau of Harry Wingate and Bessie Penn Holt.
HOLT, Wingate Harry, d. 1974, hus of Bessie Elizabeth Penn.
JOHNSON, George Thomas, b. 1917, hus of Dorothy Ann Faunce.
JOHNSON, George Thomas, Jr. b. 1940, d. 1980, son of George T. and Dorothy Faunce Johnson.
JOHNSON, James Allison, SSGT USA WW II, b. Sep 30, 1912, d. Jul 2, 1978.
JOHNSON, Peggs S., b. 1958, d. 1986.
JOHNSON, Vickie Lynn, b. Jun 26, 1961, d. Feb 12, 1971, dau of Geo. T. and Dorothy Faunce Johnson.
KLEAR, Anna Sarah, b. Jan 18, 1928, d. Sep 18, 1991, wife of Maurice Raymond "Buddy" Strine, dau of Paul and Jane Klear.
LIDDY, Mary Agnes, d. Mar 15, 1987, wife of John A. Coyle.
LOWE, Gerard Robert, b. Jun 30, 1929 NY, d. Aug 21, 1989, hus of Patricia Mary Nolan, son of Christopher Joseph and Margaret C. Lowe.

LYLES, Mary Agnes, 56, d. Dec 27, 1990, wife of __ Hawkins, dau of Edward C. and Bertha R. Lyles.
LYON, Flora Elizabeth, b. Jul 9, 1910, d. Jul 3, 1991, wife of Nicholas Hill, dau of Joseph Dixie and Mary Agnes Lyon.
MARTIN, Dorothy Marie, 56, d. Oct 20, 1992, dau of Harry Jos. and Mary Virginia Gross Martin.
MASON, James Henry, b. Feb 15, 1900, d. Mar 30, 1988, son of Samuel Mason.
MATTINGLY, Leonard J., b. Apr 27, 1925, d. Nov 1, 1988, hus of Edith __.
MORELAND, James William, b. Dec 11, 1932, d. Mar 24, 1989, hus of Evelyn "Susie" __, son of Fred Albert and Mary Agnes Countiss Moreland.
NEAL, Joseph Thomas, b. Sep 24, 1914, d. Jul 25, 1993 DC, hus of Mary Blanche __, d. Nov 8, 1983, son of Sheron Young and Margaret Wright Neal.
NELSON, Paul Benjamin, b. Oct 24, 1932, d. Jul 15, 1992, son of Benjamin and Rosalie Short Nelson.
NORRIS, James A. "Jesse", b. May 24, 1911, d. Jun 10, 1990, hus of Agnes Peach, son of James I. and Leila C. Yates Norris.
OLIVER, Joseph Berry, Jr. b. Feb 26, 1926, d. Jul 1, 1991, hus of Marie Virginia __, son of Joseph Berry and Mary Cecelia Wedding Oliver.
PENN, Bessie Elizabeth, b. Apr 17, 1906, d. Apr 7, 1993, wife of Wingate Harry Holt, dau of Ida Elizabeth Penn.
PILKERTON, Elizabeth Ann "Bet", b. Apr 24, 1909, d. Aug 1, 1991, wife of Philip C. Quade, dau of William and Esther Pilkerton.
PILKERTON, Margaret Ann, b. Nov 11, 1910, d. Jan 8, 1994, wife of Bernard Melvin Wood, dau of Zachariah and Catherine Ann Bowles Pilkerton.
PILKERTON, William A., Sr., d. Jan 1983, m. 1919 Helen Mae Wood.
POVLICH, William Joseph "Willie", b. Jul 6, 1915 MI, d. Feb 2, 1993, m. 13 Aug 1938 Ag-

St. Mary's Queen

nes Elizabeth Yergovich, son of John and Eva Katrafeld Povlich.
QUADE, Philip C., d. Mar 25, 1988, m. 14 Apr 1926, Elizabeth Ann Pilkertn.
QUEEN, John Mitchell, b. Mar 11, 1922, d. Feb 26, 1993, son of John Edw. and Effie Somerville Queen.
RALEY, Floyd Aloysius, b. Mar 24, 1934, d. May 24, 1984, m. 26 Nov 1955 Dorothy Russell, son of Benj. 'Clyde' and Louise Cecelia Knott Raley.
RALEY, Thomas Arthur, b. Mar 31, 1910, d. Mar 7, 1986, son of Daniel and Minnie Iowa Hazel Raley, m. 25 Jun 1944 Margaret Lucille __, b. Feb 18, 1920, d. Jun 25, 1981.
ROSENBERGER, Dorothy Allen, b. Jul 5, 1924, d. Jul 18, 1988, wife of Donald T. Moore, dau of Allen and Clara Rosenberger.
SMITH, James Walter, Sr. b. Aug 1, 1929, d. Feb 14, 1991, hus of Mary A. __, son of James R. and Elva M. Smith.
SOMERVILLE, Frederick Rudolph "Rudy", b. Jul 14, 1937, d. Aug 6, 1993 VA, m. 1965 Norma Elaine Green, son of Joseph Dellie and Susie Anna Frederick Somerville.
SOMERVILLE, Leonidas Ralph, b. Oct 24, 1948, d. Nov 13, 1993, m. 24 Nov 1979 Janice Darlene Armstrong, son of Joseph Blaine and Catherine Cecelia Somerville.
SPEARS, Mamie Rosetta, b. Aug 7, 1902, d. Jun 27, 1991, wife of John P. Nelson, Sr., dau of Cornelius and Annie Spears.
STEVENS, Warren Bernard, b. Feb 13, 1921, d. Apr 13, 1993, m. 5 Jul 1943 Macie Theresa Barnes, son of Frank and Priscilla Stewart Stevens.
STRINE, Maurice Raymond "Buddy", d. 1977, hus of Anne Sarah Klear.
TENNYSON, Robert Milan "Bobby" b. Jan 25, 1945, d. Jun 1, 1990, hus of Betty Hall, son of Raymond "Rip" and Thelma Eileen Tennyson.
THOMAS, Annie Elizabeth, b. Jul 13, 1924, d. Jun 16, 1993, wife of Gorman Thomas, dau of Louis and Mary Marshall Thomas.
THOMPSON, Robert Lee, b. Feb 10, 1907, d. Dec

12, 1989, son of James Bruce and Eleanora Thompson.
TRENT, Mary Cecelia, d. 1963, wife of Frank Saint Berry.
WALTHER, Mark John, b. Aug 21, 1956 SC, d. Apr 10, 1988 SC, son of John M. and Frances Walther.
WHEELER, Mary Susan "Susie", b. Jun 12, 1941, d. Mar 4, 1993, m. 1958 Joseph Leonard "Teddy Bear" Latham, dau of Lathan and Maude Russell Wheeler.
WOOD, Bernard Melvin, d. Jan 1976, hus of Margaret Ann Pilkerton.
WOODS, Raymond Joseph, b. Sep 15, 1908 CT, d. Sep 10, 1991, hus of Iva McGuire, son of James T. and Catherine Driscoll Woods.
YOUNG, Alice C., b. Jun 4, 1923, d. Apr 10, 1992 DC, wife of Clarence Leo Young, dau of William Pickney and Agnes Yorkshire Young.
YOUNG, John Alexander, d. Aug 19, 1979, hus of Mary Catherine Barnes.
YOUNG, Keith Eugene, b. Jan 11, 1985, d. Dec 14, 1991, son of Vanessa Elaine Young and Keith Eugene Bond.
YOUNG, Vanessa Elaine, b. Apr 8, 1967, d. Dec 14, 1991, dau of William Edgar Jr. and Dorothy Cecelia Curtis Young.
YOWAISKI, Wallace Clark, Sr. b. Aug 17, 1918, d. Oct 27, 1992 DC, hus of Jane Elizabeth Fish, son of Francis and Mary Hill Yowaiski.

ST. MICHAEL'S CATHOLIC CEMETERY
Ridge, Md.

BARONIAK, George Frank, d. May 5, 1969, hus of Margaret Kalhasy.
BIRCH, Frank Ford, b. May 8, 1905, d. Jan 1, 1989, hus of Asulia Huntsman, son of Raymond and Mary Edith Ford Birch.
BOHANAN, Francis Donovan, b. ca 1900, d. Oct 1964, m. 1928 Mary Lloyd.
BRADBURN, Clara "Essie", 92, b. Feb 12, 1897, d. 1989, wife of __ Wilkerson, dau of Jefferson V. and Bertie Sisson Bradburn.
BRADBURN, Mark Aloysius, b. May 21, 1915, d. Jun 19, 1992, m.(1st) Olive Margaret Hammett, (2d) Doris Louise Smith, son of Clarence and Pauline Wilkerson Bradburn.
BRADBURY, Queenie Victoria, b. Oct 20, 1903, d. Jun 26, 1989, wife of George M. Willis, dau of John Francis and Mary Ridgell Bradbury.
CARROLL, Agnes Teresa, b. Feb 25, 1914, d. Feb 27, 1990, wife of Benjamin I. McKay, dau of Charles Ignatius and Mary Henrietta Norris Carroll.
COCCIA, Victoria, b. Feb 19, 1923 DC, d. Nov 21, 1992, m. 19 Jul 1942 DC, John Linwood Nelson, dau of Michael and Mickaella Fidele Coccia.
COCIMANO, Mary Helen, b. May 20, 1955 DC, d. Apr 26, 1993 DC, wife of William Frederick Lettau, dau of Antonio Rodney "Tony" and Annie Marie Dress Cocimano.
COOPER, Louis Stephen, b. Feb 24, 1920, d. Jul 16, 1993, m. 17 Jan 1948 Anna Marie Raley, son of Joseph Walter and Mary Magdaline Lumpkins Cooper.
COOPER, Paul Vincent, b. Dec 18, 1911, d. Jul 9, 1989, son of Joseph Walter and Mary M. Lumpkins Cooper.
COOPER, William E."Billy", Jr. b. Dec 13, 1976, d. Feb 22, 1990, son of Wm. E. and Alice Tippett Cooper; gson of Phillip R. and Bertille Cooper; Cpt. Wm. Taft and Mary E. Tippett.
CULLISON, Nellie E., b. Aug 12, 1898, d. Sep 29, 1992, m. (1st) Anthony D. DeLozier, (2d)

___ DeMarr, dau of William and Ida Ridgell Cullison.
DAMERON, Madeleine Amanda, b. Oct 23, 1912, d. Oct 7, 1989, wife of ___ Stewart, dau of James Spencer and Edna Brown Dameron.
DEAN, Amanda Elizabeth, b. Jul 21, 1904, d. Nov 7, 1992 DC, wife of Raymond Englebert McKay, dau of Charles Edgar and Jennie Ridgell Dean.
DELOZIER, Anthony D., d. Jan 12, 1948, m. 26 Dec 1920 Nellie E. Cullison.
DELOZIER, Margaret Almedia, b. Jan 30, 1932, d. Aug 4, 1990, wife of Charles L. "Pete" Trossbach, dau of Anthony D. and Nellie E. Cullison Delozier.
DRURY, Donald Franklin, Sr. b. Apr 13, 1923, d. Nov 1, 1989, hus of Ruth S. ___, son of James Raub, Sr. and Rose Somers Drury.
DUNBAR, Joseph Melvin, b. Oct 2, 1902, d. Mar 16, 1991, son of Joseph S. and Mary Dameron Dunbar.
ELIFF, Robert 'Ryan', Sr. b. Sep 8, 1898, d. Feb 26, 1990, hus of Mary Evelyn ___, son of Thomas H. and Elvie E. Norris Eliff.
EPPERSON, Hilary Samuel, USN Ret., b. Nov 25, 1923 VA, d. Sep 28, 1993, m. 3 Nov 1975 Shirley Burnett Dean, son of Andrew and Leah Hensley Epperson.
FENHAGEN, Leola Mary, b. Jul 12, 1907, d. Mar 29, 1993, wife of Joseph Irving Price, dau of James Harry and Mary Eva Goddard Fenhagen.
FENHAGEN, Loubertus John, b. ca 1900, d. Dec 4, 1984, hus of Helen Morgan.
FULLER, William Stanley "Stan", b. Jul 25, 1935 AK, d. Nov 25, 1991, son of Julian Alban and Evelyn Marie Connevey Fuller. Mem. Serv.
FUNK, Laura Naomi, b. Aug 2, 1903, d. Nov 5, 1989, wife of Raymond C. Taff, dau of Isaac Martin and Mary Louise Funk.
GATTON, John Edw., Sr. b. Oct 20, 1939, d. Apr 9, 1988, son of Thomas and Lucille Gatton.
GOODE, Sylvia Rebecca, b. Oct 19, 1908, d. Sep 13, 1989, wife of Cpt. Frederick T. Goode, Jr., dau of Percy and Maude Ridgell Goode.

St. Michael's

GREEN, Joseph C., d. Jun 17, 1990, hus of Lillian D. ___.

GUY-GIBSON, Elizabeth Ann, b. Feb 23, 1928, d. Jul 11, 1990 DC, dau of Mr. and Mrs. Reed Cooksey.

HAMMETT, John Abell, b. May 3, 1920, d. Dec 8, 1988, hus of Betty B. ___, son of Alfred F. and Mary Teresa Wilkerson Hammett.

HAMMETT, Mary Ellen, b. Dec 24, 1896, d. Mar 12, 1990, wife of Joseph J. Ridgell, dau of Ignatius and Mary Ellen Wilson Hammett.

HAMMETT, Mary Rosalie, b. Nov 16, 1902, d. Jun 22, 1990, wife of William Otto Trossbach, dau of Daniel Alfred and Ida Bohannan Hammett.

HOOPER, William Warren Clarke "Billy", b. Apr 8, 1923, d. Dec 30, 1992, son of Silas Gilbert and Edna Mae Clarke Hooper.

HUNTSMAN, Asulia, 89, d. May 11, 1993, wife of Frank Ford Birch.

KALHASY, Margaret, b. Jul 24, 1922 PA, d. Dec 28, 1992, m. 14 Aug 1940 George Frank Baroniak, dau of Joseph and Mary Muri Kalhasy.

KNOTT, William Bryan, d. 1971, hus of Alice Josephine Taylor.

LONG, Mary Wilhelmina, b. Sep 25, 1917, d. Jan 13, 1991, wife of ___ Gay, dau of Daniel Thomas and Amy Wood Long.

MAJORS, Leslie Andrew, b. Nov 6, 1904 OH, d. Oct 26, 1991, hus of Dorothy Gray Williams, son of Joseph and Julia Anna Majors.

MALESKY, Mary Rita, b. Mar 25, 1914 PA, d. Apr 9, 1991, wife of ___ Hutchins, dau of Joseph and Catherine Wasicki Malesky.

MAYOR, Louis Hamilton, b. May 13, 1908, d. Nov 4, 1992, m. 27 Nov 1927 Mary A. Naumann, son of Edward and Mary Hammett Mayor.

McCOY, Frederick Louis, b. Apr 25, 1915, d. Jan 22, 1990, hus of Elizabeth "Beth" Crowley, son of Joseph S. and Ella Schade McCoy.

McKAY, Raymond Englebert, d. Mar 12, 1974, hus of Amanda Elizabeth Dean.

MERCURE, Leo Henry, b. Oct 20, 1930, d. Jun 9, 1989, hus of Mary Dean, son of Leo and Blanche Forcher Mercure.

MESSICK, Louis Elijah, b. Mar 26, 1917, d. Feb 18, 1989, hus of Beverly Viant, son of Mahoney and Sabre Moore Messick.
MESSICK, Roger Martin, b. Oct 26, 1914, d. Nov 12, 1988, hus of Katherine Ridgell, son of Mahoney and Sabre Moore Messick.
MOFFETT, Richard George, b. Dec 14, 1914 NY, d. Jan 1, 1992, hus of Henrietta M. Bean, son of Richard James and Emily Mae McNally Moffett.
NAUMANN, Mary Adelaide, b. Oct 26, 1912 VA, d. Jul 3, 1992, wife of Louis H. Mayor, dau of Charles and Mary Edwards Naumann.
NORRIS, Charles Edward, b. Jun 28, 1934, d. Apr 25, 1992, hus of Gloria Margaret Forrest, son of Enoch and Sadie Zedek Norris.
NORRIS, James Edward, Sr. b. Jul 18, 1912, d. Mar 8, 1990, hus of Burnette Ridgell, son of Joseph Neal, Sr. and Eva S. Mayor Norris.
NORRIS, Natalie Elizabeth "Nanny", 77, d. Jul 3, 1992, wife of __ MacKinzie, dau of Joseph Neal, Sr. and Eva Sedalia Mayor Norris
NORRIS, Thomas E. "Sonny", b. Feb 5, 1943, d. Apr 9, 1991, hus of Wanda Lea Dement, son of Louis Andrew and Evelyn Wood Norris.
NORRIS, William E., Jr. d. 1978, hus of Patricia Winifred Ridgell.
NORWOOD, Dr. Dwight Lawrence, b. Apr 10, 1916 MA, d. Jun 10, 1989, hus of Alice Lee Pierce, son of Loren D. and Ellen Sullivan Norwood.
ORNDORFF, Shirley Ann, b. Aug 14, 1933 DC, d. Sep 13, 1990 VA, wife of Vernon E. Taff, dau of Cecil Pine and Ethel Mary Herbough Orndorff.
PULLMAN, Thomas M., b. Nov 13, 1918, d. Nov 4, 1988, hus of Reath A.___, son of Ernest H. and Frances Berry Pullman.
RALEY, J. Frank, Sr. b. Feb 13, 1904 Balto, d. Nov 17, 1990, hus of Ruth Zimmerly, son of James Harry and Eugenia Smith Raley.
RALEY, Paul Robert, b. Jan 30, 1930, d. Dec 4, 1990, son of Stanley Lee, Sr. and Sadie Ellen Coulter Raley.
RIDGELL, Bernette Agnes, b. Jul 30, 1917, d. Jan 19, 1993, m. 1937 James Edward Norris,

St. Michael's

Sr., dau of Robert and Lula Norris Ridgell.
RIDGELL, James "Tiny", b. Jul 15, 1935, d. Feb 5, 1990, hus of Corinne A. Soper, son of Wm. Allen Ridgell and Hattie Gatton Ridgell Combs.
RIDGELL, Katherine, d. 1981, wife of Roger Martin Messick.
RIDGELL, Patricia Winifred, b. Mar 17, 1917, d. Jan 29, 1993, m. 20 Aug 1935 Wm. E. Norris, Jr., dau of Thomas and Eulie Tennyson Ridgell.
ROACH, James Henry, b. Feb 16, 1907, d. Jul 1, 1991, hus of Mary L. Hammett, son of George C. and Estelle Clarke Roach.
ROCK, Mary Billie, b. Jul 27, 1939, d. Jul 25, 1992 DC, wife of Melvin Charles Yost, Sr., dau of William C. and Mary Henderson Rock.
ROLLINS, Robert Hall, b. Oct 31, 1919 DC, d. Jan 1, 1992, hus of Mabel G. Shorter, son of Robert Harrison and Marion E. Pumphrey Rollins.
STONE, Edna Cecelia, 74, d. Jul 10, 1987, wife of James Howard Raley.
STONE, James Arthur, b. Aug 8, 1910, d. Apr 14, 1993, son of Arthur and Helen Norris Stone.
TAYLOR, Alice Josephine, b. Nov 25, 1903, d. Dec 23, 1992, m. 1971 William Bryan Knott, dau of Clarence and Kathrine Raley Taylor.
TAYLOR, Joan Beverly, b. Nov 27, 1951, d. Feb 4, 1989, wife of George Robert Aud, dau of Emerson R. and Grace E. Taylor.
TENNYSON, Catherine Marie, b. Sep 19, 1910, d. Dec 28, 1991, wife of James Lloyd Bean, dau of late Louis Edw. Tennyson and Irene Tennyson Wheatley.
TITUS, Charles Chester "Chuck", b. Apr 9, 1927 WI, d. Apr 4, 1990, hus of Cecelia "Flip" Ridgell, son of Joseph C. and Henrietta Karst Titus.
TROSSBACH, John Linwood, b. Jun 29, 1906, d. Apr 26, 1993, hus of Mary Adelaide Norris, son of John Baptist and Blanche Brady Trossbach.
TROSSBACH, Mary Alberta "Bertie", b. Mar 5, 1896, d. May 18, 1988, wife of Calvert Fran-

cis Long, dau of Joseph M. and Maggie Cullison Trossbach.

TROSSBACH, Mary Elizabeth, b. Jun 29, 1904, d. Oct 27, 1988, wife of James W. Carroll, dau of John Baptist and Annie Blanche Brady Trossbach.

VIANT, Beverly June, b. Nov 8, 1921 MI, d. Jun 25, 1991 FL, wife of Louis Elijah Messick, dau of William T. and Lydia Senical Viant.

WALDSCHMITT, Joseph A., b. Oct 3, 1917 PA, d. Jun 21, 1988, hus of Alice Richard, son of Augustus and Margaret Hoffman Waldschmitt.

WELCH, Earl Joseph, b. Dec 29, 1908, d. Jun 16, 1991, hus of Carrie E. Ryce, son of Joseph E. and Rose Stone Welch.

WILKERSON, Annie Ruth, b. Jan 10, 1894, d. Jun 10, 1988, wife of __ Wise, dau of Dant and Ida Greenwell Wilkerson.

WILKERSON, Foster J., b. Sep 20, 1909, d. Dec 15, 1992, son of Dant and Ida Greenwell Wilkerson.

WIMBERLY, Robert Bryan, Jr. b. Jul 22, 1970, d. Jun 3, 1989, son of Robert B. and Mary Lou Wimberly; gson of George B. and Helen L. Quade; William C. and Peggy A. McMurray; ggson of William Bryan and Alice J. Knott.

YEATMAN, Herbert Everett, Sr. b. Oct 26, 1918, d. Nov 7, 1991, hus of Bernadette Grace Clark, son of William and Mildred Cullison Yeatman.

ST. NICHOLAS CEMETERY
Rt. 235
Lexington Park. Md.

Information on this cemetery was furnished to me by Mr. Richard A. Everett.

This Catholic church was built by May 6, 1796 and named for St. Nicholas, patron saint of Nicholas L. Seawell, who sold the land it was erected on. The Navy bought this land in 1940 and St. Nicholas Chapel is still in use. The cemetery is intact, but the gravestones have been laid flat over the graves and covered, and the land left as a permanment park. The Navy compiled this grave site list before the markers were covered.

There are 36 plots with wood crosses, 15 with wood stakes, 1 with iron marker, 1 with iron pipes at both head and foot, 1 with a tin marker, 3 with stones, 2 with uncut headstones, and 3 with uncut head and footstones. None of these grave markers have inscriptions. There are two grave sites with G. A. R. iron markers (Grand Army of the Republic) but no other identification.

ABELL, George W., d. Jul 30, 1903.
ABELL, Joseph Edwin, d. Oct 12, 1896.
ABELL, Mary V., d. Feb 3, 1935.
ABELL, Philip, d. Aug 11, 1811, age 42 yr 4 mo 3 days.
ABELL Susanna, b. 1872, d. 1873.
ABELL, Wm. W., b. Mar 4, 1868.
ARMSWORTHY, A. E., b. Mar 6, 1847, d. Dec 15, 1870.
ARMSWORTHY, Bertha D., b. Sep 6, 1885, d. May 21, 1914.
ARMSWORTHY, Viola D., b. May 12, 1912, d. Jul 6, 1912.
BADEN, Joseph, b. 1887, d. 1888.
BARNES, Bessie M., b. Dec 3, 1902, d. Aug 25, 1924.
BARNES, Christina, b. Oct 24, 1905, d. May 9,

1906.
BARNS, John C., b. Apr 1, 1878, d. Feb 27, 1916.
BATES, James, b. 1870, d. 1889.
BEAL, Alex L., d. Jan 3, 1867.
BEAL, Eliza H., b. Aug 12, 1840, d. Oct 14, 1870.
BEAL, Ellen E., b. Mar 19, 1814, d. Sep 12, 1867.
BEAL, Henry S., b. May 7, 1852, d. Apr 17, 1915.
     One Stone
-BEAL, Ignatius, b. Nov 29, 1865, d. Dec 15, 1868.
-BEAL, India P., b. Nov 29, 1865, d. Sep 4, 1867.
     One Stone
-BEAL, James M., b. May 4, 1869, d. Nov 17, 1870.
-BEAL, Ellenor E., b. Jun 8, 1861, d. Mar 24, 1871.
BEAN, Ann E., b. Mar 31, 1851, d. Apr 11, 1910.
BEAN, Annie J., b. Oct 1, 1872, d. Dec 14, 1939.
BEAN, John S., b. Oct 5, 1845, d. Oct 22, 1920.
BEAN, Jos. A., b. Feb 28, 1839, d. Jan 6, 1916.
BEAN, Joseph Arthur, b. Sep 21, 1921, d. Jan 3, 1933.
BEAN, Margaret, Aug 19, 1847.
BEAN, Mary E., b. Feb 12, 1907, d. Aug 18, 1910.
BEAN, Thomas E., cross with backward S.L.S.
     One Stone
-BEAN, Thos. N., d. Mar 23, 1811.
-BEAN, Edward, age 11 yers.
-BEAN, Aloysius, age 11 yers.
-BEAN, Virginia, age 14 mos.
BEAN, Wm. C., b. Apr 30, 1910, d. Aug 25, 1928.
BISCOE, Martha M., on wood cross.
BLACKSTONE, Mary G., b. Aug 17, 1858, d. Feb 17, 1884.
BOHANAN, Hattie, b. Feb 19, 1874, d. Jan 2, 1880.
BOHANAN, Ida, b. Apr 15, 1881, d. Feb 28, 1882.
BOHANAN, John T., b. Feb 8, 1877, d. Jan 3,

St. Nicholas

1883.
BOHANAN, Katie, Nov 20, 1875.
BOHANAN, Willie T., b. Mar 13, 1874, d. Dec 18, 1882.
BOND, Julius A., d. Nov 15, 1873.
BRADDOCK, Joseph B., d. Mar 26, 1881.
BROME, Sarah R., b. Sep 10, 1820, d. Aug 25, 1853.
BROWN, Frank V., b. 1873, d. 1940.
BROWN, Hellen K., b. Apr 18, 1881, d. Jun 9, 1925.
BURROUGHS, Margaret J., d. Nov 4, 1833.
L.R.C. on wood cross.
M.E.C. and W.H.C. on wood crosses side by side.
CAMERON, Maria E., b. Aug 31, 1878, d. Jul 4, 1920.
CARROLL, Edwin Coad, d. Oct 12, 1896, 10y 8 m.
CARROLL, Elizabeth A., d. Oct 11, 1892, age 75 y.
CARROLL John J., b. Dec 22, 1825, d. Sep 24, 1886, hus of Anne E. Cooper.
CASEY, Migonette M., May 30, 1891.
CAWOOD, J. Clark, b. Sep 6, 1853, d. Feb 16, 1896.
CECIL, Joseph F., d. Feb 1, 1854.
CECIL, Maria L., d. Mar 1, 1899.
CECIL, Marion E., d. Aug 20, 1879.
CECIL, Mary Maude, d. Aug 12, 1897, age 23.
CECIL, Wm. W., b. Sep 23, 1836, d. Apr 23, 1914.
CHAPMAN, Chas. H., CO H USC.
CISSELL, George, b. Sep 12, 1780, d. Mar 27, 1832.
COMBS, A. Virginia, b. Apr 21, 1827, d. Mar 9, 1869.
COMBS, Albert F., b. Feb 6, 1863, d. Oct 12, 1872.
COMBS, Arthur Cornelius, b. Nov 30, 1849, d. Apr 19, 1929.
COMBS, Col. Cornelius, d. Nov 10, 1865.
COMBS, Harriet P., Dec 13, 1877.
COMBS, J. Edwin, b. Mar 2, 1864, d. Mar 8, 1869.
COMBS, L. Cornelius, d. Jun 19, 1899.
COMBS, M.E. on wood cross.

Side by Side
-COMBS, Martin E., b. Jan 30, 1850, d. Sep 24, 1917.
-COMBS, Sarah E., b. Sep 6, 1849, d. Oct 7, 1907.

COMBS, Mary E., b. Apr 30, 1829, d. Feb 20, 1866.
COMBS, Mary Margaret, b. Dec 17, 1854, d. Jan 20, 1933.
COMBS, Mary S., b. Mar 4, 1846, d. Jun 21, 1929.

Side by Side
-COMBS, Perry C., d. Mar 28, 1861.
-COMBS, Angeline Tarleton, d. Mar 5, 1848.

COMBS, Philip I. Ford, b. May 26, 1816, d. Oct 29, 1878.
COOPER, Ann E., b. Apr 4, 1830, d. Aug 23, 1895, wife of John J. Carroll.

COX PLOT
-COX, Charles P., b. Feb 4, 1883, d. Apr 23, 1920.
-COX, Charlotte, b. Apr 24, 1854, d. Dec 3, 1895.
-COX, James A., b. Oct 4, 1880, d. Sep 17, 1888.
-COX, James T., d. Aug 6, 1902.
-COX, Jos. G., b. May 5, 1877, d. Sep 7, 1917.
-COX, Lucy A., b. Jan 19, 1892, d. Sep 19, 1893.
-COX, Lucy M., b. Feb 27, 1884, d. Nov 23, 1888.
-COX, Peter C., b. Jan 19, 1892, d. Sep 19, 1893.

CURTIS, Anna M., b. 1910, d. 1914.
DEROSE, FR. Sabastian, bur in St. Nicholas Chancel in 1812.
DILLAHAY, William, d. Jun 17, 1855.
DYSON, Francis T., b. 1855, d. 1910.
DYSON, Mamie, d. May 30, 1903, age 29.
DYSON, Mary E., b. 1892, d. 1923.
DYSON, Mary Jane, Oct 3, 1932.
EDGESTON, Bernard, b. Feb 2, 1918, d. Oct 24, 1918.
EDGESTON, John Albert, b. Jun 1840, d. Mar 13, 1919. American Legion Marker.

St. Nicholas

FENHAGAN, Charles J., b. Dec 8, 1853, d. Jun 1, 1910.
FENHAGAN, Edward, b. Nov 27, 1821, d. Oct 20, 1892.
FENHAGAN, Jane E., b. Nov 21, 1820, d. Jun 7, 1891.
FENHAGAN, John, d. Dec 2, 1890.
FORD, Robert, b. Mar 14, 1814, d. Mar 28, 1871.
Side by Side
-FORD, Wm. Frank, b. Feb 25, 1840, d. Apr 12, 1918.
-FORD, Alice Pembroke, b. Apr 23, 1847, d. Sep 30, 1920.
-FORD, Laura Mabel, b. Jan 1, 1887, d. Jul 27, 1936.
FREEMAN, Bena (Lena?), Sep 25, 1852, inscription "Sweet Little Lena Enright".
Side by Side
-FREEMAN, John D., Jr. d. Jan 2, 1854.
-FREEMAN, Maria P., d. Oct 4, 1852.
Side by Side
-FREEMAN, John Wesley, b. Dec 8, 1853, d. May 16, 1935.
-FREEMAN, Mary Alma, b. Apr 12, 1857, d. Apr 18, 1930.
-FREEMAN, E. Olivia, b. Dec 25, 1827, d. Aug 18, 1893.
FLOWER-BEAN-BEAL Plot
-BEAN, Robert, b. 1759, d. 1843, son of Alexander Bean and Anne Heard.
-BEAL, Philomena P., b. 1836, d. 1843.
-FLOWER, Gustavus, b. 1796, d. 1830, son of Jeremiah and Mary.
-FLOWER, James Alexander, 1826, son of Gustavus and Jane.
Monument in plot.
-BEAL, Jane, b. 1806, d. 1861, relict of (1) Gustavus Flower, (2) George Beal, dau of Robert Bean and Sarah Lowe.
-FLOWER, William Gustavus, b. 1854, d. 1863, son of John Bennett and Mary Ellen Bean Flower.
GOODRICH, Emma J., b. Apr 16, 1850, d. Jan 1, 1926.
GOODRICH, Stephen C., b. Dec 1, 1954, d. Feb

19, 1926.
GOUGH, John Henry, b. Nov 11, 187-, d. Mar 19, 1814, hus of Amanda E. __, b. Mar 5, 1877.
GOURLEY, Mary Ann, d. Feb 8, 1873.
GREENWELL, Celestia, b. Nov 17, 1821, d. Jun 18, 1878.
GREENWELL, Gertrude Wise, d. Oct 8, 1841.
HAMMETT, David, no dates.
HAMMETT, James Gibbons, b. Aug 22, 1884, d. Feb 25, 1897.
HAMMETT, John B., b. Nov 8, 1803, d. Jan 20, 1874.
HAMMETT, Joseph, b. Sep 27, 1882, d. Sep 26, 1894.
HAMMETT, Richard P., b. & d. Oct 21, 1914.
HAMMETT, Rosa Jane, b. Nov 26, 1886, d. Sep 20, 1894.
HAMMETT, Rosa L., b. Apr 29, 1892, d. Oct 12, 1900.
HAMMETT, Sallie E., b. Jan 25, 1864, d. Jul 2, 1894.
HAMMILL, Joan Elizabeth, b. Jul 14, 1932 VA, d. Jan 30, 1992, wife of Alexander L. Vinson, dau of Chester R. and Maude E. Soules Hammill. Memorial Service.,
HAYDEN, on wood marker.
HAYDEN, Arthur Clifton, b. Oct 9, 1894, d. May 21, 1895.
HAYDEN, Irene, b. Aug 22, 1868, d. Aug 5, 1902, wife of __ Richards.
HAYDEN, James T., b. Aug 16, 1826, d. Dec 20, 1908.
HAYDEN, Mary E., d. Oct 21, 1891.
HAYDEN, Myrtle Estella, b. Mar 14, 1892, d. Aug 11, 1902.
HAYWOOD, James C., b. Aug 31, 1891, d. Nov 30, 1909.
HAYWOOD, Joshua E., b. 1862, d. 1932.
HAYWOOD, Laura C., b. 1873, _____
HEATHERLAND, Elizabeth, age 70 yrs.
HILLIS, P., The faithful nurse. (next to A.E. Armsworthy)
HILTON, Genevieve, d. Aug 25, 1918, age 75 yr.
Single Stone
-HILTON, John Louis, b. Apr 30, 1857, d. Oct

St. Nicholas

3, 1918.
-HILTON, Mary Jane, b. Feb 8, 1857, d. Aug 26, 1918.
HILTON, Wm. L., b. Nov 9, 1806, d. Dec 29, 1856.
     Side by Side
-JARBOE, Catharine, d. Nov 24, 1826.
-JARBOE, Col. James, d. 1846.
     Side by Side
-JARBOE, Elizabeth, d. Sep 6, 1810.
-JARBOE, Robert, d. Mar 31, 1803.
JARBOE, Jeff B., b. 1838, d. 1906, m. 1872 Maggie E. __, d. Oct 27, 1884, age 39, bur next to her 6 children.
-JARBOE, Bettie May, d. Jan 16, 1876.
-JARBOE, Willie A., b. Feb 1, 1874, d. Nov 11, 1882 of diphtheria.
-JARBOE, Cora Lee, b. Nov 17, 1876, d. Nov 19, 1882.
-JARBOE, Jefferson McKee, b. Jul 8, 1878, d. Nov 3, 1882.
-JARBOE, Maggie May, b. Mar 28, 1880, d. Nov 4, 1882.
-JARBOE, stillborn daughter, Nov 5, 1883.
JARBOE, Marie, b. Jul 28, 1887, d. Nov 6, 1919.
JARBOE, Robert, d. Mar 21, 1803, age 51 yrs 2 mos 18 das.
JOY, Marion, no dates.
KENNEDY, Jas. P., d. 1876.
LEAVERTON, Mary N., b. Jul 14, 1877, d. Feb 26, 1912.
     Side by Side
-LLOYD, B. Harrison, d. Dec 20, 1930.
-Five wood crosses
-LLOYD, Eliza, b. 1853, d. Jun 8, 1912.
R.H.M., on marble footstone, wood stake at head of grave.
MAGILL, Charles Sidney, b. Jan 1849, d. Jan 1, 1901.
McKAY, Sarah Eliza, d. Oct 3, 1870.
McKAY, Robt. H., b. Mar 16, 1879, d. Feb 2, 1916.
MURPHY, Maggie, d. 1876.
NORRIS, J. S., d. Oct 19, 1918. Wood Marker.
OWENS, Eliza A., b. Oct 6, 1853, d. Mar 17,

1919.
OWENS, Samuel, b. Apr 11, 1897, d. Jun 7, 1915.
OWENS, Sarah F., b. Mar 25, 1846, d. Dec 9, 1906.
OWENS, Stephen, b. Apr 11, 1888, d. Nov 26, 1913.
PARTRIDGE, Jas. A., b. 1821. (headstone br.)
PARTRIDGE, Jas. M., d. Sep 7, 1863.
PARTRIDGE, Urban H., d. Feb 9, 1863.
PASCHAULT, Catherine Kirwan, no dates.
PASCHAULT, Mrs. Mary L., d. Aug 2, 1853.
PASCHAULT, Mary Lenora, no dates.
PEAK, Ellen, d. Sep 1, 1850.
PEAK, John, d. Apr 2, 1833.
PEAK, Lewis B., b. Feb 4, 1830, d. Oct 4, 1863.
PEAK, Willie, d. Dec 29, 1855.
PEAK, Willie E., b. Oct 9, 1860, d. Jul 25, 1861.
POMEROY, Mary I., b. 1861, d. 1929.
PRICE, John A., b. Feb 28, 1848, d. Feb 14, 1902.
PRICE, Mrs. Lester and son, b. Apr 13, 1900, d. Dec 23, 1938.
RALEY, John B.,b. Feb 8, 1940, d. Apr 6, 1911. (As shown on Navy drawing).
READ, Willie K., d. May 26, 1882.
                Side by side
 -READMOND, Foley, b. Oct 12, 1886, d. Sep 25, 1887.
 -REDMOND, Lillie, b. May 5, 1897, d. Nov 7, 1897.
 -REDMOUND, Daisy, b. Apr 22, 1894, d. Jul 7, 1905.
READMOND, Jefferson J., b. Apr 11, 1829, d. Apr 8, 1896.
READMOND, Mary S., b. Aug 19, 1855, d. Oct 9, 1912.
RICHARDS, Aubrey, b. Mar 9, 1899, d. Aug 8, 1902, bur with mother Irene Hayden Richards in Hayden plot.
RUSSELL, Mary R., d. May 19, 1853.
SANNER, Elizabeth, d. Nov 22, 1829.
SEWALL family bur in railed plot behind church,

St. Nicholas   297

no markers.
SIVAK, Michael, b. Aug 15, 1863, d. May 21,
   1921.
SMITH, Ernest E., no dates.
SMITH, Sarah Ann, b. Nov 18, 1875, d. Apr 9,
   1913.
STONE, Ann Louisa, d. May 5, 1885.
STONE, Edward, b. Aug 15, 1867, d. Jun 25,
   1926.
STONE, Edwin, b. Apr 28, 1917, d. Jun 10, 1917.
STONE, Frank, d. Apr 24, 1897, age 86 y.
STONE, James Merton, b. Nov 26, 1897, d. Mar
   31, 1916.
              Next three side by side.
-TARLTON, Johny L., Aug 18, 1853.
-TARLTON, Lula A., d. Feb 20, 1856.
-TARLTON, Wm. T., d. Feb 16, 1856.
                 Side by Side.
-TARLTON, Ann, d. Aug 31, 1856.
-TARLTON, Elijah, d. Jan 10, 1850.
-TARLTON, Rebecca, d. Apr 25, 1853.
                 Side by Side
-TARLTON, Wm., Apr 11, 1812.
-TARLTON, Catherine, d. Mar 10, 1857.
TAYLOR, Sarah Eliza, b. Mar 2, 1812, d. May
   23, 1855.
                  One Stone
-THOMAS, Francis, b. 1835, d. Dec 20, 1876.
-THOMAS, Susan R., b. 1837, d. Apr 15, 1868.
THOMPSON, Maria L., b. Aug 29, 1843, d. Dec
   12, 1862.
UNCLES, Mrs. V., d. 1885.
UNDERWOOD, Elizabeth, d. Feb 14, 1826.
UNDERWOOD, Jeremiah, d. Sep 8, 1821.
L.N.V., wood cross.
WALSH, Jeffery, d. Oct 3, 1870.
WASHINGTON, Estelle, b. Mar 15, 1889, d. Jun
   8, 1905.
G.W., wood cross-located next to Estelle Wash-
   ington
WHEELER, Elizabeth, b. May 7, 1920, d. Jul 14,
   1921.
WHEELER, Evelyn V., b. Oct 6, 1917, d. Nov 18,
   1917.
WHEELER, Mary Eliza, b. Feb 10, 1876, d. Mar

7, 1909.
WHEELER, Mary Jane, b. Jun 22, 1846, d. Jul
   11, 1871.
WHERRITT, Elizabeth J., b. Feb 11, 1836, d.
   Jun 30, 1856.
WHERRITT, William, b. Mar 1831, d. Nov 1848.
WISE, Henry A., b. Oct 4, 1842, d. May 29,
   1899.
WISE, John F., d. Oct 27, 1895.
WISE, John Jackson, b. Nov 11, 1847, d. Aug 8,
   1849.
WISE, Marietta, b. Oct 28, 1850, d. Oct 23,
   1854.
WISE, Philip F.C., b. Aug 2, 1854, d. Oct 29,
   1877.
BROKEN METAL MARKER, b. 1797, d. 1860.

ST. PAUL'S METHODIST CHURCH
Rt. 5,
Leonardtown, Md.

ABELL, Edward B., b. 1814, d. Dec 16, 1861, son of Ignatius and Ann Abell.
ATTAWAY, Ann, d. Jun 8, 1850, wife of __ Tippett.
BARNHART, Ann, b. 1860, d. 1940, wife of __ Large.
BENNETT, Elizabeth, b. Aug 3, 1876, d. Jan 8, 1960, wife of __ Porter.
BENNETT, Emma Siegert, b. 1888, d. 1946.
BENNETT, James Archibald, b. May 18, 1868, d. Mar 2, 1957.
BENNETT, Leila Maude, b. Apr 23, 1874, d. Mar 31, 1949.
BENNETT, Mary Carolyn, b. Sep 1, 1883, d. Nov 5, 1965.
BENNETT, Mary Emily, b. Dec 1, 1842, d. Sep 11, 1916.
BENNETT, Mary Jane, b. Aug 17, 1870, d. Jan 26, 1964.
BENNETT, Richard H., b. Aug 4, 1866, d. Jun 30, 1928.
BENNETT, Steuart, b. Dec 25, 1903, d. Nov 5, 1974.
BENNETT, Thomas W., b. 1832, d. Sep 29, 1902.
BISCOE, Ida M., b. Apr 22, 1862, d. May 25, 1888, dau of Wm. and Elizabeth Biscoe.
BLAND, Patricia Mae, b. Aug 18, 1942 WV, d. Apr 19, 1993, wife of Ronald Wayne Cooley, dau of Claude and Gladys Bland.
BRUBACHER, Alida Mary, b. Feb 6, 1900 MN, d. Mar 21, 1990, dau of Robt. Henry and Johanna Hubin Brubacher.
BRUBACHER, Leona Susan, b. Feb 11, 1907 MN, d. Jun 22, 1990, dau of Robt. Henry and Johanna Hubin Brubacher.
BRUBACHER, Robert H., b. 1870, d. 1952, hus of Johanna Hubin.
BRUBACHER, Victor N., b. Oct 25, 1895, d. Mar 4, 1962, son of Robert and Johanna Brubacher.
COLTON, Elizabeth, d. Jan 19, 1832.
CONNELLY, John Parran "J.P.", Sr., b. 1901, d.

Jun 25, 1976, m. 1935 Mary 'Ethel' __.
CONNELLY, William Ford, b. 1890, d. 1938.
COWAN, Fred Fletcher, b. 1893, d. 1979.
CURRY, James Burton, Jr. b. Jun 22, 1926, d. Feb 19, 1993, m. 16 Aug 1952 Marjorie Louise Snapp, son of James B. and Harriett Marie Langley Curry. Memorial Service.
DAVENPORT, Philip J., b. Jul 28, 1914, d. Jul 11, 1976, hus of Fay A. __.
DAVENPORT, Zoe Z., b. 1876, d. 1968.
DEVERS, Archie N., b. 1892, d. 1965.
DEVERS, Rose M., b. 1897, d. 1974.
DILLOW, Joseph William, b. Nov 10, 1838, d. Dec 14, 1838, son of Thos. and Eleanor Dillow.
DILLOW, Thomas Henry, b. Jan 20, 1840, d. Mar 2, 1844, son of Thos. and Eleanor Dillow.
ELLIS, John Paul, d. 1967.
ENSS, Abram, b. Jul 21, 1860, d. May 9, 1917.
ENSS, Art, b. 1879, d. 1929.
ENSS, Eliza, b. 1852, d. 1930.
EWELL, Harrison, b. 1865, d. 1936, hus of Sadie G. __, b. 1869, d. 1945.
EWY, John, b. 1857, d. Oct 5, 1912.
FARGO, William A., b. 1875, d. 1948.
FAUSSETT, John, b. Mar 17, 1823, d. Jul 19, 1899.
FOXWELL, Anne M., b. May 16, 1848, d. Dec 27, 1918.
FOXWELL, Benjamin, b. Sep 21, 1835, d. Oct 31, 1904.
FOXWELL, Charles W., b. 1863, d. 1932, hus of Agnes A. Sanner.
FOXWELL, Harry Norris, b. Jun 24, 1897, d. Nov 18, 1898, son of Thomas F. and Rachel Foxwell.
FOXWELL, Ida Adele, d. Nov 27, 1972, wife of I. Stanley Johnson, dau of Thos. F. and Rachel Sanner Foxwell.
FOXWELL, J. V. B., b. 1888, d. 1891.
FOXWELL, James V., b. 1868, d. 1904.
FOXWELL, John T., b. 1866, d. 1917.
FOXWELL, Lillian, b. 1892, d. 1915.
FOXWELL, Mary A., b. 1812, d. 1894.
FOXWELL, Mary B., b. 1841, d. 1844.

FOXWELL, Mildred, b. 1890, d. 1980, wife of __ Jones.
FOXWELL, Mollie E., b. 1870, d. 1910.
FOXWELL, Rosalie, d. Jan 1, 1980, wife of William Hiles Pardoe.
FOXWELL, Sallie E., b. 1870, d. 1895.
FOXWELL, Sally, Feb 2, 1852, d. Aug 24, 1882, wife of T. Frank Tyler.
FOXWELL, Sarah J., b. 1838, d. 1894.
FOXWELL, Shadragh, d. May 19, 1845.
FOXWELL, Stephen, d. Feb 21, 1877, hus of Lovey Cannon Paul.
FOXWELL, Thomas F., b. Sep 25, 1842, d. Oct 8, 1919, m. 3 Dec 1878 Rachel R. Sanner.
FOXWELL, Willard S., b. 1893, d. 1917.
FREEMAN, William Columbus, b. Jul 4, 1859, d. Jun 3, 1951, hus of Kate R. McAdam.
GREEN, Bea Davis, b. Aug 18, 1908, d. Sep 29, 1955.
GRISWOLD, Julius A., b. Dec 16, 1850, d. May 27, 1888.
HAMSON, Nora, b. Jan 10, 1913, d. Jan 21, 1993, m. 29 Oct 1946 William Gordon Gillingham, dau of Frank and Mary Frances Chaney Hamson.
HAYWARD, Richard N., b. Jun 30, 1935, d. Oct 4, 1968.
HEARD, Bernard F., b. 1894, d. 1966.
HUBIN, Johanna, d. 1953, wife of Robert Henry Brubacher.
JARBOE, Charles G., b. Oct 8, 1875, d. Dec 6, 1956.
JARBOE, Mary Rebecca, b. Jan 19, 1853, d. Jan 2, 1925.
JESTER, Daniel Maruel, b. Aug 8, 1894, d. Dec 28, 1975, hus of Mary Langley.
JOHNSON, Ignatius Stanley, b. Feb 1876, d. Jun 5, 1940, hus of Ida Adele Foxwell, son of Hillery and Ann Marie Thompson Johnson.
JONES, Charlotte, d. Oct 25, 1918.
JONES, Harry M., b. 1872, d. 1957.
JONES, Harry S., b. 1917, d. 1948.
JONES, Harvey, d. 1881.
JONES, Laura, b. 1888, d. 1889.
JONES, Laura B., b. 1850, d. 1925, wife of __ Harding.

JONES, Milton W., b. 1874, d. 1957.
JONES, Stephen M., b. 1873, d. 1942.
JONES, Virginia B., b. 1889, d. 1980, wife of Harry S. Jones.
JONES, William H., b. 1832, d. 1904.
KNIGHT, Michael Harlan, b. Sep 4, 1954, d. Aug 21, 1993 DC, son of Robert Harlan and Elizabeth Carskadon Knight. Memorial Svc.
LACKEY, Earl Lee, 70, d. Dec 12, 1992.
LANE, Ernest, b. 1881, d. 1968.
LANE, Ethel C., b. 1880, d. 1979.
LANGLEY, Mary, b. 1901, d. 1976, wife of Daniel Maruel Jester.
LINVILLE, Nannie Lucille, b. Nov 24, 1902, d. Jun 25, 1989, wife of John Lesley Thomason, dau of A. J. and Nannie Bagly Linville.
LOKER, Robert Combs, b. May 14, 1909, d. Jan 14, 1978.
LUCAS, Clarence Percy, b. 1903, d. 1965.
MacCARTEE, Daisy V., b. Oct 18, 1889, d. Oct 26, 1970.
MARSHALL, Edith C., b. 1898, d. 1960, wife of Arthur L. Marshall.
MATHEWS, Sarah Ann, b. 1830, d. 1854, wife of Edward A. Mathews.
MATHEWS, infant twins, children of Edw. A. and Sarah Mathews. No date.
McADAM, Kate R., b. Feb 6, 1881, d. May 7, 1961, wife of William C. Freeman.
NEAL, Benjamin D., b. 1894, d. 1932.
NEAL, Henry, b. Dec 25, 1810, d. May 3, 1880.
NEAL, Susan E., b. Nov 18, 1817, d. Oct 21, 1866.
NORRIS, Charles F., b. Apr 14, 1831, d. Mar 12, 1884, hus of Rosa Anne __, b. Mar 3, 1837, d. Dec 20, 1871.
NORRIS, Charles F., b. Nov 7, 1856, d. Nov 18, 1889, son of C. F. and R. A. Norris.
NORRIS, Edmonia, b. Apr 21, 1867, d. Sep 10, 1884, dau of C. F. and R. A. Norris.
NORRIS, Emily Ida, b. Dec 14, 1854, d. Apr 20, 1880, dau of C. F. and R. A. Norris.
NORRIS, Ignatius W., b. Oct 16, 1821, d. Mar 13, 1863.
NORRIS, Lydia T., b. Nov 22, 1857, d. Apr 12,

St. Paul's   303

1872, dau of J. Washington and Hannah
Norris.
NORRIS, Mary Elizabeth, b. Nov 15, 1853, d.
Feb 1, 1952, dau of C. F. and R. A. Norris.
NORRIS, Rosa Anne, b. Dec 21, 1858, d. May 21,
1952, dau of C. F. and R. A. Norris.
PARDOE, William Hiles, b. 1892, d. Nov 17,
1973, hus of Rosalie Foxwell.
PAUL, Lovey Cannon, b. May 23, 1808, d. Sep 6,
1887, wife of Stephen Foxwell.
RICHARDSON, L. Roger, b. 1896, d. 1970.
ROBERTS, Charles B., b. 1871, d. 1953, hus of
Eliza C. __, b. 1873, d. 1948.
ROSS, Hannah, b. Feb 1, 1833, d. Oct 13, 1901,
wife of Alfred J. Smith.
SANNER, Agnes A., b. Feb 2, 1860, d. 1945,
wife of Charles W. Foxwell, dau of Abel and
Serena Foxwell.
SANNER, Rachel R., b. May 5, 1855, d. Oct 3,
1943, wife of Thomas F. Foxwell, dau of Abel
and Serena Ann Sanner.
SANNER, Rosena, b. Feb 27, 1862, d. 1899, wife
of __ Foxwell, dau of Abel and Serena Sanner.
SANNIFER, Ruby Corinne, b. Aug 16, 1909 MS, d.
Sep 18, 1991, wife of Raymond Paul Reynolds,
dau of Andy W. and Cora Young Sannifer.
SMITH, Alfred J., b. Mar 8, 1832, d. Apr 5,
1898, hus of Hannah Ross.
SMITH, Maggie J., b. 1869, d. 1886, dau of
Alfred J. and Hannah Ross Smith.
SMITH, Willard H., b. Nov 6, 1872, d. Aug 22,
1949, son of Alfred J. and Hannah Smith.
SNAPP, Marjorie Louise, b. Apr 10, 1931 VT, d.
Jul 12, 1991, wife of Jas. B. Curry, dau of
Albert M. B. and Margarite Snapp. Mem. Svc.
SYKES, Fred H., b. Oct 10, 1931, d. Jan 15,
1936.
THOMPSON, John Lesley, b. 1894, d. 1979, hus
of Nannie 'Lucille' Linville.
TIPPETT, Rev. Benjamin, d. Oct 2, 1836.
TIPPETT, Eleanor, d. Jul 24, 1840.
TYLER, Frank Foxwell, b. Oct 16, 1878, d. Jul
2, 1879, son of T. Frank and Sally Foxwell
Tyler.
TYLER, Omar Frank, b. Jul 26, 1877, d. Sep 7,

1877, son of T. Frank and Sally Foxwell Tyler.
WHEELER, Henson, b. Dec 22, 1789, d. Mar 22, 1849, hus of Lovy __, b. Mar 4, 1784, d. Dec 26, 1855.
WHEELER, John M., b. 1815, d. Feb 12, 1913, hus of Leah Ann __, b. Jul 21, 1817, d. Aug 25, 1875.
YATES, Albert W., d. Sep 20, 1859 of typhoid, age 16 yrs, son of William and Julia Yates.
YATES, Edgar F.J., b. Oct 5, 1830, d. Oct 19, 1832, son of William and Julia Yates.

ST. PETER CLAVER CATHOLIC CEMETERY
St. Inigoes, Md.

St. Peter Claver Church was named in honor of a 17th century Jesuit priest who was born in Barcelona, Spain in 1580 and died of the plague in 1654, at age 74. He took the name "Slave of the Slaves Forever". St. Peter Claver is the Patron Saint of missionaries working with black people. The church and cemetery opened in 1918. The Oblate Sisters of Providence, a Baltimore Order of Black Sisters, opened a parochial school in 1924, which is now closed.

BARNES, Della Ann, b. Oct 1, 1906, d. Jul 20, 1989, wife of Bernard Barber, dau of Joseph Clyde and Rachel Somerville Barnes.

BARNES, Florence Cecelia, b. Apr 16, 1924, d. Apr 2, 1991, wife of C. Leonard Bryan, dau of Joseph Shepaly and Mary Rozenia Edgeston Barnes.

BARNES, Helen Cecelia, b. Dec 5, 1925, d. Sep 21, 1993, wife of Henry James Dowsey, dau of Emery and Milinda Lee Barnes.

BARNES, Mary Eulalia, 80, d. Nov 13, 1970, m. (1st) George Marshall of DC, (2d) Henry Johnson, dau of Daniel and Josephine Mason Barnes.

BARNES, Roger Lamont, Sr. b. Jun 26, 1953, d. Sep 22, 1990, hus of Grace D. __, son of Corbert M. and Margaret E. Gant Barnes.

BARNES, Theodore Jerome, b. Jan 9, 1917, d. Aug 24, 1991, hus of Edna Rowena Bolts, son of John E. and Annie Elizabeth Taylor Barnes.

BENNETT, Laura Rose, b. Apr 12, 1901, d. Sep 7, 1989, dau of James and Sarah Forrest Bennett.

BISCOE, Hilda Regina, b. Oct 17, 1909, d. Aug 3, 1991, wife of Richard James Hewlett, dau of Joseph Adam and Roxy Langley Biscoe.

BISCOE, Josephine M., b. Apr 12, 1913, d. Aug 7, 1993, m. Balto 16 Feb 1936 John Westley Holley, dau of John and Annie Loker Biscoe.

BISCOE, William McKinley, b. May 3, 1898, d. Jan 7, 1991, son of Nicholas and Mary Clara Young Biscoe.

BRISCOE, George William, b. Feb 12, 1920, d.

May 4, 1992, hus of Martha Elizabeth __, son of George and Katie Gross Briscoe.
BUTLER, Earl Leroy, b. Jan 24, 1912, d. Jul 10, 1989, son of Lucas Wm. and Geneva Martha Butler.
CALVIER, Russell, b. NC, d. Sep 19, 1974, hus of Ethel Lois Willis.
CARROLL, George Samuel, b. Jul 3, 1900 PA, d. Mar 9, 1988, m. 1922 Lillie Butler, son of Joseph C. and Susie Harris Carroll.
CHASE, James Albert, b. May 2, 1916, d. Jul 7, 1989, son of Albert and Agnes Lee Chase.
CLINTON, James Alfred, b. Jul 1, 1913, d. Aug 16, 1989, hus of Dorothy __, son of Alexander and Liza Chesley Clinton.
FENWICK, Minnie Toney, b. Dec 15, 1918, d. Aug 10, 1988.
GANT, Edward Luke "Big Baby", b. Jun 11, 1898, d. Aug 16, 1992 Balto, hus of Pricilla Anne Walton, son of James and Sarah Gant.
GORDON, Bertha Irene, b. Feb 14, 1908, d. Mar 18, 1991, dau of Zachariah and Isabella Conway Gordon.
GRAYSON, William Ralph, b. May 1, 1906 VA, d. Feb 24, 1990 DC, hus of Celeste Biscoe, son of John and Laura Williams Grayson.
HAWKINS, Benjamin Ignatius, b. Dec 6, 1911, d. Aug 24, 1993, hus of Margarite __, d. Dec 21, 1980, son of James and Rose Johnson Hawkins.
HAWKINS, Steve Benjamin II, b. Nov 14, 1989, d. Nov 15, 1989 DC, son of Frank S. Hawkins and Ann Loretta Dove; paternal gson of Benjamin A. Hawkins.
HEWLETT, Shawn Garrett, b. May 23, 1962, d. Aug 26, 1988, son of Charles A. and Doris Corbin Hewlett.
JOHNSON, Henry K., 25, d. Oct 4, 1970 Balto, hus of Alice B. __, son of Joseph P. and Mary L. Johnson.
JOHNSON, Joseph P. "Bogy", 58, d. Dec 31, 1972, hus of Mary L. __.
LANGLEY, Joseph Ethelbert "Bert", b. Nov 14, 1920, d. Feb 4, 1989, hus of Marguerette __, son of John Henry and Daisy Barnes Langley.
McCLANE, Samuel Augustus, b. Jun 30, 1923, d.

Oct 12, 1989, hus of Bernice Martin, son of Nola Green.
SEWELL, Frank Joseph, b. Apr 4, 1913, d. Aug 23, 1991 Balto, hus of Cecelia Marshall, son of George and Mary Barnes Sewell.
SMITH, Beulah Lorraine, b. Aug 6, 1906 IN, d. May 29, 1992, wife of Edward J. Bennett, dau of Abraham and Hanna Kiel Smith.
TOLSON, Grace, b. May 1, 1897, d. Mar 31, 1993, wife of Douglas Carroll, dau of Charlie and Louvinia Whalen Tolson.
WHEELER, Elizabeth "Betty" Anthony, b. Oct 2, 1937 RI, d. Feb 20, 1993, wife of __ Morgan, dau of Bryon and Dorothy Bass Wheeler.
WILLIS, Ethel Lois "Dolly", b. Sep 1, 1900 GA, d. May 9, 1993, m. 1916 Russell Callier, dau of Charles and Mary Harris Willis.
YOUNG, Lawrence McClain, Jr. b. Feb 26, 1954, d. Sep 16, 1990, son of Lawrence M. and Margaret I. Young.
YOUNG, Praishaw Nicole, b. Mar 17, 1988, d. Aug 11, 1989 DC, dau of Chester Leroy and Savannah Ann Webb Young; gdau of Frank and Sheila Ann Webb; Milton and Mary Fluellen; ggdau of George P. Curtis.

TRINITY EPISCOPAL CHURCH
St. Mary's City, Md.

This is a very old cemetery that has been in use since the early 1800's. I walked through it many years ago, before becoming interested in genealogy, and found many old tombstones with fascinating inscriptions. Unfortunately, I took no notes then and have had no opportunity to return. Most of the following are obituaries taken from the local paper in the past few years.

ABELL, Elizabeth Knighton, b. Sep 5, 1923 Balto, d. May 9, 1988, wife of Roy Robert Cameron, dau of William T. and Lydia Mortimer Abell.
ALLRED, Clarence Oteroa "Duke", 90, d. Oct 24, 1992, m. 1932 Marie Franklin.
ARN, Suetta, d. 1970, 1st wife of Blair Ridington Evans.
BARONIAK, Katherine B., b. Oct 30, 1912, d. Feb 11, 1991, dau of John and Anna Baroniak.
BARONIAK, Olga Helen, b. Jan 30, 1917, d. Jan 31, 1992, dau of John Frank and Anna Mattey Baroniak.
BEAN, Elizabeth 'Jeanne', b. Jun 30, 1923 IL, d. Nov 29, 1991 FL, wife of __ Norris, dau of Lemuel Perry and Mabel Charlotte Bean.
BISCOE, Ann, b. 1747, d. 1818, m. (1st) C. C. Egerton, (2d) Mordecai Jones.
BRANNOCK, Beverly Belle "Bev", b. Dec 7, 1929 DC, d. Mar 17, 1993, wife of Roderick Burnham "Stubs" O'Neil, dau of Verne Clinton and Thelma Louise Snelling Brannock.
CLARKE, Gregory Hamilton, b. Sep 26, 1968, d. Dec 21, 1992, hus of Stacy Harmon, son of Christine McGehee Clarke and George E. "Ned" Clarke; stepson of Margaret Dunbar Clarke; gson of Cpt. and Mrs. Wm. McGehee of Va.
COOK, Jean Carson, b. Mar 11, 1990, d. Mar 21, 1990, dau of John Paul and Anne Randolph Loker Cook; gdau of Wm. M. and Beverly Corder Loker; late John P. Cook, Sr. and Barbara Taylor Raley; ggdau of Dorothy Taylor.

COWEN, Lois, d. Jan 27, 1987, wife of James Robert Donhiser.
COX, Thomas Emory, b. Dec 3, 1924, d. Aug 18, 1990, hus of Virginia B.___, son of Thomas M. and Anna B. Cox.
DAVIS, Rebecca, b. ca 1794, d. Mar 5, 1853, wife of Dr. Caleb Morris Jones.
DONHISER, James Robert, b. Jun 5, 1915 PA, d. Mar 2, 1993, hus of Lois Cowen, son of John and Theresa Lang Donhiser.
DUNBAR, Laura Marie, b. Oct 5, 1910, d. Apr 8, 1992, wife of Tynan Leonard Courtney, dau of John Franklin and Josephine Rosalie Bean Dunbar.
EVANS, Blair Ridington, 79, b. 1909 PA, d. Oct 12, 1988, m. (1st) Suetta Arn, (2d) Mary Scott, son of Gaffney Dallas and Edith Ridington Evans.
FORREST, Clarence Louis, b. Dec 1, 1946, d. Oct 30, 1991, hus of Mary Jane Walter, son of Ernest Matthew and Jeanette Allan Greenwell Forrest.
GARNER, Helen, 87, d. Jun 7, 1993, wife of J. Spence Howard.
GREENWELL, Jeanette Allan, b. Oct 15, 1913, d. Jun 25, 1990, m. (1st) Ernest Forrest, (2d) Herman Tucker, dau of Albert and Amy Greenwell.
HAYDEN, Mildred, b. Mar 16, 1918, d. Dec 16, 1990, wife of Andrew Louis Mattingly, Sr., dau of James Brady, Sr. and Susie Edna Lucas Hayden.
HOGABOOM, Robert Edward, Gen USMC, b. Nov 13, 1902 MA, d. Nov 11, 1993, m. (1st) Jean Lowe (d. 1979), (2d) Maurine Holbert, son of George Edward and Mary Ada Meyerhof Hogaboom.
HONKONEN, Meimi Katrina, b. Jan 21, 1915, d. Mar 31, 1989, wife of William Wise Unkle, dau of Matti and Anna Eleanor Mackie Honkonen.
JENKINS, Edith, b. Aug 28, 1910, d. Jul 17, 1989, wife of Theodore Meyers, dau of William E. and Grace Rogers Jenkins.
JONES, Dr. Alexander, 23, d. Jan 22, 1841.
JONES, Dr. Caleb Morris, 89, d. Feb 17, 1878,

hus of Rebecca Davis, son of Mordecai Jones.
JONES, Elizabeth, 79, d. Sep 5, 1876, wife of
Mordecai Clinton Jones.
JONES, Mordecai, b. 1747, d. 1829, 2d hus of
Ann Biscoe Egerton.
KEEN, Margaret Evelyn, b. Dec 31, 1903, d. Dec
5, 1988, dau of Edward O. and Augusta Koller
Keen.
KOHUT, Lorena Kathleen, b. Jul 20, 1940 DC, d.
Jan 1, 1989 TX, wife of John E. Baldwin, dau
of George C. and Hilda Hammett Kohut.
LANGE, Elizabeth Ann, b. Mar 18, 1948, d. Jun
28, 1990, wife of Kenneth Chan, dau of
Steven M. Sr. and Roberta A. Pratt.
McKENNY, Louise, b. Jun 5, 1908 WA, d. Dec 14,
1990, wife of __ Heagy, dau of Col. Henry J.
and Amy Concklin McKenny.
MEYERS, Theodore Thomas, b. Feb 1, 1935 DC, d.
Sep 28, 1992, m. 31 Aug 1973 Sylvia Gray,
son of Theodore and Edith Jenkins Meyers.
MOORE, Pembroke, b. Aug 11, 1892, d. Dec 13,
1989, hus of Antoinette Jarboe, son of Willard and Rosa Pembroke Moore.
MORRIS, Elizabeth, b. Nov 12, 1922 DE, d. Mar
26, 1990, wife of William A. Chapman, dau of
Thomas B. and Elizabeth Steelman Morris.
NAUMANN, Hattie Elizabeth, b. Jul 16, 1900, d.
Oct 18, 1988, wife of George Wm. Pratt, dau
of Charles Edw. and Salinda Coates Naumann.
NORRIS, Lloyd Elmer, b. Jan 12, 1912, d. Apr
10, 1987, m. (1st) Ida Marie __, (2d) Kathryn L. __.
PRATT, George William, d. 1950, hus of Hattie
Elizabeth Naumann.
RUDASILL, Leroy Undsworth, b. Jun 2, 1912 DC,
d. Jul 7, 1990, hus of Violet T. __, son of
Herndon Barbour and Mary Martha Rudasill.
SCHEIBLE, Lloyd William, b. May 9, 1913 DC, d.
Dec 27, 1992 NC, hus of Ernestine Anna
Schaffer, son of Wm. C. and Viola Frances
Clarke Scheible.
SMITH, Richard Louis, Sr. b. May 15, 1905, d.
Feb 2, 1991, hus of Mary Edna Taylor, son of
George Louis and Virginia Ruth Abell Smith.
STEELE, David Truman, b. Aug 22, 1922, d. Mar

25, 1988, hus of Nan Clapp, son of Heath McClung and Florence Truman Steele.
STOKES, James Marzell, b. Nov 21, 1919, d. Sep 5, 1988, hus of Caroline B. __, son of Ernest and Ethel Stokes.
TAYLOR, Agnes Regina "Susie", b. Aug 27, 1951, d. Dec 11, 1991, wife of Joseph Howard Gatton, dau of Donnell and Mary Agnes Taylor.

METHODIST/EPISCOPAL SOUTH CHURCH CEMETERY
Mechanicsvlle, Md.

BULLER, David, b. Feb 13, 1855, d. Jul 25, 1909.
FOWLER, William H., d. Feb 15, 1884, 69 yrs.
JONES, Effie J., b. Jun 8, 1860, d. Sep 20, 1880, 3rd dau of Joseph and Matilda Jones.
JONES, George S., b. Oct 30, 1865, d. Oct 13, 1880, 3rd son of Joseph and Matilda Jones.
JONES, J. Benj., b. Sep 13, 1855, d. Oct 26, 1888, son of Joseph and Matilda Jones.
THORNE, Ann M., b. May 21, 1807, d. Apr 3, 1878.

PRIVATE CEMETERIES
St. Mary' County, Md.

There were many private cemeteries, some of which were used until the 20th century and at least one is still being used. No one knows how many there were or where they are. The following is a listing of a few that have been identified.

PRIVATE CEMETERY
Point-No-Point, Md.

In 1980, these tombstones were leaning against trees in the private yards at the end of Holly Point Road on the shores of the Chesapeake Bay at Point-No-Point. They had been retrieved from the edge of the Bay twenty years before, after the graves had eroded into the Bay. Many of the stones are badly worn and some of the readings are uncertain.

FORREST, John W., d. Oct 23, 1850, age 3 yrs 6 mos, son of John W. and Ann W. Forrest.
HALL, Ann, d. Oct 2, 18(5?)1, age 28 yrs.
HALL, Leah, d. Mar 22, 1815.
HALL, Philip, d. Mar 30, 1852 (?) age 65 yrs.
HOLMES, Levina, d. Jan 28, 1841, age 62 yrs.
MADDOX, Mary, b. Jun 21, 1800, d. May 2, 187-.
PRICE, Ann, d. Sep 14, 1828 in her 37th yr.
PRICE, Chloe W., d. Oct 30, 182(8?).
PRICE, James W., d. Nov 9, 1823, age 2 yrs 6 mos 5 days.
PRICE, William P., d. Jan 5, 1826, age 1 yr 8 mos and 17 days.
PRICE, William P., d. Nov 13, 1860, age 72 yrs 3 mos 5 days. Erected by Dr. John Wesley Forrest, Aug 20, 1862.
WHITE, C. C., d. Jan 1, 1802, age 41 yrs.
WHITE, George, d. Feb 15, 1832, age 58 yrs.
WHITE, Tunsell, d. Feb (8?), 18(02?) 35 yrs.

MEREDITH CAPPER FARM
Dameron, Md.

DUNBAR, Alexander, d. Jul 4, 1843, age 25 yrs, son of John A. and Mary Dunbar.
DUNBAR, Ann, d. Nov 10, 1814, age 38 yrs, (1st) wife of John A. Dunbar.
DUNBAR, John A., b. Oct 11, 1779, d. Jul 29, 1820, age 60 yrs 9 mos and 18 days.
DUNBAR, John Richardson, b. Feb 27, 1804, d. Jul 15, 1851, son of John A. and Ann Dunbar.
DUNBAR, Mary, d. Jul 20, 1826, age 48 yrs, (2d) wife of John A. Dunbar.
SANNER, Frances S., d. Jan 19, 1820, age 35 yrs, wife of Jon. Sanner.
THOMAS, Ann D., d. Oct 17, 1830, in 29th yr.

BARD'S FIELD
Ridge, Md.

LOKER, __, d. Jun 29, 1848, age 5 yrs 7 mos 17 das.
LOKER, Eliza Ann, d. Mar 21, 1847, age 45 yrs 10 mos and 25 days, consort of Wm. H. Loker.
LOKER, Lucinda Evalina, d. May 16, 1855, age 25 yrs 5 mos and 5 days.
LOKER, Pamela, d. Dec 18, 1823, age 27 yrs 2 mos and 19 days.
LOKER, Rebecca, d. Sep 15, 1824, age 61 yrs 7 mos and 3 days.
LOKER, Thomas, d. Jun 29, 1847, age 2 yrs 5 mos 17 days, son of Wm. and E.A. Loker.
LOKER, Thomas B., d. Jul 6, 1821, age 2 mos and 2 days.
LOKER, Thomas W., d. Aug 5, 1834, age 2 yrs 10 mos 5 days, son of Wm. H. and E. A. Loker.
LOKER, Wm. Howe, b. May 18, 1801, d. Jan 4, 1853, age 51 yrs 7 mos and 17 days.
LOKER, Wm. M., d. Oct 10, 1837, age 1 yr 7 mos, son of Wm. H. and E. A. Loker.

"FENWICK'S FREE" Farm
St. Inigoes, Md.

BIRCH, Wilmer W., b. Dec 10, 1867, d. Apr 11,

1891, eldest son of Wm. and Susan E. Birch.
BIRCH, William, d. Feb 9, 1879, age 39 yrs 5 mos and 29 days.
JOHNSON, Mary Virginia, b. Jul 7, 1849, d. Jul 9, 1874.
TYLER, Allen Stewart, b. Aug 19, 1874, d. May 5, 1886, son of Allen and Alice Tyler.
TYLER, David A., b. Oct 15, 1837, d. Mar 25, 1865.
TYLER, David W., b. Apr 23, 1804, d. May 30, 1875, age 71 yrs 1 mo and 7 days.
TYLER, Ernest Clyde, b. Sep 30, 1868, d. Jul 10, 1873, eldest child of Allen C. and Alice Tyler.
TYLER, John Wesley, b. Apr 11, 1847, d. Nov 13, 1880, youngest son of David W. and Sarah Tyler.
TYLER, Sarah, d. 1863, wife of David W. Tyler.
TYLER, Solomon J., b. Mar 11, 1836, d. Jul 21, 1865.

FRESH POND NECK
Hayes Beach Road
Scotland, Md.

ARTIS, Mary Ann, d. Apr 19, 1838 in 11th yr.
ARTIS, Jane R., d. Feb 9, 1856, age 19 yrs 11 mos.
BEAN, Mary, b. Nov 25, 1788, d. Nov 19, 1855.
BEAN, Samuel, d. Jan 24, 1831, age 42 yrs.
BENNETT, Joseph, d. Aug 19, 1815, age 62 yrs.
BENNETT, Susana, d. Feb 28, 1806, age 49 yrs.
BENNETT, Wm., d. May 10, 1818, age 36 yrs 1 mo and 4 days.
CRANE, Susan J., d. Aug 22, 1811, age 36 yrs, wife of George Crane.
CRANE, Susanna, d. Jan 18, 1839, age 30 yrs, wife of George Crane.
GREENWELL, Wilford, d. Oct 30, 1810.
GREENWELL, William, d. Oct 30, 1801.
SMITH, Ann, d. Jan 22, 1814 in her 36th yr.

HAMMETT GRAVEYARD
San Souci Shopping Center
Lexington Park, Md.

HAMMETT, James McKelvey, will 1874.
WATTS, Rebecca, wife of James Hammett.
HAMMETT, John S. W., son.
HAMMETT, Joseph R., son.
No dates.

       KIRK'S PLANTATION
         Scotland, Md.

BISCOE, Thomas K., b. May 14, 1806, d. Jun 19, 1849.
DUNBAR, Ann Eugenia, b. Nov 15, 1841, d. Jul 3, 1852, age 10 yrs 9 mos 29 days.
DUNBAR, Leonora, d. Oct 22, 1853, age 7 yrs 10 mos and 6 days.
HALL, Ann L., b. Jan 15, 1795, d. Aug 3, 1837.
LANGLEY, James L., d. Apr 11, 1800, age 45 yrs.
LANGLEY, Laura Ann, d. Jun 16, 1837, age 18 yrs.
LANGLEY, Rebecca, d. Sep 3, 1834, age 50 yrs.
LANGLEY, T. Napoleon, b. Apr 22, 1822, d. Sep 28, 1883.
LANGLEY, Walter, d. Feb 9, 1845 in 69th yr.
LANGLEY, William A., d. Oct 13, 1822, age 5 yrs and 5 mos.
M.B.L. footstone.

   VALLANDINGHAM FAMILY CEMETERY
         Clements, Md.

MATTINGLY, Thomas Shircliffe, b. Mar 10, 1938 DC, d. Apr 10, 1992, son of Dorothy Hope Vallandingham Mattingly Milford and James Vernon Mattingly, Sr.
VALLANDINGHAM, Bernard Ignatius, b. Sep 29, 1921, d. March 29, 1988, son of Stephen Lawrence and Julia Marie Bowles Vallandingham.
VALLANDINGHAM, L. Harrison, b. Jul 14, 1951, d. Dec 23, 1992 CA, son of Jas. Howard and Lucy Harrison Vallandingham.
VALLANDINGHAM, Mary Gertrude, b. Jan 7, 1916, d. Sep 5, 1988, wife of Francis J. Weiland, (he bur St. Aloysius RCC, Leonardtown, Md),

dau of Stephen L. and Julia Bowles Vallandingham.

TIPPETT-EVANS FARM PRIVATE CEMETERY
Near Great Mills, Md.

TIPPETT, Benjamin, Jr., b. 1805, d. Mar 13, 1876, son of Benjamin and Eleanor Hayden Tippett.
TIPPETT, Susan H., bur 1870.
TIPPETT, Rev. Zackariah H., 86, d. Mar 18, 1886.
The above are brothers and sister.

TIPPETT, Benjamin Sr., d. 1836, bur Meeting House Hill Methodist Cem., Leonardtown, Md., hus of Eleanor Hayden.

FROM BIBLE RECORDS IN THE "THE GENERATOR"

DRURY-RAILEY FAMILY

DRURY, Thomas T., b. 1819, d. 1870, m. 26 Nov 1846 Martha Ann Lydamon, b. Aug 3, 1825, d. 1889.
RAILEY, James W., b. 1816, d. Feb 3, 1875 hus of Mary E. __, b. 1836, d. Mar 1, 1898.
DRURY, Georgia Winfield, b. Feb 12, 1853, d. Aug 8, 1911, son of Thomas T. and Martha A. Lydamon Drury, m. 8 Dec 1880 Georgiana Victoria Railey, b. Dec 18, 1859, d. Feb 2, 1937, dau of James W. and Mary E. Railey. Their children:

Mary Edith	b. 29 Jan 1883
	d. 13 Mar 1975
Cora Elizabeth	b. 27 Aug 1885
	d. 28 Sep 1965
Theodore L.	b. 24 Jun 1887
	d. 13 Jun 1955
Clarence Desrubes	b. 14 May 1890
	d. 1 Oct 1964
James Raub	b. 12 Aug 1891
	d. 12 Oct 1964
Joseph Clyde	b. 23 Jun 1894
	d. 25 Sep 1957
Nettie Anastatia	b. 6 Aug 1895

Georgia Esstill

Mary Lillian Esstill

George Lloyd

d. 26 Jun 1982
b. 14 Oct 1897
d. 27 Jun 1898
b. 13 Oct 1901
  Alive in 1982
b. 8 Feb 1904
d. 7 Jul 1972

BOHANAN-FISH-SANNER FAMILY

BOHANAN, George Fish, b. Nov 16, 1875, d. Jan 12, 1883 of diptheria, oldest son of J. Frank and Sallie Fish Bohanan.
COMBS, Therisy, b. Feb 24, 1800, d. Apr 13, 1844, 1st wife of Abel Sanner, dau of Nathaniel and Helen Combs.
FISH, Eliza Agnes, d. Mar 11, 1887 age 17 yrs.
FISH, Elizabeth Jane, d. Sep 22, 1863.
FISH, George F., d. Mar 29, 1880 of pneumonia, age 25 yrs.
FISH, George W., d. Jun 18, 1892 age 68 yrs, hus of Sarah Jane Johns.
FISH, J. Albert, d. Sep 5, 1883 age 18 yrs.
FISH, John Allen, d. Jun 14, 1851.
FISH, M. Alice, d. Sep 24, 1924 age 72 yrs 5 mos, m. 26 Nov 1884 Alfred G. Sanner, dau of Geo. W. and Sarah Jane Fish.
FISH, Marion, d. Aug 4, 1869, age 2 yrs 5 mos 1 wk, dau of Geo. W. and Sarah Jane Fish.
FISH, William F., d. Sep 12, 1871 age 14 yrs 2 wks 1 da, son of Geo. W. and Sarah Jane Fish.
JOHNS, Sarah Jane, d. Sep 21, 1875 age 45 yrs, m. 30 Dec 1846 George W. Fish of Balto.
SANNER, Abel, b. Nov 18, 1805, d. Mar 16, 1876, m. (1st) 14 Jan 1828 Therisy Combs, (2d) 6 Sep 1847 Serena Ann Sanner, son of John and Elizabeth Sanner.
SANNER, John Quincy, b. Apr 11, 1841, d. Sep 12, 1842, age 1 yr 5 mos 1 da.
SANNER, Lorida A.R., b. Mar 25, 1833, d. Nov 12, 1866 age 33 yrs 7 mos 13 das, m. 6 Oct 1853 William T. Shorter, dau of Abel and Therisy Combs Sanner.
SANNER, Martha Elizabeth, b. Aug 4, 1828, d. Mar 17, 1854, dau of Abel and Therisy Combs

Sanner.
SANNER, Philip D., b. May 19, 1854, d. May 27, 1854 age 9 das, son of Abel and Serena Ann Sanner.
SANNER, Richard B., b. Jun 12, 1852, d. Jul 1906, m. 20 Dec 1877 Nannie T. Jones, son of Abel and Serena Ann Sanner.
SANNER, Robert Lee, b. Sep 28, 1866, d. Apr 16, 1885, son of Abel and Serena Ann Sanner.
SANNER, Serena Ann, b. Feb 18, 1825, d. Oct 12, 1887, 2d wife of Abel Sanner, dau of John and Margaurette Sanner.
SANNER, William H., b. Aug 23, 1831, d. Aug 25, 1831, age 2 das, son of Abel and Therisy Combs Sanner.
SHORTER, Sarah G., d. Oct 14, 1873 age 8 yrs 7 das, dau of Wm T. and Lorida A.R. Shorter.

MISC. BURIALS-ST. MARY'S COUNTY

While composing these lists I found old death records (before 1900), showing date of death, but not burial place. If a memorial service was held in St. Mary's County or the exact place of death is known it is assumed the burial was also there.

BAIR, Eugene Arthur, Sr. b. May 16, 1932, d. Oct 22, 1991 FL, m. DC 17 Mar 1951 Gertrude Colbert, son of Robert F. and Regina Goucher Bair. Mem. svc. at Mattingly Funeral Home, Leonardtown, Md.
BALL, Clarence Eugene, b. Jan 1, 1935, d. Jul 24, 1993 DC, m. 1968 Henrietta Lawrence, son of Michael William and Gladys Marie Johnson Ball, bur Bethesda Meth. Cem. Valley Lee, Md.
BALDWIN, Lois, b. Apr 22, 1908, d. Jul 3, 1993, wife of Bjorn Egeli. Memorial Service.
BANNISTER, Rev. Alfred Jeffrey, 44, b. PA, d. Nov 9, 1988, hus of Sylvia __, bur Zion Baptist Church Cem., Lexington Park, Md.
BARBER, Mary Regina "Dolly", b. Jan 29, 1927, d. Jul 31, 1991, wife of J. Albert Anderson, dau of Ninian and Pauline Barber, bur Immaculate Conception Cem., Mechanicsville, Md.
BARNES, Colbert Matthews, Jr. b. Oct 7, 1931, d. Aug 25, 1993 DC, m. 10 Jan 1959 Marguerite Elizabeth Thompson, son of Colbert and Irene Biscoe Barnes, bur St. Luke UME Cem., Scotland, Md.
BENJAMIN, Gerald "Ben", Sr., USN, b. Jul 15, 1934 NJ, d. Jul 12, 1988, hus of Dora Harris. Services at NAS, Patuxent River, Md.
BENNETT, Auline Thelma, b. Jan 30, 1919, d. Jan 14, 1993, wife of __ Hayward, dau of Jos. Edw. and Gladys Mary Eliza Biscoe Bennett, bur Bethesda United Meth. Ch., Valley Lee, Md.
BERRY, Annie Elizabeth, b. Sep 21, 1922, d. Dec 13, 1991, wife of __ Young, dau of Milton and Annie Gray Berry, bur Galilee Cem., Mechanicsville, Md.
BERRY, Augustus William, b. Apr 17, 1906, d.

Aug 18, 1992, hus of Mary Thomas, son of Milton and Annie Gray Berry, bur Galilee Cem., Mechanicsville, Md.

BISCOE, Enoch M., d. Feb 21, 1975, m. 16 Jun 1947, Mary Catherine Mercer, bur Bethesda United Methodist Cem., Lexington Park, Md.

BLACKWELL, Sister Evangeline Sylvia, b. Mar 25, 1947, d. Jul 1, 1988, dau of __ Blackwell and Catherine B. Travers, bur St. Luke UME Cem., Scotland, Md.

BOZZIE, Delores Veronica "Dee", b. Aug 28, 1944 DC, d. Dec 16, 1991, m. 14 Jan 1961 George Edward Anthony, Sr., dau of Francis Guy and Viola Mae Wright Bozzie. Mem. svc. at Mattingly Funeral Home, Leonardtown, Md.

BRENNER, Nettie, b. Mar 26, 1913 Balto, d. Mar 28, 1993, m. Dec 1940 Samuel Millison, dau of Harry and Jessie Wolf Brenner. Inurnment serv.

BUCKLER, Kathy Irene, b. Jul 14, 1958, d. Nov 6, 1993, wife of __ Nowell, dau of Joseph and Florence Buckler. Memorial service at Our Lady of the Wayside Church, Helen, Md.

BURTON, Joseph Wallace, b. Nov 6, 1913, d. Apr 13, 1989 Veterans Home, Charlotte Hall, Md.

BUTLER, Mary Gladys, b. Feb 9, 1931, d. Jun 24, 1992, m. 8 Apr 1948 Thurman Davis, dau of James and Mary Butler, bur First Missionary Bapt. Church Cem., Lexington Park, Md.

BUTLER, William A. H., b. Apr 4, 1910 OH, d. Nov 24, 1991, hus of Elizabeth Kershaw, son of Henry Reese and Cora B. Stetson Butler. Mem. svc. at Brinsfield Funeral Home, Leonardtown, Md.

CARSON, Marietta Charlotte, b. Mar 26, 1922 PA, d. Apr 14 1989, wife of Albert Graves, dau of Philip and Clara Carson. Private svc.

CAWOOD, Charles Richard Rejan, USMC, b. Apr 15, 1933, d. Jul 17, 1992, son of Charles and Elna Shade Cawood. Memorial svc. at St. Mary's City, Md.

CHAMBERS, Rev. Alfred, b. Sep 11, 1907 GA, d. Sep 2, 1988, hus of Idonia __, son of Jesse and Eunice Chambers, bur First Baptist Cem., Lexington Park, Md.

Misc. Burials   325

CLARK, Ignatius of near Ridge, Md., b. 1750,
d. 1789, m. (2d) Frances ___.
CLARKE, John Ralph, Jr. b. Feb 22, 1954 DC, d.
Nov 26, 1989, son of John R. and Shirley A.
Hutcheson Clarke. Mem. svc. at Mattingly
Funeral Home, Leonardtown, Md.
CLARKE, Mrs. Nannie, d. Jan 26, 1892 at Bayside near St. Inigoes, age about 55 yrs.
COFFMAN, Francis Hunter, b. Mar 25, 1941 WV,
d. Sep 21, 1993, m. 13 Oct 1962 Cumberland,
MD, Marie Elaine Brehan, son of Clarence and
Gladys Hill Coffman, memorial services Brinsfield Funeral Home, Leonardtown, Md.
COURTNEY, Alice Roosevelt, b. Oct 13, 1905 WV,
d. Jun 25, 1993, wife of John Wm. Sander,
dau of Ulysses and Mollie Lazzell Courtney.
Mem. Svc. First Presby. Ch., Lexington Pk.,
MD.
COURTNEY, Joseph Columbus, b. Feb 19, 1931, d.
Dec 6, 1989, hus of Julia 'Mary' Haskell,
son of James Cornelius and Julia Dorothy
Hill Courtney, bur True Holiness Church Cem.,
Park Hall, Md.
CRIDDLE, Theodore Bruce "Ted", b. Sep 5, 1939
WV, d. Jul 1993, son of Osber C. and Georgia
Puckett Criddle. Memorial service Jul 21,
1993 at St. Mary's Airport, Hollywood, Md.
DEMENT, Joseph Adolph, b. Sep 18, 1924, d. Jan
14, 1991, hus of Virginia Mae ___, son of
Thomas Adolph and Daisy G. Dement. Private.
DENTON, Myrtle Louise, b. Jan 13, 1928, d. Oct
13, 1993, wife of R.W. Bohnke, dau of George
Edward, Sr. and Louise Simmons Denton, services at Mattingly-Gardiner Funeral Home,
Leonardtown, Md.
DiGIORGIO, Joseph Aloysius, b. Apr 20, 1918 LA,
d. Dec 26, 1991 NY, son of Victor and Mary
Cristoforo DiGiorgio, bur Seafarers Haven
Cem., Valley Lee, Md.
DOVE, Charles Edward, b. Dec 8, 1918, d. Apr
3, 1988, hus of Lottie C. ___, son of Joseph
Thomas and Mary Ellen Dove, bur True Holiness
Church, Park Hall, Md.
DOVE, Maggie Ardena, b. Feb 12, 1929, d. Jun
28, 1992 DC, wife of ___ Purnell, dau of Jos-

eph and Mary Cutchember Dove, bur St. Lukes UME Cem., Scotland, Md.
DROZAK, Frank P., MM WW II, b. Dec 24, 1928 AL, d. Jun 11, 1988 VA, hus of Marianne Rogers, son of Alexander C. and Alice Jordon Drozak, bur Seafarers Haven Cem., Valley Lee, Md.
DYSON, Rose Rebecca, b. Dec 15, 1927, d. Jan 30, 1992, wife of Louis M. Brooks, dau of late Jos. I. Dyson and Rachel Rebecca Hills, bur True Holiness Cem., Park Hall, Md.
FISHER, Elizabeth S., b. May 9, 1974, d. Feb 3, 1993, dau of Stephen S. and Sarah L. Yoder Fisher; gdau of Isaac B. and Sarah M. Swary Fisher; Levi J. and Lizzie Zook Yoder, bur Woodburn Hill Cem., Mechanicsville, Md.
FORE, John Allen, 73, d. Mar 11, 1992 DC, hus of Frances H. MacWather. Memorial service.
FORE, John Samuel, b. Jun 24, 1948 DC, d. Feb 27, 1993, hus of Carol Ann Unger, son of John Allen and Frances MacWather Fore. Memorial service.
GANDY, Pauline, b. Nov 10, 1896 SC, d. Jul 13, 1989, m. (1st) __ Green, (2d) __ Frazier, dau of Henry and Sereatha Williamson Gandy. Memorial service.
GILLUM, Ernest K., b. Sep 18, 1960, d. Jan 1, 1991, son of James M. amd Mary S. Lee Horstman. Mem. Svc. at Brinsfield Funeral Home, Leonardtown, Md.
GOLDSBOROUGH, Louvinia Ann, b. Nov 3, 1932, d. Oct 29, 1993, m. 18 Jun 1993 Troy Gruber, dau of James Roland and Ruth Cynthia Mattingly Goldsborough. Mass at Holy Angels RCC, Avenue, Md.
GORMLEY, John E., USA WW II, b. Jul 21, 1905 DC, d. Mar 21, 1992, hus of Willie C. __. Private services.
GRANT, Helen, b. Aug 13, 1907 WV, d. Oct 12, 1992, wife of __ McEachern, dau of Olin and Olivia Pierce Grant. Private service.
HAKE, William Elmer, b. Oct. 5, 1914 PA, d. Apr 14, 1991 DC, hus of Dora Diamond, son of William G. and Cecelia Neely Hake. Mem. svc. at Brinsfield Funeral Home, Leonardtown, Md.
HALL, Robert Kennelumn "Kenny Boots", b. Apr

29, 1957, d. Apr 25, 1993, m. 1992 Brenda
Lee Fleming, son of John William Jr. and
Gertrude Loraine Lacey Hall. Services at
Holy Angels RCC, Avenue, Md.
HALL, Rose Mary, b. Jul 10, 1928, d. May 31,
1993, m. (1st) __ Fenwick, (2d) Elbert Yates,
dau of Webster William and Mary Hawkins Hall,
bur True Holiness Church Cem., Park Hall, Md.
HANSON, Michael Timothy, USN, b. Aug 2, 1958,
d. Nov 5, 1991, son of Jennings and Mary
Anne Welsh Hanson. Mem. svc. at Brinsfield
Funeral Home, Leonardtown, Md.
HARDING, Gwynn Marie, infant, d. Feb 18, 1989,
dau of Jas. Richard and Roberta Lee O'Don-
nell Harding; gdau of Jas. R. and Sue Hard-
ing; Mr. and Mrs. Robt. J. O'Donnell; pater-
nal ggdau of Mrs. Gertrude Cusic and Mrs.
Mary Agnes Harding; maternal ggdau of Mrs.
Dorothy Jordan. Private.
HASKELL, Julia 'Mary', b. Nov 14, 1924 SC, d.
Jan 23, 1992 DC, wife of Joseph Columbus
Courtney, dau of Samuel and Lessie Edward
Haskell, bur True Holiness Church, Park
Hall, Md.
HAUF, Kevera "Kay", b. Mar 2, 1920 Balto, d.
May 20, 1992, wife of Brenton Ellsworth My-
ers, dau of Albert and Marvene Stansbury
Hauf. Memorial service at residence.
HAWKINS, Betty Lorraine, b. Aug 4, 1933, d.
Jul 3, 1993, m. 18 Jun 1955 Joseph Mason
Curtis, dau of Benjamin and Margaret Hewlett
Hawkins, bur Zion Meth. Cem., Lexington Park,
Md.
HENDERSON, James Marion, Jr. b. Nov 5, 1918
DC, d. Jun 28, 1993, hus of Myrtle R. Les-
zear, son of James M. and Mary R. Taylor
Henderson. Memorial service.
HENDERSON, Roberta Kay, b. Nov 24, 1950 MN, d.
Oct 4, 1993 FL, m. 10 Sep 1976 Cdr. Willain
Washer, dau of Robert and Jean Henderson.
Mem. svc. Patuxent River NAS, Md.
HILL, Julia Ann, b. Nov 16, 1930 VA, d. Jun 10,
1991, m. 1955 John Lee James, dau of Calvin
and Ellen V. Johnson Hill, bur First Baptist
Church Cem., Lexington Park, Md.

HILL, Julia Dorothy, b. Jul 28, 1903, d. Nov 20, 1989, wife of John Goldring, dau of Andrew I. and Lottie A. Hill, bur True Holiness Cem., Park Hall, MD.
HISLOP, Robert Edward, Sr. b. Jul 22, 1935 DC, d. Jul 13, 1993, m. 25 Nov 1966 Eileen Mary Bromley, son of Randall and Edith Wry Hislop. Memorial Service.
HOCK, Allen Anton, 44, d. Nov 5, 1991, service at Mattingly Funeral Home, Leonardtown, Md.
HORTON, Ronald Edward, b. Jan 6, 1955, d. May 15, 1992, son of John William, Jr. and Catherine J. Horton, bur St. Luke UME, Scotland, Md.
INMAN, Edwin G., LT CDR, d. May 4, 1991, hus of Anna Marie __. Mem. svc. Patuxent River NAS, Md.
JENIFER, Dora Elizabeth, b. Feb 6, 1893, d. Dec 23, 1991, wife of William Edward Whalen, dau of John and Gertrude Jenifer, bur Mt. Calvary Meth. Church Cem., Laurel Grove, Md.
JENKINS, Joseph, d. Jan 16, 1796, 22 yrs 4 mos 12 das, bur St. Inigoes RCC, Md.
JENKINS, Mary Ruth, b. Jul 6, 1926, d. Apr 27, 1989, m. (1st) __ Waring, (2d) William Rich Chesley (bur All Faith Episcopal Ch., Huntersville, Md), dau of Elmer and Edith Wyvill Jenkins, memorial Mass May 1, 1989 at Immaculate Conception Church, Mechanicsville, Md.
JERNINGHAM, Dr. Henry, d. Nov 1772/Jan 1773, of Bushwood Plantation.
JOHNSON, Leo Delbert, USN WW II, b. Apr 4, 1916 OR, d. Oct 13, 1992, hus of Zoe C. __, son of Hiram and Mary Edwards Johnson. Mem. svc. at Brinsfield Fun. Home, Leonardtown, Md.
JONES, Alexander Claxton, b. Aug 22, 1840, d. May 8, 1863, tombstone at Cornfield Harbor.
JONES, George S., 17, d. Oct 10, 1880, bur Mechanicsville, Md., son of Joseph H. and Matilda Jones.
JOWLES, Peregrine, 17--/18--, m. (1st) Dryden Chesldine, (2d) __ Forbes, bur The Plains, Golden Beach, Md.
LANE, Dorothy Gray, b. Jun 25, 1907 VA, d. Mar 18, 1987, wife of __ Croson, dau of Alfred

Clews and Virginia Tillett Lane. Private.
LAWRENCE, Elois Haywood "Buddy" "Reds", b. Aug 15, 1923 NC, d. Jan 31, 1992, m. 1979 Ark, Pamela May Shealy, son of Elijah and Lela Black Lawrence. Memorial svc. at Mattingly Funeral Home, Leonardtown, Md.
LAWRENCE, Henrietta, b. Dec 22, 1928, d. Jul 23, 1993, wife of Clarence Eugene Ball, dau of John P. and Nellie S. Barnes Lawrence, bur Bethesda Meth. Cem., Valley Lee, Md.
LITTLEJOHN, Carrie Bell, b. Feb 9, 1920 SC, d. Jun 22, 1992 NYC, wife of Pat Jeffries, dau of George Littlejohn and Ernestine Littlejohn Tate, bur First Missionary Bapt. Church Cem., Lexington Park, Md.
LUSK, Valerie Lynda, b. Sep 9, 1938 PA, d. Jun 21, 1989, wife of Paul W. Chapin, dau of William and Ethel M. Lusk. Private svc.
MADJESKI, Henry Robert, Sr. CPO USN Ret., b. Feb 29, 1924 NJ, d. Oct 7, 1993, m. 13 Feb 1949 Elizabeth Temple Morris, son of Henry and Helen Sczygiel Madjeski. Memorial svc. at Patuxent River NAS, Md.
McGUIGAN, Mary Christine, b. Dec 24, 1919, d. Dec 2, 1988, wife of Bernhard H. Mueller, dau of Michael and Susan McGuigan, bur St. Paul's Lutheran Cem., New Market, Md.
MONGELLI, Mrs. Anna Elizabeth, b. Sep 20, 1937 NY, d. Jul 24, 1989, wife of Frank A. Mongelli, bur Seafarer's Haven Cem., Valley Lee, Md.
MONROE, James Garlton, b. May 12, 1914 NC, d. May 4, 1988, hus of Mollie Lou __, son of John Martin and Victora March Monroe, bur First Baptist Cem., Lexington Park, Md.
MOSES, Anna Katherine, b. Feb 13, 1908 PA, d. Nov 8, 1992, wife of Edgar Filmore Vandivere, Jr., dau of Richard and Della Walter Moses. Memorial service.
MYERS, Brenton Ellsworth, d. Dec 15, 1990, m. 25 Jan 1946 Kevera Hauf.
NAYLOR, Jewel Mary, b. Oct 25, 1904 IN, d. Jul 17, 1988, wife of John Raymond Luskey, dau of Frank and Lydia Naylor. Private funeral service.

O'NEIL, James Alexander, b. Feb 14, 1935 NC, d. Dec 14, 1993, hus of Wanda Kathleen Manuel, son of James Newsom and Louise Ford O'Neil, mem. serv. at Brinsfield Funeral Home, Leonardtown, Md.
ORSINI, Victor Anthony, b. Dec 9, 1902 NYC, d. Oct 24, 1988, hus of Marion Frances __, son of Raffaele and Christina DeBrino Orsini, memorial service.
PITCHER, Frank Holden, b. Oct 27, 1904 IL, d. Sep 17, 1988, mem. svc. at Mattingly Funeral Home, Leonardtown, Md.
PURNELL, George Sylvester, d. Apr 4, 1985, m. 15 Sep 1930 Rosetta Shuebrooks, bur St. Lukes UME Cem., Scotland, Md.
RALEY, Thomas Stanley (Brother Paschal), b. Aug 14, 1947, drowned Pt. Lookout Sep 22, 1965, son of James Morris and Mary Lou Johnson Raley, bur Xavian Brothers Cem., Leonardtown, Md.
REEVES, Wylie David, b. Apr 6, 1933 WV, d. Dec 14, 1990, hus of Barbara May __, son of Wylie F. and Charlotte May Reeves. Private.
REGNER, Sven Gosta, 87, last member of his family, b. Sweden, d. Mar 2, 1992, bur Seafarers Haven Cem., Valley Lee, Md.
REHM, Ernest Daniel, M.D., d. Mar 30, 1982, m. 1936 OH Thelma Louise Rutschow. Mem. svc.
RUTSCHOW, Thelma Louise, b. Dec 2, 1915 OH, d. Nov 23, 1992, wife of Ernest Daniel Rehm, dau of Carl and Caroline Louise Pautz Rutschow. Mem. svc. at Mattingly Funeral Home, Leonardtown, Md.
SANDER, John William, b. Oct 21, 1901 WV, d. Apr 3, 1993, hus of Alice Roosevelt Courtney, son of Christian and Ida Hibbard Sander. Memorial svc., Lexington Park, Md.
SCHULZ, David William, b. Jun 16, 1980 NY, shot Dec 10, 1993, son of Richard Lee and Gail Frances Silver Schulz. Svc. at Mattingly Funeral Home, Leonardtown, Md.
SHEALY, Pamela May, b. July 23, 1927 SC, d. Nov 11, 1991, wife of Elois Haywood Lawrence, dau of Walter, Sr. and Rosa Eva Mitchell Shealy, private services.

Misc. Cemeteries

SKOK, William Lawrence, b. Feb 28, 1938 OH, d. Nov 23, 1988, hus of Dorothy ___, son of Lawrence and Amelia Skok. Service at Mattingly Funeral Home, Leonardtown, Md.
SMITH, James Jefferson "Jeff", Jr. b. Jan 4, 1910, d. May 30, 1988, son of Jas. J. and Amanda Smith, bur Bethesda Methodist Cem., Valley Lee, Md.
SOTHORON, Henry, d. Jan 20, 1832, age 60, at his residence near Benedict, Md., bur The Plains Cem., Golden Beach, Md.
ST.CLAIR, Mary Elizabeth, b. Feb 16, 1935, d. Oct 25, 1989, wife of James Clement Burch, Sr., dau of Bernard and Mary Letha Norris St. Clair, service at Immaculate Conception Church, Mechanicsville, Md.
STONESTREET, John Carroll, b. Jun 2, 1941, d. Aug 20, 1993, son of Joseph Elmer and Mabel Jenkins Stonestreet. Private services.
SWIHART, Imogene Cretoria, b. Oct 17, 1917, d. Aug 5, 1993, wife of Kenneth I. Thomas, dau of Francis M. and Agnes Ethel McAninch Swihart, bur Victory Bapt. Ch., Mechanicsville, Md.
TAYLOR, John, b. Apr 4, 1947, d. Jul 19, 1991, son of late Wilson Scarborough Taylor and Alice Taylor Hill, bur First Bapt. Church Cem., Lexington Park, Md.
THOMAS, Anna, b. Nov 27, 1900, d. Sep 30, 1989, dau of Mr. and Mrs. Alex Thomas, bur True Holiness Cem., Park Hall, Md.
TURNER, Pearl Elizabeth, 78, b. Balto, d. Jul 31, 1991, dau of Alexander and Henrietta Turner, bur St. Lukes UME Cem. Scotland, Md.
VANDIVERE, Edgar Filmore, Jr. 78, b. TN, d. Apr 2, 1991, hus of Anna Katherine Moses. Memorial service.
VAN PELT, Robert E., b. Nov 6, 1910, d. Jul 23, 1992 Charlotte Hall Vets Home, son of Robert E. and Etta Johnson Van Pelt.
WHALEN, Mary Alberta, b. Mar 4, 1912, d. Feb 16, 1993, m. 1933 Alexander Key, dau of Chas. and Alberta Whalen, bur Mt. Calvary Meth. Cem., Laurel Grove, Md.
WHITE, Kenneth E., b. Oct 19, 1915 Blackfoot

Ind. Res., d. Nov 5, 1989, serv. at Mattingly Funeral Home, Leonardtown, Md.

WILDMAN, Howard Daniel, b. Dec 11, 1902 DC, d. Mar 30, 1993 DC, hus of Marion H. __, son of Albert and Augusta Artes Wildman. Mem. svc.

WILSON, Rose Elizabeth, b. Dec 25, 1918, d. Feb 10, 1991, wife of William E. Young, dau of Nelson and Alice Gray Wilson, bur Galilee Cem., Mechanicsville, Md.

WOODS, Anamae, b. Jul 25, 1924 IN, d. Jun 19, 1993, wife of __ Latta, dau of Charles and Nellie Lemmon Woods. Private inurnment.

YEATMAN, Michelle, b. Mar 10, 1959, d. Dec 4, 1989, wife of Jos. Patrick Adams, dau of Robert Paul Yeatman and Margaret Dunbar Clarke. Private.

YOUNG, Martha Lee, b. Jan 29, 1912, d. Feb 2, 1991, wife of Robert Locker Noel, dau of Johnny and Elvira Price Young, bur First Baptist Church Cem., Lexington Park, Md.

YOUNG, Mary Violet, b. Jun 8, 1894, d. Jun 3, 1989, wife of Joseph H. Yorkshire, dau of Frank and Hattie Young, bur Immaculate Conception Cem., Mechanicsville, Md.

ST. MARY'S COUNTIAN DEATHS

ABELL, Addie L., d. Jul 7, 1974.
ABELL, Benedict Irving, d. Feb 4, 1977.
ABELL, Elizabeth, d. Jun 1859 of lung cong. age 2 yrs.
ABELL, Emma Pauline, d. May 23, 1965.
ABELL, Francis Edgar, d. Aug 8, 1970.
ABELL, Harry Benedict, Sr. d. Jun 6, 1976.
ABELL, Robert McGuire, d. Feb 16, 1975.
ABELL, Sophiah (male), d. Sep 1859 of whooping cough, age 5 mo.
ADAM, Anna, 100, b. Feb 26, 1893 Budapest, Hungary, d. Dec 21, 1993, wife of Frank Adam (d. 1945).
ADAMS, Eleanor, b. 1760, d. 1778, m. 1778, Ignatius Joy II, dau of James and Jane Brinan Adams.
ADAMS, James, b. 1737, d. 1795, m. 1756 Jane Brinan.
ADAMS, John Carroll "Jack", b. Dec 8, 1901, d. Feb 4, 1993, hus of Lena Groomes, son of Benjamin Franklin and Lucy Agnes Pope Adams.
ADAMS, Mary Adelaide, b. Nov 1879, d. Nov 26, 1901, 1st wife of Wm. "Alfred" Johnson, dau of Benj. F. Adams.
AUD, Clarence M., d. Apr 10, 1971.
AUD, Joseph Reginold, Jr. b. Oct 26, 1951, d. Sep 28, 1991 VA, son of J. "Reggie" and Beatrice T. Pilkerton Aud.
BAILEY, Thomas A., d. Nov 16, 1972.
BAKER, Jonathan Jennings, d. Apr 1962, hus of Lillian Gertrude Goddard.
BARNES, John Spencer, d. Nov 22, 1976.
BEAN, Christopher Philip, 33, d. Feb 26, 1991 DC, son of Robt. G. and Joanne Bean.
BEAN, Robert Jenifer, d. Jan 20, 1892, youngest child of Robert J. and A. M. Bean.
BELL, Paul Archibald, b. Nov 15, 1916, d. Nov 22, 1986.
BELL, T. Webster, Sr., d. Nov 21, 1987, hus of Mary Catherine Sterling.
BELL, Thomas, married, sailor, d. Apr 1860 of consumption, age 35 yrs.
BENNETT, Marie Elizabeth, d. 1814, wife of

Caleb Jones.
BILLINGSLEY, Dr. J.A.T., 55, d. Jul 10, 1885, m. 19 Feb 1867 at All Faith Episcopal Church Elizabeth "Betty" C. Briscoe.
BILLINGSLEY, Mary Alice, d. Mar 11, 1891 at Church Home Hosp. Balto, age 21 yrs 6 mos 11 das.
BIRCH, Joseph Francis, b. Dec 15, 1953, d. Jul 7, 1987, son of Theodore B. and Mary Delores Birch.
BOWLES, Leonard T., Sr. b. May 27, 1925, d. Apr 11, 1985.
BOWMAN, Laura Virginia, b. Apr 1, 1903, d. Feb 10, 1989, wife of John E. Bowman.
BRISCOE, Ann, d. after 1740, m. (1st) John Davis, (2d) Samuel Wood, dau of Philip and Susannah Swann Briscoe.
BRISCOE, Elizabeth "Bettie", 74, d. Jul 27, 1911, wife of Dr. J. A. T. Billingsley.
BRISCOE, Edward, b. 1685, d. Feb 19, 1726, hus of Susannah Gerard Slye, son of Philip and Susannah Swann Briscoe.
BRISCOE, George, d. March 9, 1720/21, son of Philip and Susannah Swann Briscoe.
BRISCOE, James, b. 1693, d. 1752 in Fred. Co., Md., hus of Ann Sothoron, son of Philip and Susannah Swann Briscoe.
BRISCOE, James Sothoron, d. 1774, hus of Mary __, son of James and Ann Sothoron Briscoe.
BRISCOE, John, b. 1678, d. 1734, hus of Eleanor Williamson, son of Philip and Susannah Swann Briscoe.
BRISCOE, Judith, d. ca 1740, m. (1st) Charles Aschom, (2d) Thomas Brooke, dau of Philip and Susanah Swann Briscoe.
BRISCOE, Philip, b. 1680, d. 1745, hus of Elizabeth __, son of Philip and Susannah Swann Briscoe.
BRISCOE, Philip, b. 1719, d. Jul 17, 1745, hus of Nancy Foster, son of Philip and Elizabeth Briscoe.
BRISCOE, Sarah, d. 1734, dau of Philip and Susannah Swann Briscoe, m. (1st) Thomas Truman, (2d) William Stevens Howard of Edmund.
BRISCOE, Sarah Catherine, b. 1818, d. Mar 26,

1885.
BRISCOE, Susanna, d. ca 1740, wife of ___ Compton, dau of Philip and Susannah Swann Briscoe.
BROWN, Betty Ann, b. Jul 13, 1938 DC, d. Jul 28, 1993, wife of Carroll W. Wine, Jr., dau of George William and Mary Cecelia Daras Brown.
BROWN, Matilda, 29, d. Feb 9, 1834, wife of William Jarboe, dau of Robt. Brown of DC.
BRYANT, John Benjamin, d. Jan 20, 1892, age 1 yr and 11 mos, son of John and Elizabeth Bryant.
BUCKLER, Thomas Harry, 84, d. Dec 15, 1993, Alexandia, VA, m. 1939 Esther Marie ___.
BURROUGHS, Elizabeth, d. Aug 1859, 3 mos.
BURROUGHS, John S. "Buddy", d. Oct 27, 1988 Ft. Washington, Md., hus of Katherine E. ___.
BURROUGHS, John William Henry, b. ca 1824, m. (1st) 6 Jan 1846, Ann Maria Jarboe, (2d) Ann Stone, widow w/3 children, son of John and Ruth Ann Mills Burroughs.
CAMALIER, B. Harris, d. Dec 21, 1969.
CAMPER, Olevia, d. May 1860, age 1 day.
CARROLL, Kate, d. Apr 1859 of infantile fits, age 8 das.
CAVANAUGH, Marie A., b. Jun 13, 1916, d. Nov 4, 1988.
CLARKE, Matthias, War of 1812 Vet, b. Oct 23, 1766, d. Washington Co., Md., son of Robert and Mary Clarke.
CLEMENTS, Frances E., b. Jun 10, 1916, d. Aug 13, 1988.
CLEMENTS, Sarah V., d. Feb 21, 1976.
CLEMENTS, William M., d. Nov 28, 1967.
COHEN, Julia, b. Dec 31, 1897, d. Sep 5, 1988, wife of Harry Merson, dau of Michael Henry and Esther Lopez Cohen.
COLLINS, William, 23, bur Jan 23, 1871.
COLLISON, Samuel, bay pilot, d. Nov 1859 of dropsy, age 78 yrs, widower.
COMBS, Blanche, d. Jan 4, 1960.
COMBS, E.A. (f), d. Dec 1859 of consumption, age 16 yrs.
COMBS, James Nathaniel, b. Jan 31, 1926, d.

Sep 14, 1981.
COMBS, John Cornelius, d. Jan 19, 1863.
COMBS, Mary, widow, d. Nov 1859 of pneumonia, age 44 yrs.
COMBS, William S. P., d. Dec 1859 of scrofula, age 15 yrs.
CONNELLY, Charles F., Sr. d. Nov 4, 1970.
CONNELLY, Frances Regina, d. Apr 3, 1976.
CONNELLY, Margaret R., b. Mar 19, 1922, d. May 7, 1985.
COOMBS, Ira John, b. Mar 3, 1924, d. Jul 1, 1981.
CRELLY, Thomas Sagrif "Tom", Sr. b. Mar 22, 1902 OH, d. Feb 10, 1993, hus of Marian Short, son of Thomas John and Julia Agnes Kale Crelly.
CUSIC, Daisy Ann, d. Mar 7, 1972.
CUSIC, Pearl E., b. Jul 20, 1898, d. Dec 21, 1983.
CUSIC, Richard Thomas, b. Feb 17, 1927, d. Jul 23, 1986.
DAVIS, Benjamin Lee, b. Oct 4, 1913, d. Jan 31, 1983.
DAVIS, Frances, 87, d. Feb 19, 1993 Balto, wife of Francis C. Horney, dau of Andrew J. and Kathryn Dent Davis.
DAVIS, Harold E., b. May 2, 1916, d. Aug 24, 1982.
DAVIS, Patricia Lynn, d. Aug 23, 1974.
DAVIS, Sophiah, (m), married, d. Sep 1959 of consumption, age 30 yrs.
DELAHAY, Veva, b. Jan 22, 1906, d. Jul 22, 1984.
DEL VECCHIO, John V., 82, b. NYC, d. Feb 11, 1991, m. (1st) Vivian E. Mears (d. 1974), (2d) Betty Bryant Langley.
DENT, George, b. Dec 21, 1756, d. Oct 15, 1842, hus of Elizabeth Temperance Mills.
DENT, John K., Sr., 62, b. Balto., d. Jan 10, 1993, Balto, hus of Kathleen Gibson.
DeROSA, Richard Joseph, Jr. b. Dec 15, 1958, d. Jan 25, 1980.
DIXON, Harry Oswald, Sr. b. Aug 31, 1901, d. Feb 2, 1987.
DOUGLAS, Shirley Ann, 1932-1989

DOWNS, Andrew W., d. Jul 28, 1969.
DOWNS, Catherine, d. Jul 5, 1989, Oxen Hill.
DOWNS, Mollie, d. Aug 6, 1877.
DRESHER, Ralph Edward, USN Korea, b. Aug 23, 1936 Balto, d. Jul 23, 1993, hus of Myrtle Josephine Baron, son of William Elmer and Beatrice Ann Knott Dresher.
DRURY, Edna Evangeline, b. Feb 26, 1927, d. Jan 30, 1993, wife of __ Inman, dau of Wilson L. and Mary Louise Adams Drury.
DRURY, Mrs. Mary, d. Jan 19, 1863.
DRURY, Mary A., d. Dec 1859, age 3 mos.
DRURY, Mary Rosa, d. Oct 21, 1963.
DRURY, Theadore, d. Jun 13, 1955.
DUKE, Monsignor Frederick H., b. Dec 7, 1914, d. Feb 17, 1992, Balto, son of Benj. Hooper and Grace Dent Duke.
DUNN, Pearl Agnes, d. Jan 12, 1970.
EDELEN, Mrs. Ann, d. Sep 16, 1853.
EDELIN, James S., d. Jan 1860 of consumption, age 54 yrs.
EDLEY, Catherine, d. Jul 10, 1818 age 37 yrs, 1st wife of Joshua Thompson.
EISENSCHMIDT, Henry, 77, USA WW II, d. Jul 31, 1993.
ELLIS, Mrs. Elizabeth, retired school teacher, d. Sep 2, 1993, Potomac, Md.
EVANS, Clara Priscilla, d. Mar 1, 1857, m. (1st) McKelva Armsworthy, (2d) James Nelson Evans.
EVANS, Edward E., d. Jul 8, 1968.
EVANS, Eleanor S., b. Jun 1850, d. Jan 14, 1885, wife of James T. Hazel.
EVERETT, Sister Mary Angel, nee Mary Estelle, b. Jul 5, 1893, d. May 1, 1986 DC, dau of Louis Arthur and Mary Elizabeth Raley Everett.
FARR, Joseph Lewis, d. Dec 29, 1977.
FARRELL, James Allen, d. Mar 24, 1974.
FEARNS, Francis William, d. Mar 5, 1975.
FENWICK, Cuthbert I., b. Jul 31, 1901, d. Dec 30, 1984.
FENWICK, Robert Ignatius, Sr. b. May 12, 1949, d. Aug 11, 1993, m. 1969 Joyce Louise Caple, son of Nelson William and Annie Christine

Courtney Fenwick.
FLETCHER, John Riley IV, b. Dec 30, 1909, d. Jul 4, 1987, hus of Mildred Elizabeth Milburn.
FOOTE, John Sherwood "Jack", b. Aug 7, 1922 DC, d. Feb 22, 1993 TX, hus of Doris __.
FORD, Alice M., d. Jul 13, 1880, m. 20 Nov 1865 Hayden Martin Henry Yates.
FORD, J. J., 43, d. Sep 19, 1889.
FORD, Joseph S., b. Oct 29, 1811, d. Nov 8, 1881, m. 11 Oct 1847 Elenor C. Hayden Yates.
FORD, Teresa, d. Jun 28, 1896, wife of __ Greenwell.
FORD, Mrs. Teresia, d. Jul 2, 1853.
FORREST, Lydia, b. Jun 1, 1771, d. Feb 24, 1815, m. 14 Jun 1797 John Johnson of VA, dau of Zachariah and Ann Edwards Forrest.
FRAZIER, Russell V., b. Nov 11, 1916, d. Mar 7, 1980.
FREEMAN, Mrs. Antonette, d. Nov 1859 of inflamation, age 40 yrs.
FREEMAN, Miss Priscilla Johns, b. 1848, d. 1944, dau of Samuel Hambleton and Priscilla Perry Douglas Freeman.
GATTON, Eleanor, d. Sep 8, 1965, wife of __ Bell.
GILL, Dr. Joseph E., d. Jul 29, 1965.
GLICK, Grace, 90, d. Apr 5, 1993, wife of Earl Merryman.
GOLDSBOROUGH, Sally, widow, d. Nov 1859 of pneumonia, age 90 yrs.
GOODRICH, John, b. May 2, 1808, d. Sep 6, 1861, m. 27 Mar 1845 Susan Milburn Price Bean.
GOUGH, Joseph Marion, Sr. d. Jun 11, 1971.
GOUGH, Nellie Rosalie, d. Nov 12, 1972.
GRAHAM, Barbara Jane, b. Dec 4, 1950 DC, d. Dec 21, 1989 DC, wife of Thos. E. Hewitt, dau of James C. and Carolyn Russell Graham.
GRAVES, Anita H., b. Jul 14, 1907, d. Nov 13, 1987.
GRAVES, Joseph Harold, b. Sep 23, 1936, d. Feb 27, 1980.
GREENWELL, Elizabeth, lady, widow, d. Jun 1859 of liver dis., age 68 yrs.
GREENWELL, Rev. Hezekiah, S.J., b. 1891, d.

1941, son of John Philip and Mary Estelle
Cawood Greenwell.
GREENWELL, Mrs. Monica, d. Sep 11, 1853.
GREENWELL, Nellie, d. Dec 20, 1881.
GREENWELL, Philip, b. 1894, d. 1986, son of
John Philip and Mary Estelle Cawood Greenwell.
GREER, Mary Buelah, b. Mar 27, 1906, d. Aug 2,
1993, m. 1924 H. Rhodock Scott, dau of late
John Greer and Mary McCarthy Greer Scott.
GUY, Claude Byron, b. Jan 12, 1912, d. Jul 20,
1983.
GUY, Mary E., widow, d. Jul 1859 of old age,
age 78.
GUY, Mary Lou, b. Aug 5, 1935, d. Jul 5, 1986.
GUYTHER, George, b. ca 1735, d. 1797.
GUYTHER, Henry, b. 1808, d. 1872 Balto, m.
(1st) Sarah Jane Shadrick.
GUYTHER, John Shadrick, b. 1835, d. 1919.
GUYTHER, Olive, b. 1883 Balto, d. 1971.
GUYTHER, William, b. ca 1766, d. 1820.
HALL, Dallas Franklin, b. Apr 2, 1938, d. Oct
3, 1987.
HALL, Susan Helen, d. Dec 23, 1970.
HAMMETT, Annie Weston, 30, d. Jul 24, 1892,
wife of D. Whit Jones, dau of McKelvie Hammett.
HAMMETT, John P. "Jack", b. Jun 18, 1921, d.
Jun 18, 1986.
HAMMETT, Olivia, 15, d. Jul 24, 1892, dau of
McKelvie Hammett.
HAMMETT, William I., d. Mar 13, 1966.
HARRIS, James B., d. Jan 27, 1973.
HATCHER, John F., d. Nov 26, 1874 DC, age 40,
m. 26 Mar 1862 Johanna Elizabeth Everett.
HAYDEN, Edith A., b. Dec 12, 1874, d. Aug 10,
1878, dau of Stephen Hayden.
HAYDEN, Eleanor Rose, b. Aug 17, 1922, d. May
26, 1977.
HAYDEN, Elenor C., b. Feb 16, 1810, d. after
1847, m. (1st) 26 Oct 1830 William Yates,
(2d) 1847 Joseph S. Ford.
HAYDEN, Harriet E., d. Aug 11, 1853, wife of
William Hayden.
HAYDEN, Ignatius, d. Aug 3, 1867.

HAYDEN, Miss Jane Sophia, d. Jul 2, 1853.
HAYDEN, John, d. Feb 11, 1866, brother of Stephen Hayden.
HAYDEN, John R. A., d. Jun 18, 1883, son of Stephen Hayden.
HAYDEN, Joseph Ignatius, d. Aug 1860.
HAYDEN, Margaret Lillie May, b. May 5, 1871, d. Sep 12, 1871, dau of Stephen Hayden.
HAYDEN, Mariah, d. Feb 17, 1877, consort of Stephen Hayden.
HAYDEN, Mary Doris, b. Oct 18, 1932, d. Sep 22, 1991, wife of Arthur St. Clair, dau of Elmer and Marie Buckler Hayden.
HAYDEN, Mrs. Monica, d. Mar 29, 1852.
HAYDEN, Stephen, b. Nov 8, 1841, d. after 1874, m. 17 May 1866 Scharlotte __.
HAYDEN, William, papa Hayden, d. Aug 25, 1845.
HAYDEN, William, d. May 30, 1865, hus of Nancy __.
HAYDEN, William H., d. Sep 17, 1877, hus of Sally __.
HAYDEN, Willie, b. Feb 7, 1868, d. Nov 21, 1886, son of Stephen and Scharlotte Hayden.
HAZEL, James T., b. ca 1836, d. Dec 12, 1885, m. 26 Apr 1870 Eleanor S. Evans, son of Jeremiah and Margaret Hill Hazel.
HILL, Andrew Richard, b. May 1, 1911, d. Nov 14, 1992, hus of Alice Taylor, son of Andrew Jackson and Lottie L. Armstrong Hill.
HILL, Ida C., d. Jan 15, 1974.
HILL, Kathryn Cecelia, b. May 16, 1941, d. Nov 16, 1986.
HOPEWELL, Timothy Dewayne, b. Jul 19, 1966, d. Jul 15, 1991, son of late Richard J. Hopewell and Dorothy C. Carroll Barnes.
JARBOE, Ann Maria, b. Mar 26, 1827, d. Feb 11, 1870, 1st wife of John William Henry Burroughs.
JARBOE, J. F. (male) married, farmer, d. Nov 1859 of typhoid, age 33 yrs.
JARBOE, Lucy, d. Sep 8, 1894.
JARBOE, Mary Jane, 56, d. Jun 22, 1887, relict of Mathew Jarboe.
JARBOE, Mathew, 54, d. Jan 28, 1876.
JARBOE, Mathew, 58, d. Jun 23, 1842, DC.

JARBOE, Minnie, d. Feb 9, 1894, age 22 yrs 6 mo 9 das, dau of Charles W. and Catherine Jarboe.
JARBOE, Peter, d. 1698, hus of Ann Nevitt.
JARBOE, Sophia, 56, d. Apr 30, 1875, wife of J. Alexander Jarboe.
JARBOE, Stephen Adams, d. Dec 28, 1884, age 7 yrs 4 mos 21 das, 2d son of Capt. J. T. and Mary J. Jones Jarboe of 3rd Dist.
JARBOE, William I., d. of pneumonia, age 5 yrs. (Beacon 1/2/1861)
JENKINS, William, b. 1663, d. 1755, hus of Mary Courtney, son of Thomas Jenkins of Wales.
JENNINGS, Rev. Henry, d. 1715, hus of Elizabeth Beale.
JESSUP, William, d. 1727, m. ca 1693 Agnes Hopewell.
JOHNSON, Bennet, b. 1793/94, d. 1844 DC, hus of Mary Ann Power.
JOHNSON, Charles Llewellyn, d. Dec 13, 1864, aged 26 years. (St. Mary's Beacon)
JOHNSON, Henry, d. Feb 6, 1825, age 37 years. (Nat'l Intelligence 2/21/1825)
JOHNSON, Capt. Joseph, 83, d. Jul 1, 1843 DC, native of St. Mary's County.
JOHNSON, Leonard Otis, d. Aug 17, 1986.
JOHNSON, Margaret C. "Maggie" b. Feb 19, 1856, d. Jul 31, 1928, wife of Jas. E. Mattingly, dau of Uriah Johnson.
JOHNSON, Miss Mary, d. Jun 19, 1857, age 70.
JOHNSON, Mary 'Lucy', b. Feb 24, 1870, d. Dec 24, 1962, wife of Joseph Frederick Long, dau of Hillery and Ann Marie Thompson Johnson.
JOHNSON, Mary Priscilla, b. Dec 27, 1819, d. June 10, 1873, wife of Enoch Richard Evans.
JOHNSON, Philip, b. 1788/89, d. Oct 23, 1835, hus of Mary Thomas.
JOHNSON, Richard B., b. 1825, d. May 6, 1876, hus of Eliza ___, son of Joseph and Mary Ann Drury Johnson.
JOHNSON, Miss Sarah, d. Nov 13, 1828 near Leonardtown, aged 17 years.
JOHNSON, Wayne Daniel, b. 1990, d. Feb 3, 1992, son of David Wayne and Mitzi Lee Williams

Morton Johnson.
JOHNSON, William, d. by 1659, 1st hus of Emma Langworth.
JOHNSON, William, b. 1813, d. Feb 7, 1844, son of Joseph and Mary Ann Drury Johnson.
JOLLY, Edward, d. 1675, hus of Margaret __.
JONES, Agnes Ruth, d. Sep 1899, age 8 mos 8 das, twin sister of Ellen Esther Jones, d. Aug 17, 1899, age 7 mos 18 das, children of Samuel E. and Annie E. Jones.
JONES, Capt. Alexander, b. Jul 14, 1809, d. Feb 14, 1889 Balto, MD, m. (1st) Mary Ann Shaw, (2d) 7 Mar 1850 Isabella C. Shaw, sister of Mary Ann, son of Caleb and Maria Bennett Jones.
JONES, Mrs. Ameline, 43, b. ME, d. Feb 1870 in childbirth.
JONES, Ann, b. Feb 29, 1792, d. Apr 18, 1879 in 6th Dist., wife of Henry Jones.
JONES, Asbury, 50, d. Mar 1870.
JONES, Betty A., 23, d. May 30, 1870, dau of Dr. Robt. E. Jones.
JONES, Caleb, d. 1814, hus of Maria Elizabeth Bennett.
JONES, Edmund, d. Sep 13, 1870, age 6 yrs 10 mos, son of Edmund and Nannie Jones.
JONES, Effie Jenette, 19, d. Sep 20, 1880, dau of Joseph Henry and Matilda Jones of 5th Dist.
JONES, Miss Elinor, d. Mar 27, 1830.
JONES, Elizabeth, bur Oct 11, 1868.
JONES, Ernest Marion, d. June 14, 1882 of pneumonia, age 11 yrs 6 mos, son of William H. and Laura A. Biscoe Jones.
JONES, George Marshall, b. Jun 10, 1907, d. Aug 18, 1988, son of George and Grace Jones.
JONES, George Morris, b. Jun 18, 1825, d. Jun 22, 1825.
JONES, Henrietta Cornelia, b. Oct 16, 1822, d. Jun 8, 1887 at residence of Thomas Loker.
JONES, Capt. William Caleb, lost at sea by 1889, son of Capt. Alexander Jones.
JOY, Elizabeth, widow, d. Jul 1879 in 6th District, aged 55 years.
JOY, Ignatius II, b. 1759, d. 1783, m. Eleanor

Adams, son of Ignatius and Joan Joy.
JOY, Ignatius III, b. 1781, d. Mar 16, 1838, m. 11 Jan 1807 Dorothy Drury, son of Ignatius II and Eleanor Adams Joy.
JOY, Ignatius IV, b. May 20, 1812, d. Aug 4, 1887, m. 1 Feb 1853 Mary Edley Morgan, son of Ignatius III and Dorothy Drury Joy.
JOY, Josephine Rebecca, b. Nov 1855, d. Feb 27, 1913, wife of John Hansen Wathen, dau of John M. and Eleanor Johnson Joy.
JOY, Margaret D., d. May 1860 of burns, age 5 yrs.
KING, Carolyn Jean, died Aug 30, 1986.
KING, Richard K., d. Jul 8, 1989.
KNOTT, William Henry, b. Aug 11, 1894, d. Jul 31, 1977, hus of Mary Dixon, son of Jas. H. and Georgianne Davis Knott.
LACEY, Ernest J., Sr. d. Apr 18, 1971.
LANCASTER, John J., Jr. b. Jun 25, 1923, d. Jul 30, 1991, hus of Gloria __, son of John and Genevieve Clarke Lancaster.
LANGLEY, Mary E., widow, seamstress, d. Nov 1859 of rup. blood vessel, age 48 yrs.
LASCHALT, James Francis, b. May 5, 1954, d. Aug 25, 1974, hus of Darlene __, son of Bernard and Helene Laschalt.
LATHAM, Aleatha I., d. May 18, 1975.
LATHAM, Martha, 32, d. Apr 29, 1887 of consumption, wife of A. D. Jarboe, had 1 child, dau of Thomas and Margaret Latham.
LEARY, Ellen, d. Oct 9, 1967, wife of __ Ellis.
LEIGH, Ellen, d. Jan 1860, age 3 yrs.
LOKER, Elizabeth, d. Jul 1859 of summer compl. age 9 mos.
LONG, Madeline Roe, b. Jun 8, 1893, d. Sep 3, 1969, wife of Hiram Hewitt, dau of Joseph Frederick and Mary 'Lucy' Johnson Long.
LONG, Mary Louise, b. Nov 14, 1910, d. Apr 25, 1981, m. (1st) __ Guy, (2d) __ Love, dau of Joseph Fred. and Mary 'Lucy' Johnson Long.
LYNCH, Thomas, widower, farmer, d. Feb 1860 of pneumonia, age 82 yrs.
LYON, Hiram Wilford, Sr. 83, d. Jun 25, 1993, m. (1st) Ruth L. __, (2d) Annie Fooks.

MAGILL, Ellen C., d. Feb 1860 of brain infl. age 16 yrs.
MARINER, Bryon Wallace, Jr. b. Jan 1, 1946 TX, d. Apr 22, 1993, hus of Emily __, son of Bryon W. and Shirley Mariner.
MARSHALL, William Xavier, 58, d. May 29, 1971, hus of Elizabeth Curtis.
MASON, Derek Lee, b. Jun 28, 1970, d. Dec 2, 1987.
MASON, Joseph Henry, USA, b. May 8, 1907, d. Oct 17, 1991 DC Vet Hosp., m. 15 Oct 1948 DC Blanche __, son of William Nelson and Elizabeth Thompson Mason.
MATHANY, Ellen, widow, d. Dec 1859 of pneumonia, age 56 yrs.
MATTHEWS, William Brooke, Sr. 56, d. Jul 26, 1993, hus of Lucy Moreland, son of George Henry and Agnes Lyon Matthews.
MATTINGLY, Agnes N., d. Jun 8, 1977.
MATTINGLY, Andrew J., d. Jun 8, 1968.
MATTINGLY, Annie E., b. Mar 15, 1911, d. Jan 17, 1988.
MATTINGLY, B. Kingsley, b. Mar 3, 1904, d. Mar 7, 1993 VA, hus of Dorothy A. __, son of A. Kingsley and Odie Bond Mattingly.
MATTINGLY, Beatrice M., b. Feb 20, 1910, d. May 26, 1986.
MATTINGLY, Bessie A., d. Apr 16, 1967.
MATTINGLY, Catherine P., d. Sep 30, 1965.
MATTINGLY, Charles Brendon, b. Sep 22, 1933, d. Mar 17, 1984.
MATTINGLY, J. Moakley, b. ca 1872, d. Jan 29, 1974, son of W. L. J. and Sophia Mattingly.
MATTINGLY, J. Moakley, Jr. d. Feb 3, 1978.
MATTINGLY, Joseph "Teeny", b. Oct 22, 1935, d. Feb 12, 1982.
MATTINGLY, Lester A., d. Oct 7, 1963.
MATTINGLY, Mary Amanda, d. Apr 18, 1975.
MATTINGLY, Mary Louise, b. Jan 16, 1908, d. Feb 3, 1981.
MATTINGLY, Philip King, 21, d. Jan 21, 1971.
MATTINGLY, Sophia, b. Sep 8, 1902, d. Sep 2, 1985, wife of __ Gough.
MATTINGLY, Mrs. Sophia, d. 1864 aged about 50.
MAXWELL, Mrs. Louisa, d. Sep 20, 1853.

McGHIN, Otis James, Jr. 47, d. Apr 8, 1993 Balto, hus of Melanda Fiest, son of late Otis J. McGhin and Lahoma Harbin McGhin Coppins.
McKAY, Mamie, d. Jun 7, 1947.
MILBURN, infant, d. May 7, 1848, dau of James C. and Jane Milburn.
MILBURN, Ann Maria, b. May 7, 1835, d. Apr 24, 1837, dau of William P. and Jane Robertson Milburn.
MILBURN, Susan, b. 1817/18, d. Dec 30, 1862, m. (1st) __ Price, (2d) __ Bean, (3) John Goodrich.
MILBURN, William P., d. Sep 16, 1837, m. 7 Feb 1832 Jane Robertson.
MILES, George Schley, b. Aug 22, 1898, d. Oct 4, 1979.
MILES, Mary Cecil, b. Jan 2, 1896, d. Nov 4, 1982.
MILLARD, Miss Mary, d. Sep 23, 1853.
MILLS, John J., d. Feb 18, 1856, hus of Catherine "Kitty" __, 77, d. Mar 16, 1876.
MOORE, John, d. Dec 1859 of sore throat, age 6 yrs.
MORGAN, George C., d. Jan 14, 1863.
MORGAN, Mary Edley, b. 1837, d. 1912, wife of Ignatius Joy IV.
MORGAN, Thomas W., d. Feb 23, 1856.
MORGAN, William Leo, Sr., d. Oct 5, 1983, hus of Mary Helen __.
MORRIS, Mary, b. Aug 9, 1750, d. Nov 22, 1825.
MORTON, James Arthur, b. 1988, d. 3 Feb 1992, son of Mitzi Lee Williams Morton Johnson, stepson of David Wayne Johnson.
NELSON, Alvin Francis, Jr. b. 1938, d. Feb 2, 1967.
NORRIS, Celestia, d. Mar 21, 1853.
NORRIS, Estelle P., d. Sep 25, 1976.
NORRIS, John H., 79, d. Mar 25, 1988 Inverness, FL, hus of B. Lorena Sevier, brother of John Berkman Norris.
NORRIS, Linda, b. Jun 22, 1951, d. Oct 25, 1978.
NORRIS, W. Wilson, b. Nov 14, 1916, d. Apr 13, 1985.
NOTTINGHAM, Rebecca, b. ca 1782, d. 1855.

NOWAK, Edward Martin, b. Jul 3, 1926 MA, d. Jan 14, 1993, m. 11 Aug 1960 Jacqueline Lee Whitfield, son of Martin and Jennie Kosaszka Nowak.
O'BRIEN, Patricia Ellen, d. May 7, 1992 in Severna Pk., Md, wife of Robert Walters, dau of Paul and Mary O'Brien.
O'CONNOR, Sean Paul, b. Nov 20, 1982, d. Jul 28, 1992 WA, son of Michael and Peggy Bogie O'Connor; gson of Patrick J. and Mary J. O'Connor; James and Betty Bogie.
OLIVER, Mary Robinson, b. 1864 Balto, d. 1897.
OWENS, Benjamin F., d. Mar 17, 1972.
OWENS, John J., b. St. Mary's County, d. Oct 1993, Harrisonburg, Va.
OWENS, Julia Mae, b. Jul 8, 1926, d. Feb 7, 1982.
OWENS, Marie Bernadette, d. Nov 3, 1977.
OWENS, William Edward, d. Jun 15, 1971.
PALMER, Mary Elizabeth, b. May 7, 1903, d. Dec 1, 1989, dau of Edwin Jefferson and Lydia Faunce Palmer.
PEMBROKE, George W., married, farmer, d. Apr 1860 of apoplexy, age 47 yrs.
PILKERTON, M. Blanche, d. Nov 15, 1971.
PILKERTON, W. Melvin, d. Jul 5, 1974.
PLATER, Spencer Edward, Jr. b. Dec 20, 1961, d. Aug 24, 1989, son of Spencer E. and Margaret E. Plater.
POPE, James Jerry, Sr. b. Apr 20, 1910, d. Jan 9, 1980.
PRICE, William Leo, d. Jun 4, 1954, hus of Mary Alberta Holt (she is bur in Charles Mem. Gdns.)
QUADE, Grace I., d. Oct 1, 1970.
QUADE, James Carroll, Sr. d. May 6, 1962.
QUADE, James Melvin, b. Nov 12, 1922, d. May 5, 1993, son of Jos. Lansdale and Anna Gertrude Williams Quade.
QUADE, Leonard Earl, d. Mar 27, 1971.
QUADE, Mary Elizabeth, d. Jul 10, 1976.
RALEY, Dominic, d. Jan 28, 1930, hus of Alice J. Taylor.
RALEY, James Joseph 'Woodrow', b. Mar 8, 1917, d. Apr 25, 1989, m. 27 Oct 1938 Frances

King, son of Alvah and Mary Magdaline Henderson Raley.
RALEY, Joseph Matthew II, b. Aug 9, 1949, d. Mar 26, 1969, son of Joseph M. and Blanche Catherine Payne Raley.
RICHARDS, Gwen "Richie", b. Oct 13, 1896 South Wales, d. Mar 12, 1993, m. 16 Oct 1916 Ont., Can. John Henry Richardson, dau of Harry and Margaret Brown Richards.
RIDGELY, Elizabeth, b. Oct 31, 1903, d. Apr 16, 1991 VA, m. (1st) Whitney Leary, (2d) Miodrag Blagojevich.
ROBB, Cornelia, d. Feb 16, 1884, wife of F. Biscoe Jones, dau of James Robb of Balto.
ROBERTS, Miriam G., d. Jun 19, 1968.
ROBINSON, Ellen H., b. May 3, 1916, d. Apr 12, 1979.
ROBINSON, Pius Benedict, d. May 31, 1966.
ROSWELL, William, b. 1637, d. 1695, 3d hus of Emma Langworth.
RUSSELL, Charles A., d. Jan 2, 1854, m. 29 Jan 1833 Ann L. Hayden.
RUSSELL, Jane L., d. Apr 8, 1846.
RUSSELL, Mrs. Jinnie, d. Sep 18, 1853
RUSSELL, Jos. Archie, d. Oct 24, 1967.
RUSSELL, Sarah Jane, b. Oct 10, 1834, d. Feb 27, 1855, dau of Charles A. and Ann L. Hayden Russell.
RUSSELL, R. Spaulding, d. Mar 26, 1968.
SANGER, George F., Sr. d. Sep 10, 1976.
SHADRICK, John, b. ca 1794, d. 1854, hus of Rebecca Nottingham.
SHADRICK, Sarah Jane, b. June 17, 1817, d. May 25, 1837, m. 12 Aug 1834 Henry Guyther, dau of John and Rebecca Nottingham Shadrick.
SHANKS, Richard F., 57, d. Jan 1, 1994 La Plata, Md., son of Johnnie L. Shanks.
SMITH, Agnes 'Lillian' Mrs., b. Jan 7, 1901, d. May 25, 1986.
SMITH, Bernard Leo, d. Oct 5, 1965.
SMITH, W. Benedict, d. Apr 9, 1977.
SPARKS, James D., d. Nov 12, 1988.
SPENCER, Alex. S., married, farmer, d. Oct 1859 of consumption, age 45 yrs.
SPRINGER, Sarah J., married, d. Jul 1859 of

heart disease, age 21 yrs.
SPRINGER, William, 77, d. Jun 24, 1991 Balto, hus of Lorraine Millicent.
STERLING, Ernest Abell, d. Apr 16, 1973.
STERLING, William O. E., Jr. b. Oct 24, 1952, d. Aug 16, 1984.
STONE, Mrs. Catherine, d. Apr 1860 of pneumonia, age 63 yrs.
STONE, Elizabeth Ann, d. Jul 14, 1972, wife of Richard A. McNey.
STONE, John E., Jr., 64, d. Jan 3, 1994 FL, bro. of Mary Lee Stone Breasmen.
STONE, Capt. Thomas, b. 1677, d. 1727, hus of Martha Hoskins.
SWANN, Capt. James, d. May 1708, 1st hus of Judith Compton, son of Edward and Susannah Swann.
SWANN, John, b. 1657, d. 1727, hus of Elizabeth Young, son of Edward and Susannah Swann.
SWANN, Susannah, d. 1740, wife of Col. Philip Briscoe, dau of Edward and Susannah Swann.
TAYLOR, Alice J., b. Nov 26, 1903, d. Apr 26, 1935, wife of Dominic Raley.
TAYLOR, Clarence T., b. May 17, 1896, d. Jul 1, 1952.
TAYLOR, Katie R., b. Oct 20, 1875, d. Nov 29, 1955.
TENNYSON, Andrew R., b. Mar 12, 1981, d. May 10, 1983.
THOMAS, Sidney P., d. Oct 1859 of sore throat, age 2 yrs.
THOMAS, Timothy Allen, b. Jan 2, 1967, d. Aug 15, 1993 DC, son of Walter Aloysius and Ethel Bernice Green Thomas.
THOMPSON, Elizabeth Evangeline, b. Dec 14, 1798, d. Dec 26, 1874, m. 5 Jul 1827 Maurice Shanks.
THOMPSON, Gertrude Ella, b. Sep 11, 1916, d. Nov 20, 1992, wife of Arlandus Leonard Johnson, dau of Mitchell and Marie Lawrence Thompson.
THOMPSON, Mary S., d. Mar 4, 1969.
THORNTON, Harriet, lady, d. Mar 1860, paralytic, age 59 yrs.
THRIFT, Anita C., d. Jul 13, 1975.

THRIFT, Maurice T., d. Feb 15, 1963.
THROWER, Evelyn Ward, b. Mar 25, 1907 NC, d. May 5, 1993, wife of __ Sengstack, dau of Wm. and Ethel Knowles Thrower.
TIPPETT, Lewis E., d. Apr 6, 1987.
TIPPETT, Terance David, d. Mar 12, 1977.
TRAVERS, Sarah A., married, d. May 1860 of consumption, age 33 yrs.
TURNER, Thomas, d. 1662, 2d hus of Emma Langworth.
VALLANDINGHAM, Julia B., d. Jul 11, 1971.
VAN RYSWICK, Mildred, b. May 5, 1906, d. May 11, 1983.
VU, Emilie Thi Nicole, b. May 3, 1991, d. Jul 29, 1993, dau of Ank and Vickie Elsesser Vu; gdau of Samuel and Alma Elsesser; Li Thi Nguyen and Tien Duy Vu.
WALZ, Arthur Frederick, Sr. b. Mar 17, 1908 PA, d. Jun 25, 1993 FL, hus of Beatrice Winn, son of Frederick and Ella Shover Walz.
WATHEN, John Hansen, b. Sep 2, 1848, d. Jan 19, 1929, hus of Josephine Rebecca Joy, son of James Francis and Susanna Radford Wathen.
WATHEN, John Richard, b. Jun 1, 1904, d. Nov 9, 1977.
WATTS, Dennis Leighton, d. May 17, 1985.
WELSH, Charlotte C., d. Aug 22, 1965.
WELSH, Evelyn Edith, b. May 29, 1909, d. Feb 7, 1993, wife of Thomas Jos. Tighe, dau of Edgar and Ruth Dolly Welsh, body donated to Uniformed Services University.
WERNECKE, Richard Louis "Dick", b. Apr 6, 1933 WI, d. Nov 25, 1991, hus of Margaret Richardson, son of Raymond Carl and Della Heinemann Wernecke.
WILLIAMS, Mitzi Lee, b. 1969, d. 3 Feb 1992, m. (1st)__ Morton, (2d) David Wayne Johnson, dau of Melinda Williams.
WILLIAMS, Sarah, seamstress, d. Nov 1859 of unknown cause, age 36 yrs.
WILSON, Joshua, merchant, d. Sep 1859 of rheumatism, age 22 yrs.
WOODBURN, Bertha Ann, d. Sep 18, 1970.
WOODBURN James M., d. Mar 29, 1969.
WOODBURN, Joseph Leonard "Mike", b. Oct 3,

1916, d. Jun 23, 1983.
WOODBURN, Mary Lillian, b. Jul 1, 1918, d. Feb 10, 1982.
YATES, Alma Teresa and Letecia Ann, b. Jun 25, 1880, one d. Jul 11th, the other Jul 13th 1888, twin daus of Hayden M. H. and Alice M. Ford Yates.
YATES, Hayden Martin Henry, b. Aug 29, 1838, d. after 1880, m. 20 Nov 1865 Alice M. Ford.
YATES, Martin B. S., d. Apr 1860, age 3 mos.
YATES, Mary Frances, d. Nov 5, 1877.
YATES, Rachel A., b. Oct 11, 1844, d. May 4, 1854, dau of William and Elenor C. Hayden Yates.
YATES, William, b. Feb 13, 1805, d. Aug 27, 1845, m. 26 Oct 1830 Elenor C. Hayden.
ZACHERY, Zachariah, d. Feb 4, 1842,

ST. MARY'S ROMAN CATHLIC CHURCH
Bryantown, Charles County, Md.

BARNES, Lucy, b. Mar 20, 1954, d. Dec 16, 1992, wife of John Matthews, 2d child of Emmett and Hortense Barnes.
BREWER, Clinton Michael, b. ca 1960 DC, d. accident Mar 12, 1992, son of Charles T. and Betty Jane Brewer.
BUCKLER, Henry Lawrence, Sr. b. Dec 27, 1919, d. Jul 16, 1993, hus of Margaret R. __, son of Horace and Agnes Buckler.
BUCKLER, Joseph Earl, d. 1970, hus of Alice Jennette Cusic.
BUCKLER, Kenneth Ocea, Sr. b. Jul 22, 1942, d. Aug 13, 1991, hus of Kelly Jo __, son of Joseph Earl and Alice Cusic Buckler.
BUCKLER, Sue Ellen, b. Sep 2, 1956, d. Apr 23, 1991, wife of Charles Andrew Goelling, Sr., dau of Thomas Leo and Beatrice Irene Buckler.
CHING, Marie L., b. Jul 14, 1894, d. May 18, 1992, wife of Jefferson Costen, dau of Joseph H. and Ada L. Holmes Ching.
ESTEP, James Edward, b. Sep 24, 1955, d. Sep 011, 1992, son of Albert Victor and Mary K. Gough Estep; gson of Harry and Kathleen Gough; Victor and Belle Estep.
FARRELL, Nellie Eleanor, b. Jan 1, 1905, d. Oct 22, 1991, m. (1st) Joseph A. Quade, (2d) Robert J. Quade, dau of Charles and Susan Knott Farrell.
FLORA, Sarah Virginia, b. Aug 24, 1917, d. Jul 23, 1989, wife of Joseph Howard Roache, dau of Charles E. and Cora V. Flora.
GARNER, Alfred William, 16, bur Sep 16, 1869.
GOLDSMITH, Benjamin George, Sr., b. May 1, 1932, d. Jan 25, 1992, hus of Agnes Virtie Montgomery, son of George Almer and Mary Gertrude Burch Goldsmith.
HILL, Lala Ann, b. May 18, 1901, d. Dec 5, 1989, wife of William M. Moran, dau of Chapman and Margaret Hill.
HOWE, George Henry, USAF Korea/Vietnam, b. Aug 21, 1930 VA, d. Apr 21, 1993, hus of Hannelore A.F. Franz, son of Thomas J. and Mar-

garet R. Burch Howe. Memorial Service.
JENKINS, Agnes Cecelia, b. May 4, 1925, d. Jul
29, 1991, wife of Carl George Kilhoffer, dau
of Sidney A., Sr. and Mary Etta Jenkins.
JOHNSON, Alex., d. Jun 13, 1816, aged 49 yrs.
KNOTT, Spencer, b. Jan 6, 1916, d. after 1960,
hus of Joan R. __.
KOLLER, William Robert, b. Dec 31, 1921, d. Dec
22, 1990, son of Wenzel and Mary Koller.
PERRY, Mary Lee, RN, b. Nov 5, 1917, d. Apr
12, 1992 FL, wife of Adrian E. Farrell, dau
of Bernard Lee and Annie Bishop Perry.
QUEEN, John Yates, Jr. b. Jul 10, 1928, d.
May 26, 1993, m. 25 Sep 1948 Mary Elizabeth
Hicks, son of John and Carrie Queen.
RYBIKOWSKY, Joseph Anthony, WWII, b. Nov 26,
1918 Balto, d. Jun 9, 1992, hus of Thelma
Blackwell, son of Casper Rybikowsky.
WELCH, William Kenneth, b. Jul 3, 1910, d. Mar
11, 1992, hus of Blanche __, son of Louis
and Ella Goldsmith Welch.
WINDSOR, Robert Vincent, b. Mar 17, 1909, d.
Dec 27, 1991, hus of Ida Natalie Barry, son
of Ignatius and Elizabeth Jenkins Windsor.

TRINITY MEMORIAL GARDENS
Waldorf, Charles Co., Md.

ADKINS, Jerry Wayne, b. Jun 6, 1935 VA, d. Dec 18, 1990, 1st hus of Louise Quade Haverkamp, son of Raymond and Lena Adkins.
BAILEY, Joseph Clinton, b. Jun 9, 1924 NC, d. May 2, 1991, hus of Dorothy Ireen Curlis, son of Myron and Annie Beaver Bailey.
BLANKENSHIP, Mary Elizabeth, b. Aug 3, 1915 VA, d. Mar 26, 1991, wife of __ Emick, dau of Samuel K. and Verna M. Garrett Blankenship.
BOHLE, Eleanora, b. Aug 21, 1913, d. Feb 20, 1993 FL, wife of Cmdr. Rupert D. Phillips, dau of Egon and Anna Blank Bohle.
BOHLE, John Egon, b. Jan 11, 1908 PA, d. May 22, 1991, hus of Louise M. Buckler, son of Egon and Anna Blank Bohle.
BOSWELL, Verna May "Jerri", b. Oct 14, 1947 DC, d. Jan 20, 1991, wife of Raymond Joseph Harrington, dau of Edward L., Sr. and Mary Elizabeth Bryant Boswell.
BUCKLER, Annie A., b. Mar 10, 1906, d. Sep 23, 1990, wife of Joseph Floyd Downs, dau of Thomas and Essie Williams Buckler.
BUCKLER, Dorothy Rebecca, b. Jul 9, 1919, d. Nov 7, 1990, wife of Edmond J. Taylor, dau of William Matthew and Mary Delia Tippett Buckler.
BUCKLER, Earl Leo, b. Aug 20, 1939, d. Oct 23, 1991, son of Charles Gilbert and Mary Helen Herbert Buckler.
BUCKLER, Edward 'Louis', b. Jul 22, 1918, d. Jun 10, 1993, hus of Lenora Cecelia nee Buckler, son of Daniel and Grace Buckler.
BUCKLER, Lenora Cecelia, b. Jul 3, 1915, d. Sep 2, 1993 VA, m. 1935 Edward 'Louis' Buckler, dau of George Christopher and Carrie Estelle Buckler.
BURCH, George Philip, b. Apr 13, 1917, d. Jul 30, 1993, son of Joseph Benjamin and Lucy Dent Carrico Burch.
BURCH, Joseph Christopher, b. Oct 20, 1911, d. Jun 8, 1990, hus of Frances B. Barron, son of James Edward and Kate Langley Burch.

BURROUGHS, Mary Helen, b. Sep 14, 1930, d. Jun 10, 1993, m. DC 1952 James Aloysius Dean, dau of Andrew and Mary Ida Caywood Burroughs.
BUSHELL, Curtis Junior "Curt", b. Apr 24, 1922 IL, d. Dec 20, 1993, m. (1st) Lillian Virginia Peaire, m. (2d) 7 Jan 1989 Mary Lucille Magill (bur St. John's RCC, Hollywood, Md), son of Sylvester and Amanda Irene Neeley Bushell.
BUSSLER, Gorman James, b. Dec 24, 1903, d. Jun 17, 1991, hus of Virginia O. ___, son of William James and Ada Cecelia Pope Bussler.
BYRUM, William R. "Jack", b. Nov 1, 1918 NC, d. Sep 13, 1991, son of Charles and Norsis Hasket Byrum.
CANTER, Mary Louise, b. Jul 31, 1923, d. Nov 30, 1988, wife of Levin Oliver Ryce.
CARR, Stuart K. J., Sr. b. Feb 7, 1902, d. Jul 7, 1990, hus of Aline Herbert, son of James H. and Eliza S. Wood Carr.
COE, Zeta Blanche, b. Nov 25, 1923 NY, d. Oct 24, 1988, wife of Oscar Lee Hilley, dau of Fred and Mary Smith Coe.
COPSEY, Thomas Eugene, Jr. b. Jan 15, 1947, d. Sep 25, 1993, m. 30 Aug 1968 Mary Helen Sponsher, son of Thomas E. and Carrie Cecilia Canter Copsey.
COX, Nellie Margaret, b. Dec 6, 1920, d. Dec 4, 1992, wife of John Wm. Grubb, Sr., dau of James B. and Anna E. McCrobie Cox.
CURRY, Frances, b. Sep 6, 1914 VA, d. Dec 27, 1991 FL, wife of Gregory Stea, dau of George B. and Luva Cave Curry.
CUSIC, Mamie M., b. Aug 8, 1909, d. Mar 7, 1990, wife of Raymond A. Buckler, dau of Otis and Effie Montgomery Cusic.
DOUGHERTY, David Allen, Sr. b. Dec 16, 1941 DC, d. Nov 30, 1992, hus of Caroline L. Linton, son of James Edward and Carrie Louise Estes Dougherty.
DOWNIE, Dorothy, b. Oct 28, 1895 NY, d. Oct 31, 1989, wife of Gould M. Brown, dau of James and Fannie Harkness Downie.
DOWNS, Lillie Mae, b. Jul 19, 1902, d. May 9, 1991, wife of F. Leonard Harding, Sr., dau

of Joseph and Effie Herbert Downs.
FOLEY, Daniel Woodrow, b. Jul 23, 1916 VA, d. Dec 15, 1990, hus of Elizabeth A. __, son of Ace B. and Martha Ann Brammer Foley.
FREEMAN, Deanna M., b. May 3, 1990, d. Dec 4, 1990, dau of Darrell and Judy Ann Freeman; gdau of Oren and Frances Freeman; John and Evelyn Latham.
GASS, Mary Jane, b. Aug 12, 1915, d. Feb 12, 1980, wife of Joseph Lester Thompson, dau of Joseph 'Carroll' and Ella Mae Cullins Gass.
GATEAU, John, b. Mar 29, 1969, d. Aug 18, 1991, son of George and Patricia Gateau.
GRUBB, John William, Sr. USN WW II, b. Nov 9, 1911, d. Oct 7, 1993, hus of Nellie Margaret Cox, son of Franklin and Ida Jane Shreve Grubb.
HALL, William Jennings, Sr. b. Mar 5, 1910, d. May 24, 1993, hus of Marianna Tippett, son of Amos Lee and Bette Catteron Hall.
HEFLIN, Mary Washington, b. Jul 4, 1929 VA, d. Apr 15, 1991, wife of Frank Turner, Jr., dau of Walter and Effie E. Jones Heflin.
HENDERSON, Margaret Frances, b. Jul 2, 1931 NC, d. Jun 2, 1990, wife of __ Bray, dau of late Wavreless Henderson and Susie Ann Etta Gamble.
HEWITT, Mary, b. Apr 14, 1928, d. Aug 28, 1992, wife of Jerome Richardson, dau of Hiram and Madeline Roe Long Hewitt.
HIGGS, Grace Elizabeth, b. Jun 16, 1926, d. Nov 22, 1993, wife of Albert E. Lemke, dau of Charles Dudley, Sr. and Amy Rosalie Kagle Higgs.
HILLEY, Oscar Lee, b. Jul 20, 1917 GA, d. Oct 29, 1993, m. 26 Jul 1946 Zetta Blanche Coe, son of John and Cora McGarity Hilley.
HUDSON, Linda Louise "Lou", b. May 28, 1947 DC, d. Jun 11, 1992, wife of Thos. E. Fincham, dau of Charles David and Evelyn L. Huntt Hudson.
HYNSON, Charlie Alexander, b. Jul 29, 1907 VA, d. Apr 30, 1990, hus of Elizabeth Rice, son of Thomas and Clara Bound Hynson.
JOHNSON, George Frederick, b. Dec 5, 1929, d. Nov 6, 1987, hus of Marion E. __, son of

Leonard and Imelda Wathen Johnson.
JONES, Catherine Marie, b. Dec 22, 1965 DC, d. May 26, 1990, wife of Donald Craig Ellison, dau of Stephen H. and Patricia M. Sullivan Jones.
JOSNAK, Pauline Frances, b. Nov 9, 1914 IL, d. Aug 24, 1988, wife of Oswald Henry Brubacher, dau of Joe and Pauline Kristovitsch Josnak.
KELLER, Lavern Woodrow, b. Jan 9, 1915 PA, d. Mar 23, 1991, son of Harry and Anna May Keller.
KELLOGG, Helen, 88, b. IL, d. March 17, 1988, m. 14 Feb 1924 Frederick Thos. Marshall.
KIDD, Margaret Mae, b. Feb 18, 1942 WV, d. Jun 26, 1993, wife of Warren L. Hunter, dau of Denver R. and Ethel Quillen Kidd.
LeBLANC, J. Arthur, b. Oct 25, 1926 NY, d. Feb 1, 1989, hus of Louise __, son of Arthur J. and Valerie Pededieu LeBlanc.
LETCHER, Frank, b. Jun 1, 1901 Austria-Hungary, d. May 21, 1988, hus of Ruth I. __.
LINDLEY, Marjorie, b. Apr 24, 1920 GA, d. Oct 7, 1992, wife of Rev. David D. Liles, dau of Harry and Florence Dallas Lindley.
MARSHALL, Frederick Thomas, b. Nov 4, 1889, Chicago, IL, d. Jan 16, 1991, hus of Helen Kellogg, son of Wm. Geo. and Anna Howson Marshall.
MARTIN, Howard H., b. Jan 28, 1914 NY, d. Oct 11, 1988, son of Robert Ode and Elizabeth Hill Martin.
McCLAVE, John Henry, b. Apr 25, 1918 KY, d. Jun 1, 1991, son of Russell C. and Sophia Newman McClave.
McKENZIE, Elizabeth Mae, b. Sep 2, 1930 DC, d. Jul 31, 1993, wife of late Robert E. Benett, Sr., dau of Louis, Sr. and Haidee Grist McKenzie.
MORGAN, Charles Donald, b. Jul 30, 1954, d. Jul 1, 1990, son of John Woodley and Hattie Alberta Bowles Morgan.
MULLER, Martha, b. Mar 30, 1891 GER, d. Mar 22, 1990, wife of Paul Erich Zell, dau of Rudolf and Adele Muller.
NUNN, Freddie Allen, b. Mar 13, 1940 VA, d.

Trinity Memorial 357

Mar 8, 1991, hus of Pamela __, son of Ralph and Linda Lynch Nunn.
PAUL, Victor H., d. Jun 18, 1983, m. 5 Apr 1940 Elizabeth Neale Bowen.
PEAIRE, Lillian Virginia, b. Sep 2, 1918, d. Jun 19, 1988, 1st wife of Curtis J. Bushell.
PILKERTON, Mary Christine, b. Jun 21, 1939, d. Oct 2, 1990, wife of David A. Raley, dau of Joseph R. and Dorothy R. Smith Pilkerton.
POSEY, Paul, b. Apr 10, 1903, d. Mar 16, 1993 DE, hus of Yvonne F. __, son of Harrison and Jane Marion Rye Posey.
RALEY, Kevin Joseph, b. Nov 7, 1967, d. Dec 16, 1991, m. 16 Jun 1990 Maria Josephine Romano, son of David Augustus and Mary Christine Pilkerton Raley.
ROLFE, Harold J., b. Oct 7, 1905 SC, d. Jan 5, 1992, hus of M. Ruby __, son of Albert Garfield and Bertha Walker Rolfe.
ROLLINS, Marion, b. Dec 5, 1907 DC, d. Jun 11, 1988, wife of Charles Frederick Bartz, dau of Wallace W. and Anna May Steele Rollins.
RUPPRECHT, Cynthia E. King, b. May 28, 1968, d. Jul 12, 1992, wife of Herbert T. Coffman, dau of Philip H. Rupprecht and Patricia Ann Bell.
RUSSELL, Sidney Louis, b. May 8, 1926, d. Apr 22, 1991, hus of Hilda Lee, son of James Bernard and Mary Agnes Morgan Russell.
RYCE, Levin Oliver "Lev", b. May 5, 1918, d. Jun 20, 1993, m. 1941 Mary Louise Canter, son of Thomas S. and Mary M. Oliver Ryce.
SCARICOMAZZI, Julia Ann, b. Sep 13, 1935 PA, d. Jul 25, 1993, wife of Michael M. Garrow, dau of John and Florence Filomama Scaricomazzi.
SCHMOOKLER, Mrs. Annie Bernice, R.N., b. Oct 8, 1912 NEB, d. Mar 30, 1992.
SCHNEIDER, Ivan Elwood, Sr. b. Feb 10, 1904 WV, d. Dec 31, 1992, m. MD 11 Jun 1932 Evelyn Meekling, son of George and Florence Marks Schneider.
SIMMONS, Bette, b. Dec 8, 1936 DC, d. Jul 1, 1990, wife of Milton E. McNey, Sr., dau of Irvin C. and Annie Ruth Linkins Simmons.

SMIROLDO, William, Sr. b. Oct 27, 1938 DC, d. Aug 10, 1993, hus of Patricia M. Hartnett, son of Onofrio Sam and Carmela Italiano Smiroldo.
SORRELLS, Irene Virginia, b. Dec 19, 1932, d. Oct 2, 1993, wife of Richard E. Howard, dau of Edgar Edward and Lucille Conner Sorrells.
SPAIN, Garland S., 64, b. VA, d. Jun 7, 1993, hus of Margaret Anne Fish.
SPAULDING, James Carroll, Jr. b. Jun 27, 1959, d. Jun 7, 1990, son of James C. and Mary Catherine Spaulding.
SPAULDING, Stephen Michael, Jr. b. Dec 14, 1971, d. May 29, 1990, son of Stephen M. and Sally A. Mauney Spaulding; gson of James C. and Catherine Spaulding; Forest E. Sr. and Gladys M. Fortner; maternal ggson of Henry L. McKenzie.
SPEAKE, June Marie, b. May 11, 1937 DC, d. May 13, 1990 DC, wife of Richard R. Risko, dau of John Wm. Sr. and Teresa Ann Scott Speake.
SPEAKE, Olive E., b. Nov 8, 1922, d. May 1, 1992, wife of Jas. R. Willett, dau of John M. and Mettie Mitchell Speake.
STANLEY, Charlotte C., b. Oct 22, 1935, d. Jun 7, 1992, wife of Frank D. Dawson, dau of Cleo C. and Beth Pierce Stanley.
STARR, Mary Ruan, b. Oct 16, 1907 GA, d. Jul 13, 1992, wife of David D. Briell, Sr., dau of William Lemmon and Rebecca Tinsley Starr.
STASCH, Stephen Allen, b. Jun 30, 1956, d. Aug 4, 1993, son of Otto Herman and Mary Christine Williams Stasch.
THOMPSON, William Mack, b. May 4, 1924 VA, d. Dec 9, 1993, m. 28 Sep 1945 Lillian Mae Bortner, son of Alex and Allie Flanary Thompson.
TOYE-WATTS, Aaron Tyrone, 5 mos, d. Jan 20, 1993 DC, son of Aaron Tyrone Watts and Regina Mae Toye.
TURNER, Mary Ruth, b. Feb 20, 1951, d. Dec 12, 1992, dau of Frank and Mary Washington Heflin Turner.
VON GLAHN, Mildred Anna, b. Dec 16, 1914 NY, d. Jan 12, 1992, wife of James M. Warvin,

dau of Wm. H. and Margaret Dunckley Von Glahn.
WALKER, Daniel Joseph Thomas, infant, d. Feb 16, 1993, son of Daniel C. and Laurie Ann Garner Walker; gson of Lawrence and Helena Garner; Chet and Jeanne Walker; ggson of Weddie H. Garner.
WELCOMER, Hannah Catherine, b. Oct 24, 1919 PA, d. Feb 21, 1992, wife of John Clark Grumbine, dau of Harvey and Catherine Baker Welcomer.
WHITE, David Omar, b. Mar 12, 1930 OH, d. Aug 20, 1993, hus of Eileen Antoinette Ebbers, son of Ervin E. and Mary Merz White.
WINDSOR, Russell James, b. Sep 4, 1934, d. Aug 9, 1992, hus of Shirley J. __, son of John R. and Sophie C. Peacock Windsor.
WINKWORTH, Iris W., b. Jun 9, 1923 MI, d. Jul 4, 1992, wife of Douglas E. Brandel, dau of Joseph H. and Ida Winkworth.
WOODRING, Nellie Mae, b. Aug 18, 1907 VA, d. Apr 17, 1991, wife of Arthur Reese, dau of Grant and Cynthia Ellen Woodring.

CEDAR HILL CEMETERY
Suitland, Pr. Georges Co., Md.

ABELL, James Albert, b. Feb 28, 1909, d. Jan 25, 1991, son of James Clyde and Mary Gertrude Abell.
ABLETT, Viola Marie, d. Nov 8, 1966, m. DC Bernard John McKeon.
ALLEN, Selma F. Elizabeth, b. Nov 9, 1902 Balto, d. Nov 13, 1991, dau of William Henry and Ann Margaret Misiel Allen.
BARLOWE, Edward Sanders "Essie", WW I, b. Oct 11, 1897 VA, d. Apr 4, 1990, hus of Mary __, son of William and Catherine Barlowe.
BEAVERS, Lillian Mary "Granny", b. Sep 12, 1904 DC, d. May 28, 1993, m. DC 1943 Francis Martin Raynor, dau of Charles F. Sr. and Lula Frances Hager Beavers.
BLANFORD, Barbara Cecelia, b. Sep 11, 1898, d. Dec 18, 1990, wife of Walter F. Eno, Sr., dau of Charles and Ella Blanford.
BUCKLER, Lena Mary, b. Nov 12, 1902, d. Aug 10, 1988, wife of Zack B. Pilkerton, dau of Richard L. and Sadie Burroughs Buckler.
BURROUGHS, Bessie, b. Apr 13, 1910, d. Sep 29, 1992, wife of Phillips Burton, dau of James William and Mary Jane Thompson Burroughs.
CLINTON, Evelyn, b. Apr 17, 1900 MA, d. May 11, 1988, wife of Lee Hoffman.
CULVER, Doris Virginia, b. Jul 18, 1925 DC, d. Oct 1, 1993 DC, wife of late Charles Ray Rister, Sr., dau of Clair K. and Ethel L. Cowen Culver.
DIETZ, Frieda Louise, b. Sep 15, 1912 DC, d. Nov 19, 1990, wife of __ Kolarsk, dau of John and Sophia Dietz.
DRURY, Alice Magdalen, b. Feb 7, 1898, d. May 17, 1992, wife of Joseph Lydney Wathen, dau of Robert French and Florence Hayden Drury.
FAUVER, Eva Virginia, b. Apr 26, 1908 VA, d. Aug 17, 1993, m. NC 16 Oct 1938 Donald Howard McGarity, dau of Stephen and Minnie Stout Fauver.
FILTER, Lorraine E., b. Jun 16, 1920, d. Dec 7, 1988, wife of Carl Frederick Filter.

FOWLER, Lucy Louise, b. Jun 23, 1905, d. Mar 17, 1988, wife of Lawrence L. Parlett, Sr., dau of John A. and Pearl Love Fowler.
GIDDENS, Dorothy Mildred, b. Jul 11, 1896 NC, d. Mar 6, 1988, dau of George Lullen and Sarah Rich Giddens.
GIDDENS, Sarah Elizabeth, b. Aug 5, 1903 NC, d. Apr 27, 1989, wife of Hamilton Myers Mc-Cully, dau of George Lullen and Sarah Jane Rich Giddens.
GRINDER, Raymond Edward, b. Dec 1, 1928 DC, d. Feb 12, 1990, hus of Helen Elizabeth Brown, son of Raymond M. and Theodora Pilkerton Grinder.
GRINDER, Raymond M., d. 1964, hus of Theodora Catherine Pilkerton.
HAMILTON, Donovan Kenneth, b. Nov 5, 1912 PA, d. Apr 21, 1988, son of Wilbert H. and Maud L. Hamilton, cremation.
HARRISON, Charter Gray, Sr., d. 1988, hus of Iris Watts.
HEDRICK, Marvin G., b. Feb 22, 1907 WV, d. Feb 13, 1993, hus of Nellie P. __, son of Chas. G. and Nora A. Rohbaugh Hedrick.
HICKS, Agnes Guinnette, b. Oct 24, 1914, d. Mar 22, 1993, wife of Howard N. Kramer, dau of Wm. Carlton and Violet M. Burroughs Hicks.
HODGES, Aloysius Coade II, b. Apr 30, 1898, d. Nov 9, 1992 NM, hus of Helen Forsythe, son of Thos. Gonsalvo and Virginia Gibson Hodges.
JARBOE, Raymond Warren, b. Jan 16, 1899 DC, d. Mar 3, 1954 DC, m. DC Sep 1926 Agnes May Raley, son of John Warren and Mary Elizabeth Hebb Jarboe.
JOHNSON, Amy C., b. Apr 13, 1905, d. Apr 23, 1987, wife of __ Jenkins, dau of Steven and Rose Burch Johnson.
KIDWELL, Harold James, b. Jun 25, 1909 DC, d. Oct 17, 1992, son of Wm. and Augusta Kidwell.
KING, Mary G., b. Oct 25, 1913 PA, d. Dec 5, 1990 DC, wife of Jack W. King.
KNOTT, Karen, b. Mar 22, 1945 DC, d. Mar 23, 1966 Pr. Geo. Co., MD, dau of Joseph Morgan and Vivian Ward Knott.
LEWIS, Hugh Vernon, d. Feb 1964, hus of Mary

Elise Tolley.
MARSHALL, Violet May, b. Mar 5, 1908, d. Nov 6, 1988, wife of Christopher Daniel Bartelmes, Jr., dau of John and Minnie Pearson Marshall.
McDEVITT, Alice Philemenia Pickrel, 72, b. VA, d. Dec 22, 1991, wife of James Smith, dau of Francis J. and Theresa McDevitt.
McKAY, Carolyn Lillian, b. Aug 16, 1908, d. Jan 15, 1991, wife of Joseph Warren Evans, dau of William and Blanche Stone McKay.
McKEON, Bernard John "Barney", b. Apr 24, 1905 MA, d. Mar 23, 1991, m. 8 Nov 1966 Viola Marie Ablett, son of John Benedict and Mary Elizabeth Higgins McKeon.
MILLER, Dorothy, b. Oct 21, 1914 DC, d. Jun 2, 1993, m. 30 Jun 1939 DC Henderson Alvah Raley.
OLIVER, William Edward, b. Jul 4, 1917, d. Jun 27, 1984 DC, m. DC 3 Dec 1940 Ethel Raley.
PILKERTON, Theodora Catherine, b. May 3, 1902, d. Sep 27, 1992, wife of Raymond M. Grinder, dau of Zachariah and Catherine Bowes Pilkerton.
RALEY, Agnes May, b. Dec 23, 1907, d. Mar 3, 1954 DC, wife of Raymond Warren Jarboe.
RALEY, Mary Violet, b. May 15, 1904, d. Jul 4, 1988, m. Anthony "Tony" Barbagallo (chged name to Barbra), dau of Daniel and Minnie Iowa Hazel Raley.
RANDALL, Alvah K. "Dinks", b. Dec 17, 1909 DC, d. Jun 30, 1991, hus of Anna S. __.
ROBEY, Mary Elizabeth, b. Dec 13, 1953 DC, d. Sep 9, 1991, wife of __ Burch, dau of Richard G. and Eleanor H. Robey.
SARTAIN, Dolores Aubrey "Teeny", b. May 23, 1919 DC, d. May 13, 1991, wife of John Grey Williams, dau of Theodore Bertram and Beatrice Gertrude Sartain.
SARTAIN, Ethel Elizabeth, b. Sep 23, 1899 DC, d. Nov 19, 1991, dau of Edward W. and Jennie A. Henley Sartain.
SCHAEFER, Joseph William "Boots" Sr., b. Feb 11, 1910, d. Apr 12, 1992, hus of Edna Genevieve Owens, son of Joseph Michael, Sr. and

Mary Agnes Creamer Schaefer.
SCHAEFER, Joseph William, Jr., b. Jun 26, 1931 DC, d. Sep 10, 1991, hus of Alma Jean Shaw, son of Jos. Wm. and Edna Genevieve Owens Schaefer.
SHERWOOD, Mary J., 85, b. VA, d. Feb 10, 1940 DC, wife of John R. Dewey, dau of Mrs. Ellen Sherwood. Sec 20, Lot 224, Site 4, no marker.
SMITH, Irma Virginia, b. Apr 17, 1916 DC, d. Nov 27, 1993, wife of Arthur Berry Richardson, dau of Samuel and Molly E. Shewbridge Smith.
SPRINGER, Gertrude Elizabeth, b. Jan 15, 1900, d. Jul 26, 1992, wife of Walter Chapman Slye, dau of Benjamin M. and Mockey Jeannette Combs Springer.
TOLLEY, Mary Elise, b. Apr 17, 1917, d. Oct 19, 1992, wife of Hugh Vernon Lewis, dau of Alphans and Sarah Elise Creighton Tolley.
VALLANDINGHAM, Helen Marie, b. Jan 19, 1903, d. Mar 23, 1992 FL, m. (1st) Ely Shapiro, (2d) Charles Dennison, dau of Stephen and Monica Lawrence Vallandingham.
WANNALL, William Howard, Sr. b. Apr 11, 1903 DC, d. Aug 27, 1993, m. 2 Nov 1947 Bernadette W. Quade, son of Walter Howard and Rose Conway Wannall.
WATTS, Iris, b. Sep 12, 1918 DC, d. Oct 31, 1991, wife of Charter Gray Harrison, Sr., dau of Hollingsworth Lowman and Anna Gibbs Watts.
WELCH, Margaret A. "Peggy", b. NC, d. Apr 1, 1993, wife of Reed W. Osman. (Was a great grandmother.)
WILKERSON, Irene Mae, b. Jul 26, 1934, d. Nov 21, 1991, wife of ___ Molino, dau of Benjamin F. Sr. and Agnes Shorter Wilkerson.
WILLIAMS, John Grey, d. Dec 26, 1972, hus of Delores Aubrey Sartain.
WOOD, Charles E., Jr. b. Mar 7, 1924 DC, d. May 26, 1992, son of Charles E. and Grace Jenny Englebretsen Wood.
WOOD, Grace, b. Jan 27, 1916 NY, d. Mar 23, 1991, wife of Carl M. Loffler, Sr., dau of James C. and Emily Jackson Wood.

WOODRUFF, Sarah Elizabeth, b. Jul 26, 1909 VT, d. May 6, 1990, wife of George V. Hinson, dau of Jay Vance and Ada F. Mason Woodruff.
YEATMAN, William E., b. Feb 18, 1908, d. Jun 8, 1988, hus of Matilda __, son of William and Mildred Yeatman.

FORT LINCOLN CEMETERY
Brentwood, St. George's Co., Md.

BRADY, Edith Maybell, b. Jan 16, 1905 MD, d. Dec 24, 1992 FL, wife of Roger H. McKenney, dau of Bernard Emit and Celestina Cerina Salter Brady.
BRYANT, Mary Frances, b. Jan 22, 1960 DC, d. Dec 10, 1992, wife of George "Frankie" Norris, Jr., dau of John Eldridge and Betty Mae Matthews Bryant.
FERBER, Thelma Louise, b. Sep 18, 1914 DC, d. Oct 4, 1991, wife of Frank Lee Johnson, Sr., dau of Frederick and Clara Wilson Ferber.
GEMMILL, Richard Hoover, b. May 18, 1910 PA, d. Sep 10, 1991, son of Raymond and Elizabeth Hoover Gemmill.
HAMMETT, Barbara Ellen, b. Nov 13, 1911, d. Jul 21, 1992, wife of Andrew Francis Scheible, dau of Edmund and Ellen Davis Hammett.
LOCKHART, Bernice Esther, 71, d. Mar 11, 1992, wife of William H. Palmer, dau of John and Elsie Ward Lockhart.
LUTHER, Henry E., USA WW II, b. Jul 12, 1917 TN, d. Aug 1, 1991, son of Henry and Rovirtie Meyers Luther.
MERCHANT, Lillian Alberta, b. Dec 29, 1914 DC, d. Mar 9, 1988, wife of Ralph Stuart, dau of Jas. F. and Catherine Windsor Merchant.
PALMER, William H., Sr. d. Oct 4, 1991, hus of Bernice Esther Lockhart.
REID, Edwin Luther, b. Mar 22, 1910 DC, d. Oct 20, 1992, m. 14 Dec 1935 Thelma Osborne, son of John and Orra Milstead Reid.
SHIPE, Leona, b. Jun 28, 1917 VA, d. Dec 18, 1991, wife of Charles E. "Bee" Mattingly.
SPECHT, Vernon Justin, b. Jul 20, 1909, d. Sep 15, 1988, m. 1936 Doris Tackett, son of Franklin S. and Gertrude Niswanner Specht.
STONE, Edward Leonard, 59, d. Sep 26, 1991, twin son of Leonard and Virginia Stone.
STUART, Ralph, d. 1969, hus of Lillian Alberta Merchant.
TAYMAN, Dorothy Evelyn, 74, d. Mar 24, 1993, wife of John Adrian Long, bur Historic

Gardens section.

THOMASSON, Norma Marion "Granny", b. Oct 5, 1899 DC, d. Jul 2, 1993, wife of William Earl Wannall, dau of Merriweather Lucian and Ida Elizabeth Bass Thomasson.

WILSON, Dorothy Louise, b. Jun 19, 1900 DC, d. Sep 17, 1991, wife of __ Buchholz, dau of Thomas G. and Katherine Smith Wilson.

WASHINGTON NATIONAL CEMETERY
Suitland, Pr. Georges Co., Maryland

ABELL, John 'Raymond', b. Mar 23, 1904, d. Jan 22, 1987 FL, hus of Martha Vogt, son of Francis Eugene and Annie Lucinda Adams Abell.

ABELL, Joseph Ignatius, b. Sep 22, 1919, d. Jun 22, 1992, hus of Marion Poe, son of Francis Eugene and Annie Lucinda Adams Abell.

ABELL, Mary 'Noema', b. Feb 12, 1909, d. Mar 4, 1992, wife of Charles A. Becker, Sr., dau of Francis Eugene and Annie Lucinda Adams Abell.

BECKER, Charles A., Sr., d. Aug 23, 1980, m. 1930 Mary Noema Abell.

BOULDING, Bonnie Mae, b. Mar 1, 1905 NC, d. Feb 24, 1993, wife of Harry Hopkins Cooper.

BOWLES, Minnie Cecelia, b. Feb 12, 1922, d. Mar 20, 1989, wife of Lawrence S. Hill, Sr.

CLATTERBUCK, Robert Bruce, b. Feb 10, 1948 VA, d. Apr 27, 1992, son of Silas B. and Mary C. Clatterbuck.

COOPER, Harry Hopkins, d. 1961, hus of Bonnie Mae Boulding.

POE, Marion, d. Jun 3, 1985, wife of Joseph Ignatius Abell.

WILLETT, Kathleen V., b. Aug 14, 1912, d. Mar 21, 1993, wife of Albert F. Hancock, dau of Guy and Ella May Sanders Willett.

MISC. MARYLAND STATE CEMETERIES

ASHLEY, Martha, d. Nov 23, 1985, wife of Joseph Lawrence Henderson, bur Wesley Chapel Cem., Rock Hall, Md.

BADEN, Joseph H., USA WW II, b. Jul 31, 1914, d. Aug 20, 1993, son of Halbert D. and Lucy V. Murphy Baden, bur St. Peters, Waldorf, Md.

BAKER, Jonathan Jennings, d. April 1962, hus of Lillian Gertrude Goddard, bur Rockville Cem., Rockville, Md.

BEAN, Louis Thomas, b. Jul 12, 1925, d. Nov 10, 1991 DC, hus of Margaret Trueman, son of John and Violet Goodwin Bean, bur Immanuel Meth. Cem., Baden, Md.

BIGELOW, Grace Lillian, b. Feb 12, 1895 WI, d. Jul 22, 1988, wife of George L. Howland, dau of Bert and Eva Riffenberg Bigelow, bur Hillcrest Mem. Cem., Annapolis, Md.

BISHOP, Teddy Wayne, b. Sep 20, 1941 CT, d. Sep 20, 1991, hus of Janet Kay __, son of Elmer E. and Lois B. Bishop, bur Resurrection Cem., Clinton, MD.

BOWEN, Myrtle, b. Mar 27, 1901 Balto, d. Nov 29, 1992, wife of George Edward Denton, Sr., dau of Calvin Wright and Nannie Maria Bowen Simmons, bur Central Cem., Barstow, Md.

BOWIE, Mary F., b. May 5, 1905, d. Dec 24, 1990, wife of __ Dodd, dau of John R. and Sara A. Bowie, bur Nanjemoy Bapt. Church Cem., Nanjemoy, Md.

BOWLING, Louise Daisy, b. Dec 21, 1921, d. Mar 7, 1992, wife of John W. Winstead, dau of Thomas W. and Marie Simpson Bowling, bur Dentsville Meth. Cem., Dentsville, Md.

BURKE, Robert William, IV, b. Dec 12, 1988, d. Jul 16, 1993, son of Robt. W. Burke of Bowie and Margaret F. Graham Burke of California, MD; gson of Mary Forster; Donald Graham; Robert E. Burke, Jr., bur Sacred Heart Cem., La Plata, Md.

BUYS, Katherine, 43, d. Nov 9, 1988 in car accident, m. (1st) __ Gallagher, (2d) Robert G. Durbin, dau of James H. and Katherine Moss Buys, bur Christ Episcopal Church Cem.,

Port Republic, Md.
BYRNE, Sara Evelyn, b. Apr 15, 1904 Balto, d. Dec 6, 1992, wife of Albert D. Pearce, dau of Murray Leonard and Edna Belle Almond Byrne, bur Loudon Park Cem., Baltimore, Md.
CONNEE, Elsie Mae, b. Jan 7, 1931 NC, d. Nov 1, 1993, wife of __ Poisson, dau of Elmer, Sr. and Lillie Mae Counts Connee, bur Meadowridge Mem. Pk., Elkridge, MD.
COOKSIE, Dorothy Cash, b. Jun 11, 1911, d. Nov 28, 1990, wife of Thomas H. Swann, Sr., dau of Thomas Ford and Nellie Cooksie, bur Trinity Episcopal Cem., Newport, Md.
DAVIS, Henry Harry, Sr., USA WW II, b. Feb 12, 1912, d. Aug 29, 1993, son of Harry and Lulu Spencer Davis, inurnment at Springhill Cem., Easton, Md.
DeBOLT, Mart LeRoy, 88, d. Jul 12, 1989, hus of Susan M. __, bur Southern Mem. Gardens., Dunkirk, Md.
DeFEUDIS, Rosa, b. Oct 28, 1912 Andrea, Italy, d. Jul 8, 1988, wife of Joseph Casamassima, dau of Francesco and Apolonia Alicino DeFeudis, bur Resurrection Cem., Clinton, Md.
DELLA, Ellen Marguerite, d. Oct 9, 1984, wife of Port Miller, bur La Plata United Meth. Cem., La Plata, Md.
DeMOOR, Denise, b. Jun 7, 1922 Belgium, d. Jul 22, 1992, wife of Joseph E. Montpetit, dau of Alfonse and Bertha DeMoor, bur Gate of Heaven Cem., Silver Spring, Md.
DOWNS, Frank Francis, b. Sep 20, 1907 DC, d. Sep 5, 1992, hus of Nellie M. Clifton, son of Wilmer Francis and Mary Louise Petit Downs, bur St. Barnabus Episcopal Cem., Oxen Hill, Md.
DYSON, Janie Catherine, 80, d. Sep 20, 1993 Balto, wife of John A. Dyson, bur Lorraine Park Cem., Balto., Md.
GARNER, William Irving, b. May 2, 1921 DC, d. Jul 21, 1991, hus of Mary Disharoon, son of Herman P. and Daisy Parker Garner, bur Resurrection Cem., Clinton, Md.
GALLAGHER, Leslie Ann, d. Nov 9, 1988 in car accident, dau of __ Gallagher and Katherine

Buys Gallagher Durbin, bur Christ Episcopal Church Cem., Port Republic, Md.
GARNER, Francis Leroy, b. Jun 16, 1941, d. Nov 3, 1992, son of Thadeus Eugene and Weddie H. Wink Garner, bur Resurrection Cem., Waldorf, Md.
GATTON, Lola Mae, b. Dec 31, 1929, d. Sep 1, 1992, wife of R. W. "Butch" O'Hara, bur Glen Haven Mem. Pk., Glen Burnie, Md.
GODDARD, Heloise Jane, 96, d. Jan 20, 1992, wife of __ Miller, dau of Charles and Alice Constdant Goddard, bur St. Paul's Episcopal Cem., Baden, Md.
GODDARD, Lillian Gertrude, b. Sep 9, 1905, d. Nov 10, 1992, wife of Jonathan J. Baker, dau of Benj. R. and Frances M. Owens Goddard, bur Rockville Cem., Rockville, Md.
GOLDSMITH, Henry Samuel, b. Apr 13, 1913, d. Mar 2, 1993, hus of Isabelle C. Alvey, son of Samuel and Cora Indiana Ching Goldsmith, bur Benedict, Md.
HAMMETT, Lawrence M., Jr. b. Jul 21, 1930, d. May 19, 1992, hus of E. Jean __, son of Lawrence and Alberta C. Combs Hammett, bur St. Columbia RCC Cem., Oxen Hill, Md.
HAMOR, Hoyt Herman, Sr. b. Oct 10, 1935 ME, d. Dec 24, 1992, hus of Helen A. Davis, son of Jas. E. and Lucy H. Hamilton Hamor, bur Nanjemoy Bapt. Church Cem., Nanjemoy, Md.
HARPER, Timothy Ryan, b. Feb 16, 1952, d. Mar 11, 1993, son of late Jewell Raymond Harper and Hester Ryan Harper Essex, bur Parklawn Cem., Rockville, Md.
HAYDEN, Alice May, b. Mar 9, 1908, d. Mar 1989 Mont. Co., Md., wife of Christopher 'Sheldon' Johnson, dau of Charles Maguire and Anna May Raley Hayden, bur Gate of Heaven Cem., Silver Spring, Md.
HAYDEN, Catherine Cecelia, b. Jun 30, 1912, d. May 12, 1993, wife of George Edward Burch, dau of Thomas L. and Margaret Abell Hayden, bur. St. Ignatius RCC, Chapel Point, Md.
HENDERSON, Joseph Lawrence, 86, b. St. Geo Isl, d. Aug 12, 1992, hus of Martha Ashley, son of Jos. A. and Sadie M. Robrecht Hender-

son, bur Wesley Chapel Cem., Rock Hall, Md.
HENDERSON, Mary Magdaline, b. Aug 23, 1896, d. Feb 13, 1976, wife of Alvah Raley, bur Resurrection Cem., Clinton, Md.
HIGGS, Mary Maude, b. Dec 2, 1913, d. Nov 7, 1991, wife of Joseph Donald Hurry, dau of James Mitchell and Julia Mae Bush Higgs, bur Wicomico Mem. Park, Wicomico, Md.
HINKEY, Irene Amos, b. Jan 27, 1890 Balto, d. Oct 2, 1989, wife of William White, dau of John and Martha Hinkey, bur Hebrew Congregation Cem., Balto., Md.
HURRY, Joseph Donald "Scoogie", b. Nov 4, 1908, d. Jul 9, 1989, hus of Mary Maude __, son of Jos. D. and Agnes M. Raley Hurry, bur Wicomico Mem. Park, Wicomico, Md.
INMAN, Earl, 67, d. Dec 8, 1992, son of Louis and Thelma Henly Inman. Memorial service at Bowen's Inn, Solomons, Md.
JENKINS, Julie, 11, bur Oct 8, 1870 Balto.
JOHNSON, Christopher 'Sheldon', b. Sep 12, 1908, d. Jan 1988 Mont. Co., MD, hus of Alice May Hayden, son of Charles Llewellyn and Agnes Adele Hayden Johnson, bur Gate of Heaven Cem., Silver Spring, Md.
JOHNSON, Fr. Joseph M., b. Jan 27, 1883, d. Nov 7, 1973 PA, son of Geo. E. and Johanna Long Johnson, bur Chapel Pt. Jesuit Cem., Chapel Point, Md.
JOHNSON, Myrtle, b. Mar 8, 1912, d. 1971, m. (1st) William "Bill" Abell, (2d) Benjamin Patterson, dau of Francis "Frank" and Rose F. Spaulding Johnson, bur Resurrection Cem., Clinton, Md.
JUSTICE, Mrs. Elizabeth "Bess" S., b. Feb 2, 1906 PA, d. Oct 10, 1988, memorial service at Cobb Island Baptist Church, Md.
KANE, Blanche Minnette, b. Nov 1, 1913, d. May 19, 1993 DC, wife of Harry Campbell, dau of George and Frances Gunn Kane, bur Harmony Mem. Park, Landover, Md.
LANGLEY, Harry Lee, USN, 70, d. Jun 30, 1989, hus of Minnie Kay __, bur Methodist Cem., Solomons, Md.
LORE, Joseph Cobb, Jr. b. Dec 31, 1900, d. Mar

1, 1993, hus of Virginia Bell, bur Middleham Chapel, Calvert Co., Md.
MADDEN, Thomas Joseph, b. Dec 29, 1913 Balto, d. Jul 3, 1992, hus of Gertrude B. Bradunas, son of Thomas and Rose McKenna Madden, bur St. Stanislaus Cem., Balto, Md.
MATTINGLY, Mary Catherine, b. Jun 27, 1906, d. Jun 4, 1992, wife of Samuel Ellwood Wilson, dau of James and Hortense Hayden Mattingly, bur St. Peters Cem., Waldorf, Md.
MAYOR, Mary Catherine, b. Feb 24, 1921, d. Dec 3, 1991, wife of Claude E. Shifflett, Sr., dau of Edward, Jr. and Margie Moore Mayor, bur Parklawn Cem., Rockville, Md.
McGUIGAN, William Thomas, b. Sep 26, 1933 DC, d. Oct 24, 1993, m. 1956 Nancy Mattingly, son of George Chester and Elizabeth Louise Bailey McGuigan, bur St. Charles Cem., Glymont, Md.
McLEAN, Archibald Joseph, USN, b. Jun 2, 1926 VT, d. Jun 1, 1992, hus of Dolores J. Elsbernd, son of Robert Alexander and Rose Ann Dandurand McLean, bur St. Peters RCC, Waldorf, Md.
MIDDLETON, J. Rudolph, b. Jan 30, 1921, d. Sep 5, 1993, son of Henry D. and Bertha E. Cooke Middleton, bur St. Peters RCC, Waldorf, Md.
MILLER, Ardith Elizabeth, b. Nov 4, 1915 MN, d. Oct 22, 1993, wife of Enos Ray Pumphrey, dau of Clyde and Ruth Marie Miller, bur Resurrection Cem., Clinton, Md.
MILLER, Port, b. Mar 14, 1905 WV, d. Jan 17, 1992 DC, m. Sep 1947 Ellen Marguerite Della, son of Phillip and Ellen McGraw Miller, bur La Plata United Meth. Cem., La Plata, Md.
MONTGOMERY, Ruth, b. Jul 28, 1929, d. Mar 21, 1993, wife of Thomas Weldon Sweeney, dau of Stephen and Martha Burch Montgomery, bur Brookfield Meth. Cem., Upper Marlboro, Md.
MONTPETIT, Joseph E., d. 1967, hus of Denise DeMoor, bur Gate of Heaven Cem., Silver Spring, Md.
MORGAN, Lillian Maude, 87, d. Dec 7, 1990, wife of John Melvin Langley, bur Our Lady of the Sea Cem., Solomons, Md.

MUSSER, Thomas W., Sr. b. Dec 18, 1920 MD, d. Aug 1, 1992, son of Henry M. and Mary Burdett Musser, bur Parklawn Mem. Pk., Gaithersburg, Md.
NUTTER, Luella N., b. May 2, 1908, d. May 10, 1993, wife of __ Waters, dau of John and Bertha Nutter, bur Green Acres Mem. Pk., Salisbury, Md.
PAYNE, Miss Bessie Bowen, ret., d. Jun 5, 1970, dau of Jos. and Nellie Bowen Payne, bur Woodlawn Cem., Baltimore, Md.
PEARCE, Albert D., d. Apr 18, 1969, m. 27 Sep 1927 Balto, Sara Evelyn Byrne, bur Loudon Park Cem., Baltimore, Md.
PERDUE, Morton Stanford, b. Mar 25, 1922 VA, d. Nov 7, 1992, hus of Marion S. __, son of Joseph Lee and Lucy Altic Perdue. Mem. svc. at Huntt Funeral Home, Waldorf, Md.
PERKINS, Elizabeth Ann, b. May 2, 1931 DC, d. Aug 7, 1992, wife of Joseph B. Bowles, Jr., dau of Turner and Mary Elizabeth Downey Perkins, bur Resurrection Cem., Clinton, Md.
PHOEBUS, Margaret, b. May 1, 1912 P.A. Co., d. Dec 15, 1989, wife of Sherman Dryden, Jr., dau of Isaac Fred and Sadie Green Phoebus, bur Princess Anne Co., Md.
RALEY, Alvah, b. Dec 10, 1892, d. Apr 30, 1976, hus of Mary Magdaline Henderson, son of Daniel and Minnie Iowa Hazel Raley, bur Resurection Cem., Clinton, Md.
RANSOM, Ruby V., b. Dec 19, 1917 VA, d. Aug 28, 1991, wife of Henry Herman Hoffman, dau of Joseph J. and Annie L. Goode Ransom, bur Old Fields Episcopal Cem., Hughesville, Md.
RENEHAN, Mrs. Sarah A., 65, bur May 24, 1901, Howard Co., Md.
RICHARDSON, Virginia Pearl, b. Jul 21, 1915, d. Feb 3, 1989, wife of Floyd J. Redmiles, dau of Andrew Jerome and Ruth Adams Richardson, bur Immanuel Meth. Cem., Baden, Md.
RIDGELL, Lionel Benedict, b. Mar 5, 1910, d. Sep 1, 1988, eldest child of Clarence H. and Hattie L. Norris Ridgell, bur Resurrection Cem., Clinton, Md.
ROACH, Florence, 78, d. May 3, 1993, wife of

Courtney R. Thomas, svc at St. Jane Frances de Chantal Church, Bethesda, Md.

RALEY, FR. Will F., Episcopal Rector, d. Aug 14, 1991, bur St. Marks Cem., Silver Spring, Md.

ROBERTSON, Richard Dix, b. Sep 16, 1929 Capt'l. Hgts., MD, d. May 7, 1993 Balto, m. 14 Jun 1972 Marguerite Elaine Morrison, son of Henry and Sarah Hall Robertson, bur Gate of Heaven Cem., Silver Spring, Md.

ROBINSON, Edna Elizabeth, b. Jan 28, 1916, d. Oct 26, 1991, wife of Peter Claude Morgan, dau of Benjamin and Ethel Robinson, bur Our Lady Star of the Sea Catholic Cem., Solomons, Md.

ROE, Ruth E., b. Mar 1, 1906 NY, d. Jul 29, 1991, m. 22 Jul 1930 Esley N. Schwartz, dau of Edward A. and Anna S. Roe, bur Parklawn Cem., Rockville, Md.

SADLER, John, b. Feb 25, 1916, d. Sep 27, 1964, hus of Hazel Raley, bur Gate of Heaven Cem., Silver Spring, Md.

SAUBLE, Lena Maria, b. Apr 21, 1907, d. Jun 15, 1993 DC, wife of Cleveland Lee Dodd, dau of Wesley and Irene Koontz Sauble, bur La Plata United Meth. Cem., Dentsville, Md.

SECREST, Harry Clair, b. Aug 23, 1932 PA, d. Aug 27, 1992, hus of Marie Thomas, son of Harry Morgan and Martha Secrest, bur Southern Mem. Gdns., Dunkirk, Md.

SEWELL, Frank Joseph, b. Apr 1, 1913, d. Aug 23, 1991 Balto., hus of Cecelia Marshall, son of George and Mary Barnes Sewell, bur St. Peter Claver Cem., Balto., Md.

SIMMONS, Myrtle, b. Mar 27, 1901 Balto, d. Nov 29, 1992, wife of George Edw. Denton, Sr., dau of Calvin Wright and Nannie Marie Bowen Simmons, bur Central Cem., Barstow, Md.

ST. CLAIR, Agnes Louise, b. Aug 10, 1904, d. Feb 21, 1993, m. 1933 William Wilson Penn, dau of James Walter and Frances Rebecca Goode St. Clair, bur Trinity Epis. Ch., Newport, Md.

SWANN, Anna, b. Feb 19, 1906, d. Jul 19, 1970, m. (1st) Jun 1928 T. W. Wills, Jr. (2d) Feb 1958 J. Julius Johnson, dau of Harold Serviss and Elizabeth Peabody Hayes Swann, bur St. Agnes Church Cem., Chapel Point, Md.

TALBOT, Bessie Virginia, b. Nov 16, 1907 DC, d. Oct 3, 1993, wife of Ernest Gibson, dau of Charles E. and Elsie Mae Gill Talbot, bur Resurrection Cemetery, Clinton, Md.

TARLETON, Malcolm Everett, b. Jun 27, 1908, d. Dec 22, 1988, hus of Mary Louise Ellis, son of Samuel Cleveland and Maggie Purcell Tarleton, bur Glen Haven Cem., Glen Burnie, Md.

TIPPETT, Alma, d. Jan 9, 1981 at Cheltenham, Md., wife of Harvey B. Lanier.

TYDINGS, Warren Edward, Sr., b. Oct 10, 1911 Balto, d. May 22, 1993, m. 1936 Anna Marie Quirk, son of Richard Edward and Edith Mayhew Tydings, bur Gate of Heaven Cem., Silver Spring, Md.

VERMILLION, Mildred G., b. Jun 16, 1914, d. Jul 26, 1992, wife of Benjamin F. Wilkerson, dau of Henry and Katie McKenzie Vermillion, bur St. Thomas Episcopal Cem., Croom, Md.

WALKER, Hugh Vernon, b. Jul 26, 1923 NC, d. Aug 25, 1992 Balto, m. 24 Jun 1982 DC, Mary ___, son of Wiley and Narcissus Gaultney Walker, bur Lincoln Mem. Cem., Suitland, Md.

WENK, Charles Worthy, 56, d. Jul 15, 1991, hus of Leona A. ___, bur Sacred Heart Catholic Cem., La Plata, Md.

WHITE, John M. "Big Mike", b. Feb 5, 1937, d. Dec 28, 1993, son of Thomas Ernest, Sr. and Edna Pearline Tayman White, bur Resurrection Cem., Clinton, Md.

WHITED, Larry E., 45, d. Sep 17, 1993, hus of Jeanne ___, bur Resurrection Cem., Clinton, Md.

WILLETT, Teresa, b. Feb 3, 1918, d. Aug 31, 1991, wife of Henry Estevez, dau of James Harrison and Rosalie Willett, bur St. Joseph RCC, Pomfret, Md.

WILLIAMS, June Betty, b. Feb 6, 1921, d. Aug 3, 1988 DC, wife of George B. Wiggin, bur St. Peters Cem., Lusby, Md.

WILSON, Rose Wheeler, 103, b. Harford Co., MD, d. Jan 27, 1993, bur St. Ignatius RCC, Hickory, Harford Co., Md.

WOOD, Stephen R. "Joe", Sr. b. Sep 2, 1913, d. Aug 10, 1993, bur Glen Haven Mem. Park, Md.

WOODBURN, Helen Augusta, 84, d. Jun 20, 1993, wife of Littleon Gray, bur United Meth. Cem., Solomons, Md.

WREN, Edgar A., b. Mar 26, 1916 PA, d. May 23, 1992, hus of Teresa K. __, son of Francis and Elizabeth Ham Wren, bur St. Joseph RCC, Pompret, Md.

YOUNG, Elsie Violette, b. Jun 6, 1899, d. May 9, 1992, dau of Samuel L. and Bertha Stafford Young, bur Asbury Meth. Cem., Barstow, Md.

YOUNG, Harry Lee, Sr., USA Korea, b. Dec 31, 1931, d. Oct 22, 1991, hus of Gladys Pauline Hall, son of Roy and Nellie Wilkerson Young, bur Resurrection Cem., Clinton, Md.

OUT OF MD. MISC. CEMETERIES

ADAMS, Lucille Frances, b. Sep 8, 1904 OK., d. Nov 17, 1993, wife of __ Carver, dau of Benjamin and Anna Howry Adams, inurnment in Hydro Masonic Cem., Hydro, Ok.

ADAMS, Mary Lillian, b. Sep 8, 1903, d. Feb 27, 1992, m. (1st) 1929 DC, George A. Simpson, (2d) 1955 James W. Brush (d. May 24, 1966), dau of Benjamin F. and Lucy Agnes Pope Adams, bur Mt. Olivet Cem., D.C.

ALDRIGE, William Keating, d. 1969, hus of Dorothy Louise Miller, bur Chesterfield Cem., Centerville, VA.

BABLE, Erwin Clair, b. Jan 2, 1910 PA, d. Mar 11, 1993, m. 15 Jul 1932 Martha Johanna Beike, son of Jas. and Ada Blair Bable, bur Rochester, PA.

BEAVERS, Raymond James, b. Aug 14, 1904, d. Aug 15, 1990, hus of Mary E. Holley, bur Ft. Myers, FL.

BOWLES, Ronald A., 37, d. Sep 21, 1991 FL, hus of Christine __, son of Roy Bowles, Sr. bur Highland Mem. Pk., Ocala, FL.

BRAHLER, Miss Helen T. "Aunt Helen", b. Nov 18, 1910 DC, d. Mar 29, 1992, dau of George and Catherine G. Giebel Brahler, bur St. Mary's Cem., DC.

BRICK, Helen Cecelia, b. Jul 4, 1915 MN, d. Sep 1, 1991, dau of Thomas B. and Elizabeth A. Harty Brick, bur Sacred Heart Cemetery, Owantoma, MN.

BUNCH, Edward Lloyd, b. Jan 9, 1912 DC, d. Nov 28, 1989, m. (1st) Jessie C. __, (2d) Elizabeth "Betty" Coppage (bur St. Geo. Epis., Valley Lee, Md.), son of Jesse Lee and Mary Alice Bunch, bur Monticello Mem. Gdns, Charlottesville, VA.

BURSEY, William Craig, b. Oct 17, 1920 DC, d. Jun 17, 1991, hus of Allie Florence __, bur Prospect Hill Cem., Front Royal, VA.

BUSSLER, Julia, b. Jan 21, 1950, d. Feb 7, 1992 PA, m. 1974 Rick Wagner, only child of Gorman and Virginia Oden Bussler, bur Westover Bapt. Cem., PA.

CATON, Robert D., 24, d. Oct 10, 1993 PA, son of Jerry G. and Lucy May Ridgell Caton, private interment.
CAMERON, Sister Eleanor Marie "Beatrice", b. Jun 7, 1909, d. Apr 13, 1992, bur Sisters of Charity, Nazareth, KY.
CAMPBELL, John William, b. May 26, 1915, d. Sep 23, 1992, hus of Eva Agnes Bell, son of William C. and Ollie Sanders Campbell, bur Meth. Cem., Faun Grove, PA.
CLAGETT, Lee Preston, b. Jan 18, 1915 DC, d. Apr 22, 1991, hus of Martha A. Glass, son of Adelbert Henry and Sarah Kane Clagett,bur Columbia Gdns., Arlington, VA.
CLARKE, Lavinnah, b. Jul 16, 1768, Ridge, Md., d. Jan 22, 1827 SC, wife of William Taylor, dau of Robert and Mary Clarke.
CODY, Marie Antoinette, b. Jun 13, 1919 NY, d. Nov 4, 1988, wife of __ Cavanaugh, bur PA.
COFFMAN, Pearl Mae, d. Dec 26, 1986, wife of Lake Vernon Weasenforth, bur Davis Cem., Ridgeville, WV.
COMBS, William Elmer, Sr. USA WW II, b. Nov 21, 1915, d. Jan 20, 1992 FL, hus of Maye Tyndall, son of Wm. Parren and Blanche Victoria Redmond Combs, bur Serenity Gardens, Largo, FL.
CONNELLY, Betty, b. May 6, 1928, d. Aug 9, 1993 CO, wife of Robert Thompson, Sr., dau of William Ford Connelly and Della Reed Connelly Clements, svcs. at Holy Trinity RCC, Denver, CO.
CONNELLY, Helen Beatrice, 86, d. Aug 4, 1992 PA, wife of Mearl J. Landis, dau of late William Ford Connelly and Della Reed Connelly Clements, bur Mt. Olivet Cem., Fairview Township, PA.
CONNELLY, James F., 68, d. Feb 12, 1989 FL, hus of Willeen __, son of William Ford and Della Reed Connelly Clements, bur Miami, FL.
COFFEE, Edna David, b. Aug 17, 1922 VA, d. Oct 21, 1993 VA, wife of Marc Alexander Wolicki, dau of David Gentry and Blanche Coffee, service at Ft. Myer Chapel, Ft. Myer, VA.
COURSEY, Cpt. Charles I. "Bud", Sr. 70, b. St.

Mary's Co, d. Aug 29, 1991, hus of Cecelia Howard, son of Raymond and Lavina Johnson Coursey, bur Haleyville Meth. Cem., Port Norris, NJ.

CRYER, Mary Antoinette, b. Nov 16, 1921 DC, d. May 30, 1991, wife of Lewis E. Tippett, Sr., dau of Jas. Walter and Elizabeth Ann Donoghue Cryer, bur Mt. Olivet Cem., DC.

CRYER, William Rudolphus "Rhodie", b. Jul 4, 1900 DC, d. Jun 21, 1972, m. (1st) DC, Marie Schultz, (2d) Alberta Stone Cryer, son of William B. and "Lula" Johnson Cryer, bur Prospect Hill Cem., DC.

DAHL, Richard William, b. Jun 29, 1964, d. Dec 24, 1993 FL, son of Wayne L. and Dolores "Dolly" Dahl, bur Florida Hills Mem. Gdns., Spring Hill, Fl.

DALTON, Daisy, b. Dec 16, 1905 GA, d. Oct 8, 1993, wife of Benjamin Fincher Morton, dau of Pleatus and Nancy Dutton Dalton, bur Green Lawn Cem., Jacksonville, FL.

DAVIS, Rebecca B., b. Apr 22, 1903 DC, d. Apr 19, 1992, wife of Charles J. Shaefer, dau of David and Mary Botkin Davis, bur Chapel Hills Gdns. Cem., Zephyrhills, FL.

DAVIS, Thomas William, b. Feb 23, 1906, d. Jul 10, 1993, hus of Margaret Alice Hatcher, son of Cyrus and Mary Hughes Davis, bur Lloyd Cem., Ebensburg, PA.

DOCKUM, Faye Joyce, b. Aug 26, 1931 NY, d. Oct 23, 1993, wife of __ Stone, dau of Charles Edward and Bertha Lillian Norton Dockum, bur Greenmount Cem., Whitehall, NY.

DOYLE, Teresa A., 33, d. Dec 10, 1993 VA, wife of Keith Reich, dau of Norman and Margaret Doyle, bur Hillsboro Cem., Loudoun Co., VA.

DUKE, Sister Benedicta, nee Angela, b. Oct 1, 1903, d. Jun 12, 1992, dau of Benj. Hooper and Grace Dent Duke, bur Sisters of Charity, Nazareth, KY.

EATON, Albert John, b. Jun 28, 1912 NH, d. Aug 23, 1991, hus of Marjorie Campbell, bur Congressional Cem., Auburn, NH.

ELLINGWOOD, Lawrence Elden, b. Feb 25, 1926 ME, d. Jul 1, 1991, son of Lester and Marion

Dodge Ellingwood, bur Portland, ME.
FAY, George Thomas, USA WW I, b. Jul 12, 1896 NY, d. Oct 23, 1991, son of James and Bridget Malony Fay, bur Long Island Nat'l Cem., Farmingdale, NY.
FIESTER, Irene Ruth, b. Dec 9, 1891 IA, d. May 24, 1993 FL, m. 1912 John Lee Wilkinson, bur Rock Creek Cem., DC.
FRANCISCO, Roger Benton, Sr. USN WW II, b. Apr 9, 1926 NY, d. Sep 4, 1993, m. 26 Dec 1947 NY, Carol Elizabeth Corbin, son of Wallace and Lena M. Windus Francisco, bur Fairlawn Cem., Scio, NY.
GEORGE, Genise Marie "Gigi", b. Sep 6, 1961 Guam, M.I., d. Dec 15, 1993, dau of Chester LeRoy and Mary Katherine Ley George; gdau of Thelda Ent George of Ogden, UT; Richard M. Ley, FL, inurnment D.C.
GHEEN, Ruth Elizabeth, b. Aug 1, 1928 VA, d. Aug 7, 1988, wife of Arthur Ernest Tinsman, dau of Rufus N. and Robena Herndon Gheen, bur Culpepper Nat'l Cem. Culpepper, Va.
GREENWELL, Sister Mary Estelle, nee Grace Greenwell, b. May 15, 1900, d. Feb 15, 1991 KY, dau of John Philip and Mary Estelle Cawood Greenwell, bur Sisters of Charity, Nazareth, KY.
HARDING, Helen Geraldine, b. Sep 1, 1909 IN, d. Oct 21, 1988, wife of __ Brown, dau of Ambrose O. "A.O." and Lillie Means Harding, bur Nat'l Mem. Park Cem., Falls Church, Va.
HARRIS, Willard Allen, Sr. b. Apr 24, 1912 WV, d. Apr 28, 1993, m. 1932 DC, Ida Mae Newton, son of Otha Dillon and Lillie Belle Alderton Harris, bur Andrew Chapel Meth. Cem., Vienna, VA.
HOLLIN, Mabel, b. Apr 3, 1925 KY, d. Jul 22, 1988, wife of __ Humfleet, dau of Charley and Annie Shearer Hollin, bur Grandview Cem., Mentor, Ky.
HUG, Christian Alden "Chris", LT USN, b. Jun 20, 1962 IL, d. Aug 1, 1993, m. IL 28 Jun 1986 Andrea Marie Prout, son of Gerald Floyd and Brenda Carol Larson Hug, bur All Saints RCC, Des Plaines, IL.

Out of State Misc.

JIMERSON, William Joseph, b. May 14, 1968 TN, d. June 30, 1991, son of Larry Joe and Barbara Elaine Jimerson, bur East View Cem., Union City, TN.
JOHNSON, Lewis, b. 1801/02, bur Aug 18, 1872 in DC, son of James and Mary Johnson.
KANE, Rita M., b. Jul 9, 1922 DC, d. Sep 17, 1992, dau of Timothy Patrick and Catherine Costella Kane, bur Mt. Olivet Cem., Washington, DC.
LALLANDE, John Berkeley "Jack", Sr. b. Sep 14, 1911 NY, d. Sep 25, 1993, m. DC, 1935 Helen Ray, son of Rathbone Turner and Katherine Edwards Kimball Lallande, bur Rockville Cem., Washington, DC.
LAWRENCE, Sister Mary Thoma, nee Alice Elizabeth, b. Aug 26, 1920, d. Aug 2, 1990 KY, dau of Geo. L. and Pauline Long Lawrence, bur Sisters of Charity, Nazareth, KY.
LEE, Inja, b. Mar 15, 1934 Korea, d. Feb 23, 1988 VA, wife of Charles M. Raley, bur Herndon, VA.
LOTT, Elizabeth Margaret, b. Dec 6, 1893, d. Apr 6, 1992, dau of William and Kristina Gunther Lott, bur St. Stephen's Episcopal Cem., Allentown, PA.
MARSTON, Coburn, Lt. Col., b. Oct 7, 1920 MA, d. May 13, 1992, hus of Margaret Frances __, son of Roy L. and Mary Emery Marston, mem. services at Ft. Myers, VA.
MATTINGLY, Elsie Elizabeth, b. Jul 10, 1905, d. Apr 3, 1991 Alex. VA, wife of Flourney C. Roberts, dau of Walter and Elizabeth Morris Mattingly, bur Fairfax Mem. Pk, Fairfax, VA.
MAYOR, Joseph Henry, b. Jun 2, 1928, d. Jun 5, 1992 VA, hus of Geraldine Page, son of Jos. Leonard, Sr. and Myrtle Ridgell Mayor, bur Lively Baptist Church Cem., Lively, VA.
McGINN, Elma Frances, b. Sep 16, 1927 MA, d. Aug 24, 1993 MA, m. 29 Dec 1948 Raymond S. Loyd, dau of George W. and Nora Delahay McGinn.
McKAY, Valrea Leila, b. Oct 16, 1907 PA, d. May 10, 1991, wife of Calvin L. Albaugh, dau of Herman Scott and Minnie Graham McKay, bur

East Hickory Cem., Tionesta, PA.
MEYER, Olga Paulina, b. May 2, 1893, Hamburg, Germ., d. Oct 21, 1991, wife of __ Miller, dau of August and Elise Jergens Meyer, bur Union Ridge Cem., Chicago, IL.
MILLER, Dorothy Louise, b. Feb 19, 1914 TN, d. Oct 3, 1991, wife of William Keating Aldridge, dau of John Madison and Mary Lenora Miller, bur Chesterfield Cem., Centerville, VA.
MISTLER, Sophia Maryanne, b. Jan 4, 1929 L.I., NY, d. Feb 21, 1993, m. 1946 Howard Raymond Sexton, dau of Geo. S. and Sophie McKessler Mistler, bur L.I., NY.
MONTAMED, Fereydoun, 75, b. Persia, d. Jul 13, 1993 VA, hus of Rouhangiz __ of Persia, bur Williamsburg Mem. Park, VA.
MORTON, Benjamin Fincher, d. Oct 7, 1978, hus of Daisy Dalton, bur Green Lawn Cem., Jacksonville, FL.
MOSS, Annie Bell, b. Feb 1, 1892 VA, d. Nov 8, 1988, m. 1912 John W. Lancaster, dau of George and Ann Smith Moss, bur First Baptist Church Cem., Farmville, Va.
NEAL, J. Edward, b. Oct 28, 1926 VA, d. Aug 1, 1993 FL, hus of Nadine __, mem. srv. Seminole, FL.
NORRIS, George Bernard, Sr. b. Dec 29, 1929 DC, d. Jul 15, 1988 VA, son of Bernard M. Jr. and Lucille Kershaw Norris, bur Pleasant View Cem., Augusta Co, VA.
ORR, John Ellis, 72, C. Elec. Mate, USN WW II, d. Oct 20, 1993 DC, hus of Audrey Carrington, son of John Herbert and Lydia Cornelia Orr, bur Old Trinity Church, Church Creek, NY.
PERRIE, Phillip Joseph, b. Sep 5, 1968 KS, d. Oct 21, 1991, son of Clinton "Joe" and Elizabeth Jane Perrie, bur Kechi Cem., Wichita, KS.
QUESENBERRY, Warren, b. March 16, 1932 VA, d. Apr 15, 1988, hus of Elsie __, son of Delmer and Gracie Quesenberry, bur Dickerson Cem., Floyd Co., VA.
RAY, Helen, d. Jun 7, 1976, wife of John

Out of Md. Misc.

Berkeley Lallande, Sr., bur Rockville Cem., Washington, DC.
RICHARDSON, Marshall Lee, Sr. b. Nov 29, 1929 VA, d. Oct 20, 1991, hus of Nellie J. Sexton, son of Edward C. and Pearl H. Rush Richardson, bur Detrick Cem, Fort Valley, VA.
SCHAEFER, Charles J., d. Oct 10, 1990,, hus of Rebecca B. Davis, bur Chapel Hill Gdns. Cem., Zephyrhills, FL.
SCHLAG, William Albert, Sr. d. Jun 21, 1993, hus of Susan __, bur St. Mary's Cem., Alexandria, VA.
SCULLY, Leone Isabell, b. Aug 24, 1905 Canada, d. Nov 5, 1993, dau of John J. and Margaret Harrington Scully, bur White Haven Mem. Pk., Perinton, N.Y.
SHIPE, Robert Bernard "Bob", b. Sep 4, 1948 WV, d. Dec 5, 1993 El Toro fishing boat sinking, m. 20 Nov 1983 Teresa Marlene "Teri" Miller, son of Robert and Eulalia Cox Shipe, bur Peterstown, WV.
SHULTZ, Todd Martin, b. Aug 3, 1963 TN, d. Jun 11, 1993 Patuxent River NAS, MD., m. 1986 TN Michelle D.__, son of Walter D. and Geraldine Shultz, bur TN Valley Mem. Gdns, Powell, TN.
SIMPSON, George A., Sr. d. Feb 12, 1937, 1st hus of Mary Lillian Adams, bur Mt. Olivet Cem., Washington, D.C.
SIMPSON, Smith "Smitty", b. Jun 8, 1934 DC, d. Oct 30, 1993 FL, hus of Fay B. __, son of Eunice C. Simpson of SC, service at David C. Gross Funeral Home, St. Petersburg, FL.
SMITH, Ora Kate, b. Oct 14, 1904 GA, d. Apr 6, 1993, wife of William Law Starr, dau of William and Annie Ware Smith, bur DeLand Mem. Gdns, DeLand, FL.
STANDFORD, Alverta Marie, b. Mar 21, 1921, d. Jan 12, 1991, wife of Homer Clyde Malcolm, dau of Norman Elmer and Myrtle Wilgus Standford, bur Greenlawn Mem. Pk., New Castle, DE.
STARR, William Law, d. 1977, hus of Ora Kate Smith, bur DeLand Mem. Gdns, DeLand, FL.
TAYLOR, William, b. ca 1753 Ridge, Md. d. 1822 SC, hus of Lavinnah Clarke.

THOMPSON, Mary Jane, b. Nov 3, 1895, d. Oct 20, 1988, wife of Robert Wesley Oliver, dau of Geo. Clarence and Mary Agnes Wible Thompson, bur Oak Hill Cem., Fredericksburg, VA.
TINSMAN, Arthur Ernest, d. 1982, hus of Ruth Elizabeth Gheen, bur Culpepper Nat'l Cem., Culpepper, VA.
WATHEN, Myra Lynette "Aunt Bert", b. Sep 29, 1894, d. Mar 16, 1992, wife of William B. Hutchinson, dau of Oscar and Millie Mattingly Wathen, bur Mt. Olivet Cem, Washington, DC.
WATTS, John Gilliam, b. Apr 4, 1939 NC, d. May 9, 1993, son of David and Mary Murray Watts, bur United Meth. Cem., Shady Grove, Va.
WEASENFORTH, Lake Vernon, b. Aug 23, 1901 Grant Co. WV, d. Nov 10, 1992, hus of Pearl Mae Colfman, son of William H. and Alice B. Brown Weasenforth, bur Davis Cem., Ridgeville, WV.
WHITCOMB, Sara "Sally", 87, d. Sep 2, 1993 ME, m. (1st) James E. Knowlton, (2d) 25 Jul 1981 Edward G. Sylvester, dau of Arthur R. and Mabel Stowe Whitcomb, bur Hillside Cem., Sunset Deer Isle, Me.
WHITE, Frank Stewart, Jr. b. Feb 1, 1924 MA, d. Oct 5, 1993, hus of Ruby Jane Jolin, son of Frank S. and Gertrude Sandstrom White, bur Rockridge Cem., Sharon, MA.
WILDMAN, Mildred Elizabeth, b. Mar 24, 1897 DC, d. Oct 6, 1993, dau of Albert and Augusta Artis Wildman, inurnment Washington, DC.
WILLS, Nellie Evanola, b. Nov 15, 1896 VA, d. Jul 20, 1993, m. Dec 1914 Cecil Truette Sandidge, dau of Thomas Lafayette and Carrie Etta Bryant Wills, bur Spring Hill Cem., Lynchburg, VA.
YARBER, Arline Eugene, b. Dec 29, 1914 NC, d. Apr 12, 1989, bur Tanglewood Cem., Linville, NC.
YOUMANS, Rexford T., b. Oct 23, 1922 AL, d. Oct 25, 1993 FL, hus of Ida ___. Memorial services at Our Lady of Martyrs Ch., Sarasota, FL.

MARYLAND VETERANS CEMETERY
Rt. 301
Cheltenham, Pr. Georges Co., Md.

ALLEN, William Earnest "Bill", Sr. b. Jul 2, 1924 GA, d. Sep 17, 1993, m. 15 Dec 1956 GA, Geraldine Wilkes, son of Earnest Dewie and Ethel Leona Switzer Allen.

AMAN, Martha K., b. Jun 6, 1899 VA, d. Sep 2, 1993, wife of Homer Joseph Wilson, dau of William and Annie Carroll Aman.

BALDWIN, Mary Frances, b. Dec 5, 1925, d. Oct 24, 1992, wife of Andrew Thomas Davis, Jr., dau of Andrew Edward and Roberta Josephine Cassell Baldwin.

BARBARICH, Dr. Michael, d. 1978, hus of Emma I. __, 70, d. Nov 1, 1989 AR.

BLAS, Isabel, b. Jun 24, 1919 Guam, d. Nov 16, 1992, wife of Johnny C. Flores, dau of Jose Cruz and Ana Garcia Blas.

BOWMAN, Charles Henry, 37, b. DC, d. Oct 10, 1992, son of John Walter, Sr. and Mary Helen Butler Bowman.

BRADHAM, John Aaron, USN 1953-1957, b. Nov 28, 1934 DC, d. Nov 22, 1993, son of William and Bertha Lee Bradham.

BRAGG, Odus Clark, USA, b. Apr 20, 1923 WV, d. Mar 14, 1992, son of Clark J. and Mary Dove Taylor Bragg.

BRIXEY, Roy Joseph, b. Sep 2, 1918 IA, d. Sep 13, 1989, son of Harry and Dorothea Filmer Brixey.

BROBST, Thomas Hagan, Sr. b. Jul 11, 1931 Chi. IL, d. Oct 20, 1991, hus of Karen E. Gilbert, son of Merril F. and Esther Brunsell Brobst.

BROWN, William Barry, Jr. b. Jan 1, 1922, d. Sep 25, 1992, hus of Helen E. __, son of William B. and Lucy M. Christman Brown.

CALLAHAN, Kenneth Edward, b. Jul 11, 1928 Balto, d. Jul 3, 1992, son of Austin Belle Callahan and Mary Alban.

CARTER, John Henry "Johnny", b. Mar 6, 1921, d. Feb 4, 1992, hus of Mignonette Fenwick, son of Thomas Wm. and Mary Helen Short Carter.

CHESSER, Floyd Miller, USA WW II, b. Apr 29, 1926, d. Sep 11, 1993 DC, m. 13 May 1949 Edith Gatton, son of Richard and Agnes Miller Chesser.

CLARK, James Albert "Jimmy", Jr. b. Sep 25, 1949 MO, d. May 20, 1993 Balto, son of James and Florence C. Lawrence Clark.

CLEMENTS, Scott Franklin, b. Aug 7, 1929, d. Mar 3, 1993, m. 1956 Catherine Marie Pilkerton, son of Chas. Reginold and Lillian Mary Russell Clements.

COHEN, Amy Wyvel, b. May 10, 1898, d. Aug 29, 1991, wife of Walter E. Nair, dau of late William W. Cohen and Grace M. Baird.

COLLINS, Tyler Steven, infant, d. Nov 28, 1991, son of James Colbourn Jr. and Judith Ann Wise Collins; gson of Jas. C. and Shirley Harvey Collins; Walter and Joan Russell Wise.

COOMBS, Willard Lee, b. Jul 7, 1921, d. Mar 24, 1989, hus of Helen Marie __, son of Mr. and Mrs. Harry L. Coombs.

CRAIG, Donald Edward, b. Jan 4, 1936 PA, d. Jun 27, 1993, m. 5 Apr 1957 Kathryn Isabell McConnell, son of Donald and Alice Blacey Craig.

DAVIS, Andrew Thomas, Jr. b. Feb 17, 1927, d. Feb 10, 1991, hus of Mary Frances Baldwin, son of A. T. and Frances Grant Stone Davis.

DAVIS, William C., d. Apr 26, 1993, hus of Mary Duty. (Had 17 great grandchildren)

DELANGHE, Henri "Harry", 65, b. Belgium, d. Feb 24, 1993, hus of Mary Alma Martin.

DEL BROCCO, Louis, b. Jan 18, 1922 PA, d. Dec 24, 1990, hus of Gloria __, son of Joseph and Vincenza Del Brocco.

DENT, James Arther "Lee", b. Nov 8, 1924, d. Feb 8, 1993, hus of Mae __, son of Francis Bernard and Nanny Rebecca Tolbert Dent.

DiMICHELE, Emiddio, Jr. USA, b. Nov 22, 1927 NJ, d. Dec 22, 1993, hus of Marian L. __, son of Emiddio and Francisca Manfroni Di Michele.

DORAU, Heidemarie Erika, b. Mar 6, 1950 Berlin, GER, d. Mar 15, 1993, m. 20 Apr 1968 Joseph Gilbert Johnston, dau of Paul Gunter

and Erika Noack Dorau.
DORSEY, George William "Leck" b. Jul 20, 1933, d. Mar 11, 1991, hus of Mary Eva Knott, son of John and Harriet Anne Johnson Dorsey.
DUNN, Billy Carroll, b. Oct 22, 1934 AL, d. Apr 10, 1987, hus of Janet A. ___, son of Sanford and Voncile Dunn.
EASTER, Roy S. "Pop", 81, b. DC., d. Nov 14, 1993, m. (1st) Bernadette "Bern" ___, (2d) Louise Stanford.
ENNIS, Wilson E., Sr. b. Nov 18, 1932 DE, d. Aug 23, 1990, hus of Mary Evelyna ___, son of Mr. and Mrs. Dallas Ennis.
FARMER, Albert Mark, USA WW II, b. Jan 25, 1918 SC, d. Jan 16, 1992, son of Samuel and ALberta Alexander Farmer.
FRYE, George Leonard, Sr. b. Jul 18, 1915, d. Aug 27, 1992, hus of Mary Agnes Windell, son of James Henry and Leathy Ellen Schrob Frye.
GLEASON, Margaret Ann, b. Sep 28, 1923 MI, d. Jan 10, 1990, wife of George J. Kapanoske, dau of John O. and Mildred Mueller Gleason.
GREGG, Ruth Althea, b. May 12, 1921 NC, d. Nov 4, 1992 VA, m. 19 Jun 1943 Edward William Fitzwater, dau of William and Bessie Warren Gregg.
GRINDELL, Laurice Wayne, b. Jan 20, 1938 ME, d. Mar 20, 1993, m. 1983 Norma Jean Anderson, son of Earl C. and Vivian Alice Varney Grindell.
GUY, Margaret Ann, b. Oct 16, 1937, d. Apr 24, 1993, m. 14 Nov 1954 John Williams Withers, dau of late Everard Guy and Virginia Elizabeth Farrell Ryce.
HAMMETT, Mildred, b. Mar 1, 1901, d. Nov 5, 1991, wife of J. Brennan Norris, dau of Richard Thomas and Margaret A. Hammett.
HARDESTY, Levin Wilford, b. Jan 7, 1927, d. Sep 18, 1988, hus of Mary Ethel ___.
HAYDEN, Tilden Sebastine, USN WW II, b. Sep 25, 1895, d. Jul 5, 1991, hus of Mary Philene Wise, son of Edward Henry and Susan Ellen Thomas Hayden.
HEIMER, William James, USA WW II, b. Aug 23, 1920, d. Oct 3, 1992, hus of Frances Cecelia

Torcisi, son of Edgar and Blanche Ridenour Heimer.
HEJNA, Lydia Helen, b. Nov 11, 1908 OK, d. Feb 16, 1990, wife of Castos S. Michos, dau of Joseph and Mary Simunek Hejna.
HIGGS, Edward, d. Oct 21, 1990, hus of Dorothy __, son of Preston and Maude Burroughs Higgs.
HILL, Thomas Raymond, Jr. USA WW II, b. May 4, 1922, d. Apr 25, 1992 DC, hus of Mary Cecelia __, son of Raymond and Annie Burroughs Hill.
HOPKINS, Jesse Lawrence, b. Jul 10, 1903 MO, d. Feb 19, 1990, hus of Nina L. __, son of George Thomas and Lucinda Thomas Hopkins.
JAMESON, James Edelen, b. Jun 10, 1916, d. Aug 10, 1992, hus of Margaret __, son of John W. and Florence R. Chrismond Jameson.
JAMESON, Lawrence Sylvester, b. Mar 22, 1926, d. May 6, 1991, hus of Margaret G. Murphy, son of Rudie and Mary M. Jameson.
JEWETT, Monroe Allen "Jack", b. Sep 27, 1923 Richmond, VA, d. Jan 4, 1993, hus of Lillian "Totsy" __, son of Emmett Lee and Rosa Belle Crouch Jewett.
KAPANOSKE, George Joseph, Sr. b. Nov 17, 1918 MI, d. Jan 6, 1991 CO, hus of Margaret Ann Gleason, son of Joseph George and Barbara Lewandowski Kapanoske.
KELLEY, Joseph Edward, b. Sep 7, 1925 NY, d. Mar 25, 1988, hus of Doris E. Kelly, son of Joseph E. and Catherine Reagan Kelley.
KESKINEN, Elma Ethel, b. Mar 26, 1917 MA, d. Mar 20, 1991, wife of __ Phillips, dau of Laurie and Elma Keskinen.
KLING, Gladys Cordella "Liz", b. May 26, 1927 PA, d. Sep 22, 1990, wife of Wayne D. Hetrich, dau of Leroy Filmer and Grace Mildred Shingler Kling.
KNIGHT, Richard Dale "Rick", b. Jul 10, 1948 WV, d. Jun 10, 1991, hus of Joan Williams, son of Richard K. and Ann C. Knight.
KNIGHT, Richard Kyle, b. Jan 7, 1982, d. Oct 3, 1993, son of Richard D. Knight and Joan W. Williams, step-son of Stanley J. Williams, gson of James F., Sr. and Grace W.

Stafford of Cumberland, Md; Mr. and Mrs. Richard K. Knight of Milton, FL.
KNOX, Shirley Teresa, b. Nov 9, 1932 RI, d. Nov 3, 1992, m. 27 Feb 1952 Troy Eugene Gruber, Sr., dau of Col. Thomas and Patricia McCaughery Knox.
KOZLOWSKI, Edward Joseph, b. Sep 30, 1919, d. Oct 8, 1990, hus of Lois Davis, son of Joseph and Emily Dziemczseski Kozlowski.
LOVING, Harold Richard, Jr. b. Jul 31, 1947 DC, d. Oct 4, 1992, hus of Wyona B. Benthall, son of H. R. and Joyce Edna VanHeeton Loving.
MACIEJEWSKI, John M., USA WW II, b. Jul 29, 1903 PA, d. May 7, 1992, hus of Mary __.
MARJORAM, Gerard Arthur, USA WW II, b. Mar 31, 1906 Grasse, FR, d. Jan 25, 1991, hus of Maurine E. __, son of Edw. A. and Bridget O'Connell Marjoram.
MASON, Windale Jerome, b. Dec 15, 1968, d. May 4, 1992, son of John and Susie Curtis Mason, gson of Robt. and Susie Curtis; Violet Swales Robinson.
MATTHEWS, Helen Josephine, b. Oct 6, 1922 IL, d. Jul 27, 1989, wife of Sidney Hugh Matthews.
MAYS, Raymond Stanley "Ray", Sr. b. Jul 23, 1920 Balto, d. Feb 2, 1993, son of William T. Sr. and Amy Teresa Turner Mays.
MERCHANT, James Carlin, b. May 26, 1910 DC, d. Sep 17, 1989, son of James F. and Catherine Windsor Merchant.
MESSICK, Harry Gray, Jr. b. Oct 6, 1916, d. May 6, 1990, hus of Louise B.__, son of Harry G. and Frances Copsey Messick.
MILGRIM, Leonard, b. Feb 19, 1925, d. Jan 23, 1993, m. 23 Dec 1946 Frances Manuel, son of Benjamin and Trudy Largen Milgrim.
MORGAN, Mabel Ann, b. Jan 29, 1924, d. May 3, 1992, wife of George D. Lewellen, dau of John W. and Mrytle Russell Morgan.
O'KANE, Thomas Eugene, b. Apr 24, 1933, d. Sep 22, 1988, m. 28 Jan 1966 RI, Stella Agnes Stuckey, son of Joseph Hugh and Anna O'Kane.
OUTLAND, Joseph McLain, b. May 13, 1917 VA, d. Mar 23, 1987.

OWENS, John Milton "Billy", b. Feb 19, 1910, d. Aug 30, 1989, hus of Etta V. __, son of William Freeman and Anna Elizabeth Owens.
PARROTT, James Landers, d. Dec 16, 1987, hus of Mary Ethel Sydnor.
PEGRAM, Paul Revere, b. Aug 2, 1922 WV, d. Aug 31, 1991, hus of Jessie D __, son of John Whitney and Lona Ann Lyons Pegram.
PERRIGO, Elmer McKinley, b. Apr 14, 1896 VA, d. Mar 27, 1989, hus of Louise S. __, son of Elmer and Rose Ketcherson Perrigo.
REILLY, Robert Edward, b. May 8, 1920 PA, d. May 17, 1992, hus of Dolores C. __, son of Peter J. and Catherine Faith Reilly.
REYNOLDS, Christina, b. Mar 14, 1929 ENG, d. Feb 28, 1988, wife of __ Hufford, dau of Mr. and Mrs. Edward Reynolds.
REYNOLDS, Dean Windsor, b. Apr 2, 1919 NY, d. Nov 1, 1990, hus of Marjorie H. __, son of Millard R. and Bertha E. McClure Reynolds.
RIDGEWAY, George Kenneth, Sr. USN, b. Aug 28, 1927 DC, d. Sep 6, 1991, hus of Ellen L. __, son of Fenton Stanley and Johanna Sophia Ridgeway.
ROGERS, Thomas Henry, USN WW II, b. Mar 21, 1922, d. Sep 27, 1988, son of Charles Edw. and Mary Johnson Rogers.
ROMINGER, Elizabeth L. "Betty", b. Jun 20, 1909 NC, d. Feb 18, 1993, wife of Harry J. Caputo, dau of Lee and Alice Rominger.
SAMS, George Edward, USA WW II, b. Jun 14, 1914 WV, d. Dec 30, 1992, hus of Velma Louise Michael, son of Geo. E. and Myrtle Fields Sams.
SCRIBER, Mary Martha, b. Aug 11, 1921, d. Jan 27, 1989, wife of Francis Joseph Carter, Sr. dau of Hawkins and Kola Share Scriber.
SCRIBER, Robert Hawkins, b. Aug 1, 1906, d. Jan 3, 1992, hus of Alberta Tolson, son of Hawkins and Kola Barber Scriber.
SHIPE, Robert, USA WW II, b. Oct 31, 1922, d. Apr 7, 1992, hus of Eulalia Cox, son of John and Nellie Land Shipe.
SMALLWOOD, John Andrew "Smally", b. Mar 2, 1916, d. Aug 23, 1991, son of John Maurice

and Marie Elizabeth Hill Smallwood.
SMITH, Albert Hollingsworth, b. Apr 13, 1943 CT, d. Dec 19, 1988, hus of Lynn H. __, son of Francis H. and Alice Thiffault Smith.
SMITH, James Edgar, b. Dec 12, 1921 FL, d. Aug 30, 1991, hus of Alice Philemenia McDevitt, son of Jas. Edw. and Elizabeth Shields Smith.
SMITH, Jane Rebecca, b. May 6, 1901 DC, d. Mar 12, 1991, wife of Andrew Barbagallo, dau of Parker W. and Laura V. Satterfield Smith.
SPARSHOTT, Robert Emery "Sparky", USA Vietnam, b. Sep 30, 1946 DC, d. Jun 9, 1992, hus of Susan Frances Yeroshefsky, son of Anne Isabelle Adams Nivens and late Emery Robert Sparshott.
STILLEY, Calvin Linzy, b. Aug 27, 1925 DC, d. Apr 11, 1988, son of Sidney and Maddie Craddock Stilley.
STONE, Charles Benedict, Sr. USA, b. Jun 5, 1927, d. Dec 6, 1993, hus of Margaret L. Richardson, son of Benedict Neal, Sr. and Alice M. Evans Stone.
STUCKEY, Stella Agnes, b. Feb 9, 1922 PA, d. Jun 12, 1992, wife of Thomas Eugene O'Kane, dau of Joseph Martin and Nellie Washtella Dickey Stuckey.
SYDNOR, Mary Ethel, b. Dec 7, 1926 Phila,PA, d. Aug 5, 1993, m. MD 10 May 1947 James Landers Parrott, dau of Bradley George and Audrey Mary Jones Sydnor.
THORNBURG, Ruby Elizabeth, b. Jul 1, 1908 NC, d. Feb 15, 1989, wife of John D. Allgood, dau of George and Martha Davidson Thornburg.
TIPPETT, Samuel J., b. May 6, 1921, d. Jun 26, 1992, hus of Catherine L. Kidwell, son of Samuel B. and Ethel Smith Tippett.
VANCE, Lois Jane, b. Apr 3, 1924 KY, d. Jul 28, 1989, wife of Eugene Miller Nuss, dau of Melvin and Mabel Neubaure Vance.
VAN KIRK, Norman Eugene "Weaser", b. May 12, 1922 Balto, d. Feb 2, 1993, hus of Lola May Buckmaster, son of William Frederick and Alice Nevada Whipple Van Kirk.
VINCENT, Bernard John, b. Jun 16, 1933 Balto, d. Nov 12, 1991, son of Harry Vincent and

June Oliver.
WALKER, Solomon Brooks, Jr. WW II, b. Jun 14, 1907 CT, d. Mar 21, 1990, hus of Mamie Sue __, son of Mr. and Mrs. Solomon B. Walker.
WASHBURN, Gladys E., b. Apr 26, 1913 NC, d. Feb 18, 1992 FL.
WEBB, Eileen Mae, b. May 18, 1929 KY d. Sep 2, 1993, wife of William W. Webb, Sr., dau of Milford Hartwell and Florence Evans Webb.
WHEAT, Dr. Gordon A., b. Jan 23, 1920, d. Mar 4, 1991, hus of Betty Ann Fletcher, son of Mervin and Carrie Ironmonger Wheat.
WHITE, Clarence Albert, Jr. b. Jan 6, 1919, d. Sep 7, 1991, hus of Elizabeth I. Gwynn, son of Clarence A. and Margaret Elizabeth White.
WILSON, Homer Joseph, TEC 4 USA WW II, b. May 16, 1905 WV, d. Mar 14, 1993, m. 1946 Martha Kaman, son of Eugene and Elizabeth Ball Wilson.
WINDELL, Mary Agnes, d. Jan 20, 1985 AL, m. 10 Mar 1972 VA, George Leonard Frye.
WISE, Mary Philene, b. Dec 12, 1901, d. Sep 9, 1988, wife of Tilden S. Hayden, dau of George and Cora Lee Mordic Wise.
WITHERS, John William, b. Jan 4, 1930 DC, d. Apr 20, 1991, hus of Margaret Anne Ryce, son of William Parker and Leona Belle Withers.
WITHERS, Leona Belle, b. Apr 2, 1899 IN, d. Feb 16, 1989, wife of William Parker Withers.
WOLFRAM, Andrew, Jr. b. Jul 12, 1909 Hurnberg, GER, d. Sep 11, 1989, hus of Hilda B. __, son of Andrew and Josephine Dorfman Wolfram.
WOOD, Bernice Elizabeth, b. Feb 21, 1921, d. Feb 27, 1991, wife of __ Moore, dau of William Howard and Effie Wood.
WOOD, Frank E., USN WW II, b. Aug 15, 1922 VA, d. Jul 22, 1993, m. 5 June 1961 Katherine London Mock, son of James and Florence Pullen Wood.
WRIGHT, George Littleton, Jr. b. Nov 7, 1923 VA, d. Dec 2, 1991, son of George L. and Katie Edmonia Wright.

GARRISON FOREST VETERANS CEMETERY
Owings Mills, Baltimore Co., Md.

TURNER, Francis Legrant, USA WW II, b. May 30, 1916, d. Oct 26, 1991, hus of Blanche Patricia ___, son of John Henry and Mary Eliza Turner.

WOOD, Martha E., b. Jul 4, 1914, d. Apr 16, 1992 Balto, wife of John Francis Bailey, Sr. dau of Henry A. and Martha L. Graves Wood.

CIVIL WAR DEATHS
of U. S. 7th Regiment Colored Troops
from St. Mary's County

BRISCOE, Pvt. George W., d. Oct 18, 1866.
BROWN, Pvt. Philip, d. Jul 27, 1864 Jax., FL.
BUTLER, Pvt. Peter, 20, d. of wounds rec'd Nov 15, 1864.
CURTIS, Pvt. George, 20, d. Sep 18, 1866.
EDGERTON, Pvt. Thomas, 25, d. Jan 17, 1864 at Benedict, MD.
ELGIN, Pvt. Frederick, 18, d. Sep 6, 1864, Jax., FL.
ENNELS, Pvt. Columbus, d. Sep 10, 1866, Indianola, TX.
HARRIS, Pvt. James, d. Feb 3, 1864.
HENSON, Pvt. Noble H., 22, d. aboard hospital ship "Thomas Powell", Feb 8, 1865.
SOTHORAN, Pvt. James, 25, d. Sep 12, 1864, Bermuda Hundred, VA.
TAYLOR, Pvt. William H., 30, d. Jul 1, 1864, Beaufort, SC.

ARLINGTON NATIONAL CEMETERY
Arlington, Virginia

ALLEN, Kathryn Adala, b. Feb 7, 1935, d. Nov 21, 1989, wife of Frayne C. Lydick, USAF, dau of late Robert Allen and Catherine Dorsey Allen Stienke.

AQUINO, Robert Arquica, USN, b. Sep 29, 1952, d. Oct 16, 1992, hus of Mia Baylon, son of David Aquino of Lexington Pk., Md. and Flordlige Arquica Aquino of Philp. Islands.

BARRY, Lynn Forbes, CMDR USN Ret., b. Jul 12, 1919 DC, d. Sep 28, 1993, m. 27 Dec 1952 Betty Jean Gauger, son of Gavin and Elizabeth Forbes Barry. Inurnment Sep 30, 1993.

BATEMAN, Mildred, b. Apr 27, 1923, d. Jul 24, 1993, m. 17 May 1974 Cedric Boss Snyder, dau of Robert and Louise Buchanan Bateman. Committal service.

BAXTER, Thurston H., COL USAF Ret., b. May 12, 1905 IL, d. Oct 22, 1988, hus of Mina "Pat" O'Bryan, son of Leslie Ernest and Ida Heiderschied Baxter.

BEERS, Lottie Marie, 61, d. Nov 7, 1993, wife of Albert Ross Bochert, Sr., dau of James and Catherine Beers.

BERG, Leonard H. "Pat", USN, 72, b. MN, d. Mar 24, 1992, m. (1st) Jean Ruth __, (d. Nov 16, 1981), (2d) E. Jane __, son of Oscar Wilhelm and Elizabeth Kosel Berg.

BERNAZZANI, Ralph Anthony, USN, b. Sep 6, 1919 MA, d. Apr 11, 1989, son of Antonio and Mabel Lewis Bernazzani.

BOAZ, Monroe Thomas, Jr. USN, b. Jul 14, 1953 TX, d. May 14, 1988, hus of Gail Evans, son of Monroe T. and Jacqueline Hedglin Boaz, pat gson of Mr. and Mrs. Lee Gordon; mat gson of Mr. and Mrs. Harry Hedglin.

BRAUN, John Edward, "J.B.", USN, b. Oct 14, 1936 TX, d. Oct 18, 1991, m. Jun 1988, Anne Lorraine Cuozzo, son of Julius and Minnie Tracy Braun.

BROCKHOFF, Rudolph Edward, b. Aug 3, 1926 OH, d. Mar 21, 1990, hus of Ruby P. Staten, son of Frank and Anna Loesing Brockhoff.

BUCK, David Allen, AT1 USN, b. Nov 3, 1957 PA, d. Jan 10, 1992, m. May 1990 Janice Lohwater, son of James R. Sr. and Bruna Cinelli Buck.
BUSTARD, Rodger Lee, USA, b. Jun 23, 1970 CA, d. Nov 4, 1991 LA, son of John E. and Karen L. Bustard.
CANDELA, Pompeo Benjamin, M.D., d. Jan 5, 1966, m. 3 Oct 1930 Gwendolen Catherine Cormack.
CARROLL, William Joseph, Jr., LCDR USN Ret. b. Jul 11, 1947 DC, d. Sep 30, 1993, m. 9 Jun 1973 Deborah Ruth Anderson, son of Gerald J. and Dorothy Creel Carroll.
CORMACK, Gwendolen Catherine, b. Jan 24, 1903 Yukon, Can., d. March 25, 1992, wife of Dr. Pompeo Benjamin Candela, dau of John and Agnes Spears Cormack.
COYKENDALL, Frederick Walter, LCOL USA, b. Aug 23, 1916 NY, d. May 7, 1992, m. 14 May 1947 Belgium, Evonne Palmans, son of Fred and Sarah Williams Coykendall.
DAVIS, Lee Edward, USN, b. Sep 23, 1941 MA, d. Mar 31 1992, m. 1963 FL Terry L. Pepper, son of Warren L. and Ethel A. Fitzgerald Davis.
DEARSTINE, Bernard J., Sr., d. Dec 14, 1955, m. DC 20 Feb 1920 Eva May Lilley.
DORSEY, Catherine Regina, b. Dec 16, 1919, d. May 19, 1991, wife of Oscar Steinke, Jr., dau of Peter Alfonso and Mary Elizabeth Langley Dorsey.
DOVE, Mary, d. May 28, 1971, wife of __ Bragg.
FABANS, Donald Richard, b. Jul 27, 1936 IL, d. Oct 21, 1988, hus of Sara E. __, son of Sidney and Jane T. Fabans.
FREY, Leonard, b. Mar 11, 1922 DC, d. Jun 30, 1991, son of Harlen and Adelaide Murray Frey.
FURLONG, Myra, CAPT. USA, b. May 11, 1901 N.S., Can, d. Mar 12, 1992, wife of Col. Henry R. Sanford, dau of Edward and Currie Furlong.
GIBSON, Roy Edgar III, USN, b. Apr 22, 1941 FL, d. Apr 3, 1989, hus of Deborah C. Kressmann, son of Roy E. and Virginia Armour Gibson.
GILBERT, John T., MAJ USAF, 67, d. Oct 7, 1992, 2d hus of Helen Blume.
GUETHLEIN, George John, USN Ret., b. Mar 30,

1924 OH, d. Dec 22, 1992 DC, m. 14 Feb 1953
Edna Lucille Fletcher, son of George and
Louise Mueller Guethlein.
HAMEL, Marie Josephine, b. Apr 28, 1924, d.
Nov 3, 1992 at Charlotte Hall Vet. Home, Md.,
wife of Morris John Tretick, dau of Joseph
and May Hamel.
HEMMER, George Arthur "Mike", SGT USAF, b. Nov
10, 1924 MA, d. Jun 29, 1991, son of George
M. and Marguerite Hemmer.
HOWLAND, Jack Wayne, 68, d. Aug 26, 1991, hus
of Mary Ann ___.
INGRAM, Isom Irvin, LCMDR USN, b. Apr 6, 1940
AL, d. Jul 17, 1993, m. 3 May 1963 Terryl
Anne Harper, son of Col. Fortney Hurst, Sr.
and Isabelle Huffman Ingram.
JACOB, John Willie, USA WW II, b. Jan 3, 1917
GA, d. Feb 10, 1991, son of Willie and A-
manda Appling Jacob.
JAMES, Brian Joseph, MAJ USMC, b. Aug 14,
1957 Balto, d. Jul 22, 1992, m. 20 Feb 1982
FL, Deanna Lynn Batton, son of Frederick and
Aline Potruzski James.
JOHNSON, Carol, 91, b. DC, d. Apr 19, 1991,
wife of Joseph F. Schaeffer, dau of Alfred
and Lula Yost Johnson.
JOHNSTONE, Robert Bernard, CMDR USN, b. Dec
28, 1922 NY, d. Nov 10, 1993, m. 15 Feb 1946
Ester Louise Bowman, son of Thomas and Ethel
Stillwell Johnstone.
JONES, Jamie, USN, d. Jan 24, 1984, m. 1940
Inez Annette Purdie.
JONES, William Joseph, USA WW II, b. Dec 14,
1921 DC, d. Jun 21, 1991, hus of Mary Chris-
tine ___, son of Edward Herbert and Carrie
Lancaster Jones.
KARR, Verlin R. "Dan", b. Jan 21, 1916 WV, d.
Apr 2, 1991 FL, hus of Regina J. ___, son of
Daniel J. and Ernestine Moore Karr.
KEATING, Elizabeth Gladys, b. Sep 3, 1903
Eng., d. Jul 14, 1989, wife of V. Consul
Wallace Eugene Moeisner, dau of William and
Catherine E. Keating.
KING, Leo Richard, USN, b. Aug 4, 1925 Balto,
d. Jun 12, 1991, hus of Constance V. Sowers-

by, son of Leo Peter and Dorothy Shawen King.
LEE, Frank Alex, Jr., USN, b. Dec 28, 1921 MS, d. Jul 13, 1989, m. 1948 Emma Jane Medford.
LeFAIVRE, Edward Norris, COL USMC Ret., b. Oct 11, 1920 Balto, d. Jun 28, 1992, hus of Ann Augsburger, son of John and Bertha Lacey Le Faivre.
LERETTE, Earle Livingstone, Sr., COL USA Ret., b. Sep 28, 1913 MA, d. Oct 6, 1993, m. Sep 1940 Panama CZ Mary E. Corbin, son of William P. and Elizabeth M. Livingstone Lerette.
LILLEY, Eva May, b. Feb 14, 1898, d. May 4, 1992, wife of Bernard J. Dearstine, dau of Charles H. and Alverta Beall Lilley.
MANN, Harry, b. Oct 1, 1915 NY, d. Jan 20, 1992, hus of Melba S. __, son of Harry and Georgette Winterberger Mann.
MATTINGLY, Robert A., Jr. d. 1966, m. 1943 Ft. Knox, KY, Thelma Loretta Welty.
McKENNA, Bertha Mary, b. Jun 17, 1904 NY, d. Jun 17, 1988, wife of Harold L. McKenna.
MEDFORD, Emma Jane, b. Oct 1, 1923 MD, d. Jan 23, 1992, wife of Frank Alex Lee, Jr., dau of William Elwood and Helen Porter Medford.
MERRITT, Everett L., USMC, 78, b. PA, d. Jan 7, 1991, hus of Elaine __, son of Harry and Agnes Merritt.
MILLER, Henry Louis, Sr. RADM USN, b. Jul 18, 1912 AK, d. Jan 25, 1993, m. 17 May 1939 CA, Lucille Dean of AL, son of Frank and Mary Miller.
MILLER, Lillian 'Louise', b. Jun 24, 1920 DC, d. Feb 13, 1992 DC, m. 1940 Thomas Frederick Ewell, LCol. USAF, dau of Thomas Allen and Naomi Watson Miller.
MILLS, Marcia, b. Feb 12, 1931 NY, d. Mar 26, 1988, m. 1949 Roger M. Boh, Jr., USN, dau of George A. and Mary Moser Mills.
MOORE, Ralph Layton, Jr., CMDR USN Ret., b. Nov 2, 1921 PA, d. May 16, 1988, hus of Eleanor Reigle, son of Ralph L. and Geneva Van Dyke Moore.
MURRAY, Catherine Virginia, 100, b. Aug 20, 1892, d. Sep 25, 1992, m. (1st) William Harrison Moore, (2d) Thomas Watson Dixon, dau

of Edward and Virginia Carrico Murray.
NAGLE, Gerald John, d. Sep 9, 1955, hus of E. Pauline Pilkerton.
PENDRIS, Mary Ann, b. April 15, 1913 PA, d. Apr 14, 1988, m. 11 May 1947 DC, Taylor Lemkuhl, Sr., dau of Michael and Techla Choma Pendris.
PILKERTON, E. Pauline, b. Mar 24, 1912, d. Mar 19, 1993, wife of Gerald John Nagle, dau of Zachariah and Catherine Bowles Pilkerton.
PURDIE, Inez Annette, b. Jan 17, 1916 LA, d. Apr 17, 1992, wife of Jamie Jones, dau of Joseph and Delia Robinson Purdie.
SHAW, Robert John, USN, b. Jun 1, 1955 MO, d. Nov 19, 1991, hus of Donna Jean Bennett, son of Frederick and Lois Lapthorne Shaw.
SHEWACK, Elizabeth, b. Jul 6, 1909, d. May 28, 1988, wife of Stephen Shewack.
SPRANGER, David, USMC, b. Apr 3, 1938, d. Jan 25, 1989, m. 1966 Margaret "Peggy" __, son of Henry H. and Grace Lawrence Spranger.
STELPFLUG, Walter S., USAF, d. Mar 21, 1987, hus of Madeline Wilkinson.
STRICKLAND, Harold T., USAF, d. Jul 20, 1993 MS, hus of Mary A. __.
SVEC, Willis William "Bill", SGT USAF, b. Feb 14, 1930 Balto, d. Dec 5, 1991, hus of Rita M. __, son of George and Maud Leverton Svec.
TRETICK, Morris John, d. Jul 1966, hus of Marie Josephine Hamel.
WALLING, Irie Francis, USAF and USN WWII Vet., b. May 9, 1927 LA, d. Jun 7, 1988, hus of Betty Garland, son of Ira Francis and Mary Swinney Walling.
WELTY, Thelma Loretta, b. Oct 27, 1922 DC, d. Jul 15, 1992, wife of Robert A. Mattingly, Jr., dau of George Henry and Lottie Mae Adams Welty.
WILKINSON, Madeline, b. Aug 11, 1923, d. Feb 3, 1992, m. 1952 Walter S. Stelpflug, dau of Thos. Spencer and Clara Estelle Bradburn Wilkinson.
WILLIAMSON, Hetty Kathleen, USN, b. Aug 4, 1942 MI, d. Jun 6, 1988, m. (1st) __ Olsen, (2d) __ Schultheis, dau of Allen Williamson

and Margaret Dora Williamson Baskette.

FLORIDA NATIONAL CEMETERY
Bushnell, Sumter Co., Florida

ZAGORAC, Albert Charles, b. Dec 11, 1937 MO, d. Mar 8, 1993 DC, m. 1977 Cynthia Yvonne Wise, son of Joseph and Mary Ruth Novich Zagorac.

SURNAME INDEX

Note: Names followed by a ? are possible maiden names or possible previous married names.

ABELL, 1 9 18 19 23 26 30 36 47
65 103 104 106 108-111 113
120 150 160 167 179 185 199
200-202 204 205 213 215 216
218 221 224 230 253 257 265
289 299 309 333 361 369 374
ABELL?, 17 24-26 39 71 72 104-
107 110 161 162 165 184 188
201 216 229 230 268 311 373
ABLETT, 361 363
ADAM, 333
ADAMS, 69 73 78 81 108 162
185-187 191 194 197 199 201
202 233 332 333 343 381 387
ADAMS?, 31 109 159 187 194 228
278 337 343 369 376 395 405
ADKINS, 353
AIREY?, 69
ALBAN, 389
ALBAUGH, 385
ALBRIGHT, 191
ALDERTON?, 384
ALDRIDGE, 386
ALDRIGE, 381
ALEXANDER, 47
ALEXANDER?, 391
ALICINO?, 372
ALLAN?, 310
ALLEN, 361 389 401
ALLEN?, 21 70 401
ALLGOOD, 65 395
ALLRED, 309
ALLWINE, 191
ALMOND?, 372
ALSHIRE, 22
ALTIC?, 376
ALVEY, 1 9 22 69 81 113 114 202
206 233 234 373
AMAN, 389
AMERICA?, 15
AMMANN, 10
ANDERSON, 9 30 75 95 130 234
253 255 256 323 391 402
ANDERSON?, 63 278
ANGEL?, 337
ANGERAME, 197
ANGEVINE, 202
ANGLE, 197
ANGLE?, 197
ANTHONY, 202 324
ANTONOVITCH, 73
APPLING?, 403

AQUINO, 401
ARCHER, 97
ARMOUR?, 402
ARMSTRONG, 114 281
ARMSTRONG?, 146 340
ARMSWORTHY, 167 202 289 294 337
ARMSWORTHY?, 69
ARN, 309 310
ARNDT, 253
ARNOLD, 114
ARQUICA?, 401
ARTES?, 332
ARTIS, 317
ARTIS?, 388
ASCHOM, 334
ASHLEY, 371 373
ASHTON?, 89 157
ATKINSON?, 173
ATLAS, 277
ATTAWAY, 299
ATTAWAY?, 31
AUD, 42 78 163 185 189 202 211 287 333
AUD?, 78 111 163 195
AUGSBURGER, 404
AWKWARD, 75
AYOTTE?, 222
BABLE, 381
BACON, 218
BADALAMENTI, 63
BADEN, 289 371
BADEN?, 191
BADONIEC, 11
BAECHTOLD, 65
BAGLY?, 302
BAHL, 28
BAILEY, 28 97 114-117 121 123 132 136 152 154 179 234 277 278 333 353 397
BAILEY?, 30 45 70 140 375
BAIR, 323
BAIRD, 32 390

BAKER, 9 14 81 87 116 333 371 373
BAKER?, 21 38 359
BALDWIN, 311 323 389 390
BALDWIN?, 194
BALIUS, 9 10
BALL, 95 99 101 323 329
BALL?, 96 170 396
BALLARD, 167
BALSBAUGH, 41
BALTA, 197
BAME?, 20
BANAGAN, 114 116 117 128
BANKINS, 202 209
BANKS, 10 40
BANKS?, 183
BANNISTER, 9 323
BANOVAK?, 159
BARBAGALLO, 195 196 363 395
BARBARICH, 389
BARBAS?, 35
BARBER, 10 13 19 69 75 81 86 96 202 264 305 323
BARBER?, 23 48 69 76 133 215 256 394
BARBRA, 363
BARLEY, 167 172
BARLOWE, 361
BARNARD, 69
BARNARD?, 177
BARNES, 10 32 47 65 75 77 95 104 111 112 117 120 157 159 167 168 202 228 234 273 277 278 281 282 289 305 323 333 340 351
BARNES?, 15 32 95 104 226 306 307 329 377
BARNHART, 3 299
BARNS, 47 104 290
BARON, 337
BARONIAK, 283 285 309
BARRETO, 202
BARRETT, 29

BARRETT?, 110
BARRON, 353
BARRY, 139 144 352 401
BARTELMES, 363
BARTO, 160
BARTOL, 161
BARTZ, 357
BASKETTE, 406
BASS?, 28 307 368
BASSFORD, 202 203 221
BASSFORD?, 43
BAST, 77
BASTIAN?, 64
BATEMAN, 234 401
BATES, 290
BATTON, 403
BAULT, 75
BAUMGARTNER, 222
BAVELY?, 79
BAXTER, 203 401
BAXTER?, 278
BAYLESS, 197
BAYLEY?, 148
BAYLON, 401
BEACH?, 175
BEAL, 69 95 290 293
BEALE, 341
BEALL, 10
BEALL?, 56 404
BEAN, 10 104 168 170 185 188 203 277 286 287 290 293 309 317 333 338 345 371
BEAN?, 29 132 185 189 293 310
BEANDER, 203
BEATTY, 97
BEAUREGARD, 75
BEAVER?, 353
BEAVERS, 195 361 381
BECK, 81
BECKER, 27 369
BECKERT, 75 78
BEECHAM, 47
BEERS, 401

BEIKE, 381
BEITZEL, 117
BEITZELL, 117 135 142
BEITZELL?, 128
BELAKAVITCH?, 163
BELL, 195 203 204 277 333 338 357 375 382
BELL?, 15 63 277 329
BELLINI, 203
BELT, 10
BENDER?, 73
BENETT, 356
BENJAMIN, 61 323
BENNETT, 10 29 98 168 176 221 235 269 299 305 307 317 323 333 342 405
BENNETT?, 177 342
BENTHALL, 393
BENTZ, 10 168
BENTZ?, 170
BERG, 401
BERGER?, 2
BERNAZZANI, 401
BERRY, 21 277 282 323 324
BERRY?, 45 286
BERTRAND, 203
BEST?, 43
BEVAN, 104
BIEBER?, 25
BIGELOW, 371
BILLINGSLEY, 47 334
BIONDI, 65
BIRCH, 283 285 316 317 334
BIRD?, 43
BIRTWISTLE, 81
BISCHOP, 235
BISCOE, 10 62 64 65 75 96 185 191 192 269 290 299 305 306 309 318 324
BISCOE?, 76 96 311 323 342
BISHOP, 65 371
BISHOP?, 352
BITTINGER?, 67

BLACEY?, 390
BLACK?, 329
BLACKISTON, 104 203
BLACKISTONE, 3 5 21 63 159 235
BLACKISTONE?, 5
BLACKSTONE, 290
BLACKWELL, 39 95 185 190-192 194 324 352
BLACKWELL?, 189
BLAGOJEVICH, 347
BLAIR, 3 116-118 145 179
BLAIR?, 188 381
BLAKE?, 97
BLAKISTONE, 3 4
BLAND, 299
BLANFORD, 361
BLANK, 253
BLANK?, 353
BLANKENSHIP, 10 11 353
BLAS, 389
BLED, 47
BLUME, 402
BOAZ, 401
BOCHERT, 401
BOCKSKO, 159
BOGIE, 104 346
BOGIE?, 346
BOH, 404
BOHANAN, 283 290 291 320
BOHANNAN?, 3 285
BOHANNON?, 197
BOHLE, 253 353
BOHNKE, 325
BOIS, 4
BOLLING, 118
BOLT, 11
BOLT?, 95 96
BOLTS, 305
BOND, 11 47 81 86 95 99 103 168 169 175 235 277 282 291
BOND?, 344
BONDS, 11 41
BONN, 235
BOOTH?, 176
BORG, 64
BORTNER, 358
BOSTWICK, 118
BOSWELL, 353
BOTKIN?, 383
BOULDING, 369
BOULTON?, 106
BOUND?, 355
BOWEN, 357 371
BOWEN?, 371 376 377
BOWERS?, 14
BOWES, 185
BOWES?, 363
BOWIE, 195 196 371
BOWIE?, 35
BOWLES, 11 27 28 63 69 82 104 106 118 136 159 199 203 213 228 230 235 251 253 255 256 259 334 369 376 381
BOWLES?, 9 22 216 253 257 280 318 319 356 405
BOWLING, 4 11 118 371
BOWMAN, 104 122 144 277 334 389 403
BOYD, 47 65 67 169 254 277
BOYER, 81
BOYLE, 16
BOYLE?, 16
BOZZIE, 324
BRADBURN, 65 185 186 203 235 240 283
BRADBURN?, 160 164 170 405
BRADBURY, 283
BRADDOCK, 291
BRADHAM, 389
BRADUNAS, 375
BRADY, 1 169 173 367
BRADY?, 287 288
BRAGG, 160 389 402
BRAHLER, 381
BRAMAKULAM, 26

BRAMMER?, 355
BRANDEL, 359
BRANNOCK, 309
BRANSON, 11 235
BRAUN, 169 401
BRAUN?, 171
BRAWLEY, 203
BRAXTON, 24
BRAXTON?, 24 62
BRAY, 355
BRAZEAU, 179
BREASMEN, 348
BREAU, 106
BRECKENRIDGE?, 26
BREEDEN, 87
BREHAN, 325
BRENNER, 324
BREWER, 59 203 351
BRICK, 203 210 381
BRIDGES, 11
BRIDGETT, 11 36 253 260
BRIELL, 358
BRIGHTWELL?, 257
BRILL, 169
BRINAN, 333
BRINAN?, 333
BRINDLE, 11
BRISCOE, 11 37 41 47 48 75 169 177 178 186 188 267 269 273 275 278 305 306 334 335 348 399
BRISCOE?, 42 76 177
BRISLIN?, 96
BRITTON?, 21
BRIXEY, 389
BROBST, 389
BROCKHOFF, 401
BROME, 291
BROMLEY, 328
BROOKBAND?, 98
BROOKBANK, 48 235
BROOKE, 235 334
BROOKS, 11 104 204 214 254

BROOKS (cont.)
 273 326
BROOKS?, 33 34
BROTHERTON, 29
BROWN, 11 12 33 36 42 62 63 65
 70 118 132 137 143 159-161
 169 178 183 186 195 200 204
 215 235 269 271 291 335 354
 362 384 389 399
BROWN?, 19 36 54 117 160 162
 284 347 388
BRUBACHER, 93 299 301 356
BRUBACHER?, 93
BRUFF, 4
BRUMBAUGH, 12 204
BRUMBAUGH?, 227
BRUNSELL?, 389
BRUSH, 381
BRYAN, 191 305
BRYANT, 4 5 335 367
BRYANT?, 5 336 353 388
BRYNOR?, 16
BUBNIAK?, 79
BUCHANAN?, 401
BUCHHOLZ, 368
BUCK, 402
BUCKLER, 9 12 16 39 95-97 119
 208 235 243 257 277 278 324
 335 351 353 354 361
BUCKLER?, 207 262 340
BUCKMASTER, 81 82 395
BULLARD, 48
BULLER, 313
BULLOCK, 179 180
BULLOCK?, 180
BUNCH, 191 381
BUNDICK?, 6
BURCH, 4 48 119 120 153 162
 204 211 220 254 267 277 278
 331 353 363 373
BURCH?, 32 33 183 220 254 255
 351 352 362 375
BURDETT?, 376

BURGESS, 104
BURGESS?, 193
BURKE, 195 204 254 371
BURKETT, 75
BURKS, 218
BURNS, 168 169
BURNS?, 170
BURNSIDE, 35
BURR, 82
BURRICK, 21
BURRIS, 12 17
BURROUGHS, 1 12 48 49 57 95
    120 123 204 235 236 254 257
    267 268 291 335 340 354 361
BURROUGHS?, 52 57 256 361
    362 392
BURSEY, 381
BURTON, 324 361
BUSH, 12 16 40 49 65 236 273
BUSH?, 12 55 181 374
BUSHELL, 218 354 357
BUSSLER, 179 182 186 354 381
BUSSLER?, 254
BUSTARD, 402
BUTLER, 2 12 19 39 49 105 117
    120 159 179 197 204 236 278
    279 306 324 399
BUTLER?, 17 36 72 124 144 185
    204 254 266 389
BUYS, 371
BUYS?, 373
BYRD, 12
BYRNE, 372 376
BYRUM, 354
CACCIVIO, 12
CAGNEY, 159 160
CALDWELL, 75 76
CALLAHAN, 389
CALLIER, 307
CALLIHAM, 76
CALLIS, 82
CALVARY?, 186
CALVERT, 61

CALVIER, 306
CAMALIER, 13 159 335
CAMALIER?, 163
CAMERON, 7 151 164 204 291
    309 382
CAMPBELL, 76 273 374 382 383
CAMPBELL?, 27
CAMPER, 335
CANDELA, 402
CANNOLES?, 194
CANNON?, 301 303
CANTER, 13 354 357
CANTER?, 354
CAPLE, 337
CAPPS, 32
CAPUTO, 394
CAREERRY, 159
CAREY, 13 25 65
CARGILL, 262
CARPENTER, 49 236
CARPENTER?, 51
CARR, 354
CARRICO?, 353 405
CARRINGTON, 386
CARROLL, 22 77 169 197 236
    283 288 291 292 306 307 335
    402
CARROLL?, 6 340 389
CARSKADON?, 302
CARSON, 98 324
CARSON?, 64 309
CARTAGENA, 78
CARTAGENA?, 78
CARTER, 13 16 28 31 38 63 64
    120 274 389 394
CARTER?, 34 120 154
CARTWRIGHT, 35
CARVER, 381
CARY, 168 170
CASAMASSIMA, 372
CASEY, 291
CASH?, 372
CASIMANO, 186 188

CASSELL?, 389
CASTER, 269
CATON, 382
CATTERON?, 355
CAVANAUGH, 335 382
CAVE?, 354
CAWOOD, 49 62 254 291 324
CAWOOD?, 339 384
CAYWOOD, 49
CAYWOOD?, 354
CECIL, 69 186 189 204 291
CECIL?, 69
CHAFFINS, 210
CHAKALES, 13
CHALISSERY, 26
CHAMBERS, 5 186 324
CHAMNESS, 170
CHAN, 311
CHANCE, 205
CHANDLER, 205
CHANEY?, 301
CHAPIN, 329
CHAPMAN, 291 311
CHAPMAN?, 45
CHASE, 13 76 179 278 306
CHAUNG, 13
CHERRY, 65
CHESELDINE, 4 59 115 117 120 121 127 144 145 154 161 236 263
CHESELDINE?, 37 114-116
CHESLDINE, 328
CHESLEY, 1 49 121 328
CHESLEY?, 306
CHESSER, 61 101 163 390
CHESSER?, 36 191
CHING, 49 351
CHING?, 170 373
CHISLEY, 96
CHOMA?, 405
CHOPORIS, 179 180
CHRISMOND?, 392
CHRISTMAN?, 389

413

CHRISTMAS?, 218
CHUNN?, 243
CINELLI?, 402
CISSELL, 291
CLAGETT, 49 382
CLAPP, 312
CLARK, 28 49 170 288 325 390
CLARK?, 64
CLARKE, 4 13 14 121 196 205-207 212 213 222 236 309 325 332 335 382 387
CLARKE?, 185 215 219 222 285 287 311 343
CLARKY, 49
CLATTERBUCK, 369
CLEMENTS, 41 61 159 160 164 170 206 221 335 382 390
CLEMENTS?, 41
CLEO?, 40
CLIFTON, 372
CLINE, 14
CLINTON, 306 361
CLYBURN, 206
COAD, 121
COADE, 121
COATES, 78 185 236
COATES?, 185 279 311
COATS, 236
COCCIA, 283
COCIMANO, 283
CODY, 382
COE, 354 355
COFFEE, 382
COFFMAN, 160 325 357 382
COFFMAN?, 66
COHEN, 335 390
COLBERT, 323
COLE, 104 236
COLEMAN, 14
COLEMAN?, 75
COLES, 14
COLFMAN, 388
COLLEARY, 69

COLLINS, 14 76 121 122 254 335 390
COLLINS?, 115 120
COLLISON, 206 335
COLONNA, 1
COLTON, 208 254 299
COMBS, 10 13 14 34 69 70 72 82 91 104 105 108 109 111 160 170 186 191 199 206 228 236 287 291 292 320 335 336 382
COMBS?, 14 23 91 107 189 216 320 321 364 373
COMPTON, 335 348
COMUNTZIS?, 180
CONCKLIN?, 311
CONNEE, 372
CONNELLY, 97 160 162 170 174 299 300 336 382
CONNELLY?, 163 170 382
CONNER?, 358
CONNEVEY?, 284
CONROY?, 31
CONSTANTINIDES, 14
CONSTDANT?, 373
CONWAY?, 306 364
COOK, 14 76 206 212 309
COOK?, 10 212 270
COOKE, 50
COOKE?, 375
COOKSEY, 170 285
COOKSIE, 372
COOLEY, 299
COOMBS, 70 180 336 390
COOMBS?, 12 183
COONEY?, 165
COOPER, 46 54 122 236 254 259 283 291 292 369
COOPER?, 6 25 109 162
COPPAGE, 191 381
COPPINS, 345
COPSEY, 13 14 81 105 206 211 231 236 254 262 354
COPSEY?, 16 205 212 393

CORBIN, 384 404
CORBIN?, 306
CORDER?, 2 309
CORMACK, 402
CORNTHWAITE, 97
COSGROVE, 14
COSTELLA?, 385
COSTELLO, 14
COSTEN, 351
COULTER?, 286
COUNCELL?, 43 157
COUNTESS, 14 36
COUNTISS, 122 254
COUNTISS?, 9 41 151 267 280
COUNTS?, 372
COURSEY, 382 383
COURTNEY, 65 101 199 310 325 327 330 341
COURTNEY?, 338
COWAN, 170 173 300
COWEN, 310
COWEN?, 361
COX, 34 206 292 310 354 355 394
COX?, 14 27 34 70 387
COYKENDALL, 402
COYLE, 278 279
CRADDOCK?, 191 395
CRAGER, 14
CRAIG, 390
CRAIG?, 95
CRANE, 170 317
CRANE?, 174
CRANSTON?, 185
CRAWFORD, 14 39
CRAWFORD?, 39
CREAMER?, 364
CREASEY?, 59
CREECH?, 61
CREEL?, 54 402
CREGGER, 15
CREIGHTEN, 160
CREIGHTON, 180
CREIGHTON?, 364

CRELLY, 336
CRIDDLE, 325
CRISMOND, 122 144
CRISMOND?, 143
CRISTOFORO?, 325
CRITCHFIELD, 191
CROLL, 278
CRONKITE, 41
CROOK, 185
CROPPER, 1
CROSON, 328
CROSS, 4 5
CROSWELL, 180
CROUCH, 15
CROUCH?, 392
CROWDER, 101 122
CROWLEY, 285
CRUMP?, 69
CRYER, 5 69 70 72 105 111 159-162 179 180 182 183 254 255 260 262 383
CRYER?, 30 31 160 180 181 263
CUFFEE?, 97
CULLINS, 122 123 127 149 236
CULLINS?, 20 355
CULLISON, 69 122 197 283 284
CULLISON?, 16 72 284 288
CULVER, 361
CUMMINGS, 98 278
CUNNINGHAM, 2 206
CUOZZO, 401
CURLIS, 353
CURRUTHERS, 7
CURRY, 9 24 42 98 253 255 300 303 354
CURRY?, 96 104
CURTIS, 15 23 30 45 105 117 122 159 206 213 236 278 292 307 327 344 393 399
CURTIS?, 2 282 393
CUSHMAN?, 54
CUSIC, 181 206 207 219 228 254 255 261 265 268 327 336 351

CUSIC (cont.) 354
CUSIC?, 267 351
CUSICK, 207
CUSTIS?, 68
CUTCHEMBER, 15 44 186 269
CUTCHEMBER?, 13 326
CYRUS, 63
DAFFRON, 105 108
DAHL, 383
DAILEY, 269
DALA?, 22
DALLAM?, 2
DALLAS?, 356
DALTON, 383 386
DALTON?, 169
DALY, 278
DAMERON, 191 284
DAMERON?, 284
DANDURAND?, 375
DANOS, 118
DARAS?, 335
DARE, 82 91
DARNEY, 97
DARST?, 83
DAUGHERTY, 170
DAUTRICH, 170
DAVENPORT, 300
DAVID, 207 215
DAVIDSON, 170
DAVIDSON?, 395
DAVIES, 15
DAVIS, 1 2 15 16 35 50 59 65 82 95 105 122 123 170 177 181 191 207 217 223 236 237 310 311 324 334 336 372 373 383 387 389 390 393 402
DAVIS?, 1 2 22 54 95 145 187 223 261 343 367
DAWKINS, 169 171 177 206 207
DAWKINS?, 206
DAWSON, 237 358
DAWSON?, 51

DAYE, 44
DEADMAN?, 122
DEAKINS, 82 89
DEAN, 16 35 61 81-84 87 88 90
    98 120 123 127 130 170 176
    181 186 207 224 229 255 265
    284 285 354 404
DEAN?, 59 91 176
DEANE, 122 123
DEAR, 70
DEARSTINE, 402 404
DEBBIS, 45
DEBOLT, 372
DEBRINO?, 330
DECORDANI, 105
DEFEUDIS, 372
DEFREITAS, 131
DEGENKOLB?, 28
DELAHAY, 255 263 336
DELAHAY?, 253 263 385
DELANGHE, 390
DELBROCCO, 390
DELLA, 372 375
DELOZIER, 16 283 284
DELROSSI, 123 153
DELVECCHIO, 336
DEMARR, 284
DEMENT, 191 192 286 325
DEMOOR, 372 375
DEMOSS, 16
DENIS, 70
DENNIS, 16 207
DENNISON, 364
DENT, 3-5 16 19 83 89 171 175
    178 273 336 390
DENT?, 13 38 55 58 170 336 337
    353 383
DENTON, 325 371 377
DEROSA, 336
DEROSE, 292
DERWENT?, 59
DESSENBERGER, 12
DEVAUGHN, 43

DEVERS, 300
DEWEY, 105 364
DEXTER, 76
DIAMOND, 326
DICANDY, 237 244
DICKENS, 11 186 187 195 269
DICKENS?, 186
DICKERSON, 17 123 155 278
DICKEY?, 395
DIEHL, 95
DIETZ, 361
DIGGS, 123
DIGIORGIO, 325
DIHLMANN?, 18
DILL, 95
DILLAHAY, 237 292
DILLARD?, 260
DILLON, 83
DILLOW, 181 207 208 300
DIMICHELE, 390
DINENNA, 180
DINGEE, 17 123 154 255
DISHAROON, 372
DISHMAN?, 89
DIXON, 2 17 95 98 208 254 255
    336 343 404
DIXON?, 58
DIZE, 65
DOCHERTY?, 2
DOCKUM, 383
DODD, 371 377
DODD?, 34
DODGE?, 384
DODSON, 17 171 208 229
DODSON?, 17
DOHRMAN, 83
DONALDSON, 49-51 192
DONGHI?, 12
DONHISER, 310
DONOGHUE?, 383
DONOVAN?, 164
DOOLEY, 17
DORAU, 390 391

DORFMAN?, 396
DORNALL, 17 24
DORNALL?, 24
DORSEY, 4-6 15 95 98 123 171 177 208 237 273 391 402
DORSEY?, 38 112 401
DOUGHERTY, 354
DOUGLAS, 17 336
DOUGLAS?, 7 338
DOVE, 306 325 326 402
DOVE?, 61 145 389
DOWNES, 255
DOWNEY?, 376
DOWNIE, 354
DOWNS, 17 105 115 116 123 124 160 208 237 337 353-355 372
DOWNS?, 37 42
DOWSEY, 305
DOYEN, 192 193
DOYLE, 383
DRESHER, 76 337
DRESS?, 283
DRISCOLL, 18
DRISCOLL?, 9 282
DROSCHAK?, 76
DROZAK, 326
DRURY, 5 105 107 124 208 215 237 255 260 284 319 337 343 361
DRURY?, 194 241 242 258 265 341-343
DRYDEN, 376
DUBREUIL, 208
DUCKETT, 18
DUCKETT?, 108
DUDLEY, 18
DUFOUR, 18
DUGAN, 64 208
DUKE, 157 160 169 171 337 383
DUKE?, 27 63 191
DUNBAR, 284 310 316 318
DUNBAR?, 309 332
DUNCAN, 273

DUNCKLEY?, 359
DUNN, 5 6 337 391
DUPONT, 208
DURBIN, 371 373
DUTTON?, 383
DUTY, 390
DUY?, 349
DYER, 105 124
DYSON, 15 18 28 40 44 70 76 124 186 237 269 278 292 326 372
DYSON?, 15 40 95 151 202
DZIEMCSZESKI?, 393
EAMIGH?, 12
EARNSHAW, 29
EASTER, 391
EATON, 383
EATON?, 32
EBBERS, 359
ECHOLS, 186
ECHOLS?, 186
EDELEN, 237 337
EDELIN, 124 337
EDGERTON, 399
EDGERTSON?, 75
EDGESTON, 292
EDGESTON?, 305
EDLEY, 337
EDLY, 237
EDMONDS, 51
EDMUNDSON, 18
EDSON, 51 57
EDWARD?, 327
EDWARDS, 2 6 40 51 55 110 181 183 191-193 208 237
EDWARDS?, 69 165 286 328 338 385
EGARTON, 51
EGELI, 323
EGERTON, 309 311
EGERTON?, 75
EICHNER, 172
EISENSCHMIDT, 337
EISGRAU, 76

ELDER, 128 181
ELGIN, 399
ELIFF, 284
ELLINGWOOD, 383 384
ELLIOTT, 83 90 230
ELLIS, 19 124 125 138 148 151 253 255 300 337 343 378
ELLIS?, 12 44 145 197
ELLISON, 356
ELSBERND, 375
ELSESSER, 349
ELSESSER?, 349
ELY, 183
EMERY?, 385
EMICK, 353
EMORY, 216
ENGLEBRETSEN?, 364
ENGLES, 18
ENGLES?, 18
ENNELS, 28 208 399
ENNELS?, 78
ENNIS, 391
ENO, 361
ENRIGHT?, 293
ENSS, 300
ENT?, 384
EPPARD, 181
EPPERSON, 284
ERICH, 105
ERVIN, 208
ERWIN, 172
ERZSEBET, 207
ESCH, 167 172
ESLIN, 187
ESSEX, 373
ESSTILL?, 320
ESTELLE?, 337 353
ESTEP, 208 255 260 351
ESTES?, 354
ESTEVEZ, 378
ETHERTON, 208
ETHRIDGE, 65
EVANS, 43 70 82-84 101 104 106
EVANS (cont.) 110 125 147 172 208 209 214 309 310 337 340 341 363 401
EVANS?, 64 69 182 222 257 277 395 396
EVERETT, 289 337 339
EWELL, 300 404
EWY, 300
FAASS, 18
FABANS, 402
FABEY, 18
FABRIZIO, 209
FANNIN?, 195
FARGO, 300
FARMER, 18 44 391
FARR, 15 125 160 187 237 337
FARRELL, 19 106 107 125-127 129 133 137 143 147 159 160 212 337 351 352
FARRELL?, 21 127 391
FAUNCE, 19 126 278 279
FAUNCE?, 279 346
FAUSSETT, 300
FAUVER, 361
FAY, 384
FEARNS, 337
FEATHERS, 106
FEENEY, 126 148
FELDMAN, 192 194
FELLENCHER, 209
FENHAGAN, 293
FENHAGEN, 284
FENHAGEN?, 71 191
FENNER, 12
FENWICK, 16 17 19 65 76 126 160 163 202 209 278 306 327 337 338 389
FENWICK?, 150 197 266 269
FERBER, 367
FERGUSON, 19 126 141 209 221 225
FERRALL, 209
FERRARI, 105

FERREIRA?, 131
FERRELL?, 112
FERRIS, 36
FICKLIN, 255
FIDELE?, 283
FIELDS, 65
FIELDS?, 394
FIEST, 345
FIESTER, 384
FILMER?, 389
FILOMAMA?, 357
FILTER, 361
FINCH, 70 209
FINCH?, 70
FINCHAM, 355
FISH, 282 320 358
FISH?, 189 320
FISHER, 76 326
FITTALL?, 43
FITZGERALD, 187 188
FITZGERALD?, 206 402
FITZGIBBON?, 159
FITZPATRICK, 64
FITZPATRICK?, 26
FITZWATER, 391
FIX, 138
FLANARY?, 358
FLEISSNER, 76
FLEMING, 327
FLETCHER, 83 338 396 403
FLIPPO?, 42
FLORA, 255 351
FLORES, 389
FLOWER, 293
FLOYD, 104 147 209 210
FLOYD?, 208 255
FLUELLEN, 307
FOLEY, 181 355
FOLLIN, 39
FOLSE?, 153
FONNER, 19 28
FOOKS, 343
FOOTE, 338

FOOTE?, 61
FORBES, 51 237 278 328
FORBES?, 401
FORCHER?, 285
FORD, 19 106 109 126 145 192 210 237 273 293 338 339 350 372
FORD?, 109 283 330 350
FORE, 326
FORREST, 65 67 70 286 310 315 338
FORREST?, 305
FORSTER, 371
FORSYTHE, 362
FORT, 84 85
FORT?, 85
FORTIN, 11
FORTNER, 358
FORTNEY, 256
FORTNEY?, 179
FOSTER, 334
FOWLER, 19 29 51 237 238 255 256 313 362
FOWLER?, 20
FOX, 95 96
FOX?, 19
FOXWELL, 66 119 300 301 303
FOXWELL?, 303 304
FRANCIS, 126
FRANCISCO, 384
FRANCK, 185
FRANCK?, 185
FRANKLIN, 19 101 309
FRANKLIN?, 40 61 62
FRANKS, 192 193
FRANZ, 351
FRAZIER, 19 326 338
FREDERICK, 126 134
FREDERICK?, 281
FREEMAN, 126 127 132 210 293 301 302 338 355
FREEMAN?, 147
FRENCH, 14

FRERE, 278
FREY, 402
FRITZ, 29
FROESCH, 149
FRYE, 391 396
FRYER, 19
FULKS, 19 20
FULLER, 51 277 278 284
FULTON, 84 86
FUNCH?, 22
FUNK, 284
FURLONG, 402
GALLAGHER, 75 96 371 372
GALLAGHER?, 373
GALLANT, 106
GALLION?, 44
GAMBLE, 355
GAMS, 76
GANDARA, 2
GANDY, 326
GANT, 306
GANT?, 305
GANTT, 51
GARCIA?, 389
GARDINER, 20 70 161 181
GARDINER?, 18
GARDNER, 61 127
GARLAND, 405
GARNER, 20 51 52 112 123 127
    203 210 223 224 227 230 310
    351 359 372 373
GARNER?, 23 25 51 58 268 359
GARRETT, 22
GARRETT?, 353
GARROW, 357
GASPAROVIC, 70
GASPAROVIC?, 70
GASS, 20 23 116 122 127 355
GASS?, 189
GASSMAN, 63
GATEAU, 355
GATTON, 20 40 42 59 70 84 106
    125 127 135 137 147 210 284

GATTON (cont.)
    312 338 373 390
GATTON?, 21 26 62 147 287
GAUGER, 401
GAULT?, 1
GAULTNEY?, 378
GAUS, 210
GAY, 185 285
GAY?, 185
GEADY, 238
GEMMILL, 367
GENGE, 192
GENUS, 24
GEORGE, 77 210 384
GERLICH, 172
GERLICH?, 161 172
GERRARD, 47
GHEEN, 384 388
GIBBONS, 262
GIBBONS?, 1 16 31
GIBBS, 18 210 215
GIBBS?, 18 364
GIBSON, 4-6 28 52 63 101 115
    116 120 127-129 134 138 336
    378 402
GIBSON?, 134 362
GIDDENS, 362
GIDDINGS, 194
GIEBEL?, 381
GILBERT, 389 402
GILL, 124 338
GILL?, 378
GILLETTE, 170
GILLIAMS, 172
GILLINGHAM, 301
GILLUM, 326
GILPEN?, 98
GLADDEN, 269
GLADDEN?, 271
GLADSTONE, 52
GLADSTONE?, 144
GLASS, 20 382
GLEASON, 391 392

GLICK, 338
GODDARD, 20 33 70 84 106 111 192 202 211 216 238 333 371 373
GODDARD?, 38 71 195 284
GODWIN, 106 111
GODWIN?, 40 111
GOELLING, 351
GOETZ, 118
GOLD, 43
GOLDBERG?, 181
GOLDEN, 20 238
GOLDER, 63 64
GOLDRING, 278 279 328
GOLDSBOROUGH, 20 21 44 71 107 108 110 129 160 161 168 211 224 226 238 326 338
GOLDSBOROUGH?, 27 221 254
GOLDSMITH, 351 373
GOLDSMITH?, 72 105 111 352
GOOD, 52 150
GOODE, 52 105-107 127 129 133 151 153 284
GOODE?, 128 376 377
GOODRICH, 293 338 345
GOODWIN, 32 129 192 211 224
GOODWIN?, 185 201 223 371
GORDON, 21 22 96 107 306 401
GORDON?, 12 78
GORHAM, 203
GORMAN?, 118
GORMLEY, 326
GOUCHER?, 323
GOUGH, 21 52 77 107 124 161 172 187 189 211 238 294 338 344 351
GOUGH?, 218 351
GOULD, 84
GOURLEY, 294
GOWENS?, 261
GRAFF, 29
GRAGAN, 129 133 139
GRAHAM, 192 193 338 371

GRAHAM?, 371 385
GRANADOS, 211
GRAND, 161
GRANT, 326
GRANT?, 390
GRASON, 3 6 129
GRAVES, 13 21 26 34 44 83-85 87 95-97 107 110 129 130 132 211 238 239 256 324 338
GRAVES?, 19 45 62 83 87 95 165 397
GRAY, 21 63 96 161 211 239 256 265 279 311 379
GRAY?, 161 181 228 277 285 323 324 328 332
GRAYSON, 306
GRAYSON?, 142
GREEN, 21 27 28 41 59 96 107 256 281 285 301 307 326
GREEN?, 10 348 376
GREENE, 6 186 187
GREENE?, 19 189
GREENFIELD, 239
GREENSFELDER, 152
GREENWELL, 21 22 66 85 91 103 105 107 108 130 161 163 173 180 211 212 216 230 239 294 310 317 338 339 384
GREENWELL?, 70 160 161 215 219 221 270 288 310
GREER, 12 339
GREER?, 339
GREEVES, 52
GREGG, 391
GREGORY, 22
GREIG, 84 85
GRESHAM, 157
GREY, 21
GRICE, 93
GRINDELL, 391
GRINDER, 77 362 363
GRIST?, 356
GRISWOLD, 301

GROOMES, 333
GROOMS?, 28
GROSS, 269 270
GROSS?, 280 306
GROVE?, 97
GRUBB, 354 355
GRUBER, 326 393
GRUMBINE, 359
GUENTHER, 20
GUETHLEIN, 402 403
GUMTOW, 39
GUNN?, 157 227 374
GUNNELL, 182
GUNTHER?, 385
GUSTAFSON, 173
GUY, 20 22 38 72 125 130 161 164 212 239 256 261 267 339 343 391
GUY-GIBSON, 285
GUY?, 20 36 41 153 179 197 267 268
GUYTHER, 111 339 347
GWYNN, 396
HABIG, 206 212
HADDOW?, 278
HAGER?, 361
HAKE, 326
HALES, 82
HALL, 22 38 52 121 123 130 147 195 197 222 254 281 315 318 326 327 339 355 379
HALL?, 9 19 33 130 181 255 377
HALLMARK, 22 31
HAM?, 379
HAMEL, 403 405
HAMILL, 130
HAMILTON, 362
HAMILTON?, 373
HAMLET, 22
HAMMER, 14 22 37 44
HAMMERSLY, 130 147
HAMMETT, 22 44 66 70 71 85 108 130 170 173 200 212 283

HAMMETT (cont.)
285 287 294 318 339 367 373 391
HAMMETT?, 40 42 199 285 311
HAMMILL, 294
HAMOR, 373
HAMSON, 301
HANCE?, 278
HANCOCK, 96 179 239 256 262 369
HANCOCK?, 262
HANDY, 75 239 240
HANEY, 66
HANOBECK, 200
HANSBOROUGH, 11
HANSEN, 22
HANSEN?, 33
HANSON, 108 193 327
HARBIN?, 345
HARBISON, 173
HARDEN, 130 161 162 181
HARDEN?, 22 71 108 114 125 162
HARDESTY, 391
HARDIN, 131 181
HARDING, 96 256 301 327 354 384
HARDING?, 96
HARDMAN, 187
HARKNESS?, 354
HARMON, 309
HARPER, 22 373 403
HARPER?, 254 373
HARRELL, 18
HARRINGTON, 353
HARRINGTON?, 97 387
HARRIS, 22 23 37 161 169 173 174 213 240 323 339 384 399
HARRIS?, 19 162 193 210 257 306 307
HARRISON, 38 52 131 174 235 240 362 364
HARRISON?, 318

HARROVER, 85
HARSH, 85
HART, 77
HARTER, 213
HARTLINE?, 63 64
HARTNETT, 23 131 358
HARTY?, 203 381
HARVEY?, 390
HASKELL, 70 325 327
HASKET?, 354
HASSHAW, 23
HATCHER, 339 383
HATCHER?, 67
HAUF, 327 329
HAUKLAND, 97
HAVERKAMP, 353
HAW, 174
HAWKINS, 23 96 131 197 240 273 280 306 327
HAWKINS?, 267 271 277 327
HAWKS?, 43 97
HAYDEN, 9 23 33 36 52 53 58 85 122 131 132 145 150 197 203 206 213 214 229 240 253 256-258 260 268 294 296 310 319 339 340 347 350 373 374 391 396
HAYDEN?, 12 30-32 52 54 57 58 78 79 81 163 174 248 258 296 319 338 347 350 361 374 375
HAYES?, 69 378
HAYFORD, 71
HAYS?, 259
HAYWARD, 214 301 323
HAYWOOD, 270 294
HAYWOOD?, 330
HAZEL, 61 181 240 257 262 265 337 340
HAZEL?, 148 265 266 281 363 376
HAZELL, 132
HAZZARD, 101
HEAGY, 311

HEALY, 71 257 264
HEARD, 10 77 78 85 104 108 118 132 184 214 240 293 301
HEARD?, 118 221
HEASLY?, 112
HEATHERLAND, 294
HEBB, 15 23 77 108 132 137 157 214 257 260
HEBB?, 18 30 177 216 260 362
HEBRON?, 25
HEDGLIN, 401
HEDGLIN?, 401
HEDRICK, 362
HEFFERMAN, 18
HEFLIN, 355
HEFLIN?, 358
HEH, 212
HEIDERSCHIED?, 401
HEIMER, 391 392
HEINEMANN?, 349
HEINZ, 33
HEINZMAN, 193
HEJNA, 392
HELCOMB?, 194
HELMS, 61
HEMMER, 403
HEMMING, 162 214
HENDERSON, 101 193 194 327 355 371 373 374 376
HENDERSON?, 63 208 266 287 347
HENDNICK?, 186
HENDRICK, 67 181
HENDRICK?, 195
HENDRICKSON?, 269
HENLEY?, 363
HENLY?, 374
HENNEN, 16
HENRICKSON, 206
HENSEL, 96
HENSLEY, 13
HENSLEY?, 284
HENSON, 399

HENZEL, 96
HERBERT, 1 20 23 30 53 115 124
    126 132 133 139 152 161 181
    214 240 241 257 279 354
HERBERT?, 116 241 242 257 353
    355
HERBOUGH?, 286
HERMANN, 181
HERN, 187
HERNDON?, 384
HERRIMAN, 53
HERRIMAN?, 48 56
HERRMANN, 185 187
HERTZLER, 93
HESS, 6
HESSE, 133
HESSE?, 148
HETRICH, 392
HEWITT, 23 71 73 159 161 191-
    193 338 343 355
HEWITT?, 1
HEWLETT, 305 306
HEWLETT?, 327
HIBBARD?, 330
HICKEY?, 72
HICKS, 208 214 352 362
HIDALGO, 63
HIGGINS, 133 195
HIGGINS?, 363
HIGGS, 23 34 53 54 96 104 181
    187 214 355 374 392
HILBERT, 34
HILDEBRAND, 193
HILDEBRAND?, 193
HILDENBERG?, 75
HILEMAN?, 14
HILL, 17 23 24 36 54 71 96 118
    125 129 133 134 136 137 143
    149 153 174 215 219 221 226
    240 277 279 280 327 328 331
    340 351 369 392
HILL?, 36 128 129 146 282 325
    340 356 395

HILLEY, 354 355
HILLIS, 294
HILLS, 77 326
HILTON, 294 295
HINKEY, 374
HINSON, 365
HINTON, 64
HINZ, 77
HINZMAN, 96
HISLOP, 328
HOBB?, 135
HOBBS, 101 102
HOCK, 328
HODGES, 108 128 134 141 163
    362
HODGES?, 160
HOFFMAN, 24 85 361 376
HOFFMAN?, 73 190 288
HOFMANN, 161
HOFTIEZER, 85
HOGABOOM, 310
HOGAN, 44
HOLBERT, 310
HOLLAND, 270 279
HOLLAND?, 105 188
HOLLEY, 77 161 273 274 305 381
HOLLIN, 384
HOLLY, 108 134 150 273 274
HOLLY?, 179
HOLMES, 6 7 108 134 315
HOLMES?, 351
HOLSINGER?, 216
HOLT, 17 24 27 32 96 97 134 154
    215 226 240 278-280 346
HOLT?, 14 32 40
HOLTON, 24 62 134
HOLTON?, 45
HOLTZ, 85 92
HONKONEN, 310
HOOD, 24 134 138
HOOPER, 13 24 85 86 215 285
HOOVER?, 367
HOPEWELL, 340

HOPKINS, 215 392
HOPKINS?, 23
HOPPA?, 27
HOPPER, 212 215
HOPSON, 33
HORNE, 174
HORNEY, 336
HORSTMAN, 326
HORTON, 328
HORVATH, 207 215
HOSKINS, 348
HOUCK, 117 134 135
HOUGH, 95 97
HOUSER, 174
HOWARD, 181 310 334 358 383
HOWARD?, 191 215
HOWE, 24 135 174 215 257 351 352
HOWELL, 24 25 61 189
HOWELL?, 40 62 189
HOWLAND, 84 86 371 403
HOWLIN, 97
HOWRY?, 381
HOWSON?, 356
HUBIN, 299 301
HUBIN?, 299
HUDSON, 181 182 192 355
HUDSON?, 182 192
HUFF, 63
HUFFMAN?, 403
HUFFORD, 394
HUG, 384
HUGHES, 25 51 189 192 193
HUGHES?, 383
HUMFLEET, 384
HUNT, 25 161
HUNTER, 356
HUNTER?, 45
HUNTINGTON, 25 31 54 135 240
HUNTSMAN, 283 285
HUNTT, 161 162 215
HUNTT?, 355
HUPP?, 61

HURLBURT, 174
HURRY, 135 257 374
HURST, 403
HURST?, 11
HURT, 172 178 182
HUSEMAN, 6 135 143 148
HUTCHESON, 205
HUTCHESON?, 325
HUTCHINS, 107 108 285
HUTCHINSON, 388
HUTSON, 135 136
HUTTON, 144
HYNSON, 355
INGERSOL?, 76
INGLIS, 97 98
INGRAM, 403
INMAN, 328 337 374
INSLEY, 32 86 87 215
IRONMONGER?, 396
ISAAC?, 93
ITALIANO?, 358
JACKSON, 25 45 86 89 142 165 215 241 274
JACKSON?, 75 197 364
JACOB, 403
JACOBS, 25
JAMES, 108 327 403
JAMES?, 98 103
JAMESON, 211 392
JARBOE, 70 71 162 205 211 215 226 241 295 301 311 335 340 341 343 362 363
JARBOE?, 70 161
JARVIS, 97
JAYNES, 25
JEFFERIES, 41
JEFFRIES, 329
JENIFER, 6 274 328
JENKINS, 1 13 25 112 135 147 241 310 328 341 352 362 374
JENKINS?, 311 331 352
JENNINGS, 341
JENNINGS?, 52

JERGENS?, 386
JERNINGHAM, 328
JESSUP, 341
JESTER, 301 302
JETER, 25
JEWEL?, 139
JEWETT, 392
JIMERSON, 385
JOHNS, 98 320
JOHNSON, 1 6 9 17 20 25 26 28 29 36 40 43 64 71 77 81 86 87 105 108 109 111 113 133 135 137 138 140 160-165 170 174 180 182 192 193 200 201 208 215-217 219 220 222 223 233 240-244 246 247 250 251 253-261 263-268 278 279 300 301 305 306 317 328 333 338 341 342 345 348 349 352 355 356 362 367 373 374 377 385 403
JOHNSON?, 7 16 23 34 79 105 141 160 185 202 216 223 242 244 245-247 255 257 262 265 306 323 327 330 331 343 383 391 394
JOHNSTON, 54 390
JOHNSTONE, 403
JOLIN, 388
JOLLY, 342
JONES, 10 18 19 26 35 39 66 70 76 81 84-87 89 90 97 98 109 135 136 161 212 216 217 242 256 260 261 301 302 309-311 313 321 328 334 339 342 347 356 403 405
JONES?, 2 15 21 22 43 63 70 86 89 91 123 161 341 355 395
JORDAN, 109 216 327
JORDAN?, 12
JORDON, 77 79 136 187 269 270
JORDON?, 270 278 326
JOSNAK, 356
JOWLES, 328
JOY, 20 25 26 44 59 81-83 85 88 89 92 135 136 200 216 241-243 295 333 342 343 345 349
JOY?, 9
JUROVATY, 71
JUSTICE, 374
KAGLE?, 355
KAHL?, 27
KALE?, 336
KALHASY, 283 285
KAMAN, 396
KANE, 25 77 95 216 227 374 385
KANE?, 382
KANNARKAT, 26
KAPANOSKE, 391 392
KAPY?, 58
KARR, 403
KARST?, 287
KATRAFELD?, 281
KATTERLA, 36
KAUFMAN, 6 174
KAUFMANN, 109
KEATING, 26 403
KEATLEY, 187
KEATLEY?, 187
KEECH?, 52
KEELING, 97
KEEN, 98 311
KEENAN, 136
KEISTER, 97
KELLER, 96 193 194 356
KELLEY, 217 392
KELLOGG, 356
KELLY, 217 392
KELLY?, 79
KEMP, 88
KENADY, 26 27
KENNAN, 136
KENNAN?, 118
KENNEDY, 115 136 295
KENNETT, 136
KENNY, 127
KENYON, 97

KERN, 181
KERSHAW, 324
KERSHAW?, 386
KESKINEN, 392
KETCHERSON?, 394
KETTERMAN?, 79
KEW?, 195
KEY, 23 27 274 331
KEY?, 47
KIDD, 27 356
KIDWELL, 35 362 395
KIDWELL?, 44
KIEL?, 307
KILGO, 162
KILHOFFER, 352
KIMBALL, 188
KIMBALL?, 385
KINDER, 27
KING, 64 162 174 217 242 343 347 362 403 404
KING?, 216 357
KIRBY, 88
KIRBY?, 88
KIRCHNER, 217
KIRK, 54 217
KIRST, 88
KIRWAN?, 296
KLEAR, 21 25 159 160 162 279 281
KLEGIN, 27
KLING, 392
KNIGHT, 16 27 43 136 157 174 217 242 302 392 393
KNIGHT?, 161
KNIGHTON?, 209 309
KNOPE, 27 38
KNOTT, 2 6 11 12 23 27 32 54 70 71 97 109 133 136 162 183 187 188 190 195 197 207 217 242 261 265 266 285 287 288 343 352 362 391
KNOTT?, 18 29 32 109 125 162 183 195 204 218 241 242 254

KNOTT? (cont.) 255 261 266 281 337 351
KNOWLES?, 349
KNOWLTON, 388
KNOX, 393
KOGER, 2
KOHL, 69
KOHUT, 311
KOLARSK, 361
KOLLER, 352
KOLLER?, 311
KOONTZ?, 377
KOPEL, 36
KORBEKA, 188
KOSASZKA?, 346
KOSEL, 217
KOSEL?, 401
KOSTKOWSKI, 27
KOZLOWSKI, 393
KRAMER, 362
KRAUSE, 103 109
KRESSMANN, 402
KRISTOVITSCH?, 356
KRUG, 217
KRUPINSKY, 30
KUCHER, 114
KUEHN, 27
KUHSE, 27
LABOU?, 188
LACEY, 27 28 125 133 136 137 148 216-218 254 343
LACEY?, 134 146 148 153 279 327 404
LACKEY, 302
LACY, 118 137
LAFLAME?, 188
LAIGLE, 77
LAKE, 28
LAKEARN?, 188
LALLANDE, 385 387
LAMB?, 67
LAMDIN?, 174
LANCASTER, 132 137 270 343

LANCASTER (cont.)
 386
LANCASTER?, 55 403
LAND?, 394
LANDAU, 218
LANDIS, 382
LANE, 302 328 329
LANG, 66 71
LANG?, 310
LANGE, 311
LANGFORD?, 196
LANGLEY, 29 162 198 218 301
 302 306 318 336 343 374 375
LANGLEY?, 29 300 305 353 402
LANGSTER, 28
LANGWORTH, 342 347 349
LANIER, 378
LANIFER, 218
LANTZ, 61
LAPTHORNE?, 405
LARGE, 299
LARGEN?, 393
LARR?, 182
LARSON, 193
LARSON?, 384
LASCHALT, 343
LASSERE, 172
LASSERRE, 161
LASSERRE?, 161
LATHAM, 77 105 108-110 112
 137 153 176 218 242 243 282
 343 355
LATHAM?, 22 31 154 215 216
 267
LATHROUM, 218 243
LATTA, 332
LAVADA?, 151
LAVENDER, 196
LAWRENCE, 18 26 28 43 88 113
 127 135 137-139 149 185 186
 188 270 323 329 330 385
LAWRENCE?, 18 348 364 390
 405

LAWSON, 201
LAYTON?, 97
LAZURE, 28
LAZZELL?, 325
LEACH, 180 182 241
LEACH?, 180
LEARY, 343 347
LEAVERTON, 295
LEBLANC, 356
LECLERE, 261
LECOMPTE, 170
LEDLEY?, 98
LEE, 28 134 138 182 191 218 270
 357 385 404
LEE?, 95 266 273 305 306 326 389
LEFAIVRE, 404
LEIGH, 343
LEIZEAR, 193
LEMKE, 355
LEMKUHL, 405
LEMMON?, 332
LENNETT?, 271
LEOPARD, 5
LERETTE, 404
LESZEAR, 327
LETAU, 66
LETCHER, 356
LETTAU, 66 283
LEVERTON?, 405
LEVIN, 28
LEWANDOWSKI?, 392
LEWELLEN, 393
LEWIS, 28 101 197 254 362 364
LEWIS?, 1 2 401
LEY, 384
LEY?, 384
LIDDY, 278 279
LILES, 356
LILLEY, 402 404
LINCOLN?, 51 57
LINDLEY, 356
LINDSEY, 28
LINEHAN?, 211

LINGER, 193
LINK?, 191
LINKINS?, 357
LINTON, 6 7 354
LINVILLE, 302 303
LIPPERT, 19 28
LITTEN, 28
LITTLEJOHN, 329
LITTLEJOHN?, 41 329
LIVINGSTON, 28 174
LIVINGSTONE?, 404
LLOYD, 79 185 218 243 258 261 283 295
LLOYD?, 264
LOCHNER, 218
LOCKE?, 63
LOCKHART, 367
LOCKWOOD, 11
LOE, 28
LOESING?, 401
LOFFLER, 364
LOGALBO, 186 188
LOGAN, 29
LOHWATER, 402
LOICHOT?, 181
LOKER, 109 112 170 174 302 309 316 342 343
LOKER?, 305 309
LOMAX?, 4
LONG, 18 29 36 37 61 62 124 131 138 139 162 200 218 235 243 253 258 261 262 285 288 341 343 367
LONG?, 44 70 121 124 138 154 255 256 258 260 265 268 355 374 385
LONGMORE, 109
LONGMORE?, 34
LONGWORTH?, 61
LOPEZ?, 335
LORD, 188
LORE, 174 374
LOTT, 385

LOUDEN, 61
LOUIS?, 160
LOVE, 162 163 243 256 262 264 343
LOVE?, 26 50 241 256 362
LOVELESS?, 10
LOVING, 29 393
LOWE, 265 279 293 310
LOWERY, 54
LOWERY?, 57
LOYD, 385
LUCAS, 302
LUCAS?, 86 310
LUFFEY, 29
LUKAC, 197 198
LUMPKINS?, 283
LUNCEFORD, 54
LUNDREGAN, 88 89
LUPUS, 262
LUSBY, 29
LUSK, 329
LUSKEY, 329
LUTHER, 367
LYDAMON, 319
LYDAMON?, 319
LYDICK, 401
LYLE?, 224
LYLES, 30 54 274 280
LYNCH, 35 54 75 77 343
LYNCH?, 113 357
LYON, 29 54 55 139 279 280 343
LYON?, 7 56 344
LYONS?, 4 394
MACCARTEE, 302
MACDONNELL, 182
MACFARRON?, 75
MACIEJEWSKI, 393
MACK, 4 29 139 274
MACKIE?, 310
MACKINZIE, 286
MACKUBIN?, 57
MACWATHER, 326
MACWATHER?, 326

MACWILLIAMS, 218 223
MADDEN, 375
MADDOX, 11 55 83 89 136 139 186 218 226 315
MADDOX?, 11 52 56-58 132
MADISON, 15
MADJESKI, 329
MADOX, 162
MADSEN, 174 175
MAGDLIN?, 216
MAGEE, 212
MAGELSSON, 29
MAGILL, 82 89 218 295 344 354
MAGNER?, 33
MAHALIE?, 273
MAHER, 223
MAHONEY?, 76
MAHORNEY, 29 43
MAJORS, 66 285
MAKIN?, 78
MALASPINA, 29 30 32
MALCOLM, 387
MALESKY, 285
MALONY?, 384
MALUEQ?, 79
MANFRONI?, 390
MANIGAULT, 30
MANKIN?, 5
MANN, 64 194 404
MANNING, 106 109
MANUEL, 330 393
MANUELITIS?, 14
MARCH?, 329
MARCUM, 64
MARINE, 164
MARINER, 344
MARINI, 30
MARJORAM, 393
MARKS?, 357
MARLE?, 17
MARQUEZ, 211
MARSH, 97
MARSHALL, 30 97 182 188 204

MARSHALL (cont.) 253 262 302 305 307 344 356 363 377
MARSHALL?, 41 194 281
MARSTON, 385
MARTIN, 59 62 89 93 182 205 219 274 280 307 356 390
MARTIN?, 61 160 188
MARVASO, 12
MASKEE, 30
MASON, 30 89 109 139 188 219 262 280 344 393
MASON?, 15 22 28 161 187 262 277 305 365
MASSIE?, 69 73
MATHANY, 344
MATHEWS, 302
MATITIAVICH?, 183
MATSON, 28
MATTEY?, 309
MATTHEWS, 109 139 219 344 351 393
MATTHEWS?, 91 367
MATTINGLY, 7 13 25 30 31 40 42 43 45 71 88 103 107 109 110 114 117 124 135 138-141 143 151 152 162 163 168 175 180 182 206 219 223 237 241-246 251 254 255 258 260 262-265 267 280 310 318 341 344 367 375 385 404 405
MATTINGLY?, 23 25 36 135 144 162 164 180 182 208 215 229 241 242 253 256 257 259 268 318 326 388
MAUCK, 70
MAUNEY?, 358
MAUPAI, 141
MAXWELL, 344
MAYHEW?, 378
MAYNARSKY, 71
MAYOR, 31 66 71 72 285 286 375 385

MAYOR?, 286
MAYS, 393
MAYWOOD?, 95
MAZUCHOWSKI, 30
MAZUR?, 18
MCADAM, 301 302
MCALLISTER?, 78
MCANINCH?, 331
MCCABE, 31
MCCALL, 168 170 175
MCCALLUM, 175
MCCARTHY?, 218 339
MCCAUGHERY?, 393
MCCLANE, 306
MCCLAVE, 356
MCCLURE?, 394
MCCONNELL, 390
MCCORMACK, 190
MCCORMICK, 141
MCCOWAN?, 98
MCCOY, 285
MCCRADY, 89
MCCRAE?, 42
MCCROBIE?, 354
MCCULLY, 163 362
MCDANIEL, 89
MCDANIELS, 90
MCDERMOTT?, 77
MCDEVITT, 363 395
MCDONALD?, 189
MCEACHERN, 326
MCELHINEY, 175
MCFARLAND, 154
MCFARLEN, 97
MCGARITY, 361
MCGARITY?, 355
MCGEE, 219 221
MCGEE?, 189
MCGEHEE, 309
MCGEHEE?, 309
MCGHEE, 35
MCGHIN, 345
MCGHIN?, 345

MCGINN, 385
MCGOWAN, 195
MCGRATH, 126 141
MCGRAW?, 375
MCGREEVY, 175
MCGUIGAN, 25 31 329 375
MCGUIRE, 282
MCGUYRE, 165
MCKAY, 187 188 219 226 260 264 283-285 295 345 363 385
MCKAY?, 31
MCKEEN?, 25
MCKENNA, 404
MCKENNA?, 375
MCKENNEY, 66 195 196 367
MCKENNIE, 246
MCKENNY, 311
MCKENZIE, 22 356 358
MCKENZIE?, 378
MCKEON, 361 363
MCKESSLER?, 386
MCLANE, 39
MCLAUGHLIN, 77
MCLEAN, 375
MCLEOD, 89
MCLERAN?, 12
MCMURRAY, 288
MCNALLY?, 286
MCNEELY, 195
MCNEY, 12 162 163 348 357
MCNEY?, 17
MCPHERSON?, 26 260
MCQUADE, 264
MCTHOMPSON, 219
MCWHIRT, 174 175
MCWILLIAMS, 31 34 141 142 147 182
MCWILLIAMS?, 157
MEADE, 31
MEANS?, 384
MEARS, 336
MECK, 32
MEDFORD, 404

MEDLEY, 25 142 246
MEEKLING, 357
MELENDY, 192
MELVIN, 82
MENDELIS?, 161
MERCER, 324
MERCHANT, 367 393
MERCURE, 285
MEREDITH, 31
MERRITT, 404
MERRYMAN, 182 196 338
MERSON, 335
MERTZ, 163
MERZ?, 359
MESSICK, 66 101 286-288 393
MESSINA?, 186
MEUSHAW?, 114
MEYER, 386
MEYERHOF?, 310
MEYERS, 77 310 311
MEYERS?, 37 367
MICHAEL, 394
MICHOS, 392
MIDDLETON, 102 264 375
MIDDLETON?, 181
MIEDZINSKI, 32 210 219 220
MIEDZINSKI?, 17
MIESOWITZ, 72
MILANO, 89
MILBURN, 25 95 97 110 175 188 191 193 194 241 246 247 338 345
MILBURN?, 37 338
MILES, 32 142 220 222 262 264 267 345
MILES?, 11
MILFORD, 318
MILFORD?, 163
MILGRIM, 393
MILLARD, 163 345
MILLER, 12 32 63 160 163 363 372 373 375 381 386 387 404
MILLER?, 27 38 194 390

MILLICENT, 348
MILLISON, 324
MILLS, 30 32 49 51 55 110 142 163 171 172 175 194 220 277 336 345 404
MILLS?, 183 335
MILSTEAD, 32
MILSTEAD?, 367
MINNICK, 63
MISIEL?, 361
MISTLER, 386
MITCHELL, 32 163 264
MITCHELL?, 330 358
MOCK, 396
MOEISNER, 403
MOFFETT, 286
MOLDEN, 32 274
MOLINO, 364
MONEYMAKER, 63
MONGELLI, 329
MONROE, 329
MONTAMED, 386
MONTEDONICO, 262 264
MONTFORT, 7
MONTGOMERY, 351 375
MONTGOMERY?, 354
MONTPETIT, 372 375
MOONEY?, 39
MOOR, 66
MOORCONES, 77 79
MOORE, 30 32 38 40 98 101 102 142 175 182 281 311 345 396 404
MOORE?, 7 286 375 403
MORAN, 220 351
MORDIC?, 396
MORELAND, 241 247 280 344
MORELAND?, 258
MORGAN, 15 32 33 35 43 55 89 92 110 126 140 142 143 152 163 182 204 220 247 248 260 264 270 271 284 307 343 345 356 375 377 393

MORGAN?, 42-44 64 95 149 264 265 269 271 357
MORGUL?, 18
MORONEY, 188
MORRIS, 22 33 89 116 118 122 128 133 134 139 143 144 220 311 329 345
MORRIS?, 64 143 144 385
MORRISON, 377
MORSE, 189
MORTIMER?, 309
MORTON, 345 349 383 386
MORTON?, 342 345
MORVICK, 159
MOSER?, 404
MOSES, 329 331
MOSHER, 87 89 220
MOSS, 79 386
MOSS?, 371
MOSSMAN, 2
MOTTLER, 66
MUELLER, 329
MUELLER?, 391 403
MUGG, 220
MULLEN, 120 144 153
MULLER, 356
MULLINS?, 62
MURI?, 285
MURPHY, 33 144 220 295 392
MURPHY?, 371
MURR, 217
MURRAY, 163 404 405
MURRAY?, 264 388 402
MUSSER, 376
MYERS, 43 327 329
NAGLE, 405
NAIR, 390
NAKRASEIVE, 163
NALLEY, 33
NALLEY?, 18 206
NASH?, 168
NAUGHTON, 265
NAUMANN, 285 286 311

NAYLOR, 20 329
NEAL, 112 280 302 386
NEALE, 144 182 248
NEALE?, 24 139 357
NEALON, 188
NEELEY?, 354
NEELY?, 326
NEILL, 89
NEILSON?, 187
NELSON, 7 10 33 41 42 55 66 69 72 97 144 159 195 248 263-267 280 281 283 345
NELSON?, 23 28 42 106 182 256 267
NEMECEK?, 194
NEUBAURE?, 395
NEVITT, 144 341
NEWELL, 33
NEWELL?, 44
NEWKIRK, 33 61
NEWMAN?, 356
NEWTON, 16 33 41 110 206 209 215 219-221 384
NEWTON?, 13 16 205 207
NGUGEN?, 349
NICHALSON, 66 67
NICHOLSON, 221
NIGHTMAN?, 39
NILES?, 19
NILSEN, 182
NISWANNER?, 367
NIVENS, 395
NOACK?, 391
NOEL, 332
NOLAN, 10 23 33 75 76 204 221 279
NOLAN?, 13
NOLLAN?, 278
NORDSTROM, 161
NORRIS, 9 33 38 41 72 73 77 78 89 106 107 110 111 121 124 130 144 145 162 163 203 205 212 219 221 222 228 265 280

NORRIS (cont.)
   345 367 386 391
NORRIS?, 9 14 41 72 112 125 149
   163 164 201 205 211 219 228
   283 284 287 331 376
NORTON?, 383
NORWOOD, 286
NOTTINGHAM, 345 347
NOTTINGHAM?, 347
NOVICH?, 406
NOVOTNY, 72
NOWAK, 346
NOWELL, 324
NOY, 111
NOYES, 78
NUNN, 356 357
NUSS, 395
NUTHALL, 163 164
NUTTER, 376
O'BRIEN, 75 78 346
O'BRYAN, 401
O'CONNELL?, 265 393
O'CONNOR, 346
O'CONNOR?, 254
O'DONNELL, 327
O'DONNELL?, 71 327
O'HARA, 265 373
O'HEARN, 76
O'KANE, 393 395
O'MOORE, 145
O'MOORE?, 126
O'NEIL, 309 330
OBERAITIS, 222
ODEN?, 381
OELLER?, 253
OGDEN, 89
OLIVER, 20 33 34 55 56 145 197
   280 346 363 388 396
OLIVER?, 29 55 357
OLIVERA, 175
OLSEN, 405
OLSON, 33 89 91
OREM?, 23

ORNDORFF, 286
ORR, 386
ORSINI, 187 188 330
ORTON?, 194
OSANTOWSKI, 17
OSBORNE, 367
OSMAN, 364
OSTER, 98
OTT, 33
OTT?, 127
OUTLAND, 393
OWEN, 33 34 86 89
OWEN?, 34
OWENS, 34 72 145 146 255 265
   295 296 346 363 394
OWENS?, 24 35 44 135 364 373
PADDY?, 230
PADGET?, 175
PADGETT, 175 182
PAGE, 106 385
PAGE?, 96
PAHEL, 14
PAHEL?, 14
PAINTER, 34
PALMANS, 402
PALMER, 146 346 367
PALMER?, 195
PARCEL, 195
PARDOE, 301 303
PARENT, 222
PAREZO?, 197
PARHAM, 34
PARHAM?, 34
PARKER, 34 56 146
PARKER?, 372
PARKS?, 82 185
PARLETT, 362
PARLETT?, 20
PARRAN?, 168
PARRIS, 61 62
PARRISH, 63
PARROTT, 394 395
PARSONS, 248

PARTIN, 34
PARTRIDGE, 296
PASCHAULT, 296
PASSARELLI, 163 164
PASSMORE, 34
PATTERSON, 56 374
PATTERSON?, 52
PAUL, 301 303 357
PAUTZ?, 330
PAYNE, 14 31 34 146 164 182 183 216 222 229 248 253 258 260 265 376
PAYNE?, 16 181 208 258 261 268 347
PEABODY?, 378
PEACH, 280
PEACOCK, 34 40 146 222
PEACOCK?, 359
PEAIRE, 354 357
PEAK, 222 296
PEARCE, 372 376
PEARSON, 97 98 102
PEARSON?, 363
PECK, 270
PEDEDIEU?, 356
PEGG, 32 62
PEGG?, 226
PEGRAM, 394
PEMBROKE, 346
PEMBROKE?, 293 311
PENDRIS, 405
PENN, 56 274 279 280 377
PENN?, 279
PENNINGTON, 56
PENNISI, 16 35
PEPPER, 402
PERDUE, 376
PERDUE?, 270
PERISHO, 37
PERKINS, 13 376
PERRIE, 386
PERRIGO, 394
PERRY, 145 222 352

PETER, 222
PETERSON, 176
PETIT?, 372
PETRIE?, 4
PFIEL, 89
PHIEL, 89
PHILIPPY, 35
PHILLIPS, 2 194 353 392
PHILLIPS?, 24 64
PHOEBUS, 376
PICHARD?, 32
PICKENS, 218
PICKREL?, 363
PICKRELL, 175
PIE, 7
PIERAS, 35
PIERCE, 139 286
PIERCE?, 139 326 358
PILKERTON, 35 38 77 106 125 127 136 146 147 179 181 182 220 222 254 265 268 280-282 346 357 361-363 390 405
PILKERTON?, 11 20 26 34 36 70 71 255 256 267 279 333 357 362
PINES, 7
PINGLETON, 89
PINKNEY?, 57
PITCHER, 330
PLATER, 35 222 274 277 346
PLOWDEN, 35 126 130 134 147 222 248
POE, 38 102 183 195 196 369
POE?, 122 195
POFF, 56
POGUE, 6 7
POISSON, 372
POLZ, 14
POMEROY, 296
POMEROY?, 227
POMPIZZI, 45
PONTON, 248
POORMAN, 35

POPE, 182 183 197 346
POPE?, 183 333 354 381
PORRETTI, 35
PORTER, 3 222 299
PORTER?, 404
POSEY, 18 35 357
POTEETE, 104 111
POTRUZSKI?, 403
POTTER, 20 79 102 193 196
POTTER?, 79
POTTS, 79
POVLICH, 280 281
POWELL, 35
POWELL?, 39 63 225
POWER, 248 341
PRATT, 142 147 311
PRICE, 15 24 35 44 65 67 78 147 175 248 284 296 315 345 346
PRICE?, 65 178 332 338
PRINGLE, 196
PRITCHARD, 104 111
PROCTOR?, 14
PROUT, 384
PRYOR, 35
PUCKETT?, 325
PUGH, 175
PUGH?, 99
PULLEN?, 396
PULLIAM, 62
PULLIAM?, 62
PULLMAN, 286
PUMPHREY, 375
PUMPHREY?, 287
PURCELL, 197
PURCELL?, 62 73 378
PURDIE, 403 405
PURDY, 72
PURKS, 56
PURNELL, 325 330
PUSSLER, 171 175 176
QUADE, 9 33 36 37 39 40 63 111 130 135 137 147 148 153 201 222 223 265 279-281 288 346

QUADE (cont.) 351 364
QUADE?, 34 40 129 136 139 146 153 265 353
QUAID, 248
QUARLES, 98
QUEEN, 281 352
QUESENBERRY, 386
QUIGLEY, 181 183
QUILLEN?, 356
QUILLIAM, 62
QUIRK, 378
RABBITT, 78
RADCLIFFE, 194
RADFORD?, 349
RAILEY, 223 319
RAINEY?, 97
RALEY, 2 12 14 25 36 148 182 197 207 216 223 231 248 254 257 261 265 266 281 283 286 287 296 309 330 346-348 357 362 363 374 376 377 385
RALEY?, 10 40 162 186 219 254 257 258 260 261 287 337 373 374
RAMSEY, 176 183
RANDALL, 71 72 363
RANDOLPH, 63 64 188
RANDOLPH?, 309
RANSOM, 376
RAPP, 176
RASMUSSEN, 43
RASPA, 78
RATLEDGE, 176
RATLIFF, 64
RATLIFF?, 64
RAUTERBERG, 148
RAVAGO, 36
RAWLINGS?, 44
RAY, 386
RAYNIAK, 78
RAYNOR, 361
READ, 296

READMOND, 89 90 223 296
REAGAN?, 392
REAM, 98
REANEY, 6
REANY, 5
RECOS, 56
REDDIN?, 35
REDMAN, 185 187-189 193
REDMAN?, 10 69 72 161 186
REDMILES, 376
REDMOND, 36 37 56 67 78 176 224 228 296
REDMOND?, 228 382
REDMOUND, 296
REED, 36 56 267
REED?, 32 382
REEDER, 2 176 249 256
REEDER?, 47 51 58
REESE, 359
REEVES, 7 56 330
REGIS, 199
REGNER, 330
REHM, 330
REICH, 383
REID, 36 191 254 367
REIGLE, 404
REILLY, 394
REINTZELL, 11 36
REITH?, 44
RENEHAN, 126 148 376
RENSCHKE, 133 148
RETTSTATT, 98
REVELY?, 173
REY?, 211
REYNOLDS, 303 394
REYNOLDS?, 188
RICE, 23 31 36 355
RICE?, 23 63
RICH?, 1 35 123 362
RICHARD, 288
RICHARDS, 184 294 296 347
RICHARDS?, 134 190
RICHARDSON, 22 148 173 192

RICHARDSON (cont.)
 193 303 347 349 355 364 376 387 395
RICHARDSON?, 15 70
RIDDELL, 78
RIDENOUR?, 392
RIDGELEY, 1
RIDGELL, 67 203 285-287 376
RIDGELL?, 31 72 197 283 284 287 382 385
RIDGELY, 347
RIDGEWAY, 394
RIDINGTON?, 310
RIFFENBERG?, 371
RILEY?, 24
RINEHART?, 14
RINGLING, 181
RIOUX?, 104
RIPPIE, 56
RISKO, 358
RISTER, 361
RITCHIE, 224
RIVERS, 160
ROACH, 103 111 270 287 376
ROACHE, 351
ROBB, 347
ROBERTS, 36 37 47 85 189 269 303 347 385
ROBERTSON, 345 377
ROBERTSON?, 9 345
ROBESON, 90
ROBEY, 363
ROBIDAS?, 208
ROBINSON, 30 37 90 183 189 347 377 393
ROBINSON?, 346 405
ROBRECHT, 102 192
ROBRECHT?, 373
ROCK, 114 138 148 287
ROE, 377
ROE?, 355
ROESSLER, 37
ROGERS, 37 161 326 394

ROGERS?, 310
ROHBAUGH?, 362
ROITH, 78
ROLFE, 357
ROLLER, 224
ROLLINS, 197 287 357
ROMANO, 357
ROMINGER, 394
ROOKER?, 191
ROOSEVELT?, 325 330
ROSE, 176 277
ROSENBERGER, 281
ROSS, 303
ROSS?, 303
ROSSETTA?, 2
ROSSI, 27
ROSSON, 224 228
ROSWELL, 347
ROTH, 176
ROWE, 7 90
ROWZE?, 33
RUDASILL, 311
RUDD, 79
RUDIGIER, 33
RUDROFF?, 34
RUEGER, 18
RUHLMAN?, 76
RULE?, 171 177
RUMBOL?, 176
RUPPRECHT, 357
RUSH, 134
RUSH?, 387
RUSKIN, 72
RUSSAVAGE, 111
RUSSELL, 17 22 27 29 36 37 55
    56 64 72 115 122 125 140 145
    148 149 154 164 183 193 194
    200 205 207 208 210 211 224
    230 249 250 259 266 281 296
    347 357
RUSSELL?, 7 20 26 55 63 122 188
    204 209 223 258 259 265 282
    338 390 393
RUSTIN, 266
RUTSCHOW, 330
RYAN, 26 266
RYBIKOWSKY, 352
RYCE, 37 98 288 354 357 391
RYCE?, 119
RYDER, 125
RYE?, 357
RYON, 111
SADLER, 377
SAINTCLAIR, 7 15 40 109 130
    149 150 225 331 340 377
SAINTPETER?, 78
SALTER, 224
SALTER?, 367
SALVIOLI, 69
SAMARAS, 64
SAMBOS?, 64
SAMPLES, 208
SAMPSON, 10
SAMS, 394
SAMSON, 111
SANCHEZ, 78
SANDER, 325 330
SANDERS?, 369 382
SANDIDGE, 27 176 388
SANDSTROM?, 388
SANFORD, 402
SANGER, 347
SANNER, 176 296 300 301 303
    316 320 321
SANNER?, 67 189 300
SANNIFER, 303
SAPP, 37 38
SARGENT?, 56
SARTAIN, 363 364
SASSER, 2
SATTERFIELD?, 196 395
SAUBLE, 377
SAULK?, 61
SAUNDERS, 19 67 176 189 210
SAUNDERS?, 194
SAXON, 78

SAXTON, 188 224 250
SAYLER?, 31
SAYRE, 195
SAYRES, 38
SCANLON, 38
SCARICOMAZZI, 357
SCHADE?, 285
SCHAEFER, 363 364 387
SCHAEFFER, 403
SCHAFFER, 311
SCHEFERE?, 66
SCHEIBLE, 311 367
SCHERER, 137 149
SCHERNE, 72 73
SCHILLER, 32
SCHINDLER, 111 211 224
SCHLAG, 387
SCHLANG, 164
SCHMOOKLER, 357
SCHNEIDER, 357
SCHONHART?, 141
SCHORN, 73
SCHROB?, 391
SCHUELE, 164
SCHUHART, 56 57
SCHULTHEIS, 405
SCHULTZ, 383
SCHULZ, 330
SCHWARTZ, 377
SCHWIENTECK, 5
SCOFIELD, 96
SCORAH, 149
SCOTT, 38 149 150 250 310 339
SCOTT?, 192 358
SCRIBER, 14 38 146 150 224-226 394
SCRIBER?, 122 217
SCRIVENER, 189
SCULLY, 225 387
SCZYGIEL?, 329
SEAN?, 97
SEARIGHT, 270
SEAWELL, 289

SEBASTIAN, 38
SECORA, 38
SECREST, 377
SEEK, 25
SELF, 111
SELLERS, 38
SELLMAN, 57
SELLS, 28
SENGSTACK, 349
SENICAL?, 288
SENSENBACH, 4
SESTAN, 183
SEVIER, 345
SEWALL, 296
SEWELL, 98 307 377
SEWELL?, 13 186
SEXTON, 38 64 197 198 386 387
SEXTON?, 13
SEYMOUR, 150
SHADE, 78 198
SHADE?, 324
SHADRICK, 339 347
SHAEFER, 383
SHAFFER, 38 64
SHAIKEWITZ, 38
SHANKS, 347 348
SHANNONHOUSE?, 185
SHAPIRO, 364
SHARE?, 394
SHATZER, 43
SHAW, 7 67 342 364 405
SHAWEN?, 404
SHAY, 35
SHEA, 225
SHEAFFER, 196
SHEALY, 329 330
SHEARER?, 384
SHEKELL, 57
SHELER, 193 194
SHELTON?, 34
SHENTON, 90
SHEPHERD, 64 69 73 174 176 188

SHEPPARD, 26
SHERCLIFFE, 250
SHERCLIFFE?, 234
SHERELL?, 30
SHERIDAN, 98
SHERKLEY, 242 250
SHERKLEY?, 241 260
SHERWOOD, 364
SHERWOOD?, 25
SHEWACK, 405
SHEWBRIDGE?, 364
SHIELDS, 51
SHIELDS?, 395
SHIFFLETT, 375
SHIFLETT, 21
SHINGLER?, 392
SHIPE, 367 387 394
SHIRCKLIFF, 176
SHIRLEY, 38 39
SHOEMAKER, 9
SHORT, 7 39 77 79 150 152 264 266 336
SHORT?, 277 280 389
SHORTER, 193 194 287 320 321
SHORTER?, 364
SHOTWELL, 39
SHOVER?, 349
SHREVE?, 355
SHREY, 63 64
SHUEBROOKS, 330
SHULTZ, 387
SHUPE, 39
SIEGERT?, 299
SILVER, 176
SILVER?, 330
SIMMONS, 203 357 371 377
SIMMONS?, 325
SIMMS, 250
SIMONCHI?, 71
SIMONS, 39
SIMPKINS, 102
SIMPSON, 48 131 150 381 387
SIMPSON?, 84 371

SIMS, 90
SIMUNEK?, 392
SIPKO?, 111
SISSON, 67
SISSON?, 283
SIVAK, 197 198 297
SIZEMORE, 39
SKIDGEL, 176
SKOK, 331
SLACUM, 64
SLADE, 189
SLOCHAZKI?, 19
SLUSS?, 198
SLUSSER, 192
SLYE, 57 334 364
SMALL?, 39
SMALLWOOD, 39 225 394 395
SMALLWOOD?, 204
SMIROLDO, 358
SMITH, 39 44 57 67 83 88 90 96 98 105 111 150 164 176 177 183 195 196 221 250 281 283 297 303 307 311 317 331 347 363 364 387 395
SMITH?, 95 105 168 192 286 354 357 368 386 395
SMOOT, 189
SNAPP, 300 303
SNELLING?, 309
SNIDER, 201 225
SNYDER, 21 79 401
SOBOLEFT, 178
SOCHOWSKI, 75
SOLOMON, 57
SOMER----, 250
SOMERS, 65 67
SOMERS?, 284
SOMERSET?, 57
SOMERVILLE, 10 22 37 39 40 78 111 133 177 183 202 224 225 231 250 267 274 281
SOMERVILLE?, 10 13 42 75 277 281 305

SOMMERKAMP, 83
SOMMERVILLE?, 262
SONESTOGARD?, 104
SOPER, 287
SOPER?, 154
SORRELLS, 358
SOTHORAN, 399
SOTHORON, 57 274 331 334
SOTHORON?, 334
SOUDER, 67
SOULES?, 294
SOWERSBY, 403 404
SPAIN, 358
SPALDING, 162
SPARKES, 90
SPARKS, 40 347
SPARSHOTT, 395
SPAULDING, 40 106 111 164 183 225 250 358
SPAULDING?, 106 256 374
SPEAKE, 358
SPEARS, 40 225 281
SPEARS?, 13 39 402
SPECHT, 367
SPEDDEN, 83 85 90
SPEEKS, 274
SPENCER, 90 92 177 225 347
SPENCER?, 372
SPINNER, 225
SPITALER, 36
SPONSHER, 354
SPRANGER, 405
SPRINGER, 186 187 189 347 348 364
SPRINGIRTH?, 39
SPURLOCK, 163
SQUIRES, 177
STAFFORD, 393
STAFFORD?, 379
STAHL, 57
STAHL?, 96
STAKE?, 204 227
STALKER, 34
STALLMAN, 73
STANDFORD, 387
STANFORD, 391
STANLEY, 146 358
STANSBURY?, 327
STANTON, 103
STARKWEATHER, 90
STARR, 358 387
STASCH, 358
STATEN, 401
STATESMAN, 270
STAUFFER, 93 96
STAUFFER?, 93
STEA, 354
STEELE, 311 312
STEELE?, 357
STEELMAN?, 311
STEINKE, 402
STELPFLUG, 405
STEPHENS, 195 196
STEPHENS?, 196
STEPHENSON, 189
STERLING, 333 348
STERLING?, 277
STERNKOPF, 175
STETSON?, 324
STEVENS, 12 79 215 225 226 281
STEWART, 13 40 62 63 75 150 171 177 183 226 284
STEWART?, 171 253 281 317
STIENKE, 401
STILLEY, 395
STILLWELL?, 403
STODDARD?, 29
STODDERT, 57
STOKES, 312
STOLTZFUS, 93
STONE, 7 29 40 73 87 90 105 107 108 111 150 151 164 177 183 202 211 215 219 226 231 250 251 287 297 335 348 367 383 395
STONE?, 169 215 288 348 363

STONE? (cont.)
    383 390
STONESTREET, 331
STOUT?, 193 361
STOWE?, 388
STREBE, 189
STRICKLAND, 40 61 62 405
STRINE, 279 281
STRINGER, 177
STRIPPEY, 36
STRONG?, 186
STROUD, 62 90 91
STUART, 367
STUART?, 58
STUCKEY, 393 395
SUCCHI?, 30
SUEHLE?, 192
SUITE, 40 151
SUITE?, 37
SULLIVAN, 2 64
SULLIVAN?, 164 187 286 356
SUMMERVILLE, 226
SUMMITS?, 38
SUMSTINE, 78
SUNDERLAND, 226
SUTER, 46
SUTHERLAND, 64
SUTPHIN, 59
SUTTON?, 27
SVEC, 405
SWAINE, 226
SWALES, 111 157 164 226 227
SWALES?, 39 157 393
SWANN, 48 51 57 140 151 242
    251 257 266 348 372 377 378
SWANN?, 135 267 334 335
SWARY?, 326
SWEENEY, 20 40 41 43 151 227
    375
SWEENEY?, 16
SWIDERSKI, 41
SWIFFLETT, 205
SWIHART, 331
SWINNEY?, 405
SWITER?, 41
SWITZER?, 389
SYDNOR, 227 394 395
SYKES, 303
SYLVESTER, 388
TABBS, 251
TACKETT, 367
TAFF, 284 286
TAGUE, 31
TALBERT?, 77
TALBOT, 21 41 378
TALBOT?, 16
TANEY, 111 164 251
TARLETON, 73 198 378
TARLETON?, 292
TARLTON, 151 297
TASE?, 35
TASKER, 33 41
TATE, 41 114 329
TAVEY, 227
TAWNEY, 62
TAYLER?, 180
TAYLOE, 182
TAYLOR, 11 17 41 64 82 83 86
    91 104 112 183 217 227 260
    285 287 297 309 311 312 331
    340 346 348 353 382 387 399
TAYLOR?, 40 188 189 193 198
    305 309 327 331 389
TAYMAN, 367
TAYMAN?, 378
TAYSOM?, 22
TEACHEM, 183
TEMPLE?, 329
TENNESON, 111
TENNISON, 98 234 251 254 258
    266 267
TENNISON?, 257 259
TENNYSON, 41 264 267 268 281
    287 348
TENNYSON?, 25 33 45 130 264
    287

TERRY, 270
TESAR?, 176
TESERMAN, 41
TEXIERA, 41
TEXTOR, 37
THARPE, 67
THEODOSSIOU, 64
THI?, 349
THIFFAULT?, 395
THOMAS, 2 10 17 31 37 41 42 57
  79 102 104 112 123 134 151
  153 169 177 196 227 251 264
  267 268 274 275 281 297 316
  324 331 341 348 377
THOMAS?, 7 24 51 76 78 105 135
  198 267 279 391 392
THOMASON, 302
THOMASSON, 368
THOMPSON, 2 19 31 34 42 57 58
  79 91 129 132 150-152 157 159
  180 183 187 189 194 201 202
  204 210 227 228 251 254 256
  258 259 267 270 271 281 282
  297 303 323 337 348 355 358
  382 388
THOMPSON?, 28 32 33 42 73 96
  110 111 126 139 151 160 162
  180 192 211 215 230 241 258-
  260 301 341 344 361
THORINGTON?, 12
THORNBURG, 395
THORNE, 64 313
THORNTON, 348
THRALL, 123
THRIFT, 163 348 349
THROCKMORTON, 177
THROWER, 349
THUMBSUR, 67
TIARE?, 167
TIBURZI, 195
TIGHE, 349
TILLETT?, 329
TINSLEY, 177

TINSLEY?, 358
TINSMAN, 384 388
TIPPETT, 42 115 143 152 170 177
  183 203 211 228 251 255 283
  299 303 319 349 355 378 383
  395
TIPPETT?, 107 256 262 283 353
TITUS, 287
TODD, 67
TOKLEY, 10
TOLAND, 123 152
TOLBERT?, 390
TOLLEY, 363 364
TOLSON, 39 194 275 307 394
TONEY, 76 188
TONEY?, 69 306
TORCISI, 392
TORNEY, 79
TOSTENSON?, 193
TOUTE, 31 42
TOWNSEND, 55
TOYE, 26 358
TOYE-WATTS, 358
TRACY, 82 91
TRACY?, 401
TRAN, 64
TRAUB, 42
TRAVERS, 271 324 349
TRAYNOR, 228
TREADWELL, 70
TRENT, 112 277 282
TRETICK, 403 405
TRIBLE, 91
TRICE?, 191
TRIGGER, 91
TROSSBACH, 42 106 284 285
  287 288
TROSSBACH?, 106 198
TRUEMAN, 371
TRUMAN, 334
TRUMAN?, 312
TRUXILLO, 153
TUCKER, 91 228 310

TUCKER?, 195
TUITE, 182
TURLEY, 30 43
TURLEY?, 43
TURLINGTON, 20
TURNER, 43 58 153 164 183 194
    228 331 349 355 358 397
TURNER?, 2 38 44 49 171 254
    393
TUTT, 43
TUTWILER, 129
TWILLEY, 62 102 204
TWILLEY?, 64 193 196
TYDINGS, 378
TYDINGS?, 29
TYER, 150 154
TYLER, 275 301 303 304 317
TYLER?, 118
TYNAN?, 71
TYNDALL, 382
UGLOW, 67
UHLER, 228
UNCLES, 297
UNDERWOOD, 38 43 297
UNGER, 326
UNKLE, 26 43 72 73 310
USILTON, 185
USILTON?, 185
USUAL?, 96
VALDENAR, 67
VALLANDINGHAM, 37 73 129
    130 133 147 153 163 179 251
    267 318 319 349 364
VALLANDINGHAM?, 61 71 139
    318
VANAERNAM, 179
VANCE, 395
VANCE?, 38
VANDALSUM, 224 228
VANDERGRIFT, 105
VANDERGRIFT?, 105
VANDEVANTER, 27 43
VANDIVERE, 329 331

VANDYKE?, 404
VANHEETON?, 393
VANHOUSEN, 43
VANKIRK, 395
VANMETER, 64
VANPELT, 43 331
VANRYSWICK, 349
VANSISE, 91
VANWART, 98 251
VANWERT, 119 153 206 228
VARNER, 43
VARNEY?, 391
VAUGHT?, 76
VAUPEL?, 178
VERGIE?, 11
VERMILLION, 378
VERNON?, 27
VIANT, 286 288
VIETCH?, 189
VINCENT, 395
VINSON, 294
VOGT, 369
VONGLAHN, 358 359
VONHEIN, 58
VU, 349
WADE, 278
WAGNER, 43 381
WAGONER?, 64
WAHLER, 187 190
WAIKART, 194
WAITE?, 170
WALCH, 29
WALDSCHMITT, 288
WALKER, 15 77 122 143 228 267
    359 378 396
WALKER?, 39 357
WALLACE, 38 43 84 91 95 98
    130 228
WALLACE?, 30 64 90 219
WALLING, 405
WALLIS, 43 44
WALLY, 164
WALSCH?, 42

WALSH, 297
WALTEMEYER, 7
WALTER, 119 153 310 389
WALTER?, 329
WALTERS, 346
WALTHER, 282
WALTON, 103 113 306
WALZ, 349
WANNALL, 364 368
WARD, 44 177 194
WARD?, 5 43 349 362 367
WARE, 44
WARE?, 387
WARING, 58 328
WARING?, 1 47 52 54
WARNER, 69
WARNER?, 217
WARREN, 275
WARREN?, 391
WARRENTON, 228
WARVIN, 358
WARWICK, 219
WASHBURN, 396
WASHER, 327
WASHINGTON, 297
WASHINGTON?, 77 95 355 358
WASHTELLA?, 395
WASICKI?, 285
WASSER?, 12
WATERS, 76 98 211 269 376
WATHEN, 16 26 44 136 146 153 162 164 165 183 199 228 229 258 267 268 343 349 361 388
WATHEN?, 9 21 125 162 356
WATSON, 44 177 229
WATSON?, 404
WATTS, 79 112 177 318 349 358 362 364 388
WATTS?, 70 104 130 169
WAUGH?, 20
WEART?, 36
WEASENFORTH, 382 388
WEAVER, 93

WEBB, 7 112 307 396
WEBB?, 307
WEBER?, 27
WEBSTER?, 208
WEDDING?, 182 280
WEEKS, 82 89 91
WEEMS, 275
WEILAND, 318
WELCH, 251 252 264 268 288 352 364
WELCH?, 35 195
WELCOMER, 359
WELLS, 7 95 99 177 213 229
WELLS?, 213
WELSH, 56 349
WELSH?, 327
WELTY, 404 405
WENGER, 93
WENK, 378
WENTZELL, 181
WERNECKE, 349
WEST, 44 58 67
WESTON?, 339
WESTURA, 184
WHALEN, 44 271 328 331
WHALEN?, 10 18 307
WHEAT, 396
WHEATLEY, 234 287
WHEELER, 91 112 120 123 137 153 154 229 282 297 298 304 307
WHEELER?, 89 378
WHERRITT, 298
WHIPPLE?, 395
WHITAKER, 92
WHITCOMB, 388
WHITE, 10 19 34 112 229 315 331 359 374 378 388 396
WHITE?, 65 67
WHITED, 378
WHITFIELD, 346
WHITINGER, 229
WHITTINGHAM?, 119

WIBLE, 20 44 85 92 229 231
WIBLE?, 223 388
WICK?, 217
WICKER, 154
WIDMAN, 229
WIELAND, 229
WIENER?, 57
WIGGIN, 378
WIGGINGTON, 192 194
WIGGINS, 271
WIGGINTON, 109 112
WIGGS?, 13
WILDMAN, 332 388
WILES, 13 41
WILEY, 190
WILGUS?, 387
WILKERSON, 224 230 283 288 364 378
WILKERSON?, 22 283 285 379
WILKES, 389
WILKINS, 79
WILKINSON, 154 384 405
WILKINSON?, 17
WILLENBORG, 62 64
WILLENBORG?, 63
WILLETT, 358 369 378
WILLIAM?, 116
WILLIAMS, 26 42 44 97 154 177 179 187 194 230 252 258 268 285 349 363 364 378 392
WILLIAMS?, 12 15 26 36 73 110 179 253 258 259 306 341 345 346 353 358 402
WILLIAMSON, 334 405
WILLIAMSON?, 326 406
WILLIS, 64 283 306 307
WILLIS?, 64
WILLOUGHBY, 22 44
WILLS, 44 135 377 388
WILLS?, 176
WILMER, 161
WILSON, 16 44 45 67 87 112 253 332 349 368 375 378 389 396

WILSON?, 32 185 285 367
WIMBERLY, 288
WINDELL, 391 396
WINDSOR, 45 58 352 359
WINDSOR?, 367 393
WINDUS?, 384
WINE, 335
WINFIELD?, 319
WINK?, 373
WINKFIELD?, 224
WINKLE?, 43
WINKWORTH, 359
WINN, 92 349
WINSTEAD, 371
WINTERBERGER?, 404
WINTERS, 71
WISE, 2 62 68 92 109 112 123 134 150 154 168 169 171 177 178 185 230 288 298 390 391 396 406
WISE?, 19 29 31 145 150 168 185 261 294 390
WITBURN, 61
WITHERS, 391 396
WOFFORD, 31
WOLF?, 324
WOLFE, 58
WOLFORD, 178
WOLFRAM, 396
WOLICKI, 382
WOOD, 21 45 64 68 99 165 203 212 230 252 257 263 265 268 280 282 334 364 379 396 397
WOOD?, 51 285 286 354
WOODBURN, 95 99 110 112 114 132 154 185 210 230 231 260 268 349 350 379
WOODBURN?, 72 129 135 224 231 241 253 257 266
WOODLAND, 17 62 154 274
WOODLAND?, 4 17 24
WOODLEY, 229 231
WOODLEY?, 229

WOODRING, 359
WOODROW?, 356
WOODRUFF, 365
WOODRUM, 51
WOODS, 92 282 332
WOODS?, 39
WOODSON, 62
WRAY, 19
WREN, 208 379
WRIGHT, 79 396
WRIGHT?, 79 280 324
WRIGHTSON, 67 68
WRY?, 328
WUNDER, 45
WYVILL?, 328
WYWICK, 45
YARBER, 388
YATES, 25 31 45 112 115 154 155 165 184 231 267 268 275 304 327 338 339 350
YATES?, 53 107 165 182 241 280
YEATMAN, 68 288 332 365
YEATMAN?, 78
YERGOVICH, 281
YEROSHEFSKY, 395
YINGLING?, 98
YODER, 25 326
YODER?, 326
YORKSHIRE, 45 332
YORKSHIRE?, 32 44 282

YOST, 287
YOST?, 403
YOUMANS, 388
YOUNG, 4 6 11 13 21 23 45 46 58 92 112 155 157 178 186 210 226 231 254 267 268 277 282 307 323 332 348 379
YOUNG?, 10 14 17 23 34 45 97 179 256 267 277 303 305
YOUNGBLOOD, 12
YOUNGE, 275
YOUNGER, 46
YOWAISKI, 282
ZACHERY, 350
ZAGORAC, 406
ZALUTE?, 50
ZAWISLAK, 79
ZEDEK?, 286
ZELL, 356
ZELLER, 165
ZENZ?, 162
ZHAN, 73
ZIDEK?, 197
ZIMMERLY, 286
ZIMMERMAN, 93
ZIMMERMAN?, 93
ZISSIS, 14
ZOOK?, 326
ZORNEK, 145
ZORNEK?, 145

www.ingramcontent.com/pod-product-compliance
Lightning Source LLC
Chambersburg PA
CBHW071222230426
43668CB00011B/1273